Inhibitory Processes in Attention, Memory, and Language

Inhibitory Processes in Attention, Memory, and Language

Edited by

Dale Dagenbach

Department of Psychology
Wake Forest University
Winston-Salem, North Carolina

Thomas H. Carr

Department of Psychology
Michigan State University
East Lansing, Michigan

ACADEMIC PRESS
A Division of Harcourt Brace & Company
San Diego   New York   Boston   London   Sydney   Tokyo   Toronto

Academic Press, Inc.
525 B Street, Suite 1900, San Diego, California 92101-4495

United Kingdom Edition published by
Academic Press Limited
24–28 Oval Road, London NW1 7DX

Library of Congress Cataloging-in Publication Data

Inhibitory processes in attention, memory, and language / edited by
    Dale Dagenbach, Thomas H. Carr
        p.   cm.
    Includes bibliographical references and index.
    ISBN 0-12-200410-8
    1. Attention.   2. Memory.   3. Psycholinguistics.   4. Cognitive
neuroscience.   I. Carr, Thomas H.
    BF321.I54   1994
    153.1 --dc20   93-31495
                                                                      CIP

PRINTED IN THE UNITED STATES OF AMERICA
94 95 96 97 98 99   BB   9 8 7 6 5 4 3 2 1

Contents

1

The Neurology of Inhibition: Integrating Controlled and Automatic Processes
Robert Rafal and Avishai Henik

2

A Model of Inhibitory Mechanisms in Selective Attention
George Houghton and Steven P. Tipper

3

Categories of Cognitive Inhibition with Reference to Attention
Raymond M. Klein and Tracy L. Taylor

4

Temporal Allocation of Visual Attention: Inhibition or Interference?
Kimron L. Shapiro and Jane E. Raymond

5

On the Ability to Inhibit Thought and Action: A Users' Guide to the Stop Signal Paradigm
Gordon D. Logan

6

Directed Ignoring: Inhibitory Regulation of Working Memory
Rose T. Zacks and Lynn Hasher

7

Mechanisms of Inhibition in Long-Term Memory: A New Taxonomy
Michael C. Anderson and Robert A. Bjork

8

Inhibitory Processes in Perceptual Recognition: Evidence for a Center-Surround Attentional Mechanism
Dale Dagenbach and Thomas H. Carr

9

Inhibitory Processes in the Recognition of Homograph Meanings
Greg B. Simpson and Hyewon Kang

10

Phonological Inhibition in Auditory Word Recognition
Kathleen M. Eberhard

11

Inhibition in Interactive Activation Models of Linguistic Selection and Sequencing
Gary S. Dell and Padraig G. O'Seaghdha

Contributors

Numbers in parentheses indicate the pages on which the authors' contributions begin.

Michael C. Anderson (265)   Department of Psychology, University of California, Los Angeles, California 90024

Robert A. Bjork (265)   Department of Psychology, University of California, Los Angeles, California 90024

Thomas H. Carr (327)   Department of Psychology, Michigan State University, East Lansing, Michigan 48824

Dale Dagenbach (327)   Department of Psychology, Wake Forest University, Winston-Salem, North Carolina 27109

Gary S. Dell (409)   Department of Psychology, University of Illinois at Urbana-Champaign, Champaign, Illinois 61820

Kathleen M. Eberhard (383)   Department of Psychology, University of Rochester, Rochester, New York 14627

Lynn Hasher (241)   Department of Psychology: Social and Health Sciences, Duke University, Durham, North Carolina 27706

Avishai Henik (1)   Department of Behavioral Sciences, Ben-Gurion University of the Negev, Beer-Sheva 84105, Israel

George Houghton (53)   Department of Psychology, University College London, London WC1E 6BT, United Kingdom

Hyewon Kang (359)   Department of Psychology, University of Kansas, Lawrence, Kansas 66045

Raymond M. Klein (113)   Department of Psychology, Dalhousie University, Halifax, Nova Scotia, Canada B3H 4J1

Gordon D. Logan (189)   Department of Psychology, University of Illinois at Urbana-Champaign, Champaign, Illinois 61820

Padraig G. O'Seaghdha (409)   Department of Psychology, Lehigh University, Bethlehem, Pennsylvania 18105

Robert Rafal (1)   Department of Neurology and Center for Neuroscience, University of California, Davis, Davis, California 95616

Jane E. Raymond (151)   Department of Psychology, University of Calgary, Calgary, Alberta, Canada T2N 1N4

Kimron L. Shapiro (151)   Department of Psychology, University of Calgary, Calgary, Alberta, Canada T2N 1N4

Greg B. Simpson (359)   Department of Psychology, University of Kansas, Lawrence, Kansas 66045

Tracy L. Taylor (113)   Department of Psychology, Dalhousie University, Halifax, Nova Scotia, Canada B3H 4J1

Steven P. Tipper (53)   Department of Psychology, McMaster University, Hamilton, Ontario, Canada L8S 4K1

Rose T. Zacks (241)   Department of Psychology, Michigan State University, East Lansing, Michigan 48824

Preface

Communication within the nervous system involves the excitation and inhibition of neurons. Exactly how these processes interact to control and guide behavior has been the subject of intense speculation in cognitive models at various points in time from the earliest models of attention to the present. Pillsbury (1908, *Attention*. New York: Macmillan) provided a prescient discussion of the roles of facilitation and inhibition in attention in which he dissected Müller's conclusion that attention is a process based on facilitation, and Wundt's conclusion that selective attention was accomplished by the active inhibition of unattended information. Pillsbury favored an account in which both processes were at work. We find ourselves in sympathy with his conclusion for reasons elaborated throughout this volume.

Although early psychologists were acutely aware of the possible importance of inhibition in cognitive processes, the notion seems to have been somewhat lost in successive generations of theorists. The models of cognitive processes that emerged in the 1960s and 1970s tended to describe mental functioning mainly in terms of facilitation. Inhibitory processes typically were mentioned merely as a possibility, if at all.

This is no longer the case. Over the past decade, there has been a renewed interest in understanding the role of inhibitory processes in cognition and in finding ways to disentangle inhibitory and facilitatory effects. This interest may reflect a number of different factors, including the appearance of theoretical arguments suggesting that inhibitory processes might explain important aspects of cognitive performance. The discovery of various experimental paradigms that seem to yield reliable evidence of inhibition has also been an important contributing factor. Finally, this being the "Decade of the Brain," we might speculate that the desire to have what is known about the way the nervous system works reflected in our cognitive models may be a relevant factor in renewed interest in inhibitory processes as well.

Given this renewed interest, it seemed appropriate to ascertain what had been learned since Pillsbury's discussion. The genesis of this particular volume occurred several years ago as we described our own findings regarding inhibition at various conferences. The topic, regardless of the quality of the presentations, seemed to generate considerable interest. Moreover, many of those who stopped to chat with us about it at these conferences had stories of their own to tell about inhibition. Many others, it seemed, had stories to tell about trying to obtain inhibitory effects, but failing. We thought the various questions they asked us about the relationship between the inhibitory effects that we had observed and those that others were then describing deserved better answers than any we were able to provide. ("Beats me" loses its elegance after a while.) Our hope was that bringing some of the various reports on inhibitory mechanisms or components of cognitive processes together under one cover would facilitate the process of determining what commonalities exist in terms of the experimental conditions under which inhibitory effects can be observed, and in terms of the functions that inhibitory processes may serve in various cognitive domains.

We have enjoyed reading the chapters for this volume as they came in, and we learned a great deal about inhibition in cognitive processes as we read them. Some of the questions that we began with have been answered, some are now better framed and potentially more resolvable, and some new and extremely interesting ones have arisen. We hope that our readers have the same experience.

Dale Dagenbach
Thomas H. Carr

1

The Neurology of Inhibition
Integrating Controlled and Automatic Processes

Robert Rafal and Avishai Henik

> *I always think that inhibition is a sculpturing process. The inhibition, as it were, chisels away at the diffuse and rather amorphous mass of excitatory action and gives a more specific form to the neuronal performance at every stage of synaptic relay.*
>
> Sir John Eccles (1977)

I. INTRODUCTION

The newborn infant is a bundle of reflexes, the toddler a distractible dynamo impulsively reacting to the outside world. During development, primitive reflexes disappear and behavior becomes guided more by internally generated goals. This behavioral maturation depends on the maturation of the cerebral cortex: Frontal lobe pathways, the last to mature, are not fully myelinated until adolescence.

It is a cardinal principle of neurology that disease processes affecting higher centers—especially the cerebral cortex—are revealed by the reappearance of primitive reflexes. The knee jerk of a normal person is tonically inhibited; it can become hyperactive after damage to the spinal cord, which interrupts descending inhibitory pathways from the motor cortex. The sucking and rooting reflexes of infants disappear after the nursing years, but can reappear in a patient with Alzheimer's disease. Presumably, these primitive reflexes remain hardwired in the nervous

INHIBITORY PROCESSES IN ATTENTION, MEMORY, AND LANGUAGE

system but are inhibited after infancy—until a cortical insult causes them to be disinhibited.

Implicit here is the notion that reflexes, by definition automatic, can be inhibited, and that the nervous system routinely goes about its business through an orchestration of reflexes and endogenous processes which can inhibit them. It is not clear whether the preceding tonic and hardwired inhibition of primitive reflexes can be related directly to the question of strategic or voluntary control of automatic cognitive processes. These examples do, however, emphasize that there is no biological imperative to assume that automatic or reflexive processes cannot be inhibited, or that they should be defined by this criterion.

This is a notion that is rather new in cognitive science (Kahneman & Treisman, 1984). Much theorizing about controlled and automatic processing (e.g., Hasher & Zacks, 1979) is predicated on a dichotomy in which automatic processes are entirely involuntary and cannot be controlled by voluntary effort. Automatic processes are construed as being carried out without intention; once started they run on to completion, they cannot be stopped and their products cannot be ignored.

The current volume reflects a growing appreciation within cognitive science that inhibitory processes are a vital part of skilled performance, and that their understanding is central to the issues of automaticity and control. In this chapter we look at what is known about the neural basis for some selected inhibitory processes in attention. One goal will be to develop a biologic framework for understanding the issues of automaticity and control, and the role that inhibitory processes play in orchestrating them. We proceed from a perspective which views the attention system of the human brain as "anatomically separate from the data processing systems that perform operations on specific inputs" (Posner & Petersen, 1990, p. 26). This perspective views attention in terms of the "operation of a separate set of neural areas whose interaction with domain specific systems . . . is the proper subject for empiric investigation" (Posner & Petersen, 1990, p. 26).

Posner and Petersen (1990) have outlined a framework for understanding the attention system of the human brain in terms of two interacting systems: A *posterior system* which orients to objects in the external world and which generates perceptual awareness, and an *anterior system* which orients to the meaning of percepts and which guides selection for action. The organization of this chapter follows this framework. The first part of the chapter reviews some of what has been learned recently about inhibitory mechanisms in spatial orienting. We then consider preliminary efforts to apply this framework to understanding inhibitory mechanisms in word processing and review some recent work being done on the neurology of the Stroop effect and semantic priming.

II. INHIBITORY MECHANISMS IN SPATIAL ORIENTING

We start by focusing on a simple cognitive act: the orienting of attention to a location in the visual field to detect a luminance change there. When Posner first began to examine this issue in humans in the mid-1970s, his intent was to develop it as a framework for cognitive processes in general. This framework considers cognition in terms of opponent processes, which include both facilitory and inhibitory components (Posner, 1978; Posner & Snyder, 1975). Spatial attention was selected as a model system because it fostered an active contact with a converging strand of research in neuroscience. Because this is a simple cognitive act that we share with other animals, there is a growing literature in neurophysiology which is beginning to link this behavior to its neural substrates. The paradigm for measuring covert shifts of visual attention that Posner developed (Posner, 1980) was designed to be simple enough to relate to studies done in animals. This simplicity also made it possible to examine brain mechanisms for orienting attention in humans through the study of brain-injured individuals, and, more recently, to trace the development of these mechanisms in infants (Clohessy, Posner, & Rothbart, 1991; Johnson, 1990; Rothbart, Posner, & Boylan, 1991). The past decade has revealed quite a bit about the neural basis for visual orienting in humans. This section of the chapter will review what has been learned about the neurology of some inhibitory processes that operate in visual selective attention.

The orienting of attention to a point of interest is usually accompanied by overt movements of the head, eyes, or body. This is so whether attention is summoned exogenously, as in turning toward a movement seen out of the corner of the eye, or is deployed endogenously, as when we decide to look both ways before crossing the street. In everyday life there are constantly competing demands on attention by the outside world as well as from internally generated goals. The need for mechanisms to arbitrate between these competing demands is obvious—so that they can be integrated to provide coherent and adaptive behavior.

This section begins by summarizing evidence that there are separate neural systems for reflexively orienting attention to external signals, and others which allocate attention under endogenous control. Studies in normal and brain-injured humans have identified subcortical brain regions critical for reflexive orienting, and cortical regions important for endogenously controlled orienting. They also suggest some degree of independence between the neural structures that control covert attention and those which regulate eye movements. The section ends by considering some of the interactions that have been identified between these systems and the special role that inhibitory processes may play in coordinating them. Three major inhibitory processes in spatial attention, and their neural substrates, have been identified:

1. Inhibition of responding to signals at unattended locations;
2. Endogenous inhibition of visual reflexes; and
3. Reflexive inhibition of detection of subsequent visual signals (inhibition of return).

A. Differences between Exogenous and Endogenous Orienting

In a typical spatial attention experiment using the precuing method, the subject is asked to respond, by pressing a key, to the appearance of a target at a peripheral location. The target is usually preceded by a cue which may summon attention to target location (valid cue), to the wrong location (invalid cue), or may have only an alerting value and provide no spatial information (neutral cue). In most studies, the dependent variables are response latency (the time from the target to the subject's response, reaction time) or accuracy (when subjects are asked to report which of several target letters appeared on a given trial). Orienting of attention results in increased efficiency of target processing at cued locations (valid cue) relative to uncued locations (a neutral or invalid cue). By manipulating the time interval between the cue and target, and measuring the effect of cue validity as a function of the stimulus onset asynchrony (SOA), the timecourse of covert attention movements can be measured.

Experiments of this kind have indicated that orienting to a spatial location has both facilitory and inhibitory components (Posner, 1980). Compared to a "neutral cue" condition, performance at the attended location is facilitated whereas processing and responding to signals at other locations are less efficient. These effects have been demonstrated in a variety of situations including detecting supra threshold luminance changes (brightening or dimming; Posner & Cohen, 1984), signal detection studies of near threshold stimuli (Bashinski & Bacharach, 1980), discrimination tasks (Egly & Homa, 1991; Henderson, 1991), and using event-related potentials recorded from the scalp (Rugg, Milner, Lines, & Phalp, 1987; Hillyard, Luck, & Mangun, in press).

The type of cue used can be selected to examine exogenously triggered or endogenously deployed attention. For example, an arrow presented at the center of a display which points to the right or left, and which predicts the likely location of the target with an 80% probability, can be used to study endogenous orienting. Because the target never appears at the center (where the arrow is presented), any effect that the cue has on performance must be ascribed to an endogenously generated set based on its symbolic meaning. In contrast, a peripheral luminance change that precedes the target, but which does not predict the likely target location (i.e., a cue on the right which is equally likely to be followed by a target on the left as on the right), can be used to study exogenous orienting. Because the subject is given no reason to expect the target at the location of the cue, any effect the cue has may be ascribed to a more reflexive or automatic process.

Jonides (1981) identified four properties that distinguish endogenous and exogenous orienting, and which characterize exogenous orienting as being more automatic and reflexive:

1. Endogenous orienting is vulnerable to the effects of a concomitant memory load, whereas exogenous orienting is not affected by such cognitive demands.
2. Endogenous orienting can be suppressed voluntarily, whereas exogenously triggered orienting cannot.
3. Exogenous orienting is not dependent on the likelihood of a peripheral signal, whereas endogenous cueing is strongly influenced by the subjects' expectations.
4. Exogenous signals appear to produce stronger orienting effects (as measured by the size of the validity effect of the precue).

Müller and Rabbit (1989a, 1989b) also claimed that exogenous orienting is more resistant to interuption and suggested that it occurs more rapidly than endogenous orienting. Moreover, Briand and Klein (1987) suggested that these two modes of orienting produce different effects on perception: Endogenously oriented attention has similar effects on feature and conjunction search, whereas exogenously oriented attention has a larger effect on conjunction than on feature search.

One approach to determining whether exogenous and endogenous orienting are mediated by different physiologic systems is to determine whether the timecourse of facilitation and inhibition differs in the two types of orienting. Because exogenous attention orienting is often considered to be more reflexive or automatic (Hasher & Zacks, 1979; Logan, 1985), one reasonable expectation would be that exogenously triggered orienting might occur more quickly, and that it might produce facilitation of detection at the stimulated location without producing inhibition at other locations (because it might be expected to occur without encumbering limited capacity, voluntary or controlled processes). Other investigators have marshaled evidence in support of these predictions. In those studies endogenous cueing was accomplished with central arrows which predicted the likely target location. However, exogenous cueing was a peripheral visual signal which also *predicted likely target location* (Jonides, 1981; Müller & Rabbit, 1989b; Briand & Klein, 1987). Thus, the peripheral cues *also summoned attention endogenously*. It is possible that such peripheral cues reflect the *conjoint* action of both endogenous and exogenous orienting.

To prevent confounding exogenous and endogenous effects, a peripheral signal can be used that does not predict the target location, that is, the cue validity is 50%, and the target is as likely to appear in the contralateral visual field as at the cued location. The results for 14 normal subjects, tested in two cueing conditions, are shown in Figure 1

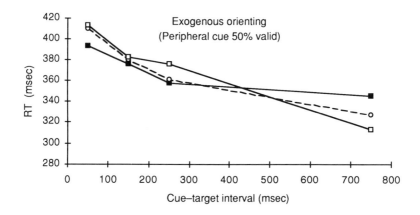

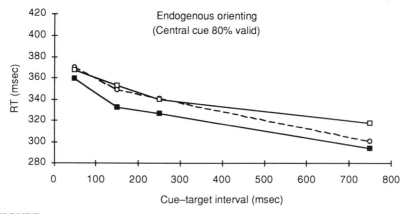

FIGURE 1

Effect on mean detection RT of orienting of nonpredictive peripheral cues (top) and to predictive central cues (bottom). The task is a simple RT key press response to the appearance of the target. Detection RT in msec is shown as a function of cue–target interval for valid (solid squares), neutral (open circles, dashed line), and invalid (open squares) cue conditions.

(Sciolto, 1990). The central cues were arrows which predicted the likely target location with an 80% probability. The peripheral cues consisted of brightening one of the two boxes for 200 msec. The peripheral cue did not predict the likely target location. Peripheral and central cueing were tested in separate blocks. For both kinds of cues, one-third of trials in each block had a neural cue consisting of the brightening of the center box for 200 msec. The intertrial interval was 1500 msec. Mean detection reaction time (simple key press) is shown as a function of the cue–target interval for valid cue (closed squares), invalid cue (open squares), and neutral cue (dashed line). Certain similarities between exogenous and endogenous cueing patterns are noteworthy:

1. Both types of cues produce both facilitation (or benefits) at the cued location and inhibition (or costs) at the contralateral location.

2. For both types of cueing, the facilitory effects occur before the appearance of inhibition, being evident at the 50-msec interval for both peripheral and central cues. In this kind of detection reaction time experiment, the timecourses of these facilitory effects are not much different between peripheral and central cues. Studies using discrimination tasks, however, typically find that facilitation by peripheral cues is larger and occurs earlier than with central cues (Jonides & Mack, 1984; Müller & Rabbitt, 1989b).

Some differences between exogenous and endogenous orienting shown in Figure 1 are also noteworthy:

1. With peripheral cueing, the advantage at the cued location is superseded, after a few hundred msec, by an inhibition at the cued location resulting in longer RTs (reaction times). No such inhibition is seen with endogenous shifts of covert attention. This phenomenon has been called the *inhibition of return* (Posner, Cohen, & Rafal, 1982; Posner & Cohen, 1984; Posner, Rafal, Choate, & Vaughn, 1985), or the *inhibitory aftereffect* (Tassinari, Aglioti, Chelazzi, Marzi, & Berlucchi, 1987; Tassinari, Biscaldi, Marzi, & Berlucchi, 1989). In this circumstance, where the cue is not predictive of target location and the subject has no incentive to maintain attention there, the reflexive orienting to the cue is brief and the inhibition of return effect is readily apparent. Quite a bit has been learned about the neural basis and function of this intriguing inhibitory phenomenon, and this will be an important part of our story.

2. With endogenous cueing, the facilitory effect appears to be more sustained and the contralateral inhibition (costs) are later in evolving.

3. Reaction times are generally slower in the peripheral cue condition of this experiment, especially at the shorter cue–target intervals. This relative slowing seen with peripheral cues turns out to be an artifact caused by the persistence of inhibition of return, which carries over

from trial to trial. This does not occur when peripheral and central cues are mixed within blocks, when longer cue–target intervals are used, or when multiple target locations are possible (Egly, Rafal, & Henik, 1992).

In summary, when a detection task is required, both kinds of cues produce a rapid facilitation at the cued location, with costs at the uncued location developing later. According to the framework for distinguishing automatic from controlled processes (Posner & Snyder, 1975), endogenous and exogenous orienting seem to involve both processes (because they both produce earlier facilitation followed by later inhibition). These data also do not support the notion that exogenous orienting produces earlier and larger effects than does endogenous orienting. However, the timecourse for these two forms of orienting, as they seem to evolve in this experiment, should not be interpreted too literally. When discrimination tasks are used, both the timecourse and the size of exogenous versus endogenous orienting differ quite substantially (Egly et al., 1992).

Returning to the theme of inhibition, precuing studies have revealed several potential inhibitory processes:

1. The "cost" of orienting at unattended locations.
2. Inhibition of exogenously triggered reflexive orienting by endogenous mechanisms for voluntary control of visual attention.
3. Inhibition of return, which is activated by peripheral visual signals.

B. Costs of Orienting and the Phenomenon of Extinction

In this kind of paradigm the "benefit" in performance provided by the valid cue condition compared to a neutral cue provides a measure of facilitation, whereas the "cost" of an invalid cue compared to the neutral condition provides a measure of inhibition at unattended locations. However, dependence on neutral cues to measure these components independently can be problematic (Jonides & Mack, 1984). When less efficient processing is found at an unattended location, does this simply reflect less availability of resources which are deployed elsewhere? Or is there also active inhibition of processing there? If there is active inhibition, does it act early in processing to degrade perceptual sensitivity, or does it operate at a later stage of selection for action? Studies in normal and injured human brains provide evidence that covert orienting does have both facilitory and inhibitory components, and that both early and late selection may be affected.

Spatial orienting has been shown to influence early, visual evoked brain potentials recorded from the scalp of normal humans over ventral occipital areas. Facilitory effects were reflected in an augmentation of the N_1 component of the response evoked by a visual target, whereas inhibitory effects were reflected in a decrease in the P_1 response (Hillyard et al., in press). These findings are consistent with findings both from single unit recordings in monkeys (Moran & Desimone, 1985) and from positron emission tomography (PET) studies in normal humans (Corbetta, Miezin, Dobmeyer, Shulman, & Petersen, 1991), which have shown attentional modulation early in visual processing in the prestriate cortex.

Perhaps the most direct and dramatic evidence that orienting attention can cause an active *inhibition* at unattended locations comes from observing neurologic patients with lesions of the parietal lobe who manifest a clinical sign called *extinction*. Figure 2 shows one conventional way that examination for extinction is performed. The patient is asked to keep the eyes fixed on the examiner's face and to report objects which the examiner presents in one or both visual fields. The patient shown in Figure 2 had recently suffered a stroke in his right hemisphere, and he frequently failed to notice things on his left. When shown one fork in his left visual field, the patient turned toward it and reported it, so he is not blind in the field contralateral to the lesion. He also had no trouble reporting the fork when it was presented in the right visual field. In Figure 2, bottom, two forks are presented simultaneously, one in each field. The patient orients only to the one on the right and does not notice the one on the left. When asked, he is quite certain that nothing happened on that side, and that he only saw one fork.

This failure to detect bilateral simultaneously presented stimuli is called *extinction*. It can be elicited even with simple features such as movement. The patient can report that the examiner is wiggling a finger in either visual field, but when the examiner wiggles fingers in both fields at once, the patient does not see the movement in the field contralateral to the lesion. Detection of a brisk movement like this is commonly thought not to require attentional resources. It seems likely that extinction reflects some kind of active inhibition.

In the covert orienting experiment described earlier, patients with parietal lesions—even those who do not show clinical extinction on conventional examination—show an "extinction-like-reaction-time pattern" (Posner, Inhoff, Friedrich, & Cohen, 1987; Posner, Walker, Friedrich, & Rafal, 1984, 1987). That is, detection reaction time in the field opposite to the lesion (contralesional field) is not much slowed if a valid cue is given, but there is often a striking slowing of RT to detect a target in that field after an invalid cue has first summoned attention to the good (ipsilesional) field. These results show that patients with neglect may be able to move their attention toward the contralesional field. However, they have great difficulty in disengaging from the current focus of attention to orient in the contralesional direction.

FIGURE 2

Extinction in a patient with a stroke in the right hemisphere. He was able to report an object in either visual field when shown by itself; therefore he does not have a hemianopia, that is, he is not blind in either field. When presented two forks (bottom), one in each visual field, he fails to detect the one on the left; that is, there is extinction of the visual stimulus in the contralesional field. However, when he is shown two different objects (top), he orients first to the key on his right, then to the comb on his left.

If the "extinction-like-reaction-time pattern" found in these patients reflects an active inhibitory process, does the reaction time "cost" seen in normal subjects in this paradigm also reflect active inhibition? There is now converging evidence from patients and normal subjects that the cost of orienting in normal subjects is not phenomenologically different from the more dramatic extinctionlike phenomenon seen in patients with neglect (Friedrich, Walker, & Posner, 1985; Sieroff, Pollatsek, & Posner, 1988).

What is inhibited in "extinguished" stimuli? Certainly *detection* is impaired in patients with extinction, that is, the ability to report awareness of the signal—defined, operationally, as the ability to make an arbitrary response to it (Posner, Snyder, & Davidson, 1980). Is it the case that all perceptual processing of the extinguished object is inhibited? If not, to what level is information about the extinguished object processed? In the top panel of Figure 2 the patient is being shown two *different* objects and he promptly identifies both, first the key on his right and then the comb on his left. Information in the unattended field clearly is processed sufficiently for the visual system to know that it is different from its counterpart in the ipsilesional field. Figure 2 shows that extinguished objects are processed to an extent that information about their identity is available to brain mechanisms that transduce perception into action—even though the subject reports being unaware of the stimulus.

Baylis, Rafal, and Driver (1993) have recently extended this clinical observation in five patients with extinction. The patients were presented colored letters either unilaterally or bilaterally and asked to report what they saw on each side. The critical trials were those in which bilateral targets were presented and in which the patient reported seeing "nothing" in the contralesional field. In one condition, they were asked to name only the letter(s) (*X* or *E*), and in another, to report only the color(s) (red or green). This study confirmed that extinction occurred much more frequently when the bilateral stimuli were identical *in the attribute to be reported*. On blocks in which the task was to report the name of the letter, extinction was not ameliorated if the stimuli were of different colors, and vice versa for the color report blocks.

Berti and Rizzolatti (1992) have also provided evidence from neglect patients that extinguished objects are processed to a categorical level of representation. Their subjects categorized line drawing of pictures presented in their ipsilesional field. Their performance was better not only when the same picture was presented simultaneously in the contralesional, extinguished visual field, but also when the picture in the contralesional field was a different object in the same category as the target object in the ipsilesional field.

Even under conditions of extinction in which the patient reports that a signal in the neglected field was not present, some kinds of information from the neglected stimulus are processed as efficiently as in the non-neglected field. McGlinchey-Berroth, Milberg, Verfaellie, Alexander, and Kilduff (1993) showed that pictures presented to the patients' neglected field produced just as much priming in a lexical decision task (for centrally presented letter strings) as did pictures in the good field ipsilateral to the lesion. Cohen, Ivry, Rafal, and Cohn (1994) showed that flanker interference in a color discrimination task is just as robust when flankers are presented to the extinguished field as to the good field. The emerging evidence suggests that clinical extinction involves an active inhibitory process that operates at a late level of selection. It is not perceptual or categorical processing that is inhibited, but access to awareness and the attendant ability to make overt responses. This is now thought to be the business of the anterior attention system. Thus parietal lesions affect attention such that visual information is not available to the anterior attention system, and it seems likely that this channel of information is actively inhibited at unattended locations.

III. NEURAL MECHANISMS FOR EXOGENOUS AND ENDOGENOUS ORIENTING

Studies of patients with focal brain lesions suggest that there are separate neural systems for regulating reflexive orienting to exogenous signals and others for voluntary spatial orienting under endogenous control. We first review some of these studies before turning to evidence that endogenous mechanisms for regulating spatial orienting can influence inhibitory control over reflexive or automatic orienting to exogenous signals. This strand of neuropsychologic research has shown that reflexive orienting is mediated by an ancient visual pathway to the midbrain, whereas endogenous orienting is under cortical control.

These findings help address a puzzle of evolutionary biology. The encephalization of visual function in the cerebral cortex is a relatively new development in phylogeny. The geniculostriate pathway is fully developed only in mammals. The demands of increasingly complex visual cognition presumably generated the evolutionary pressures leading to the development of a completely new, parallel visual pathway in mammals. In lower vertebrates, vision is mediated by input through the retinotectal pathway to the superior colliculus of the midbrain. What function does the phylogenetically older midbrain pathway serve in humans?

There is converging evidence for a special role of the midbrain pathway in reflexive orienting in humans from three sources: (1) patients with lesions of the midbrain have been studied to define what visually guided behaviors are impaired; (2) patients with hemianopia due to lesions of the visual cortex have been examined to determine what visually guided behaviors are preserved when only the midbrain visual pathway is available; and (3) extrageniculate vision has been studied in normal subjects by comparing the orienting of attention into the temporal and nasal hemifields. This last approach exploits a difference in the normal anatomy of cortical and subcortical visual systems: The phylogenetically older midbrain pathway is asymmetrically represented, with the temporal hemifield receiving more visual information (see Rafal, Henik, & Rhodes, 1991; Figure 1).

A. Exogenous and Endogenous Covert Orienting and Lesions of the Midbrain and Tempero-Parietal Junction

The progressive degenerative disorder PSP affects subcortical nucleii of the diencephalon, midbrain, cerebellum, and brain stem. Because the basal ganglia and the substantia nigra are involved, the clinical picture shares many features with Parkinson's disease. In addition, however, there is degeneration, unique to this disease, involving the midbrain superior colliculus and the adjacent peri-tectal region. This pathology results in the distinctive paralysis of voluntary eye movements, especially pronounced in the vertical plane. The study of these patients affords a special opportunity to understand the function of the midbrain extra-geniculate pathways in regulating human visually guided behavior.

The midbrain pathology of this disease produces not only a compromise of eye movements, but also results in a striking and distinctive global derangement of visually guided behavior (Rafal, 1992). Although visual acuity is not affected, patients with PSP *behave as if they were blind*, even at a stage in the disease when their eyes are not totally paralyzed. They do not orient to establish eye contact with persons who approach them or engage them in conversation, nor do they look down at their plates while eating, but rather grope for their food without looking.

Rafal, Posner, Friedman, Inhoff, and Bernstein (1988) used the same design for comparing reflexive and voluntary orienting described for normal subjects (See Figure 1) in patients with PSP (except that a neutral cue condition was not used). Vertical and horizontal covert shifts of attention were measured using both central and peripheral cues. Compared to neurologic control patients with Parkinson's disease, valid cues were less efficient in summoning attention in the vertical plane (in which eye movements were also more affected), especially with exogenous cueing. These findings are consistent with a specific midbrain role in reflexive covert orienting as well as in generating eye movements.

Recent work has compared exogenous and endogenous orienting in patient groups with focal cortical lesions: lesions of the dorsolateral prefrontal cortex, the parietal lobe, and the tempero-parietal junction including the superior temporal gyrus (Senechal, unpublished data, 1994). In these patient groups with lateralized lesions, the effectiveness of a cue (exogenous and endogenous) in summoning attention into the contralesional field was compared to the ipsilesional field. The results, shown in Figure 3, give the data from the *valid cue condition*. The three cortical lesion groups are shown and are compared to the findings in PSP patients. The difference in detection RT between contralesional field and ipsilesional field is shown for the two types of cues. Detection RT is slower for targets occurring in the bad field (contralateral to the cortical lesion) in all groups. The critical findings here concern differences between the two types of cues that indicate which kind of cue is more effective in summoning attention in the direction affected by the lesion. As may be seen in Figure 3, there were no differences in the efficiency of exogenous and endogenous cues in summoning attention for patients with lesions of the parietal lobe or dorsolateral prefrontal cortex. In the PSP patients, as discussed earlier, exogenous cues were less effective than endogenous cues in summoning attention, reflecting

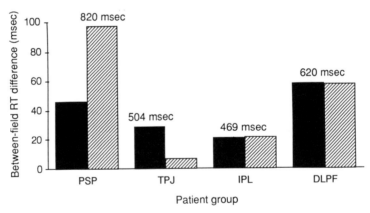

FIGURE 3

The difference in RT between affected and unaffected visual fields for the valid condition is shown for exogenous (cross-hatched) and endogenous (solid) orienting for each patient group. PSP = progressive supranuclear palsy; TPJ = tempero-parietal junction lesion; IPL = inferior parietal lobule lesion; DLPF = dorsolateral prefrontal cortex lesion. To provide some index of the relative general impairment of the four groups, the mean RT for each group is shown above the columns.

a deficiency in exogenous orienting. The opposite pattern is evident in patients with lesions of the tempero-parietal junction. In that group there is a relative deficiency in orienting endogenous attention. It is of interest that it was this same group of patients who had been shown previously to have a deficit in generating the endogenous P300 brain-related potential (Knight, Scabini, & Woods, 1989). The dissociation between the PSP and the tempero-parietal junction patient groups provides further evidence for separate brain systems for exogenous and endogenous orienting.

B. Reflexive and Voluntary Saccades: Fronto-Collicular Inhibition

The patient studies reviewed so far have concerned covert orienting of attention. We now turn to studies that demonstrate that there may also be separate systems for reflexive and voluntary saccadic eye movements. We first describe findings in hemianopic patients which confirm that visual signals, presented to the patient's blind visual hemifield, do produce a reflexive activation of the oculomotor system of the midbrain. We will then turn to a study that shows that lesions of a specific region of the dorsolateral prefrontal cortex for controlling voluntary saccades also produce disinhibition of this midbrain orienting reflex.

1. Blindsight: Saccade Inhibition by Signals in the Hemianopic Field

What visuomotor function is preserved when *only* the retinotectal pathway is competent to process visual input? Humans who become hemianopic due to destruction of the primary visual (striate) cortex are rendered clinically blind in the entire hemifield contralateral to the lesion, and cannot see even salient signals, such as a waving hand, within the scotoma (the blind area). They are unable to report such events and deny any awareness of them. In no other animals, including monkeys, do striate cortex lesions produce such profound and lasting blindness. It is thus clear that the geniculo-striate pathway in humans is dominant over the phylogenetically older retinotectal pathways. It is perhaps not surprising that the neuroscience community came to view the older pathway as being vestigial in humans, providing little service to normal vision.

Yet, it is remarkable how well these patients compensate for their visual loss. With time, they get about beautifully and their function in everyday life gives only an occasional hint that they have lost half their visual field. Recent studies in hemianopic human patients have provided some evidence that this remarkable compensation may be mediated, in part, by preserved retinotectal visual pathways. These pathways process information that, although not accessible to conscious awareness, can nevertheless trigger orienting responses toward the hemianopic field. This "blindsight" has been demonstrated by requiring hemianopic subjects to move their eyes or reach toward signals that they cannot "see" and by employing forced-choice discrimination tasks (Weiskrantz, 1986). The physiologic mechanisms mediating blindsight remain uncertain, and the role of the retinotectal pathway is controversial. In some patients there is "residual vision," which could be mediated by spared geniculostriate fibers, and which could reflect degraded cortical vision near the perceptual threshold. Other investigators propose that blindsight reflects processing of visual input from retinotectal afferents to the superior colliculus.

Figure 4 shows an experiment used to demonstrate that blindsight can be mediated by extrageniculate visual pathways (Rafal, Smith, Krantz, Cohen, & Brennan, 1990). It shows that a peripheral visual signal, for which the individual has no conscious awareness, reflexively activates the midbrain oculomotor system. This experiment studied patients who had suffered an occipital stroke destroying the geniculo-striate pathway; they were blind in the visual field opposite the lesion and could not report the presence or absence of stimuli presented there. They maintained fixation on the middle of a video display, and on each trial made a response to the appearance of a target in the *intact* hemifield. Blindsight was inferred from the effect which resulted from the presentation of an unseen distractor in the blind hemifield (which had the same eccentricity and luminance change as the saccade target), simultaneous with or immediately preceding the target.

The results (Figure 5) showed that unseen distractor signals presented to the blind, temporal (but not nasal) hemifield of hemianopic patients increased the latency of saccades directed to targets presented in the intact visual field. These results provide direct evidence that there is a reflexive activation of retinotectal pathways to prime the oculomotor system, and that this activation, possibly by inhibition of the contralateral superior colliculus, slows saccades to the opposite field.

In contrast to the hemianopic patients, the performance of normal subjects in this task was interesting. The normal control subjects did not show any inhibitory effect of the distractor. These subjects always saw both the target and distractor. They were instructed, in one block, to saccade always to the left, and in another to saccade always to the right. They were told to ignore the distractor. In this experiment, where they knew the location of the signal to which they had to respond and the one that they had to ignore, they seemed able to inhibit the effects of the distractor; the distractor had no effect on their saccade latency. This difference between hemianopic patients and normal subjects is striking. The results in the patients demonstrate a midbrain mediated reflexive orienting to signals that the patient cannot see. The results in

Fixation

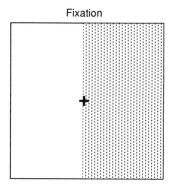

Target and distractor   or   Target only

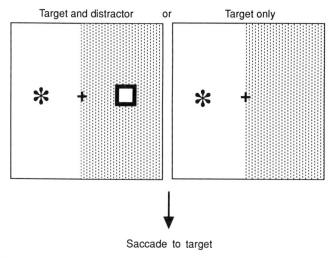

Saccade to target

FIGURE 4

Experiment for a patient with right hemianopia. The hemianopic field is depicted by stippling. The task was to make a saccade to the asterisk on the left (in the intact field) as soon as it was seen to brighten. The patient did not see the box on the right. On some trials the box on the right brightened—the distractor. On blocks in which the right eye was patched the distractor was in the nasal hemifield; on blocks in which the left eye was patched the distractor was in the temporal hemifield. In this experiment the effect of the unseen distractor on saccade latency was measured compared to the no distractor condition.

the normal subjects seem to indicate that for this reflex to be manifest, it may be *necessary that the individual not be able to see the distractor.* When the subjects become aware of the distractor, they are then able to *inhibit this primitive midbrain reflex.* This interpretation is supported by studies in normal subjects by Lambert and Hockey (1991). They found that the attention-capturing effect of perceptually salient cues tended to diminish with practice, whereas the attention-capturing ef-

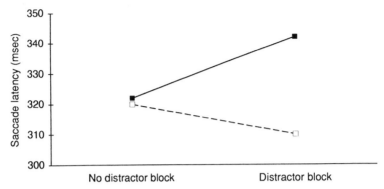

FIGURE 5

Mean latency for saccades to targets in the intact field for five hemianopic patients in the distractor and no distractor conditions. In one session the distractor in the blind hemifield was nasal (open square, dashed line) and in another it was temporal (solid square, solid line) to fixation.

fects of *less* salient peripheral cues did not. Lambert and Hockey suggested that subjects may need to be consciously aware of the cue in order to suppress orienting to it.

If this interpretation is correct, then it should be possible for normal subjects to inhibit reflexive orienting only when they can predict its location and develop a strategic set to inhibit signals there. To test this notion, Rafal, Henik, and Smith (1991) tested normal subjects under monocular conditions in a task in which the subjects made saccades to targets which appeared unpredictably on the right or left. Attention was summoned by noninformative peripheral precues, and the benefits and costs of attention were calculated relative to a central precue condition (similar to the experiment shown in Figure 1). Both the benefits and costs of orienting attention were greater when attention was summoned by signals in the temporal hemifield. This study confirms that the midbrain reflex found in hemianopics does occur in normal subjects. The fact that this reflexive effect was not manifest in the normal control subjects in the hemianopic study seems to suggest that this primitive reflex can be modulated under circumstances where a strategic set can be employed to inhibit it.

2. Effect of Frontal Eye Field Lesions on Reflexive and Voluntary Saccades As shown in Figure 3, our studies of patients with dorsolateral prefrontal cortex lesions did not reveal a defect in covert orienting specific to either endogenous or exogenous cueing. In another recent study, however, we showed that lesions of one specific area of the frontal lobes, the frontal eye fields, do affect *saccade* latency, and that these lesions have opposite effects on endogenously activated and visually guided saccades to external signals. In this experiment, exogenously triggered saccades were made to peripheral targets appearing either contralateral or ipsilateral to the lesion. Endogenously generated saccades were made in response to an arrow in the center of the display which pointed toward the field either contralateral or ipsilateral to the lesion (Rafal, Henik, & Rhodes, in press).

As shown in Figure 6, endogenous saccades were slower to the contralesional field, whereas exogenously triggered saccades were faster to the contralesional field. These results indicate that frontal eye field lesions have two separate effects on eye movement: (1) The frontal eye fields are involved in generating endogenous saccades and lesions in this region and therefore increase their latency; (2) The frontal eye fields have inhibitory connections to the colliculus, and lesions in this area result in disinhibition of the colliculus and a consequent decrease in latency for reflexive saccades to exogenous signals. Does this result reflect a more efficient detection due to the work of an uninhibited colliculus or does it reflect an uninhibited oculomotor reaction? When the same subjects were asked to make key press responses to peripheral targets, they had *slower* RTs for targets appearing in the contralesional field. That is, using the same display, opposite effects were found for

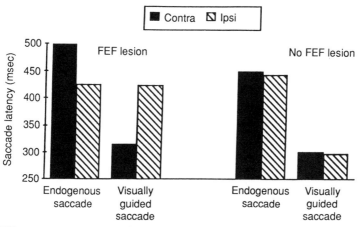

FIGURE 6

Mean saccade latencies for nine patients with lesions of frontal eye field, and for seven control patients with prefrontal cortex lesions not involving frontal eye fields. For the patients with frontal eye field lesions, saccade latencies are longer for endogenously generated saccades to the contralesional field, and shorter for visually guided saccades toward the contralesional field.

saccade and key press responses. Responses were faster to contralesional signals specifically when the response was a saccade.

Pashler, Carrier, and Hoffman (1993) found converging evidence in
normal subjects that exogenously triggered saccades are automatic and
do not tap resources requiring cortical involvement, whereas endogenously generated saccades do. Endogenous saccades result in a psychological refractory period for other tasks, and exogenously triggered
saccades do not.

C. Can Reflexive Covert Orienting Be Inhibited?
Effects of Normal Aging

The last section showed that visual signals reflexively activate the
oculomotor system through midbrain pathways, and that this reflex can
be inhibited by the frontal eye fields. Is this also the case for covert shifts
of attention? Can reflexive covert orienting of attention also be inhibited? That is, if subjects are instructed to actively inhibit these signals—
not just to ignore them, but to move their attention away from them—
are they able to do so? One way of looking at this question is with
experiments in which a peripheral cue predicts that a target will appear
in the *opposite* visual field. In one such experiment (Posner et al., 1982)
a peripheral cue was valid on 20% of trials: The cue instructed the
subject to expect the target in the visual field *opposite to the cue*. The
subjects were neurologically normal young adults. Results showed that
for short cue–target intervals of 50–200 msec, detection RT was faster at
the location of the cue, even though the task conditions gave the subjects a strong incentive to inhibit orienting to the cue signal and to shift
their attention toward to contralateral hemifield instead. Warner, Juola,
and Koshino used a modification of this paradigm to show that, with
practice, subjects were able to inhibit this reflexive orienting of attention to the cue (Warner, Juola, & Koshino, 1990).

In a comparison of peripheral and central cues, Folk and Hoyer
(1992) showed that older individuals oriented attention to both kinds of
cues just as effectively as did younger subjects. We have examined the
effects of normal aging on the ability to *inhibit* reflexive orienting to
peripheral signals using 10 young adults (mean age = 27) and 10 older
subjects (mean age = 69). The results for the young subjects are shown
on the top of Figure 7, and the data for the older subjects are shown on
the bottom. In this experiment, a faster detection RT for targets at the
cued location (solid lines) indicates that the subject had oriented to that
location at the time the target appeared. A faster detection RT for targets
appearing in the field contralateral to the cue (dashed lines) indicates
that the subject was successful in inhibiting the reflexive orienting to

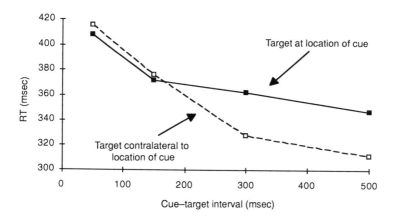

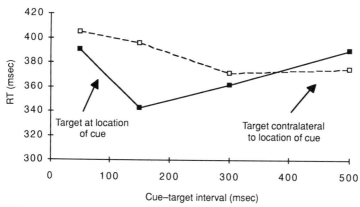

FIGURE 7

Reflexive orienting toward and endogenous orienting away from a peripheral cue in younger (top) and older (bottom) adults.

the cue, and in reorienting toward the opposite hemifield where the target was expected.

Figure 7 (top) shows that the younger subjects had a small reflex orienting effect which was present only at the shortest (50 msec) interval. By the 300 msec interval, detection RT is quicker for targets in the field contralateral to the cue. The older subjects (bottom) have a much more robust and prolonged reflex orienting effect. Detection RT is faster for targets appearing at the location of the cue through the 300 msec cue–target interval. Only at the longest (500 msec) interval do these subjects show evidence for having reoriented way from the cue.

This result confirms that there is an automatic orienting, a so-called visual grasp reflex, toward a peripheral signal. Attention is summoned, at least briefly, to the stimulated location even when the individual has an incentive to try to ignore it (Yantis & Jonides, 1990; Folk, Remington, & Johnston, 1992). These findings also suggest that it is possible to study how endogenous mechanisms inhibit and regulate this reflex, what neural structures mediate this control, and how they are affected by age and disease processes.

One possibility is that the effects of aging result from a decline in noradrenergic projections to the prefrontal cortex. Aged monkeys, impaired on delayed alternation tasks, have reduced catecholamine in the prefrontal cortex (Goldman-Rakic & Brown, 1981). In humans, noradrenergic deficiency affects covert orienting of visual attention, both in normal adults treated with catecholamine blocking drugs (Clark, Geffen, & Geffen, 1989), and in a subgroup of Alzheimer's disease patients with catecholamine depletion (Freed, Corkin, Growdon, & Nissen, 1988).

Having dissected the neurology of externally and endogenously triggered attention shifts and eye movements, the job now is to figure out how they work together in regulating normal orienting behavior. We are beginning to get a picture of what these neural structures are, and how each, with its own evolutionary history and place in ontogeny, contributes to adaptive orienting. How these subsystems are integrated and coordinated is a key question for understanding both normal and deranged orienting behavior. Inhibitory processes help regulate this complex network for spatial orienting to integrate flexible and efficient responses to the outside world with the ongoing goals of voluntary behavior. When these inhibitory processes are working as they should, we seem to handle the competing demands of the outside world and those needed for planned activity so seemlessly that these subsystems seem to be one. Damage to the brain reveals how important these inhibitory processes are in making these subsystems work together, and just how dependent we are on them for coherent thought and action. Now we consider inhibition of return (Figure 1). As we will see, this is a midbrain reflex that may play a key role in integrating and coordinating reflexive and voluntary spatial orienting.

D. Inhibition of Return

1. Its Relationship to Attention and Eye Movements   When attention is summoned by a peripheral luminance change, the initial facilitation of detection at the cued location is followed (as shown in Figure 1) by a slowing of detection at the same location. Posner and Cohen (1984) called this inhibitory effect the *inhibition of return*. Because inhibition of return does not occur when covert attention is allocated endogenously, Posner and Cohen (1984) suggested that it may reflect sensory processes rather than being related to the deployment of attention. A number of other observations, however, are not consistent with a low-level process of sensory masking or habituation. The effect is quite long lasting (3 sec or more; Tassinari et al., 1989). If an eye movement is made after the cue signal, the inhibition does not move with the retina but seems to tag the location in the environment (Posner & Cohen, 1984). Indeed, if the stimulated object moves, inhibition of return moves with it, even into the opposite hemifield (Tipper, Driver, & Weaver, 1991).

Because inhibition of return is activated during reflexive orienting of attention and not with endogenous shifts of covert attention, Maylor (Maylor, 1985; Maylor & Hockey, 1985) proposed that inhibition of return is specifically associated with exogenously triggered orienting of attention. However, in addition to summoning covert attention, visual signals also activate the oculomotor system as was evident in our study of hemianopic patients. This oculomotor activation may be quite independent from any other effect on covert attention. It is possible, then, that inhibition of return occurs following visual signals not because it is a specific manifestation of a separate neural system for exogenous covert orienting, but because it is the result of activation of the oculomotor system independent of covert orienting (exogenous or endogenous).

A number of lines of converging evidence now suggest that inhibition of return is generated by activation of the oculomotor system. First, although inhibition of return does not occur after endogenously deployed shifts of covert attention, it does occur after an endogenously generated saccade (Posner et al., 1985; Rafal, Calabresi, Brennan, & Sciolto, 1989). If a saccade was made to a peripheral location and the eyes are then moved back to the center, key press responses were delayed to signals presented at the location to which the saccade had just been made. Moreover, simply preparing an endogenous saccade was sufficient to generate inhibition of return, even when no saccade was actually made, and even when no peripheral signal occurred prior to the target (Rafal et al., 1989).

Next we review evidence that the neural substrate for generating inhibition of return involves the midbrain retinotectal pathway, and evidence from developmental studies that also link inhibition of return to midbrain structures necessary for making saccadic eye movements.

2. Neural Substrates for Generating Inhibition of Return   The importance of the retinotectal pathway in generating inhibition of return was demonstrated by converging evidence from two sources: (1) it was deficient in PSP patients with midbrain degeneration, and (2) it was more efficiently activated in normal subjects by signals presented to the temporal hemifield. The temporal-nasal hemifield asymmetries have been demonstrated in normal subjects as well as in individuals who do not have functioning visual cortex, that is, neurologic patients with strokes of the occipital lobe and newborn infants.

In these studies, brightening of a peripheral box was used to summon attention. On half the trials, however, this first cue was then followed by brightening of a center box which summoned attention back to the center. The target then appeared with equal probability either at the first cued location, or in the uncued contralateral visual field. Inhibition of return was measured as a slower detection RT for targets at the location of the first cue. In the PSP patients, inhibition of return was compared in the vertical and horizontal planes. In the normal subjects, we compared inhibition of return in temporal and nasal hemifields under monocular viewing conditions. The PSP patients showed no inhibition of return in the vertical plane (Posner et al., 1985), as shown in Figure 8. In normal subjects (Rafal et al., 1989), signals presented to the temporal hemifield generated a larger inhibition of return (Figure 9). These converging results suggest that inhibition of return is mediated by midbrain extrageniculate visual pathways.

3. Development of Inhibition of Return   The newborn human infant is a collicular creature in terms of its visual function. Under monocular viewing, for example, newborns will orient predominantly to signals presented in the temporal hemifield (Lewis & Maurer, 1992; Lewis, Maurer, & Blackburn, 1985; Rothbart et al., 1991). Perceptual processing

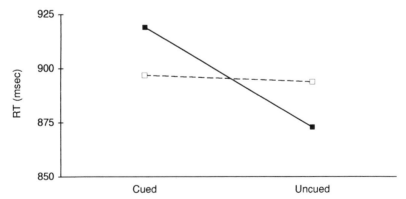

FIGURE 8

Mean RT in experiment comparing inhibition of return in the vertical (open square, dashed line) and horizontal (solid square, solid line) plane in six PSP patients. Inhibition of return is manifest as slower detection RTs for targets appearing at the recently cued location and is not activated by cues in the vertical plane.

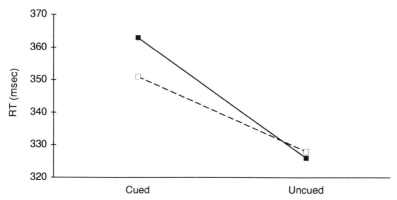

FIGURE 9

Mean RT in experiment comparing inhibition of return in temporal (solid square, solid line) and nasal (open square, dashed line) hemifields of normal subjects. Inhibition of return is manifest as slower detection RTs for targets appearing at the recently cued location, and is larger when the cue is presented to the temporal hemifield.

of stimuli in the nasal hemifield does not emerge until about 2 months of age.

Developmental studies of inhibition of return in human infants (Clohessy et al., 1991; Harmon, Posner, & Rothbart, 1992) also suggest a linkage between inhibition of return and the eye movement system. The ability of visual signals at different eccentricities to activate inhibition of return matures in concert with the development of the infant's ability to execute accurate saccades to targets at these varying eccentricities. As an infant gets older, the amplitude of accurate saccades to peripheral targets increases. At any given age, the eccentricity of signals that are effective in activating inhibition of return is restricted to the amplitude to which accurate saccades can be made. Recently, Valenza, Simion, Umilta, and Paiusco (1992) showed that newborn infants have inhibition of return following orienting saccades to precues.

4. Can Inhibition of Return Be Inhibited? Inhibition of return is activated reflexively through primitive midbrain pathways. How automatic is this reflex? Can it be inhibited voluntarily when it is not appropriate to the task at hand? Berger (1992) compared the influence of peripheral signals in activating inhibition of return at attended and unattended locations. Normal subjects made simple RT key press responses on detecting a target which followed a predictive (80%) central arrow cue (on 33% of trials the central cue was a neutral diamond shape). On each trial, 500 msec after the central arrow cue, a peripheral box brightened at the location cued by the arrow, in the opposite field or in the center of the display. Each of these peripheral cue types occurred with equal probability, and they were not predictive with regard to the location of the forthcoming target. Subjects were instructed to keep the eyes fixed, to allocate attention as indicated by the central arrow, and to "ignore" the peripheral box brightening. The target occurred either simultaneously with the peripheral cue, 100 msec after its onset, or 750 msec after its onset. For our purposes of examining inhibition of return, only the data from the 750 msec peripheral cue–target interval are shown in Figure 10.

Figure 10 shows that subjects did use the predictive value of the central arrow to allocate their attention. Detection RT was fastest when the target appeared at the locations cued by the arrow, and slowest when the target appeared in the field opposite the locations cued by the arrow. Figure 10 also shows the effect of each type of peripheral cue within each central cue condition. Regardless of whether the peripheral box brightened at the attended location or unattended location, it was equally effective in activating inhibition of return. That is, inhibition of return was generated by signals occurring at an attended location, and was manifest even though attention was maintained at that location. We have evidence, then, that inhibition of return is activated automatically, and that its effects occur independent of where attention is voluntarily allocated. The results shown in Figure 10 did not give any evidence that

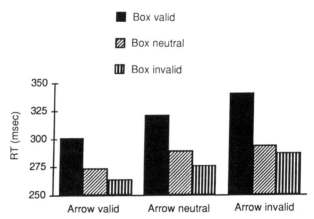

FIGURE 10

Mean detection RT in msec for targets occurring at the attended (valid arrow) condition compared to unattended (invalid arrow) condition and neutral arrow conditions. For each arrow cue condition the effects of each peripheral box cue (valid, neutral, and invalid) are shown for targets occurring 750 msec after onset of the peripheral box cue. Inhibition of return is generated regardless of whether the peripheral cue occurs at attended or unattended locations.

the magnitude of inhibition of return is suppressed at the attended location; that is, there is no evidence that subjects in this experiment were able to voluntarily suppress inhibition of return at a location at which they were expecting a target. In a more recent experiment, however, in which the arrow cue was presented immediately before the target, some reduction of inhibition of return was found. So while inhibition of return is a very autonomous reflex, it may be possible to inhibit it with voluntary effort.

Can inhibition of return be inhibited when the location of the forthcoming target is certain? Is it a bias to be less responsive to one location relative to others? To answer these questions, an experiment was done to determine whether inhibition of return would be produced even when a target signal could only occur at one location—a situation where there is the strongest incentive to maintain attention at only one location. Normal subjects made simple RT key press responses to signals that always occurred at the same place; in half the subjects all targets occurred in the left field, and in half they were presented in the right field. Targets occurred on half the trials, and the other half of the trials were catch trials. Each trial began either with brightening of a peripheral box where the target could occur, or with brightening of a box at the center of the display. This first cue was followed by brightening of the center box 500 msec after onset of the first cue. On trials in which a target appeared, it occurred 500–1000 msec after onset of the central brightening second cue. Results showed that detection RT was slower when the first cue was a peripheral brightening than when it was a central brightening. That is, inhibition of return occurred even when there was no alternative location at which a target could occur, and the subject had a strong incentive to maintain attention at that location.

E. What Is Inhibited by Inhibition of Return?

In their initial description of inhibition of return, Posner and Cohen (1984) suggested that it was a mechanism for integrating attention and eye movements which served to favor novelty in visual scanning. One way in which it might accomplish this is to produce a motor bias which affects the way the eyes move next.

The biasing of motor responses seems to be a property of collicular processing. For example, it has been shown that when adults are presented with bilateral signals under monocular viewing conditions, they exhibit a strong bias to saccade to the temporal hemifield; yet when the same signals are presented in a temporal order judgment task, no temporal bias is evident (Posner & Cohen, 1980; Shulman, 1984). Similarly, when the effect of inhibition of return on responses to bilateral simultaneous stimulation was examined, the same dissociation was found between perceptual and oculomotor tasks: Inhibition of return biased the direction of a saccade toward the location that had not been recently stimulated, but had no influence on temporal order judgments (Posner et al., 1985). Inhibition of return may simply be a motor bias which does not affect perceptual processing at the tagged location.

In some recent experiments we tested whether the effect of inhibition of return was specifically on the direction of the next saccade (Rafal, Egly, & Rhodes, in press). As in the previous experiments, a peripheral cue was followed by a central brightening and then by a target which occurred with equal likelihood either at the first cued location or in the opposite field. Normal subjects were tested in two conditions: prosaccade and antisaccade. In one block, their task was to make a saccade to the peripheral target; in another block, they made a saccade to the field opposite the target. The results showed that when the target appeared at the recently cued location, saccade latency was longer in *both* saccade tasks. That is, inhibition of return delayed the latency of the response to a signal appearing at the tagged location—even when that response was to make a saccade to a novel location. Taken together the evidence seems to indicate that inhibition of return may bias motor responses, but the bias is not specific to the direction of saccades, rather, it appears to tag a location (or an object appearing there) and affects subsequent responses to events occurring there.

Other observations, however, suggest that inhibition of return may not be adequately understood strictly in terms of location tagging. There are circumstances in which it can bias the direction of a saccade. Dobkin and Abrams (1992) and Rafal et al. (in press) showed inhibition of return to affect the latency of endogenous saccades (from a central arrow) toward the cued location. The findings of Posner et al. (1985) mentioned earlier also demonstrate that inhibition of return can bias saccade direction when bilateral targets are presented. So neither a location tagging or a alternation bias account can adequately accommodate all the emerging data. It may be that inhibition of return is not a unitary phenomenon. Tipper, Weaver, Jerreat, and Burak (1994) have recently advanced a perspective in which inhibition of return has evolved with the increasing demands of visual cognition during phylogeny. They propose that inhibition of return may have both a more primitive location-based operation, and a more sophisticated and phylogenetically newer object-based operation. In lower vertebrates, it may have been a tectal reflex to bias exogenously triggered orienting. Its behavior in humans, however, suggests a more sophisticated mechanism. Its long duration (3 sec or more (Posner et al., 1985; Tassinari et al., 1989) and the observation that the inhibitory effect can move with an object at a tagged location (Tipper et al., 1991) suggest something more than a primitive subcortical reflex. We suggest that inhibition of return may be activated either by visual stimulation or by endogenous oculomotor pathways from the cortex. The location tag generated by the colliculus might then also be made available to cortical, object-based representations. The behavior of these two inhibition of return phenomenon might be quite different depending on how inhibition of return is generated, and what level of representation is tapped by the task at hand.

F. What Is the Function of Inhibition of Return?

In their initial description of inhibition of return, Posner and Cohen (1984) suggested that it was a mechanism for integrating attention and eye movements which served to favor novelty in visual scanning. It may also be important for coordinating responses to exogenous and endogenous information. In everyday life, exogenous sensory signals are constantly competing with endogenous control for access to the oculomotor apparatus. An inhibitory mechanism for mediating between them is required. There are adaptive advantages to orienting automatically to new sensory signals occurring in the visual periphery. However, it is also necessary to be able to control visual attention and eye movements endogenously under voluntary guidance. Although automatic orienting in response to new and salient events occurring in our visual periphery serves an important defensive and social function, its tight linkage with the generation of inhibition of return may permit us to search our environment strategically, under voluntary control, without continual distraction by repeated extraneous stimulation.

IV. SUMMARY OF INHIBITORY EFFECTS IN SPATIAL ORIENTING

We have looked at three kinds of inhibitory processes involved in spatial selection. One occurs at unattended locations and biases behavior by acting at a late level of selection for action. Clinical extinction, associated chiefly with posterior association cortex lesions, may represent a striking amplification of this inhibitory effect. Inhibition of return is a location and object tagging mechanism generated reflexively by midbrain oculomotor pathways. It induces a bias for novelty in exploratory behavior, and helps to arbitrate between the competing external and internal demands on attention. The third type of inhibitory process, mediated by cortical mechanisms for endogenous control over attention and eye movements, inhibits midbrain-mediated reflexive orienting.

This last kind of inhibitory process is perhaps the most relevant to the understanding of skilled performance. It is this kind of inhibition that is involved in the efficient control of automatic processes in the service of goal-directed behavior. These inhibitory mechanisms are the business of the anterior attention system of the brain which mediates mental activities related to effort, vigilance, and a working memory scratch pad accessible to conscious awareness. The remainder of this chapter will attempt to apply the framework developed for spatial attention to these higher cognitive processes of the anterior attention system involved in the skilled use of language.

It is important to keep in mind that brain systems for spatial attention have their own unique evolutionary history: a subcortical pathway mediating primitive reflexes overlaid by a cortical system for voluntary endogenous orienting. Because we turn now to language skills, a domain that is unique to human beings, we should not expect to find the same kind of biologic implementation. Nevertheless, as with models of spatial attention, those of word processing also incorporate separate automatic-reflexive and voluntary-controlled mechanisms. These also involve facilitation and interference, and time variables play a major role in the emergence of strategic controlled processing. Moreover, similar to the domain of spatial attention, the controllability of automatic processing has been a controversial issue.

V. INHIBITORY MECHANISMS IN WORD PROCESSING

Attention can be oriented not only to events occurring on the sensory surface—as in the case of spatial orienting— but also to internal representations such as words, images, or memories. Posner (1978) suggested that the spatial attention system can be regarded as a model system. We now turn to words and their meanings, and attempt to apply the same framework used for visual attention. We will look at some aspects of language processing which appear to be automatic and others which are under voluntary control. Toward this end, we will examine the neurology of two phenomena used to study the orienting of attention in language or word processing: the Stroop effect and semantic priming. We will consider both normal performance and the effects of disease processes such as Parkinson's disease, schizophrenia, and focal lesions of the cerebral cortex.

Skilled reading, like any other skilled performance, should reflect mastery or the ability to manipulate the processed material and to accommodate to situational demands and constraints (see Logan, 1985, for a similar view). This means that skilled performance should reflect both automaticity and control. Automaticity may be manifested by the fact that reading draws nothing, or very small amounts, from limited mental resources, and control may be manifested by the ability to ignore a word or inhibit its processing as the prevailing conditions require.

A. The Stroop Effect

One of the most cited examples for automaticity and uncontrollability is the Stroop effect (see MacLeod, 1991, for a recent review). Subjects are asked to name the ink color of a word and ignore the meaning of the word (e.g., when presented with the word *green* in red they are supposed to answer "red"). Ink color naming is slower when the ink color and the word meaning are incongruent (e.g., *green* in red) than when they are congruent (e.g., *red* in red), or when they are neutral (e.g., *xxx* or a noncolor word in red). That is, the irrelevant word interferes with processing the ink color. Word reading is initiated without intention, and apparently in spite of the subjects' attempts to suppress it. In experiments that employ successive presentations of single words, the interference effect (reaction time difference between neutral and incongruent conditions) is relatively large and stable, whereas the facilitation effect (reaction time difference between congruent and neutral conditions) is small and may not reach significance. Here, we consider a number of converging lines of evidence that the facilitory and interference effects, measured in this kind of Stroop paradigm, are separable phenomena which can be dissociated both in normal subjects and by brain injury.

The Stroop effect is considered to be a good example of automatic word reading because the word, which is irrelevant, cannot be shut off and intrudes on the subject even though he or she make an effort to ignore it. The automatic processing of words in skilled readers accounts for why reading seems so effortless. Clearly, automaticity here is an important aspect of skilled performance. We would like to emphasize, however, that skill should be evidenced not only in the unintended reading of the irrelevant word, but also in the ability to inhibit such processing when necessary for the task at hand. This ability to control reading would be manifested here in a reduced Stroop effect or a reduced interference. Moreover, the idea that this ability is tied to skill level suggests that such an effect should be stronger with skilled readers than with unskilled readers.

To determine the effects of language competence on facilitory and inhibitory components of the Stroop effect, Tzelgov, Henik, and Leiser (1990) investigated inhibition of word reading with Hebrew-Arabic bilinguals. The expected language (i.e., the irrelevant dimension) and congruency were manipulated in two separate groups of bilinguals. One group was Arabic speakers, who were also fluent in Hebrew. The other group was Hebrew speakers who also knew Arabic. In one session, 80% of the stimuli were in one language and only 20% were in the other language. In a second session, subjects were exposed to the reversed proportion of trials. Subjects were influenced by this manipulation only in their preferred language. That is, they were able to inhibit the Stroop effect in the expected (80%) language only when it was their native language. They were unable to show this reduction in the effect in their second language. As can be seen in Figure 11, all subjects showed Stroop effects when stimuli were presented in either Hebrew or Arabic. However, for Arabic speakers, the effect, in Arabic, was smaller when Arabic was expected (76 msec) than when unexpected (121 msec—i.e., when Hebrew was expected), and the opposite was true for Hebrew stimuli (122 msec when Arabic was expected and 109 msec when unexpected). Hebrew speakers showed the opposite pattern. For them, the effect, in Hebrew, was smaller when Hebrew was expected (100 msec) than when unexpected (136 msec—i.e., when Arabic was expected), but no difference due to expectations for Arabic stimuli (61 msec when Hebrew was expected and 56 msec when unexpected).

These results provide evidence for both automaticity (i.e., Stroop effect) and control (i.e., reduction of Stroop effect under certain conditions). The reduction in the Stroop effect was present in the native language, but not in the second language. The ability to suppress word reading processes which are usually automatic is thus dependent on the

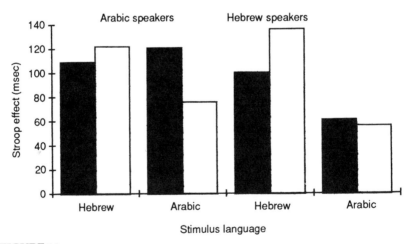

FIGURE 11

Stroop effect (incongruent minus congruent) in msec for Hebrew and Arabic under different language expectations. Dark bars = expected language Hebrew; white bars = expected language Arabic.

degree of language competence, and may be an important aspect of skilled performance in general.

The reduction of the Stroop effect may occur when specific expectations are induced. Tzelgov, Henik, and Berger (1992) tested this in a monolingual situation by manipulating the proportion of neutral trials in order to induce different expectations as to the forthcoming stimulus. If subjects can inhibit reading the irrelevant words, they should be in a better position to do so when there is a large proportion of words that deserve the application of such inhibition than when there is just a slim chance that such a stimulus will appear, on a given trial. We found that the larger the proportion of neutral words, the larger the interference effect. This manipulation did not affect the facilitory component. When subjects were expecting a large proportion of color words (i.e., only a small proportion of neutral trials), they were able to inhibit processing of the interfering word. Because in most Stroop experiments the proportion of neutrals is relatively small, it is likely that the magnitude of the interference effect reported in many studies is an underestimate of the potential interference from word reading.

From these effects of language competence and proportion of neutral words, it is clear that it is possible to inhibit at least partially some of the automatic effects of word reading. Note that the effects of these particular manipulations seem to influence the interference effect specifically without affecting facilitation effects. Although subjects do seem to be able to inhibit automatic word reading to some degree, it bears emphasis that automatic word reading was not completely eliminated in any of these studies.

Logan (1980) and Logan and Zbrodoff (1979) reported that increasing the proportion of congruent (vs. incongruent) stimuli augmented the Stroop effect (see also Cheesman & Merikle, 1986; Eglin & Hunter, 1990). Logan (1980) suggested that the color's name acted as a prime. In several studies, Tzelgov and Henik (1990, 1992) manipulated the proportion of congruent (vs. incongruent) trials and the proportion of neutral (noncolor word) trials orthogonally. Changing the ratio of congruent to incongruent trials affected mainly the facilitory component, whereas changing the proportion of neutral trials influenced only the interference component. It seems that when one changes the ratio of congruent to incongruent trials, one changes the informative nature of the irrelevant dimension (the word); when there are many congruent trials, it pays to pay attention to them because this may facilitate color processing. A similar kind of modulation of interference effects, based on expectation of the likelihood of incongruent information, has also been reported in flanker interference tasks (Gratton, Coles, & Donchin, 1992).

Stroop effects are usually taken as examples for automatic, uncontrolled word reading. Yet, it is clear that people are able to inhibit word reading to a certain degree. Word reading seems automatic because it interferes with color naming and cannot be suppressed completely. However, it can be controlled, at least to a certain degree, when advanced information about the nature of the stimuli is provided. Moreover, inhibition of word reading requires language proficiency. Individuals who are not proficient in a language may show the Stroop effect if they are familiar with the stimulus language but they are not able to inhibit word reading in that language. Developmental studies show that the Stroop effect increases and then decreases as age and reading experience increase (Schadler & Thissen, 1981; Schiller, 1966). Word reading becomes automatic gradually, as reading skill develops, but later on it may be reduced at will. Thus it seems that both automaticity and control are important features of skill. However, we would like to emphasize that the more advanced phase of skilled performance is not automaticity but control.

B. Biological Aspects of the Stroop Effect

What neural mechanisms are related to the Stroop effect? Perret (1974) reported an enlarged Stroop effect due to left hemisphere lesions, and suggested that the frontal lobe is involved in inhibiting reading of the irrelevant word. On the other hand, studies using lateralized presentations to test for hemispheric asymmetries in normal subjects have produced inconsistent results (see MacLeod, 1991, for a review).

Several authors (e.g., Brown & Marsden, 1988; Hietanen & Teravainen, 1988) have reported that Parkinson's disease (PD) patients showed deficient performance on the Stroop task. Stern, Tetrud, Martin, Kutner, and Langston (1990) found that young people who had parkinsonism induced by the toxic drug MPTP also had a deficient ability to inhibit word reading. Henik, Singh, Beckley, and Rafal (in press) measured both Stroop facilitation and interference in early onset and late onset Parkinson's disease patients. The RT interference effect of the patients was not different from the age-matched controls, but the *facilitory* effect was *larger* in both patient groups. The fact that early and late onset PD patients showed an enlarged facilitory effect suggested that the basal ganglia has a role in inhibiting automatic cognitive processes. Older patients with late onset Parkinson's disease also showed a significantly larger interference effect in their error rates, than their age-matched controls. This effect may not be related to basal ganglia damage but to a dementing process affecting the cerebral cortex in the older patient group. The differential effect of brain injury on the facilitation and interference effects also points to these processes being separable. These results converge with the dissociation between the facilitory and the interference components of the Stroop effect found in normal subjects; namely, the influence of the neutral proportion on the interference component and the lack of its influence on the facilitory component.

Investigations of cognitive deficiencies in Parkinson's disease patients have implicated dysfunction not only of the basal ganglia but also of the frontal cortex (e.g., Taylor, Saint-Cyr, & Lang, 1986). These patients seem to be deficient on various tasks that require frontal lobe involvement. Brown and Marsden (1988) discussed the problem of these patients in terms of employing external versus internal cues. In their study, subjects were asked to report the color of the ink or the content of the word in separate blocks of trials. The reported dimension changed between blocks of trials that were presented in a given session. Parkinson's patients performed poorly unless reminded frequently what the relevant dimension was. That is, when the patients were provided with external cueing as to their current task, their performance (on a Stroop task) did not depart from controls. In contrast, when such cues were not supplied, the Stroop effect was larger than in the control group (see also Robertson & Flowers, 1990, for a similar result with a movement task). The emerging view is that Parkinson's disease impairs the ability to inhibit certain automatic processes (possibly guided by external cues) and to select other processes (possibly internally motivated).

Carter, Robertson, and Nordahl (1992) reported that in a Stroop task, schizophrenic patients showed elevated facilitory effects and normal interference effects compared with a group of controls. A follow-up study (Carter, Robertson, Nordahl, & Chaderjian, 1993) replicated this result, and also found some differences related to illness subtypes. Whereas patients with the undifferentiated subtype of the disorder showed increased facilitation and normal interference, patients with the paranoid subtype of the disorder showed normal facilitation and increased interference. Whatever the specific pattern of deficiency, it seems that the schizophrenic patients showed reduced ability to suppress processing of the irrelevant word or to inhibit response tendencies to it.

Fronto-striatal dysfunction has been implicated in schizophrenia. Early and his colleagues (Early, Posner, Reiman, & Raichle, 1989a, 1989b; Early, Reiman, Raichle, & Spitznagel, 1987) reported a hypermetabolism of the left globus pallidus in unmedicated schizophrenic patients. They concluded that the fronto-striatal loop, which includes the basal ganglia, the medial frontal lobe (in particular, the anterior cingulate gyrus), and the dorsolateral prefrontal cortex, constituted an anterior attention system that is deranged in schizophrenia. The dorsolateral prefrontal cortex appears to have a role in maintaining information on line to enable delayed response (Goldman-Rakic, 1987). Studies using PET have implicated the anterior cingulate gyrus in selection of semantic information both in a Stroop experiment (Pardo, Pardo, Janer, & Raichle, 1990) and in generation of word meaning (Petersen, Fox, Posner, Mintun, & Raichle, 1988; Petersen, Fox, Snyder, & Raichle, 1990). The anterior attentional system is necessary for maintaining focused attention on selected information and, at the same time, suppressing other information so that the planned behavior can be carried out.

As in Parkinson's disease, the evidence in schizophrenia suggests a reduced ability to control or inhibit automatic processes (e.g., Callaway & Naghdi, 1982), to ignore extraneous stimulation, and to carry out willed intentions (Frith & Done, 1988). We might tentatively conclude that some of the symptoms of these patients groups in the Stroop and similar language tasks reflect dysfunction in a fronto-striatal circuit which normally modulates automatic cognitive operations.

C. Semantic Priming

One widely used method for studying the human semantic system is the semantic priming technique (see Neely, 1991, for a recent review). In a typical experiment the subject is presented with two successive stimuli called the prime and target, respectively. The subject is usually asked to respond overtly only to the target. The response may be determining whether the target constitutes a word, or it may be naming the target stimulus. An interesting effect that appears under these conditions is the semantic priming effect or the relatedness effect (Meyer & Schvaneveldt, 1971, 1976; Neely, 1977; Schvaneveldt & McDonald, 1981; Smith, 1979; Smith, Theodor, & Franklin, 1983). Briefly, it can be described as greater speed and accuracy of performance in responding to a target word (e.g., *DOCTOR*) when it follows a semantically-related prime (e.g., *NURSE*) than when it follows an unrelated prime (e.g., *GOD*).

Students of the semantic system have suggested that concepts are represented as nodes that are linked together to form a semantic network. The act of reading a word involves the activation of certain nodes in a semantic network which is structured around a principle of semantic or associative relatedness (e.g., Collins & Loftus, 1975). A common assumption is that the presentation of a word results in an activation of a node in the semantic network and this, in turn, causes a spread of activation to semantically related words. Because the spread of activation decays over time, it affects nodes that are close together and may have no effect (or an insignificant effect) on nodes that occupy distant areas in the network. Moreover, both the activation of lexical representation and the spread of activation to related concepts are often assumed to be obligatory or automatic (Collins & Loftus, 1975; Posner & Snyder, 1975). Automaticity is reflected in the fact that the occurrence of priming is not dependent on conscious attention or a subject's intentions, though such factors may mediate the magnitude of priming, especially at relatively long time intervals (SOA) between prime onset and target onset (Balota, 1983; Carr & Dagenbach, 1990; Dagenbach, Carr, & Wilhelmsen, 1989; Fischler, 1977; Marcel, 1980; Neely, 1977).

As with spatial orienting and the Stroop effect, semantic priming effects are both facilitatory and inhibitory. Neely (1977) showed that attended concepts were facilitated whereas unattended concepts were inhibited. In keeping with Posner and Snyder's two-process theory of priming (1975), Neely found that facilitation—but not inhibition—occurs when the interval between prime and target is short (less than 250 msec), whereas inhibition dominates at longer intervals. Moreover, similar to the ability of subjects to endogenously orient attention to a certain location in space, subjects were able to orient strategically to a category in preference to another category. For example, if the prime was the category name *bird*, subjects were able to attend to the category of *furniture*. This resulted in facilitation of targets that were examples of the furniture category and inhibition of targets that were examples of the bird category. The appearance of this pattern under long, but not under short, SOAs is consistent with the idea that it takes time to orient attention and to overcome the influence of the preexisting category organization that produces automatic priming.

Selection is also needed while processing ambiguous words. Simpson and Burgess (1985) reported that the presentation of an ambiguous word *bank* produced activation of both the dominant (*money*) and the subordinate (*river*) meanings. The dominant meaning was available first, and for a longer period of time, than the subordinate meaning. Simpson and Burgess suggested that processing ambiguous words involved both passive and active processes, and that selection of one meaning required inhibition of the other. They discussed their results within the framework of automatic and controlled processing: The passive, automatic processes activated both meanings which were manifest at short SOAs; later focusing attention on the dominant meaning was responsible for maintaining the facilitation for the dominant meaning and for inhibition of the subordinate meaning. Recently, Frost and Bentin (1992) suggested that the specific pattern of meaning activation and decay may be language dependent. They reported that in Hebrew the subordinate meaning was still maintained under the long SOA condition. This difference in the longevity of priming effects may be related to differences between English and Hebrew syntax; namely, in Hebrew, words are often not disambiguated until the end of the sentence, whereas in English ambiguity is resolved earlier in the sentence.

A whole sentence can also serve as the prime. Typically, subjects are presented with a sentence that contains an ambiguous word followed by a target for naming or lexical decision. The sentence may be biased in the direction of one of the meanings of the ambiguous word and the target word may be related to one of the meanings or to neither. Both meanings may be activated initially in spite of the context supplied by the sentence (e.g., Onifer & Swinney, 1981), but the dominant meaning can be selectively activated when the sentence is sufficiently constraining (Tabossi, 1988). Simpson and Krueger (1991) showed that the sentence may restrict the activation of either meaning. They also showed that the pattern of activation for the dominant and the subordinate meanings for unbiased sentences were similar to that which appeared in the single word prime situation (Simpson & Burges, 1985). In contrast, a biased sentence can cause the activation of one of the meanings (dominant or subordinate) and not the other. It seems that under various circumstances the presentation of an ambiguous word activates more than one meaning automatically; but context can inhibit some of the activation and restrict it to the context relevant meaning only.

In summary, the presentation of a word automatically activates its meaning and also spreads to related concepts. However, this initial pattern of activation may be molded and changed according to situational constraints in order to create a functionally efficient pattern. We again see the interplay between automatic and controlled processes, and a principle underlying skilled performance and strategic operations in general.

D. Priming Effects in Schizophrenia

As with the Stroop effect, priming has also been considered in relation to the symptomatology of schizophrenia (e.g., Frith, 1981; Maher, 1983). The abnormal associative intrusions that appear in schizophrenic speech may be due to deficient selection processes, and these may be manifest as abnormal priming effects. Maher, in particular, suggested that the priming effect should be augmented in these patients due either to their inability to inhibit activations which are not context relevant, or to a deficient decay which is abnormally protracted. Kwapil, Hegley, Chapman, and Chapman (1990) reported that schizophrenic subjects showed a larger facilitory effect, but no difference in the inhibitory effect, when compared to normal or bipolar patients. Henik, Priel, and Umansky (1992) have studied schizophrenic and normal control subjects under long and short SOAs and found no such differences between groups. Schizophrenic subjects seemed to present a somewhat less reliable priming effect under the short SOA condition (240 msec). They also showed a larger priming effect under the long SOA condition (1840 msec), but that was not significantly different from the controls.

Taking the available Stroop and priming evidence together, it appears that schizophrenics are unable to exert the same kinds of internal control over processing word stimuli that normal individuals exert. It is possible that the deficit in control reflects dysfunction of the anterior attention system. Given the discrepancies between different studies, however, more research is needed before any firm conclusions are reached with respect to the exact pattern of schizophrenic performance in word processing tasks requiring internal control.

E. Suppressing the Spread of Activation

Both the activation of a node and the spread to semantically related nodes are often considered to be automatic. It is becoming clear, however, that each of these can be affected independently by manipulating attention or in cases of brain injury. This strand of research has manipulated the degree and type of processing required of the *prime* word on lexical decisions for either indentical (identity priming) or semantically related (semantic priming) target words. If both the activation of the prime word's node and the spread to semantically related nodes are automatic and cannot be inhibited, then manipulations of the processing of the *prime* word should not lessen the priming effect in either case.

Semantic priming effects have been consistently found when the prime word requires no response (Neely, 1977; Smith et al., 1983), when it is read aloud (Henik, Friedrich, & Kellogg, 1983), when a lexical decision is made on the prime word (Fischler, 1977; Tweedy, Lapinski, & Schvaneveldt, 1977), or when semantic judgment is required (Smith et al., 1983). However, the effect is not found when the area surrounding the prime is searched for a visual probe (Hoffman & MacMillan, 1985), or when the prime word is searched for a specific letter (Friedrich, Henik, & Tzelgov, 1991; Henik et al., 1983; Smith et al., 1983). This pattern of effects is the same for English and Hebrew and does not change due to manipulation of the SOA (Henik, Friedrich, Tzelgov, & Tramer, submitted).

In contrast to semantic priming (*BUTTER–BREAD*), identity priming (*BREAD–BREAD*) was preserved even when the prime task was to search for a specified letter (Friedrich et al., 1991). Snow and Neely (1987) manipulated the prime–target similarity and found that changes in the proportion of physically similar trials (i.e., trials in which the prime and the target were identical in meaning and case), did not influence the indentity priming effect. In contrast, semantic priming was reduced significantly when most trials consisted of physically similar pairs of stimuli. The same was true when shadowing was employed as a secondary task (Posner, Sandson, Dhawan, & Shulman, 1989): Although identity priming was not affected by the secondary task, semantic priming was. A similar dissociation between identity and semantic priming was reported by Dagenbach, Carr, and colleagues (Carr & Dagenbach, 1990; Dagenbach et al., 1989) in a masked prime paradigm.

In summary, priming appears to involve two dissociable stages: one is the automatic activation of the representation of the word itself, and the other is the spread of activation to associated concepts, possibly under attentional modulation (see also Besner, Smith, & MacLeod, 1990; Smith, Besner, & Miyoshi, 1992). Under various situations the spread of activation in the network may be either actively suppressed or not maintained due to the withdrawal of limited resources away from the semantic level.

F. Neural Substrate for Word Processing

Positron emission tomography studies have demonstrated several cortical sites involved in word processing (Petersen et al., 1988; Posner, Petersen, Fox, & Raichle, 1988; Howard et al., 1992). This technique measures increases in local brain blood flow (assumed to reflect increased neural activity) during ongoing language tasks. Passive presentation of words or pronounceable nonwords activates a region of the medial occipital cortex. The left superior and middle temporal regions are activated when reading aloud visually presented text or repeating auditorily presented words. Tasks requiring active generation of semantically related words activates the dorsolateral prefrontal cortex, and activation of the anterior cingulate gyrus (probably the left) is manifest in relation to effort focused on the semantic task. This approach has lead to a cognitive-anatomical model of word processing having several components (Carr, 1992; Petersen et al., 1988; Posner et al., 1989). A posterior word form system located in the ventro-medial occipital lobe is postulated for early visual processing of written words. An anterior attention system includes the inferior dorsolateral prefrontal cortex involved in semantic processing, and the anterior cingulate gyrus, which is active in effortful attention to word meaning.

This cognitive-anatomical model has been consistent with some lesion studies associating Broca's aphasia and reduced semantic priming; the "posterior" aphasic syndrome, such as Wernicke's aphasia, does not appear to affect priming. Milberg, Blumstein, and colleagues conducted several lexical-decision priming experiments with aphasic patients (Blumstein, Milberg, & Shrier, 1982; Milberg & Blumstein, 1981; Milberg, Blumstein, & Dworetzky, 1988). Wernicke's aphasia patients showed priming effects similar to normal controls whereas Broca's aphasia patients showed an inconsistent pattern. The authors have suggested that Wernicke's patients are equipped with intact semantic representations which may be activated automatically but are inaccessible to conscious semantic decision tasks. Broca's aphasia patients "have a processing deficit in automatically accessing the lexical representation of words" (Milberg & Blumstein, 1981, p. 138). However, Katz (1988) demonstrated a priming pattern in Broca's aphasia patients similar to that of normal controls. Chenery, Ingram, and Murdoch (1990) compared high and low comprehension aphasia patients and reported that all subject groups manifested priming (note however, that while there was a significant effect of prime type in a simultaneous comparison of four prime types—superordinate related, function associate related, unrelated, and nonword—pairwise comparisons of these four conditions did not yield any significant effect).

In a recent priming study, Henik, Dronkers, Knight, and Osimani (1993) used an anatomical, rather than behavioral, criterion for patient selection. Both identity priming and semantic priming were measured in four groups of brain-injured patients with chronic focal lesions of the anterior and posterior association cortex (matched for lesion volume and other relevant clinical variables: left anterior, left posterior, right anterior, and right posterior), as well as in a group of age-matched controls. All of the lesions in the patients involved lateral association cortex in the middle cerebral artery territory. None of the lesions were posterior cerebral artery strokes and they did not involve ventral or medial occipital prestriate cortex. Thus, the word form area suggested by Carr (1992), Petersen et al. (1988), and Posner et al. (1989), and which may be implicated by the identity priming, was spared in these patients. These experiments manipulated the SOA (250 vs. 1850 msec) and the nature of prime–target relatedness. In one experiment, the related condition consisted of associative pairs (*DOCTOR–NURSE*), and in another experiment, it consisted of identical pairs (*NURSE–NURSE*).

Patients with left hemisphere lesions, whether anterior or posterior, showed impaired semantic priming. Identity priming, on the other hand, was preserved and was indistinguishable from that shown by age-matched controls and patients with focal right hemisphere lesions. The deficiency of semantic priming in the two left hemisphere lesion groups was not influenced by lesion location (anterior vs. posterior to the Rolandic fissure) or SOA. The net priming effects (RT difference between unrelated and related, or identical, trials) are depicted in Figure 12. As can be seen, although the groups differ in terms of semantic priming they are comparable with respect to their identity priming.

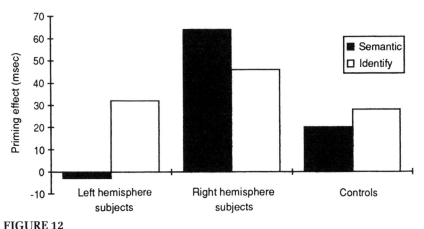

FIGURE 12

Priming effect (unrelated minus related or identical), in msec, for three groups of subjects in semantic (DOCTOR-*NURSE*) and identity (*NURSE-nurse*) priming experiments.

Our data show that semantic priming relies not only on an intact anterior system but also on an intact parieto-temporal region of the left hemisphere. Although lexical entries are accessible in spite of these brain injuries (identity priming), spread of activation is deficient (semantic priming). It is possible that spread of activation in patients with left hemisphere lesions is not eliminated completely but reduced to an ineffective level. If so, semantic priming might be reinstated in the left hemisphere lesioned patients under conditions which optimize control in normals. For example, a higher proportion of related trials may reinstate the semantic priming effect in patients just as it enhances it in normals. With normal subjects, the semantic priming effect that was eliminated when the prime was searched for a letter (Friedrich et al., 1991; Henik et al., 1983), was reinstated when the proportion of related trials was larger (Henik, Friedrich, Tzelgov, & Tramer, in press).

Experiments with normal subjects (Nakagawa, 1991) provided converging evidence for a special role of the left hemisphere in semantic priming, and for the role of the anterior attention system in mediating the inhibitory component of semantic priming. In these experiments, a prime word was presented in the center of the display and the target in either the left or right visual field. Inhibition of unrelated word meanings was found only when the target was presented in the right visual field, that is, to the left hemisphere. Moreover, this inhibitory effect for right visual field targets was eliminated when the subject's attention was occupied by a concomitant verbal shadowing task.

As with orienting to locations, orienting to words and their meanings can be activated automatically and without attention. However, attention to a certain meaning or level of processing can modulate subsequent processing of the word. Focused attention facilitates processing of meanings relevant to the context in which the word is encountered, and brings about inhibition of unattended concepts.

In what ways do the anterior and posterior attention systems interact with one another? In her studies of semantic priming, Nakagawa (1991) found that spatial orienting and semantic priming had independent and additive effects. On the other hand, some preliminary work in our laboratory relating Stroop effects to spatial orienting have indicated some interactions. Stroop interference was augmented when the color word occurred at an attended location, and was diminished when it occurred at an unattended location.

VI. CONCLUDING REMARKS

Inhibitory processes are ubiquitous and a biologic imperative. The brain goes about the business of coordinating reflexive responses with goal-directed behavior through inhibitory mechanisms. In reviewing both spatial orienting and orienting internally to representations in memory, we have seen that these inhibitory processes serve to provide a coherent experience of the world, as well as flexibility and efficiency in skilled performance. We have learned quite a bit about the neural inhibitory mechanisms involved in spatial orienting, and are beginning to learn more about the psychobiology of inhibitory processes involved in verbal learning and thinking.

This chapter has emphasized the inhibitory processes that operate quite late in attentional selection. It is well to recall Eccles' emphasis that inhibition influences information processing at "every stage of synaptic relay." It is now known, for example, that lesions of human dorsolateral prefrontal cortex result in disinhibition of tactile and auditory evoked responses which are manifest within 20–40 msec of stimulation (Yamaguchi & Knight, 1990). So prefrontal cortex not only tonically inhibits primitive reflexes, it also tonically inhibits sensory processing at the level of the thalamus (Skinner & Ynigling, 1977) to influence all subsequent perception and action.

Our understanding of the human mind has benefited from the information processing approach developed in the last few decades. Continuing progress requires an appreciation of the brain processes underlying the human mind. Any sensible account of human cognition will benefit from an appreciation of the human brain as having both a phylogenetic and ontogenetic history, and having as its *modus operandi* the opponent operation of facilitory and inhibitory mechanisms.

REFERENCES

Balota, D. E. (1983). Automatic semantic activation and episodic memory encoding. *Journal of Verbal Learning and Verbal Behavior, 22,* 88–104.

Bashinski, H. S., & Bacharach, V. R. (1980). Enhancement of perceptual sensitivity as the result of selectively attending to spatial locations. *Perception and Psychophysics, 28,* 241–248.

Baylis, G., Rafal, R., & Driver, J. (1993). Attentional set determines extinction following parietal lesions. *Journal of Cognitive Neuroscience, 5,* 453–466.

Berger, A. (1992). *Competition between endogenous and exogenous covert orienting of attention.* Unpublished master's thesis, Ben-Gurion University of the Negev.

Berti, A., & Rizzolatti, G. (1992). Visual processing without awareness: Evidence from unilateral neglect. *Journal of Cognitive Neuroscience, 4,* 345–351.

Besner, D., Smith, M. C., & MacLeod, C. M. (1990). Visual word recognition: A dissociation of lexical and semantic processing. *Journal of Experimental Psychology: Learning, Memory and Cognition, 16,* 862–869.

Blumstein, S. E., Milberg, W. P., & Shrier, R. (1982). Semantic processing in aphasia: Evidence from an auditory lexical decision task. *Brain and Language, 17,* 301–315.

Briand, K. A., & Klein, R. M. (1987). Is Posner's "beam" the same as Treisman's "glue"?: On the relation between visual orienting and feature integration theory. *Journal of Experimental Psychology: Human Perception and Performance, 13,* 228–241.

Brown, R. G., & Marsden, C. D. (1988). Internal versus external cues and the control of attention in Parkinson's disease. *Brain, 111,* 323–345.

Callaway, E., & Naghdi, S. (1982). An information processing model for schizophrenia. *Archives of General Psychiatry, 39,* 339–347.

Carr, T. H. (1992). Automaticity and cognitive anatomy: Is word recognition "automatic"? *American Journal of Psychology, 105*(2), 201–37.

Carr, T. H., & Dagenbach, D. (1990). Semantic priming and repetition priming from masked words: Evidence for a center-surround attentional mechanism in perceptual recognition. *Journal of Experimental Psychology: Learning, Memory and Cognition 16,* 341–50.

Carter, C. S., Robertson, L. C., & Nordahl, T. E. (1992). Abnormal processing of irrelevant information in chronic schizophrenia: Selective enhancement of Stroop facilitation. *Psychiatry Res, 41,* 137–46.

Carter, C. S., Robertson, L. C., Nordahl, T. E., & Chaderjian, M. C. (1993). Abnormal processing of irrelevant information in chronic schizophrenia: The role of illness subtype. *Psychiatry Research 48,* 417–426.

Cheesman, J., & Merikle, P. M. (1986). Distinguishing conscious from unconscious perceptual processes. *Canadian Journal of Psychology, 40,* 343–367.

Chenery, H. J., Ingram, J. C., & Murdoch, B. E. (1990). Automatic and volitional semantic processing in aphasia. *Brain and Language, 38,* 215–232.

Clark, C. R., Geffen, G. M., & Geffen, L. B. (1989). Catecholamines and the covert orientation of attention in humans. *Neuropsychologia, 27,* 131–139.

Clohessy, A., Posner, M. I., & Rothbart, M. K. (1991). The development of inhibition of return in early infancy. *Journal of Cognitive Neuroscience, 3,* 346–357.

Cohen, A., Ivry, R., Rafal, R., & Cohn, C. (1994). *Response code activation by signals in the neglected hemifield.* Manuscript submitted for publication.

Collins, A. M., & Loftus, E. (1975). A spreading activation theory of semantic processing. *Psychological Review, 82,* 407–428.

Corbetta, M., Miezin, F. M., Dobmeyer, S., Shulman, G. L., & Petersen, S. E. (1991). Selective and divided attention during visual discriminations of shape, color, and speed: Functional anatomy by positron emission tomography. *Journal of Neuroscience, 11*, 2383–2402.

Dagenbach, D., Carr, T. H., & Wilhelmsen, A. (1989). Task-induced strategies and near-threshold priming: Conscious effects on unconscious perception. *Journal of Memory and Language, 28*, 412–443.

Dobkin, R. S., & Abrams, R. A. (1992). Inhibition of return: Effects of attentional cueing on eye movement latencies. In *Program of the 33rd Annual Meeting of the Psychonomics Society*, (p. 45).

Early, T. S., Posner, M. I., Reiman, E. M., & Raichle, M. E. (1989a). Left striato-pallidal hyperactivity in schizophrenia. Part II: Phenomenology and thought disorder. *Psychiatric Developments, 2*, 109–121.

Early, T. S., Posner, M. I., Reiman, E. M., & Raichle, M. E. (1989b). Hyperactivity of the left striato-pallidal projection: 1. Lower level theory. *Psychiatric Developments, 7*, 85–108.

Early, T. S., Reiman, E. M., Raichle, M. E., & Spitznagel, E. L. (1987). Left globus pallidus abnormality in never-medicated patients with schizophrenia. *Proceedings of the National Academy of Sciences, 84*, 561–563.

Eccles, J. C. (1977). *The understanding of the brain* (2nd ed.). New York: McGraw-Hill.

Eglin, M., & Hunter, A. (1990). Cueing efficiency in a Stroop-like task with visual half-field presentation. *Perception and Psychophysics, 18*, 459–468.

Egly, R., & Homa, D. (1991). Reallocation of visual attention. *Journal of Experimental Psychology: Human Perception and Performance, 17*, 142–59.

Egly, R., Rafal, R. D., & Henik, A. (1992, November). *Exogenous and endogenous orienting of visual attention in detection and discrimination tasks*. Paper presented at the meeting of the Psychonomic Society, St. Louis, MO.

Fischler, I. (1977). Expectancy and associative facilitation in a lexical decision task. *Journal of Experimental Psychology: Human Perception and Performance, 3*, 18–26.

Folk, C. L., & Hoyer, W. J. (1992). Aging and shifts of visual spatial attention. *Psychology and Aging, 7*, 453–465.

Folk, C. L., Remington, R. W., & Johnston, J. C. (1992). Involuntary covert orienting is contingent on attentional settings. *Journal of Experimental Psychology: Human Perception and Performance, 18*, 1030–1044.

Freed, D. M., Corkin, S., Growdon, J. H., & Nissen, M. J. (1988). Selective attention in Alzheimer's disease: CSF correlates of behavioral impairments. *Neuropsychologia, 26*, 895–902.

Friedrich, F. J., Henik, A., & Tzelgov, J. (1991). Automatic processes in lexical access and spreading activation. *Journal of Experimental Psychology: Human Perception and Performance, 17*, 792–806.

Friedrich, F. J., Walker, J. A., & Posner, M. I. (1985). Effects of parietal lesions on visual matching: implications for reading errors. *Cognitive Neuropsychology, 2*, 253–264.

Frith, C. D. (1981). Schizophrenia: An abnormality of consciousness. In G. Underwood & R. Stevens (Eds.), *Aspects of consciousness* (pp. 437–443). New York: Academic Press.

Frith, C. D., & Done, D. J. (1988). Towards a neuropsychology of schizophrenia. *British Journal of Psychiatry 153*, 437–443.

Frost, R., & Bentin, S. (1992). Processing phonological and semantic ambiguity: Evidence from semantic priming at different SOAs. *Journal of Experimental Psychology: Learning, Memory and Cognition, 18*, 58–68.

Goldman-Rakic, P. A. (1987). Circuitry of primate prefrontal cortex and regulation of behavior by representational memory. In J. Mills & M. V. B. (Eds.), *Handbook of physiology: The nervous system V* (pp. 373–417). Bethesda, MD: Williams and Wilkins.

Golman-Rakic, P. S., & Brown, R. M. (1981). Regional changes in monoamines in cerebral cortex and subcortical structures of aging rhesus monkeys. *Neuroscience, 6,* 177–187.

Gratton, G., Coles, M. G. H., & Donchin, E. (1992). Optimizing the use of information: Strategic control of activation of responses. *Journal of Experimental Psychology: General, 121,* 480–506.

Harmon, C., Posner, M. I., & Rothbart, M. K. (1992). Spatial attention in 3-month olds: Inhibition of return at 10 and 30 degree eccentricities. *Infant Behavior and Development, 15,* 449.

Hasher, L., & Zacks, R. T. (1979). Automatic and effortul processes in memory. *Journal of Experimental Psychology: General, 108,* 356–388.

Henderson, J. M. (1991). Stimulus discrimination following covert attentional orienting to an exogenous cue. *Journal of Experimental Psychology: Human Perception and Performance, 17,* 91–106.

Henik, A., Dronkers, N. F., Knight, R. T., & Osimani, A. (1993). Differential effects of semantic and identity priming in patients with left and right hemisphere lesions. *Journal of Cognitive Neuroscience, 5,* 45–55.

Henik, A., Friedrich, F. J., & Kellogg, W. A. (1983). The dependence of semantic relatedness effects upon prime processing. *Memory & Cognition, 11,* 366–373.

Henik, A., Friedrich, F. J., Tzelgov, J., & Tramer, S. (in press). Capacity demands of "automatic" processes in semantic priming. *Memory & Cognition,*

Henik, A., Priel, B., & Umansky, R. (1992). Attention and automaticity in semantic processing of schizophrenic patients. *Neuropsychiatry, Neuropsychology and Behavioral Neurology, 5,* 161–169.

Henik, A., Rafal, R., & Rhodes, D. (in press). Endogenously generated and visually guided saccades after lesions of the human frontal eye fields. *Journal of Cognitive Neuroscience.*

Henik, A., Singh, J., Beckley, D., & Rafal, R. (in press). Disinhibition of automatic word reading in early and late onset Parkinson's disease. *Cortex.*

Hietanen, M., & Teravainen, H. (1988). The effect of age on disease onset and neuropsychological performance in Parkinson's disease. *Journal of Neurology, Neurosurgery and Psychiatry, 51,* 244–249.

Hillyard, S. A., Luck, S. J., & Mangun, G. R. (in press). The cuing of attention to visual field locations; Analysis with ERP recordings. In H. J. Heinze, T. F. Munte, & G. R. Mangun (Eds.), *Cognitive electrophysiology: Event-related brain potentials in basic and clinical research.* Boston: Birkhausen.

Hoffman, J., & MacMillan, F. (1985). Is semantic priming automatic? In M. I. Posner & O. S. M. Marin (Eds.), *Attention and performance XI.* Hillsdale, NJ: Lawrence Erlbaum.

Howard, D., Patterson, K., Wise, R., Brown, W. D., Friston, K., Weiller, C., & Frackowiak, R. (1992). The cortical localization of the lexicons. Positron emission tomography evidence. *Brain, 115,* 1769–1782.

Johnson, M. H. (1990). Cortical maturation and the development of visual attention in early infancy. *Journal of Cognitive Neuroscience, 2,* 81–95.

Jonides, J. (1981). Voluntary versus automatic control over the mind's eye's movement. In J. B. Long & A. D. Baddeley (Eds.), *Attention and performance IX* (pp. 187–203). Hillsdale, NJ: Lawrence Erlbaum.

Jonides, J., & Mack, R. (1984). On the cost and benefit of cost and benefit. *Psychological Bulletin, 96,* 29–42.

Kahneman, D., & Treisman, A. M. (1984). Changing views on attention and automaticity. In R. Parasuraman & D. R. Davies (Eds.), *Varieties of Attention* (pp. 2201–2211). New York: Academic Press.

Katz, W. F. (1988). An investigation of lexical ambiguity in Broca's aphasics using an auditory lexical priming technique. *Neuropsychologia*, *26*, 747–752.

Knight, R. T., Scabini, D., & Woods, D. L. (1989). Prefrontal cortex gating of auditory transmission in humans. *Brain Research*, *504*, 338–342.

Kwapil, T. R., Hegley, D. C., Chapman, L. J., & Chapman, J. P. (1990). Facilitation of word recognition by semantic priming in schizophrenia. *Journal of Abnormal Psychology 99*, 215–221.

Lambert, A., & Hockey, R. (1991). Peripheral visual changes and spatial attention. *Acta Psychologia (Amst)*, *76*, 149–163.

Lewis, T. L., & Maurer, D. (1992). The development of the temporal and nasal visual fields during infancy. *Vision Research*, *32*, 903–911.

Lewis, T. L., Maurer, D., & Blackburn, K. (1985). The development of young infants' ability to detect stimuli in the nasal visual field. *Vision Research*, *25*, 943–950.

Logan, G. D. (1980). Attention and automaticity in Stroop and priming tasks: Theory and data. *Cognitive Psychology*, *12*, 523–553.

Logan, G. D. (1985). Skill and automaticity: Relations, implications, and future directions. *Canadian Journal of Psychology*, *39*, 367–386.

Logan, G. D., & Zbrodoff, N. J. (1979). When it helps to be misled: Facilitative effects of increasing the frequency of conflicting stimulis in a Stroop-like task. *Memory & Cognition*, *7*, 166–174.

MacLeod, C. M. (1991). Half a century of research on the Stroop effect: An integrative review. *Psychological Bulletin*, *109*, 163–203.

Maher, R. A. (1983). A tentative theory of schizophrenic utterance. In B. A. Maher & W. B. Maher (Eds.), *Progress in Experimental Personality Research* (pp. 1–52). New York: Academic Press.

Marcel, A. (1980). Conscious and unconscious perception: Experiments on visual masking and word recognition. *Cognitive Psychology*, *15*, 197–237.

Maylor, E. A. (1985). Facilitory and inhibitory components of orienting in visual space. In M. I. Posner & O. S. M. Marin (Eds.), *Attention and performance XI*. Hillsdale, NJ: Lawrence Erlbaum.

Maylor, E. A., & Hockey, R. (1985). Inhibitory component of externally controlled covert orienting in visual space. *Journal of Experimental Psychology: Human Perception and Performance*, *11*, 777–787.

McGlinchey-Berroth, R., Milberg, W. P., Verfaellie, M., Alexander, M., & Kilduff, P. T. (1993). Semantic processing in the neglected visual field: Evidence from a lexical decision task. *Cognitive Neuropsychology*, *10*, 79–108.

Meyer, D. E., & Schvaneveldt, R. W. (1971). Facilitation in recognizing pairs of words: Evidence of a dependence between retrieval operations. *Journal of Experimental Psychology*, *90*, 227–243.

Meyer, D. E., & Schvaneveldt, R. W. (1976). Meaning, memory structure and mental processes. *Science*, *192*, 23–27.

Milberg, W., & Blumstein, S. (1981). Lexical decision and aphasia: Evidence for semantic processing. *Brain and Language*, *14*, 371–385.

Milberg, W., Blumstein, S., & Dworetzky, B. (1988). Phonological processing and lexical access in aphasia. *Brain and Language*, *34*, 279–293.

Moran, J., & Desimone, R. (1985). Selective attention gates visual processing in the extrastriate cortex. *Science*, *229*, 782–784.

Müller, H. J., & Rabbitt, P. M. A. (1989a). Spatial cueing and the relation between the accuracy of "where" and "what" decisions in visual search. *Quarterly Journal of Experimental Psychology*, *41A*, 747–773.

Müller, H. J., & Rabbitt, P. M. A. (1989b). Reflexive and voluntary orienting of visual attention: Timecourse of activation and resistance to interruption. *Journal of Experimental Psychology: Human Perception and Performance, 15*, 315–330.

Neely, J. H. (1977). Semantic priming and retrieval from lexical memory. *Journal of Experimental Psychology: General, 106*, 226–254.

Neely, J. H. (1991). Semantic priming effects in visual word recognition: A selective review of current findings and theories. In D. Besner & G. Humphreyes (Eds.), *Basic processes in reading: Visual word recognition* (pp. 264–336). Hillsdale, NJ: Lawrence Erlbaum.

Onifer, W., & Swinney, D. A. (1981). Accessing lexical ambiguities during sentence comprehension: Effects of frequency of meaning and contextual bias. *Memory & Cognition 9*, 225–236.

Pardo, J. V., Pardo, P. J., Janer, K. W., & Raichle, M. E. (1990). The anterior cingulate cortex mediates processing selection in the Stroop attentional conflict paradigm. *Proceedings of the National Academy of Sciences, U.S.A., 87*, 256–259.

Pashler, H., Carrier, M., & Hoffman, J. (1993). Saccadic eye movements and dual-task interference. *Quarterly Journal of Experimental Psychology, 46A*, 51–82.

Perret, E. (1974). The left frontal lobe of man and the suppression of habitual responses in verbal categorical behavior. *Neuropsychologia, 12*, 323–330.

Petersen, S. E., Fox, P. T., Posner, M. I., Mintun, M., & Raichle, M. E. (1988). Positron emission tomographic studies of the cortical anatomy of single-word processing. *Nature, 331*, 585–589.

Petersen, S. E., Fox, P. T., Snyder, A. Z., & Raichle, M. E. (1990). Activation of extrastriate and frontal cortical areas by visual words and wordlike stimuli. *Science, 249*, 1041–1044.

Posner, M. I. (1978). *Chronometric explorations of mind*. Oxford: Oxford University Press.

Posner, M. I. (1980). Orienting of attention. *Quarterly Journal of Experimental Psychology, 32*, 3–25.

Posner, M. I., & Cohen, Y. P. C. (1980). Attention and the control of movements. In G. E. Stelmach & J. Requin (Eds.), *Tutorials in motor behavior* (pp. 243–258). Amsterdam: North Holland.

Posner, M. I., & Cohen, Y. P. C. (1984). Components of visual orienting. In H. Bouma & D. Bouwhuis (Eds.), *Attention and performance X* (pp. 531–556). London: Lawrence Erlbaum.

Posner, M. I., Cohen, Y. P. C., & Rafal, R. D. (1982). Neural systems control of spatial orienting. *Philosophical Transactions of the Royal Society of London, B298*, 187–198.

Posner, M. I., Inhoff, A. W., Friedrich, F. J., & Cohen, A. (1987). Isolating attentional systems: A cognitive-anatomical analysis. *Psychobiology, 15*, 107–121.

Posner, M. I., & Petersen, S. (1990). The attention system of the human brain. *Annual Reviews of Neuroscience, 13*, 25–42.

Posner, M. I., Petersen, S. E., Fox, P. T., & Raichle, M. E. (1988). Localization of cognitive operations in the human brain. *Science, 240*, 1627–1631.

Posner, M. I., Rafal, R. D., Choate, L., & Vaughn, J. (1985). Inhibition of return: Neural basis and function. *Cognitive Neuropsychology, 2*, 211–228.

Posner, M. I., Sandson, J., Dhawan, M., & Shulman, G. L. (1989). Is word recognition automatic? *Journal of Cognitive Neuroscience, 1*, 50–60.

Posner, M. I., & Snyder, C. R. R. (1975). Facilitation and inhibition in the processing of signals. In *Attention and performance V* (pp. 669–681). New York: Academic Press.

Posner, M. I., Snyder, C. R. R., & Davidson, B. (1980). Attention and the detection of signals. *Journal of Experimental Psychology: General, 109,* 160–174.

Posner, M. I., Walker, J. A., Friedrich, F. J., & Rafal, R. (1984). Effects of parietal injury on covert orienting of visual attention. *Journal of Neuroscience, 4,* 1863–1874.

Posner, M. I., Walker, J. A., Friedrich, F. J., & Rafal, R. D. (1987). How do the parietal lobes direct covert attention? *Neuropsychologia, 25,* 135–146.

Rafal, R. D. (1992). Visually guided behavior in progressive supranuclear palsy. In I. Litvan & Y. Agid (Eds.), *Progressive supranuclear palsy: Clinical and research approaches.* Oxford: Oxford University Press.

Rafal, R., Calabresi, P., Brennan, C., & Sciolto, T. (1989). Saccade preparation inhibits reorienting to recently attended locations. *Journal of Experimental Psychology: Human Perception and Performance, 15,* 673–685.

Rafal, R., Egly, R., & Rhodes, D. (in press). Effects of inhibition of return on reflexive and endogenous saccades: Alternation bias or location tagging? *Canadian Journal of Experimental Psychology.*

Rafal, R., Henik, A., & Smith, J. (1991). Extrageniculate contributions to reflexive visual orienting in normal humans: A temporal hemifield advantage. *Journal of Cognitive Neuroscience, 3,* 323–329.

Rafal, R. D., Posner, M. I., Friedman, J. H., Inhoff, A. W., & Bernstein, E. (1988). Orienting of visual attention in progressive supranuclear palsy. *Brain, 111,* 267–280.

Rafal, R., Smith, J., Krantz, J., Cohen, A., & Brennan, C. (1990). Extrageniculate vision in hemianopic humans: Saccade inhibition by signals in the blind field. *Science, 250,* 118–121.

Robertson, C., & Flowers, K. A. (1990). Motor set in Parkinson's disease. *J Neurol Neurosurg Psychiatry 53,* 583–592.

Rothbart, M. K., Posner, M. I., & Boylan, A. (1991). Regulatory mechanisms in infant development. In J. Enns (Ed.), *The development of attention: Research and theory.* Amsterdam: North Holland.

Rugg, M. D., Milner, A. D., Lines, C. R., & Phalp, R. (1987). Modulation of visual event-related potentials by spatial and nonspatial visual selective attention. *Neuropsychologia, 15,* 85–96.

Schadler, M., & Thissen, D. M. (1981). The development of automatic word recognition and reading skill. *Memory & Cognition 9,* 132–141.

Schiller, P. (1966). Developmental study of color-word interference. *Journal of Experimental Psychology 72,* 105–108.

Schvaneveldt, M. S., & McDonald, J. E. (1981). Lexical ambiguity, semantic context, and visual word recognition. *Journal of Experimental Psychology: Human Perception and Performance, 7,* 673–687.

Sciolto, T. (1990). *Timecourse of exogenous and endogenous orienting in detection.* Unpublished undergraduate honors thesis, Brown University, Providence, RI.

Senechal, S. (1994) [   ]. Unpublished data.

Shulman, G. L. (1984). An asymmetry in the control of eye movements and shifts of attention. *Acta Psychologia, 55,* 53–69.

Sieroff, E., Pollatsek, A., & Posner, M. I. (1988). Recognition of visual letter strings following injury to the posterior visual spatial attention system. *Cognitive Neuropsychology, 5,* 427–449.

Simpson, G. B., & Burgess, C. (1985). Activation and selection processes in the recognition of ambiguous words. *Journal of Experimental Psychology: Human Perception and Performance, 11,* 28–39.

Simpson, G. B., & Krueger, M. A. (1991). Selective access of homograph meanings in sentence context. *Journal of Memory and Language,*

Skinner, J. E., & Yingling, C. D. (1977). Central gating mechanisms that regulate event-related potentials and behavior: A neural model for attention. In J. E. Desmedt (Ed.), *Attention, Voluntary Contraction and Event-Related Cerebral Potentials* (pp. 30–69). Basel: S. Karger.

Smith, M. C. (1979). Contextual facilitation in a letter search task depends on how the prime is processed. *Journal of Experimental Psychology: Human Perception and Performance, 5*, 239–251.

Smith, M. C., Besner, D., & Miyoshi, S. (1992). On the demise of automaticity. In *The 33rd Annual Meeting of the Psychonomics Society* (pp. 239–251). St. Louis, MO.

Smith, M. C., Theeodor, L., & Franklin, P. F. (1983). The relationship between contextual facilitation and depth of processing. *Journal of Experimental Psychology: Learning, Memory and Cognition, 9*, 697–712.

Snow, N., & Neely, J. H. (1987). Reduction of semantic priming from inclusion of physically or nominally related prime–target pairs. In *Annual Meeting of the Psychonomics Society*, Seattle, WA:.

Stern, Y., Tetrud, J. W., Martin, W. R., Kutner, S. J., & Langston, J. W. (1990). Cognitive change following MPTP exposure. *Neurology 40*, 261–264.

Tabossi, P. (1988). Accessing lexical ambiguity in different types of sentential contexts. *Journal of Memory and Language,*

Tassinari, G., Aglioti, S., Chelazzi, L., Marzi, C. A., & Berlucchi, G. (1987). Distribution in the visual field of the costs of voluntarily allocated attention and the inhibitory aftereffects of covert orienting. *Neuropsychologia, 25*, 55–72.

Tassinari, G., Biscaldi, M., Marzi, C. A., & Berlucchi, G. (1989). Ipsilateral inhibition and contralateral facilitation of simple reaction time to nonfoveal visual targets from noninformative visual cues. *Acta Psychologia, 70*, 267–291.

Taylor, A. E., Saint-Cyr, C. J., & Lang, A. E. (1986). Frontal lobe dysfunction in Parkinson's disease: The cortical focus of neostriatal outflow. *Brain, 109*, 845–883.

Tipper, S. P., Driver, J., & Weaver, B. (1991). Object-centred inhibition of return of visual attention. *Quarterly Journal of Experimental Psychology, 43*, 289–298.

Tipper, S. P., Weaver, B., Jerreat, L., & Burak, A. (in press). Object and environmental-centered inhibition of return of visual attention. *Journal of Experimental Psychology: Human Perception and Performance.*

Tweedy, J. R., Lapinski, R. H., & Schvaneveldt, R. W. (1977). Semantic-context effects on word recognition: Influence of varying the proportion of items presented in the appropriate context. *Memory & Cognition, 5*, 84–89.

Tzelgov, J., & Henik, A. (1990). Controlling Stroop effect. In *31st Annual Meeting of the Psychonomics Society*. New Orleans, LA.

Tzelgov, J., & Henik, A. (1992). *Controlled processing in the semantic network*. No. Israel Foundations Trustees.

Tzelgov, J., & Henik, A., & Berger, A. (1992). Controlling Stroop effects by manipulating expectations for color words. *Memory & Cognition, 20*, 727–735.

Tzelgov, J., Henik, A., & Leiser (1990). Controlling Stroop interference: Evidence from a bilingual task. *Journal of Experimental Psychology: Learning, Memory and Cognition, 16*, 760–771.

Valenza, E., Simion, F., Umilta, C., & Paiusco, E. (1992). Inhibition of return in newborn infants. In *Fifth Conference of the European Society for Cognitive Psychology*, Paris, September 12–16.

Warner, C. B., Juola, J. F., & Koshino, H. (1990). Voluntary allocation versus automatic capture of visual attention. *Perception and Psychophysics, 48*, 243–251.

Weiskrantz, L. (1986). *Blindsight: A case study and implications*. Oxford: Oxford University Press.

Yamaguchi, S., & Knight, R. T. (1990). Gating of somatosensory input by human prefrontal cortex. *Brain Research, 521*, 281–288.

Yantis, S., & Jonides, J. (1990). Abrupt visual onsets and selective attention: Voluntary versus automatic allocation. *Journal of Experimental Psychology: Human Perception and Performance, 16*, 121–134.

A Model of Inhibitory Mechanisms in Selective Attention

George Houghton and Steven P. Tipper

I. INTRODUCTION

The complex environments encountered and internally represented by many organisms contain numerous objects toward which action could be directed, or which the organism may need to avoid. Given the simultaneous presence of many objects of different adaptive value, and affording a variety of different responses, it is extremely important for coherent, organized behavior that actions be selectively directed toward one object at a time. In this chapter we propose that the means by which internal goal states mediate the interaction between perception and action is the mechanism of selective attention.

For a complete understanding of selective attention, investigations have to take place at a number of different levels (Marr, 1982). For example, the precise adaptive function of attention must be specified within the context of an organism's normal interactions with the world, as well as the kinds of representations on which attentional processes act. Algorithms for executing attentional processes need to be specified and tested experimentally. Experimental evidence may be drawn from the cognitive level, where performance by human subjects is carefully analyzed in laboratory tasks (Broadbent, 1958; Kahneman, 1973; Posner, 1978), and from the neurophysiological level, where the activity of single cells, or an animal's performance after lesions, can be assessed during attentional tasks (Moran & Desimone, 1985; Picton, Stuss, & Marshall, 1986; Posner & Driver, 1992).

The interaction between the cognitive and neurophysiological levels of investigation provides mutual constraints for models of attention. However, most models derived from experimental results are informal (e.g., Tipper, 1985), and hence it is often difficult to detect inconsistencies in logic, or to demonstrate that the informal theory is sufficiently precisely specified to constitute an effective explanation of the data under consideration. Such models therefore need to be made maximally explicit, for instance by being specified mathematically and instantiated in computer programs which can work out the predictions of the model in detail. In this chapter we develop a preliminary neural network model of certain aspects of voluntary selective attention which is consistent with our views regarding the central purpose ("why") and method ("how") of selective attention.

Section II discusses our overall approach to selective attention (our "computational theory," using Marr's (1982) term) and considers a variety of data in support of it. In Section III we develop a neural network model that formalizes certain aspects of the theory presented in Section II, and in Section IV we show how the model accounts for a variety of existing data.

II. THEORIES OF ATTENTION

In discussing theories of selective attention, and the place of our theory in relation to others, it is useful to identify two dimensions of variation: the locus of selection in the pathway from perception to response (e.g., late vs. early), and the kind of mechanism used in selection (e.g., amplificatory, "the spotlight," or inhibitory or both). We first consider the issue of the locus of selection, which we believe to be central to the issue of the functional role of attention, and then consider the nature of the mechanisms involved.

A. Locus and Function of Selective Attention

With regard to the issue of the locus of selection, two positions have emerged which we refer to as the *precategorical* and *postcategorical* positions. The precategorical view proposes that attention is critical for perceptual processes, that without attention only low levels of analysis can take place, for instance detecting edges and motion (Triesman & Gelade, 1980). More specifically, it proposes that attention is necessary for the categorization of objects, hence the term precategorical. The postcategorical position proposes that perceptual processes, including grouping and (implicit) categorization, are largely automatic, at least for familiar stimuli. Selection acts on objects (or perceptual groups) for the purposes of controlling action towards them.

The models of Koch and Ullman (1985) and LaBerge and Brown (1989) are of this type. For example, LaBerge and Brown's model describes three properties of selective attention. First, selection takes place at early levels of perceptual input, allowing one object to enter a limited capacity identification system; second, attentional modulation of low-level stimulus attributes is carried out by reference to their location; and third, selection is based on excitation, where the perceptual features of a stimulus receive facilitated transmission into the identification system. In contrast, the model we describe is qualitatively different on all of these dimensions. Our model proposes that selection can take place after perceptual grouping and semantic analysis, that attention accesses object-based representations, and that a central mechanism in the selection process is active inhibition of distracting information.

The position we take in this chapter is based on the computational level of analysis emphasized by Marr (1982). Such an analysis specifies the functions for which a particular system has evolved, considering both biological goals and the environment in which such goals are to be achieved. In other words, attention must be considered in the global context of an organism's self-organization of its behavior, in pursuit of its socially and biologically acquired goals (Luria, 1973; Norman & Shallice, 1986). Thus we suggest that in the context of an organism's encounters with its familiar, natural environments, the role of attention in low-level perceptual analysis may be quite limited. Schema-based expectations may facilitate the perception and comprehension of a scene without the need to focus attention serially on each object in the scene (Biederman, Mezzanotte, & Rabinowitz, 1981; Palmer, 1975; Friedman, 1979; Treisman, 1986). Indeed, if attention is necessary for object perception, it is difficult to see how it can be moved from object to object in the first place. Furthermore, the constraints provided by information distributed throughout a scene (such as objects appearing in conjunction with other objects, being supported by them, having the ability to occlude other objects, having a typical locus in the scene, etc.) reflect the identity of an object and take part in the construction of its internal representation. These "normal" conditions contrast with the highly nonpredictable decontextualized situations encountered in the typical experimental study of attention.

It is thus likely that highly efficient parallel perceptual analysis takes place in familiar situations. As Neumann (1987) noted, the brain processes an immense amount of perceptual information (from many modalities) in parallel, and thus information handling limitations in the nervous system may not be critical at the level of perceptual analysis, but rather at more central levels, specifically in the linking of perception and action, and the perceptual control of effector systems: one hand cannot raise two beer glasses to the mouth for drinking, just as one visual object naming system cannot name two objects at once.

Apart from such general considerations, experiments with the negative priming paradigm (Tipper, 1985; discussed in more detail later) have shown clear *semantic* effects of distractors. In these priming studies, an ignored picture of a cat can affect the subsequent processing of a semantically related word such as *dog* (Tipper & Driver, 1988). Note that there is no physical resemblance between the picture and the word, so any interactions between them must be at semantic levels. Other work has demonstrated that the semantic properties of ignored objects can influence the concurrent processing of a target stimulus (Stroop, 1935). In the priming studies of Tipper and his colleagues, the distracting stimuli are usually presented very briefly and subjects are typically unable to report awareness of the objects' identity. It is argued from such evidence that the prime display is analyzed in parallel by the visual system to semantic levels, but that the selective attention mechanism only allows information from an object possessing the target property into the response systems (and into awareness). Information relating to the distractor is inhibited and this in some way retards later responses to semantically related items (this inhibitory element will be discussed further).

It may be objected here that it is pointless to construct representations of multiple objects in parallel, only to have to suppress information from most of them for the purposes of generating coherent thought and action. We would argue, however, that the identification of objects is facilitated by their occurring in familiar contexts with other known objects (Biederman, 1972; Biederman, Mezzanotte, & Rabinowitz, 1982). In addition, we suggest that interactions with complex real world environments *require* object-based representations of distractor objects, rather than free-floating features. Consider reaching for potato chips from a bag placed in the middle of a table. Also on the table are a variety of bottles, glasses, ashtrays, and so on that one must reach around or over. Successful behavior could not be achieved if only the target stimulus was fully represented and distractors were only analyzed in terms of low-level features. Rather, we propose that to achieve the behavioral goal, the accommodation of a detailed form of an action to the nontarget objects is required, such as when reaching around or over obstacles. Such indirect actions can only be guided by object- or action-centered representations (see Tipper, Weaver, & Houghton, in press). Thus human perceptual systems have evolved to produce internal representations of both objects forming the focus of current goal-directed behavior and those providing the context.

We therefore propose that the role of attention in overall behavior lies not so much in the creation of an internal representation of the environment, but rather in the linking of the appropriate action with the appropriate object in contexts which may afford an arbitrary number of such linkages, the great majority of which, at any time, will be disruptive to the organism's goal-seeking behavior (Luria, 1973). In the model presented here, we suppose processing of visual inputs to be taking place in parallel, up to categorical levels, without the intervention of attentional processes, and that selection involves the "binding" of information in target object representations (e.g., location, form, etc.) to variables associated with response schemas (Arbib, Iberall, & Lyons, 1987; Arbib, 1990). Object representations *compete* for control of action by binding the parameters of action schemas, and selective attention acts to modulate this competition in favor of target objects.[1]

B. Amplification and Inhibition in Selective Attention

Whatever the location and function of selection, we can consider two mechanisms by which it may be achieved: amplification and inhibition (enhancement and suppression, respectively). Spotlight models of attention are based on amplification and argue that selection of a target from a distractor is primarily an excitatory process. Attention is directed toward some part of the input field, like the beam of a spotlight, and information within the beam is amplified, allowing it to receive further processing beyond that of initial preattentive analysis. The initial representations activated by ignored inputs passively decay back to resting levels (Broadbent, 1970; Van der Heijden, 1981). Such a model appears to suggest no role for inhibitory mechanisms. An alternative account, one which we develop here, argues that the remarkably efficient selection

[1]The adaptive value of the capacity to select out one object from an array of potential targets is perhaps most clearly illustrated in the phenomenon of predatory attack (see Curio, 1976). In terms of our model, this requires that the typical predator select one target prey and bind the parameters of the attack response to the movements of the target. Many prey animals move together in groups (e.g., schools of fish) and it has been found that the attack response of predators becomes disorganized and less successful when confronted with such groups (as opposed to isolated prey). Hunting success has been found to vary inversely with school size for some predatory fish (Neill & Cullen, 1974) and the reason for this seems to be that the copresence of multiple, highly similar potential targets disrupts the selective coupling of the attack response. As response to this, some predators have evolved the tactic of breaking up fish schools, thereby increasing the number of isolated stray individuals, which are then selected for attack. We would hypothesize that this is because the absence of distractors near strays facilitates the sustained selection necessary for pursuit and capture. It is thus possible that schooling behavior has evolved in part to exploit limitations in the attentional systems of predators.

found in experimental tasks may be better accounted for by a dual mechanism consisting of the previously described excitatory component, supplemented by an inhibitory component that acts to suppress competing information derived from the analysis of the distractor. We show in the model how such combined processes of excitation and inhibition can rapidly differentiate the internal representations of the target and distractor objects (Tipper, 1985).

The point may be made that postulating a dual mechanism is unparsimonious, if all one is ultimately doing is separating out information-bearing signals by selective gain control—all that is needed for this is either an amplificatory mechanism or an inhibitory one, but not both. We would argue, however, that a dual (opponent) mechanism is advantageous for at least two reasons. First, any gain control mechanism implemented in biological (i.e., neural) hardware can only operate within finite limits, and thus the rate at which one signal can be boosted with respect to another (remaining constant) must have some finite upper bound. A dual mechanism, acting in parallel, can boost a target signal while suppressing a distractor, thereby effectively doubling the rate at which target and distractor (signal and noise) can be pulled apart. The second reason is perhaps less obvious. Any signals in a biological information processing system must have a limited dynamic range—maximum and minimum amplitudes. Suppose we arbitrarily scale this range in the interval [0,1], with 0 representing the floor and 1 the ceiling. It may happen that this system is simultaneously presented with two signals, T and D, and that both are at high levels, say 0.9 on our scale. Suppose that one signal, T, is to be "attended." In this case a "spotlight" mechanism can induce a maximum signal amplification of about 12% ($T = 1.0$, $D = 0.9$), at which point the target signal T saturates. This gap is unlikely to be sufficient to prevent debilitating interference from D, which remains at high amplitude. Clearly what is needed in such a case is some ability to suppress D to a significant extent. The converse argument holds for low amplitude signals, where selective amplification would be more effective than inhibition of low amplitude distractors. A system with both components would thus be maximally effective over the entire dynamic range, exhibiting more rapid selection of targets and better performance in situations of low signal-to-noise ratios.

The emphasis we place here on the ability to inhibit distracting information is not new. According to Wundt (1904),

> The basic phenomenon of all intellectual achievement is the so-called concentration of attention. It is understandable that in the appraisal of this phenomenon we attach importance first and therefore too exclusively to its positive side, to the grasping and clarification of certain presentations. But for the physiological appraisal it is clear that it is the negative side, the inhibition of the inflow of all other disturbing excitations . . . which is more important. (p. 481)

From this perspective, the excitation-spotlight metaphor is perhaps better regarded as representing the "view from consciousness," that is, it is how things appear to the conscious mind, which deals only with the results of selection in the control of thought and action. The actual mechanisms of selection, and the levels of preattentive analysis, may bear little resemblance to what is suggested by such an introspective viewpoint. We now consider some of the experimental evidence for the importance of late, inhibitory processes in selective attention.

Evidence for inhibitory mechanisms in selective attention comes from both physiological and cognitive research. Within the neurophysiological paradigm, Moran and Desimone (1985) demonstrated that when a stimulus was ignored while attention was directed to another stimulus, the response of the cell in whose receptive field the ignored stimulus was located was suppressed. They suggested that suppression of distractors may be the primary mechanism of selection in these cortical regions (V4 and the inferior temporal lobe). Electrophysiological techniques have also provided evidence for the inhibition of distractors. Arsten et al. (1983) demonstrated that naloxone improves selectivity by increasing the suppression of distractors in the frontal lobe, rather than by changing the analysis of the attended targets. Much neuropsychological evidence points to the role of areas of the prefrontal lobes in the direction and maintenance of attention, and to a strong inhibitory component in this function. For instance, on reviewing an extensive body of evidence on the subject, Fuster (1980) concludes:

> [N]europsychological evidence . . . points to the essential role of the orbitomedial prefrontal cortex in the suppression and control of [sources of] interference . . . [T]hat role may be considered inhibitory and part of . . . the selective attention that the animal must direct and maintain for the proper conduct of the behavioral sequence. (p. 187)

Fuster further remarks that the mechanisms by which prefrontal attentional systems interact with other cortical areas (e.g., posterior sensory areas) are unknown. It seems likely that progress in this area will depend not only on further physiological investigation, but also on the development of much more detailed models of selective attention that can be interpreted physiologically.

Much of the cognitive evidence for inhibition of distractors arises from the negative priming paradigm (Dalrymple-Alford & Budayr, 1966; Neill, 1977; Tipper, 1985). If the internal representations of a to-be-ignored object are associated with inhibition during selection and execution of the responses to the target object, the processing of a subsequent stimulus requiring the inhibited representations should be impaired. Therefore, in a priming procedure, when an ignored stimulus in a prime trial is subsequently presented as a probe for rapid identification, reaction time (RT) to name this probe should be increased.

In the procedure illustrated in Figure 1 for example, subjects were instructed to attend to the red object (solid line) and ignore the green object (broken line). In the ignored repetition condition the ignored prime (green object) reappeared as the red object in the probe. As predicted by the inhibition hypothesis, RTs were longer in this situation than in the control condition where there was no relationship between the objects in the prime and probe displays. Such a result is consistently observed in negative priming tasks, and the evidence for the active inhibition of distractors thus obtained is now quite substantial and has been observed with a wide variety of experimental stimuli. These stimuli include:

1. Words (Beech, Baylis, Tipper, McManus, & Agar, 1991; Hoffman & MacMillan, 1985; Fuentes & Tudela, 1992; Hung & Tzeng, 1989; Tipper & Driver, 1988; Yee, 1991)

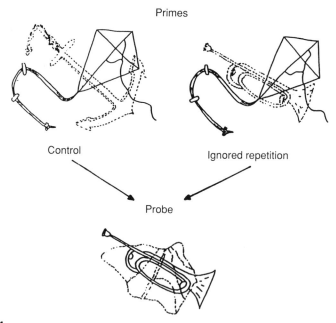

Figure 1

Sample displays from a study demonstrating negative priming. Subjects were required to name the red object (solid line) while ignoring a green distractor (broken line). In the control prime display, the target and distractor were unrelated to the subsequent probe, but in the ignored repetition condition, the ignored prime was the same as the subsequent probe target. Negative priming was revealed by longer reaction times to name the probe after presentation of the ignored repetition prime than after presentation of the control prime. The probe target was superimposed over a neutral, meaningless distractor.

2. Stroop color words (Beech, Agar, & Baylis, 1989; Beech, Baylis, Smithson, & Claridge, 1989; Beech & Claridge, 1987; Beech, Powell, McWilliams & Claridge, 1989, 1990; Benoit et al., 1992; Dalrymple-Alford & Budayr, 1966; Enright & Beech, 1990; Lowe, 1979, 1985; McLaren & Bryson, 1988; Neill, 1977; Neill & Westberry, 1987; Tipper, Bourque, Anderson, & Brehaut, 1989)
3. Local-global letters (Briand, in preparation; Baylis & Tipper, unpublished)
4. Letters (Hasher, Stoltzfus, Zacks, & Rympa, 1991; McDowd & Oseas-Kreger, 1991; Neumann & DeSchepper, 1991, 1992; Tipper & Cranston, 1985; Tipper, MacQueen, & Brehaut, 1988)
5. Pictures (Gernsbacher & Faust, 1991; McLaren, 1989; Tipper, 1985; Tipper & Driver, 1988; Tipper, Weaver, Cameron, Brehaut, & Bastedo, 1991)
6. Color (DeSchepper, Khurana, O'Connell, & Wilson, in preparation)
7. Random shapes (DeSchepper & Treisman, 1991)

Furthermore, negative priming has been obtained when report of the target locus is required, as opposed to target identification tasks (Tipper, Brehaut, & Driver, 1990; Tipper & McLaren, 1990; Tipper, Weaver, Kirkpatrick, & Lewis, 1991), and when the target and distractor stimuli are presented in different perceptual modalities (Driver & Baylis, 1993; Greenwald, 1972). The effects have also been observed when subjects engage in real-world tasks such as reaching towards stimuli (Tipper, Lortie, & Baylis, 1992). Similar patterns of results in the latter procedure are observed in both humans and infrahuman primates (Taffe, Moore, Tipper, & Baylis, 1991).

A central concern in this work has been the investigation of the locus of the inhibitory processes in the pathways from stimulus to response. As previously described, the evidence is clear that inhibition can act on semantic (categorical) level representations (indeed, the finding of negative priming effects between semantic associates is used as evidence that distractors are processed to semantic levels without necessarily reaching awareness). Other studies, in which subjects make different types of responses to prime and probe trials (Tipper et al., 1988), indicate that the inhibitory effects are not associated with specific motor responses. We might conjecture that inhibition is associated with those aspects of the stimulus most relevant to the goals of the organism. In tasks involving naming responses, this is semantic identity. However, when analysis of color (DeSchepper et al., in preparation) or the production of specific reaching responses (Tipper et al., in press) are central components of the task, then inhibition can be associated with the perceptual property in the former case, and with action-centered representations in the latter case. Thus, the inhibitory effects may not be associated with one particular level of internal representation, but might act flexibly to coordinate the link between perception and action at whatever level is optimal given the current task and stimulus situation. One important consequence of this position is that, because organisms typically interact with objects, it is most parsimonious for attention to access object-based representations (rather than, say, simple spatial coordinates; see Duncan, 1980, for elaboration of this point). Experimental evidence has, indeed, supported such a contention. The inhibitory component of the selection mechanism is associated with objects, so that as objects move through space, inhibition can move with them—that is, it is not tied to a location (Tipper et al., 1990; Tipper, Driver, & Weaver, 1991).

The proposed function of inhibitory mechanisms in our conception is that they assist in the efficient foregrounding of target information and reduce interference from competing distractors. If this is so, and if the degree of negative priming found is an indication of the strength of the inhibitory process, then we would predict an inverse relationship between interference and negative priming: less negative priming should indicate weaker inhibitory processes and hence greater interference. Evidence for such a relationship has been observed from a number of sources which have investigated individual differences in selective attention. It is well established that some populations have particular difficulty responding to stimuli when distractors are present, appearing to be unable to efficiently select. If inhibition is a mechanism of selection, then it may be predicted that such populations have less effective inhibitory mechanisms and will show less negative priming. Experiments investigating a variety of populations known to have selection difficulties support this suggestion. Thus, reduced negative priming has been observed in the following populations:

1. Children (Tipper et al., 1989)
2. Children with attentional deficit disorder (McLaren, 1989)
3. The elderly (Hasher et al., 1991; McDowd & Oseas-Kreger, 1991; Tipper, 1991)
4. Obsessionals (Enright & Beech, 1990)
5. Subjects who report high cognitive failure (Tipper & Baylis, 1987)
6. Schizophrenics (Beech et al., 1989)
7. High schizotypes (Beech & Claridge, 1987)
8. Depressed patients (Benoit et al., 1992)
9. Alzheimer's patients (Mueller & Baylis, in preparation)

Similarly, Gernsbacher & Faust (1991, Experiment 3) showed that subjects who scored low on story comprehension tests seem to be less able to suppress to-be-ignored stimuli than were control subjects (as indexed by the degree of interference caused by to-be-ignored stimuli on a subsequent response).

In the opposite direction, Beech et al. (1990) have shown that chlorpromazine (a dopamine blocking neuroleptic that reduces the symptoms of schizophrenia) increases negative priming. The results related to schizophrenia are of particular interest in that some recent models of schizophrenia suggest that one element of the schizophrenic syndrome involves loss of selectivity due to weakened inhibitory filtering systems. For instance, Swerdlow and Koob (1987) suggest that in schizophrenia, loss of inhibitory processes means that "appropriate filtering and amplification of cortical information cannot occur . . . and irrelevant and relevant cognitive or emotional activity are not segregated" (p. 204). The notion of "relevance" must surely be defined in relation to the subject's goal or drive states. In a similar vein, Gray, Feldon, Rawlins, Hemsley, and Smith (1991) postulate that the schizophrenic syndrome involves "the weakening of inhibitory processes crucial to conscious attention," which allows "the intrusion into awareness of aspects of the environment not normally perceived" (Gray et al., 1991, p. 2). The authors further suggest that in normals, selection is for goal-relevant stimuli, and therefore schizophrenics suffer a deficit in the ability to filter incoming (or endogenously generated) information on the basis of goal-derived targets. Further investigation of this intriguing area would clearly benefit from the development of explicit models of inhibitory filtering in normal subjects. We hope the following model will make a useful contribution.

Thus far we have discussed only evidence for inhibitory processes being associated with nontarget (distractor) items. There is evidence from other sources that attended items become actively suppressed when attention is switched. This is illustrated, for example, by the phenomenon of inhibition of return (Posner & Cohen, 1984), whereby responses to stimuli at previously attended locations are retarded, following a switch of attention, compared to items at new (never-attended) locations. This suggests that as a spatial attentional target is switched, the shift of attention involves inhibition of the last attended location. Similar results have been found involving conceptual entities and objects, rather than simply locations. For instance, in work on text comprehension, it has been found that when a text requires the switching of attentional focus from one protagonist to another, responses related to the previous focus become retarded (Gernsbacher, 1989). Within the attentional literature per se, evidence for object-centered inhibition of return is reported by Tipper et al. (1991), who show that when attention is cued to a *moving* object and then removed from it, a subsequent response made to that object is retarded relative to a response made to a different object. Because the objects are moving continuously, the inhibitory effect cannot be tied to a location, but instead moves with the object. These studies show that inhibition can be associated not only with distractor objects, but also with conceptual entities which have been previously attended. The work on text comprehension indicates that the inhibition of attended items occurs at the point at which the last attended item becomes a potential distractor, that is, when a shift of focus is required. It is of some interest to our work to consider whether these disparate inhibitory effects, involving both attended and unattended items, might arise from a single underlying mechanism. This issue has been raised before (see, e.g., Tipper et al., 1991; Gernsbacher & Faust, 1991), but thus far no explicit candidate mechanisms have been proposed.

This concludes the informal overview of our theory of attention and its current empirical basis. Thus far no precise mechanism has been proposed to account for the negative priming effects, or the active suppression of attended items, beyond general statements concerning inhibition becoming associated with internal representations and processes (Tipper, 1985; Gernsbacher & Faust, 1991). Proposals made in the experimental literature fail to provide answers to numerous questions, such as: What is the source of the inhibitory processes? How do they locate their targets (i.e., know relevant from irrelevant information)? How are they are initiated? How are they terminated? What is their timecourse more generally? The following model attempts to remedy this situation by proposing a detailed model of the dynamics of selective attention. The basic premises of the model, that selection is important in behavioral control, that it is object based, and so on, are derived from the extensive experimental literature just described. These premises are supplemented by a formalized selection mechanism which accounts in detail for a variety of previously obtained results. The proposed mechanism also motivates new experiments and contains nonobvious properties which we believe may contribute to the integration of different areas of research.

III. A MODEL OF THE DYNAMICS OF SELECTIVE ATTENTION

The previous discussion outlines the basic conception of selective attention, which the model described in this section attempts to develop more formally. We see the purpose of our modeling efforts as being threefold:

1. Increased theoretical precision. We believe the previously cited data provide ample evidence for inhibitory selection mechanisms act-

ing on central (object-based) representations. However, current proposals regarding the nature of the mechanisms remain vague and intuitive. Thus ongoing empirical investigations need to be linked to a parallel program of theoretical development if a detailed understanding of the relevant phenomena is to be attained. We intend the model presented here to be a first step toward a precise mechanistic account of central selection processes, as employed in a wide variety of perceptual and cognitive tasks.

2. Increased predictive power. As well as providing more detailed accounts of known results, precise models can be expected to generate predictions that cannot be derived from intuition-bound formulations.

3. Theoretical integration. We believe it is possible that the phenomena of negative priming, inhibition of return, and cognitive inhibition more generally, may reflect different facets of a single type of underlying control mechanism (Houghton, 1993). To make this case convincingly, we need to show in detail what such a mechanism might look like and how it would function in specific circumstances to generate the attested data.

As described, our model asserts that a central function of selective attention is in the goal-based modulation of perceptual input to schemas guiding action and thought. This conception is shown diagrammatically in Figure 2.

We suppose the visual system to be delivering up multiple object-based representations of the external world in parallel. The representations contain a variety of information regarding location, form, identity, and so on. The informational content of each object representation is bound together to form a unity distinct from other entities. If some part of this information changes, it remains linked to the same object representation (or "object file"; Kahneman & Treisman, 1984), so that, in the case of a change of positional information, the entity is perceived to move rather than to be a series of distinct objects at different locations. (What transformations an object can undergo while still being perceived to be the same object, even, say, with a changed identity, is clearly an important empirical and theoretical issue, but one which we will not address here. We simply take it for granted that the visual system automatically attempts to organize spatio-temporally distributed features into objects on the basis of grouping (gestalt) principles developed through evolution.)

On the motor side, we follow other authors (e.g., Norman & Shallice, 1986; Arbib et al., 1987; Arbib, 1990) in proposing that many basic motor responses are packaged in the form of motor "schemas," such as reaching and grasping, naming, pointing at, and so on, by which the

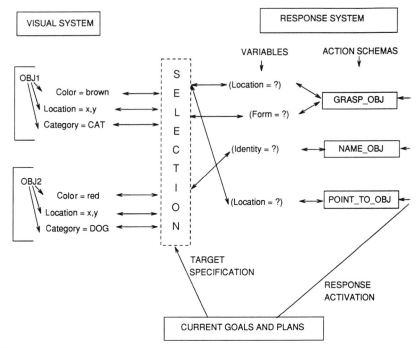

Figure 2

Schematic outline of the model showing attention as a gating mechanism at the perception–action interface. Attentional targets are specified top-down in relation to current
goals and plans. These higher-level planning systems are also responsible for the activation of action schemas which have variables associated with them (Norman & Shallice,
1986). Variables are bound from information specified in perceptual representations
(though other sources of binding information, e.g., memory, are possible). The attentional
mechanism is object centered and foregrounds information contained in specific object
representations, although selection can take place on the basis of featural targets.

agent acts on particular objects in its environment. These schemas are
activated or suppressed by central planning and execution systems
(Norman & Shallice, 1986). Schemas, representing general classes of
actions, have parameters associated with them which, on any occasion
of use, must be bound to information derived from perceptual or memory systems (Arbib, 1990). The binding of the schema parameters adapts
the action to the details of its current goal and context. Thus the actions
of grasping and lifting need information concerning (at least) the location (relative to the effector), form, and likely weight of a target object.
We refer to this setting of variable parameters in action schemas as *binding*. We propose that information capable of binding these variables
potentially will be available from a number of candidate objects in the

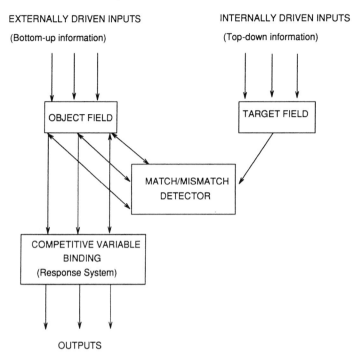

EXTERNALLY DRIVEN INPUTS

(Bottom-up information)

INTERNALLY DRIVEN INPUTS

(Top-down information)

OBJECT FIELD

TARGET FIELD

MATCH/MISMATCH DETECTOR

COMPETITIVE VARIABLE BINDING
(Response System)

OUTPUTS

Figure 3

The interrelations between the four subsystems in the implemented model.

visual field. Coherent action toward a particular object requires that all the relevant parameters of the response schema be bound to properties of that object alone. We will refer to this *coherent* binding of a set of response variables to target objects as *coupling*. Our model proposes that successful perceptuo-motor coupling requires the intervention of a strategically controlled selective attention mechanism which sets up goal-derived targets. Information from objects matching the attentional target is selectively enhanced, whereas information from nonmatching objects is suppressed. We propose that the process of variable binding is a parallel competitive one in which all relevant information from analyzed objects feeds into the binding arena in a cascade fashion. The foregrounding of information connected to the target object provides it with sufficient advantage in the competition for binding that responses become successfully coupled to the target object.

We will now describe the selection mechanism in more detail. The principal components of the mechanism are (1) the object field, (2) the target field, and (3) the match/mismatch field. Their overall organization is shown in Figure 3.

The basic mode of action in the model is that information from both (internally driven) targets and (externally driven) perceptual object representations meet in the match/mismatch field. This system generates signals that feed back into the object field leading to the foregrounding of any objects matching the target specification. The following description of the model begins with an informal account of the organization and function of the various fields of the model, followed by a mathematical specification of the implementation used in the simulation studies.

A. Object Field

We model object representations to a first approximation as a set of linked nodes or units, as familiar from connectionist theory. Each unit represents some or other aspect of the informational content of the representation. We assume these object representations are built up automatically by the visual system in its normal functioning, the various "features" of an object being bound together to form a unified representation. The novel proposal of this model compared to typical connectionist formulations, is that the components of the object representation have an "opponent processing" type character.[2] It is commonplace in network models utilizing lateral inhibition (Grossberg, 1980; Kohonen, 1984) that individual units generate excitatory feedback onto themselves. Our model includes this self-excitatory feedback (generated via an excitatory "on-cell"), but supplements it with an inhibitory feedback loop generated by an inhibitory "off-cell." Thus, when activated, each node coding for some aspect of an object (a "property" node) sets up a combined excitatory–inhibitory feedback signal from its associated on- and off-cells. (Given the function of these cells in the model, we refer to them collectively as the *gain-control subsystem*. The basic circuit is shown in Figure 4.

We refer to the inhibitory feedback loop as the *off-channel*, and the excitatory loop as the *on-channel*. Likewise, we shall refer to the gain-control unit in the off-channel as the *off-cell*, and the analogous unit in the on-channel as the *on-cell*. In the model, we propose that these feedback signals are roughly equally weighted so that, left to itself, the gain-control feedback sums to 0.

We propose that units representing properties of the same object are linked by excitatory weights, representing the fact that the perceptual

[2]The general idea of opponent processing has a long history in neurophysiology and psychology, for instance, in vision (Hurvich & Jameson, 1957), emotion and motivation (Solomon & Corbit, 1974), and learning and memory (Schull, 1979; Wagner, 1981). Grossberg (1980,1983) suggests a neural net realization of an opponent-type mechanism that he terms a *gated dipole*. The dipole is differently constructed from our opponent circuit, but shares a number of functional properties, including the ability to show "rebound" behavior.

PROPERTY UNIT

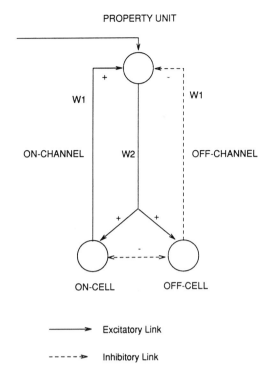

Figure 4

Figure 4

A single opponent-circuit. Activity in a property unit (representing the presence of some feature in the input) activates two balanced feedback circuits, one excitatory and one inhibitory (the gain-control subsystem, GCS). The activity level of the property cell can be suppressed or enhanced by changing the balance of activity in the GCS. The dependence of the activity in the GCS on the activity level of the property cell means that the feedback intensity is automatically controlled. The symbols w_1, w_2 represent model parameters.

system has grouped these properties together to form the object representation. We further propose, however, that links have been formed among units in the gain-control subsystem, so that within a given object representation all the off-cells excite each other and inhibit the on-cells, and all the on-cells excite each other and inhibit the off-cells (Figure 5).

When the property cells of such an assembly are activated, they generate a stable pattern in the gain-control subsystem that echoes the pattern in the property cells, neither enhancing nor suppressing it. However, as we shall see, if some additional signal increases the activation of some subset of on-cells (even just one), this will enhance the activity of all the property cells within the object representation by the familiar process of spreading activation (and, in this case, inhibition of off-cells). On the other hand, if an on-cell is selectively inhibited (or the

PROPERTY UNITS

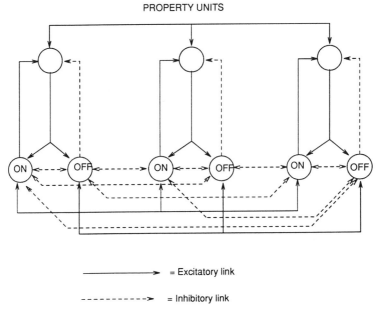

————————————➤ = Excitatory link

- - - - - - - - - ➤ = Inhibitory link

Figure 5
A set of units in an "object assembly." An object assembly is made up of a linked set of opponent circuits of the type illustrated in Figure 4. The links between the on- and off-channels of the opponent system allow for the spread of activation or inhibition through the assembly. Thus, for instance, the representation of a whole object can be suppressed if just one of its component parts is inhibited.

activation of its companion off-cell is enhanced), then, by an analogous spreading inhibition mechanism acting through the linked off-channels, the activity of all the property cells within the object representation will be reduced. As we will show, this foregrounding–backgrounding mechanism is self-stabilizing, so that when an object assembly in the "balanced" state is perturbed by an external influence to the gain-control subsystem, it will move toward a new equilibrium pattern of activation and stay there, as long as the perturbation remains. Importantly, the equilibrium pattern may be anywhere within the space allowed by the activation range, rather than just at its extremes (i.e., with all units at maximal or minimal values).

B. Target Field

Activation of nodes in the target field is taken to represent the properties of an internally generated attentional target (or template). The content of the target specification is taken to be derived from an organism's current goals. Though able to represent sensory qualities of to-be-attended items (such as color), the target field is strictly separate from the sensory fields involved in making up the object representation. We intend that this architectural separation correspond to a physiological separation in the brain, with the target field corresponding to areas of the prefrontal lobes. A similar notion appears in the work of Näätänen (1985), who refers to what we call the target specification as the *attentional trace*.

The specification of the target leads to the biasing of the influence of perceptual information on response systems, allowing coupling of response parameters to properties of individual objects. In this way, internal goal states mediate perceptuo-motor interactions. In an experimental context, activation of targets will be due to the subject explicitly following the experimental protocol. For instance, if the subject is told to name the red object, then the activated schema in Figure 2 will be NAME-OBJ and the target property will be "red." In the implemented model, the target is thus a preset level of activity in units representing the target property (see Figure 6).

C. Match/Mismatch Field

The model proposes that the influence of top-down attentional targets on perceptuo-motor interactions is mediated by the generation of match/mismatch signals from a system which receives inputs from both internal target specifications and from perceptual systems (Figure 6). Objects having properties that fail to match the target specification (on the appropriate stimulus dimension) receive feedback to their gain-control subsystem which "breaks the symmetry" between excitation and inhibition (in the on–off channels), shifting the balance in the inhibitory direction. This inhibitory shift begins in the circuit representing the property on which selection is made (e.g., color), but by the spreading inhibition mechanism described earlier leads to the suppression of all the properties associated with the object. Objects matching the target receive an excitatory boost which begins in the circuit coding the target property and spreads via the on-channels throughout the object representation. A role for match/mismatch systems in goal-driven attention has been posited by a number of authors (e.g., Näätänen, 1982, 1985; Duncan & Humphreys, 1989; Humphreys & Müller, 1993). Näätänen (1985) reviews a number of studies of event-related potential (ERP) supporting the existence of matching operations in selective attention. Näätänen (1985) postulates that a component of the ERP known as the *processing negativity* is "generated by a cerebral matching process

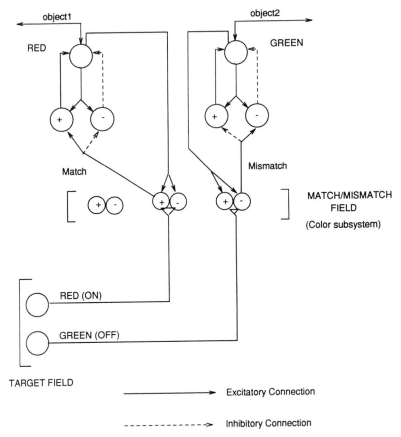

Figure 6

Figure showing the links between the object, target, and match/mismatch fields. Two objects are being represented, one red and one green (only the color circuits of the representations are shown). The attentional target is red, leading to the target unit representing red to be on. The target unit representing green is off. Signals from color cells in the object and target fields met in the match/mismatch field generating feedback signals to the gain-control systems of the object representations. Entities with properties matching the target specification have the balance in their gain-control systems shifted in the positive direction, whereas mismatching entities are shifted in the negative direction, leading to the rapid foregrounding of target objects. It should be noted that match/mismatch signals are held to be generated only from within a subfield related to the featural dimension of the target (color in this case).

between the sensory input and the attentional trace" (p. 366). In the modeling domain, Humphreys and Müller (1993) describe a network model of visual search that involves the matching of perceptual inputs with an internal template. One important reason for postulating the existence of matching operations (rather than a simpler mechanism based on direct interactions between target and perceptual systems) is that organisms "know" when they have detected targets—search behaviors are interrupted and other actions (approach, retreat, etc.) are initiated. Signals from match systems can thus play a role in regulating behavior.

The match/mismatch field (MMF) is divided up into a number of property subfields corresponding to subfields in the object property representation (for instance, a color subfield, a location subfield, a shape subfield, etc.). A target property such as *red* will be matched against specific inputs to the color subfield from the object representations (Figure 6). A match causes feedback to the gain-control system of the matching object, which leads to an excitatory imbalance in the gain-control feedback. A mismatch causes an analogous inhibitory imbalance. No signals are generated from match/mismatch subfields which code for properties of a different type than the target property (e.g., color targets are not matched against the location properties of perceptual inputs).

D. Response Binding

Inputs to the response-binding field are derived from property nodes in the object field. Recall that the idea behind the binding field is that response (action) schemas are associated with variable parameters which must be given specific values to guide the precise execution of the response. Many variables which might be bound simultaneously (e.g., form and position) are likely to be independent (uncorrelated) in an organism's experience, and must be supplied independently from the same target object. The object-based selection, which the current model postulates, allows properties to be selected in coherent bundles, although a target may be selected from distractors on only one individuating dimension (examples follow). This raises the important question of how variable binding is to be represented in a network. In the present model we use the brute force method of assuming that for any response variable there exists a set of nodes capable of representing all values of that variable. Within connectionist terms, this representation might be "distributed," with different values being represented by nonorthogonal (overlapping) patterns across the set of units, or "local," with orthogonal patterns representing each value. In the simulations presented here, the output variable is the category of the target needed by a naming response. Each category is represented orthogonally by a single node, and the model learns associations between patterns of activity over the property nodes of the object field and nodes representing (reportable) categorization decisions. Copresence of multiple objects leads to multiple activation of categories, and hence to competition within this field of category nodes. We will show how the selective foregrounding–backgrounding achieved by the model provides the object matching the target with sufficient advantage in this competition to determine the categorization response. Details of the construction of the links between the property and (response) category units are given in the discussion of the simulations.

E. A Neuropsychological Interpretation of the Model

We intend the various components of the model just described to correspond to anatomically localizable neural systems. Any such mapping from theoretical to neural systems must of course be tentative, but we believe there are reasonable grounds for suggesting the following arrangement. The object field we take to correspond to the large areas of posterior cerebral cortex responsible for the coding of visual information. This coding appears to be distributed over numerous parieto-occipital areas, some dedicated to particular stimulus dimensions (e.g., color in V4). At the highest level, regions in the inferior temporal lobes are also implicated (Mishkin, Ungerleider, and Macko, 1983). As yet unknown grouping mechanisms must act to bind these distributed codes into coherent perceptual unities (objects). We suggest that the gain-control subsystem (on- and off-cells) may be implemented locally within the cortex or may involve interaction with the thalamus by a cortico-thalamo-cortical loop regulating cortical activity. On neuroanatomical grounds, the latter proposal implicates the pulvinar nucleus of the thalamus.

We locate the target field in prefrontal cortex, which is seen by many authors as the center of nervous system "self-control," responsible for the highest levels of planning and goal-directed behavior (see, e.g., Luria, 1973; Fuster, 1980; Stuss & Benson, 1986; Goldman-Rakic, 1987; Shallice, 1988). Such ideas invariably involve a central role for selective attention (Fuster, 1980, 1989). Areas of the prefrontal lobes (e.g., principal sulcus, inferior convexity) are known to be able to maintain visual representations (Fuster, 1980; Goldman-Rakic, 1987), and these areas have reciprocal connections with the preceding posterior visual areas (Goldman-Rakic, 1988). A number of authors have speculated that these areas are involved in the integration of perceptual information in guiding nonroutine behavioral responses, that is, those responses requiring attention (Fuster, 1980; Goldman-Rakic, 1987).

Motor schemas are generally associated with regions of the frontal cortex, such as the premotor cortex and supplementary motor area (Arbib, 1990), and we suppose that the binding of response parameters must take place in such areas. Our model thus proposes that the throughput of sensory information from posterior to frontal (motor) regions is gated by prefrontal selection targets. The remaining issue is that of precisely how prefrontal and posterior systems interact, a notable gray area in all of the preceding works referred to. Our model postulates that the interaction takes place via a matching process, and it seems possible that this could take place by direct cortico–cortical interactions between prefrontal and posterior systems, utilizing the reciprocal pathways known to exist (Goldman-Rakic, 1988). However, there appears to be other possibilities, such as an interaction with the loop from sensory cortex through the limbic system (including the hippocampus) and back to the cortex, as postulated in the visual learning model of Mishkin and his associates (Mishkin, 1982; Mishkin & Appenzeller, 1987). This model appears to attribute attentional modulation of visual learning to prefrontal interaction with this reafferent loop. This idea is consonant with our model, so long as prefrontal inputs are considered to gate activity in the loop such that activity in nommatching channels leads to suppression of associated sensory registers. In this regard it is interesting to note that Goldman-Rakic (1987) remarks that areas of the prefrontal cortex "project to the presubiculum . . . [which] represents a major output of the hippocampus to other cortical structures . . . Accordingly, the prefrontal terminals in this area are in position to gate the output of the hippocampal formation" (p. 389).

We now briefly describe the mathematical implementation of the model used in the simulation studies described in Section IV.

F. Formal Specification of the Model

The model is implemented as a neural network using components familiar from such works as Grossberg (1980), Kohonen (1984), and Rumelhart and McClelland (1986). Each unit in the model is associated with a scalar variable referred to as its *activation value*. Activation values vary in the range $[-1, 1]$ with a resting level of 0. Negative activation values represent sub-baseline states. Nodes are connected by weighted links and communicate by the spread of activation along the links. Links may have positive (excitatory) or negative (inhibitory) values. Only positive activation levels are propagated. The rule of propagation is the familiar one whereby (positive) activation values are multiplied by the weights in the connecting pathways. The *net input* to a given unit is typically the sum of the (positive and negative) inputs it receives along its input pathways. Net inputs are converted into momentary activation values by an *activation function*. The main activation function used in this model is of the "leaky integrater" type, which integrates input activations over space and time but "leaks" due to passive decay.

The function is used by all the units in the object field (property units, and on- and off-units) and by units in the response-binding field. It is given formally by

$$a_i(t+1) = \begin{cases} \delta a_i(t) + (1 - a_i(t))f(net_i(t)) & \text{if } net_i > 0 \\ \delta a_i(t) + (1 + a_i(t))f(net_i(t)) & \text{if } net_i < 0 \end{cases} \tag{1}$$

where a_i is the activation level of unit u_i, and net_i is the net input to u_i, and δ is a "decay" parameter. Because we use negative activation values to represent states of suppressed responsiveness (which should not be thought of as the inverse of excited states, or as the possession of "negative activation"), we in fact use two "decay" parameters: δ^+, representing passive decay from excited states (i.e., $\delta = \delta^+$ if $a_i > 0$), and δ^-, representing spontaneous recovery from suppressed states (i.e., $\delta = \delta^-$ if $a_i < 0$). In *all* the reported simulations $\delta^+ = 0.5$ and $\delta^- = 0.9$, spontaneous recovery being slower than passive decay. To ensure that activations remain bounded, the function $f(x)$ should be some suitable S-shaped "squashing" function, with output in the range $[-1,1]$, and the property $f(0) = 0$. In the reported simulations we use

$$f(x) = \frac{2}{1 + e^{-x}} - 1 \tag{2}$$

which has an appropriate sigmoidal shape with asymptotes at -1 and 1. We note in passing that we have run the model using other activation functions of a similar type, and have not found it to make any difference to the phenomena discussed here.

Because negative activation values represent states of suppressed responsiveness, such values clearly are not propagated. Thus each unit has an output function,

$$o_i(t) = \max(0, a_i(t)) \tag{3}$$

that is, the output is 0 unless the activation value is positive. This will be assumed in all the following equations, where a_i should be taken to represent the output activation value [i.e., $a_i(t) = o_i(t)$].

The behavior of different nodes depends essentially on their net inputs from outside sources. In the assemblies of nodes forming object representations, we have three types of node (see Figure 4): u^p, representing some property, u^{on}, the on-cell, and u^{off}, the off-cell. Their net inputs, net^p, net^{on}, and net^{off} are given respectively by

$$net_i^p = I_i^{ext} + w_1(a_i^{on} - a_i^{off}) \tag{4}$$

$$net_i^{on} = w_2 a_i^p + w_3 \sum_{j \in A} a_j^{on} - w_4 \sum_{j \in A} a_j^{off} + mm_i^{on} \tag{5}$$

$$net_i^{off} = w_2 a_i^p + w_3 \sum_{j \in A} a_j^{off} - w_4 \sum_{j \in A} a_j^{on} + mm_i^{off} \tag{6}$$

where I_i^{ext} is the external input to property unit u_i^p; a^p, a^{on}, and a^{off} are the activations of the property, on- and off-units respectively; w_1, w_2, w_3, and w_4 are weight parameters; A is the set of nodes in the assembly; and mm_i^{on} and mm_i^{off} are signals from the match field [defined in Eqs. (11), (12)]. The external input signal I_i^{ext} is derived from sources outside the model and is set to a value of 1.5. Given the activation function used [Eq. (1)], this is sufficient in itself to drive the activation of a property node to a value of about 0.75. Therefore, in the simulations reported in the following section, the establishment of property node activation levels above or below this value is due to the selection mechanism.

The parameters w_1 and w_2 govern the strength of the interaction between property units and the gain-control cells, and vice versa (Figure 4). Thus, w_1 is the magnitude of the weight of the feedback links from the on- and off-cells to the property unit in an opponent circuit, and w_2 is the weight from property units to gain-control units. Having just one weight parameter in each direction (instead of two independent ones) means that the circuit is inherently "symmetrical" (though this is, in fact, not strictly necessary for the model to function). In all the simulations, $w_1 = 1.3$ (except where it is purposefully manipulated) and $w_2 = 1$. We have not systematically investigated the effects of changing the relative values of these weights or of using nonsymmetrical weights.

The parameters w_3 and w_4 govern the strength of the lateral interactions among the gain-control (on–off) cells. Their values are not fixed but depend on the number of property nodes in the object assembly. These weights control the strength of the feedback within the on–off channels, and it is important that the total feedback any node receives via these channels does not grow too large. Otherwise, for instance, the activity in a channel could become self-sustaining because of the positive feedback. It is also desirable in the implementation to keep the *total* input weight to any gain-control cell from other cells within an assembly constant, independent of the number of other such cells that happen to be in the assembly. This means that the strength of the feedback any gain-control cell receives is independent of the number of cells in the object assembly. Normalization can be achieved locally if each cell is thought of as having a total input "weight," which it distributes evenly among its inputs. Thus the actual values of the parameters w_2 and w_3 are given by

$$w_3 = \frac{W_{tot}^+}{|A|} \tag{7}$$

$$w_3 = \frac{W_{tot}^-}{|A|} \tag{8}$$

where $|A|$ is the number of nodes in the assembly. The parameter W_{tot}^-

represents the total inhibitory weight to a cell (i.e., from off-cells to on-cells, and vice versa), and W_{tot}^+ is the total excitatory weight (from on-cells to on-cells, and off-cells to off-cells).

Units in the match/mismatch field receive input from object property units and from target units. The field contains two classes of units: match units and mismatch units. Only units coding properties of the same class as the current target property can be activated; for example, if targets are specified by location, only the location subfield of the match/mismatch system will be active. Match units of the active subfield fire when they receive inputs from both object and target field cells (i.e., target and property are the same). Mismatch units fire when they receive inputs only from property cells (target and property are different). In the implementation, the activation values of match/mismatch cells are proportional to the strength of the input from the property node, modulated by the strength of the target activation. Formally, for all match/mismatch units u_i^{m+} and u_i^{m-} in the appropriate selction subfield,

$$a_i^{m+} = a_i^{tar} a_i^p \tag{9}$$

$$a_i^{m-} = (1 - \text{sign}(a_i^{tar}))a_i^p \tag{10}$$

where a_i^{m+}, a_i^{m-}, a_i^{tar}, and a_i^p are the activations of the ith match, mismatch, target, and property units, respectively (i.e., for simplicity, units at corresponding locations in the property, target, and match fields code for the same feature). From Eqs. (9) and (10), we see that when $a_i^{tar} = 1$, then $a_i^{m+} = a_i^p$ and $a_i^{m-} = 0$. That is, when a target node is active, the strength of the match signal (a_i^{m+}) generated from the corresponding input property node is equal to the activation level of that node. The mismatch (a_i^{m-}) signal is 0. When $a_i^{tar} = 0$, then $a_i^{m+} = 0$ and $a_i^{m-} = a_i^p$. That is, when there is no target input, the mismatch signal is equal in magnitude to the activation of the property node, and the match signal is 0. When $a_i^p = 0$ (i.e., there is no sensory input to a match/mismatch channel) no signals are generated, whether there is target node input or not, that is, sole activation of a target specification does not give rise to activation in corresponding sensory registers (property nodes). This assumption is probably incorrect, judging by physiological indicators of heightened activity in cortical regions corresponding to a to-be-attended stimulus, even in the absence of the stimulus itself (see, e.g., Roland, 1982). The model could be altered to reflect this "expectancy" priming (which would make selection more efficient), but this would not appear to have any bearing on the issues which concern us in this chapter.

The match/mismatch signals project to the gain-control cells associated with the property unit whose activation caused the match or mismatch. Match signals inhibit the off-cell and excite the on-cell, mismatch signals inhibit the on-cell and excite the off-cell. Formally,

$$mm_i^{on} = a_i^{m+} - a_i^{m-} \tag{11}$$

$$mm_i^{off} = a_i^{m-} - a_i^{m+} \tag{12}$$

where mm_i^{on} and mm_i^{off} are the match/mismatch inputs to the ith on- and off-cells, respectively [see Eqs. (5), (6)] and a^{m+} and a^{m-} denote the activation levels of match and mismatch cells, respectively [Eqs. (9), (10)].

The following tabulation lists the given model parameters and provides typical values used in the following simulations:

$$I_i^{ext} = 1.5$$

$$\delta^+ = 0.5$$

$$\delta^- = 0.9$$

$$w_1 = 1.3$$

$$w_2 = 1.0$$

$$W_{tot}^+ = 1.3$$

$$W_{tot}^- = 1.3$$

IV. MODEL SIMULATIONS

This section provides detailed examples of the dynamical properties of the model and simulates data from a number of paradigms, including interference effects and negative priming.

A. Selection and Interference

The simulations in this section illustrate the basic dynamics of selection in the model. The case considered is the generation of an overt categorization response (naming) to one of two simultaneously presented line drawings of common objects. The naming target is distinguished from the distractor by its possession of some criterial attribute—this attribute will generally be the object's color. (This is the display type used in, e.g., Tipper, 1985.)

To implement such simulations, the network was trained to associate sets of properties with object categories. In terms of Figure 3, weights were learned between distributed (i.e., correlated) patterns of activity in the object field and activity in single nodes representing categories in the response system (Figure 7). These weights were learned using the

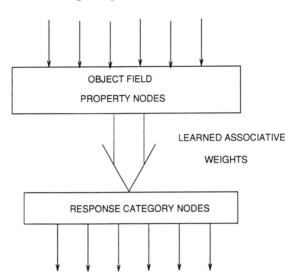

Figure 7

Weights linking nodes in the object and category fields are learned using the delta rule supervised learning algorithm. After learning, a distributed pattern of activity in the object field, representing a single object, gives rise to a single (orthogonal) categorization decision. The presence of multiple, simultaneously analyzed objects can give rise to competing bindings of the categorization response.

delta rule associative learning procedure (Rumelhart & McClelland, 1986), though the model is not tied to the use of this particular algorithm. After learning, presentation of an object is represented by activity over a particular set of property nodes. This activity feeds through the learned weights generating a pattern of activity on the category nodes, considered here to represent the binding of the naming response to a particular category (Figures 2 and 3). If multiple objects are present in the input, it will be expected that multiple category bindings will be coactivated and that selection, therefore, will have to take place to generate a coherent response to the target.

The property nodes are organized into a number of property subfields, according to stimulus dimension. The dimensions used include location, position, size, shape, animacy, and function. These dimensions are important in the matching process, as match/mismatch signals are only directly generated within the selection dimension subfield. Some of the nodes in the object field stand for contingent properties of the particular object presented (e.g., color and position). These properties, although bound into the object assembly, are irrelevant with regard to the categorization response. Other activated nodes stand for defining characteristics of the object (i.e., characteristics present during training of the property to category mapping). Patterns of activity over such property nodes are assumed to encode semantic (categorization-relevant) features, and may be thought of as a distributed representation of the semantic classification of the object. In the following simulations, object assemblies consist of nine or ten property nodes, of which five are always category relevant, the remainder code for color and position. The generation of an overt (conscious) classification response thus involves the mapping of the distributed semantic representation (in which different objects of correlated categories might share nodes) onto a local representation of category (in which different categories are orthogonal to each other). Thus nodes representing, say, *ANIMATE HUMAN MALE TWO-LEGS*, would give rise to a peak of activity in a category node representing the category *MAN*, with relatively little activation of the other category nodes. In the simulations reported here, there were 50 property nodes in the object field and 12 category nodes in the response (parameter-binding) field. Given the replication of the property node structure in the gain-control and match fields, this yields a total of 262 nodes.

We now illustrate the way in which the mechanism just described realizes the central function of selection of objects and the concomitant coherent binding of response parameters in situations in which a target object is accompanied by one or more distractor. In the following simulations the objects presented will be thought of as colored line drawings, with the selection cue being color (Tipper, 1985). The simulations are produced by activating property nodes for both objects (say, a red cat and a green guitar), which are linked in two assemblies, as previously discussed. The process of linkage (object grouping) is not explicitly modeled here, but is assumed to take place during lower level perceptual processes (as stated earlier, this model of attention is object based). Concurrently, in the target field, a node representing the target property (say, the color red) is activated. Activation from the object field feeds through the learned connections to the category field (as discussed previously) giving rise to two competing response tendencies. Selection is achieved by virtue of the fact that internal targets and externally driven activations come together in the match/mismatch field. In the particular example under consideration, the target *red* generates a match with the property "red," which forms part of the object assembly representing the cat, and a mismatch with the property "green," which forms part of the guitar representation. As discussed previously, the match/mismatch signals break the symmetry in the gain-control feedback within the object field. The match signal from *red* causes the opponent mechanism to generate net excitatory feedback to the property "red," which spreads through the relevant object assembly (via the on–off nodes), giving a boost to all property nodes within it. Conversely, the mismatch with the

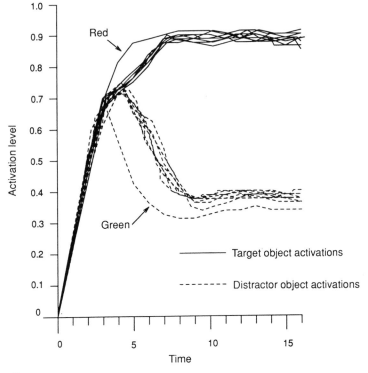

Figure 8

Attentional separation of target and distractor objects using color as the dimension of selection. As input arrives in the object field the two assemblies briefly attain similar activation levels, but eventually the nodes representing target (RED) and distractor (GREEN) colors are respectively enhanced and suppressed by virtue of matching or failing to match the internal target (RED). This activation gap then spreads through to the rest of the property nodes in the respective assemblies by the linked on–off channels described in the text.

property node "green" tips the balance in its gain-control feedback in favor of the off-channel. This heightened off-activation spreads from the node coding for green to the rest of the relevant assembly via the lateral connections between the gain-control units (Figure 5).

To illustrate this process, Figure 8 shows the activation values of nodes in the object field when two objects are simultaneously presented, one of which is to be responded to (selected) on the basis of possessing some criterial property (color, in this case). The target object is in the color *red* and the distractor is in *green*. At stimulus onset, all activated property nodes increase their activation levels together. At a certain point, however, the feedback from the match system starts to influence the pattern of activity. First of all, the nodes which give rise to the match/mismatch signals (*red* and *green*) become separated, *red* being amplified and *green* suppressed. This amplification/suppression rapidly spreads to the rest of their respective assemblies, leading to the separation of the two sets of nodes.

It should be noted at this point how the model does not cause the representation of the distractor to fall below background levels (i.e., to disappear). This is partly due to the fact that the activation of the property nodes drives the activity in the gain-control feedback channels—as the activity level of a property node falls it generates less inhibitory feedback onto itself. The resting level represents the equilibrium activation between the external driving input and the self-generated inhibitory feedback. The model thus provides an implementation of an automatically self-adjusting gain-control mechanism, which allows the strength of the inhibitory feedback to be continually responsive to distractor activation levels.

The effect of this separation of target and distractor inputs on responding is shown in Figure 9. To begin with, there is an equal tendency to bind the response to both input patterns, preventing any response being made (two categories cannot be named at once). However, as the target and distractor activations in the object field become separated, this leads to one categorization decision becoming dominant. Although we have not attempted to implement a specific response generation mechanism, we suppose that there is some minimal dominance of one binding over another, which is required before a response can be confidently initiated. Thus, reaction time will correlate positively with the time taken for a clearly dominant response binding to emerge. These simulations show how the model implements the idea that the selective attention acts to bias the competition for control of the parameters of the response systems.

The strength of the gain-control feedback in the on–off channels, which leads to these results, is dependent not only on the strength of the input from the property nodes but also on the values of the weights in the on- and off-channels, which are set to be equal (in magnitude) and opposite [parameter w_1 in Eq. (4)]. From this it seems clear that the degree of separation achieved at asymptote between target and distractor will be a function of the magnitude of these weights. Because it is this activation advantage which allows a dominant response tendency to emerge, it follows that this selection gradient will be reflected in the response system.

This is illustrated in Figure 10, which shows the timecourse and asymptotic values of the activation difference between target and distractor for different values of the magnitude on the feedback parameter w_1. As can be seen, the greater the value of w_1, the greater and more

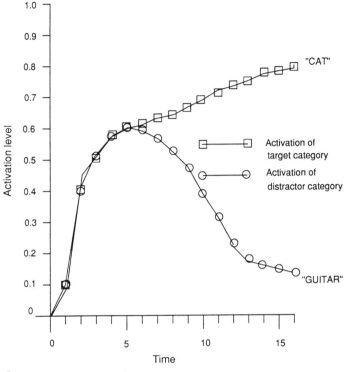

Figure 9

Activation levels of nodes representing the binding of the identification (naming) response to a particular category in response to the object field activation pattern shown in Figure 8. The attentional separation of target and distractor representations leads to the dominance of information from the target in the categorization decision. Because this information is "consistent," a clear categorization emerges.

rapid is the separation achieved between response strength to target and distractor. In other words, higher values of w_1 lead to more efficient selection. As previously discussed, there is known to be wide individual variation in selection ability, as well as systematic differences between various groups. The model thus suggests possible mechanistic sources for these differences. There are other manipulations which may be made, giving a variety of individual selection profiles. For instance, for the model to function, it is not necessary that the feedback weights (w_1) have equal magnitudes in the on–off channels. Greater strength in the off-channel, for instance, leads to an overall dampening effect.

A familiar finding in studies of interference is that greater similarity beween target and distractor leads to greater interference (Estes, 1972; Bjork & Murray, 1977; La Heij, 1988; Duncan & Humphreys, 1989;

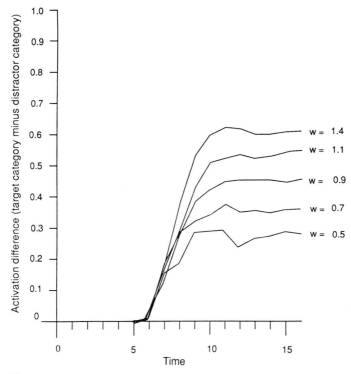

Figure 10

Difference in activation level between target and distractor categories (response binding) over time for different magnitudes of the opponent-circuit feedback parameter w_1. Higher values of w_1 produce more rapid separation of target and distractor categories as well as higher asymptotic values.

LaBerge & Brown, 1989).[3] This increase in interference is found in the model if it is assumed that two separate objects can share property nodes, that is, if the same property node can be bound into more than one object assembly. Thus, in a display showing a cat and a dog, individual nodes representing properties such as *ANIMATE HAS-FOUR-LEGS* would form part of two assemblies simultaneously. These nodes would thus receive positive (excitatory) feedback from the other nodes

[3]We note that distractor interference effects are complex. Although distractor interference can be greater when the distractor is related to the target (Klein, 1964; Stroop, 1935) and such interference is determined both by semantic properties and response set (La Heij, 1988; La Heij, Dirkx, & Kramer, 1990), other work has shown facilitation from related distractors (La Heij, Van Der Heijden, & Schreuder, 1985; Underwood, 1980). One explanation is that there are multiple representations associated with the ignored object, for example, for its perceptual, semantic, and response properties. The effects of these representations may be to facilitate or inhibit performance, depending on task demands.

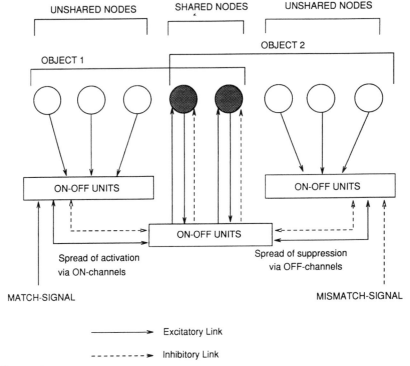

Figure 11

An example of two object assemblies sharing nodes. Each assembly consists of five nodes with two nodes being shared with the other. The assembly labeled OBJECT 1 is shown as matching a selection target (on some dimension) and thereby receiving a match signal to its gain-control subsystem. The nonmatching object (OBJECT 2) receives a mismatch input, flipping its gain-control system into inhibitory mode. The two shared nodes, being part of both assemblies, are thus subject to both amplificatory and suppressive influences spreading from the nodes that are unique to each object.

forming part of the object assembly matching the target, and negative feedback from the nonmatching object. (See Figure 11.)

This combination would be expected to yield an activation level in the shared nodes that would be higher than that achieved by the unshared nodes in the distractor, yet lower than that achieved by the unshared nodes in the target. Because the activation of these shared nodes can spread via the on-channels to other components of the distractor assembly, we predict that the general level of activation of a distractor will be a positive function of its degree of correlation with the target, thus giving rise to greater interference in the binding process.

To illustrate this phenomenon, the selection process just described was run with a series of distractor objects varying in their degree of similarity to the target and implemented as the sharing of category-relevant property nodes. As before, in each trial two object assemblies were simultaneously activated representing two objects differing in color. Selection was based on the activation of a node in the target field specifying only the color of the object to be named. All parameters were unchanged. In the simulations, the shared features between target and distractor were always of the criterial kind (i.e., the shared features were relevant to the categorization decision). Although sharing noncriterial features would be expected also to produce interference (by the same process as that described), these features themselves would not directly contribute to the activation of competing responses. Thus the more difficult case for the model is to generate a coherent response in the presence of distractors with shared criterial features, and it is crucial to demonstrate that it is capable of such performance. The dependent variables looked at were the difference in the activation levels achieved by target and distractor objects in the object field, and the subsequent level of interference in the binding process. Figure 12 shows the difference in the mean activation levels achieved by object field nodes for four levels of correlation between object assemblies. Each curve is labeled with the percentage of shared active nodes in the two assemblies, given for both criterial (category-relevant) features ($c1$) and total (criterial and noncriterial features ($c2$).

As the correlation rises the mean activation gap achieved between target and distractor objects decreases. This decreased activation gap between sets of property nodes is reflected in the category-binding field in the form of a poorer signal-to-noise ratio for the target category. This greater interference simply reflects the fact that, in this model, overt categorization is implemented as a process of orthogonalization (correlated object-field pattern vectors are mapped to orthogonal categorization vectors). The greater the correlation between two distinct simultaneously presented inputs, the more difficult this becomes (i.e., the patterns become harder to separate).

Earlier we presented two general arguments regarding why inhibition is likely to be an important component of any biological selection process. To make this point further, we emphasize that it would be impossible to achieve this separation of patterns with shared nodes without the ability to specifically suppress the features unique to the distractor (i.e., without the inhibitory component of the gain-control mechanism). If the model contained only a facilitatory mechanism boosting target activation, then enhancement of the shared properties in the target assembly would spread unopposed through *both* assemblies, leading to enhancement of the distractor and the inability to selectively respond. In general, it is difficult to see how any model which uses correlated, distributed representations (thereby allowing sharing of nodes in object

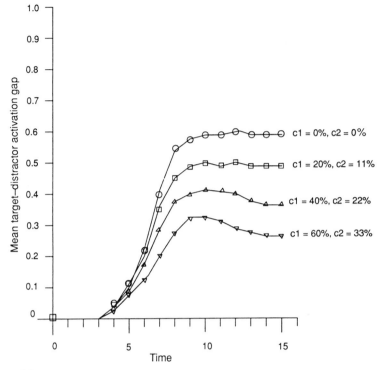

Figure 12

Simulation of similarity effects on efficiency of selection. The greater the similarity between two (categorically distinct) objects (in terms of shared nodes in the two assemblies), the greater the interference caused by the distractor, as measured here by the difference in the mean activation values achieved by the nodes composing the target and distractor object assemblies. Each curve in the figure is labeled by two percentage correlation values, c_1 and c_2. The former gives the percentage of category-relevant active nodes that the target and distractor share, and the latter the percentage of overall active nodes (including, e.g., nodes representing location).

representations) could achieve effective selection without the active inhibition of nontarget related features counteracting the spread of activation from the attended object. We additionally note that these features may be arbitrarily many, and, as is the case in these simulations, may not be related in any way to the endogenously generated selection feature (and thus cannot be directly inhibited by a mismatch signal). It is thus hard to escape the conclusion that the specific inhibition of such features must be due to a spreading inhibition mechanism (as proposed by Tipper, 1985), with its source in the dimension on which selection is being made.

Previous discussions of this idea (e.g., Neumann & DeSchepper, 1991) have considered spreading inhibition as analogous to spreading activation, and have not addressed the issue of how it is that inhibition *can* spread. Activation can spread because excitatory links are, so to speak, transitive. If a node u_1 excites a node u_2, and u_2 excites u_3, then activation of u_1 will eventually spread to u_3. If the links in this chain are inhibitory, however, then activation of u_1 will inhibit u_2, the effect of which will be to *disinhibit* u_3, the exact opposite of what is required. Hence, spreading inhibition cannot operate in a manner strictly analogous to the typical mechanism of spreading activation. The model presented here contains an effective solution to this problem, the only one we are aware of.

B. Negative Priming

We now consider how the model accounts for the basic facts of the negative priming phenomenon discussed earlier (Tipper, 1985). In this paradigm, a priming selection trial, which might be represented in the model by Figures 8 and 9, is followed by a probe trial. In the probe selection trial, the target item might be the same as in the priming trial (repeated prime condition), the same as the distractor item in the priming trial (ignored prime condition), or different from both (novel probe condition). It is commonly found that reaction times to the ignored prime condition (i.e., when the current target item was the previously ignored distractor) are slower than in the novel probe condition. Reaction times are fastest to the repeated prime. In the following simulations we will only be interested in the comparison between the ignored prime (IP) and the novel probe (NP) conditions. We assume that the repetition priming effect is due to factors which we do not attempt to model here, such as increased connection strength in selected perception–action pathways, or in the lowering of selected response thresholds. Repetition priming appears to last for some time (at least a matter of hours, possibly much longer) and can withstand any number of intervening events, whereas the negative priming effect does decline over time (Neill & Valdes, 1992), and appears not to survive the making of intervening responses (Neill & Westberry, 1987; Tipper et al., 1991).

Previous informal accounts of the negative priming phenomenon (Tipper, 1985; Tipper & Cranston, 1985) stipulate that during selection, distractors are actively inhibited, and the inhibition is evident in the retarded responding in the IP condition. This informal account does not stipulate *to what extent* distractor items are inhibited while they are present. For instance, are their internal representations suppressed below resting levels? Our formal model makes specific proposals in this regard. As illustrated in Figures 8 and 9, which show how the model achieves selection and coherent responding, it is not necessary for the model to "obliterate" any internal trace of the distractor object in order to respond properly to the target; that is, it is not necessary to suppress its representation below resting levels. Indeed, we do not believe it is appropriate to postulate that the distractor is suppressed below resting levels for a variety of reasons. As discussed earlier, nonattended objects in the world form a background, the representation of which facilitates both recognition of particular objects (by providing contextual information) and effective action toward them (by allowing the adaptation of actions to unpredictable details of the physical context). Further evidence that the unattended field is not only not deleted but is actively monitored comes from the orienting response. Organisms exhibit orienting responses to salient or potentially significant events in the unattended field to the extent that ongoing, useful activity (e.g., eating) may be disrupted. A particularly relevant example of orienting to the background is when we notice the *offset* of an unattended background noise, whose presence we had ceased to be conscious of. It is difficult to see how the offset of an unregistered signal is likely to be noticeable. There is also experimental evidence of distractor objects (associated with specific responses) being processed even to the point of incipient response generation, as indicated by electromyogram recordings in appropriate effectors (Erikson, Coles, Morris, & O'Hara, 1985). All such considerations support the notion that the unattended field is analyzed and continually monitored as a background to focal actions. This would not be possible if selectively attending to one part of the afferent field effectively obliterated all else. Our model thus does not postulate that the representation of distractors is suppressed below resting levels (Figure 9), and we consider such a proposal to be, in the general case, untenable.

This apparently raises something of a quandary. Suppose that Figure 9 represents the priming trial in a negative priming experiment and that at the end of the trial the display is terminated and the distractor disappears. The object field nodes constituting its internal representation now no longer receive external input. We might expect that their activation values would then decay back to resting levels, given the decay term in the activation function [Eq. (1)]. On the basis of this it would be difficult to predict any kind of negative priming when the probe display appears in the IP condition. We might even predict a modicum of facilitatory priming based on any residual activation in the relevant units at the onset of the probe display.

However, this is not in fact what happens. As noted earlier, the equilibrium activation level achieved by any property unit constitutes a balance between its net input and the spontaneous tendency to decay to resting levels. This level is lower for units in distractor representations than for the units in targets because, in the distractor assembly, the activity in the linked opponent circuit is concentrated in the off-channel, counteracting the effect of the excitatory external input, and reducing the overall net input. Once the external excitatory input is terminated, however, the net input to a property unit in a distractor representation consists of just inhibitory feedback from the off-channel, driven by the activation of the property units themselves. We can see this from the net input equation for a property node u_i^p, Eq. (4), repeated here.

$$net_i^p = I_i^{ext} + w_1(a_i^{on} - a_i^{off})$$

Thus for a property node u_i^p in a distractor assembly, when the external input is terminated, then $I_i^{ext} = 0$, $a_i^{on} < 0$ (on-channel is suppressed during selection), and $a_i^{off} > 0$ (off-channel is boosted). Thus at the offset of the prime display, $net_i^p = -w_1 a_i^{off} < 0$. The effect of this switch of the net input from excitatory to inhibitory is to cause an inhibitory "rebound" in the activation values of the property units constituting the distractor representation. This process is illustrated in Figure 13, which shows what happens to the property nodes in the object field for a display of two objects, one of which is selected for responding and one of which is ignored.

The two curves in the figure represent the mean activation values of all the nodes in each of the two object assemblies (the assemblies are orthogonal in this case). As can be clearly seen, at the offset of the display, while the representation of the target object gradually decays back toward resting levels,[4] the representation of the distractor returns to a resting equilibrium value via a different route involving an excursion into the negative activation region representing suppressed responsiveness.[5] We propose that it is this postoffset inhibitory rebound in the

[4]To try to model what happens when displays are terminated, it is necessary to add two further processing assumptions to the model. The first is that the assembly of nodes representing an object percept should immediately start to decay as an assembly; that is, the lateral connections linking the on–off cells in each assembly should decay back to 0, so that the property cells are no longer grouped in an object percept. In the implementation, after stimulus offset $w_{ij}(t + 1) = 0.9w_{ij}(t)$, where w_{ij} is the weight linking any two on- and/or off-cells. If the weights do not decay, activity within, say, the off-circuit of the distractor, can be self-maintaining, generating long-term negative priming, akin to an object-shaped "hole" in perception. There would also be disastrous interference between successively presented objects which share nodes, producing a summed assembly containing all input properties. The second assumption is that at stimulus offset, activity of the target node passively decays at the usual rate. Without this assumption, decay of the target–object representation is considerably slower, due to continued match field input.

[5]This "rebound" behavior at offset of external input is typical of opponent mechanisms, and is largely responsible for their attraction in explaining a variety of phenomena (see, e.g., Solomon & Corbit, 1974; Houghton, in press).

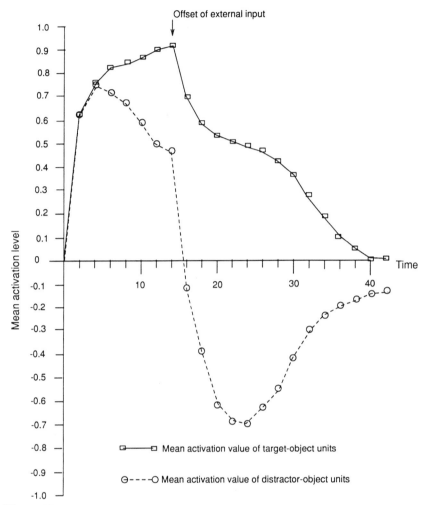

Figure 13

Showing how the model can accommodate the negative priming effect with the need for the distractor representation not to be suppressed below resting levels while there is external input. The two curves show the mean activation values over time of the units in two object assemblies, activated by an external display in a selection task. In particular, the dashed curve shows the mean activation of a distractor stimulus. At offset of the external input, the representation of the distractor does not passively decay to resting level but suffers an inhibitory rebound.

activation of the distractor representation that causes negative priming. If the distractor is re-presented as a target during the time the nodes constituting its internal representation are in this suppressed state, then reaction times will be retarded relative to a novel probe (whose constituent nodes will be at resting level activations). Thus the model successfully accommodates negative priming with the need for the representation of distractor inputs to be maintained above resting level. Moreover, no special mechanism is required to achieve this. The inhibitory component of the selection mechanism, being based on self-feedback via the opponent system, is automatically self-regulating so that ignored distractors reach equilibrium activation levels above resting level (but below that of the target). It is this same opponent mechanism that is responsible for the postoffset rebound (negative priming) found when the distractor input is suddenly terminated (or, conversely, if attention is suddenly switched from a target; see the simulation of inhibition of return in the following section).

The effect of the inhibitory rebound at prime offset on subsequent representation in the probe is shown in Figures 14 and 15. These figures show the mean activation values achieved by target and distractor assembly nodes in a priming trial followed by a probe trial (the curves are actually the means of 10 runs of the model using different sets of input objects and some random variation of the parameters, w_1, δ^+, and δ^-). As before, each assembly contains one node representing color (red or green). The target object is red in both the prime and probe trials, and the distractor is green. One consequence of this is that in the ignored prime condition, the ignored distractor must change color. Figure 14 shows the novel probe (NP) condition in which the target in the probe trial is unrelated to either of the objects in the priming trial. In this case, there is little difference between the prime and probe conditions. The target is separated from the distractor while both are on (presentations here are fairly brief and maximal separation is not achieved while the input is still on). After stimulus offset (when responses are actually made in such experiments), there is clear dominance of the target over the distractor (which is, of course, inhibited). Response binding in the probe trial is thus not significantly different than the prime.

By contrast, Figure 15 shows the situation in the critical ignored prime condition. Here the target in the probe display is the same category as the previously ignored distractor. In this case, the inhibitory rebound at the offset of the prime interferes with the re-representation of the stimulus as a target. Indeed, at probe onset, the distractor achieves a higher initial activation than the target which takes time to establish dominance. Interestingly, at probe offset, the decay of the target representation is more rapid than in the novel probe condition. This is because, in the ignored prime condition, the establishment of recirculating activation in the on-channels of the target is badly interfered with by the residual activation in the off-channel, established when the probe target was the previous distractor. In the novel probe condition, it is this

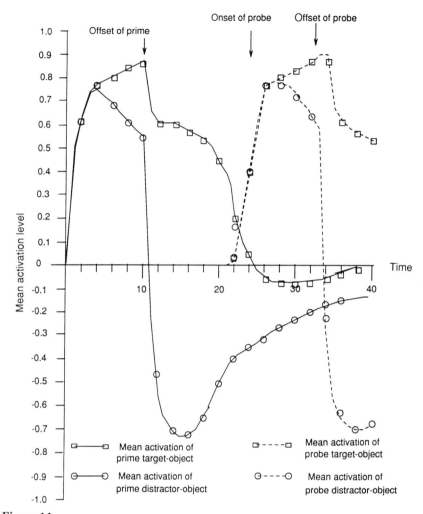

Figure 14

Full simulation of a negative priming trial with both a prime and a probe display. This figure shows the mean activation of object assembly nodes in the NP (novel probe) condition. Selection is achieved equally well in both the prime and probe sections of the task.

self-reinforcing on-channel activity that enables the target to maintain its activation after display offset, despite receiving no further external input and having a passive decay rate (δ^+) of 0.5. The off-channel activation affecting the new target is, in addition, supported by some residual strength, at the onset of the probe, in the link from the distractor color (green) to the target (as previously noted, in the IP condition, the

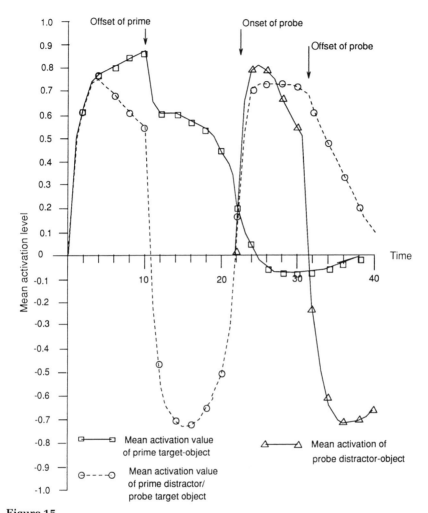

Figure 15

Full simulation of a negative priming trial with both a prime and a probe display. This figure shows the mean activation of object assembly nodes in the IP (ignored prime) condition, that is, where the target in the probe is the previously ignored distractor. In this condition, selection of the target in the probe trial is clearly impaired relative to both the prime trial and to the selection of a novel probe (control condition) shown in the Figure 14.

probe target has changed color from green to red in the probe trial). The idea that negative priming might involve interference in the formation of what we call object assemblies has been previously put forward by Allport, Tipper, and Chmiel (1985).

Thus the model claims that for brief stimulus exposures, negative priming in the IP condition involves both increased interference from the distractor while the display is on (compared to the NP condition) and in addition a "weaker" (more rapidly fading) internal representation of the previously ignored target. Given longer exposure this "weakness" is eventually overcome. Our account of the negative priming effect is thus that the suppressed activation of an ignored distractor found at the offset of a display results in a later response to that distractor, suffering greater interference from copresent objects. This emphasis on the role of interference is very important because it suggests that in the ignored prime condition, negative priming might not be observed if there is no distractor present in the probe stimulus, because there would then be no interference. As is clear from Figure 15, the fact that the representation of the ignored distractor is suppressed at probe onset does not actually prevent that representation from rapidly reaching a significant activation level. What is slowing coherent response binding is the difficulty in selecting the previous distractor as the new target, which requires the suppression of a probe distractor that has an initial activation advantage.

This effect of the distractor can best be shown by comparing the activation of competing categorical response bindings when there either is or is not a distractor present in the probe display in both the IP and NP conditions. Figure 16 shows the difference in the activations of units representing the target and distractor categories during the probe display for each of four conditions: ignored prime, with and without distractor (IP +D, IP −D), and novel probe, with and without distractor (NP +D, NP −D).

Positive values of the curves indicate that the correct (target) category is more highly active. Negative values indicate that the incorrect (distractor) category is more highly active. As can be seen, there is a considerable difference in activation in both IP and NP conditions depending on whether or not a distractor is present. The only time when the incorrect categorization decision shows an advantage is in the IP +D condition. In the absence of a distractor, correct categorization in the IP condition is rapid and effective, though there is still some lag relative to the novel probe condition.

Allport et al. (1985, Experiment 9; see also Lowe, 1979) tested the four probe conditions simulated here and found that in the absence of a probe distractor, RTs in the ignored prime condition were faster than to both the IP +D condition *and* the NP +D condition, in accordance with the model. They also found, however, that the IP −D probe produced faster responding than the corresponding NP −D probe; that is, in the absence of a distractor there was *facilitation* of the ignored prime relative to the novel probe, which we have not replicated in the model (the

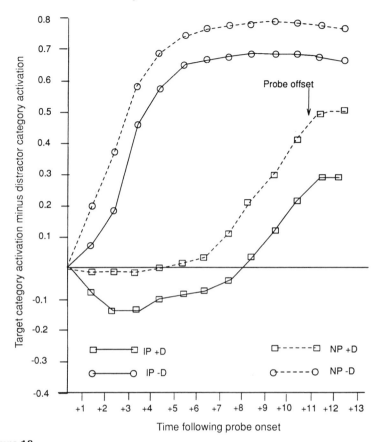

Figure 16

Negative priming as the effect of increased interference in response binding from the distractor during the probe. Each curve shows the difference in activation between the unit in the response binding field representing the correct (target-matching) category and the unit representing the incorrect (distractor) category during presentation of the probe. The four conditions are IP +D: ignored prime with distractor, IP −D: ignored prime without distractor, NP +D: novel probe with distractor, and NP −D: novel probe without distractor. In the ignored prime trials, the to-be-attended item was the distractor on the previous (prime) trial.

NP −D curve in Figure 16 shows the fastest rise and highest asymptote, which we take to be negatively correlated with RT). Thus our model gives the correct ordinal positions for three of the four conditions, but cannot account for the facilitation of the ignored prime (relative to the NP −D condition) in the absence of a distractor. It seems possible (as is argued by Allport et al., 1985) that this facilitation is produced by the prior encoding of the IP −D target in the prime, allied to the fact that in the absence of the distractor, coupling of noncategorical (e.g., color) features with categorical features is not necessary for selection and identification. Responses can therefore be made simply on the basis of the facilitated categorical features. However, as mentioned earlier, we have not tried to account for facilitatory effects generally, as we believe them to be due to different mechanisms.

Thus our model does not include any perceptual facilitation in the formation of an object assembly due to prior encoding of that object. There is nothing in the model, however, which rules out such facilitatory processes, and it seems clear that this explanation for the facilitation of ignored primes could be implemented within our current scheme, for instance by requiring the links in an object assembly to build up over time. Prior formation of links (during the prime) could then facilitate their (re-)formation during the probe. Alternatively, as noted earlier (Figure 9), our model shows activation of response bindings related to the distractor which could form the basis of a small positive priming effect. We should add though that this issue is a little confused empirically. For instance, Tipper et al. (1990) found no priming effects when the probe had no distractor. Others (e.g., Yee, 1991) have found negative priming in the absence of probe distractors. This suggests that whatever the source of facilitatory priming due to ignored distractors, it is fairly weak and probably varies with the task.

We have carried out other simulations with the model investigating, for instance, the effects of parameter variance on the timecourse of the negative priming effect and the relation between efficiency of selection and degree of negative priming. The model also shows semantic spread of negative priming if ignored prime and probe target share nodes (see the preceding discussion of similarity effects in interference). At present, we are testing novel predictions derived from such simulations. Although we anticipate that the model will not remain unchanged in the light of further investigation, we believe that in its current form, it has provided a useful first attempt, suggesting new experiments and providing a much more detailed (and demonstrably effective) theory of selection and negative priming than has hitherto been available.

During work with the computer model, we noted that the rebound effect which the opponent mechanism generates is not confined to ignored inputs, but can happen to selected inputs also, if the internal target field representation suddenly changes. This generates a mismatch with the still activated, previously selected item, causing it to inhibit itself. This is an adaptively useful property, allowing rapid attention switching by automatically deselecting previously facilitated items and preventing perseverative responding. Given the apparent utility of such a process (provided for free by the model), we wondered whether there was any evidence for it in attention switching and we were put in mind of the phenomenon of inhibition of return (IOR; Posner & Cohen, 1984). We consider in the next section whether a mechanism essentially identical to the one we propose can also account for IOR.

C. Inhibition of Return

In this section, we briefly discuss another attentional phenomenon, inhibition of return (Posner & Cohen, 1984). Whereas the negative priming effect appears to be implicated in voluntary selective attention (endogenous selection), IOR arises in the context of the orienting response, the "grabbing" of attention by an external event (exogenous selection). Our main concern here will be to consider whether the IOR phenomenon can be accounted for by mechanisms similar to those we propose in our account of negative priming, and consequently whether endogenous and exogenous selection processes may be related.

In the IOR paradigm, subjects fixating a central point have their attention peripherally cued. If a target subsequently appears in the cued location within about 100 msec, RTs to the target are facilitated with respect to targets at uncued locations. Paradoxically, at longer SOAs of 300–500 msec, RTs to targets at cued locations are retarded by comparison to uncued targets (Maylor, 1985). This phase represents the inhibition of return. Posner and Cohen (1984) argued that the facilitation was due to a short-lived covert orienting response to the cued location, that is, the involuntary capturing of attention by an unexpected external event. The inhibitory effect was also found for overt orienting and appeared to require that after orienting, attention had to be removed from the cued location. According to the authors: "[I]f attention is not drawn away from a cued location, no net inhibition is found" (p. 541). They noted that the inhibitory component apparently occurs automatically (not as the result of a conscious strategy) and argued that it was independent of the facilitatory effect and possibly due to events in sensory pathways rather than to the orienting response per se.

A somewhat different view is put forward by Maylor (1985), who argues that the facilitatory and inhibitory components are not due to different processes, but rather reflect different facets of the orienting reaction. This conclusion is supported by a number of empirical studies carried out by Maylor. For instance, in one experiment (Maylor, 1985, Experiment 2) it was found that the facilitation effect was completely abolished if the subject needed to make an overt orienting response to another stimulus at the moment the cue appeared (thus preventing orienting to the cue). In this case, inhibition disappeared also, apparently being linked to the occurrence of orienting (and thus of facilitation). In addition to this, it was found (Maylor, 1985, Experiment 3) that when cueing of two locations simultaneously occurred, then facilitation was approximately halved compared to cueing to a single location. At the same time, the amount of inhibition found was also decreased in the double-cue condition, again by approximately one half. Maylor concluded that the inhibitory component, as well as the facilitatory, is thus "dependent on externally controlled orienting," and acts in tandem with the facilitation.

A recent development in this paradigm is the discovery by Tipper, Driver, and Weaver (1991) that IOR can occur not just for locations but for whole objects. These authors employed a design in which subjects' attention was cued to one of two peripheral *moving* objects (squares). Following cueing, subjects' attention was recalled to a central point. On two-thirds of the trials, a probe then appeared in one of the two squares, either the previously cued or the uncued (both of which would have moved). Stimulus onset asynchrony (SOA) between the initial peripheral cue and the probe was equiprobably 430 msec or 695 msec, and subjects had to press a key as soon as they noticed the probe. The important comparison was for the probe detection RT in the cued and uncued conditions, with slower RTs in the cued condition indicating inhibition of return to the object (which would have moved since the presentation of the peripheral cue). This result was obtained for both SOAs, indicating that the inhibitory component of the IOR phenomenon can be linked to whole objects rather than simply locations. (Unfortunately, the experiments reported did not look for the facilitatory component at shorter SOAs.) It had been previously argued that IOR is useful in a visual search through static scenes, inhibiting reexamination of already searched locations. Tipper et al. (1991) argue that "tagging fixed spatial coordinates would not permit efficient search through the dynamic scenes of everyday life, in which mobile objects' locations continually change" (p. 290) and thus that object-centered IOR is highly adaptive.

Given the preceding findings, a reasonable theory of IOR would need to account for at least the following:

1. The coupling of the facilitatory and inhibitory components of IOR, such that the inhibitory component manages to "hit" just what was previously facilitated.
2. The timecourse of the phenomenon, such that the facilitation disappears with a shift of attention and the inhibition takes over. What turns off the facilitation and turns on the inhibition?
3. The apparent positive correlations of the strength of the two components found by Maylor (1985), described earlier.

We show here how a plausible extension of our opponent-based selection mechanism to orienting can account for these findings. To do

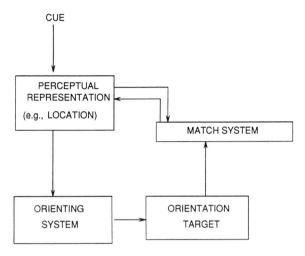

Figure 17

A functional model of the orienting response. We propose that cue detection causes the orienting system to set up an internal representation of the cue location, which then acts as a target. The presence of the internal target leads to facilitation of the cue location by feedback via the match system. The internal architecture and interactions of the target, match, and perceptual systems in the figure are identical to the target, match, and object fields (respectively) of our selection model.

this we need first to present a functional model of what happens during orienting. Our proposed model is shown in Figure 17. The cueing signal is detected by an orienting subsystem (which we propose works in dynamic, competitive interaction with the top-down attentional system in our selection model). The detection of the cue and activation of orienting sets up a representation of an orientation target, analogous to the top-down target in the selection model. (This exogenously generated target will typically suppress endogenous targets, diverting attention from ongoing goal-directed activity.) We propose that this target interacts with the cue representation in the same way as in our selection model. The cue representation (which may, of course, be an object) is composed of linked opponent circuits, and the interaction of cue and target in the match/mismatch system generates a match signal causing facilitation in the manner described earlier. (This matching would permit the organism to know when orienting is complete.) We propose that the subsequent switching away of attention involves the quenching of the activation of the previous (externally derived) orientation target and its replacement with another target (specified by an internal plan or a new external stimulus, for instance). The activation in the cue representation will persist, however (due to the previous facilitation, or to the fact that the corresponding object is still visible), but will now generate a mismatch signal from the match field (due to the change of target). This instigates an inhibitory rebound in the representation of the cued input, as occurs to the ignored distractor in our selective attention model. Such a mechanism would clearly be of adaptive value, allowing the organism to rapidly and specifically suppress previously attended (and potentiated) stimuli, thereby preventing interference and perseverative responding. (Regarding perseveration, we note in passing that the need to actively suppress highly activated representations in the control of serially ordered behavior is postulated in the "competitive queueing" models of Houghton, 1990, and Burgess & Hitch, 1992. Both these models use an opponent-type mechanism to achieve this, whereby a sequence element generates inhibitory feedback onto itself. See Houghton, 1993, for discussion of the general need for such control mechanisms in neural networks.)

We now illustrate this dynamic in a number of simulations in which we adapt our selection model to the orienting response, with minimal changes. In terms of Figure 17, the target, match, and perceptual representation systems are identical in internal structure and interactions to the target, match, and object fields of our selective attention model. We simply add the assumption that the orienting system, on being activated by a cue, creates an orientation target, represented as activity in a target node. All the parameters used in the following simulations are kept constant and are identical to those used in the previous simulations.

A simulation of the basic dynamical pattern we propose for IOR is shown in Figure 18. The curve shown represents the activation level of a location node in the object field which is activated by an external cue. On orienting to this location (realized by the instantiation of the cue location as a target), its activation is boosted. At t = 5, attention is switched away (coincident, in this case, with cue offset). This attention switching is implemented in the simulation by the replacement of the target location with another target (representing, say, the location of a central fixation point). The cue representation now no longer matches the target and quickly suffers an inhibitory rebound, in essentially the same manner as do the ignored distractors in our selection model.

As previously noted, Posner and Cohen (1984) found that the inhibitory component of IOR only occurs after attention is switched from the cued location. Figure 19 illustrates that this is also true for our model and that the effect is not contingent on cue offset coinciding with an attentional shift. In this case, attention is maintained to the cued location after cue offset (leading to facilitation). Only on attentional shift (t = 14) is the inhibitory component initiated.

It was proposed that a model of IOR should account for Maylor's finding that (in a multiple cueing task) degree of facilitation was posi-

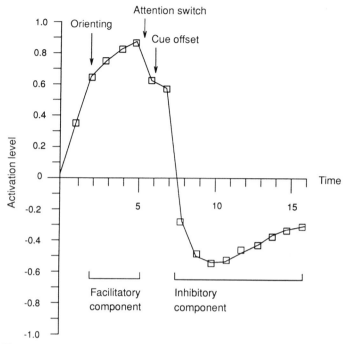

Figure 18

Simulation of the two components of the inhibition of return effect. The curve represents the activation of a single node representing the location of an external cue. Orienting (realized as the establishment of the internal target) takes place at t = 2, leading to facilitation. Attention switching (followed rapidly by cue offset in this case) at t = 5 removes the facilitation and initiates an inhibitory rebound in the location opponent circuit. This suppresses activation of the previously facilitated location.

tively correlated with degree of inhibition (less facilitation, less inhibition). In attempting to simulate this phenomenon, the question arises as to how one should represent the effect of having multiple cues in the model. We propose here that having multiple cues leads to each cue becoming more weakly represented as an orientation target. This weakened activation might, for instance, be due to competitive interactions within the orienting system. In the previous simulations, the single orientation target was given an activation value of 1 (as in all the other simulations reported here). The strength of activation of the internal target affects the degree of facilitation of matching inputs by virtue of the fact that the strength of the match signal is computed as the product of the cue signal and the target signal [Eq. (9)]. This signal, in turn, affects the degree to which the cue opponent circuit is pushed over into excitatory mode. The greater the target activation level then, the greater

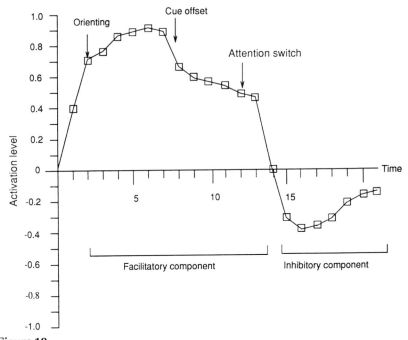

Figure 19
This figure illustrates that in the model the inhibitory rebound is initiated by attention switching, not cue offset. This is in agreement with the findings of Posner and Cohen (1984).

should be the facilitation. The question then arises whether under these circumstances increased (or decreased) cue facilitation in the model will lead to increased (or decreased) inhibition of return. Figure 20 shows that we get a positive correlation.

In this simulation, the model was run with target activation levels increasing from 0.2 to 1 in steps of 0.1. The timing of cue onset, offset, and attention switching were the same as for the simulation in Figure 18. For each run of the model, the maximum and minimum values of the cue node activation level were recorded. The maximum value was taken to indicate degree of facilitation, and the minimum value, degree of inhibition. Each vertical line on the graph joins the maximum and minimum activation values achieved for a given target activation value (shown below the line). As can be seen, both facilitation and inhibition increase in tandem as target activation strength increases. We thus attempt to account for the data by claiming that multiple cueing leads to weaker target activation (weaker cue activation per se is also possible). This theory could be independently tested if we can equate the level of

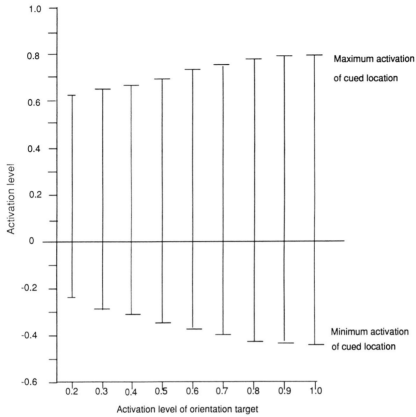

Figure 20

In simulations of inhibition of return (IOR), greater activation of the orientation target node (derived exogenously from cueing), shown along the x-axis, leads to greater facilitation of the cued location, followed by greater IOR to that location, as indexed by the degree of suppression of the sensory representation of the location. Each vertical line in the graph joins points representing maximum and minimum activation values attained by a cued location mode for a given level of internal target node activation.

target activation with other psychological variables, such as degree of focusing or concentration. The model predicts a similar pattern of results for single cues if, say, attention is divided (or concentration is low).

The simulations described show that the model provides answers to the theoretical questions about IOR we asked earlier. It explains the coupling of the facilitatory and inhibitory components (how inhibition "knows" what has previously been facilitated) by having the sources of both components joined in the opponent mechanism—it is the facilitation itself which primarily drives the inhibitory feedback. The timecourse and the dependence on attention switching for the release of inhibition is explained by the fact that, in the model, the switching of the opponent feedback circuit from net excitation to net inhibition is dependent on the generation of match/mismatch signals. The switch of attention means that the cue representation no longer matches the target and it effectively quenches itself. This account is also in line with Posner and Cohen's claim that the inhibitory component is automatic. The positive correlation found between degree of facilitation and inhibition (in multiple cueing) is explained on the assumption that it is reasonable to equate multiple cues with weaker internal activation of each one (other things being equal). Weaker targets lead to less facilitation, and thereby to a weaker inhibitory rebound.

In conclusion, our model provides a concrete demonstration that the IOR phenomenon (and hence orienting) might involve mechanisms very similar to those involved in voluntary selective attention and negative priming. In voluntary selection, the mismatch-driven opponent mechanism actively deselects nontarget items while maintaining their activation at an equilibrium value above resting levels. Offset of external inputs to a deselected item throws the system out of equilibrium, causing it to experience an inhibitory rebound manifest as negative priming. In the case of inhibition of return, the rebound is caused by an internal switch of target specification, which leads a previously selected item to automatically deselect itself, preventing it from interfering with subsequent processing. We believe this account has sufficient theoretical elegance and economy to deserve active investigation.

V. CONCLUSIONS

This chapter advances a theory of selective attention formulated at a number of levels. At the functional level, we propose that selective attention facilitates the organism's maintenance of its goal-directed behavior by gating the flow of perceptual information into response systems (conceived to encompass both action and thought), emphasizing goal-relevant information, and backgrounding irrelevant or contextual information. In neuropsychological terms, we suggest this involves the action of the prefrontal lobes in gating the flow of activation from posterior (perceptual) systems through to frontal motor planning and execution systems. In terms of mechanisms, we propose that attentional gating requires the maintenance of internal target specifications that are matched against high-level perceptual representations. Matched representations are facilitated, and nonmatching inhibited. The precise mechanism we propose for this operation allows efficient selection over the whole dynamic range of the processing substrate and implements automatic gain control of inhibitory signals, so that the strength of the inhibition continually adapts to the strength of the to-be-ignored inputs. This self-regulating feedback mechanism allows nontarget stimuli to find automatically an equilibrium activation level below that of targets, but above resting levels. The opponent mechanism realizing these properties exhibits rebound behavior, which we use to account for the phenomenon of negative priming, bringing our model into contact with established experimental paradigms. In addition, the same rebound behavior, triggered somewhat differently, allows for rapid attention switching and provides an account of inhibition of return. In conclusion, the model contains mechanisms motivated primarily on functional grounds (e.g., the provision of self-regulating inhibitory feedback), which turn out to have certain nonobvious properties enabling us to account for a range of data not previously explained in any theoretically precise or coherent manner. Future work will concentrate on further testing of the model's predictions, as well as investigate variants of and alternatives to the model itself.

REFERENCES

Allport, D. A., Tipper, S. P., & Chmiel, N. (1985). Perceptual integration and postcategorical filtering. In M. I. Posner and O. S. M. Marin (Eds.), *Attention and performance XI* (pp. 107–132). Hillsdale, NJ: Lawrence Erlbaum.

Arbib, M. A., (1990). Programs, schemas, and neural networks for control of hand movements: Beyond the RS framework. In M. Jeannerod (Ed.), *Attention and performance XIII* (pp. 111–138). Hillsdale, NJ: Lawrence Erlbaum.

Arbib, M. A., Iberall, T., & Lyons, D. (1987). Schemas that integrate vision and touch for hand control. In M. A. Arbib & R. Hanson (Eds.), *Vision, brain and co-operative computation* (pp. 489–510). Cambridge, MA: MIT Press.

Arsten, A. M. F., Segal, D. S., Neville, H. J., Hillyard, S. A., Janowsky, D. S., Judd, L. L., & Bloom, F. E. (1983). Naloxone augments electrophysiological signs of selective attention in man. *Nature, 304,* 725–727.

Beech, A. R., Agar, K., & Baylis, G. C. (1989). Reversing priming while maintaining interference. *Bulletin of the Psychonomic Society, 27,* 553–555.

Beech, A. R., Baylis, G. C., Smithson, P., & Claridge, G. (1989). Individual differences in schizotypy as reflected in measures of cognitive inhibition. *British Journal of Clinical Psychology, 28,* 117–129.

Beech, A. R., Baylis, G. C., Tipper, S. P., McManus, D., & Agar, K. (1991). Individual differences in cognitive processes: Towards an explanation of schizophrenic symptomology. *British Journal of Psychology, 82,* 479–489.

Beech, A. R., & Claridge, G. (1987). Individual differences in negative priming: Relations with schizotypal personality traits. *British Journal of Psychology, 78,* 349–356.

Beech, A. R., Powell, T. J., McWilliams, J., & Claridge, G. S. (1989). Evidence of reduced "cognitive inhibition" in schizophrenia. *British Journal of Clinical Psychology, 28,* 110–116.

Beech, A. R., Powell, T. J., McWilliams, J., & Claridge, G. S. (1990). The effect of a small dose of chlorpromazine on a measure of cognitive inhibition. *Personality and Individual Differences, 11,* 1141–1145.

Benoit, G., Fortran, L., Lemelin, S., LaPlante, L., Thomas, J., & Everett, J. (1992). L'attention selective dans la depression majeure: Ralentissement clinique et inhibition cognitive. *Canadian Journal of Psychology, 46*, 41–52.

Biederman, I. (1972). Perceiving real world scenes. *Science, 177*, 77–80.

Biederman, I., Mezzanotte, R. J., & Rabinowitz, J. C. (1981). Scene perception: Detecting and judging objects undergoing relational violations. *Cognitive Psychology, 14*, 143–177.

Bjork, E. L., & Murray, J. T. (1977). On the nature of input channels in visual processing. *Psychological Review, 84*, 472–484.

Briand, K. (in preparation). *Selective attention to global and local structure of objects: Converging measures of nontarget processing.*

Broadbent, D. E. (1958). *Perception and communication.* London: Pergamon Press.

Broadbent, D. E. (1970). Stimulus and response set: Two kinds of selective attention. In D. I. Mostotsky (Ed.), *Attention: Contemporary theories and analysis.* New York: Appleton-Century-Crofts.

Burgess, N., & Hitch, G. (1992). Toward a network model of the articulatory loop. *Journal of Memory and Language, 31*, 429–460.

Curio, E. (1976). *The ethology of predation.* New York: Springer-Verlag.

Dalrymple-Alford, E. C., & Budayr, B. (1966). Examination of some aspects of the Stroop color-word test. *Perceptual and Motor Skills, 23*, 1211–1214.

DeSchepper, B. G., Khurana, B., O'Connell, K. M., & Wilson, M. (in preparation). *What is inhibited in negative priming?*

DeSchepper, B., & Treisman, A. (1991). Novel visual shapes in negative priming. *Thirty-second Annual Meeting of the Psychonomic Society, San Francisco.*

Driver, J., & Baylis, G. C. (1993). Cross-modal negative priming and Stroop-like interference in selective attention. *Bulletin of the Psychonomic Society, 31*, 45–48.

Duncan, J. (1980). The locus of interference in the perception of simultaneous stimuli. *Psychological Review, 87*, 272–300.

Duncan, J., & Humphreys, G. W. (1989). Visual search and stimulus similarity. *Psychological Review, 96*, 433–458.

Enright, S. J., & Beech, A. R. (1990). Obsessional states: Anxiety disorders or schizotypes? An information processing and personality assessment. *Psychological Medicine, 20*, 621–627.

Eriksen, C. W., Coles, M. G. H., Morris, L. R., & O'Hara, W. P. (1985). An electromyographic examination of response competition. *Bulletin of the Psychonomic Society, 23*, 165–168.

Estes, W. K. (1972). Interactions of signal and background variables in visual processing. *Perception and Psychphysics, 12*, 278–286.

Friedman, A. (1979). Framing pictures: The role of knowledge in automatized encoding and memory for gist. *Journal of Experimental Psychology: General, 108*, 316–355.

Fuentes, L. J., & Tudela, P. (1992). Semantic processing of foveally and parafoveally presented words in a lexical decision task. *Quarterly Journal of Experimental Psychology, 45A*(2), 299–322.

Fuster, J. M. (1980). *The prefrontal cortex* [2nd ed., 1989]. New York: Raven Press.

Gernsbacher, M. A. (1989). Mechanisms that improve referential access. *Cognition, 32*, 99–156.

Gernsbacher, M. A., & Faust, M. E. (1991). The mechanism of suppression: A component of general comprehension skill. *Journal of Experimental Psychology: Learning, Memory and Cognition, 17*, 245–262.

Goldman-Rakic, P. S. (1987). Circuitry of primate prefrontal cortex and regulation of behavior by representational knowledge. In F. Plum (Ed.), Handbook of physiology: *Sec. 1. The nervous system: Vol. V: Higher cortical function* (pp. 373–417). Bethesda, MD: American Physiological Society.

Goldman-Rakic, P. S. (1988). Topography of cognition: Parallel distributed networks in primate association cortex. *Annual Review of Neuroscience, 11*, 137–156.

Gray, J. A., Feldon, J., Rawlins, J. N. P., Hemsley, D. R., & Smith, A. D. (1991). The neuropsychology of schizophrenia. *Behavioral and Brain Sciences, 14*, 1–84.

Greenwald, A. C. (1972). Evidence both for perceptual filtering and response suppression for rejected messages in selective attention. *Journal of Experimental Psychology, 94*, 58–67.

Grossberg, S. (1980). How does a brain build a cognitive code? *Psychological Review, 87*, 1–51.

Grossberg, S. (1983). Processing of expected and unexpected events during conditioning and attention: A psychophysiological theory. *Psychological Review, 89*, 529–572.

Hasher, L., Stoltzfus, E. R., Zacks, R. T., & Rypma, B. (1991). Age and inhibition. *Journal of Experimental Psychology: Learning, Memory and Cognition, 17*, 163–169.

Hoffman, J. E., & MacMillan, F. W. (1985). Is semantic priming automatic? In M. I. Posner and O. S. M. Marin (Eds.), *Attention and performance XI*. Hillsdale, NJ: Lawrence Erlbaum.

Houghton, G. (1990). The problem of serial order: A neural network model of sequence learning and recall. In R. Dale, C. Mellish, & M. Zock (Eds.), *Current research in natural language generation* (pp. 287–319). London: Academic Press.

Houghton, G. (1993). Inhibitory control of neurodynamics: Opponent mechanisms in sequencing and selective attention. In M. Oaksford & G. D. A. Brown (Eds.), *Neurodynamics and Psychology*. London: Academic Press.

Humphreys, G. W., & Müller, H. J. (1993). SEarch via Recursive Rejection (SERR): A connectionist model of visual search. *Cognitive Psychology, 25*, 43–110.

Hung, D. L., & Tzeng, O. J. L. (1989, November). Location-specific inhibitory processes in visual selective attention. *Thirtieth Annual Meeting of the Psychonomic Society*, New Orleans.

Hurvich, L. M., & Jameson, D. (1957). An opponent process theory of color vision. *Psychological Review, 64*, 384–404.

Kahneman, D. (1973). *Attention and effort*. Englewood Cliffs, NJ: Prentice Hall.

Kahneman, D., & Treisman, A. M. (1984). Changing views of attention and automaticity. In R. Parasuraman & D. Davis (Eds.), *Varieties of attention* (pp. 29–61). Orlando, FL: Academic Press.

Klein, G. S. (1964). Semantic power measured through the interference of words with color naming. *American Journal of Psychology, 57*, 576–588.

Koch, C., & Ullman, S. (1985). Shifts in selective visual attention: Toward the underlying neural circuitry. *Human Neurobiology, 4*, 219–227.

Kohonen, T. (1984). *Self-organization and associative memory*. New York: Springer-Verlag.

LaBerge, D., & Brown, V. (1989). Theory of attentional operations in shape identification. *Psychological Review, 96*, 101–124.

La Heij, W. (1988). Components of Stroop-like interference in picture naming. *Memory & Cognition, 16*, 400–410.

La Heij, W., Dirkx, J., & Kramer, P. (1990). Categorical interference and associative priming in picture naming. *British Journal of Psychology, 81*, 511–525.

La Heij, W., Van Der Heijden, A. H. C., & Schreuder, R. (1985). Semantic priming and Stroop-like interference in word naming tasks. *Journal of Experimental Psychology: Human Perception and Performance, 11*, 62–80.

Lowe, D. G. (1979). Strategies, content, and the mechanisms of response inhibition. *Memory & Cognition, 7*, 382–389.

Lowe, D. G. (1985). Further investigations of inhibitory mechanisms in attention. *Memory & Cognition, 13*, 74–80.

Luria, A. R. (1973). *The working brain.* London: Penguin.

Marr, D. (1982). *Vision.* New York: W. H. Freeman.

Maylor, E. A. (1985). Facilitatory and inhibitory components of orienting in visual space. In M. I. Posner & O.S.M. Marin (Eds.), *Attention and performance XI* (pp. 189–204). Hillsdale, NJ: Lawrence Erlbaum.

McDowd, J. M., & Oseas-Kreger, D. M. (1991). Aging, inhibitory processes, and negative priming. *Journal of Gerontology, 46,* 340–345.

McLaren, J. (1989). *The development of selective and sustained attention in normal and attentionally disordered children.* Unpublished doctoral dissertation, Dalhousie University, Halifax, Nova Scotia.

McLaren, J., & Bryson, S. (1988). Sustained and selective attention. *Canadian Psychology, 29,* Abstract No. 530.

Mishkin, M. (1982). A memory system in the monkey. *Philosophical Transactions of the Royal Society of London, B298,* 65–95.

Mishkin, M., & Appenzeller, T. (1987). The anatomy of memory. *Scientific American, 256*(6), 62–71.

Mishkin, M., Ungerleider, L. G., & Macko, K. A. (1983). Object vision and spatial vision: Two cortical pathways. *Trends in Neurosciences, 6,* 414–417.

Moran, J., & Desimone, R. (1985). Selective attention gates visual processing in the extrastriate cortex. *Science, 229,* 782–784.

Mueller, P. M., & Baylis, G. C. (submitted). *Effects of normal aging and Alzheimer's disease on attention: 2. Intertrial priming effects.*

Näätänen, R. (1982). Processing negativity: An evoked-potential reflection of selective attention. *Psychological Bulletin, 92,* 605–640.

Näätänen, R. (1985). Selective attention and stimulus processing: Reflections in event-related potentials, magnetoencephalogram, and regional blood flow. In M. I. Posner & O. S. M. Marin (Eds.), *Attention and performance* XI (pp. 355–373). Hillsdale, NJ: Lawrence Erlbaum.

Neill, S. R., & Cullen, J. M. (1974). Experiments on whether schooling by their prey affects the hunting behavior of celaphod and fish predators. *Journal of Zoology,* London, *172,* 549–569.

Neill, W. T. (1977). Inhibition and facilitation processes in selective attention. *Journal of Experimental Psychology: Human Perception and Performance, 3,* 444–450.

Neill, W. T., & Valdes, L. A. (1992). The persistence of negative priming: Steady-state or decay? *Journal of Experimental Psychology: Learning, Memory and Cognition, 18,* 565–576.

Neill, W. T., & Westberry, R. L. (1987). Selective attention and the suppression of cognitive noise. *Journal of Experimental Psychology: Learning, Memory and Cognition, 13,* 327–334.

Neumann, E., & DeSchepper, B. G. (1991). Costs and benefits of target activation and distractor inhibition in selective attention. *Journal of Experimental Psychology: Learning, Memory and Cognition, 17,* 1136–1145.

Neumann, E., & DeSchepper, B. G. (1992). An inhibition-based fan effect: Evidence for an active suppression mechanism in selective attention. *Canadian Journal of Psychology, 46,* 11–50.

Neumann, O. (1987). Beyond capacity: A functional view of attention. In H. Heuer and A. F. Sanders (Eds.), *Perspectives on perception and action.* Hillsdale, NJ: Lawrence Erlbaum.

Norman, D. A., & Shallice, T. (1986). Attention to action: Willed and automatic control of behavior. In R. J. Davidson, G. E. Schwartz, & D. Shapiro (Eds.), *Conscious and self-regulation: Advances in research:* Vol. IV. New York: Plenum Press.

Palmer, S. E. (1975). The effects of contextual scenes on the identification of objects. *Memory & Cognition, 3,* 519–526.

Picton, T. W., Stuss, D. T., & Marshall, K. C. (1986). Attention and the brain. In S. L. Friedman, K. A. Klivington, & R. W. Peterson (Eds.), *The Brain, Cognition, and Education* (pp. 19–79). New York: Academic Press.

Posner, M. I. (1978). *Chronometric explorations of mind.* Hillsdale, NJ: Lawrence Erlbaum.

Posner, M. I., & Cohen, Y. A. (1984). Components of visual orienting. In H. Bouma and D. G. Bouwhuis (Eds.), *Attention and performance* (pp. 531–554). Hillsdale, NJ: Lawrence Erlbaum.

Posner, M. I., & Driver, J. (1992). The neurobiology of selective attention. *Current Opinion in Neurobiology, 2,* 162–169.

Roland, P. E. (1982). Cortical regulation of selective attention in man. A regional cerebral blood flow study. *Journal of Neurophysiology, 48,* 1059–1078.

Rumelhart, D. E., & McClelland, J. L. (1986). *Parallel distributed processing: Vol. 1, Foundations.* Cambridge, MA: MIT Press.

Schull, J. (1979). A conditioned opponent theory of Pavlovian conditioning and habituation. In G. H. Bower (Ed.), *The psychology of learning and motivation:* Vol. 13. New York: Academic Press.

Solomon, R. L., & Corbit, J. D. (1974). An opponent process theory of motivation: 1. Temporal dynamics of affect. *Psychological Review, 81,* 119–145.

Stroop, J. R. (1935). Studies of interference in serial verbal reactions. *Journal of Experimental Psychology, 18,* 643–662.

Stuss, D. T., & Benson, D. F. (1986). *The frontal lobes.* New York: Raven Press.

Swerdlow, N. R., & Koob, G. F. (1987). Dopamine, schizophrenia, mania and depression: Toward a unified hypothesis of cortico-striato-pallido-thalamic function. *Behavioral and Brain Sciences, 10,* 197–245.

Taffe, M., Moore, B. O., Tipper, S. P., & Baylis, G. C. (1991). Action-based spatial attention in normal and hippocampal lesioned monkeys. *Society for Neuroscience Abstracts, 18,* 479.9.

Tipper, S. P. (1985). The negative priming effect: Inhibitory effects of ignored primes. *Quarterly Journal of Experimental Psychology, 37A,* 571–590.

Tipper, S. P. (1991). Less attentional selectivity as a result of declining inhibition in older adults. *Bulletin of the Psychonomic Society, 29,* 45–47.

Tipper, S. P., & Baylis, G. C. (1987). Individual differences in selective attention: The relation of priming and interference to cognitive failure. *Personality and Individual Differences, 8,* 667–675.

Tipper, S. P., Bourque, T., Anderson, S., & Brehaut, J. C. (1989). Mechanisms of attention: A developmental study. *Journal of Experimental Child Psychology, 48,* 353–378.

Tipper, S. P., Brehaut, J. C., & Driver, J. (1990). Selection of moving and static objects for the control of spatially directed action. *Journal of Experimental Psychology: Human Perception and Performance, 16,* 492–504.

Tipper, S. P., & Cranston, M. (1985). Selective attention and priming: Inhibitory and facilitatory effects of ignored primes. *Quarterly Journal of Experimental Psychology, 37A,* 591–611.

Tipper, S. P., & Driver, J. (1988). Negative priming between pictures and words: Evidence for semantic analysis of ignored stimuli. *Memory & Cognition, 16,* 64–70.

Tipper, S. P., Driver, J., & Weaver, B. (1991). Object-centered inhibition of return of visual attention. *Quarterly Journal of Experimental Psychology, 43A,* 289–298.

Tipper, S. P., Lortie, C., & Baylis, G. C. (1992). Selective reaching: Evidence for action-centered attention. *Journal of Experimental Psychology: Human Perception and Performance, 18,* 891–905.

Tipper, S. P., MacQueen, G. M., & Brehaut, J. C. (1988). Negative priming between response modalities: Evidence for the central locus of inhibition in selective attention. *Perception and Psychophysics, 43*, 45–52.

Tipper, S. P., & McLaren, J. (1990). Evidence for efficient visual selective attention in children. In J. T. Enns (Ed.), *The development of attention: Research and theory.* Amsterdam: Elsevier.

Tipper, S. P., Weaver, B., Cameron, S., Brehaut, J. C., & Bastedo, J. (1991). Inhibitory mechanisms of attention in identification and localization tasks: Timecourse and disruption. *Journal of Experimental Psychology: Learning, Memory, and Cognition, 17*, 681–692.

Tipper, S. P., Weaver, B., & Houghton, G. (in press). *Behavioral goals determine excitation–inhibition states of the internal representations of unattended objects. Quarterly Journal of Experimental Psychology.*

Tipper, S. P., Weaver, B., Kirkpatrick, J., & Lewis, S. (1991). Inhibitory mechanisms of attention: Locus, stability, and relationship with distractor interference effects. *British Journal of Psychology, 82*, 507–520.

Treisman, A. M. (1986). Features and objects in visual processing. *Scientific American, 255*, 114–125.

Treisman, A. M. & Gelade, G. (1980). A feature integration theory of attention. *Cognitive Psychology, 12*, 97–136.

Underwood, G. (1980). Attention and the nonselective lexical access of ambiguous words. *Canadian Journal of Psychology, 34*, 72–76.

Van Der Heijden, A. H. C. (1981). *Short term visual forgetting.* London: Routledge and Keegan Paul.

Wagner, A. R. (1981). SOP: A model of automatic memory processing in animal behavior. In N. E. Spear & R. R. Miller (Eds.), *Information processing in animals: Memory mechanisms.* Hillsdale, NJ: Erlbaum.

Wundt, W. (1904). *Principles of physiological psychology* (5th ed.) [originally published 1874]. Fifth edition, E. Titchener (Ed.). New York: Macmillan.

Yee, P. L. (1991). Semantic inhibition of ignored words during a figure classification task. *Quarterly Journal of Experimental Psychology, 43A*, 127–153.

Categories of Cognitive Inhibition with Reference to Attention

Raymond M. Klein and Tracy L. Taylor

I. INTRODUCTION

In contemporary psychology there is great interest in the interdisciplinary wedding of the cognitive and neural sciences.[1] In this burgeoning field of cognitive neuroscience, information from cognitive science informs the study of the ways in which cognitive computations may be implemented in the neural machinery, and, in a similar manner, knowledge of neural functioning helps to develop and constrain models of cognitive functioning. The potential for symbiosis between cognitive and neural science is particularly evident in the study of inhibition where, on the one hand, neural mechanisms provide a terminology and insight for understanding possible mechanisms of cognitive inhibition and, on the other hand, behavior-based models of cognitive functioning imply the need for inhibitory circuitry. Distinct from neural inhibition, cognitive inhibition refers to a hypothetical construct whose effects within the information processing stream are inferred to exist on the basis of observable human behavior. By reducing or blocking the

[1]The excitement of this occasion has generated interest in models of cognitive processes in which vast arrays of pseudoneural elements are richly interconnected in a neo-Hebbian network of excitatory and inhibitory links in order to simulate some aspect of human behavior. Whether one regards this approach as one method for developing neuropsychological theories or as a pretheoretical assumption/belief about how such theories ought to be expressed, neoconnectionism is and will continue to be a fruitful approach (cf. Houghton & Tipper, this volume).

INHIBITORY PROCESSES IN ATTENTION, MEMORY, AND LANGUAGE

activation level of a psychological system, pathway, or representation, inhibitory mechanisms can usually be revealed either by the hindrance or the prohibition of the achievement of some behaviorally relevant goal state. Alternatively, inhibition may be inferred from improvements in performance that result if a pathway that interferes with a goal is itself inhibited. Because such goal states generally have an attentional basis, the study of behavioral interference produced by cognitive inhibition is often studied with respect to attentional processes.

To the extent that they reflect mechanisms related to attention, three types of interference effects used to infer cognitive inhibition will be described in this chapter: Interference which results from (1) reduced access to attention, (2) reduced activation of a psychological pathway and (3) reduced ability of a system to function. In addition, in a final section, inhibition of return (IOR), which the field had assumed to be an example of inhibition acting on attention itself but which instead appears to be an example of attention acting on sensory–motor pathways, will be discussed in detail. Because of the interest in exploring the actual or metaphorical links between neural and cognitive inhibition, several classes of neural inhibition will be presented prior to our review and categorization of cognitive inhibitory mechanisms.

II. INHIBITION IN THE CONCEPTUAL NERVOUS SYSTEM

Inhibition in the peripheral nervous system had been demonstrated by Sherrington (1906), and central inhibitory processes had been proposed by earlier theorists (e.g., Hughlings Jackson, see Taylor, 1931); nevertheless, when Hebb (1949) proposed his seminal cell-assembly theory he assumed only excitatory pathways in the central nervous system. He felt that his model was already speculative enough. In 1957, however, Milner argued that Hebb's model had to include inhibition if it were to function properly, and in the years following publication of Hebb's book, Eccles and others (see Eccles, 1969, for a review) firmly demonstrated inhibitory connections in the central nervous system. For cognitive theorists who have hypothesized conceptual inhibitory processes, known neural inhibitory mechanisms have often been used to suggest properties and structural arrangements for the proposed cognitive architecture. In this section, we will describe three such arrangements: lateral inhibition, mutual inhibition, and assymetric inhibition.

Lateral inhibition was first observed in the visual system of the crab, *limulus*. In this type of system, neural units at one level of analysis (e.g., visual receptors in the crab's eye) are mutually inhibitory, with the strength of inhibition often inversely proportional to the distance between the units. Because this arrangement has the effect of enhancing the detection of regions of abrupt contrast change, lateral inhibition has frequently been incorporated into cognitive models, where inhibition is assumed to operate in situations requiring resolution of competitive interactions. Shallice (1972), for example, proposed that in order to achieve a goal, the action schema most appropriate to guide behavior in a coherent, goal-directed fashion must become dominant. All possible action schemas are mutually inhibitory, and because of this lateral inhibition, an action schema weakly activated by prior experience or input from the attentional system will quickly become dominant. Similarly, Walley and Weiden (1973), and later McClelland and Rumelhart (1981), proposed lateral inhibition among all representational units (gnostic units for Walley & Weiden, logogens for McClelland & Rumelhart) at a given level of analysis. McClelland and Rumelhart's model is illustrated in Figure 1a, where it can be seen that all letter units at the letter level are mutually inhibitory, as are all the units representing words.

In a second possible arrangement, two systems are mutually inhibitory. Kinsbourne (1973), for example, whose model is illustrated in Figure 1b, proposed that

> Each hemisphere is in a reciprocally inhibitory relationship with the other, and the paired midbrain output facilities have a similar reciprocal relationship . . . When hemispheric activity is in exact balance, attention is centered upon the median plane . . . When one hemisphere is more active than the other either because it is stimulated or because the other is depressed (for instance by a lesion), attention deviates in a direction contralateral to the more active hemisphere. (pp. 241–242)

A third arrangement is asymmetric: One system may inhibit another, but not vice versa. There are numerous pathways which appear to carry inhibition of this sort between neural subsystems. Voluntary gating of primitive reflexes by descending cortical pathways (cf. Rafal & Henik, this volume) typifies this class of inhibition. Likewise, in an information processing model with a plausible neuroanatomical basis, Fischer and Breitmeyer (1987) have proposed such an asymmetric relationship between visual attention and the system responsible for generating saccades. Their model, which is illustrated in Figure 1c, claims that when the system responsible for covert shifts of visual attention is engaged on an object in visual space, the saccadic system is inhibited, and this inhibition must be released for a saccade to occur (see Section V for further discussion of this proposal).

In the first two examples, the inhibition would appear to play a hindering, rather than a prohibiting, role. In Kinsbourne's (1973) model, for example, the relative activation of one hemisphere results in a continuous change in the distribution of attention in favor of the activated hemifield. The hemisphere suffering greater net inhibition is not, of course, incapable of processing, it is merely less efficient than if it were

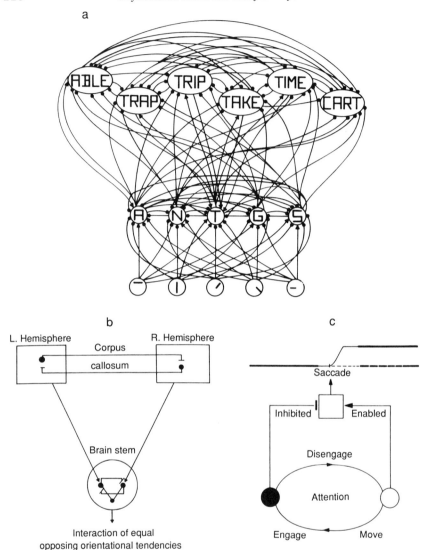

FIGURE 1

Examples of three possible inhibitory arrangements. Excitatory connections are represented by arrows; inhibitory connections by filled circles (a) or lines (b and c). (a) Lateral inhibition among units at the same level of analysis. From McClelland, J. L., & Rumelhart, D. E. (1981). An interactive activation model of context effects in letter perception: Part 1. An account of basic findings. *Psychological Review, 86,* 287–330. Copyright 1981 by the American Psychological Association. Reprinted by permission. (b) Reciprocal inhibition between processing systems. Reprinted by permission from Kinsbourne (1973), Figure 1. (c) Unidirectional inhibition. Reprinted from Fischer, B., & Breitmeyer, B. (1987), Mechanisms of visual attention revealed by saccadic eye movements, *Neuropsychologia, 25,* 73–83, with kind permission from Pergamon Press Ltd, Headington Hill Hall, Oxford OX3 OBW, UK.

not inhibited. Similarly, in models like McClelland & Rumelhart's (1981), it is assumed that inhibitory input to a unit is integrated with, and can be outweighed by, sufficient excitatory input. In contrast, it is possible that in some cases inhibition might operate more like a shutoff valve. Through maturation, learning, or prior instruction (e.g., Evarts & Tanji, 1974) for example, some reflex pathways may come under such strong voluntary control that transmission along them is prohibited rather than merely hindered by the inhibition. Likewise, the inhibition proposed by Fischer and Breitmeyer (1987) would appear to be of the prohibitive type. We believe that the distinction between hindering, where it is assumed that sufficient excitatory input can overcome the inhibition, and prohibiting, where it is assumed that the inhibition must be removed and cannot be overcome, is highly relevant in cognitive models, even if the difference, at a neural level, turns out to be one of degree rather than kind.

III. REDUCED ACCESS TO ATTENTION

Noting that many situations involve multiple inputs only some of which are relevant for a currently dominant task, James (1890) suggested that attention "implies withdrawal from some things in order to deal effectively with others" (p. 490). That unattended stimuli are hindered from gaining access to central attentional mechanisms is fundamental to Broadbent's seminal filter theory (1958) and, although they do not necessarily concur with Broadbent's placement of the bottleneck in the information processing stream, many theorists nevertheless make a similar assumption about the limited availability of attention.

Guided by such limited-capacity notions and their implications for lack of attentional access for unselected inputs, a secondary probe paradigm has been developed to assess the degree of attentional involvement required for performance of a primary task (e.g., Posner & Boies, 1971; Posner & Klein, 1973). This approach engages the attentional system with a primary task and then assesses attentional involvement at various points during information processing by requiring that subjects make speeded responses to an occasional concurrent secondary task. The extent to which the subjects' attentional resources are focused on the primary task is revealed by secondary probe performance, where attentional demands are inversely related to performance on the secondary task. Such interference in secondary task performance due to the limited capacity of attention contrasts with the interference that may occur because of competition for a peripheral (sensory or motor) system. For example, it is much more difficult to chew gum while whistling than to walk while whistling, but this difference is due to

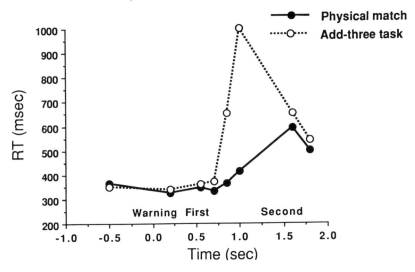

FIGURE 2

Reaction time to auditory probes presented at various times during two sequential letter matching tasks. Pairs of letters were matched on the basis of physical identity (solid
lines, filled circles) or by counting forward three letters in the alphabet from the first letter (dashed lines, open circles). Redrawn by permission from Posner and Klein (1973),
Figure 5.

competition for the same effectors rather than to competition for a
central system, making the label "attentional" inappropriate in such
cases.

The use of a dual task probe paradigm to measure interference (viz.,
the attentional requirements) during a sequential letter matching task is
illustrated in Figure 2.[2] Subjects in this study (Posner & Klein, 1973)
were presented first with a visual warning cue and then with a pair of
visual letters whose onsets were separated by 0, 1, or 2 sec. In response
to the target letter pair, subjects were required to perform one of two
tasks. One task was physical matching, where subjects were required to
indicate whether the first and second target letters shared the same identity. The other task was also physical matching, but it was based on the
identity of the letter that was three positions removed from the first
target. That is, subjects were required to count ahead three letters from

[2]The finding that stimulus–response mode changes may alter the observed interference
has been used to challenge this method for quantifying central processing limitations
(McLeod, 1978). It should be noted, however, that the pattern of results discussed in this
section is not easily explained without recourse to the notion of a central processing
limit. Moreover, if one adopts a multiprocessor viewpoint for these findings (cf. Allport
et al., 1985), then the inhibition described in this section might still be attributed to
reduced access to the task-appropriate attentional subprocessor.

the first letter target and indicate whether that new letter matched the identity of the second target letter that was presented to them. On half of the trials, an auditory probe was presented at various times during the sequence of primary task events (marked on the abcissa). The subject's secondary task was to detect and respond to the probe. When the first letter remained present during the trial and the matching task was based on the identities of the presented target letters, there was no interference with the probe during the encoding of the first letter (0–300 msec); interference began at about 500 msec after the first letter was presented (solid line in Figure 2). This interference appears to be related to the decision/response processing associated with the imminent presentation of the second letter, because when the interval between the two letters was lengthened, the interference was correspondingly delayed (Posner & Klein, 1973, Experiment 3). On the other hand, requiring the subject to count forward in the alphabet (three letters) in order to match the target letter greatly increased the probe interference effect, and accelerated its appearance (dashed line in Figure 2). Similarly, if the first letter was presented for a brief period (e.g., 50 msec), the interference began as early as 150 msec (Posner & Klein, 1973, Experiment 1), as if decreasing the quality of the stimulus information requires that attention be allocated to an encoding process that normally proceeds automatically. The point illustrated here (cf. Posner, 1978) is that the allocation of attention is not tied to a fixed locus in the processing sequence; it is, rather, a flexible process determined by strategic adaptations to task demands.

The interference described here might be attributed to an inhibitory mechanism, perhaps of the sort proposed by Shallice (1972) in which competing action systems are mutually inhibitory, but, on the basis of the evidence presented so far, the attribution of inhibition is not mandatory. The interference could be due to a more passive process. In either case, it is important to note that whatever mechanism is at work, it is *not* the case that *specific* psychological pathways are inhibited or neglected. On the contrary, because attention is occupied with one process or task, all other activities that might require access to it will suffer from its relative lack of availability; thus the effects are widespread and nonspecific.

Another method aimed at exploring the involvement of attention was introduced by Posner and Snyder (1975a). Posner and Snyder (1975a) contrasted the automatic beneficial effects of stimulating a psychological pathway with what they called the inhibitory effects suffered by nonselected pathways when one input pathway is consciously attended (see also Neely, 1977, for a particularly impressive set of findings supporting this distinction). Their use of the term inhibition (which was reinforced in Posner & Snyder, 1975b) must be qualified, because they did not mean that *specific* input pathways were inhibited (as many readers of their model incorrectly inferred). In their proposal, nonselection does not affect the accrual of information in the psychological pathway; it merely affects access of these pathways to central mechanisms.

Posner and Snyder (1975a, 1975b) presented subjects with a prime stimulus (letter or plus sign) at various intervals prior to the presentation of two simultaneous letter targets calling for a same–different decision. In one condition (low probability), the likelihood that the prime letter was a member of the target pair was very low. In another condition (high probability), the prime letter was very likely to be repeated in the stimulus. The results are shown in Figure 3. On trials when the prime letter reoccurred as the target, response latencies were shorter than in the neutral (+) prime condition. This facilitation effect grew rapidly following the onset of the prime and was more pronounced in the high probability condition. Posner and Snyder attributed the facilitation in the low probability condition to automatic pathway activation. The additional facilitation in the high probability condition was attributed to the subject turning attention toward the psychological pathway for the prime letter. On trials when the prime letter did not appear in the stimulus, subjects were slower (inhibition) than on neutral trials, but only in the high probability condition. Unlike facilitation, which begins to accrue almost immediately after the onset of the prime, inhibition does not begin to grow until about 200–300 msec after onset of the prime. This slower growth was attributed to the relatively late time by which attention can be directed to the input pathway representing the primed letter.[3] Posner and Snyder (1975a, 1975b) interpreted the apparently widespread inhibition observed in this paradigm (which accrues to all nonattended letter pathways when one is attended) as due to the lack of availability of attention.

Allocating attention to a pathway because it is likely to be stimulated is equivalent to the notion of set or expectancy, which we discuss in Section IV(C). In contrast to the paradigm introduced by Posner and Snyder (1975a), direct stimulation of the "expected" pathway is not necessary to initiate this process. Voluntary control in response to instructions and probabilities is sufficient (Neely, 1977; Posner, Nissen, & Ogden, 1978). Any inhibitory consequences associated with such perceptual expectancies could be either at the interface between perception and attention or carried into the perceptual machinery and affect the

---

[3]It must be pointed out that the interesting pattern of results described in the text, and illustrated in Figure 3, is confined to SAME responses (when the two target letters match). On DIFFERENT trials, where either one or neither of the target letters was the same as the prime, the data did not reveal the pattern of facilitation and inhibition which was observed on SAME trials. This lack of generality is problematic and might suggest that the "interesting" pattern is produced by decision diagnostics rather than attention.

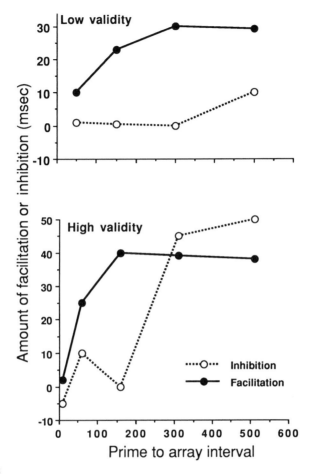

FIGURE 3

Facilitation and inhibition in simultaneous letter matching as a function of prime–array SOA. A prime (letter or +) was followed after different delays by a pair of letters. In the low validity condition the likelihood that a letter prime would appear in the array was 20%; in the high validity condition it was 80%. Results shown here were computed with reference to the neutral (prime = +) condition. Facilitation = neutral minus valid (prime is in the array); inhibition = invalid (prime is not in the array) minus neutral. Redrawn by permission from Posner and Snyder (1975b, Figure 7).

accumulation of information there. Posner and Snyder were quite explicit in proposing that the costs in their paradigm were of the former type. However, in the next section, which deals with more localized inhibitory effects, we will present some evidence that suggests a refinement of their position.

IV. REDUCED ACTIVATION LEVEL OF
A PSYCHOLOGICAL PATHWAY

In contrast to the widespread inhibitory effects associated with reduced access to attention described in Section III, in this section we selectively review some localized interference effects that have been observed in the literature and attributed to inhibitory processes. Reduced activation of specific psychological pathways exemplifies a psychological phenomenon for which the assumption of localized inhibition appears useful or necessary and is probably the most commonly assumed type of inhibition of cognitive processes.

A. Repeated Activation

Posner and Rogers (1978) used the terminology *widespread inhibitory consequences* to refer to decreased access to attention, and they contrasted this nonselective inhibitory effect with inhibition of specific pathways. They described the phenomenon of semantic satiation, in which prolonged repetition of a word produces the subjective experience of loss of meaning (for a review see Esposito & Pelton, 1971), as a possible example of pathway inhibition, but they felt that the existing data were subject to alternative explanations.

Subsequently, Smith (1984) and Smith and Klein (1990) provided evidence that inhibition develops in a repeatedly activated semantic pathway. Subjects were required to repeat a visually presented word 3 or 30 times and then perform a task requiring access to their lexical and semantic knowledge. Unlike many previous studies of semantic satiation, reaction time and accuracy, rather than subjective experience, provided the dependent variables. Interference was observed following 30 (as compared to 3) repetitions of a category name when information about that category was needed for a category membership (Smith, 1984; Smith & Klein, 1990, Experiment 2) or category matching decision (Smith & Klein, 1990, Experiment 1). Perhaps even more compelling was the demonstration that the hypothesized inhibition could produce a beneficial effect: The ability of an irrelevant flanker to interfere with the category membership decision was reduced when the flanker was in the repeated category.

Sample stimuli and findings from one of the experiments is shown in Table 1. Following 3 or 30 visual presentations and verbal repetitions of the criterion category (36 different categories were used, one of which is exemplified here), subjects were shown an uppercase and a lowercase word. Their task was to decide if the uppercase word was a member of the criterion category and to ignore the lowercase word. Evidence of

TABLE 1

Reaction Time (RT) and Errors (%E) as a Function of Number of Repetitions of the Criterion Category, Target, and Flanker Conditions[a]

Criterion category	Target	Flanker	3 Repetitions		30 Repetitions	
			RT	%E	RT	%E
Fruit	APPLE	Plum	581	6.0	629	4.5
Fruit	APPLE	Truck	603	6.4	636	5.8
Fruit	CAR	Plum	657	8.5	662	4.7
Fruit	CAR	Truck	628	3.7	640	4.6

[a] From Smith, L., & Klein, R. (1990). Evidence for semantic satiation: Repeating a category slows subsequent semantic processing. *Journal of Experimental Psychology: Learning, Memory, and Cognition, 16*(5), 852–861, Table 4. Copyright 1990 by the American Psychological Association. Adapted by permission.

satiation can be seen in two patterns. The first is a selective interference effect also observed by Smith (1984) where, collapsed across flanker condition, there is an increase in the time to classify exemplars (APPLE) of the repeated category (Fruit) after 30 repetitions (compared with 3) that is not observed with the nonexemplars (CAR). The second pattern is a reduction in the flanker effect. Following three repetitions there is a flanker effect where the categorical relationship between the target and the ignored word influences performance by facilitation of encoding and/or response processes when they are in the same category (APPLE/plum, CAR/truck) and by interference when they are not (APPLE/truck, CAR/plum). For example, following three repetitions of the category name *fruit*, when APPLE is the target, reaction time (RT) is slower with the conflicting flanker *truck* than with the congruent flanker *plum*. Similarly, when the target is CAR, the flanker *plum*, which is now conflicting, results in a slower and less accurate performance than when the flanker is *truck*. However, following 30 repetitions of the criterion category *fruit*, these flanker effects are reduced, so that with the nonexemplar targets there is actually an increase in accuracy (errors decrease from 8.5% to 4.7%) when the flanker is of the repeated category (CAR/plum), presumably because the associates of fruit (including the flanker *plum*) have been inhibited.

As described, semantic satiation fits the behavioral definition we have given for conceptual inhibition, that is, *reduced activation level of a psychological pathway*. It must be noted, however, that although Smith and Klein (1990) referred to "inhibition due to fatigue," their findings do not require the assumption of inhibitory connections. Indeed, we believe that in the case of semantic satiation, the alternative mechanism of adaptation provides an equally plausible explanation for the observed behavioral data.

B. Selection by Filtering

In contrast to the phenomenon of semantic satiation, which suggests that interference can occur when a pathway is repeatedly stimulated and selected, evidence from work on the phenomenon of negative priming reveals inhibition not for the selected pathway, but rather for stimulated pathways that are filtered out in the process of target selection.

Such filtering is required in the Stroop task where irrelevant words must be ignored while the subject attempts to name the color in which the words are printed. Interference is observed in the Stroop task when the irrelevant words are color names that differ from the correct response (ink color). This interference is usually attributed to response competition and can be explained without recourse to inhibitory mechanisms. For example, if response selection is dependent on the activation level of the correct response relative to other possible responses in a particular task (see Keele, 1973), then responses would be delayed in the conflict condition because two color names would be highly activated instead of just one (as in the control condition). On the other hand, Shallice's (1972) proposal that an action system becomes dominant by inhibiting competing action systems is also capable of explaining the interference, because it would take longer for the correct ink color name to become the dominant action system when it is being simultaneously inhibited by the colored word than when it is not.

These two views of the mechanism responsible for selection in the color-naming task (and for Stroop interference) might be distinguished by looking at what happens when activation of a previously nonselected or filtered pathway is required to perform a task. If Stroop interference is merely due to a delay in discriminating activation levels in competing pathways, one might expect the prior activation to facilitate subsequent performance. On the other hand, prior inhibition of an activated but irrelevant pathway should, by definition, make that pathway more difficult to reactivate. This latter prediction has been supported by several investigators who made the ink color of the word on one trial the same as the ignored color word of the preceding trial (Dalrymple-Alford & Budayr, 1966; Lowe, 1979, 1985; Neill, 1977). In this condition there was an increase in the magnitude of Stroop interference compared to when there was no relationship between the name of the previously ignored color word and the to-be-named ink color. For example, it takes a subject longer to say "red" to the word *blue* written in red ink if, on the previous trial, the ignored word had been *red* (as opposed to say, *green*). This inhibitory effect on an ignored pathway has been called *negative priming* (Allport, Tipper, & Chmiel, 1985; Tipper, 1985), and has been demonstrated in a variety of situations where filtering is required (see Houghton & Tipper, this volume, for a review and Moran and Desimone, 1985, for a possible neural analogue).

Much of the data on negative priming comes from two basic paradigms in which a target is selected from among distractors on a prime trial and then possible inhibitory effects are measured by examining the performance on a subsequent probe trial that may require processing within the previously ignored pathway. One such paradigm, which is discussed more fully by Houghton and Tipper (this volume), presents subjects with two different stimuli superimposed in the same spatial location on the prime task. The subject is then required to select and report the identity of the stimulus defined by a specified color. On the probe task, the identity of the stimulus in the target color may then be the same as or different from the ignored prime distractor, and negative priming is indicated when the subject is slower to report the identity of the probe target when its identity is the same as the previously ignored distractor than when it is different.

A second paradigm, and the one that is our focus here, involves selecting a target on the basis of its identity and responding on the basis of its location (cf. Tipper, Brehaut, & Driver, 1990). Tipper et al.'s (1990) basic paradigm is shown along with typical results in Figure 4. On prime trials with no distractor, the subject is presented only with a target (@), which can occur in one of four locations, and must make a spatially

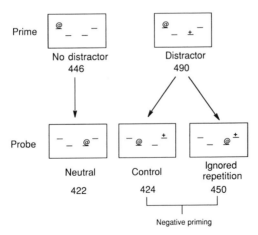

FIGURE 4

Sample trials and RTs from Tipper, Brehaut, and Driver (1990, Exp. 1a). @ = target; + = distractor.

compatible manual response to indicate which location was occupied by the target. Then, on the probe trials, the target again appears alone in any one of the three locations that had not been occupied by the target on the prime trial (neutral). On distractor prime trials, subjects are presented with both a target and a nontarget stimulus (+) in different spatial locations, and the subject must indicate where the target stimulus occurred. Then, on the probe trial, the target can occur in the same location as had been occupied by the distractor on the prime trial (ignored repetition), or else in a different location (control). On prime trials, responses are significantly slower when a distractor accompanies the target than when the target occurs alone. On probe trials, negative priming is observed: Responses to the target are slower when the target appears in the location that had been occupied by the distractor on the prime trial (ignored repetition condition) than when it occurs in a location that had not been occupied by the prime trial distractor (control condition). Importantly, Tipper and Baylis (1987) have demonstrated that negative priming is greatest in individuals who are good selectors (i.e., those who show relatively few interference effects in a filtering task), which suggests that the inhibition may be the mechanism for, rather than merely the by-product of, an attention-based selection process.

Using the example of a pike attempting to direct an attack against its stickleback prey, Tipper et al. (1990) have suggested that as the mechanism for selection, negative priming must necessarily be tied to objects. This is because in the real world, selected objects (the prey) tend to move through the environment, requiring that animals select on the basis of identity (e.g., choosing a particular stickleback) rather than on the basis of location (e.g., where that stickleback is in space). In the spatial paradigm just described, it is not possible to distinguish between coding of the inhibition in terms of location versus object because these are confounded in a static display. However, through the use of apparent motion and occlusion, Tipper et al. (1990) have provided evidence suggesting that in selective attention or filtering, the inhibition (negative priming) is tagged not to the location of an ignored distractor but rather to its object representation.

In contrast to the suggestion that negative priming represents only inhibition for object representations, a study reported by Connelly, Hasher, and Kimble (1992) demonstrates the existence and separability of both location-based and identity-based negative priming. They performed two studies using a variant of the spatial negative priming paradigm. In both studies, a letter printed in a target color and a distractor letter printed in a nontarget color each appeared randomly in one of four possible locations. In the report-identity experiment, subjects were required to report the name of the letter that was printed in the target color, and for the localization experiment, subjects were required to make a manual response to indicate the location of the letter that was printed in the target color. In both experiments, the probe target was the same color as in the prime trial, but could be (1) the same letter as had been ignored on the prime trial in a new location (identity-repetition), (2) a different letter in the same location as had been occupied by the prime distractor (location-repetition), (3) the same letter and in the same location as the prime trial distractor (identity+location repetition), or (4) a different letter in a new location (control). For the task in which subjects were required to respond with the identity of the target letter, negative priming was found for identity-repetition and for location-repetition, and these effects were additive in the identity+location repetition condition. This shows that even when location information is not needed to make a response, there is inhibition for a previously ignored location. However, for the task in which subjects were required to respond with the location of the target letter, repetition priming was found only for location-repetition. In other words, when identity is irrelevant, an ignored identity is not inhibited. This suggests a fundamental asymmetry where location suppression occurs even when it is not required, whereas identity suppression occurs only when identity forms the basis of the response (see Nissen, 1985, for a potentially related asymmetry).

This finding of dissociability between identity- and location-based inhibition suggests that selective processes can operate on attributes at different levels in the perceptual hierarchy (early attributes like location, late ones like object identity). This notion is reinforced by the Stroop studies previously mentioned. Specifically, even though the ink color and the word itself comprise a single object, in the Stroop task there is an increase in interference when the ink color of a word is the same as the previously ignored color word compared to when the ink color is unrelated to the name of the previously ignored color word, suggesting that selection can occur for the color of an object, whereas inhibition can accrue for its identity. Combined with the Connelly et al. (1992) finding, this analysis of the Stroop effect challenges the functional explanation that Tipper and colleagues (Tipper et al., 1990) have applied to negative priming.

A further and more direct challenge to Tipper's functional explanation for negative priming comes from a study conducted by Neill, Valdes, and Terry (1992). Noting that Tipper's example of the pike selecting one stickleback from among many essentially represents a problem of choosing one target from among many, Neill et al. used a spatial negative priming paradigm for which, on some of the prime trials, rather than having a target and a distractor, there were two targets and the subject was required to respond to either one of them. Reaction times on subsequent probe trials, where the target was presented in the same location as the ignored prime target, failed to reveal negative priming. This finding (which has also been demonstrated by Park & Kanwisher, in press) is difficult to reconcile with the view that negative priming is a function of selecting one of many targets. Instead it suggests that negative priming may depend on having to ignore a stimulus to which a response should never be directed.

Regardless of its functional interpretation and whether operating on object identity or on attributes like location (or both), negative priming stands as a good example of an inhibitory process that hinders the subsequent activation of a pathway. The fact that selective attention may be subserved by this inhibitory mechanism contrasts it with the pathway inhibition (or adaptation) seen for semantic satiation where lowered activation of the psychological pathway appears to represent a passive process of fatigue. However, like semantic satiation, negative priming does require that the inhibited pathway be stimulated on the prime trial (otherwise no difference would exist between ignored repetition and control conditions), and in this sense contrasts with the next two subcategories of inhibition—inhibition related to expectancies.

C. Maintaining an Expectancy

Previously, we described two paradigms that have been used to study the allocation of attention. One uses the interference observed when the primary task stimulus is not the expected one (Neely, 1977; Posner & Snyder, 1975a) to gauge the commitment of attention to an expected psychological pathway. Findings using this paradigm reveal that holding an expectancy facilitates the recognition of the expected input and interferes with the recognition of unexpected inputs. Because Posner and Snyder interpreted their findings in terms of the allocation of attention to a particular psychological pathway and the consequent lack of access to attention by other inputs, we described their paradigm and findings under the rubric of "reduced access to attention" (Section III). The other paradigm uses the interference with a secondary probe task (e.g., Posner & Klein, 1973) to gauge the attentional requirements of the primary task at the time of the secondary probe.

If, as implied by Posner and colleagues (Posner & Snyder, 1975b; Posner, 1978; Posner & Rogers, 1978), the interference effects revealed through these two paradigms reflect inhibition from the same underlying source, then, when used together, they should provide converging results. Precisely this strategy was used by McLean and Shulman (1978). They combined the two paradigms in a single experiment by occasionally presenting a secondary probe task (auditory choice RT) at various intervals following a highly informative letter prime during a primary letter matching task. Contrary to the prediction just outlined, the two interference effects dissociated. Between 100 msec and 500 msec following the letter prime, inhibition (as measured via the probe task) decreased, while during the same interval inhibition of unexpected letter pathways increased (see Figure 5). This finding implies that the inhibitory consequences of holding an expectancy are *not* as widespread as suggested by Posner.

One view of expectancies is that they involve top-down excitation of some of the same pathways that would be activated by the expected stimulus if it were actually presented (cf. Hawkins, Shafto, & Richardson, 1988). One may reasonably ask if this excitatory process is accompanied by an inhibitory one. Adopting the general view that related representational units at a given level of analysis laterally inhibit one another (see Section III), we propose that generating and maintaining an expectancy may involve:

(1) Directing attention to the task-appropriate representational system (e.g., abstract letter identities);

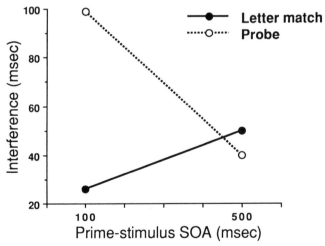

FIGURE 5

The timecourse of two interference effects during a simultaneous letter matching task with high validity primes. The SOA refers to the interval between the prime and the primary task letter array (closed circles) or a secondary auditory probe (open circles). Interference in the primary letter matching task was computed by subtracting letter matching RTs in the neutral condition (+) from that in the invalid condition (prime is not in the array). Interference in the secondary auditory probe task was computed by subtracting RT to auditory probes following a neutral cue (+) from that following a letter cue. Redrawn by permission from McLean and Shulman (1978, Figure 1).

(2) Selection of the expected pathway or logogen within that system (e.g., a particular letter); and

(3) A lowered level of activation in nonattended pathways in that system as a consequence of lateral inhibition among alternative pathways in the attended system.

Step 1, and possibly step 2, would require the sort of volitional control that would produce a general interference with other, nonprimary task activities. However, once the expected pathway is activated via volitional control, the lateral inhibitory connections within the network of similar representations would preserve the relative difference in activation levels within the task-relevant system with minimal involvement of attentional resources. Lateral inhibition of this sort would have the effect of sharpening a volitional expectancy, because as one pathway became weakly activated from top-down influences, lateral inhibition would enhance the relative activation difference between it and its neighbors and possibly help maintain that difference even after the volitional input was reduced or removed.

This proposed lateral inhibition, together with the distinction between generating and maintaining an expectancy, can explain McLean and Shulman's (1978) results as follows: They found that generation of a visual expectancy requires attention in a general sense (delayed auditory reaction time) and that this dependence on volitional control, as measured by effects on nonexpected visual stimuli, decreases (though not to zero) while the expectancy (measured in terms of costs and benefits in the letter matching task) takes hold. We suggest that attention is involved in generating the expectancy in the perceptual machinery, but that lateral inhibition among the possible *primary task* representations (e.g., letter level in the perceptual machinery) is primarily responsible for maintaining it.

Support for this suggestion comes from a study by Neill (1979) in which he discovered an intracategory inhibition effect. Neill showed that expecting an exemplar from a category (e.g., the letter *A*) produces larger costs for an unexpected member of that category (any other letter) than for an equivalently unexpected member of a different category (a digit). The general interference suffered by unexpected stimuli might be due to the fact that attention is not directed to their pathways. The additional interference suffered by items whose pathways are in the same subsystem or category as the expected one might be due to lateral inhibition among the items in this subsystem.[4]

---

[4]This proposal must be regarded as highly speculative. Although we have found no reported nonreplications of the Neill finding, neither have we found any replications. Moreover, in Neill's experiment the effect was somewhat fragile, occurring only on SAME trials (as in Posner & Snyder's inhibitory effect) and disappearing when the instructions emphasized speed of response.

Intracategory inhibition differs from negative priming in that negative priming is observed for presented stimuli that are ignored; the inhibition proposed here accrues to to-be attended inputs that, although not expected, are closely associated to the input that is expected. The underlying mechanisms, however, might be similar. For example, both may be mediated by lateral inhibition. In the case of negative priming, inhibitory feedback loops ensure that stimulated but to-be-ignored pathways are more inhibited than their nonstimulated neighbors, whereas in the case of intracategory inhibition, lateral inhibition may be confined to the highly related set, of which the expected stimulus is a member (or it may merely be greater for those items).

D. Cancelling an Expectancy

In the previous section, we introduced the possibility that inhibition of pathways might result from attentional activation: Maintaining an expectancy might involve lateral inhibition of the nonexpected pathways in the task-relevant representational system. But what happens to a previously expected and selected pathway when an expectancy is switched or disconfirmed? Posing precisely this question, Kingstone (1992; Kingstone & Klein, 1991) discovered that there is an inhibitory after effect following the real-time cancellation of a shape or form expectancy. In one study (Kingstone & Klein, 1991), the target stimuli (upright or upside down letters) could appear at one of three locations—one of which was precued at the start of each trial—where some of the possible stimuli were much more likely to occur at some locations than others (see Table 2).

When a location where a particular letter was likely had been cued, subjects presumably generated both a location and a form expectancy. Subjects were faster to respond when a target occurred at the cued location, and faster when the form at a particular location was the one likely to be presented there, an effect that was larger at the cued location than at uncued locations. This latter finding suggests that when cued to a location, subjects were expecting or preparing for a particular form. The interesting question is what happens to this expectancy when the subject realizes that the target is not at the cued location: Does the pathway for the previously expected form remain facilitated? does it return to its baseline level? or does it become inhibited? As shown in Table 2, this question was addressed in Experiment 1 by examining the location where the two shapes are equiprobable (location 3), and in Experiment 2 by examining both uncued locations. In both cases, reaction time to the previously expected form is compared to a form that is equally likely at the stimulated location. The results indicate that compared to an

TABLE 2

Design and Selected Results from Kingstone & Klein (1991)[a]

				Assuming location 1 is cued, target is			
	A	V		A	V		
				Experiment 1			
1	.8	.2		573	641		
2	.2	.8		776	698		
3	.5	.5		792	752	(40 msec)	
				Experiment 2			
	A	V	G	A		V/G	
1	.8	.1	.1	582		645	
2	.1	.8	.1	796	757		713
3	.1	.1	.8	(unlikely 39 msec)		(likely)	

[a] The columns on the left show the probability of each letter appearing at each location (rows). In the example given, it is assumed, for illustrative purposes only, that the location where A was likely was precued. The data are shown on the right side of the table and are collapsed across trials when locations 1 and 2 in Experiment 1 were cued and across all three locations in Experiment 2. The inhibition effects (in parentheses) are seen by comparing the italic latencies.

equally likely but not previously expected form, in both experiments subjects were 40 msec slower when the form they were originally prepared for was presented at an uncued location. Thus, when a shape expectancy is no longer warranted and the subject disengages from it (either to a neutral state as in Experiment 1, or to an active preparation for an alternative shape, as in Experiment 2), there is an inhibitory aftereffect which slows processing in the pathway for the previously expected form.

Although the phenomena of combined and cancelled expectancies are theoretically important and their emphasis on complex and dynamic adjustment is ecologically valid, there is a paucity of research in this area. As such, at this point, we are unable to draw out the implications for the generality of the proposed inhibitory effects or their possible relationship to other inhibitory mechanisms.

V. REDUCED ABILITY OF A SYSTEM TO FUNCTION

We now turn from attentionally mediated inhibition of specific pathways within cognitive subsystems to inhibitory effects on the cognitive subsystems themselves. In this section, we focus on the interesting proposal (Fischer & Breitmeyer, 1987; see also Fischer & Weber, 1993) that when visual attention is engaged either at fixation or elsewhere in the visual field, the saccadic system is "inhibited" and that in order for a saccade to be executed this inhibition must be removed (e.g., by removing the attended stimulus and thus predisengaging attention). This proposal, represented in Figure 1c, implies that disengaging attention is a prerequisite for a saccadic eye movement and, as pointed out earlier, the inhibitory relationship between visual attention and the oculomotor system proposed by Fischer and colleagues is of the prohibitive type (see Section III).

It has been known for some time that removal of the fixation point 200 msec prior to the appearance of a visual target can dramatically reduce saccadic latencies (Fischer & Ramsperger, 1986; Saslow, 1967; Ross & Ross, 1981). If it is assumed that visual attention is normally engaged at fixation, this gap effect is consistent with the inhibitory relationship proposed by Fischer and Breitmeyer (1987), which we will call attentional predisengagement theory (APT). However, it should be noted that this finding could just as easily, and more parsimoniously, be explained by assuming that it is 'the oculomotor system itself, and not visual attention, which must be disengaged from fixation.

To demonstrate that it is the disengagement of covert attention that underlies the gap effect, it is necessary to dissociate attention from fixation. In other words, it follows from Fischer and Breitmeyer's proposal that a reduction in saccadic latency will accompany the prior removal of attended, but not unattended, stimuli (even when these are not at fixation). Kingstone and Klein (1993) conducted three tests of APT in which objective measures of attention were key aspects of the design. To determine if the gap effect could be attributed to the predisengagement of attention, rather than to the removal of fixation per se, a dual task procedure was used in which targets on the vertical meridian called for simple manual detection responses and targets on the horizontal meridian called for saccadic responses (manual and saccadic targets and responses were equally likely). Precues indicating the likely location of the manual detection targets encouraged subjects to direct attention toward an object on the vertical meridian and cost–benefit analysis (cf. Posner, 1980) of manual reaction times for this task allowed objective determination of where covert attention was engaged. The appearance of a target could be preceded by the disappearance of an object the subject was fixating, attending, or not attending. Saccadic RT was reduced when any stimulus in the visual field was extinguished 200 msec before saccadic target onset. This gap effect was always larger following fixation offsets than following peripheral offsets, but it was unaffected by whether an extinguished peripheral stimulus had been attended or unattended. These results, which were observed with both endogenous and exogenous covert orienting, show that covert visual attention plays no role in the gap effect.

The pattern of results in these experiments led to a proposal that two independent components combine to produce the gap effect (see Kingstone & Klein, 1993; Reuter-Lorenz, Hughes, & Fendrich, 1991; Ross & Ross, 1980, 1981). One component, *motor preparation*, can operate on *any* response modality and is tightly dependent on the foreperiod between a warning signal and a subsequent target. The other component, a *fixation offset effect*, operates specifically to reduce saccadic latencies by freeing the *oculomotor system* from fixation (in our experiments this effect was remarkably stable at about 35 msec). This latter effect is probably mediated by the rostral pole of the superior colliculus (Munoz & Wurtz, 1992). Cells in this region of the superior colliculus fire during active fixation and cease firing just before a saccade. When this region is chemically disabled, monkeys are unable to suppress unwanted saccades to abruptly presented targets, and saccadic latencies are extremely rapid even in the presence of a fixation stimulus. Although freeing the oculomotor system from fixation might be viewed as a disengagement operation, in contrast to the Fischer and Breitmeyer (1987) proposal, it would appear to be the *overt* (saccadic) not *covert* (attentional) orienting system whose predisengagement reduces saccadic latencies in the gap paradigm. Note that we are disputing a claim about the relationship between covert visuo-spatial attention and the oculomotor system; we are not challenging the ubiquitous fact of voluntary modulation of the relatively reflexive oculomotor machinery.

VI. INHIBITION OF RETURN: INHIBITION OF ATTENTION?

Discovered and named by Posner and Cohen (1984), inhibition of return (IOR) was originally thought to be an effect on covert orienting, in which visual attention is inhibited from returning to a recently "visited" location. Our interpretation of the accumulating evidence on this phenomenon challenges this interpretation. The paradigm typically used for eliciting IOR and some typical findings are illustrated in Figure 6.

Most targets are presented at fixation, but occasionally a target may appear at one of two peripheral locations. A precue (usually an abrupt luminance increment) conveying no information about the upcoming target's location is presented near one of the two peripheral locations at varying intervals before the appearance of the target. At short cue–target stimulus onset asynchrony (SOA), subjects detect the target faster when it appears at the cued/stimulated location. In contrast, after about 200–300 msec this effect reverses and targets at the uncued location are

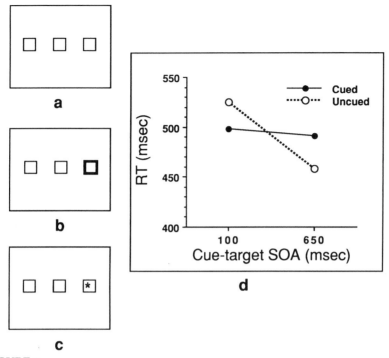

FIGURE 6

(a) The subject fixates the center box at the start of a trial. One of the peripheral boxes brightens briefly (b), and after varying delays a target (*) is presented in one of the three boxes to which the subject must make a response (c). (d) Typical finding from Posner and Cohen (1984, Figure 32.3). Redrawn by permission.

detected more rapidly. Several early findings that revealed boundary conditions for this inhibitory effect were instrumental in the genesis of an interesting functional interpretation:

(1) The inhibition is not observed following peripheral cues which are informative. Following an informative peripheral cue, orienting to the cued location should be maintained endogenously; attention is not inhibited from returning to the cued location at the longer SOAs because it is still there.

(2) When the subject makes a saccade following an uninformative peripheral cue, it is the previously stimulated display location that shows the subsequent inhibition and not the stimulated retinal location. This finding shows that the inhibition is coded in environmental rather than retinal coordinates (Posner & Cohen, 1984; Maylor & Hockey, 1985).

(3) When covert orienting to a location is generated endogenously (say in response to a central arrow cue) and then returned to fixation, the inhibitory effect is not observed (Posner & Cohen, 1984; Rafal, Calabresi, Brennan, & Sciolto, 1989). This finding which demonstrates that IOR is not merely the consequence of endogenous orienting, has been cited, together with the first point, in support of the view that endogenous and exogenous control of visual orienting may involve quite different attentional mechanisms (cf. Briand & Klein, 1987; Klein, Kingstone, & Pontefract, 1993). Whether or not one accepts this view, the finding does seem to suggest that the peripheral stimulation elicits IOR, not merely because it tends to get visual attention to a location in space (a central cue does that), but because it *is* peripheral stimulation.

These early findings led to what we will refer to as the standard interpretation: The probability manipulation gives the subject incentive to keep attention at fixation, but a peripheral cue that lacks meaning reflexively (exogenously) attracts attention, thus giving rise to the early advantage at the cued location. As endogenous control over visual orienting brings attention back to fixation, an inhibitory process develops that operates to repel attention from returning to the cued/stimulated location (where nothing of interest had been "found"). Hence the label, "inhibition of return." Under this interpretation, it is the behavior of attention[5] that is inhibited from returning to the previously "examined" region or object (cf. Tipper, Driver, & Weaver, 1991), possibly because of the buildup of inhibition within the psychological pathway representing the previously stimulated region or object.

In considering this functional explanation of inhibition of return, Klein (1988) was struck by how useful such an inhibitory mechanism might be in search tasks where each display item might require an attention-demanding "inspection" to determine if it is the target. In such a situation, a mechanism for keeping track of which display items attention had already been drawn to (so as not to waste time reinspecting previously rejected distractors) is necessary for efficient search. IOR seemed to be the ideal mechanism to perform such a tagging function. Klein tested this idea by presenting luminance detection probes immediately after the subject had performed a serial or pop-out visual search. The probes occurred on half of all trials and were presented at locations where there had been an item in the search display (ON probes) or at a

[5]Partly to test this view, Posner and Cohen (1984) and Maylor (1985) compared the effects of stimulating (cuing) both peripheral locations with the typical situation in which only one location is stimulated. They drew quite different conclusions about the nature of IOR from their somewhat discrepant data. Because there were numerous methodological differences between these studies and because in our own work the double cuing condition produces extremely variable patterns, we do not feel that any firm conclusions can yet be drawn from this potentially interesting manipulation.

location where no item had been presented (OFF probes). The rationale was simple:

> In serial search if the presumed allocation of attention to each item is followed by inhibition of return, then detection of ON-probes should be delayed compared with OFF-probes. [A] parallel search condition, in which the target is detected pre-attentively, serves as a control or baseline for most other factors. (Klein, 1988, p. 430)

These factors include masking and expectancies, which are nearly identical in serial and parallel search.

The first experiment, with relatively unpracticed subjects, led to a positive result: In serial but not in parallel search, RT to ON probes was slower than RT to OFF probes. It was decided that the finding was too important to rely on a single demonstration, so the design was replicated using a smaller number of subjects, with each contributing significantly more data. The results were pretty much the same. These findings, shown in the top two rows of Table 3, generated considerable excitement and interest. Unfortunately, however, there have been several nonreplications, including one published study by Wolfe and Pokorny (1990), and we are aware of no studies that have replicated the original finding.

In Klein's (1988) original study, subjects were not prevented from making eye movements to inspect the display. This was a motivated feature of the original experiment, because if the IOR were coded in environmental coordinates, then eye movements during search would not detract from the usefulness of inhibitory tags in facilitating search. Nevertheless, it seemed possible that the inhibitory tagging phenomenon would be observed even if subjects could not move their eyes to

TABLE 3
Probe Latencies on Target Absent Trials from Five Different Experiments[a]

Study	S/B	Parallel/Pop-out		Serial	
		OFF	ON	OFF	ON
Klein (1988, Exp. 1)	14/1	522	529	545	594
Klein (1988, Exp. 2)	5/6	497	513	495	557
Klein (unpublished, a)	9/1	440	461	472	488
Klein (unpublished, b)	13/1	428	470	465	504
Klein (unpublished, c)	10/6	458	492	482	510

[a] S/B indicates the number of subjects (S) per experiment and the number of blocks (B) contributed by each subject to each search condition (serial or parallel). As in Klein (1988), the probe latencies have been collapsed across stimulus materials (circles with gaps and circles with lines), blocks (where appropriate), and set size.

inspect the array. At around the same time, Klein and Farrell (1989) demonstrated that the pattern of search performance with circular arrays of two to ten items is almost unaffected by whether or not subjects are permitted to make eye movements. So when the design of the inhibitory tagging study was repeated using circular arrays with regular spacing and eye position monitoring with feedback to discourage eye movements, changes from the original pattern were not anticipated. The data from this experiment are shown in Table 3 (Klein, unpublished a). Reaction time to ON probes was slower than to OFF probes, but this was equally true for parallel and serial search, and most likely due to forward masking.

Although these results were puzzling, evidence that oculomotor programming might be necessary for the inhibitory tags to be laid down (see the following) was in the air, and thus the circular array experiment was repeated but without monitoring eye position (Table 3, Klein, unpublished b). Once again the original pattern was not replicated. News of Wolfe and Pokorny's (1990) nonreplication had become known by this time, and it was decided that a straightforward replication of the original paradigm was required. In this replication, the circular array was discarded in favor of the irregular rectangular array which had been used in the published experiments, and twice as many highly practiced subjects were used (compared with Klein, 1988, Experiment 2). The inhibitory tagging phenomenon was not replicated (Table 3, Klein, unpublished c). These nonreplications from the Klein laboratory, together with those from other laboratories, imply that the original result, however interesting it might have been, was the product of chance (alas a fluke).

If inhibitory tags are not laid down during visual search, then what are we to make of the functional explanation of IOR? These nonreplications of the inhibitory tagging phenomenon led Pontefract and Klein (1988) to see if they could elicit IOR in the typical cuing paradigm. In these subsequent cuing studies of IOR, a display was used like that shown in Figure 7. In all three experiments, subjects initiated each trial by pressing a thumb switch when they were fixating the middle dot of the center square. After 500 msec, an exogenous cue (brightening) was presented at the center location (Neutral-Central), at one of the peripheral locations (Cued/Uncued), or at both peripheral locations (Neutral

FIGURE 7
Display used in studies of cue-induced IOR with simple and choice reaction time.

Left-Right). After SOAs of 100 or 500 msec (run in separate blocks) a target was presented. The target was the sudden expansion or contraction of one of the three boxes. In all experiments, the target was much more likely to occur at the center box (60%) than at either peripheral box (20% each), and the cues conveyed no information.

Pontefract and Klein (1988) conducted three experiments using this paradigm, one using a choice task, one using a simple (detection) task, and one using simple and choice tasks on alternate days. The results from the peripheral target trials are shown in Figure 8. Visual inspection of these data reveal that although IOR was observed with the simple detection task, it was not observed in the choice task.[6] In response to the failure to obtain IOR using a choice task, we searched the literature for support, or disconfirmation of, this finding. At the time, Maylor (1985) was the only study to have used a choice RT task to measure IOR. Maylor (1985) found that simple manual RT, choice saccadic RT, and choice manual RT all showed slower latencies to targets at the previously cued location at the 500 msec SOA (although saccades did not show the cuing benefit at the shortest SOA, they did show a significant interaction— growth of inhibition with SOA). It is important to note that both of Maylor's choice RT tasks involved the subject making a localization response. In the saccadic task, the subject was instructed to fixate the target, whereas in the manual choice RT task, the subject was to press a left or right key to indicate where the target had appeared.

More recently, Egly, Rafal, and Henik (1992) have also reported a dissociation between simple and choice tasks with normal subjects, and so have Kingstone and Gazzaniga (1992) in a split-brain subject. It is worth noting for their choice task, Egly et al. (1992) used form discrimination; Kingstone used color discrimination; and Pontefract & Klein (1988) used size discrimination. Thus, there can be confidence in the generalization that IOR is observed with simple detection responses and may not be observed with choice RT, unless the choice involves localization (as in Maylor, 1985). Of course, there may be other choice judgments that will elicit and measure IOR; their discovery will certainly constrain theory building. However, for now, we will operate under the assumption that IOR is obtained with simple RT or location judgments (ocular or manual), but not with choice responses on a nonlocation dimension. We have considered several explanations for this pattern,

---

[6]These observations are clearly confirmed via statistical analysis of the pure choice or simple RT experiments. The IOR that is apparent in simple RT from the mixed design was not significant. However, because precisely the same cues and targets did produce a significant interaction in the pure simple design, we are confident that this is due to the reduced power of the mixed design. In the pure choice task with the 500 msec SOA, there was a trend for more errors at the cued than uncued location. This trend is reversed in the choice data from the mixed design, so we are not inclined to treat it as reliable.

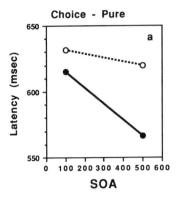
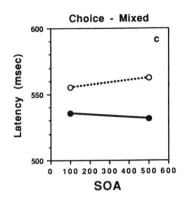
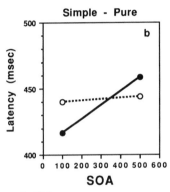
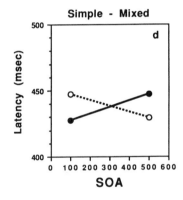

FIGURE 8

Reaction time to peripheral targets appearing at a previously cued (solid circles, solid lines) or uncued (open circles, dotted lines) location as a function of cue–target SOA. The cue in panel (a) was the brief brightening of the dot at the center of a square; in the remaining panels the cue was the brightening of the four dots at the corners of a square (see Figure 7). In both simple and choice RT tasks the target was a change in the size of a square.

but before presenting these, it is appropriate to describe the results of several recent experiments that strongly implicate oculomotor programming in the generation of IOR.

Rafal et al. (1989) performed an incisive set of experiments, the results of which constrain models and explanations of IOR (Table 4). They used endogenous cues (arrows at fixation) and exogenous cues (peripheral luminance changes) to direct or prepare eye movements or to generate attention shifts. On some trials, the eyes or attention were

TABLE 4
Summary of the Findings of Rafal et al.'s (1989, Experiment 4) Exploration of the Conditions which Produce Inhibition of Return[a]

| | Cue type | |
Condition	Peripheral	Central
Saccade-execute	YES	YES
Saccade-ready	YES	YES
Attention	YES	NO

[a] YES indicates that inhibition was significant at the cued (previously fixated, prepared to fixate, attended) location.

drawn back to fixation, or the saccade preparation was "cancelled" and a simple detection target was presented at the previously cued or uncued location. In the eye movement conditions, they found delayed response to the detection target when it was presented at locations that subjects had either planned to fixate or actually had just fixated, with these effects independent of the nature of the cue. In contrast, when the precues were used to direct attention and the subjects were instructed to keep their eyes fixed, the inhibitory effect was observed following peripheral cues but *not* following central cues. Because exogenous cues tend to activate the oculomotor system, whereas central cues do not (Klein, 1980; Klein & Pontefract, in press), the set of conditions which produces inhibition of return suggests that it is a consequence of prior saccadic programming.[7]

We have considered three explanations for the failure of IOR to be measured or observed via choice response. One maintains the standard interpretation of IOR but asserts that the effect is lost in the extra time required to make a choice response. In other words, attention is inhibited from returning, but it moves in parallel with the accumulation of information at the target location and by the time it returns to that location, evidence is still accumulating, so that the additional time needed for attention to return has no impact on response times. This explanation is difficult to mesh with the vast array of data showing that attentional cuing effects are usually as large, if not larger, with choice RT than with simple RT (e.g., see Klein & Hansen, 1990, for a direct comparison; Posner, Snyder, & Davidson, 1980, are often cited for the contrary observation, but their finding is atypical.)

[7] Indirect support for this conclusion can be drawn from Maylor (1985, Experiment 2), who was able to eliminate IOR by requiring the subject to make a small saccade at the time of the cue, precisely because such a manipulation might make it difficult for the saccadic system to generate a program to foveate the cue.

A second possibility depends on the similarity between the cue stimulus and the task-relevant information in the target stimulus (cf. Folk, Remington, & Johnston, 1992). In a typical IOR experiment, both the cue and the target are defined by a luminance increment. In Egly et al. (1992), the cue was the brightening of a peripheral box and the target was the appearance of a letter. The fact that two different forms were presented was irrelevant; only the luminous flux in the appearance of the letter was necessary for the detection response. However, in the choice task, the fact of luminous flux in the target might be useful for locating the target form, but not for making the form decision. In the foraging metaphor, having found a luminance increment that was not the target, the system might be reluctant to classify the next luminance increment in the same region as the target. But when the target is not specified by luminous flux, then no inhibition will be observed. In the experiments presented here, this explanation is a bit more difficult to accept because whether the task was simple or choice RT, the size changes didn't involve any net change in overall luminance, although the cues did. In order to make a similar case in this experiment, one would have to resort to the idea that the detection of a local luminance change was inhibited, whereas the discrimination of the type of change was not, and then attribute the difference to the nature of the cue (luminance). Likewise, recall Rafal et al. (1989) demonstrated that IOR is observed following endogenously generated preparation to make an eye movement. In this condition, there was no peripheral stimulation, and yet IOR was observed with a subsequent detection stimulus. Because the IOR observed in this condition cannot be attributed to cue–target similarity, there is little reason to adopt this principle to explain the choice data.

A third explanation, and the one we currently favor, is that IOR is a reluctance to respond to an event at the inhibited location; in other words, IOR is more closely associated with responding than with attention.[8] Eye movements and choice responses that involve localization would obviously be affected. However, choice responses on dimensions other than location are assumed to involve the focusing of the attention/decision system on a visual representation appropriate for making the

[8]Maylor (1985) has also argued that IOR is operating at a response level. In her Experiment 3 it was reported that immediately after a peripheral cue, temporal order judgments for a subsequent stimulus pair were modulated in the expected direction (as if the stimulus at the cued location were perceived earlier than the stimulus at the uncued location). However, after a delay long enough for IOR to be measured with a speeded response task, there was no reversal of this effect. Following the time-honored notion that the direction of attention influences the relative arrival times in conscious experience (cf. Stelmach & Herdman, 1991, for a recent demonstration), Maylor's observation implies that cuing, but not IOR, is an attentional phenomenon. This finding is not often cited, perhaps because Maylor only reported the data from two subjects.

decision (e.g., form, color, size) and not on a map of spatial locations. This explanation does make the ad hoc assumption that, normally, detection responses are implicitly "to a spatial location." In essence, there is a criterion shift for responding that something has happened at a particular location. Unlike the allocation of attention in cuing paradigms (cf. Hawkins et al., 1990), this shift does *not* affect the processing efficiency of information coming from the attended location. If it did, all choice tasks would show evidence of IOR. Its effect is only seen in simple detection or localization responses, because the criterion is changed for "responses to" stimuli from a particular location. This view of what is inhibited in IOR has the added benefit that it can be seen to be related to the conditions necessary for generating IOR in the first place: a previously activated oculomotor program to fixate a particular location. The representational system or visual map in which this inhibition is generated is also the one in which it is measured.

Although this explanation appears to be the most satisfactory of the three presented, a recent study by Abrams and Dobkin (1992) challenges our proposed explanation, and, in so doing, suggests directions for future research on IOR. Before describing this final study, it is first necessary to present a brief account of a finding which suggests that IOR may be tied to objects.

In outlining boundary conditions for IOR, we suggested that the inhibition is tied to environmental rather than retinal coordinates. Tipper et al. (1991), however, have argued that IOR is tied not to the stimulated environmental location, but rather to objects that have been cued exogenously. We would not dispute this empirical claim, and by itself we do not see it as conflicting with our interpretation of IOR. From a functional point of view, Tipper et al.'s result would suggest that responses are made toward, or in relation to, objects, making inhibitory coding in environmental coordinates adequate only when the objects are stationary. As soon as the object can move, object-centered coding would be required. According to our view of IOR, this would require the assumption that the saccadic system generates a program to fixate an object and then, when that object moves through space, the program parameters are adjusted to maintain a current program capable of fixating the object. Because, according to our proposed explanation, it is the cancellation or decay of a saccadic program that produces IOR, IOR should move with the cued object. Thus, the finding of object-centered IOR effects does require the assumption that the saccadic program is continually updated as a cued object moves through space, but this assumption is quite compatible with our proposal.

However, a potential problem for our view does arise in a follow-up study performed by Abrams and Dobkin (1992) which first sought to measure IOR using saccadic rather than manual responses, and which then extended their approach to a study of object- versus location-based IOR. In their study, a cue was flashed in the periphery and following a 200-msec interval, a flash was used to draw attention back to fixation. After 150 msec, a peripheral (flash) or a central (arrow) command signal directed the subject to make a saccade to the location that had or had not been cued previously. Saccadic latencies exhibited IOR for both the peripheral and central command signals, but the effect was greater with the peripheral signals. Abrams and Dobkin suggested that the exogenous cue resulted in inhibition of both sensory (delayed processing of the peripheral cue at the recently stimulated location) and motor (delayed execution of a saccade that had recently been activated) pathways. Saccades in response to the peripherally presented command signal were sensitive to both forms of inhibition. However, because the central arrow condition does not involve a new stimulus at the previously cued location, saccades in this condition were only sensitive to the motor inhibition. Abrams and Dobkin's (1992) suggestion of a pure oculomotor inhibition is quite consistent with our proposal, which places the source of the inhibition in oculomotor programming, and we would attribute the additional "sensory" component to inhibition in *localization* of the target. So long as the two components operate in tandem, their existence poses no problem for our explanation.

However, a puzzle arises from Abrams and Dobkin's demonstration that these two components can be dissociated if the two objects move (along a 90° arc around fixation) after the peripheral cue and before the central or peripheral saccadic command signal. In this moving condition they found no evidence of inhibition (saccades were actually 2 msec faster to the cued object) following a central signal (i.e., there was no oculomotor inhibition), yet the inhibition following a peripheral command signal was the same magnitude as the inferred sensory component previously described. Thus, in contrast to the stationary condition for which both sensory and oculomotor inhibition are seen following a peripheral command and for which an oculomotor inhibition is seen following a central command, these results suggest that in the moving condition it is only sensory inhibition that is tagged to and moves with the object. Previously, we suggested that the object-centered inhibition observed by Tipper et al. (1991) is possibly due to a recalibrated oculomotor program, requiring that as long as the localization component is present, the pure motor component should be present as well. But Abrams and Dobkin have shown that it is not. One possible escape from the predicament this dissociation presents is to assume that inhibition in the localization and oculomotor systems decays at different rates. To assess this possibility, it would be necessary to examine the timecourse of the accrual and decay of IOR measured with manual responses (as in Tipper et al., 1991) and saccadic responses to central and peripheral commands (as in Abrams & Dobkin, 1992). Whether such a study would support our explanation of IOR remains to be seen.

Converging evidence from studies of performance demonstrates that it is prior activation of the oculomotor system and not activation of covert visual attention that is necessary to produce the IOR effect, and that this inhibition is not revealed when choice responses are based on information other than location. In response to these findings, we have proposed that the inhibition may be confined to perceptual, and perhaps to motor representations used to locate objects in space. Regardless of how the story of IOR unfolds, or whether our interpretation is supported by future research, on the basis of the evidence presented here it is clear that the original functional explanation of the effect is unlikely to be correct.

VII. EPILOGUE

From our discussion of cognitive inhibitory mechanisms, it should be clear that the literature has appealed to a variety of inhibitory processes to explain interference effects arising both within the attention system itself and within the motor and perceptual pathways leading to and from attentional resources. As such, characteristics of proposed mechanisms have included both hindering and prohibitive inhibitory effects resulting from both bottom-up activation and top-down selection processes. In this chapter we have attempted to categorize these forms of conceptual inhibition according to the ways in which they have been thought to mediate the relationship between attention and behavioral interference. In this regard, studies and phenomena were selected from the literature to illustrate three broad classes of inhibition.

The first class of conceptual inhibition described widespread interference effects that result from reduced access to attention when it is already engaged. These effects have been portrayed in the literature as representing nonselective consequences of the limited capacity of attention, and are generally measured in paradigms that require subjects to respond to a secondary task while simultaneously performing an attention-demanding primary task.

The second class described inhibitory effects thought to involve the reduced activation of or within a psychological pathway. Because psychological pathways are presumed to exist throughout the structural hierarchy of a cognitive architecture, inhibition of a psychological pathway does not represent a single process, but rather represents a broad class of inhibitory processes which may result from both bottom-up and top-down influences acting at various levels within the hierarchy. As such, included within this second class were inhibition due to the repeated activation of a pathway (semantic satiation), pathway inhibition as a mechanism of selection (negative priming), and inhibition associated with maintaining and cancelling expectancies.

The third class of inhibition results in the reduced ability of a system to function. To exemplify this category of conceptual inhibition, we described a proposal in which covert attention inhibits the saccadic system, and then presented evidence to suggest that the inhibition is actually within the saccadic system itself. This demonstration of the ability to distinguish between attentional and nonattentional inhibitory mechanisms emphasizes the power of converging evidence to develop and constrain models of conceptual inhibition.

Implicitly following up on this strategy of using converging evidence, the final section was devoted to IOR. Inhibition of return was originally conceived as an inhibitory consequence of prior exogenous orienting that results in a reduced ability of attention to return covertly to the previously attended location. Challenging this conception, however, is the failure to observe the inhibition in many choice tasks and evidence which implicates saccadic programming in laying down the inhibition. As such, we have emphasized the view that IOR may be an inhibitory process which is closely tied to the saccadic system and which exerts its influence on explicit or implicit localization responses.

Many of these inhibitory mechanisms have been suggested by, and based on, metaphors of inhibition that have come to cognitive psychology through the neural sciences. Unlike in the neural sciences, however, where inhibitory mechanisms can be observed in the hardware, in cognitive models inhibition must be inferred on the basis of overt behavior. As such, there is a danger of circularity whereby investigators attribute interference effects to inhibition and subsequently define inhibition on the basis of behavioral interference. For this reason, the terms inhibition and interference are often confused in the literature. For example, does the reduced access to attention necessitate the inhibition of nonselected pathways? Is the fatigue of a psychological pathway seen in semantic satiation mediated by inhibition? If so, is it really an attentional inhibition? Although answers to such questions are not presented here, they are intended to demonstrate that there is as yet no established method for distinguishing between those forms of interference which are likely to depend on inhibitory mechanisms and those which reflect processes such as response competition or fatigue. Until such time as the neural bases of cognitive inhibitory effects are revealed or else until cognitive psychology can offer proscriptive methods for distinguishing between interference and inhibitory effects, reliance on metaphors from the neural sciences will have to continue to be informed by the power of converging evidence.

REFERENCES

Abrams, R. A., & Dobkin, R. S. (1992, November). *Inhibition of return: Effects of attentional cueing on eye movement latencies.* Paper presented at the 33rd Annual Meeting of the Psychonomic Society, St. Louis, MO.

Allport, D. A., Tipper, S. P., & Chmiel, N. (1985). Perceptual integration and postcategorical filtering. In M. Posner & O. S. M. Marin (Eds.), *Attention and performance XI* (p. 107–132). Hillsdale, NJ: Lawrence Erlbaum.

Briand, K., & Klein, R. M. (1987). Is Posner's "beam" the same as Treisman's "glue"?: On the relationship between visual orienting and feature integration theory. *Journal of Experimental Psychology: Human Perception and Performance, 13,* 228–241.

Broadbent, D. E. (1985). *Perception and communication.* London: Pergamon.

Connelly, S. L., Hasher, L., & Kimble, G. A. (1992, November). *The suppression of identity and spatial location.* Paper presented at the 33rd Annual Meeting of the Psychonomic Society, St. Louis, MO.

Dalrymple-Alford, E. C., & Budayr, B. (1966). Examination of some aspects of the Stroop colour-word test. *Perceptual and Motor Skills, 16,* 1211–1214.

Eccles, J. C. (1969). *The inhibitory pathways of the central nervous system.* Liverpool, England: Liverpool University Press.

Egly, R., Rafal, R. D., & Henik, A. V. (1992, November). *Reflexive and voluntary orienting in detection and discrimination tasks.* Paper presented at the 33rd Annual Meeting of the Psychonomic Society, St. Louis, MO.

Esposito, N. J., & Pelton, L. H. (1971). Review of the measurement of semantic satiation. *Psychological Bulletin, 75,* 330–346.

Evarts, E. V., & Tanji, J. (1974). Gating of motor cortex reflexes by prior instruction. *Brain Research, 71,* 479–494.

Fischer, B., & Breitmeyer, B. (1987). Mechanisms of visual attention revealed by saccadic eye movements. *Neuropsychologia, 25,* 73–83.

Fischer, B., & Ramsperger, E. (1986). Human express saccades: Effects of randomization and daily practice. *Experimental Brain Research, 64,* 569–578.

Fischer, B., & Weber, H. (in press). Express saccades and visual attention. *Behavioral and Brain Sciences, 16,* 553–610.

Folk, C. L., Remington, R., & Johnston, J. C. (1992). Involuntary covert orienting is contingent on attentional control settings. *Journal of Experimental Psychology: Human Perception and Performance, 18,* 1030–1044.

Hawkins, H. L., Hillyard, S. A., Luck, S. J., Mouloula, M., Downing, C. J., & Woodward, D. P. (1990). Visual attention modulates signal detectability. *Journal of Experimental Psychology: Human Perception and Performance, 16,* 802–811.

Hawkins, H. L., Shafto, M. G., & Richardson, K. (1988). Effects of target luminance and cue validity on the latency of visual detection. *Perception and Psychophysics, 44,* 484–492.

Hebb, D. O. (1949). *The organization of behavior: A neuropsychological theory.* New York: Wiley.

James, W. (1890). *Principles of psychology.* New York: Holt.

Keele, S. W. (1973). *Attention and human performance.* Pacific Palisades, CA: Goodyear.

Kingstone, A. (1992). Combining expectancies. *Quarterly Journal of Experimental Psychology, 44A,* 69–104.

Kingstone, A., & Gazzaniga, M. S. (1992, June). *Covert orienting in the split brain.* Paper presented at the Canadian Society of Brain, Behaviour, and Cognitive Science, Québec City.

Kingstone, A., & Klein, R. M. (1991). Combining shape and position expectancies: Hierarchical processing and selective inhibition. *Journal of Experimental Psychology: Human Perception and Performance, 17*(2), 512–519.

Kingstone, A., & Klein, R. M. (1993). Visual offsets facilitate saccadic latency: Does predisengagement of visuo-spatial attention mediate this gap effect? *Journal of Experimental Psychology: Human Perception and Performance, 19*(6), 1251–1265.

Kinsbourne, M. (1973). The control of attention by interactions between the cerebral hemispheres. In S. Kornblum (Ed.), *Attention and performance IV.* New York: Academic Press.

Klein, R. M. (1980). Does oculomotor readiness mediate cognitive control of visual attention? In R. S. Nickerson (Ed.), *Attention and performance VIII.* Hillsdale, NJ: Lawrence Erlbaum.

Klein, R. M. (1988). Inhibitory tagging system facilitates visual search. *Nature, 334,* 430–431.

Klein, R. M. (1989). [Inhibitory tagging in visual search: Three failures to replicate]. Unpublished raw data.

Klein, R. M., & Farrell, M. (1989). Search performance without eye movements. *Perception and Psychophysics, 46*(5), 476–482.

Klein, R. M., & Hansen, E. (1990). Chronometric analysis of spotlight failure in endogenous visual orienting. *Journal of Experimental Psychology: Human Perception and Performance, 16*(4), 790–801.

Klein, R. M., & Kingstone, A. (1993). Why do visual offsets reduce saccadic latencies? *Behavioral and Brain Sciences, 16,* 583–584.

Klein, R. M., Kingstone, A., & Pontefract, A. (1993). Orienting of visual attention. In K. Rayner (Ed.), *Eye movements and visual cognition: Scene perception and reading* (pp. 46–65). New York: Springer Verlag.

Klein, R. M., & Pontefract, A. (in press). Does oculomotor readiness mediate cognitive control of visual attention? Revisited! In C. Umilta & M. Moscovitch (Eds.), *Attention and performance XV: Conscious and unconscious processing.*

Lowe, D. G. (1979). Strategies, context, and the mechanism of response inhibition. *Memory & Cognition, 7,* 382–389.

Maylor, E. A. (1985). Facilitatory and inhibitory components of orienting in visual space. In M. I. Posner & O. S. M. Marin (Eds.), *Attention and performance XI.* Hillsdale, NJ: Lawrence Erlbaum.

Maylor, E. A., & Hockey, R. (1985). Inhibitory component of externally controlled covert orienting in visual space. *Journal of Experimental Psychology: Human Perception and Performance, 11,* 777–787.

McClelland, J. L., & Rumelhart, D. E. (1981). An interactive activation model of context effects in letter perception: 1. An account of basic findings. *Psychological Review, 86,* 287–330.

McLean, J. P., & Shulman, G. L. (1978). On the construction and maintenance of expectancies. *Quarterly Journal of Experimental Psychology, 30,* 441–454.

McLeod, P. (1978). Does probe RT measure central processing demand? *Quarterly Journal of Experimental Psychology, 30,* 83–89.

Milner, P. M. (1957). The cell assembly: Mark II. *Psychological Review, 64,* 242–252.

Moran, J., & Desimone, R. (1985). Selective attention gates visual processing in the extrastriate cortex. *Science, 229,* 782–784.

Munoz, D. P., & Wurtz, R. H. (1992). Fixation cells in monkey superior colliculus. Characteristics of cell discharge. *Journal of Neurophysiology, 67,* 1000–1002.

Neely, J. H. (1977). Semantic priming and retrieval from lexical memory: Roles of inhibitionless spreading activation and limited capacity attention. *Journal of Experimental Psychology: General, 106,* 226–254.

Neill, W. T. (1977). Inhibitory and facilitatory processes in selective attention. *Journal of Experimental Psychology: Human Perception and Performance, 3*(3), 444–450.

Neill, W. T. (1979). Switching attention within and between categories: Evidence for intracategory inhibition. *Memory & Cognition, 7*, 283–290.

Neill, W. T., Valdes, L. A., & Terry, K. M. (1992, November). *Negative priming in target localization.* Paper presented at the 33rd Annual Meeting of the Psychonomic Society, St. Louis, MO.

Nissen, M. J. (1985). Accessing features and objects: Is location special? In M. I. Posner & O. S. M. Marin (Eds.), *Attention and performance XI.* Hillsdale, NJ: Lawrence Erlbaum.

Park, J., & Kanwisher, N. (in press). Negative priming for spatial locations: Identity mismatching, not distractor inhibition. *Journal of Experimental Psychology: Human Perception and Performance.*

Pontefract, A., & Klein, R. M. (1988). *Assessing inhibition of return with Simple and choice reaction time.* Unpublished manuscript.

Posner, M. I. (1978). *Chronometric explorations of mind.* Hillsdale, NJ: Lawrence Erlbaum.

Posner, M. I. (1980). Orienting of attention. *Quarterly Journal of Experimental Psychology, 32*, 3–25.

Posner, M. I., & Boies, S. J. (1971). Components of attention. *Psychological Review, 79*, 391–408.

Posner, M. I., & Cohen, Y. (1984). Components of visual orienting. In H. Bouma & D. G. Bouwhuis (Eds.), *Attention and performance X: Control of language processes.* Hillsdale, NJ: Lawrence Erlbaum.

Posner, M. I., & Klein, R. M. (1973). On the functions of consciousness. In S. Kornblum (Ed.), *Attention and performance IV.* New York: Academic Press.

Posner, M. I., Nissen, M. J., & Ogden, W. C. (1978). Attended and unattended processing modes: The role of set for spatial location. In H. Pick & I. J. Saltzman (Eds.), *Modes of perceiving and processing information.* Hillsdale, NJ: Lawrence Erlbaum.

Posner, M. I., & Rogers, M. (1978). Chronometric analysis of abstraction and recognition. In W. K. Estes (Ed.), *Handbook of learning and cognition processes: Vol. 5. Human information processing* (pp. 143–188). Hillsdale, NJ: Lawrence Erlbaum.

Posner, M. I., & Snyder, C. R. R. (1975a). Facilitation and inhibition in the processing of signals. In P. M. A. Rabbitt & S. Dornic (Eds.), *Attention and performance V.* New York: Academic Press.

Posner, M. I., & Snyder, C. R. R. (1975b). Attention and cognitive control. In R. L. Solso (Ed.), *Information processing and cognition: The Loyola Symposium.* Hillsdale, NJ: Lawrence Erlbaum.

Posner, M. I., Snyder, C. R. R., & Davidson, B. J. (1980). Attention and the detection of signals. *Journal of Experimental Psychology: General, 109*, 160–174.

Rafal, R. D., Calabresi, P. A., Brennan, C. W., & Sciolto, T. K. (1989). Saccade preparation inhibits reorienting to recently attended locations. *Journal of Experimental Psychology: Human Perception and Performance, 15*, 673–685.

Reuter-Lorenz, P. A., Hughes, H. C., & Fendrich, R. (1991). The reduction of saccadic latency by prior offset of the fixation point: An analysis of the "gap effect." *Perception and Psychophysics, 29*, 429–437.

Ross, L. E., & Ross, S. M. (1980). Saccade latency and warning signals: Stimulus onset, offset, and change as warning events. *Perception and Psychophysics, 27*, 251–257.

Ross, S. M., & Ross, L. E. (1981). Saccade latency and warning signals: Effects of auditory and visual stimulus onset and offset. *Perception and Psychophysics, 29*, 429–437.

Saslow, M. G. (1967). Effects of components of displacement-step stimuli upon latency of saccadic eye movements. *Journal of the Optical Society of America, 57*, 1024–1029.

Shallice, T. (1972). Dual functions of consciousness. *Psychological Review*, *79*(5), 383–393.

Sherrington, C. S. (1906). *The integrative action of the nervous system*. New Haven, CT: Yale University Press.

Smith, L. C. (1984). Semantic satiation affects category membership decision time but not lexical priming. *Memory & Cognition*, *12*, 483–488.

Smith, L., & Klein, R. (1990). Evidence for semantic satiation: Repeating a category slows subsequent semantic processing. *Journal of Experimental Psychology: Learning, Memory and Cognition*, *16*(5), 852–861.

Stelmach, L. B., & Herdman, C. M. (1991). Directed attention and perception of temporal order. *Journal of Experimental Psychology: Human Perception and Performance*, *17*(2), 539–550.

Taylor, J. (Ed.). (1931–2). *Selected writings of John Hughlings Jackson*. London: Hodder & Stoughton.

Tipper, S. P. (1985). The negative priming effect: Inhibitory effects of ignored primes. *Quarterly Journal of Experimental Psychology*, *37A*, 571–590.

Tipper, S. P., & Baylis, G. (1987). Individual differences in selective attention: The relation of priming and interference to cognitive failure. *Personality and Individual Differences*, *8*, 667–675.

Tipper, S. P., Brehaut, J. C., & Driver, J. (1990). Selection of moving and static objects for the control of spatially directed action. *Journal of Experimental Psychology: Human Perception and Performance*, *16*, 492–504.

Tipper, S. P., Driver, J., & Weaver, B. (1991). Object-centered inhibition of return of visual attention. *Quarterly Journal of Experimental Psychology*, *43A*, 289–298.

Walley, R. E., & Weiden, T. D. (1973). Lateral inhibition and cognitive masking: A neuropsychological theory of attention. *Psychological Review*, *804*, 284–302.

Wolfe, J. M., & Pokorny, C. W. (1990). Inhibitory tagging in visual search: A failure to replicate. *Perception and Psychophysics*, *48*, 357–362.

4

Temporal Allocation of Visual Attention
Inhibition or Interference?

Kimron L. Shapiro and Jane E. Raymond

I. INTRODUCTION

With natural viewing, the visual images stimulating the retinae are typically rich in variations of luminance and wavelength in both the spatial and temporal domains. To derive coherent perception of and responses to such diverse and dynamic visual information, the human brain relies on a sophisticated attentional system, operating in conjunction with a number of low-level sensory mechanisms, to limit and control the flow of visual information arriving at higher cortical areas. Attentional regulation of information probably involves both excitation (i.e., enhancement of visual processing) and inhibition (i.e., reduction in visual processing). Because visual information is distributed over space and time, the excitation and inhibition exerted by attentional mechanisms must also operate over restricted spatial and temporal windows if such mechanisms are to regulate effectively visual information flow.

Although there has been considerable evidence that visual attention may be allocated over limited spatial regions of a display, there has been relatively little research investigating the allocation of attention in the temporal domain. In this chapter we consider the episodic nature of visual attention with emphasis on empirical studies that we and others have conducted. We examine specifically how activation of attentional mechanisms at one point in time appears to inhibit or interfere with

INHIBITORY PROCESSES IN ATTENTION,
MEMORY, AND LANGUAGE

subsequent visual processing. We review a number of studies in which information is presented serially within a narrowly restricted spatial area, thus isolating temporal factors from spatial ones in the allocation of attention. Because most of these studies have employed a technique known as rapid serial visual presentation (RSVP), we begin with a brief review of the application of this procedure to the study of visual attention. We then discuss the visual and attentional mechanisms that appear to be involved when subjects are required to select a single target from an RSVP sequence. Following this, we discuss RSVP studies in which subjects are required to respond to two or more serially presented targets. The general result of such studies is that the ability to detect or identify a second target is seriously impaired when the intertarget interval is less than about 500 msec. These studies provide evidence that relatively long-lasting inhibitory attentional processes are in operation after target selection. We shall see that the results of RSVP studies reveal certain similarities between temporal and spatial visual search which suggest that attention may be viewed as a combination of excitatory and inhibitory mechanisms operating within a spatio-temporally defined space.

II. RSVP TECHNIQUES

In RSVP procedures, items such as letters, digits, pictures, words, and even sentences are presented briefly in rapid succession. Item presentation rates vary from about 6 items/sec up to nearly 30 items/sec. In some studies the onset of one stimulus is simultaneous with the offset of the previous stimulus, whereas in others, a nonpatterned interstimulus interval (ISI) is used. In the former situation, the stimulus onset asynchrony (SOA) is equivalent to stimulus duration, and in the latter situation, the SOA is equal to the stimulus duration plus the ISI.

In experiments on visual attention, RSVP procedures usually consist of a sequence of between 15 and 20 items. In most cases, except studies of repetition blindness (Kanwisher, 1987), all items in the sequence are different. In single-target RSVP studies, one item in the stimulus sequence is designated as the target and is differentiated in some way (e.g., presented in a different color) from all other items. The subject's task is to identify or detect the target. In tasks where the target is partially specified, the subject is given the key, i.e. target-defining, feature and is asked to supply the response feature. For example, a subject is asked to view a sequence of different colored letters and to report the letter name (response feature) of the red (key feature) item. In other experiments, the target may be fully specified and the subject must report its presence or absence. Tasks in which the target is identified on the basis of a simple feature will be referred to as filtering RSVP tasks. Tasks in which the target is distinguished on the basis of a category (e.g., name the digit embedded in a sequence of letters) will be referred to as selective set tasks, according to the distinction made by Kahneman and Treisman (1983). From trial to trial, the target is assigned a serial position approximately midway through the sequence. This serial position is assigned a value of 0, items preceding the target are labeled as $-n$ items, and items succeeding the target are referred to as $+n$ items. Nontarget items will be referred to here as distractors.

In multiple target RSVP studies, additional targets are presented after the first target and the subject's task is to detect or identify all the targets. To simplify stimulus references, we will use the term *target* to refer to the first target in a sequence and the term *probe* to refer to subsequent targets. The serial position of the probe(s) relative to the target is systematically manipulated so that the effect of the target–probe interval on performance can be investigated. A schematic of a typical RSVP experiment is seen in Figure 1.

A. Single-Task RSVP Studies

Lawrence (1971) observed that processing a briefly exposed target letter presented singly is substantially easier than processing the same stimulus embedded in an RSVP sequence of similar stimuli. Does this decrement in target letter identification reflect a sensory or an attentional limitation? Although visual masking of the target letter by the +1 item may limit performance to some small extent, the results of single target RSVP experiments overwhelmingly suggest that visual attentional mechanisms are the limiting factor. Masking studies have shown that no significant degradation of letter identification is found when targets are presented for longer than 10 msec and when the SOA of the target and mask is longer than 30 msec (Taylor & Chabot, 1978). Yet Lawrence (1971) found significant target identification error rates when stimuli were presented as slowly as 7 items/sec (SOA = 142 msec). Perhaps the most compelling evidence to reject the idea that sensory masking can account for limitations of target identification in RSVP is that target errors are not random, as would be expected if simple sensory masking were completely obscuring perception of the target.

Analysis of the errors in single-target RSVP studies has been useful in modeling the processes involved in target identification (Botella & Eriksen, 1992; Gathercole & Broadbent, 1984; Lawrence, 1971; McLean, Broadbent, & Broadbent, 1982; Keele, Cohen, Ivry, Liotti, & Yee, 1988). Depending on the stimuli, presentation rate, ISI, and key and response features, target identification errors tend to follow three patterns: (1) a

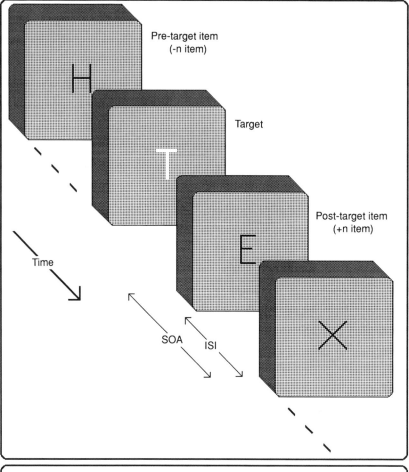

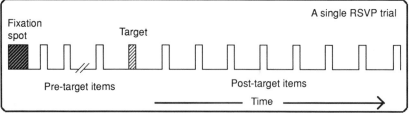

FIGURE 1

The top panel illustrates stimuli typically used in RSVP attention experiments. The target, embedded in the stimulus stream, is denoted by a key feature, in this example the color white, and subjects are required to report the target letter name. The bottom panel is a diagram of the temporal arrangement used in typical RSVP experiments.

predominance of pretarget intrusions, that is, naming the response feature from an item immediately preceding the target by n items—designated as $-n$ errors (Intraub, 1985), (2) a predominance of post-target intrusions, that is, naming the to-be-reported feature from an item succeeding the target by n items—$+n$ errors (Botella & Eriksen, 1991, 1992; Gathercole & Broadbent, 1984; Lawrence, 1971; McLean et al., 1982; Raymond, Shapiro, & Arnell, 1992a), or (3) a symmetrical pattern, that is, an approximately equal number of pre- and postintrusion errors (Botella & Eriksen, 1991, 1992; Gathercole & Broadbent, 1984; Intraub, 1985; McLean et al., 1982).

When the target-defining characteristic is featural (e.g., "name the red letter") and the SOA is relatively short, subjects typically produce only post-target intrusion errors (Botella & Eriksen, 1992; Lawrence, 1971; McLean et al., 1982). The prevalence of $+n$ errors suggests that processing of features in the target to an output stage extends beyond the time during which the target is physically present by n times the SOA. Based on the filtering notions of Broadbent (1977), the occurrence of post-target intrusion errors has been interpreted to indicate that target identification in these tasks involves a recursive process wherein early selection of the key feature initiates an analysis of the response feature (Broadbent & Broadbent, 1986, 1987; Gathercole & Broadbent, 1984; Lawrence, 1971; McLean et al., 1982). In this view, post-target intrusion errors occur when the response feature of the $+n$ item is conjoined with the key feature of the target. Keele et al. (in press) investigated the spatial versus temporal basis for the illusory conjoining of key and response features. They presented items in RSVP alternating between two locations and found that instrusion errors were more likely to occur for items that shared the target's spatial location in spite of relatively long temporal separations. Items temporally adjacent to the target but spatially separated were unlikely to produce intrusion errors. These results indicate that the attentional mechanism that determines how features are to be integrated relies on spatial coordination cues before temporal coordination cues.

Although the detect-then-identify model can neatly explain post-target intrusion errors, it has greater difficulty accounting for a symmetrical pattern of pre- and post-target intrusion errors. Such patterns have been found in picture (Intraub, 1985) and letter RSVP filtering tasks (Botella & Eriksen, 1992) and in selective set RSVP tasks (McLean et al., 1982). An alternative explanation of target intrusion errors that can adequately account for all error patterns is a late selection model in which codes associated with key and response features in each item develop concurrently and in parallel. Target identification errors may occur because either (1) analysis of key and response features proceeds at different rates (Keele & Neill, 1978), or (2) because different selection schedules are applied to the results of the parallel analyses (Duncan, 1980). According to Keele and Neill's (1978) idea, intrusion errors would occur when the target's code for the key feature and a distractor item's code for the response feature arrive simultaneously for integration into one percept. McLean et al. (1982) tested this possibility using filtering RSVP tasks with different key features. First, color was used as the key feature and target name as the response feature. In the second experiment using the same presentation rate, the roles were reversed. A predominance of post-target intrusions was found for both conditions. Although MacLean et al. (1982) interpreted this to support the early selection detect-then-identify model of target identification, these findings do not rule out a late selection account. In RSVP, the response feature per se may be processed more slowly than the key feature, or according to Duncan's (1980) selection schedule notion, the key feature may always precede the response feature in gaining entry to visual short-term memory (VSTM).

In a selective set RSVP task, Gathercole and Broadbent (1984) asked subjects either to identify a digit among a sequence of letters or to identify an animal name embedded in a sequence of nonanimal words. In both cases, Gathercole and Broadbent found a symmetrical pattern of intrusion errors. To account for these findings, they suggested that an early selection mechanism limits performance in a filtering task, but that late selection mechanisms limit performance in a selective set task. Proposing alternative task-dependent modes of processing lacks parsimony, and because late selection mechanisms can be used to account for both filtering and selective set RSVP identification errors, it seems more reasonable to suggest that both key and response features are analyzed in parallel.

Botella and Eriksen (1991, 1992) have recently reported a series of experiments which support this notion. Using a letter filtering RSVP task, they asked subjects to identify a target letter appearing in a pre-specified color by choosing from a menu of letters presented at the end of each sequence. The experimentors constrained the responses of the subjects by manipulating the availability of items on the menu and were thus able to ascertain the information subjects were able to obtain from the stimulus sequence. They found that the pattern of errors could be modified from predominantly post-target intrusions to a symmetrical pattern of intrusions through changes in the response menu, with no concurrent change to the stimuli in the RSVP sequence. The detect-then-identify model of D. E. Broadbent and his colleagues cannot account for such findings. Rather, a late-selection model in which a number of items in the stream are identified and stored would predict such an outcome.

Independent of the mechanisms that produce errors in single-task RSVP studies, it is clear that conjoining a key and response feature is complete in at least 100 msec because intrusions of items presented later than this are rare. One might assume that once a target is identified, the perceptual and attentional mechanisms would be free to begin analyzing subsequent stimuli. However, multiple-task RSVP research strongly suggests that this is not the case. Rather, it appears that large deficits in the processing of subsequent stimuli are found for as long as 600 msec after target identification is seemingly complete.

B. Multiple-Task RSVP Studies

The primary purpose of multiple-task RSVP experiments is to track the timecourse of events succeeding selection of a single target. D. E. Broadbent and M. H. P. Broadbent (1987, Experiment 3) were the first to demonstrate a long-lasting interference effect following target identification in RSVP. They used a multiple-task RSVP procedure and asked subjects to identify a target and a probe word (each defined by flanking hyphens) that were embedded at different serial positions within a sequence of unrelated lowercase words. The SOA was 120 msec with an ISI of 20 msec. The number of items between the target and probe words was varied. It was found that when target and probe were temporally adjacent, subjects could produce a correct response to either the target or the probe, but not to both. As the temporal proximity of target and probe was decreased, the probability of correctly identifying the probe word on target-correct trials increased. This rose from a low value of .1 for target–probe intervals of less than 400 msec up to an asymptote of .7 for intervals of 720 msec or longer. Results of this experiment are presented in Figure 2. Not only were subjects unable to correctly identify the probe when it was presented within 400 msec post-target, they reported frequently being unaware that it had been embedded in the stimulus stream. Broadbent and Broadbent (1987) proposed that the interference producing poor probe performance occurred at the target identification stage. They suggested that once the key feature of the target was detected, a slow identification process was initiated which produced a long-lasting interference effect.

Using a variant on the multiple-task RSVP procedure, Reeves and Sperling (1986) and Weichselgartner and Sperling (1987) also observed large deficits in the processing of post-target items. In both studies, highly practiced subjects were presented with an RSVP stream of digits and asked to identify a highlighted or boxed digit (target) and to name the next three (post-target) digits. Reeves and Sperling (1986) presented the post-target digits at a location to the right of the target and pretarget items, whereas Weichselgartner and Sperling (1987) presented all items at the same location. Both studies found that subjects' reports generally

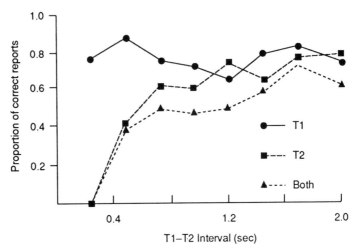

FIGURE 2

Performance on the first target and on the second target in Experiment 3 of D. E. Broadbent and M. P. H. Broadbent (1987). The proportion of trials on which both targets were correct is also shown. From "From detection to identification: Response to multiple targets in rapid serial visual presentation" by D. E. Broadbent and M. H. P. Broadbent, 1987, *Perception and Psychophysics, 42*, p. 110. Copyright 1987 by the Psychonomic Society. Reprinted by permission.

consisted of the target, the first post-target item, and items presented about 300–400 msec after the target. The items presented in the interval between 100 and 300 msec post-target were rarely reported. They noted, as did Raymond et al. (1992a), that the perceived temporal order of items recalled was nonveridical. Using this complex response requirement, it is not clear whether subjects were unable to perceptually process the items during this interval or whether they were unable to store and retrieve these items from memory for later recall. In either event, a deficit in the ability to process successive post-target items to an output stage was reported. Although Reeves and Sperling (1986) attributed this post-target processing deficit in recall to a shift in the spatial allocation of attention, similarly sized effects were observed by Weichselgartner and Sperling (1987), indicating that the post-target processing deficit occurs independently of a spatial shift in attention.

To account for the post-target processing deficit, Weichselgartner and Sperling (1987) proposed that two attentional processes were initiated by target detection. One is a fast, short-lived, automatic process producing effortless identification of the target and, occasionally, the +1 item. This process is terminated after about 100 msec and is unaffected by task difficulty. The other process is a slow, effortful, controlled process that mediates identification of items appearing between 200 and 300 msec post-target. This process is acknowledged to be affected by factors normally seen to affect attention, for example, practice, expectation, stimulus probability, and target signal-to-noise ratio. The post-target processing deficit reflects the interval after the automatic process has subsided and before the controlled process has gained sufficient power. Nakayama and Mackeben (1989) proposed a similar dual process model of attention to account for cueing effects.

III. THE ATTENTIONAL BLINK

The preceding dual-task RSVP studies demonstrate a deficit in reporting items presented during an interval of approximately 100–500 msec post-target. All these studies required target identification, but they differed in the response requirement to subsequent stimuli. However, the similarity of the timecourse of the observed deficits suggests that a common mechanism operates to inhibit or interfere with visual processing after the target. It is as if the perceptual and/or attentional mechanisms blink after target presentation. Eye blinks produce a dramatic, brief reduction in pattern vision and are only initiated *after* important stimuli are viewed. The results of the multiple-target RSVP studies just reviewed, as well as those we have conducted in our laboratory, suggest that sensory and/or attentional mechanisms may undergo a covert analogue to this overt ocular process. For this reason and for ease of reference, we have labeled the post-target processing deficit the attentional blink (AB; Raymond et al., 1992a).

In this section, we address a number of questions concerning the AB effect. For example, is the post-target processing deficit due to attentional, memory, or sensory factors? Would the effect be found with simpler stimuli and a reduced memory load of the response? Do these results simply reflect the time required to switch from one target task to another? That is to say, have these studies simply measured the psychological refractory period, or is a different inhibitory mechanism involved?

In an effort to address these issues, we developed a simplified technique for measuring the AB based on both Weichselgartner and Sperling's (1987) and Broadbent and Broadbent's (1987) methodology (Raymond et al., 1992a). Like Weichselgartner and Sperling (1987), we presented subjects with a RSVP series of single black characters (we used letters instead of digits) viewed against a gray field and presented at a rate of 11 items/sec (75 msec stimulus, 15 msec ISI). Like Broadbent and Broadbent (1987), we asked subjects to respond to two predefined targets, rather than using the memory recall task of Weichselgartner and

Sperling. The subject's task was to identify a single white letter (the target) and then to detect the presence or absence of a black letter X (probe) in the post-target stream. The target was presented at a variable serial position midway through the RSVP stream. The duration of the entire series of stimuli was between 1.5 and 2.1 sec. Subjects responded to both tasks at the end of each stream. The probe, present on 50% of trials, could appear at one of eight possible serial positions after the target. We reasoned that the simple probe task made less demand on memory than the secondary task employed by Weichselgartner and Sperling (1987). Thus, in our procedure, an inability to successfully detect the probe could be argued to be more likely due to a failure in visual processing, rather than in memory recall. We further modified the procedure by adding a control condition that enabled us to determine if the AB was due to sensory (e.g., masking) or attentional factors. In the control condition, subjects were instructed to ignore the target and merely perform the probe task. Thus the sensory information presented in both conditions was the same, but the need to attend and respond to the target was eliminated in the control condition.

The results of the experiment are shown in Figure 3 and reveal a deficit in the probability of probe detection, relative to controls, for probes presented in post-target serial positions 2 through 5, corresponding to the temporal interval between 180–450 msec after the target's occurrence. In the control condition, subjects correctly detected the probe on 85% or better of trials for all probe relative serial positions. However, for the experimental condition, the percentage of correct detection dropped below 60% for the indicated post-target interval.

According to this rationale, we can conclude that the AB is not a low-level perceptual effect (e.g., sensory masking), but is, rather, attentional in nature. We can also conclude that the AB does not likely result from a problem in memory retrieval, because it occurred even when the load on memory was minimal; that is, when the probe task required only the detection of a single letter.

As described previously, Weichselgartner and Sperling (1987) suggest that the post-target deficits seen in their experiments are due to the lack of overlap between fast and slow attentive processes initiated by the target key feature. However, two experiments (Experiments 3 and 4) by Raymond et al. (1992a) do not support such an explanation. In these experiments, we removed the stimulus letter occurring in the +1 serial position (Experiment 3) or in the +2 position (Experiment 4) in order to assess the ballistic nature of the post-target deficits. The rationale was that a ballistic process initiated by the target identification task, such as that posited by Weichselgartner and Sperling (1987), should be unaffected by the removal of any item following the target. If, on the other hand, the AB was produced as a result of confusion from stimuli occur-

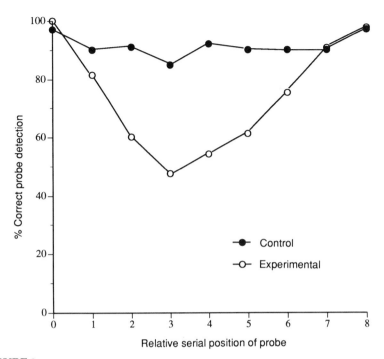

FIGURE 3

The group mean percentage of trials in which the probe was correctly detected plotted as a function of the relative serial position of the probe in Experiment 2 of Raymond et al. (1992a). Solid circles represent data obtained in the control condition in which subjects were told to ignore the target letter. Open circles represent data obtained in the experimental condition in which subjects were told to identify the target letter. From "Temporary suppression of visual processing in an RSVP task: An attentional blink?" by J. E. Raymond, K. L. Shapiro, and K. M. Arnell, 1992, *Journal of Experimental Psychology: Human Perception and Performance, 18,* p. 854. Copyright 1992 by the American Psychological Association. Reprinted by permission.

ring after the target, removal of immediate post-target stimuli should reduce the AB effect. In all other major aspects, the procedure was identical to that described for Experiment 2 of Raymond et al. (1992a). The result of this experiment was that replacement of the +1 item with an interval lacking in pattern stimulation eliminated the AB effect. In other conditions, leaving in the +1 item but replacing the +2 alone or the +2 and +3 post-target positions with the same blank interval(s) had no effect. These results provide strong indications that the AB does not result from events initiated by the target itself, but rather result from either the presence of the +1 item or the interaction of the +1 item with other items in the stimulus series, presumably the target.

A second important point addressed by this experiment is whether the AB simply reflects the time required to switch from the target task to the probe task. There is an extensive literature investigating task switching (for reviews, see Bertelson, 1966; Smith, 1967) and the resulting deficits that ensue when two tasks compete for a limited capacity mechanism. This phenomenon has commonly been referred to as the *psychological refractory period* (PRP). Pashler and his colleagues (e.g., Pashler, 1984, 1989, 1990; Pashler & Johnston, 1989) have argued that this bottleneck occurs at the level of response selection, a stage accessible by only one task at a time but required by both. Thus it is at least plausible that such a bottleneck is the root cause of the AB. However, the finding that the AB effect is eliminated when the +1 item is replaced with a blank interval strongly suggests that this is not the case. It does not seem possible that a blank interval could affect such a stage, given that the two stimuli that clearly require response selection (target and probe) are still present in the same temporal relation to one another. Moreover, because subjects responded to both targets as a group at the end of the stream, it is unlikely that the PRP bottleneck could account for the AB effect. Finally, results of experiments to be reported later in this chapter also argue against task switching as a viable explanation for the AB. In these experiments, the target task is the detection or identification of a "gap" interval between two stream elements and the probe task is the detection of the letter *X*. Because AB effects are not found under these circumstances, a PRP explanation of the AB seems untenable (Shapiro, Raymond, & Arnell, in press).

So the question must be asked: What causes the attentional blink? In our first report (Raymond et al., 1992a), we suggested that the blink resulted from the second of a two-stage process of target identification, similar to the account offered by Broadbent and Broadbent (1987). We postulated that the following sequence of events may lead to an attentional blink. During the presentation of the RSVP stream of letters, the white color of the target is detected preattentively. This information is then used to initiate an attentional response to facilitate target identification. If attention is allocated in an episodic manner, as suggested by Sperling and Weichselgartner (1990), then target identification may involve the opening and closing of a gate to regulate the flow of postreceptoral visual information to recognition centers of the brain (Reeves & Sperling, 1986). According to this model, an attentional episode begins, that is, the gate opens, when the target-defining feature is detected and continues until target identification is complete. The presentation of a new item (+1 item) immediately after the target (i.e., while the gate is still open), but before the termination of the attentional episode, will result in features of the +1 item being processed along with features of the target item. This possibility is supported by the observation that probes presented in the +1 position were detected on an average of 82% of trials in experiments in which attentional blinks were found. However, the availability of features from both the target and the +1 item in the sensory store will provide the identification mechanism with confusing information: two letter colors and two letter names. This potential confusion is noted by the system and then used to initiate a suppressive mechanism to eliminate further confusion. When confusion is not present, that is, when target identification can reach completion without interference from new stimuli, the attentional gate is merely closed and the next attentional episode can be initiated rapidly (i.e., probes can be readily detected at any time). Such would be the case when the +1 item is absent. However, when confusion is present, the attentional gate is both shut and locked, making the initiation of the next attentional episode a more time-consuming process than if a locking operation had not been conducted. The possibility of a shut-and-lock procedure when interference is present is supported by the finding (Raymond et al., 1992a, Experiment 4) that once initiated, suppression of visual processing lasts for the same amount of time whether there is a steady stream of new stimulation being presented or not (as long as the +1 item is present).

Such a theory makes two specific predictions. First, if target detection but not identification is required, no AB should be observed. Second, if the +1 item cannot be confused with the target because of categorical or featural dissimilarity, then the AB should also be absent. We now describe a series of experiments designed to investigate each prediction. To anticipate, neither prediction held, and we were required to reformulate an appropriate model to explain the AB. This model is described after all the data for which it accounts have been reported.

A. Target Manipulations

Because a serial processing, limited-capacity mechanism has formed the basis of most models of spatial visual search, it is reasonable to postulate that a similar mechanism underlies visual search in the temporal domain. In the spatial domain, such a model predicts the general outcome that spatial search becomes more difficult with increasing attentional demands of the target task. With this in mind, Shapiro et al. (in press) conducted a set of experiments manipulating the set size of the target task in an attempt to derive the relationship between attentional demands and the magnitude of the blink. In subsequent experiments, by manipulating identification versus detection requirements of the target task, we were able to assess the validity of the previously described early-processing model suggested by Raymond et al. (1992a).

The general strategy employed in the following set of experiments was to manipulate the target task while leaving all other elements of the RSVP procedure unaltered.

In a first attempt to determine if target task difficulty affected the magnitude of the blink (Shapiro et al., in press, Experiment 1), we reduced the set size of the target from 25 letters of the alphabet, as used in Experiment 2 (Raymond et al., 1992a), to a set size of 3 letters. Thus the experimental group was required to identify the (white) target letter, which was one of only three target letters, whereas the control group was required to do the probe task, but ignore the target task. In all other respects, the methods remained the same as in our previous experiments, in which the target could be any one of 25 different letters. The results of this experiment revealed significant post-target processing deficits in the experimental group, relative to controls, for the probe when it occurred in the post-target serial positions 1 through 3, corresponding to the post-target interval occurring between 0 and 270 msec. We also compared the experimental condition from this first manipulation to that of Raymond et al. (1992a) to see if there was any effect of set size and found nonsignificant differences. Contrary to what we expected, it appears that target set size did not exert an effect on the blink, or at least, not a very large effect. It is perhaps possible that both set sizes were sufficient to overload attentional capacity. However, this alternative was investigated in subsequent experiments and found lacking.

The detect-then-identify model (Broadbent & Broadbent, 1987) argues that the target task requires an attentionally demanding identification process which extends beyond the time of the target's appearance. Raymond et al. (1992a) suggested that the attentional blink effect results from the attentional system attempting to reduce confusion arising during this identification process by suppressing processing of subsequently presented information. If the attentional demand of the target requires only simple *detection*, then the detect-then-identify model would predict that performing the target task should not be affected by the occurrence of the first post-target stimulus and therefore no AB should be produced.

To test this possibility, we conducted a series of subsequent experiments in which the target tasks required simple detection, rather than identification. In our initial experiment, the target was a white letter drawn from an alphabetic set of 25 and subjects were required merely to *detect* if a white stimulus (i.e., target) appeared. The probe was a black *X* and, as in all previous experiments, subjects were required to detect it. Targets and probes were present on 50% of trials. Trials where no target was presented served as a within-subjects control condition. The results of this experiment were surprising and are shown in Figure 4. We expected to find the blink reduced, if not attenuated fully.

However, statistical analysis revealed that the group mean percentage of probe detection for the target present condition was significantly lower than the corresponding point for the target absent condition for post-target serial positions 2, 3, and 4, again indicating a significant AB effect for the post-target interval occurring between 90 and 360 msec.

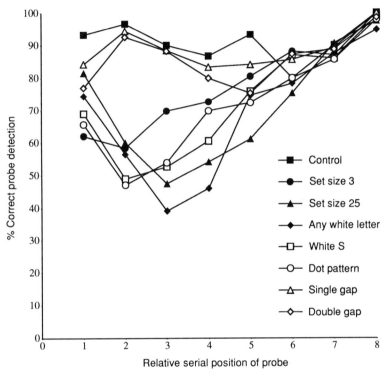

FIGURE 4

The group mean percentage of trials in which the probe was correctly detected plotted as a function of the relative serial position of the probe. Solid squares represent the control condition where the target task was ignored. Solid circles represent the set size = 3 condition where the target had to be identified. Solid triangles represent the set size = 25 condition where the target had to be identified. Solid diamonds represent the condition where the target could be any white letter of the alphabet and detection of a white "target" was all that was required. Open squares represent the condition where the requirement was detection of the presence or absence of a white S. Open circles represent the condition where the target could be a random white dot pattern and detection of the presence versus absence was required. Open triangles represent the condition where the target judgment was the presence or absence of a gap caused by the removal of one letter in the position where the target normally occurred. Open diamonds represent the condition where the target had to be identified as either a short (one letter removed from the stream) or long (two letters removed from the stream) gap.

The magnitude of the effect was not much different from the effects already described.[1]

The results of this experiment suggested that an attentional blink occurs after a target *detection* task, like that found after the target *identification* task. Although it was tempting to conclude that the results of this experiment invalidated the detect-then-identify account of why the blink is produced, we were concerned this might be a premature conclusion. We reasoned that subjects might be identifying the target even though they were instructed not to do so, that is, perhaps letter identification occurs involuntarily. Our next experiment (Shapiro et al., in press, Experiment 3A) sought to create a target task that also required target detection but would not prompt target identification.

This experiment was identical to the previous one in all respects, except that the target task now required subjects to detect a white letter *S* that was presented on 50% of trials. The subjects were informed of the target's constant identity and that there was no need to attempt identification. Again to our surprise, the results (see Figure 4) revealed just as large a blink with similar temporal characteristics as we had found in the previous experiment. Although these data suggest that even target detection causes a blink, the possibility of involuntary letter identification still remained.

We then employed a target task that required subjects to detect the presence or absence of a nonletter stimulus containing pattern information of a scale similar to that used in the letter detection tasks (Shapiro et al., in press, Experiment 4). The target consisted of five white dots positioned randomly within the area normally occupied by a letter in the RSVP stream. The probe task remained the same as in all previous experiments. The results of this experiment (see Figure 4) revealed an AB of equal magnitude to that found in previous experiments. Because involuntary naming of the nonletter stimulus seems unlikely, these results strongly suggest that detection of any pattern information produces an AB, as long as the target is followed by another patterned stimulus.

The question now was whether detection per se caused the blink or whether directing attention to a visual pattern was the necessary condition. To answer this question, we created a nonpatterned target that could be used in both a detection and an identification task. In one condition, the target task was to *detect* whether a single, short gap had occurred in the stimulus stream (Shapiro et al., in press, Experiment 5A). In a second condition (Experiment 5B), the target task was to *identify* whether a short or a long gap had interrupted the stimulus sequence.

---

[1]We quantified the magnitude of the AB effect in this and subsequent experiments by calculating the difference between 100% and the mean probability of probe detection for each possible probe position and then summing these differences.

The short and long gap conditions were created by removing either one or two letters, respectively, from the stimulus series. In the gap detection condition, gap-absent trials served as control trials. In the gap identification condition, a separate condition was conducted in which subjects ignored the gap identification task and simply performed the probe detection task.

The probability of probe detection remained uniformly high for all post-target serial positions of the probe in both the gap detection and identification experimental conditions, and differences between experimental and control conditions were nonsignificant. (See Figure 4.) The absence of an AB effect in these experiments supports the idea that the AB is produced whenever a target containing pattern information requires attention in a continuous RSVP stream, and that it is attention to or selection of this pattern information, not the detection versus identification requirement of the target task, per se, that causes the attentional blink.

Before leaving this section, we review briefly the results of another experiment where a target manipulation resulted in an attenuation in AB magnitude. Martin and Shapiro (1993) created two target conditions distinguished by the temporal predictability of the target's occurrence, rather than by its attention demands or pattern content. The target in both conditions was a white *S* and the probe was a black *X*. Subjects were required to detect both stimuli. In the unpredictable condition (a replication of Shapiro et al., in press, Experiment 3A), the target appeared in a temporally unpredictable point in the letter stream. In the predictable condition, the target was always presented at the tenth serial position in the stream. Two sessions were administered to subjects in each condition, as opposed to the one session typically employed. We found that subjects in the unpredictable condition exhibited an equal magnitude blink in both sessions. However, subjects in the predictable condition showed a significant attenuation of the AB on the second session. These findings may be interpreted to indicate that the temporally predictable aspect of the target in the predictable condition may have narrowed the temporal window over which an attention episode may extend, allowing the perceiver to exclude other, potentially confusing information occurring either before or after the target.

B. The Role of the +1 Item

Our original model of the mechanism mediating the AB postulated that visual suppression occurs in an attempt to protect the target identification process from interference from subsequent items in the stimulus stream, including the +1 item. As noted previously, we found that when subjects were asked to identify the target, they responded on a significant number of trials with the identity of the item in the +1 serial position, suggesting that an erroneous conjunction of the +1 letter identity and the target letter color had occurred. If the AB occurs because of the potential for these conjunction errors, then no AB effect should have been observed in the Shapiro et al. (in press) experiment, in which the target was a random dot pattern and the distractor items were all letters. Because subjects were required only to detect the presence of the random dot target, it seems unlikely that inappropriate conjunctions of +1 item features with target features were being made in this experiment, assuming a reasonably well-described target representation. Thus the observation of large AB effects indicates that the potential for conjunctions of target and +1 item features is not necessary for AB production. This finding, along with others reported earlier, led us to propose an interference model of the AB based on similarity relationships among items in the RSVP stream. Before describing this model in detail, the results of a series of experiments in which the role of similarity between the +1 item and other items in the stream are presented.

Using the same procedure as in Experiment 2 of Raymond et al. (1992a), these studies presented a white target letter embedded among black letter distractors. The probe was a black X and the subject's task was to identify the white letter and report whether the probe was present or absent. The difference between these and the previous experiments was the nature of the +1 item. In the first experiment, the +1 item was a number rather than a letter so that the effect of categorical dissimilarity could be evaluated. As shown in Figure 5, we found that with these stimulus conditions the AB was still present and was not significantly different in magnitude from that found when the +1 item was a letter. However, target identification error rates were significantly lower. Such a finding indicates that even when category information can be used to separate target processing from +1 item processing and thereby improve target task accuracy, AB effects still occur. In a similar dual-task RSVP experiment using letter targets and number distractors, Chun and Potter (1992) also reported large AB effects.

In a second experiment designed to examine the effect of featural dissimilarity, we presented the same RSVP series as before but with the +1 item consisting of an array of four randomly positioned black dots. The result of this experiment (see Figure 5) was that whereas the AB was still present, the magnitude of the effect was significantly attenuated compared to the condition in which the +1 item was a black letter. Although such a finding may seem contradictory with the dot-as-target experiment of Shapiro et al. (in press), it must be recalled that in the dot-as-+1 item condition, the subject's task was to select two letters: a target and a probe letter. The +1 item (a dot pattern) was not similar to

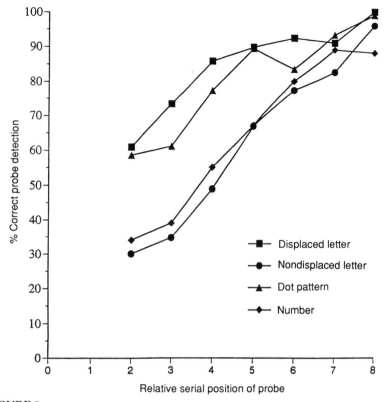

FIGURE 5

The group mean percentage of trials in which the probe was correctly detected plotted as a function of the post-target serial position of the probe. Squares represent the condition where the +1 letter was displaced spatially. Triangles represent the condition where the +1 item was a randomly constructed dot pattern. Diamonds represent the condition where the +1 letter was a number. Circles represent the condition where the +1 letter was a letter randomly chosen from the alphabet.

either target or probe, and for this reason may not have contributed to AB effects as much as its counterpart in the dot-as-target condition. In that condition, subjects were required to select a white dot pattern (target) and a black letter (probe). Because the +1 item was also a black letter, its similarity to the probe may have contributed to interference effects producing the AB. More details on the role of similarity in AB production are provided in the following model. Similar effects of featural dissimilarity of immediate post-target items have been reported by Chun and Potter (1992).

We conducted a third experiment similar to the previous two except that the +1 item was an easily resolvable letter displaced to the right of the location at which all other items were presented. Keele et al. (in press), using an RSVP paradigm, suggested that a fixed spatial location led to more conjunction errors than a spatially displaced stream. Thus we expected that a spatially displaced +1 item should yield fewer target errors because of a reduced potential for erroneous conjunctions between the target and the +1 item. However, given that Shapiro et al. (in press) found no correlation between target difficulty and the magnitude of the blink, we correctly predicted the results of this experiment to yield fewer target identification errors but a significant AB. The magnitude of the AB was reduced relative to the nondisplaced letter condition, suggesting that even when the +1 item shares featural and categorical similarity with both target and probe, its spatial dissimilarity is sufficient to attenuate the interference effects thought to underlie the AB.

C. Probe Manipulations

Previous research reported in this chapter has shown that an attentional deficit for post-target stimuli occurs as long as a very few prerequisites are met: (1) there must be attention allocated to a target containing pattern information, and (2) there must be a patterned item immediately after the target. Manipulations of the target itself and of the +1 item have been shown to produce some attenuation of the blink under certain circumstances, but the effect is completely absent only under conditions when the target or the +1 item is a temporal interval of spatially uniform stimulation. In this section we address the importance of another stream element, the probe, which will be seen to play a critical role in our current model of the AB. The probe can be viewed merely as an index of the AB (i.e., not playing a critical role in the production of the blink) only if one adopts an early-selection model where the blink occurs as a result of a visual processing mechanism shutting down to facilitate processing of the target. To look ahead for the moment, much of our recent data support a late-selection model in which the AB effect results from interference between target and probe during retrieval of information out of a short-term visual store. With this view, characteristics of the probe task should be a determinant of the AB effect.

In a first experiment to address this issue, Shapiro, Arnell, and Drake (1991) created three different probe conditions to manipulate attentional demand. The target task for all conditions required subjects to identify a white letter embedded among black distractor letters, as in a number of previous experiments. For two of the conditions, the probe task required subjects to make a featural discrimination based on the shape of a black filled square, circle, triangle, or diamond or on the color of an equal number of filled squares. In the third condition, a conjunction of color and shape defined the same number of probe possibilities. The results of this experiment, shown in Figure 6, reveal that only the shape feature probe task exhibited an AB effect. Both the color feature task and the conjunction task showed a marked absence of a post-target processing deficit, revealing a level of probe performance similar to that of controls not required to perform the target task. The results of the shape as feature condition are quite consistent with those of our standard letter X as probe condition and suggests that use of a pattern recognition system to perform the target task interferes with use of the same system to perform the probe task. Lack of an AB in the two conditions involving color discrimination suggests that color information may allow representations of an item to persist in a storage buffer for a longer time than shape information alone, thus assisting retrieval.

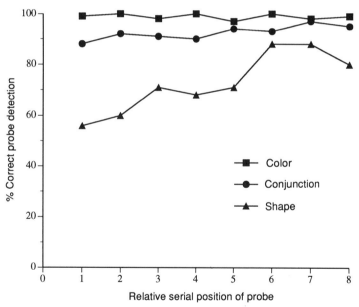

FIGURE 6

The group mean percentage of trials in which the probe was correctly detected plotted as a function of the post-target serial position of the probe. The target was a white letter embedded in a stream of black letters. Circles represent data obtained when the probe was a filled square and subjects were required to name its color. Triangles represent data obtained when the probe was a black filled square, triangle, circle, or diamond and subjects were required to name its shape. Squares represent data obtained when the probe was a filled shape and subjects were required to name both its color and shape. Only the shape conditions produced a significant AB effect.

In another experiment (Shapiro, Raymond, & Taylor, 1993), we again examined the ability of subjects to detect a shape-based probe; in this case, stimulus size served as the probe cue. As before, a white letter formed the basis of the target identification task in the experimental (dual-task) condition, but the probe was a letter the same size as the other stream letters on a third of the trials and larger or smaller than the other stream letters on two thirds of the trials. Subjects had to respond same or different to the size of the probe relative to the stimulus stream. The data for this condition and a probe-task-only control condition are shown in Figure 7. In the dual task condition, an AB effect of approximately the same magnitude as in previous experiments was observed, a finding consistent with the results of the shape-as-feature condition of the previous experiment.

Finally, we have made one additional probe manipulation that is germane to the issues under discussion. Drake (1992, Experiment 2)

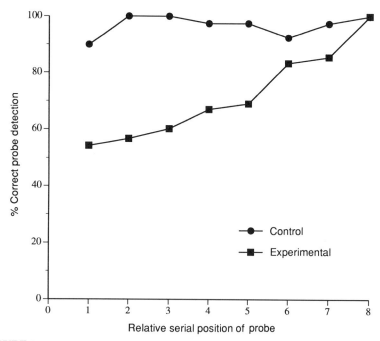

FIGURE 7

The group mean percentage of trials in which the probe was correctly detected plotted as a function of the probe's relative serial position. The probe was a letter that was either smaller or larger than the other items in the stream. Circles represent data obtained in the control condition in which subjects were told to ignore the target letter. Squares represent data obtained in the experimental condition in which subjects were told to identify the target letter.

required subjects to perform target identification (white letter) and probe (black *X*) detection tasks similar to those described previously. The probe task in this experiment, however, differed from previous manipulations in so far as the probe, when presented, was constrained to appear as the last letter in the stream. It was always followed by a sufficient number of masks to yield the standard eight post-target items. Masks were composed of randomly organized dots matched to the letters for overall average luminance. Thus the probe, when it did appear, was always the last letter in the post-target stimulus stream and the question of interest was whether this would affect probe detection in the interval where the AB normally occurs. Although a blink was observed, this manipulation revealed a significant attenuation of AB magnitude relative to the standard condition in which the probe is followed by other letters. These results are consistent with others previously discussed in that the blink seems to be reduced whenever fewer items are contained in the short-term memory buffer from which target and probe selection is made.

IV. A SIMILARITY-BASED MODEL OF THE ATTENTIONAL BLINK

In our earlier work (Raymond et al., 1992a), we proposed an inhibitory model to account for the post-target deficits observed in dual-task RSVP experiments. In this model, the attentional blink results from an inhibitory mechanism serving the function of preventing confusion during the process of target identification. Target identification is thought to involve a two-stage process. In stage 1, the target is *detected* by its key feature (e.g., the item's color). In stage 2, the target is *identified* when the key feature from stage 1 is conjoined with the appropriate response feature (e.g., letter identity). Incorrect conjunctions are revealed as target errors. The fact that most target identification errors are +1 intrusions is taken as evidence of this conjunction task and its associated difficulty. Thus, in this model, the blink is viewed as the attentional system's effort to reduce confusion during the process of target identification by ceasing to admit stimuli to a limited capacity buffer until target identification is complete.

Shapiro et al. (in press) tested this model directly by changing the nature of the target task from one of identification to detection, with the expectation that the AB would be eliminated. As described earlier, however, this change had no effect on AB magnitude. Contrary to the model's prediction, we found that the only target manipulations that modified the post-target processing deficit in a significant way were those in which the target contained no pattern information, that is, a gap versus no gap detection task, or a short versus long gap identification task. These results, along with the finding that featural spatial manipulations of the +1 item attenuated the AB effect, led us to propose a late selection interference model based on Duncan and Humphreys' (1989) similarity theory. Although their theory was proposed originally to model performance of search for targets among spatially distributed items, many aspects of the theory are applicable to search for targets among temporally distributed stimuli.

Similarity theory has three components. First, it proposes that there is a parallel stage of perceptual description that produces a structured representation of items in the visual field at a number of spatial scales. Second, these representations are matched against an internal template of the target. Third, based on the matching process, items are selected for entry into VSTM (visual short-term memory), which is limited in capacity. The model suggests that two similarity-based determinants will predict the success of visual search for a single target among spatially displaced nontargets. One determinant is similarity between target and nontargets. When similarity is low, nontargets fail to match the template and thus are less likely to gain entry into VSTM. The other determinant is similarity among nontargets. If similarity among nontargets is high, then nontarget items may be perceptually grouped and a single instance may be used to reject the entire group, reducing the number of necessary template comparisons. The theory goes on to posit that weighting in VSTM is assigned according to the goodness of the template match. Heavily weighted items are more likely to be selected for response out of VSTM than lightly weighted items. Because VSTM is limited in capacity, nontargets that are similar to targets and thus gain entry, albeit with a lighter weighting, will adversely affect search.

What additional assumption must be made in order to model dual-target temporal search, as opposed to single-target spatial search? Our model must assume that the temporal sequence of representations entering VSTM reflects the temporal sequence of items in the RSVP stream. This implies that the extent of the interference of one item on another in VSTM is a function of the same temporal ordering. Such an assumption is required to explain the limited temporal duration of the AB effect (i.e., occurring with post-target intervals between 100 and 450 msec). It is interesting to note, however, that once items are in VSTM, it appears unlikely that information regarding the temporal sequence of items is maintained (Weichselgartner & Sperling, 1987; Raymond et al., 1992a).

To account for the AB effect, we must first consider which items gain entry into VSTM. According to the goodness-of-match tenet of the theory, items meeting target or probe template criteria gain entry into VSTM and are assigned a weighting. Given the relatively high incidence of +1 intrusion errors, it is reasonable to assume that the +1 item and, similarly, the item immediately following the probe are also granted entry. Entry of the target and probe +1 items is likely due to the rapid stimulus presentation rate combined with the slowness with which the filter closes after opening to allow entry of the target and probe. Studies by Botella and Eriksen (1991, 1992) lend support for our idea that other nontarget items may occasionally gain entry in VSTM.

In the second stage of our model, two items must then be selected for response out of VSTM: one for the target task and one for the probe task. This model assumes that subjects respond to both tasks after the entire RSVP stream has been viewed. Successful retrieval from VSTM of target and probe items is viewed to depend on the number of items and their similarity.[2] The greater the number of items and the more similar the items, the less probable is successful retrieval of appropriate information. Thus the model predicts that whereas the probe stimulus may gain entry into VSTM by virtue of its match to the probe template on every trial, successful retrieval of the probe item for report may occur only on a percentage of trials for the preceding reasons. Such a model can thus account for why we have never found the probability of probe detection to approach zero. To account for the time-limited duration of the AB effect, we suggest that the probability of probe detection returns to a high value when the target item has decayed or been flushed from VSTM. Thus targets separated by more than 450 msec will not interfere with each other, as do targets separated by shorter intervals. If we assume that the target is given the highest weighting by virtue of being the first task, then the finding that there are relatively few target errors rather than an equal number of target and probe errors is also consistent with the model.

One of the fundamental results is that the AB effect is only observed when attentional selection of the target item is required (Raymond et al., 1992a) and that either a detection or identification target task requirement produces the AB effect (Shapiro et al., in press). The model assumes that unless an item is at least partially matched to a template, it cannot gain entry into VSTM. If there is only one template, that of the probe, then the number of items gaining access to VSTM is reduced and no interference effects should be observed. When both target and probe tasks must be performed, additional items gain access to VSTM and interference effects should ensue regardless of whether identification or detection of the target is required.

A second important finding is that the target must be a patterned stimulus, rather than a temporal interval, if an AB of a patterned probe is to be observed (Shapiro et al., in press). To account for this observation,

---

[2]It is possible that selection of items out of VSTM is based solely on the weighting assignments of each item and that similarity among items within VSTM is not a factor.

we propose that VSTM stores only visual pattern information and that temporal information, and quite possibly color information,[3] is stored separately (at least at the stage of processing at which AB interference effects seem to operate). Such an idea is consistent with other modular views of visual processing (e.g., Treisman & Gelade, 1980). Shapiro et al. (in press) found large AB effects when target and probe were featurally dissimilar. If AB effects reflect interference during retrieval of items out of VSTM, then this result suggests that retrieval is performed by a mechanism that is relatively insensitive to differences in visual patterns.

A third interesting finding is that the nature of the item immediately succeeding the target is a determinant of the AB effect (Raymond, Shapiro, and Arnell, 1992b). If the +1 item is replaced with a gap in pattern stimulation the AB is eliminated, and if the +1 item is featurally or spatially dissimilar from the target (and/or probe), the effect is attenuated. These findings can be accounted for by proposing that entry of +1 items into VSTM depends not only on their temporal contiguity to the target, but also on the goodness-of-match to the target or probe template. Thus, similarity determines the likelihood of the +1 items gaining entry into VSTM. Attentional blink effects are eliminated or attenuated when +1 item entry is impossible or unlikely because fewer items are in VSTM to produce interference effects.

Finally, the results of a number of experiments indicate that with the exception of the items immediately following the target and probe, the distractor items in the RSVP stream play a relatively insignificant role in AB production. This was directly measured in an experiment (described in detail in the next section) by Ward, Duncan, and Shapiro (1992) in which AB effects were observed when the stimulus stream consisted only of a brief exposed target and probe, each followed by a pattern mark made of short line segments. The model accounts for this finding because it proposes that AB effects result from interference during retrieval out of VSTM. Because distractor items are unlikely to gain entry into VSTM with anything but a very low weighting, they are unlikely to contribute significantly to interference problems. The magnitude of Ward et al.'s AB effect is somewhat less than that typically seen when the stimulus stream contains nontarget items and thus is consistent with our model.

To summarize, Raymond et al. (1992a) proposed an *inhibitory* model of the AB. This model was based on an early-selection notion that the target identification process was facilitated by ceasing to admit stimuli for processing for a limited period of time until such processing was

[3]In a dual task RSVP experiment in which the target task was to name the color of a filled square embedded in a stream of black letter distractors and the probe task was to detect the letter *X*, no AB effects were found (Shapiro, Arnell, & Drake, 1991).

completed. The results of subsequent experiments (Shapiro et al., in press) challenged this assumption in two ways. First, Shapiro et al. found that target detection yielded a blink of nearly equal magnitude in spite of the lack of identification requirement. Second, these investigators found that lack of pattern information in the target eliminated the AB. Whereas this latter finding does not necessarily deny the possibility of an early-selection account, it does favor a late-selection *interference*-based account, such as the one presently proposed, where pattern information from both the target and probe compete for retrieval on the basis of similarity.

Before leaving the discussion of the model, we would like to point out that Dixon and his colleagues (Dixon, 1986; Dixon & Twilley, 1988) proposed a location-confusion model to explain empirical findings similar to those of the present authors and discussed in this chapter. Dixon presented subjects with two 17-msec displays separated by both positive and negative variable SOAs. One "target" display consisted of a horizontal five letter array and the other a single "probe" letter. Subjects were asked to report whether or not the probe was contained in the target array with half the trials scheduled as probe "present" and half as probe "absent." When the percentage of correct judgments as a function of SOA is plotted, a U-shaped function emerges. Performance improves linearly when the probe either precedes the target array (negative SOAs) or follows the target array (positive SOAs) by increasing SOA values. Performance is worst when there is a positive 100-msec SOA.

The location-confusion model proposed by Dixon suggests a two-stage process similar to that proposed by Treisman (cf. Treisman & Gormican, 1988) to account for these results. In the first stage, perceptual attributes (e.g., location and identity) are encoded but certain attributes, particularly location, decay quickly. In a second, limited-capacity stage, identity codes must be linked with location codes prior to being passed on for report. Poor performance at short positive SOAs is explained by the occurrence of the probe interrupting second-stage processing of the target array prior to the development of effective episodic codes linking location to identity.

Dixon's paradigm does not require subjects to identify or detect targets in exactly the same way as the RSVP task requires in the studies reported by the present authors in this chapter. Nevertheless, the similarity between the paradigms and, more importantly, between the outcomes is noteworthy. However, the model proposed by Dixon and Twilley (1988) and that proposed by Shapiro et al. (in press) differ considerably. Whereas the former account is based on a failure to link codes conjoining stimulus attributes required for successful task performance, the latter account is based on identity codes competing for a retrieval mechanism sensitive to stimulus featural similarity. Evidence in support of the latter hypothesis may even be found in Dixon's report (1986, Experiment 3) where he manipulated the similarity of the items in the target array and found a significant decrement in accuracy when they were similar. A critical test of Dixon's account would be the situation where a single-letter target array preceded the probe, in which case the lack of demand to form more than one identity code should attenuate the negative effects of the purported rapidly decaying location code. However, Ward, Duncan, and Shapiro (1992) found that a masked target and probe separated by variable SOAs, but without the presence of any nontarget letters, produced as much of a decrement in subjects' ability to accurately detect the two stimuli as when the nontarget letters were present. Such an outcome suggests that location (episodic) confusion is an insufficient explanation for the deficits observed in Dixon's studies. More detail of Ward et al.'s experiment is presented in the following section.

V. RELATED PHENOMENA

A. Repetition Blindness

Temporary impairments in visual processing using RSVP have also been revealed by Kanwisher and her colleagues and have been labeled repetition blindness (RB). In these studies, subjects viewed a series of words forming a sentence or a series of letters forming a word and were asked to report the sentence or word. On half the trials, one of the items in the stream was presented twice. It was found that when an item had been repeated, the subjects tended to omit the second repetition of the item in their response, even when the omission reduced the grammaticality of the sentence or correctness of spelling (Kanwisher, 1987; Kanwisher & Potter, 1989, 1990). In other studies, a stream of unrelated words was presented and subjects were required to indicate the word they thought had occurred twice in the list (Kanwisher, 1987). Kanwisher reported that for word presentation rates between 5.4 and 8.5 words/sec, subjects showed a low probability of reporting word repetitions if one to three intervening words were presented between the first and second presentation of the repeated item (i.e., with SOAs of between approximately 150 and 750 msec). Repetition blindness was found at the level of letter groups when words were the perceptual unit in a given task, and at the level of letters when letters were presented one at a time in RSVP to spell words (Kanwisher & Potter, 1990).

Although originally studied using visually identical stimuli, it is not clear whether RB is primarily a visual phenomenon. In support of a visual basis for the effect, Kanwisher & Potter (1990) reported RB when the repeated word shared orthographic identity but had a different meaning or pronunciation than that of the first instance. Furthermore, they found that RB effects were not found for synonyms or homophones, or when words composing sentences were presented auditorily at the same rate in compressed speech (Kanwisher & Potter, 1989, 1990). If there is a visual basis for RB, the finding that RB is found for words differing in letter case indicates that it operates at a relatively late stage in processing (Kanwisher, 1987; Bavelier and Potter, 1992). Supporting the idea that RB operates on representations derived from either visual or phonological codes is a recent report of "repetition deafness" for words presented auditorily in compressed speech (MacKay & Miller, 1992). Consistent with this view is the finding that RB can be found for items that have only phonological and no visual similarity (Bavelier & Potter, 1992).

There are both similarities and differences between AB and RB effects. The similarity between the two phenomena is the timecourse of both effects: The onset and offset of each occur approximately 150 msec and 500 msec, respectively, after the occurrence of the target, although RB has been observed to last for a longer period. As far as differences go, there are two that deserve mention. Although the use of RSVP methodology is similar for AB and RB, the nature of the target task is different. As described earlier, the target in the AB procedure can be either partially or fully defined. In contrast, the target in RB is defined as the *repeated item*. Whereas certain AB target task requirements at least allow for the possibility of an early-selection mechanism to cause the blink, this cannot be the case in RB because the target is only defined after the occurrence of a second identical stimulus. This suggests the operation of a late-selection mechanism. Specifically, Kanwisher (1987) has distinguished type recognition from token individuation as a starting point for her explanation. Word "type recognition" identifies a word as a type (e.g., the word *chair*), whereas "token individuation" characterizes an item as a particular token of a given type (e.g., as the first instance of the word *chair*). Repetition blindness occurs, according to Kanwisher, when the second instance of a word follows too closely after the first and is recognized as a type, but is not individuated as a distinct token. Thus the second occurrence of the word is conjoined to the first instance, and only one token for the word is activated.

A second important difference between AB and RB resides in the relative magnitude of the interference effects. When one examines the magnitude of the AB effect over the variety of conditions investigated, the probability of probe detection in the post-target interval 180–450 msec reaches an average minimum of approximately 50%. In contrast to this, the average minimum probability of detecting the repeated item in RB approaches on the order of 20% less.

Ward et al. (1992) explored the relationship between AB and RB directly. The rationale for their experiment was that in RB, subjects are required to select virtually every item for entry into VSTM, whereas in the AB experiment, subjects need only select items well matched to target and probe. In the former case, distractor items exacerbate the retrieval process, whereas in the latter case, distractor items do not contribute substantially to the interference producing the effect. Thus target *selection* becomes a key determinant of entry and may serve to explain the difference in the outcomes of AB and RB.

The first experiment was a standard RSVP dual-target task similar to those used in our previous AB experiments. The target task was to detect either a white outlined box or the white letter X presented in blocked conditions. The probe for both conditions was the black letter X, as was used previously. The white X (identity) condition consisted of the stimulus conditions necessary for production of both AB and RB, whereas the white box (nonidentity) condition should produce AB effects only. A similar contrast was set up in the second experiment where conditions were the same but the nontarget letters were removed from the stream. Thus a given trial was composed of a target (white box or letter X) followed by a patterned mask, followed by a probe that was also masked. In this second experiment the probe either was a randomly determined X, H, K, or Y. A variable SOA between the target and probe allowed us to chart the attentional blink over the same timecourse as in Experiment 1. The results of both experiments are shown in panels A and B of Figure 8.

Experiment 1 revealed a large reduction in the probability of probe detection in both target conditions. However, the effect was considerably larger in magnitude in the condition where the target and the probe shared an identity relationship, that is, the RB condition. This outcome replicates both the AB and RB results obtained by investigators previously cited. A different pattern, however, was obtained in Experiment 2

FIGURE 8

(Panel A) The group mean percentage of trials in which the probe was correctly detected plotted as a function of the probe's relative serial position for the conditions where nontarget elements were present in the stimulus stream. Filled circles represent the control condition where subjects ignored the target task. Filled squares represent the condition where the target was defined by the presence of a box. X's represent the condition where the target was defined by the presence of the letter X. (Panel B) The group mean percentage of trials in which the probe was correctly detected plotted as a function of its relative serial position for the conditions where nontarget elements were *not* present in the stimulus stream. Filled circles represent the control condition where subjects ignored the target task. Filled squares represent the condition where the target was defined by the presence of a box. X's represent the condition where the target was defined by the presence of the letter X.

Panel A

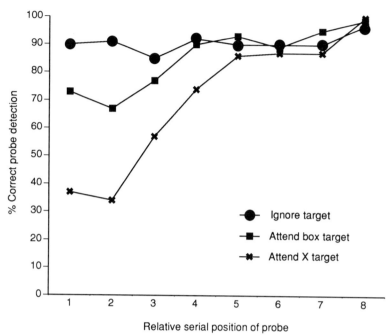

Panel B

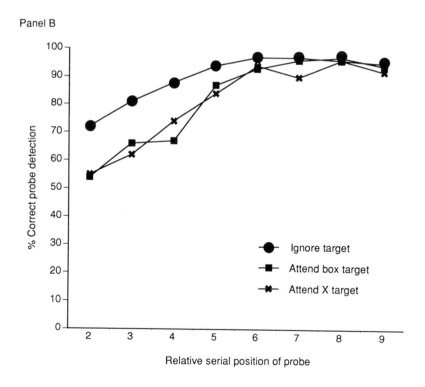

where the nontarget stream was absent. Here, the magnitude of both the identity (RB) and nonidentity (AB) conditions were equal and of approximately the same magnitude as that obtained in the AB condition in Experiment 1. The results of these experiments suggest two important conclusions: (1) AB and RB are dissociable, although similar interference processes may underlie both phenomena, and (2) the dissociability between these two processes is revealed when the target must be selected from a nontarget stream.

While we are mentioning the possibility that RB and AB may represent similar interference processes, it should be noted that other inhibitory processes mentioned in this volume also have a timecourse similar to these two processes. It has been noted by Posner and Cohen (1984) that it takes approximately 150 msec for inhibition of return (IOR) to reveal itself; prior to this time, the authors note that facilitation rather than inhibition is observed (see also Klein & Taylor, this volume). A similar timecourse is noted for negative priming (NP) where approximately 150-msec SOAs are required, prior to which time positive priming is observed (see also Houghton & Tipper, this volume). Perhaps these similarities among the various inhibitory processes reflect nothing more than the time it takes for inhibition of any kind to build. However, even if this is the case, such similarities may speak to the common purpose of inhibitory processes as they function to supplement attentional mechanisms.

B. Spatial Search

We began this chapter by asserting that attention may operate over a spatio-temporal window in order to effectively regulate the flow of visual information. Many of the principles purported to underlie temporal search were adaptations of principles derived from the results of experiments examining spatial search. Thus it is not unreasonable to expect to find results similar to those reported for purely temporal search when the RSVP paradigm is adapted to present stimulus information over the spatial domain.

In an attempt to derive this correspondence, Duncan, Ward, and Shapiro (1993) removed the nontarget elements from the stimulus stream and displaced two targets (i.e., target and probe) in space. Trials began with the subject required to fixate a central spot on a VDT (video display terminal). Subjects, depending on condition, were then required to identify either one or two targets. In the one-target condition, the number 2 or 5 could appear 1.5° either to the left or to the right of fixation (horizontal condition) *or* the letter *L* or *T* could appear the same distance above or below fixation (vertical condition). In the two-target condition, subjects had to identify a stimulus appearing in one of the two locations in *both* the horizontal and vertical plane. All targets were masked by a pattern mask. Negative and positive SOAs varying from trial to trial and ranging from −1000 to +1000 msec separated the occurrences of the horizontal and vertical target tasks. Percentages of correct identification of the target as a function of SOA for both the single- and dual-target condition are shown in Figure 9 (negative SOAs reveal performance on the first target, whereas positive SOAs reveal performance on the second target). The results indicate that the AB effect is not limited to stimuli occurring at one particular point in space. This is revealed in the blink, which is shown in the dual-target condition for positive SOAs between approximately 0 and 400 msec. Such a finding has important implications for spatial search experiments: The typical finding in such studies is that slopes of RT–display size functions indicate that serial search of a target from among nontargets requires inspection times of about 30–40 msec per item. From our data, it appears that these serial inspection times are restricted to *nontarget* inspections where items are simply rejected if they do not match target template parameters. In contrast, it appears that experiments examining

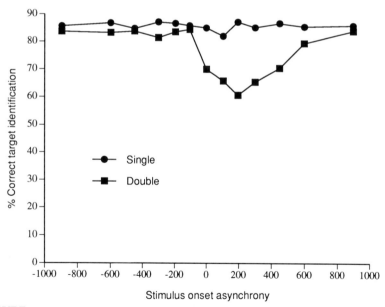

FIGURE 9

Group mean percentage of correct target identification as a function of negative (first target) and positive (second target) SOAs. Circles represent the conditions where only a single target (either number *or* letter) was identified, whereas the squares represent the condition where both targets (number *and* letter) had to be identified.

search for multiple targets, something not often examined in visual search experiments, indicate that search in the neighborhood of 400 msec per item may be required.

One final experiment recently completed by Ward, Duncan, and Shapiro (in preparation) employed virtually the identical stimulus array as that just described, but examined the magnitude of the AB effect as a function of the number of target attributes required to be judged. In this experiment, using spatially displaced stimuli, the horizontal number identification task always preceded the vertical letter identification task by a variable SOA between 0 and 1000 msec. In the first (horizontal number) task, in addition to the identity attribute, the numbers possessed a size attribute (large or small). In blocked conditions, the subject was asked to judge either the identity of the number (single-attribute condition), the size of the number (single-attribute condition), both identity and size (double-attribute condition), or neither (control condition). The identity of the letter in the second (vertical letter) task was always reported and the percentage of correct reports constituted the dependent variable to assess the degree of the AB as a function of the number of target attributes judged. The results of this experiment, as shown in Figure 10, reveal an equal magnitude blink for all conditions relative to the control condition, which showed no blink. Thus the magnitude of the AB effect does not seem to depend on the number of target attributes. This result is consistent with findings of target manipulation studies where no correlation existed between target difficulty as defined by d' estimates and the magnitude of the AB effect (Shapiro et al., in press).

To summarize this section, we can draw two conclusions concerning the relationship of temporal and spatial search in RSVP. First, AB exists with temporally presented targets displaced in space, as well as at fixed locations in space. Second, the magnitude of the AB effect for spatially displaced targets does not change regardless of whether one or two target attributes must be reported.

VI. CONCLUSIONS

We would like to end this chapter by reasserting that visual attention modulates a temporal, as well as spatial, window that constrains the processing of stimulus information. The limitations of *spatial* attention have been elaborated in other chapters in this volume as well as in many other places (see Treisman & Gormican, 1988, for a review). However, limitations affecting the *temporal* domain have been less well explicated and yet are nevertheless critical for understanding perception of a dynamic visual environment under natural viewing conditions. As we

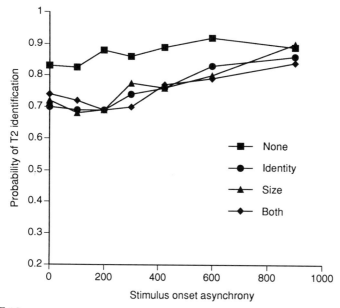

FIGURE 10

The group mean probability of T2 identification as a function of the positive (T1 occurs before T2) SOAs between T1 and T2. Square represent the condition where no attributes of T1 had to be identified. Circles represent the condition where the identity of T1 had to be identified. Triangles represent the condition where the size of T1 had to be identified. Diamonds represent the condition where both the identity and size of T1 had to be identified.

have discussed in this chapter, the inability under certain circumstances to process serially presented visual information has been revealed in the attentional blink and repetition blindness effects. Both AB and RB show that after attention has been directed to a patterned target, perception is seriously attenuated for a period of about 350 msec or longer, beginning approximately 100–150 msec after target presentation. This timecourse is typical of other phenomena discussed in other chapters in this volume, for example, inhibition of return and negative priming.

In this chapter, we raise a number of issues regarding the mechanisms mediating temporal attentional limitations. Among them are the implications of the apparent requirement that visual pattern information must be present to produce AB and RB effects. If currently popular modular views of visual processing are accepted, then the issue of whether such deficits operate within or between visual modules (e.g., color or motion) should be considered in future research. Finally, the model we propose, which is based on the similarity model of Duncan and Humphreys (1989), makes a number of predictions that require further empirical validation. Based on the available data, we have suggested that neither a PRP account nor an inhibitory account fit the pattern of accumulated data. On the other hand, an interference account based on similarity seems to provide a framework into which the effects of attending targets over time can be accommodated.

ACKNOWLEDGMENTS

The authors wish to express our sincere thanks to Judy Caldwell for her assistance with many aspects of the preparation of this manuscript. We also gratefully acknowledge the support from the Natural Science and Engineering Research Council of Canada in the form of operating grants to both authors.

REFERENCES

Bavelier, D., & Potter, M. (1992). Visual and phonological codes in repetition blindness. *Journal of Experimental Psychology: Human Perception and Performance, 18,* 134–147.

Bertelson, P. (1966). Central intermittency twenty years later. *Quarterly Journal of Experimental Psychology, 18,* 153–163.

Botella, J., & Eriksen, C. W. (1991). Pattern changes in rapid serial visual presentation tasks without strategic shifts. *Bulletin of the Psychonomic Society, 29,* 105–108.

Botella, J., & Eriksen, C. W. (1992). Filtering versus parallel processing in RSVP tasks. *Perception and Psychophysics, 51,* 334–343.

Broadbent, D. E. (1977). A hidden preattentive process. *American Psychologist, 32,* 109–118.

Broadbent, D. E., & Broadbent, M. H. P. (1986). Encoding speed of visual features and the occurrence of illusory conjunctions. *Perception, 15,* 515–524.

Broadbent, D. E., & Broadbent, M. H. P. (1987). From detection to identification: Response to multiple targets in rapid serial visual presentation. *Perception and Psychophysics, 42,* 105–113.

Chun, M. M., & Potter, M. (1992, November). *Interference in detecting multiple RSVP targets: Effects of similarity.* Paper presented at the 33rd Annual Meeting of the Psychonomic Society, St. Louis, MO.

Dixon, P. (1986). Attention and interference in the perception of brief visual displays. *Journal of Experimental Psychology: Human Perception and Performance, 12,* 133–148.

Dixon, P., & Twilley, L. C. (1988). Location confusions in visual information processing. *Canadian Journal of Psychology, 42,* 378–394.

Drake, S. H. (1992). *The effect of blank intervals on a dual-target RSVP task.* Unpublished master's thesis, University of Calgary, Calgary, AB.

Duncan, J. (1980). The locus of interference in the perception of simultaneous stimuli. *Psychological Review, 87,* 272–300.

Duncan, J., & Humphreys, G. (1989). Visual search and stimulus similarity. *Psychological Review, 96,* 433–458.

Duncan, J., Ward, R., & Shapiro, K. L. (1993). *Direct measurement of attentional dwell time in human vision*. Manuscript submitted for publication.

Gathercole, S. E., & Broadbent, D. E. (1984). Combining attributes in specified and categorized target search: Further evidence for strategic differences. *Memory & Cognition, 12*, 329–337.

Intraub, H. (1985). Visual dissociation: An illusory conjunction of pictures and forms. *Journal of Experimental Psychology: Human Perception and Performance, 11*, 431–442.

Kahneman, D., & Triesman, A. (1983). Changing views of attention and automaticity. In R. Parasuraman, R. Davies, & J. Beatty (Eds.), *Varieties of attention*. New York: Academic Press.

Kanwisher, N. G. (1987). Repetition blindness: Type recognition without token individuation. *Cognition, 27*, 117–143.

Kanwisher, N. G., & Potter, M. C. (1989). Repetition blindness: The effects of stimulus modality and spatial displacement. *Memory & Cognition, 17*, 117–124.

Kanwisher, N. G., & Potter, M. C. (1990). Repetition blindness: Levels of processing. *Journal of Experimental Psychology: Human Perception and Performance, 16*, 30–47.

Keele, S. W., Cohen, A., Ivry, R., Liotti, M., & Yee, P. (1988). Tests of a temporal theory of attentional binding. *Journal of Experimental Psychology: Human Perception and Performance, 14*, 444–452.

Keele, S. W., & Neill, W. T. (1978). Mechanisms of attention. In E. C. Carterette & M. P. Friedman (Eds.), *Handbook of perception IX* (pp. 3–47). New York: Academic Press.

Lawrence, D. H. (1971). Two studies of visual search for word targets with controlled rates of presentation. *Perception and Psychophysics, 10*, 85–89.

MacKay, D. G., & Miller, M. (1992, November). *What causes repetition deafness? A test of seven hypotheses*. Paper presented at the 33rd Annual Meeting of the Psychonomics Society in St. Louis, MO.

Martin, M. J., & Shapiro, K. L. (in preparation). *Predictable temporal location of the target attenuates the attentional blink effect*.

McLean, J. P., Broadbent, D. E., & Broadbent, M. H. P. (1982). Combining attributes in rapid serial visual presentation tasks. *Quarterly Journal of Experimental Psychology, 35A*, 171–186.

Nakayama, K., & Mackeben, M. (1989). Sustained and transient components of focal visual attention. *Vision Research, 29*, 1631–1647.

Pashler, H. (1984). Processing stages in overlapping tasks: Evidence for a central bottleneck. *Journal of Experimental Psychology: Human Perception and Performance, 10*, 358–377.

Pashler, H. (1989). Dissociations and dependencies between speed and accuracy: Evidence for a two-component theory of divided attention in simple tasks. *Cognitive Psychology, 21*, 469–514.

Pashler, H. (1990). Do response modality effects support multiprocessor models of divided attention? *Journal of Experimental Psychology: Human Perception and Performance, 16*, 826–842.

Pashler, H., & Johnston, J. C. (1989). Chronometric evidence for central postponement in temporally overlapping tasks. *Quarterly Journal of Experimental Psychology, 41*, 19–45.

Posner, M. I., & Cohen, Y. (1984). Components of visual orienting. In H. B. Bouma & D. G. Bouwhuis (Eds.), *Attention and performance X: Control of language processes*. Hillsdale, NJ: Lawrence Erlbaum.

Raymond, J. E., Shapiro, K. L., & Arnell, K. M. (1992a). Temporary suppression of visual processing in an RSVP task: An attentional blink? *Journal of Experimental Psychology: Human Perception and Performance, 18,* 849–860.

Raymond, J. E., Shapiro, K. L., & Arnell, K. A. (1992b). The role of post-target stimulation in producing "attentional blinks" in RSVP. *International Journal of Psychology, 27* (3 & 4), 44.

Reeves, A., & Sperling, G. (1986). Attention gating in short-term visual memory. *Psychological Review, 93,* 180–206.

Shapiro, K. L., Arnell, K. A., & Drake, S. H. (1991). Stimulus complexity mediates target detection in visual attention search [Abstract]. *Investigative Ophthalmology and Visual Science, 32,* Supplement, 1040.

Shapiro, K. L., Raymond, J. E., & Arnell, K. M. (in press). Attention to visual pattern information produces the attentional blink in RSVP. *Journal of Experimental Psychology: Human Perception and Performance.*

Shapiro, K. L., Raymond, J. E., & Taylor, T. (1993). The attentional blink suppresses size and shape but not colour information. (Abstract) *Investigative Ophthalmology and Visual Science, 34*(4), 1232.

Smith, M. C. (1967). Theories of the psychological refractory period. *Psychological Bulletin, 67,* 202–213.

Sperling, G., & Weichselgartner, E. (1990, November). *Episodic theory of visual attention.* Paper presented at the meeting of the Psychonomic Society, New Orleans, LA.

Taylor, D. A., & Chabot, R. J. (1978). Differential backward masking of words and letters by masks of varying orthographic structure. *Memory and Cognition, 6,* 629–635.

Treisman, A. M., & Gelade, G. (1980). A feature integration theory of attention. *Cognitive Psychology, 12,* 97–136.

Treisman, A., & Gormican, S. (1988). Feature analysis in early vision: Evidence from search asymmetries. *Psychological Review, 95,* 15–48.

Ward, W., Duncan, J., & Shapiro, K. L. (1992, November). *The attentional blink does not require selection from among a nontarget stream.* Paper presented at the 33rd Annual Meeting of the Psychonomic Society, St. Louis, MO.

Ward, R., Duncan, J., & Shapiro, K. L. (in preparation). *Target selection requiring one vs. two attributes does not affect the attentional blink.*

Weichselgartner, E., & Sperling, G. (1987). Dynamics of automatic and controlled visual attention. *Science, 238,* 778–780.

5

On the Ability to Inhibit Thought and Action

A Users' Guide to the Stop Signal Paradigm

Gordon D. Logan

I. INTRODUCTION

This chapter presents a users' guide to the stop signal paradigm. It explains the paradigm and the situations in the natural and artificial environment the paradigm is intended to capture. It explains how the inhibition that is apparent in the stop signal paradigm is similar to and different from the kinds of inhibition seen in other paradigms. It reviews theory and data in the experimental literature on stopping. It explains the race model, which is the commonly accepted theory of performance in the stop signal paradigm, and it explains how to apply the model to data.

II. THE STOP SIGNAL PARADIGM

A. What Is Stopping?

You are Guy Lafleur racing across the blue line with the puck on your stick. You wind up your famous slap shot . . . and the whistle blows. You are Pete Rose trying to hit a home run . . . and the pitch breaks out of the strike zone just as you begin your swing. You are Spaceman Spiff blasting aliens in the asteroid belt . . . and your teacher calls your attention back to the lesson. You are Gordon Logan giving the same lecture for the nth time . . . and you stumble on the word "resources." What happens? Guy stops his famous slap shot in mid swing (much to the goalie's relief). Pete checks his swing before his wrists "break," avoiding a strike. Gordon stops in midword and begins again (this time with tongue out of cheek). The school child may or may not heed the teacher's call. If his diagnosis is attention deficit disorder, he is less likely to.

What do these situations have in common? The current course of thought and action is no longer appropriate. Goals change (as they did for Guy and the school child) and the world changes—the stimuli one is reacting to change (as they did for Pete). Errors introduce new goals (error correction) that take priority over current goals (as they did for Gordon). The thing to do is to stop the current course of thought and action and begin another. In this chapter, the focus is on stopping. Stopping is the first step in reorienting to new goals and new worlds, a general requirement in all kinds of cognitive control. Stopping is a clear case of executive intervention. It gives us a chance to see executive processes in action, a chance to discern their nature.

Stopping can be studied empirically in a simple laboratory analogue called the *stop signal paradigm*: People are engaged in a primary task, and occasionally, they are presented with a signal that tells them to stop their response to the primary task. The primary task is typically a visual choice reaction time task, such as discriminating X's from O's, and the stop signal is usually a tone. Other primary tasks and stop signals work just as well. The main datum is whether or not subjects withhold their response to the primary task when the stop signal occurs—do they stop? This datum, interpreted in terms of data on timing of stimuli and responses, can reveal a surprising amount about the underlying mechanism.

B. Why Is Stopping Interesting?

Stopping is interesting theoretically because it is an internally generated act of control. It is something a person does to change the current course of thought and action and bring it into line with current goals. Stopping research focuses on the role of the person in cognitive control, whereas most research focuses on the role of the environment, asking how familiar, novel, and distinctive stimuli control a person's behavior (e.g., research on involuntary attraction of attention, research on automaticity). These foci are complementary: Stopping research addresses the control process directly and research on involuntary control addresses the things that confront the control process (i.e., the demands for attention).

I think that cognitive control can be understood generally as acts of control, just like stopping. Some acts of control are more subtle and graceful than stopping. They involve deciding to do something a little differently, like digging an edge in a little deeper to turn more sharply in skating and skiing. The parameters of action may change, but action may proceed uninterrupted. Not so with stopping. Stopping is an extreme form of control; the subject decides not to do something and action stops. The skater gives up and falls down; the skier takes a dive to stop careening down the hill. Subtle control and extreme control may differ more in degree than in kind. Both can be analyzed as acts of control that are triggered by certain circumstances and result in certain changes after some latent period.

The stop signal paradigm is advantageous because it allows a clear definition of the conditions that trigger the act of control (i.e., presentation of the stop signal) and the changes that result from executing the act (i.e., inhibition of the response). It provides a way to measure the latency of the act of control (i.e., stop signal reaction time), even though successful execution of the act produces no overt behavior (it is the absence of overt behavior that tells us that stopping was successful). Acts of control that are more subtle may be harder to observe and their latencies may be harder to measure. The disadvantage of the stop signal paradigm is that it reflects an extreme form of control that may be different in important ways from more subtle forms of control. Understanding the relation between stop signal control and other forms of cognitive control is an important goal for future research.

Stopping is interesting empirically because some important results have emerged and others are on the horizon. First, the data from young adults are consistent with the idea that a single, general mechanism underlies the ability to inhibit many kinds of thought and action. Young adults can stop a wide variety of actions very quickly. Eye movements, hand movements, key presses, squeezes, and speech can all be stopped in about 200 msec (for a review, see Logan & Cowan, 1984). The similar latencies across tasks and effector systems suggest that stopping relies on an amodal, central process.

The speed with which young adults can stop responses is impressive. It allows them very close control over their actions. The speed is even more impressive because stopping is the response to the second of two stimuli. Usually, the response to the second of two stimuli is very slow, as the burgeoning literature on dual-task interference and the psychological refractory period attests (see, e.g., Pashler, 1989; see Logan & Burkell, 1986, for an explicit comparison of stopping with dual-task performance). Somehow, stop signals seem to bypass the bottlenecks that hold back other signals (see Logan & Cowan, 1984).

Second, there are interesting changes in stopping performance over the life span that are consistent with theories of development (Bjorklund & Harnishfeger, 1990) and aging (Hasher & Zacks, 1989) that interpret the cognitive difficulties of the young and the elderly as deficits in inhibitory processing. Younger children (Schachar & Logan, 1990a) and older adults (Kramer, Humphrey, Larish, Logan, & Strayer, 1992) are slower to stop than young adults, suggesting that the stopping process is the same over the life span but increases in speed (and therefore effectiveness) as childhood progresses to adulthood and declines in speed with senescence. There may be deficiencies earlier in childhood and later in aging. The youngest children studied by Schachar and Logan (1990a) were 7-year-olds; younger children may have qualitatively different stopping processes (or qualitatively different deficiencies). The older adults studied by Kramer et al. (1992) were all healthy and active and reported no more cognitive deficits in daily life than young adult controls. Perhaps older subjects who have significant cognitive deficits in daily life would show qualitatively different deficiencies in the stop signal paradigm.

Third, stop signal inhibition may be implicated in inhibitory psychopathology. Schachar and Logan (1990a) found that hyperactive children had trouble stopping on stop signal trials. Not only were they slower to inhibit than normal controls, they were less likely to inhibit altogether, responding more often than normals on stop signal trials. It was not the case that hyperactive children were less likely to "notice" the stop signal. Schachar and Logan (1990b) ran a dual-task experiment presenting the same stimuli they used in their stop signal experiment but requiring the children to make an overt response to the "stop signal" as well as an overt response to the primary task. Hyperactive children detected the signal as often as normal controls, and showed the same refractory effect in their reaction times. Their deficiency in stopping was not a deficiency in detecting the stop signal. Interestingly, stimulant medication (methylphenidate), which improves behavioral symptoms of hyperactive children, also improves their stopping performance (Tannock, Schachar, Carr, Chajczyk, & Logan, 1989).

III. STOP SIGNAL INHIBITION

The inhibition seen in the stop signal paradigm may be different from inhibition seen in other paradigms in important ways. Stop signal inhibition requires the subject to take a deliberate action. Stop signal inhibition represents an entire process, extending from (stop signal) stimulus to (internal inhibitory) response. Moreover, stop signal inhibition cannot be understood adequately without a formal theory of the stopping process.

These factors make stop signal inhibition different from the neurologically inspired inhibition that is seen in spreading activation and connectionist models (e.g., Rumelhart & McClelland, 1986; see Dell & O'Seaghdha's chapter in this volume for a detailed discussion of inhibition in connectionist models). Neurological inhibition is negative activation; it is something that is subtracted from the current level of activation. The subtraction is intended to be understood neurally rather than cognitively. It happens as a result of the connectivity of the network; it does not require the subject to perform mental arithmetic. In these theories, subjects generally have little control over neurological inhibition. Inhibitory (and excitatory) connections are established by a long history of training and do not change during the course of the trial.

Stop signal inhibition is also different from what might be termed reactive inhibition. *Reactive inhibition* is inhibition that results from executing some process. It may be the most common kind of inhibition in the literature, challenging the ubiquitous "neurologically inspired" inhibition. Classical examples of reactive inhibition include response conflict (Berlyne, 1957), refractory effects in dual-task situations (Welford, 1952), and proactive inhibition in short-term memory (Wickens, 1970). Current examples include inhibition of return (Posner & Cohen, 1984), negative priming (Lowe, 1979; Neill, 1977; Tipper, 1985), top-down inhibition of distractors (Treisman & Sato, 1990), and a "center-surround" memory retrieval system (Carr & Dagenbach, 1990; Dagenbach, Carr, & Barhnardt, 1990). The idea behind reactive inhibition is that executing a process has a side effect that concurrent processes must overcome or leaves a residual effect that subsequent processes must overcome. The process that produces the inhibition may be engaged deliberately, but its inhibitory effect on concurrent and subsequent processes is not (usually) intended.

An important similarity is that all forms of inhibition work against some form of excitation. Neurologically, a tendency to decrease firing tempers a tendency to increase firing. In reactive inhibition, aftereffects of prior processing work against current-trial processing. And in the stop signal paradigm, the inhibitory process races against a "go" process. Stop signal inhibition is different from the others in that the excitatory and inhibitory processes are largely independent. The race model that is used to analyze stopping performance assumes that stop and go processes are independent, and the data for the most part are consistent with that assumption (De Jong, Coles, Logan, & Gratton, 1990; Jennings, van der Molen, Brock, & Somsen, 1992; Logan & Cowan, 1984; Osman, Kornblum, & Meyer, 1986, 1990). By contrast, neural inhibition works together in the same network as excitation, and reactive inhibition affects the same mechanisms and processes used for current-trial processing. These forms of inhibition are not independent of excitatory processes. Instead, they interact in complex ways. Nonlinearity has important computational consequences in neural networks and connectionist models (Rumelhart & McClelland, 1986).

Relations between stop signal inhibition and other forms of inhibition have not been studied extensively. This is surprising because the experiments should be easy to do and the logic required to interpret them should be fairly straightforward. Stop signal inhibition can be compared in conditions that either require or do not require some other form of inhibition. If that other inhibition is based on the same process as stop signal inhibition, there should be interactions. Stopping may be easier when the go task requires inhibition, because the go task inhibition may prime or prepare the inhibition required for stopping. Alternatively, stopping may be harder when the go task requires inhibition if there is a limited capacity for inhibition.

Three studies have used this logic to compare stop signal inhibition with other forms of inhibition. First, Logan (1981) compared the ability to inhibit spatially compatible and spatially incompatible responses and found no difference. Apparently, the kind of inhibition required to resolve incompatible stimulus–response relationships (Kornblum, Hasbroucq, & Osman, 1990) does not interact with stop signal inhibition. Second, Kramer et al. (1992) compared the ability to inhibit responses to targets that were flanked by distractors that were associated with compatible and incompatible responses and found that subjects found it harder to inhibit responses to incompatible displays. Apparently, the kind of inhibition required to resolve response conflict (Eriksen & Eriksen, 1974) interacts with stop signal inhibition. Third, Jennings et al. (1992) compared stop signal inhibition with inhibition of the cardiac cycle and found that successful inhibition slowed heart rate. They suggested that stop signal inhibition and cardiac inhibition may depend on the same midbrain structures. These studies only scratch the surface. There is much more research to be done.

IV. BALLISTIC PROCESSES AND THE POINT OF NO RETURN

A. Discrete Tasks

A great deal of the interest in the stop signal paradigm has been focused on the possibility that some processes are *ballistic*—they cannot be stopped. Can something as automatic as Guy Lafleur's slapshot be stopped once it begins? A great deal of the modeling has been addressed toward ways of distinguishing ballistic from stoppable (or *controlled*) processes (Osman et al., 1986, 1990; see also Logan, 1981, 1982; Logan & Cowan, 1984; Zbrodoff & Logan, 1986). Early on, it became clear that no tasks were ballistic, in that virtually all responses can be inhibited if the stop signal occurs early enough, even highly skilled responses like speaking (Ladefoged, Silverstein, & Papcun, 1973) and typing (Logan, 1982). So the focus shifted from tasks to components of tasks. Researchers asked whether components of tasks—processing stages—were ballistic or controlled (De Jong et al., 1990; Logan, 1981, 1983, 1985; Osman et al., 1986, 1990).

An important concept in research on ballistic processes is the point of no return. The *point of no return* is a cusp that divides controlled processes from ballistic ones. If the stop process finishes before the go task has reached the point of no return, the response can be inhibited. If the stop process finishes after the point of no return, the response cannot be inhibited (De Jong et al., 1990; Osman et al., 1986, 1990). Several studies have tried to find the point of no return and locate it in terms of processing stages defined psychologically or psychophysiologically. The studies agree in concluding that if there is a point of no return, it is pretty close to the effectors. They disagree on how close. It is possible to make a case that there are no ballistic processes—that the point of no return is "on the skin" (at the interface between the person and the manipulanda)—and it is possible to make a case that certain late processes are beyond the point of no return.

One set of studies modeled the stop signal paradigm as a race between stop and go processes, and used the additive factors logic (Sternberg, 1969) to locate the point of no return in terms of stages in the go task. The idea was to manipulate factors that affect reaction time to the go task and see if those factors affect the probability of inhibiting responses (see Logan, 1981; Osman et al., 1986, 1990). According to the race model, the stop process races against the go process. If the stop process finishes before the go process reaches the point of no return, the response can be inhibited. If the stop process finishes after the go process reaches the point of no return, the response cannot be inhibited. Factors that increase the duration of go task stages before the point of no return should increase the probability of inhibition; those factors provide subjects with more time to stop, and therefore make stopping more likely. Factors that increase the duration of go task stages after the point of no return should have no effect on the probability of inhibition. The time available for subjects to stop is not affected by increasing the duration of ballistic processes.[1]

---

[1]The predictions that were actually tested were more precise than the ones described here. The race model allows one to predict exactly how much the probability of inhibition should change given an increase in the duration of the controlled phase. Those predictions require a deeper analysis of the race model than I have presented so far. The interested reader is referred to the original papers or to subsequent sections of this chapter (see Section VIII).

Studies conducted in this fashion showed that discriminability (Logan, 1981; Osman et al., 1986), lexical status (Osman et al., 1986), stimulus–response compatibility (Logan, 1981), and response complexity (Osman et al., 1990) affect controlled stages of processing. The only factor that appeared to affect ballistic stages of processing was stimulus–response repetition (Osman et al., 1986). Repetition is a difficult factor to interpret, however, because it has many different effects on the information processing system and affects several stages (Kornblum, 1973). It may even change the way the task is organized (Fletcher & Rabbitt, 1978).

A study by De Jong et al. (1990) used psychophysiological measures to search for the point of no return. They measured responses at three different stages in the motor system: They measured lateralized readiness potentials on the scalp above the motor cortex, electromyograms from the responding muscles in the forearm, and the force with which subjects' hands squeezed the response manipulanda (zero displacement dynamometers). They argued that if any of these stages was past the point of no return, then it should not be possible to inhibit the response once it reached that stage. Thus, if central preparation were after the point of no return, it should not be possible to inhibit responses that show a lateralized readiness potential; if muscle activation were after the point of no return, it should not be possible to inhibit responses that show an electromyographic response; and if the squeeze itself were after the point of no return, then it should not be possible to stop a squeeze once it begins.

The data suggested that central preparation was before the point of no return; subjects could easily inhibit responses that produced lateralized readiness potentials. The data also suggested that muscle activation was before the point of no return; subjects could inhibit responses that produced electromyographic responses. Finally, the data suggested that the squeeze itself was before the point of no return. There were many partial squeezes on stop signal trials, squeezes in which less than the criterial amount of force was exerted, as if subjects stopped in the middle of squeezing. Thus, if there are processes after the point of no return, they must be very late and very brief in duration.

Jennings et al. (1992) replicated the results of De Jong et al. (1990), finding evidence of electromyographic activity on some trials on which the final response (switch closure) was inhibited. The interval between electromyographic activity and switch closure was brief, 60–80 msec, which suggests that ballistic processes must be very brief in duration and late in the processing sequence.

The electromyographic data can be interpreted differently, given a different definition of the point of no return. De Jong et al. (1990) and Jennings et al. (1992) defined the point of no return as the point at which subjects could not stop themselves from *completing* the motor response. Thus, De Jong et al. interpreted partial (subthreshold) squeezes as cases of successful inhibition, and Jennings et al. interpreted all trials that did not result in a key closure as cases of successful inhibition. However, Osman et al. (1986, 1990) defined the point of no return as the point at which subjects could not stop themselves from *beginning* the overt movement. From that perspective, the partial squeezes observed by De Jong et al. would be interpreted as cases of unsuccessful inhibition. From that perspective, if muscle activation is the point of no return, the motor response should always begin if there is electromyographic activity. De Jong et al. (1990) found no cases in which there was electromyographic activity and no (partial) squeezes; electromyographic activity was always accompanied by a measurable motor response. Osman et al. (1986, 1990) would interpret those data as evidence that muscle activation was the point of no return.

Logan and Cowan (1984) presented a mathematical analysis that corroborates the conclusion that ballistic processes must be very brief. They modeled the stop signal paradigm as a race between stop and go processes (see the following). In the full development of the model, they included two parts to the go process: a controlled phase and a ballistic phase. They showed that estimates of stop signal reaction time include not only the reaction time to the stop signal, but also the duration of the ballistic phase of the go task. They note that estimates of stop signal reaction time are on the order of 200 msec. This may be interpreted as an upper limit on the duration of ballistic processes. The repetition effect observed by Osman et al. (1986) may be interpreted as a lower limit: If repetition affected the ballistic stage by 25 msec (as Osman et al. estimate), then the ballistic stage had to be at least 25 msec in duration.

B. Continuous Tasks

Several investigators have studied the ability to inhibit continuous responses, such as arm movements, and found they are inhibited in much the same way as discrete responses. Stop signal reaction times are the same as, if not faster than, those observed with discrete responses (Henry & Harrison, 1961; Megaw, 1972; Vince, 1948). Continuous tasks, such as speaking (Ladefoged et al., 1973; Levelt, 1983) and typing (Logan, 1982; Long, 1976; Rabbitt, 1978), can also be stopped very quickly. Typically, subjects emit only a syllable or two, or a keystroke or two before stopping. Stop signal reaction times are on the order of 200–400 msec.

The possibility of ballistic processes in continuous tasks is interesting. One often gets the impression that very familiar continuous tasks, such as chopping onions or typing sentences, go on ballistically—on automatic pilot—once they are initiated. However, the data suggest there is very close control. Subjects may not be able to prevent themselves from making a few responses (e.g., uttering a few syllables or striking a few keys) before stopping, but this most likely reflects the latency of the response to the stop signal rather than a substantial ballistic component. The stopping process, once begun, takes time to finish, and in tasks like speaking and typing, subjects may have time to execute several responses between the onset of the stop signal and the completion of the stopping process. Much of the data can be interpreted that way. In typing, for example, the number of characters typed after a stop signal multiplied by the rate at which characters are typed yields values close to 200 msec (Logan, 1982), which is a typical stop signal reaction time for a discrete task. The only evidence of ballistic responding in a continuous task comes from Logan's (1982) study of typewriting, in which skilled typists tended to type out familiar verb endings (*es* and *ed*) and the word *the* together with the space that followed it. In a similar vein, however, Osman et al. (1990) found that subjects had a hard time inhibiting second and subsequent responses in preprogrammed sequences if they failed to inhibit the first.

How can we reconcile the close control over continuous tasks with our intuition that we perform continuous tasks ballistically? The facility with which people inhibit continuous tasks suggests they have very close control over their performance, but the control can be realized in several ways. One possibility is that the task is organized in a single feedback loop, in which the consequences of each response or two are monitored and used to base decisions on what to do next. In this view, the stopping process is an integral part of the feedback loop and stop signal reaction time represents the time it takes the feedback loop to operate. Another possibility is that the task is organized hierarchically in several feedback loops. Low-level processes may be controlled by local feedback loops whose parameters are set by higher level processes. The different feedback loops may have different latencies; lower level loops may be faster than higher level loops. The stopping process may act outside of this hierarchy, separate from its feedback loops. The stopping process might inhibit low-level loops directly or it may change the parameters that high-level loops pass to low-level loops. In either case, stop signal reaction time does not represent the duration of a feedback loop within the control system for the go task.

Hierarchical control seems more likely on other grounds (Dell, 1986; Lashley, 1951; Rumelhart & Norman, 1982). In typing, for example, there are several "spans" that reflect different levels of organization—typists plan phrases, words, and keystrokes (Logan, 1983; Salthouse, 1986). Vallacher and Wegner (1987) pointed out that people can think of what they are doing at several different levels. I may be pressing keys, typing words, writing sentences, explaining the stop signal paradigm, or fulfilling my obligations to Dale and Tom, the editors who asked me to write this chapter. Reason and Myceilska (1982) studied everyday errors—action slips—and found they were best explained assuming hierarchical control. Many errors involve doing the wrong low-level activity in the right way (e.g., driving directly home instead of stopping for milk). Thus, the control seen in the stop signal paradigm may operate outside the go-task control system, intervening when necessary to stop action, but otherwise quiescent. This underscores the point made earlier, that stopping is an extreme and unsubtle form of control.

C. Ballisticity, Automaticity, and Autonomy

In theory, it is important to distinguish between ballistic processes, automatic processes, and autonomous processes. Ballisticity is often a defining characteristic of automatic processes; once initiated, they run on to completion whether or not the person intends them to (Posner & Snyder, 1975; Shiffrin & Schneider, 1977). However, ballisticity is only one of several properties of automaticity: automatic processes are also fast and effortless. Automatic processes may be ballistic, but ballistic processes are not necessarily automatic. Similarly, autonomous processes are ballistic in that once initiated, they run on to completion whether or not the person intends them to. But autonomous processes can also be initiated without intention, and that is not necessarily true of ballistic processes (Zbrodoff & Logan, 1986). Ballisticity has to do with whether a process runs on to completion without intention, not with whether it begins without intention. In principle, a process begun intentionally can run on to completion ballistically.

The stop signal paradigm addresses ballisticity directly. It addresses automaticity and autonomy indirectly, through their relations to ballisticity. Thus, the stop signal paradigm may be used as part of a battery of tasks to assess automaticity and autonomy. Zbrodoff and Logan (1986) suggested using Stroop-type tasks or Eriksen-type flanker tasks to determine whether processes begin without intention, and the stopping task to determine whether a process runs on to completion without intention.

V. COMPLICATING THE STOPPING PROCESS

The stop signal paradigm, as described so far, involves a simple response to the stop signal, which is analogous to a simple reaction time task. There is only one signal and only one response to make to it. It is like blowing a whistle to stop play in a hockey game: everything stops. There is nothing to do until "the next trial," when play begins again. Some investigators have begun to explore complications of the stopping process. Some examine the change paradigm, which models situations that require doing something else after stopping, like switching from autopilot to real thinking when a student asks a question during a lecture. Others examine selective inhibition, modeling situations in which the stop signal is not always a signal to stop (e.g., when your little brother vs. your mother discovers your hand in the cookie jar) and situations in which not everything must be stopped (e.g., trying to avoid using a sore finger, trying to avoid sensitive topics in conversation).

A. Change Paradigm

The complication of the stop signal paradigm that has been explored most often is the *change paradigm*, in which the stop signal tells the subject to change from one task to another. There are three tasks: the go task, the stop task, and the change task. Subjects perform the go task unless a stop signal occurs. The stop signal triggers the stop task and the change task. It tells subjects to inhibit their response to the go task (the stop task) and make an overt response to the stop signal (the change task). The stop signal itself is the stimulus for the change task, though it need not be. The stop signal could indicate a change in the task to be performed on the go-task stimulus, but it has not done so in the studies I know. Several studies have used simple (overt) reaction time to the stop signal as the change task (Logan, 1983, 1985; Logan & Burkell, 1986). Another presented two stopping tones and had subjects stop to both tones but press different keys for each tone in the change task (Logan, 1983). Others changed the go task stimulus and had subjects respond to the new go task stimulus (Logan, 1982, 1983, 1985).

The change paradigm is interesting because there are three processes involved, not just two. The go process and the stopping process seem to function pretty much the same in the change paradigm and the stop signal paradigm. The race model provides an accurate account of go signal and stop signal processing. Reaction times to the go signal and the stop signal may be a little slower in the change paradigm than in the stop signal paradigm, but the race model fits just as well (Logan, 1982; Logan & Burkell, 1986). The goodness of fit and the similarity of parameter values are interesting because they support the assumption that stop and go processes are independent of each other, which is a key assumption in the race model. The go and stop processes are not affected much by adding another task.

Reaction times to the change task depend on what the subject does in the stop task: Change reaction times show the usual dual-task interference or psychological refractory period if the subject fails to inhibit the response to the go task. Change reaction times are elevated on signal-respond trials, and the elevation is greater the shorter the delay. However, change reaction times show no interference at all if the subject succeeds in inhibiting the response to the go task. Change reaction times are fast on signal-inhibit trials and change very little with stop signal delay (Logan, 1985; Logan & Burkell, 1986; Schachar, Marriott, Tannock, & Logan, 1993; Tannock, Schachar, & Logan, 1993).

The change task reaction times are interesting because of their implications for theories of dual-task interference. The data show that dual-task interference depends on whether or not a response was executed. This suggests response execution as the locus of the processing bottleneck that is responsible for dual-task interference (Logan & Burkell, 1986). This conclusion contrasts with Pashler's (1984, 1989) claim that stimulus–response translation processes are the locus of the bottleneck (see also De Jong, 1993). It may be possible to reconcile the views by proposing that translation is linked to execution, such that execution is a necessary (obligatory) consequence of translation. If that were the case, then the only way to prevent execution would be to prevent translation (or to inhibit via some other, peripheral mechanism). Successful inhibition would leave the stimulus–response translation processes free to deal with the response to the change task, eliminating dual-task interference, just as we observed.

The key to this proposal is the assumption that translation and execution processes are linked, so that execution is a ballistic consequence of translation. This assumption received little support in studies that searched for the point of no return (see Section IV), where there was little evidence for ballistic processes. The specific hypothesis that translation necessitates execution was addressed by Osman et al. (1990), and they found little support for it. So it is not clear how to resolve the difference between Pashler's (1984, 1989) claim and Logan and Burkell's (1986) claim about the locus of the dual task bottleneck. The finding that inhibiting a response eliminates dual-task interference is an interesting and important challenge for future research.

The change task is interesting from a clinical perspective. Schachar et al. (1993) tested hyperactive children on the change task and found their stopping performance was poorer than that of normal controls, as Schachar and Logan (1990a) found with the stopping task. Interestingly, hyperactive children were not deficient on the change task. Their overt reaction times to the change signal were not much worse than control subjects'. They appear to have trouble stopping one task, but have no trouble switching to another. This is consistent with Schachar and

Logan's (1990b) finding that hyperactive children were no more susceptible than normal controls to dual-task interference. Tannock, Schachar,
and Logan (1993) found that stimulant medication improved the stopping performance of hyperactive children in the change task, just as it
did in the stopping task (Tannock et al., 1989). There was a suggestion
that the dose-response curves were different: Whereas inhibition performance improved with dose in the simple stopping study, it improved
and then declined as the dose increased in the more complex change
study.

B. To Stop or Not to Stop

Riegler (1986) complicated the stopping task in a classical Donderian
fashion. He presented two different stop signals and compared the usual
simple stopping task, in which subjects stopped responses when either
tone sounded, with a *stop/no-stop* task, in which subjects stopped responses when one tone sounded but not when the other tone sounded
(i.e., get your hand out of the cookie jar if your mother comes, but not if
your brother comes). He found substantially longer stop signal reaction
times in the stop/no-stop condition, corresponding to single-task differences between simple reaction times and go/no-go reaction times to the
same tones.

Riegler (1986) manipulated the difficulty of the go task independently of the difficulty of the stop task. The go task involved two or four
choices. The easy conditions were much like simple stopping: stopping
was fast and independent of the go task. However, performance started
to break down in the most difficult combination of stop and go tasks—
the four-choice stop/no-stop condition. The stop and go tasks were no
longer performed independently. They interfered with each other, as if
they were competing for shared resources. This result is important because it is the first suggestion that the stopping process may suffer the
same limitations as other concurrent tasks.

C. Selective Stopping

Logan, Kantowitz, and Riegler (1986) complicated the stopping process by asking subjects to engage it selectively, inhibiting one response
but not another. Subjects performed a two- and four-choice go task and
were presented with stopping tones. In the *selective stopping* task they
were required to inhibit only the key press assigned to the right index
finger, as if it were a sore finger they were trying to avoid using. Key
presses assigned to other fingers were to be executed whether or not a

stop signal sounded. In the simple stopping task, they stopped key presses assigned to all fingers when a stop signal sounded, just as in the usual stop signal paradigm.

Subjects were able to stop selectively. The selective stopping task produced inhibition functions that were well fit by the race model. The requirement to inhibit selectively increased stop signal reaction time substantially, and the increase was greater for the four-choice task, where one response out of four had to be inhibited, than for the two-choice task, where one response out of two had to be inhibited. By contrast, in the control task, stop signal reaction times were fast and not affected much by the number of choices in the go task. Logan et al. (1986) interpreted this interaction by proposing two modes of inhibition, a global mode for the control task that inhibited all responses, and a local mode for the selective inhibition task that focused on a single response (anticipating, perhaps, the distinction between central and peripheral inhibition mechanisms made by De Jong et al., 1990; Jennings et al., 1992). Stop signal reaction time depended on the difficulty of the discrimination that the stop process had to make in selecting the response to be inhibited. The global mode should be fast because all responses are inhibited; there is no discrimination required. The local mode should be slower because it requires discrimination, and it should be slower to discriminate the greater the number of alternatives. It should take longer to discriminate one response from four alternatives than from two alternatives, following a stop signal equivalent of Hick's law.

Logan et al. (1986) performed two experiments varying the stimuli used in the go task. One experiment used letters presented in the center of the screen that were assigned randomly to the keys. The other used X's presented in four different locations that were assigned to response keys that were spatially compatible with them. The second experiment produced much faster go task reaction times than the first, but the magnitudes and the patterns of the stop signal reaction times were the same. This is important because it rules out one interpretation of the pattern of stop signal reaction times: Subjects could postpone their stopping response until they could see which response was required in the go task. This would produce longer stop signal reaction times in selective stopping than in simple stopping because simple stopping need not be postponed in the same manner as selective stopping. It would produce longer selective stop signal reaction times in the four-choice task than in the two-choice task because subjects would have to wait longer to know which response to inhibit in the four-choice task. These predictions are in accord with the data. However, postponing stopping should also produce longer stop signal reaction times in the first experiment than in the second, corresponding to the longer go task reaction times in the first experiment, and this prediction was not confirmed. The delay in selective stopping cannot be attributed to postponing the stop process to monitor the go process.

VI. AFTEREFFECTS OF INHIBITION

What are the consequences of inhibiting a response? What aftereffects does the inhibition process leave behind? Kramer et al. (1992) examined the immediate consequences of inhibition, asking whether inhibiting the response on trial n affected performance on trial $n + 1$. They found that go signal reaction time was slower on trials following successful inhibition than on control trials. The effect was significant for both young and old subjects, but it was stronger for old subjects than for young ones (50 msec vs. 21 msec). This effect is interesting and merits further investigation. It would be interesting to compare it with negative priming, which is also interpreted as an aftereffect of inhibition (Tipper, 1985).

The inhibition process does not appear to leave behind much in the way of longer term aftereffects. Logan (1985) compared repetition priming effects—the reduction in reaction time produced by presenting something twice—produced by stimuli whose responses had and had not been inhibited on first presentation, and found equivalent repetition priming. This corroborates Logan's (1990) conclusion from transfer experiments that memory for response execution does not play a large role in repetition priming.

Logan (1983) used the same materials (words on which subjects performed category and rhyme judgments) but tested recognition memory rather than repetition priming. He found equivalent memory for words associated with responses that had and had not been inhibited during the study phase, corroborating the results of the repetition priming experiments.

Experiments by Zbrodoff and Logan (1986) suggest that inhibition may leave some measurable aftereffects. They performed a stop signal experiment in which the go task was verification of simple arithmetic problems like 3 + 4 = 7, and later compared memory for problems associated with responses that had and had not been inhibited. This time, memory was worse for inhibited problems, as if subjects stopped encoding the problem into memory when they stopped trying to solve it. The differences between these results and Logan's (1983) must be due to the nature of the go tasks. Arithmetic problems may be less memorable than words, particularly words subjected to semantic orienting tasks. Arithmetic verification may be less automatic than category or rhyme judgments and therefore less likely to run on to completion ballistically.

Research on the aftereffects of inhibition has only just begun. Very little is known. Very little is even known about what to look for. This strikes me as a promising area for future research, particularly for researchers interested in relating stop signal inhibition to other forms of inhibition, which also appear as aftereffects of prior acts of control.

VII. MECHANISMS OF INHIBITION

Little is known about the mechanisms underlying the stop process, except that they take time to finish and when they finish, they stop responses. The data on young adults are consistent with the hypothesis that a single, global mechanism is responsible for inhibition in all kinds of stopping tasks; a wide variety of tasks can be stopped in about 200 msec (see Logan & Cowan, 1984, for a review). Most of the data come from simple stopping experiments, in which there is only one stop signal and it tells subjects to inhibit any and all responses. A single, global mechanism may be responsible for simple stopping performance. Selective stopping, studied by Riegler (1986) and Logan et al. (1986), may require a more complicated mechanism. A selective stopping mechanism may operate differently, depending on the nature of the selection required. More research on selective stopping will be necessary to reveal the nature of simple and selective stopping mechanisms.

Two recent psychophysiological investigations of stopping provoked speculations about the nature and number of stopping mechanisms. De Jong et al. (1990) examined event-related potentials in the electroencephalogram while subjects processed go and stop signals. Their analysis suggested two mechanisms of inhibition: a central one that operated selectively, inhibiting central preparation of the required response, and a peripheral one that operated nonselectively, inhibiting any and all responses. Two pieces of evidence suggested a central mechanism. The first was a positive deflection in the waveform of the event-related potential at frontocentral electrode sites on trials on which subjects successfully inhibited their responses (*signal-inhibit* trials) that was not present on trials on which subjects failed to inhibit their responses (*signal-respond* trials). The second piece of evidence was a difference in the amplitude of the *lateralized readiness potential*, which reflects central motor preparation. The amplitude was lower on signal-inhibit trials than on signal-respond trials, and on trials on which no stop signal was presented, as if the stopping process inhibited central motor preparation.

The peripheral mechanism was suggested when attempts to account for the observed inhibition with central mechanisms failed. Differences in both central waveforms appeared (slightly) too late to cause inhibition of muscle activation and the final response. The amplitude of the lateralized readiness potential was smaller on signal-inhibit trials, but it was still larger than the amplitude needed to trigger electromyographic activity in the responding muscles—it ought to have produced a response, but somehow the response was inhibited. Do Jong et al. (1990) argued that responses were inhibited by a peripheral inhibition mechanism that operated separately from the central processes that prepare and inhibit motor responses.

Jennings et al. (1992) monitored cardiac activity rather than cortical activity during stopping, and came to the same conclusion as De Jong et al. (1990), albeit from a different direction. Jennings et al. (1992) found that the interval between heart beats was longer on signal-inhibit trials than on signal-respond trials or trials on which no stop signal was presented. They interpreted this interaction between cardiac inhibition and stop signal inhibition as suggesting that the stop process may be controlled by the same midbrain system that controls heart rate. They argued that the midbrain system inhibited central commands for a motor response, just like De Jong et al. (1990), but this time with more direct evidence for a noncentral (noncortical) locus.

The distinction between central preparation and peripheral inhibition is consistent with current theories of motor control. Brooks (1986) and Bullock and Grossberg (1988), among others, have argued that cortical processes determine which responses are to be made and midbrain processes determine when they start and stop. Nevertheless, the evidence for central and peripheral inhibitory mechanisms is scant and depends as much on argument as on fact.

The arguments De Jong et al. (1990) made about timing depend on very small differences and required generalizations from different tasks, subjects, and paradigms, which may not be valid. The arguments about the amplitude of the lateralized readiness potential assume that the critical factor is amplitude (and not, for example, the smoothness with which the potential rises to a critical amplitude). The relation between amplitude and responding is an empirical generalization, not a theoretical premise. It may be correlated with, but conceptually different from, the critical factor that triggers the motor response.

Similarly, the arguments of Jennings et al. (1992) for a midbrain inhibition system assume that the stopping process affects cardiac control directly. The stopping process could affect cardiac control indirectly, by eliminating one of the factors that affect it. Other studies show that responding during the critical phase of the heart rate is necessary to prevent prolongation of the heart beat (Jennings & Wood, 1977). Perhaps, stop signal inhibition prolongs heart rate by removing the response that is necessary to prevent prolongation. More research will be necessary to distinguish these alternatives. The idea of two inhibition mechanisms—cortical and midbrain—is tantalizing, but it is only the beginning. There is a great deal more to the story of the nature and the locus of stop signal inhibition processes that remains to be discovered.

VIII. THE RACE MODEL

So far, I have been able to explain most of the important results in the stop signal paradigm without getting very deeply into the race model that underlies the analysis of stopping performance. Most of the conclusions were not based on the data directly, but rather were based on the data as interpreted through the race model. In order to understand how the conclusions relate to the raw data (or to the data one might collect in one's own stopping experiment), it is necessary to understand how the race model accounts for stopping performance. The rest of this chapter is intended to provide such an understanding. Up to now, the chapter has shown the benefits gained from studying the stop signal paradigm and has suggested benefits to be gained from future studies. The rest of this chapter is the gauntlet that must be run to appreciate the intricacies of those benefits or to gain similar benefits oneself. There is no avoiding the race model.

Stop signal inhibition involves a whole process—the stopping process—working against another process—the go process. The go process is easy to understand. Much of the literature in experimental psychology is dedicated to understanding go processes, and what was learned there can be adapted to our purposes. The stop process is harder to understand because it is not directly observable. When the stop process beats the go process, there is no response to observe and no latency to measure. In order to understand stop signal inhibition, we must have a theory of the stop process. That theory must tell us when the stopping process is executed, how to measure the latency of the stopping process when it is executed, which factors affect the probability and latency of stopping. This is where the race model comes in.

The stop signal paradigm is interesting because in contrast with other paradigms, there is no controversy over the basic theory. All approaches assume that performance depends on a race between the stopping process and the go process. In some cases, the race is described informally (Lappin & Eriksen, 1966; Vince, 1948). In other cases, the race is described more formally, relating the inhibition function to the distribution of reaction times in the go task (Logan, 1981; Logan, Cowan, &

Davis, 1984). Others describe the race in terms of the distributions of finishing times of stop and go processes (Colonius, 1990; Logan & Cowan, 1984; Osman et al., 1986, 1990). Still others assume specific forms for the distributions (Logan & Burkell, 1986; Ollman, 1973). But the basic theory in each case is a race between the stop and the go processes.

The race model derives from two rules that define the conditions for the outcomes of the race: (1) If the stop process is faster than the go process, the response is inhibited. Formally, if $T_g > T_s + t_d$ then the stopping process wins and the response is inhibited. T_g and T_s are the finishing times of the go process and the stopping process, respectively, and t_d is the delay between the onset of the go signal and the onset of the stop signal. (2) If the go process is faster than the stop process, the response is executed. Formally, if $T_g < T_s + t_d$ then the go process wins and the response is executed. All theories assume that T_g and T_s are independent random variables, so the outcome of the race is stochastic rather than deterministic. On some proportion of the trials, the stop process will be faster than the go process; on the remaining proportion of the trials, the go process will be faster. That proportion depends on the distributions of finishing times for the stop and go processes and on t_d, the delay between the onsets of the stop and go stimuli.

These assumptions are sufficient to account for all of the observed behavior in the stop signal paradigm. They account for inhibition functions, the effects of go task reaction time on the inhibition functions, and the speed of responses that escape inhibition (i.e., responses that occur when $T_g < T_s + t_d$). They provide three ways to estimate parameters of the distribution of stop process finishing times (i.e., stop signal reaction time). Performance in the stop signal paradigm seems well described as a race between stop and go processes (Logan & Cowan, 1984; Osman et al., 1986).

The race model succeeds because it is general. It addresses only the finishing times of the stop and go processes, and it imposes little constraint on those finishing times. All Logan and Cowan (1984) required, for example, was that the finishing times come from some distribution. The form of the distribution did not matter (see also Colonius, 1990; cf. Ollman, 1973). More importantly, the nature of the process that gave rise to the distribution of finishing times did not matter either. The only constraint was that the stopping process and the go process should function independently, and that is possible theoretically (e.g., in multiple resource theory) and appears to be the case empirically (De Jong et al., 1990; Jennings et al., 1992; Logan & Cowan, 1984).

The generality of the race model is a weakness as well as a strength. The strength is obvious: The race model accounts for the data very well.

It makes quantitative predictions that are impressively accurate. The weakness is that the race model is not a process model. The race model does not depend on the nature of the processes that race against each other, only on their finishing times. Thus, the race model itself does not give any special insight into the nature of those processes. However, the race model may be used as a tool to investigate hypotheses about the nature of the underlying processes. Hypotheses about underlying processes are often couched in terms of reaction time and to factors that affect it. The race model provides a way to measure the reaction time of the stopping process and to determine which factors affect it. Thus, the race model is not the final answer to questions about performance in the stop signal paradigm, but it is an important and apparently necessary first step toward the final answer. A process model that explains how stopping actually occurs must be built within the constraints of the race model, filling in the details of processes that the race model treats abstractly.

A. Inhibition Functions

Inhibition functions relate the probability of inhibiting or the probability of responding to stop signal delay. They are important because stop signal delay (or some transformation of delay) is the most important independent variable in the stop signal paradigm; inhibition functions plot the effect of delay. Inhibition functions are important theoretically because they reflect the outcome of the race between the stop process and the go process. The race and the distributions of finishing times for the stop and go processes determine the shape of the function. Finally, inhibition functions are important because they are the focus of most of the data analysis in stop signal experiments.

Two questions arise immediately: Should we plot probability of inhibiting or probability of responding? And what measure of delay should those probabilities be plotted against? The probability of inhibiting is 1 minus the probability of responding, so it makes no difference formally which one is plotted. Choosing a measure of delay is more difficult. As experimenters, we have control over the delays between the onset of the go signal and the onset of the stop signal, which determine the *starting times* of the underlying processes. As theorists, we wish to control the finishing times of the underlying processes. The different measures of delay approximate control over the *finishing times*. They tell us how to set the delay between stimulus onsets—how to lag the starting times—in order to achieve a certain delay between the finishing times. They are all motivated by the race model, so it is important to explain how the race model accounts for inhibition functions before explaining the differences between the measures.

The easiest way for me to explain how inhibition functions result from the race model is to begin with two simplifying assumptions: (1) the finishing time of the stopping process (*stop signal reaction time*) is constant, and (2) there are no ballistic processes. The assumption about stop signal reaction time makes the mathematics easier, but more importantly, it allows a graphic representation of the underlying processes that illustrates the relationships very clearly (see Figure 1). The assumption is bound to be wrong—no one would seriously propose a psychological process that took a constant amount of time to execute— but it turns out in practice that the correctness of the assumption is not very important. Logan and Cowan (1984) (mostly Cowan) analyzed the formal consequences of the assumption, and found that it introduced very small measurement errors. De Jong et al. (1990) analyzed the effects of violating the assumption with Monte Carlo simulations and found they were small if stop and go processes were independent. Logan and Cowan (1984) compared estimates of stop signal reaction time that assumed it was constant with estimates that assumed it was variable (see the following) and found good agreement between them. Measures that do not require the assumption often require better data (Colonius, 1990; Logan & Cowan, 1984).

The assumption that there are no ballistic processes is more controversial, as the earlier section on ballistic processes and the point of no return attested (see Section IV). Nevertheless, it is clear that if there are ballistic processes, they occur late in the sequence, close to or during motor execution. The clearest candidate for a point of no return is muscle activation, and this candidacy depends on defining the point of no return as the point beyond which subjects cannot stop themselves from *beginning* the movement (Osman et al., 1986, 1990). The point beyond which subjects cannot stop themselves from *completing* the movement is clearly after muscle activation (De Jong et al., 1990). If we define that point as the point of no return, then we can safely ignore ballistic processes. We adopt that definition for the remainder of this chapter, mostly because it makes the model easier to explain. Logan and Cowan (1984) develop the model completely, assuming that stop signal reaction time is a random variable and that there may be ballistic processes in the go task.

The top panel of Figure 1 depicts a time line that indicates the onset of the go stimulus (primary task stimulus) and the onset of the stop signal. The distribution of reaction times to the go stimulus is drawn above the time line. The constant finishing time of the stopping process is drawn as a vertical line that intersects the time line. It extends

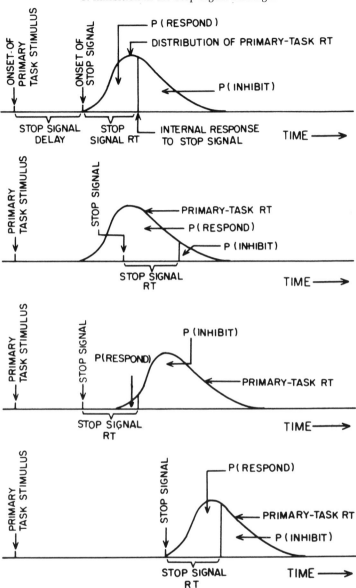

FIGURE 1

Graphic representation of the assumptions and predictions of the race model, indicating how the probability of inhibiting a stimulus—P(INHIBIT)—and the probability of responding given a stop signal—P(RESPOND)—depend on the distribution of primary (go) task reaction times, stop signal reaction time, and stop signal delay. (The representation assumes that stop signal reaction time is constant.) From "On the Ability to Inhibit Thought and Action: A Theory of an Act of Control" by G. D. Logan and W. B. Cowan, 1984, *Psychological Review*, *91*, 295–327, Figure 2. Copyright 1984 by the American Psychological Association. Reprinted by permission.

vertically above the time line, dividing the go process reaction time distribution into two parts. The part on the left side of the line represents go reaction times that win the race. They are faster than stop signal reaction time plus stop signal delay (i.e., $T_g < T_s + t_d$). The area under the distribution to the left of the line represents the probability of responding, given a stop signal at that delay. The part of the distribution on the right side of the line represents the go trials that lose the race to the stopping process. They are slower than stop signal reaction time plus stop signal delay (i.e., $T_g > T_s + t_d$). The area to the right of the line represents the probability of inhibiting at that stop signal delay.

The second panel of Figure 1 illustrates how inhibition functions are produced by varying the stop signal delay. It depicts the same time line as the top panel, with the go signal presented at the same time and the same distribution of go signal reaction times. However, this time, the stop signal is delayed. Consequently, the point at which the stopping process finishes is delayed. It appears farther to the right on the time line, cutting the go signal reaction time distribution in a different place. Compared to the top panel, the probability of responding is higher and the probability of inhibition is lower.

It is easy to see how this idea can be extended to produce a complete inhibition function. If the stop signal is presented early enough, the probability of responding will equal 0, and the probability of inhibition will equal 1. If the stop signal is presented late enough, the probability of responding will equal 1, and the probability of inhibition will equal 0. Points in between these extremes will produce a smooth function in which the probability of responding increases from 0 to 1 and the probability of inhibition decreases from 1 to 0 as delay increases. Formally,

$$P_r(t_d) = \int^{T_s + t_d} f_g(t) dt \tag{1}$$

where $P_r(t_d)$ is the probability of responding at delay t_d, T_s is the stop signal reaction time, and $f_g(t)$ is the distribution of reaction times to the go signal. The go stimulus is presented at $t = 0$. An important point to be taken from Figure 1 and Eq. (1) is that the shape of the inhibition function depends on the shape of the reaction time distribution. This relationship is emphasized when inhibition functions are plotted using the probability of responding rather than the probability of inhibiting. The "central" part of the inhibition function, where the probability of responding is around .5, depends on the mean of the reaction time distribution. The "slope" of the inhibition function depends on the variability of the reaction time distribution. The more variable the distribution, the broader and flatter the inhibition functions.

The third panel in Figure 1 illustrates the effects of mean reaction time to the go signal on the inhibition function. The stop signal is presented at the same time (i.e., the stop signal delay is the same), but the go signal reaction time distribution is delayed. Consequently, the internal response to the stop signal cuts off less of the go-signal reaction time distribution; the probability of responding is lower and the probability of inhibiting is higher.

The fourth panel of Figure 1 illustrates the major point of the race model: The inhibition function depends on the relative finishing times of the stop and go processes, not on their relative starting times. In the fourth panel, the go process reaction times have been delayed relative to the first panel, but the presentation of the stop signal has been delayed by the same amount. Consequently, the stopping process finishes at the same time, relative to the go process, as it does in the first panel. Go signal reaction time and stop signal delay are very different, but the probability of inhibition and the probability of responding given a signal are the same because the relative finishing time is the same.

The compensatory relationship between go reaction time and stop signal delay has been investigated several times. Different experimental conditions (Logan, 1981, 1982; Osman et al., 1990), tasks (Logan et al., 1984), strategies (Logan, 1981), subjects (Logan & Cowan, 1984), and subject populations (Schachar & Logan, 1990a) produce different go signal reaction time distributions and different inhibition functions, but it is generally possible to bring the functions into alignment by plotting them against some transformation of delay that takes into account the differences in go signal reaction time distributions (but see Osman et al., 1986, 1990, Experiment 2; Schachar & Logan, 1990a; Tannock et al., 1989). Simply subtracting stop signal delay from mean go signal reaction time (i.e., plotting inhibition functions against mean reaction time minus stop signal delay) is sufficient to bring most functions into alignment. When there are large differences in variability, other transformations are necessary to bring the functions into alignment (Logan et al., 1984; Schachar & Logan, 1990a). All of these transformations are intended to express the inhibition function in terms of the relative finishing times of the stop and go processes. They will be discussed more extensively later (see Section IX).

Logan and Cowan (1984) developed a complete version of the race model in which the stop process and the go process were both random variables (i.e., in which stop signal reaction time was not assumed to be constant). Their analysis is too complex to reiterate here, but the main results are straightforward. Logan and Cowan (1984) (again, mostly Cowan) treated the inhibition function as if it were a cumulative distribution (it looks like one) and related it to the distribution of stop process and go process finishing times. They showed that the mean of the inhibition function is simply the difference between the mean go signal reaction time and the mean stop signal reaction time.[2] Explicitly,

$$\overline{T}_i = \overline{T}_g - \overline{T}_s \tag{2}$$

where $\overline{T}_i$ is the mean of the inhibition function and $\overline{T}_g$ and $\overline{T}_s$ are the means of the go and stop process reaction times, respectively.

The relationship in Eq. (2) is very useful. First of all, it defines the relationship between the inhibition function and go signal reaction time; the greater the go signal reaction time, the later the inhibition function. Second, it provides an easy way to estimate stop signal reaction time. The mean of the inhibition function is subtracted from the mean go signal reaction time (i.e., $\overline{T}_s = \overline{T}_g - \overline{T}_i$).

Logan and Cowan (1984) showed that the variance of the inhibition function was equal to the sum of the variances of the stop and go processes. Explicitly,

$$\sigma^2_i = \sigma^2_g + \sigma^2_s \tag{3}$$

The relationship in Eq. (3) is very useful in interpreting inhibition functions. It allows us to separate the contribution of differences in go process variance from differences in stop process variance. Basically, the variance of the inhibition function determines how broad and flat the inhibition function appears. Under some conditions, the variance can be estimated quantitatively from the slope of the inhibition function (i.e., if the inhibition function is assumed to have a particular shape; see Logan & Cowan, 1984, pp. 313–314). In most conditions, the slope of the inhibition function can be interpreted qualitatively in terms of the variance of the go process and the variance of the stop process. Subjects with more variable go processes will produce flatter inhibition functions. Subjects with more variable stop processes will also produce flatter inhibition functions. It is possible to correct for differences in go process variance by transforming the stop signal delay appropriately. Residual differences in the inhibition function after these differences

[2]Logan and Cowan (1984) distinguished between a controlled phase and a ballistic phase in responses to the go signal. Responses could be inhibited if the stop process finished during the controlled phase; responses could not be inhibited if the stop process finished during the ballistic phase. In their analyses, the mean of the go processes was expressed in terms of both components (i.e., $\overline{T}_g = \overline{T}_c + \overline{T}_b$, where $\overline{T}_c$ and $\overline{T}_b$ are the means of the controlled and ballistic phases, respectively). However, the mean of the inhibition function was expressed only in terms of the mean of the controlled process (i.e., $\overline{T}_i = \overline{T}_c - \overline{T}_s$) and the variance of the inhibition function was expressed only in terms of the variance of the controlled process (i.e., $\sigma^2_i = \sigma^2_c + \sigma^2_s$). I do not distinguish between controlled and ballistic components of the go process in this chapter in order to keep the exposition clear and because the evidence suggests that ballistic processes may be negligible, brief enough to be safely ignored (De Jong et al., 1990; Osman et al., 1986, 1990; see Section IV).

have been removed, may be interpreted as differences in the variability of the stopping process. Schachar and Logan (1990a) used this technique to conclude that hyperactive children had more variable stopping processes than normal and clinical control children. The transformations will be discussed more extensively in Section IX.

B. Stop Signal Reaction Time

Probability and latency are the two most important measures of responses in experimental psychology. The inhibition function describes the probability that the response to the stop signal will win the race. But the internal response to the stop signal cannot be observed directly, so its latency must be estimated somehow. This is an important step in any stop signal study. Estimates of stop signal reaction time are the basis for most of the conclusions about the ability to inhibit thought and action. They are essential in comparing inhibitory ability between subjects and tasks, and in detecting deficient inhibition.

Three methods are available to estimate stop signal reaction time. The easiest to understand and the most commonly used is the one that assumes stop signal reaction time is constant, first proposed by Logan (1981). It is illustrated in Figure 1. Stop signal reaction time is the difference between the point at which the stop signal was presented and the point at which the stopping process finished. We know when the stop signal was presented from the experimental protocol. We have to estimate the point at which the stopping process finished from the observed distribution of go signal reaction times and the observed probability of responding given a stop signal. We do so by integrating the go signal reaction time distribution until the area under the integral equals the probability of responding. In Figure 1, this amounts to moving a vertical line across the distribution until the area to the left of the line equals the probability of responding, and then reading the value of the time axis at that point as an estimate of the finishing time of the stopping process. Then stop signal delay is subtracted out, and the remainder is the estimate of stop signal reaction time. Formally, stop signal reaction time is estimated by $r(t_d) - t_d$, where $r(t_d)$ is defined in terms of Eq. (1):

$$P_r(t_d) = \int^{r(t_d)} f(t)\,dt \tag{4}$$

How do we calculate stop-signal reaction time in practice? Reaction times from go signal responses on which no stop signal occurred are collapsed into a single distribution. The reaction times are rank ordered, and the nth reaction time is selected, where n is obtained by multiplying the number of reaction times in the distribution (m) by the probability of responding at a given delay [$P_r(t_d)$; i.e., $n = m \cdot P_r(t_d)$]. The nth reaction time estimates the time at which the stopping process finished, relative to the onset of the go signal. To estimate stop signal reaction time (the time at which the stopping process finished relative to the stop signal), stop signal delay (the interval between the onset of the go signal and the onset of the stop signal) must be subtracted from this value. This process is repeated for each stop signal delay for each subject. The results are then averaged over subjects within and sometimes across stop signal delays.

Stop signal reaction times estimated by this method are close to 200 msec in a variety of experimental tasks, conditions, and strategies in subjects in their late teens and early twenties (for a review, see Logan & Cowan, 1984). Stop signal reaction time is longer in younger children (Schachar & Logan, 1990a) and older adults (Kramer et al., 1992), following other life-span trends in reaction time. Hyperactive children show slower stop signal reaction times than normal and clinical control children (Schachar & Logan, 1990a; Schachar et al., 1993), and their stop signal reaction times are sped up by methylphenidate, a stimulant medication that relieves the behavioral symptoms of hyperactivity (Tannock et al., 1989; Tannock, Schachar, & Logan, 1993). Perhaps stop signal reaction time can reveal inhibitory deficiencies related to other forms of psychopathology and other clinical conditions.

Researchers have typically ignored factors affecting stop signal reaction time, being more concerned with factors affecting go signal reaction time (but see Logan et al., 1986; Riegler, 1986). This is unfortunate because the nature of processes are revealed by the factors that affect their latency, and we need to learn more about the nature of the stopping process.

Stop signal reaction times estimated by the method described in Eq. (4) tend to decrease somewhat as the stop signal delay increases (Logan & Burkell, 1986; Logan & Cowan, 1984; Logan et al., 1984). This reduction could reflect a refractory effect of processing the go signal, as if the stop process and the go process compete for common resources. De Jong et al. (1990) showed with Monte Carlo simulations that negative dependencies between stop and go tasks produce estimates of stop signal reaction time that decrease with delay. This is bad news for the race model; the reduction in stop signal reaction time with delay suggests that the stop task and go task are not independent, as the race model requires them to be.

Logan and Burkell (1986) tried to save the independence assumption and account for the decrease in terms of variability in stop signal reaction time. They argued that at short stop signal delays, nearly all stop signal reaction times would be fast enough to win the race, so the mean of the winners of the race would approximate the mean of the stop signal reaction time distribution. At longer delays, only the faster stop signal reaction times would be fast enough to win the race. Responses to the go signal win the race on a significant proportion of the trials, and they screen out the slower stop signal reaction times. Thus, the mean of the stop signal reaction times that won the race would be faster than the mean of the entire distribution because the go signal responses cut off the upper tail [this logic is developed formally in Section VII(C)]. Logan and Burkell (1986) had some success fitting means of distributions with truncated upper tails to the data. Thus, decreases in stop signal reaction time with delay need not be interpreted as evidence against the independence assumption. De Jong et al. (1990) found that high variance in (simulated) stop signal reaction times produced estimated stop signal reaction times that decreased with delay, even when stop and go processes were independent, corroborating this conclusion.

The second method for estimating stop signal reaction time assumes that it is a random variable, not a constant. The method derives from Logan and Cowan's (1984) treatment of the inhibition function as distribution. It exploits the relationship between the mean of the inhibition function and the means of the stop and go processes expressed in Eq. (2): Mean stop signal reaction time equals the difference between the mean go signal reaction time and the mean of the inhibition function. Explicitly,

$$\overline{T}_s = \overline{T}_g - \overline{T}_i \tag{5}$$

The estimate in Eq. (5) is easy to calculate. All that is required is the mean of the go signal reaction times, which is easy to compute, and the mean of the inhibition function. The mean of the inhibition function can be computed in several ways. If there is a complete inhibition function, ranging from 0 to 1, then the mean is simply $\Sigma p_i x_i$, where p_i is the probability of responding at the ith stop signal delay minus the probability of responding at the $i-1$th stop signal delay [i.e., $p_i = p(\text{respond})_i - p(\text{respond})_{i-1}$] and x_i is the ith stop signal delay. The mean can be calculated in a similar manner from a truncated inhibition function (i.e., one in which the smallest probability of responding given a signal is greater than 0, and the largest probability of responding given a signal is less than 1).[3]

It is also possible to use the median to estimate the mean of the inhibition function. This can be justified formally if the investigator is willing to assume that the inhibition function is a symmetrical distribution

---

[3]Specifically, the computation of p_i has to be rescaled to reflect the truncated range. Each value of p_i has to be divided by the difference between the maximum and the minimum probabilities of responding, that is, the probabilities of responding at the longest and shortest stop signal delays, respectively. The corrected p_i should equal $p_i/[p(\text{respond})_{\max} - p(\text{respond})_{\min}]$. In practice, it is easier to do the correction once, after summing the $p_i x_i$ values (i.e., $(\Sigma p_i x_i)/[p(\text{respond})_{\max} - p(\text{respond})_{\min}]$).

(such as the normal, the *t*, and the rectangular) so that the mean and median are guaranteed to be identical (see Logan & Cowan, 1984, pp. 313–314). Investigators not willing to make that assumption can hope that the mean and the median are not too different so that the median is a reasonable estimate of the mean. The ease of computing the median of the inhibition function may encourage tough-minded investigators to make one assumption or the other: The median is simply the point at which the probability of responding and the probability of inhibiting are .5. In principle, one stop signal delay could suffice if it were guaranteed to produce inhibition 50% of the time. More realistically, two delays are sufficient, one with the probability of responding below .5 and one with the probability above it. The median can be computed by interpolation. Logan and Cowan (1984) compared estimates based on the median to estimates based on the mean and found reasonable agreement in the three subjects they studied. Interpolation based on the two delays that surrounded the median produced estimates very close to those computed from means based on the entire inhibition function. They did not explore the possibility of extrapolating when the maximum probability of responding is less than .5 or when the minimum probability of responding is greater than .5, but estimation by extrapolation is possible in principle.

Regardless of how the mean of the inhibition function is calculated, using it to estimate stop signal reaction time is easy, and this is an important advantage. The method does not require implausible assumptions, like a constant stop signal reaction time, and this is an advantage as well. The main disadvantage is that the method provides one measure of the mean stop signal reaction time for the whole inhibition function. It does not allow separate estimates at each stop signal delay and it does not allow estimates of parameters other than the mean.

The third method of estimating stop signal reaction time was proposed by Colonius (1990; see also De Jong et al., 1990, Appendix). It involves using the observed distribution of go signal reaction times from trials on which no stop signal was presented, $f_g(t)$, and the distribution of go signal reaction times from stop signal trials on which the subjects failed to inhibit their responses (i.e., *signal-respond* reaction times), $f_r(t)$. The cumulative distribution of stop signal reaction times, $F_s(t-t_d)$, is defined as follows:

$$F_s(t-t_d) = 1 - [P_r(t_d) \cdot f_r(t)/f_g(t)] \tag{6}$$

where $P_r(t_d)$ is the probability of responding given a stop signal at delay t_d.

This method has the advantage of estimating the entire distribution of stop signal reaction times at each stop signal delay. Parameters like means and standard deviations can be calculated directly from the estimated distribution. They do not have to be estimated or approximated in other ways. The disadvantage of the method is that the quality of the estimates is very sensitive to the quality of the data. The major limitation comes from signal-respond reaction times. For reasons, which follow, stop signals typically do not occur very frequently (often on 25% or less of the trials) and signal-respond trials occur even less frequently. It is difficult to gather enough observations to get stable signal-respond distributions, particularly at the tails, and the stability of the signal-respond distributions limits the stability of the estimated distributions of stop signal reaction times.

C. Signal-Respond Reaction Times

Responses that escape inhibition are observable and their latency (*signal-respond* reaction time) can be measured directly. An adequate model of the stop signal paradigm should be able to predict signal-respond reaction times and account for factors that affect them, and the race model does just that. This prediction is important because it bears on the validity of the assumptions underlying the race model. De Jong et al. (1990) and Jennings et al. (1992) used the prediction to test the assumption that stop and go processes are independent of each other (see De Jong et al., 1990; Jennings et al., 1992; Logan & Cowan, 1984).

The way that the race model accounts for signal-respond reaction times is illustrated in Figure 1. The responses that escape inhibition are those to the left of the line representing the finishing time of the stop process. Signal-respond reaction time should correspond to the mean of the reaction times in the area to the left of the line. Formally,

$$\overline{T}_r = (1/P_r(t_d)) \int^{T_s + t_d} t \cdot f_g(t) dt \tag{7}$$

where $\overline{T}_r$ is the mean signal-respond reaction time and the other variables are as defined in Eq. (1).

Three predictions follow from this analysis. First, signal-respond reaction time should be faster than go signal reaction time. Signal-respond reaction times come from the same distribution as go-signal reaction times, but the stopping process cuts off the upper tail. The mean of the left part of the distribution has to be smaller than the mean of the whole distribution. This prediction has been confirmed every time it is tested (De Jong et al., 1990; Jennings et al., 1992; Lappin & Eriksen, 1966; Logan, 1981; Logan & Cowan, 1984; Osman et al., 1986, 1990).

Second, signal-respond reaction times should increase as stop signal delay increases. This follows because slower go responses win the race when the stop signal is delayed. It can be seen in Figure 1: The mean of the left part of the top panel is smaller than the mean of the left part in the second panel. This prediction has also been confirmed several times (De Jong et al., 1990; Jennings et al., 1992; Logan, 1981; Logan & Cowan, 1984; Osman et al., 1986). Sometimes it is violated with very short delays, when signal-respond reaction times are based on very few observations (Logan & Cowan, 1984), but it is generally true when there are sufficient observations.

Third, observed signal-respond reaction times should *equal* those predicted from the race model, using Eq. (2). This is a *point* prediction rather than a *difference* prediction or a *trend* prediction, so it is stronger than the first two. Nevertheless, it has been confirmed several times (De Jong et al., 1990; Jennings et al., 1992; Logan & Cowan, 1984). Again, it is confirmed more readily in the central parts of the inhibition function where signal-respond responses are more numerous.

How is the prediction tested in practice? Reaction times from go signal responses on which no stop signal occurred are collapsed into a single distribution. The reaction times are rank ordered, and the mean of the fastest n is computed, where n is the number of reaction times in the distribution (m) multiplied by the probability of responding at a given delay $[P_r(t_d); $ i.e., $n = m \cdot P_r(t_d)]$. The mean of the fastest n is the predicted value, to be compared with observed signal-respond reaction times. (This procedure is essentially the same as the procedure for calculating stop signal reaction time. The main difference is that here we take the mean of the fastest n reaction times, whereas in estimating stop signal reaction time, we took the nth reaction time and interpreted it as the finishing time for the stopping process.)

In a way, it is impressive that this prediction succeeds. It depends on the assumption that stop signal reaction time is constant, and that is unlikely to be true. That assumption also predicts an odd shape for the distribution of signal-respond reaction times; the fast tail should be typical of all reaction time distributions, but the slow tail should be truncated abruptly at the point at which the stopping process finishes. Observed signal-respond reaction time distributions do not look like this (see Lappin & Eriksen, 1966; Osman et al., 1986, 1990). The point prediction of mean signal-respond reaction time excludes the upper tail of the observed signal-respond distribution, so it is not influenced by outliers. This may be bad in principle, but in practice, it may actually be helpful. The prediction may be improved by excluding spurious outliers.

De Jong et al. (1990) and Jennings et al. (1992) took the prediction of signal-respond reaction times a step further. They tried to predict the latencies of partial responses on stop signal trials. De Jong et al. had subjects respond by squeezing a zero-displacement dynamometer, and defined partial responses as squeezes that did not reach the criterial amount of force (25% of maximum force). Jennings et al. defined partial responses as ones that occurred when there was electromyographic activity but no completion of the button press response. The analysis involved distinguishing between three classes of responses rather than two: complete inhibition responses, partial inhibition responses, and complete go responses. The probability of responding given a stop signal corresponds to the probability of making a complete go response [i.e., $P_r(t_d)$]. The probability of inhibition [i.e., $1 - P_r(t_d)$] corresponds to the sum of the probability of complete inhibition and the probability of partial inhibition. This is illustrated in Figure 2, which depicts the race model with two finishing times for the stopping process. The first (leftmost) distinguishes between responses that are executed and responses that are inhibited partially or completely. The second (rightmost) distinguishes between partially inhibited responses and completely inhibited responses. The idea is that partially inhibited responses were faster than completely inhibited responses, almost fast enough to be executed, but not completely. The area between those lines corresponds to the probability of partial inhibition, and the mean reaction time in that area corresponds to signal-respond reaction times for the partial responses. It can be calculated using a variation of Eq. (7). De Jong et al. (1990) and Jennings et al. (1992) made such calculations and found that the predicted signal partial respond reaction times agreed well with the observed ones.

Osman et al. (1986) developed the race model a little differently and generalized these predictions to distributions of signal-respond reaction times, not just the means. According to their analysis, distributions of signal-respond reaction times and distributions of go task reaction times from trials on which no stop signal was presented (*no-signal* reaction

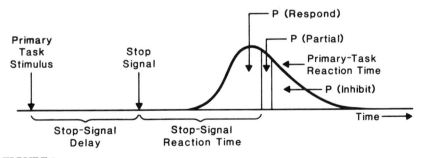

FIGURE 2

The race model extended to include partial responses. From R. De Jong, M. G. H. Coles, G. D. Logan, and G. Gratton (1990). In search of the point of no return: The control of response processes. *Journal of Experimental Psychology: Human Perception and Performance, 16,* 164–182. Copyright 1990 by the American Psychological Association. Reprinted by permission.

times) should start from roughly the same minimum value, but signal-respond distributions should reach their peaks before no-signal distributions do. Moreover, signal-respond reaction times should reach their peaks sooner the earlier the stop signal was presented. In practice, this means that the cumulative distributions of reaction times should begin from about the same point and then "fan out," with the signal-respond reaction times from the earliest stop signal delay rising first and most sharply, and no-signal reaction times rising last and most gradually. They tested and confirmed this prediction in three experiments (see also Osman et al., 1990).

IX. SETTING STOP SIGNAL DELAY

Inhibition functions depend on go signal reaction time and stop signal reaction time, as well as on stop signal delay, so choosing and setting stop signal delays is a difficult matter. At some delays, subjects will inhibit all the time and at other delays they will respond all the time. The problem is to find the intermediate delays at which the probability of responding is between 0 and 1. This part of the function is the most meaningful theoretically. All of the analytic methods reviewed previously focus on it. Several methods are available, ranging from choosing delays arbitrarily to tracking several parameters of subjects', performances and setting delays contingent on the values of those parameters.

The first issues to be decided are how many delays to use and how often to present the stop signal. The data provide a clear answer: At least three or four delays should be used. In theory, at least two are required to estimate the mean and variance of the inhibition function. In practice, subjects adapt to the range of delays they experience. If there is only one delay, they will prolong their go signal reaction times in order to maximize the probability of inhibiting (Lappin & Eriksen, 1966; Logan, 1981). Prolongation can be minimized by presenting several delays, some early enough that subjects will be able to inhibit most of the time, and some late enough that subjects will usually respond when they occur (Logan, 1981). Early and late delays break the contingency between variation in go signal reaction time and the probability of inhibiting. Subjects can still increase the probability of inhibiting by prolonging reaction time, but the effects of prolongation will be small compared to the effects of early versus late stop signal delays, so subjects may not bother with prolongation. Tracking procedures, like those of Osman et al. (1986, 1990), also break the contingency between variation in go signal reaction time and the probability of inhibition. They guarantee that stop signals will be presented at different delays whose values are unpredictable to the subject.

How often should the stop signal be presented? Again, the data are clear: The greater the probability that a stop signal will occur, the greater the probability of inhibition and the slower the reaction times to the go signal. Logan (1981) found these effects presenting stop signals on 10% versus 20% of the trials. Logan and Burkell (1986) found similar (and larger) effects presenting stop signals on 20%, 50%, and 80% of the trials. Quantitative analyses of inhibition functions, described previously, showed that the increase in probability of inhibition can be accounted for completely by the increase in go signal reaction time. It appears as if subjects place greater importance on the stopping task the more often the stop signal occurs, prolonging their go signal reaction times in order to increase the probability of inhibition. This effect can be minimized by instructing subjects appropriately and presenting stop signals relatively infrequently. There is a trade-off, because the more often stop signals are presented, the more observations there are to analyze (e.g., signal-respond reaction times), but the more often stop signals are presented, the more likely the data are to be influenced by unwanted strategies. In practice, presenting stop signals on 25% of the trials is a reasonable compromise. The stop signal occurs often enough to get reasonable data, but rarely enough that subjects do not expect it and change their go signal reaction times accordingly.[4]

How should the delays be chosen? Ideally, the delays should capture the part of the inhibition function that is most informative—the part where the probability of responding changes smoothly from 0 to 1. There are several options.

A. Arbitrary Delays

Delays may be chosen arbitrarily and fixed for all conditions and all subjects. This may seem to rely a lot on luck, but some rules of thumb,

[4]Instructions are very important in the stop signal paradigm. The main difficulty is in getting subjects to give appropriate priority to the two tasks. I usually instruct subjects about the go task first, without describing the stopping task. I tell them what they are expected to do and to do it as quickly as possible without making errors. Then I introduce the stopping task, telling them about the stop signals and what to do when a stop signal occurs. I tell them that stop signal delay is varied by the experimenter, and that some stop signals will occur so early that they will always be able to stop and some will occur so late that they will rarely be able to stop. I tell them to try to stop if they can, but not to worry about failing to stop because of the way the delays are set. I tell them to perform the go task as quickly and accurately as possible. I tell them not to let the stopping task interfere with their performance on the go task. I tell them specifically not to delay their response to the go task in order to improve their chances of stopping. I have not investigated the consequences of varying these instructions, so I do not know which parts are essential. The whole set of instructions works well, however, producing reasonable inhibition functions and reasonable reaction times. Other investigators have used explicit payoff schemes to the same end (De Jong et al., 1990; Jennings et al., 1992).

which are formalized in the other methods, can guide the selection and produce a reasonable set of delays. The shortest delay should be close to zero, the longest should not be much longer than the mean go signal reaction time, and the rest should be evenly spaced in between. The top row of Figure 3 contains inhibition functions from the simple- and choice-reaction go tasks in Logan et al. (1984) that were generated choosing arbitrary delays using these rules of thumb. The left panel in the top row plots the functions according to stop signal delay; the middle and right plot them according to transformations of delay. The arbitrary delays captured most of the inhibition function between 0 and 1.

The alternative to choosing delays arbitrarily is to choose delays contingent on some aspects of subjects' performance, such as the mean go signal reaction time, or the success or failure of the last attempt at inhibition. Delays can be set dynamically, calculating performance measures and updating delays on every trial, or they can be set in advance, based on performance measures gathered in control blocks or a control session. There are several options for setting delays contingent on performance.

B. Mean Go Signal Reaction Time Minus Delay

Delays may be set relative to mean go signal reaction time. The idea here is that stop signal delay can compensate for differences in mean reaction time, which is illustrated in the top and bottom panels of Figure 1, as discussed previously. If the mean go signal reaction time for the first of two conditions, tasks, subject groups, or whatever, is x msec faster than the second, then stop signal delays for the two that differ by x msec (with the first shorter than the second) should produce equivalent probabilities of responding. This prediction has been confirmed many times by showing that disparate inhibition functions can be brought into alignment by replotting them relative to mean go signal reaction time (Logan, 1981, 1982, 1983; Logan et al., 1984; Osman et al., 1990).

The procedure by which delays are set relative to mean go signal reaction time is as follows: First some measure of mean go signal reaction time is calculated. The mean may be estimated from similar experiments with similar subjects and stimuli, or it may be calculated subject by subject. The intervals between the delays are chosen arbitrarily. As a rule of thumb, the shortest stop signal delay should be close to zero, the largest should be close to the mean, and the others should be spaced evenly in between. Schachar and Logan (1990a) set stop signal delays equal to the mean go signal reaction time minus 0, 100, 200, 300, 400, and 500 msec. The second row of Figure 3 contains inhibition functions

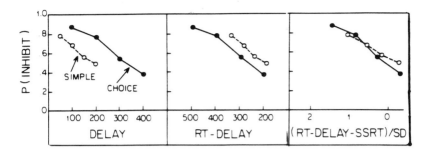

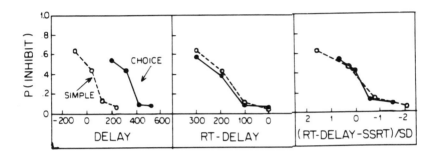

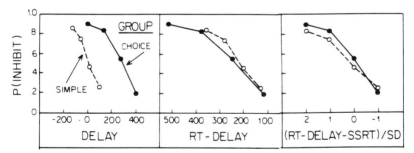

FIGURE 3

The effects of different methods of selecting stop signal delays on the inhibition functions
on data from simple and choice reaction time tasks. From G. D. Logan, W. B. Cowan, and
K. A. Davis (1984). On the ability to inhibit simple and choice reaction time responses: A
model and a method. *Journal of Experimental Psychology: Human Perception and Performance, 10,* 275–291. Copyright 1984 by the American Psychological Association.
Adapted by permission.

from the simple- and choice-reaction go tasks in Logan et al. (1984) that
were generated by selecting delays relative to mean go signal reaction
time. Mean go signal reaction time was calculated after each block, and
the delays for the next block were determined by the means from the
immediately previous block.[5] The data gathered by this procedure are
plotted in the middle panel of the second row of Figure 3; the left and
right panels represent transformations of mean minus delay. These
functions capture much of the range from 0 to 1 for both tasks.[6]

C. Relative Finishing Time as a Z Score

Inhibition functions generated by setting delay relative to mean reaction time will be aligned only if the go-signal distributions differ only
in mean reaction time. If they differ substantially in variance, then functions set relative to the mean will not produce equivalent probabilities
of responding. This can be seen in Figure 4, where the two panels depict
two go signal reaction time distributions that differ substantially in variance. Two stop signals are presented at equivalent delays in the two
conditions. Their finishing times are depicted as vertical lines intersect-
ing the go signal reaction time distributions. The figure shows that the
two stop signal delays cut off different proportions of the distributions.
They cut off the upper and lower tails off the low-variability distribution, whereas they cut off the upper and lower thirds of the high-
variability distribution. The inhibition function for the condition with
the greater variability would be flatter than the function for the condition with the lesser variability.

One solution to this problem, proposed by Logan et al. (1984) is to
plot inhibition functions in terms of a Z score that represents the relative
finishing time of the stop and go processes in standard deviation units,
using the standard deviation of the go signal reaction times to define the
units: specifically, Z relative finishing time or

[5]Delays for the first block were set arbitrarily. Schachar and Logan (1990a) used a similar
method, calculating delays relative to the mean reaction time from the previous block,
but the first block did not require subjects to inhibit responses when they heard the stop
signal. This allowed the experimenter to introduce the task gradually and emphasize the
importance of responding quickly to the go task.

[6]There is a potential for confusion in discussing this transformation and relating it to
delays defined in terms of stimulus onsets, which Schachar and Logan (1990a; mostly
Logan) fell prey to in describing the procedure for setting delays (p. 712). The transformation, called *mean minus delay*, reverses the ordering of the delays. The shortest stop
signal delay is the largest mean minus delay, and vice versa. It is important to keep this
clear in discussing how the probability of responding (or inhibiting) changes with stop
signal delay versus mean minus delay. The probability of responding increases as stop
signal delay increases and decreases as mean minus delay increases.

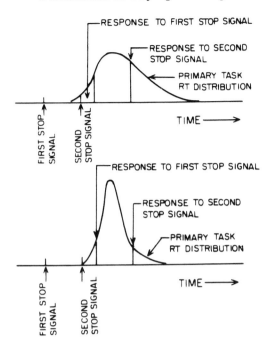

FIGURE 4

The effects of variability of go-process reaction times on inhibition functions, shown by comparing the effects of two stop signals presented at different delays on distributions with more (top panel) and less (bottom panel) variability.

$$\text{ZRFT} = (\overline{T}_g - t_d - \overline{T}_s)/S_g \tag{8}$$

where $\overline{T}_g$, t_d, and $\overline{T}_s$ are mean go-signal reaction time, stop signal delay, and mean stop signal reaction time, respectively, as defined above, and S_g is an estimate of the standard deviation of the go-signal reaction times.

The motivation for including stop signal reaction time, $\overline{T}_s$, in Eq. (8) can be seen in Figure 1. The idea is to express the relative finishing times of the stop and go processes. The mean go signal reaction time provides some estimate of the finishing time of the go process. The finishing time of the stop process, represented by the vertical line across the go signal reaction time distribution in Figure 1, is the sum of two components: stop signal delay, t_d, and stop signal reaction time, $\overline{T}_s$. The relative finishing time is the difference between these estimates [i.e., $\overline{T}_g - (t_d + \overline{T}_s)$].

In practice, ZRFT is calculated by estimating the mean and standard deviation of go signal reaction time, estimating stop signal reaction time, and choosing arbitrary delays to produce evenly spaced Z scores.

It can be calculated post hoc to bring different inhibition functions into alignment (see Logan & Cowan, 1984; Logan et al., 1984; Schachar & Logan, 1990a), or it can be calculated dynamically, estimating each of the parameters each block. The third row of Figure 3 contains inhibition functions from the simple- and choice-reaction go tasks in Logan et al. (1984) that were generated by selecting delays in terms of ZRFT, calculating the parameters of each block, and setting the ZRFTs for the next block. Stop signal reaction time was calculated for each delay, and the average over delays was used in Eq. (8). The data collected by this method are plotted in the right panel in the bottom row of Figure 3. The other two panels contain transformations of ZRFT. These functions capture much of the range from 0 to 1 for both tasks.[7]

D. Relative to Go Signal Reaction Time Distribution

The finishing time of the stop process relative to the go process may be represented as a point on the distribution of go signal reaction times. In Figure 1, it is drawn as a vertical line across the distribution. The ZRFT method tries to estimate that point as a Z score, in order to capture differences in variability as well as differences in means. However, inhibition functions will be aligned when plotted against ZRFT only if the distribution of go signal reaction times is normal or approximately normal. If it is skewed, as reaction time distributions typically are, then ZRFT will not produce perfect alignment.

One solution to this problem, attempted by Kramer et al. (1992), is to set stop signal delays relative to the go signal reaction time distribution directly. They targeted specific percentiles of the go signal reaction time distribution and set delays so that the stopping process should finish at those percentiles. Subjects were tested in four sessions, one baseline session and three sessions with the stopping task. In the baseline session, subjects performed the go task as a single task and the 20th, 40th, 60th, and 80th percentiles of each subject's reaction time distribution

---

[7]There is potential for confusion with ZRFT as well, that Schachar and Logan (1990a), this time entirely Logan, fell prey to. ZRFT reverses the ordering of delays, relative to stop signal delay. ZRFT decreases as stop signal delay increases. When calculating the ZRFT values for Figure 2 (the clinical study) in Schachar and Logan (1990a), I added stop signal delay to mean minus delay instead of subtracting it. This resulted in an artifactual horizontal separation of the inhibition functions for the different groups. When ZRFT is calculated correctly and the data are replotted, the different inhibition functions are aligned horizontally. However, even with this alignment, the inhibition function was flatter for hyperactive children than for normal controls, and that is the important point to be taken from the analysis. In fact, the difference in slope was the main basis for the conclusion that hyperactive children were deficient inhibitors. This conclusion was correct even if the figure was wrong.

were calculated. Subjects also performed a simple reaction time task, responding to the stop signal tones, which were presented on the same schedule as they would be in the stopping task itself. These simple reaction times to the onsets of the tones were used as estimates of stop signal reaction times. They were calculated for each subject and subtracted from the go signal reaction times at the target percentiles to produce stop signal delays. That is,

$$t_d = x - \overline{T}_s,$$

where x is the target percentile on the cumulative distribution of go signal reaction times, $F_g(x)$. These estimates were revised each session, using the data from the previous session to set the new delays.

This technique produced nice inhibition functions. The probability of responding was close to the value of the target percentile, except for the shorter delays where subjects responded more often than predicted. The main problem with this technique is that it does not guarantee that stop delays will be equally spaced on the time axis, as the other methods do. The skew typical of reaction time distributions means that equal intervals on the (cumulative) probability axis will generally not produce equal intervals on the time axis. Equal time intervals are important primarily for some statistical analyses (such as analysis of variance); they are not important in theory.

E. Tracking Stopping Performance

All of the techniques reviewed so far track parameters of the go task. Osman et al. (1986) developed a method for setting stop signal delays that tracks subjects' stopping performance. They used three different delays—early, middle, and late—and had a different rule for changing each delay. The middle delay was increased by 50 msec every time the subject inhibited, and decreased by 50 msec every time the subject responded. On average, subjects should respond half of the time and inhibit half of the time to delays set by this rule. The early delay was decreased by 50 msec every time the subject responded, and increased by 50 msec every time the subject inhibited twice consecutively. On average, subjects should respond 29% of the time and inhibit 71% of the time with delays set by this rule. The late delay was increased by 50 msec every time the subject inhibited, and decreased by 50 msec every time the subject responded twice consecutively. On average, subjects should respond 71% of the time and inhibit 29% of the time to delays set by this rule. Osman et al. (1986) found observed probabilities of responding that were very close to the predicted values.

The observed probabilities of responding at early, middle, and late delays do not reflect the inhibition function, however. The tracking algorithm guaranteed that each subject experienced several different values of t_d for early delay, some of the same values and some different ones for the middle delay, and another overlapping range for the late delay. In order to calculate inhibition functions, Osman et al. (1986) collapsed data across early, middle, and late delays and plotted the probability of responding at each value of t_d they used in the experiment (the tracking algorithm varied t_d in 50 msec increments). This procedure produced inhibition functions that covered the range from 0 to 1, but the number of observations was not distributed evenly across values of t_d, so many of the inhibition functions were nonmonotonic. Osman et al. (1986) smoothed the inhibition function for each subject by finding the monotonic function with the best least squares fit to the observed inhibition function. The mean of the smoothed function was calculated for further analysis. The distinction between early, middle, and late delays plays no part of this analysis, so Osman et al. (1990) dropped the early and late delays in subsequent experiments and calculated inhibition functions in the same fashion. They found that the tracking algorithm for the middle delay produced enough different values of t_d to produce inhibition functions that covered the range from 0 to 1.

The main problem with this method is the difficulty of computing inhibition functions. The fact that early, middle, and late delays do not correspond to distinct values of t_d may raise problems for data analysis (for reasons described in G. Computing Inhibition Functions).

De Jong et al. (1990) used a variation of Osman's technique. Osman et al. (1990) changed delays on every stop signal trial, but that was impractical for a psychophysiological study in which event-related potentials had to be averaged across several trials to be recovered from the data. De Jong et al. needed fixed delays. They compromised by running a practice session using the Osman et al. tracking technique, calculated the average, short, middle, and long delays, and fixed those values for the test session during which psychophysiological measures were recorded. In the data from their test session, early, middle, and late delays each corresponded to single values of t_d, so they could be interpreted directly as inhibition functions, without the subsequent curve-fitting process of Osman et al. (1986, 1990). De Jong et al. got nice looking inhibition functions from this procedure.

F. Other Contingencies

Jennings et al. (1992) produced inhibition functions of a different type by holding stop signal delay constant and varying reaction time by imposing various deadlines on go task performance. They used two stop signal delays (50 and 150 msec) and four deadlines (225, 300, 375, and 400 msec). Their analyses suggested violations of the race model with the 50-msec delay, so they focused on the 150-msec delay and compared inhibition performance across deadlines. They tested the independence assumption of the race model, for example, by comparing estimates of stop signal reaction time in the different deadlines and finding that it was nearly constant.

It is possible to present stop signals contingent on events external to the stop signal paradigm, events that are not directly involved in processing the stop signal and the go signal but are interesting nevertheless. The experiment of Jennings et al. (1992) is interesting again in this regard. Jennings et al. (1992) presented go and stop stimuli presented contingent on the phase of the subject's heartbeat, and found that responses inhibited during a sensitive period between heartbeats delayed the next heartbeat. Jennings et al. (1992) interpreted this result as suggesting that stop signal inhibition may involve the same midbrain structures as the processes that control heart rate (see also De Jong et al., 1990).

G. Computing Inhibition Functions

In theory, the different methods for choosing stop signal delays are equivalent because any one measure can be transformed into any other. In practice, however, the different methods exert different constraints on the computation and analysis of inhibition functions. Points that are equivalent under one transformation will generally not be equivalent under other transformations. If the data are grouped tightly according to values of one transformation, they may be spread across the function in some other transformation. For example, an experiment that tests all subjects at the same values of ZRFT will test different subjects at different values of stop signal delay. The actual stop signal delays will vary with the mean and standard deviation of each subject's go task reaction times and with each subject's stop signal reaction time. The tracking technique of Osman et al. (1986) is extreme in this regard. It groups observations very tightly into early, middle, and late delays, but the observations in each category are made at several different values of stop signal delay (t_d). Different subjects are unlikely to cover the same range of stop signal delays and are unlikely to have the same number of observations in the delays they happen to share.

The importance of grouping or spreading observations along the various transformations of delays depends on the data analysis techniques one wishes to employ. Standard techniques like analysis of variance require tight grouping—several levels of the delay factor with an equal number of observations at each level. They can be applied only to the transformation by which delays are selected (i.e., the transformation in which grouping is tight). Other transformations must be analyzed by other methods.

X. DETECTING DEFICIENT INHIBITION

The main use of the stop signal paradigm is to compare the ability to inhibit in different tasks, conditions, strategies, and subject populations. A major goal in these comparisons is to detect and diagnose deficient inhibition. What can go wrong with the stopping mechanism? It can become slower and more variable, and it can fail to be triggered. Each of these effects would diminish the ability to inhibit. Slower and more variable stop signal reaction times would be more likely to lose the race with the go process, decreasing the probability of inhibition. And if the stopping process failed to be triggered altogether—if it acted as if no stop signal were presented—the probability of inhibition would decrease even further.

So far, the analysis sounds straightforward: look for decreases in the probability of inhibition. The problem with that simple analysis is that there are ways to decrease the probability of inhibition without impairing the stopping process. A faster go process, for example, would be harder to stop than a slower one simply because of its speed. So a decrease in the probability of inhibition does not necessarily imply deficient inhibition. A more complex analysis is required, one that uses the race model. The idea is to try to account for differences in the probability of inhibition—differences in inhibition functions—by testing a series of hypotheses. Differences in the inhibition functions due to differences in go processes are removed, and residual differences are interpreted in terms of the stop process. Some residual differences reflect differences in the speed of the stop process; others reflect differences in the variability of the stop process or differences in the probability of triggering the stop process.

The analysis consists of three phases. First, the inhibition functions are inspected to see if they are interpretable. In order to be interpretable, they must capture some of the middle part of the inhibition function, where the probability of responding is, say, between .1 and .9. Functions in which subjects nearly always inhibit or nearly always respond are not interpretable within the race model (although the race model can inform their interpretation; see the third phase). Inhibition functions that are flat (i.e., in which the probability of inhibition does not vary with stop signal delay) are also not interpretable within the race model.

For example, subjects may withhold a certain proportion of their responses whether or not a stop signal occurred. This would flatten their inhibition functions, adding the same number of inhibited responses to each part of the inhibition function. This strategy can be detected on go signal trials; the proportion of missed responses on go signal trials can be used to correct the inhibition function (see Tannock et al., 1989).

Flat inhibition functions are diagnostic of an inhibitory deficit. Most people can inhibit responses on request and produce reasonable inhibition functions. Someone who cannot is deficient in the ability to inhibit. Flat inhibition functions could also mean poor experimental control. The stop signals could have been presented too early or too late to capture the interesting part of the inhibition function. To tell the difference, it is helpful to have a control group with stop signal delays selected in the same manner as the group in question (i.e., so as to have the same opportunity to inhibit). If the control group's inhibition function is "reasonable" (i.e., not flat), the flat inhibition functions of the group in question reflect an inhibitory deficit. If the control group's inhibition function is also flat, the delays are inappropriate.

If the inhibition functions are reasonable, the second phase of the logic begins. The race model is fitted to the data. Inhibition functions are calculated and the transformations just described are applied in an attempt to bring the functions into alignment. If the functions can be brought into alignment, then the fit is successful. The race model applies to the data set. The different tasks, conditions, strategies, or subject populations have the same stopping process with different parameters. Differences in the parameters of the fitted model are then interpreted within the race model. If mean minus delay is sufficient to bring the functions into alignment, then the differences in the inhibition functions are due only to differences in mean go signal reaction time. The stopping process is essentially the same. It is executed with the same probability and latency in the different tasks, conditions, strategies, or subject populations. If mean minus delay brings the functions into alignment, there is no inhibitory deficit.

If mean minus delay does not bring the functions into alignment, I suggest trying mean minus delay minus stop signal reaction time (i.e., the numerator of Eq. (8): $\overline{T}_g - t_d - \overline{T}_s$) as the next transformation. If the functions can be brought into alignment with this transformation, then differences in the inhibition functions are due to differences in mean go signal reaction time and differences in mean stop signal reaction time. Differences in stop signal reaction time have to be interpreted. They could reflect a specific deficit in inhibition (as in hyperactive children) or a general slowing that affects go processes as well as stop processes (as in young children; Schachar & Logan, 1990a).

If mean minus delay minus stop signal reaction time does not bring the functions into alignment, ZRFT should be tried. If ZRFT brings the functions into alignment, then the tasks, conditions, strategies, or subject populations differ in the standard deviation of go signal reaction time. There are generally differences in mean go signal reaction time and stop signal reaction time as well when ZRFT brings the functions into alignment. They need to be interpreted if they appear. Note, however, that differences in the mean and standard deviation of go signal reaction time should be interpreted differently from differences in stop signal reaction time. They reflect differences in the go task. Differences in stop signal reaction time may indicate a deficient stopping process.

If the race model cannot be fitted to the data successfully—if the inhibition functions cannot be brought into alignment by some transformation—then the third phase of the logic begins. The failed alignment means that the race model does not apply to one of the tasks, conditions, strategies, or subject populations, and it is the experimenter's job to find out which one it is. In many cases, one of the tasks, conditions, strategies, or subject populations is considered "normal" or "standard" and the other is considered as a possible deviation. Children with no psychiatric problems are considered normal in studies of psychopathology. College-age adults provide standards against which others are compared in studies of life span development.

Often, failed alignment means that one inhibition function has a flatter slope than the other even after ZRFT correction. The difference in slope reflects a deficiency in the stop process. It can be interpreted in two ways. First, it could indicate greater variability in the stop process. The slope of the inhibition function depends on the variability of the stop process as well as variability in the go process, and the ZRFT transformation only corrects for differences in go process variability [see Eq. (3)]. Subjects with more variable stop processes would produce flatter inhibition functions even after ZRFT correction. Second, a difference in slope could mean that the inhibition process was executed or triggered less often. Failing to trigger the inhibition process on a constant proportion of the trials would produce a shallower inhibition function. The lowest probability of responding would not be 0.0, as with a normal inhibition function. Subjects would respond whenever the inhibition process failed to be triggered, so the lowest probability of responding would be the probability that the inhibition process failed to be triggered, P_f. The inhibition function itself would be compressed. It would range from P_f to 1.0, compressed by a factor of $1 - P_f$. Formally,

$$P_o(t_d) = (1 - P_f) \cdot P_r(t_d) + P_f \tag{9}$$

where $P_o(t_d)$ is the observed inhibition function and $P_r(t_d)$ is the "true" inhibition function for those trials on which the stopping process is triggered by the stop signal.

A difference in slope after ZRFT correction does not discriminate between these alternatives. It may be possible to discriminate them by using stop signal delays short enough to estimate the lower asymptote of the inhibition function, which can be interpreted as a measure of P_f. Equation 9 can then be used to separate the effects of failing to trigger from the effects of increased variability; residual differences in slope not accounted for by Eq. 9 would reflect differences in variability. It may also be possible to use some other method to estimate the variability of the stop signal reaction times. The analyses of signal respond reaction times suggested by Colonius (1990) can be used to estimate the distribution of stop signal times, from which the variance can be calculated. Equation (3) can then be used to separate the effects of differences in variability from differences in triggering; slope differences that remained after subtracting out differences due to variability would reflect differences in triggering probability.

XI. STOPPING IN THE FUTURE

What lies ahead for the stop signal paradigm? I think the next important step will be to understand the nature of the stopping process. This can be done in several ways, but four deserve special mention. First, more research must be done to discover the relations between stop signal inhibition and other forms of inhibition. Relations between stop signal inhibition and behavioral measures of inhibition, such as negative priming and Stroop interference, must be worked out empirically and theoretically. Second, more research must be done on the brain systems underlying stop signal inhibition. The hypothesized distinction between central and peripheral, cortical and midbrain inhibition systems needs further investigation. Drug studies may reveal the psychopharmacology of the processes involved. Studies of patients with inhibitory problems would be interesting in this regard. Third, more research must be done on deficiencies in the stopping process. Encouraged by our work with hyperactive children, Schachar, Tannock, and I are looking for inhibitory deficits in other clinical groups. The stop signal paradigm might be used more generally to study inhibitory psychopathology, such as that evidenced by people with psychopathic personalities. It would be quite interesting to look at the stopping performance of patients with frontal lobe damage, who have trouble with inhibitory control. Fourth, more research must be done on life span developmental changes in stopping performance. It is important to look at children much younger than those Schachar and Logan (1990a) examined to learn when the ability to inhibit is first acquired and to study its early development. The work of Kramer et al. (1992) suggests that investigations of stop signal inhibition in aging may be very fruitful.

ACKNOWLEDGMENTS

I wrote this chapter while I was a visiting professor at the University of Amsterdam. I am grateful to the Developmental Psychology group for their hospitality and stimulation. I was lucky enough to get reactions from many of the people whose research has shaped the current state of stopping research. I am grateful to Ritske De Jong, Darryl Humphrey, Art Kramer, Allen Osman, Russell Schachar, Rosemary Tannock, and Maurits van der Molen for valuable comments and suggestions. They may not endorse everything I say here, but their comments made it clearer, broader, and more representative. Tom Carr and Dale Dagenbach provided excellent editorial comments, for which I am grateful.

REFERENCES

Berlyne, D. E. (1957). Uncertainty and conflict: A point of contact between information-theory and behavior-theory concepts. *Psychological Review, 64*, 329–339.

Bjorklund, D. F., & Harnishfeger, K. K. (1990). The resources construct in cognitive development: Diverse sources of evidence and a theory of inefficient inhibition. *Developmental Review, 10*, 48–71.

Brooks, V. D. (1986). *The neural basis of motor control.* New York: Oxford University Press.

Bullock, D., & Grossberg, S. (1988). Neural dynamics of planned arm movements: Emerging invariants and speed–accuracy properties during trajectory formation. *Psychological Review, 95*, 49–90.

Carr, T. H., & Dagenbach, D. (1990). Semantic priming and repetition priming from masked words: Evidence for a center-surround mechanism in perceptual recognition. *Journal of Experimental Psychology: Learning, Memory and Cognition, 16*, 341–350.

Colonius, H. (1990). A note on the stop-signal paradigm, or how to observe the unobservable. *Psychological Review, 97*, 309–312.

Dagenbach, D., Carr, T. H., & Barnhardt, T. (1990). Inhibitory semantic priming of lexical decisions due to failure to retrieve weakly activated primes. *Journal of Experimental Psychology: Learning, Memory and Cognition, 16*, 328–339.

De Jong, R. (in press). Multiple bottlenecks in overlapping-task performance. *Journal of Experimental Psychology: Human Perception and Performance.*

De Jong, R., Coles, M. G. H., Logan, G. D., & Gratton, G. (1990). Searching for the point of no return: The control of response processes in speeded choice reaction performance. *Journal of Experimental Psychology: Human Perception and Performance, 16*, 164–182.

Dell, G. S. (1986). A spreading-activation theory of sentence production. *Psychological Review, 93*, 283–321.

Eriksen, B. A., & Eriksen, C. W. (1974). Effects of noise letters upon the identification of a target letter in a nonsearch task. *Perception and Psychophysics, 16*, 143–149.

Fletcher, B., & Rabbitt, P. M. A. (1978). The changing pattern of perceptual analytic strategies and response selection with practice in a two-choice reaction time task. *Quarterly Journal of Experimental Psychology, 30,* 417–427.

Hasher, L. T., & Zacks, R. T. (1989). Working memory, comprehension, and aging: A review and a new view. In G. H. Bower (Ed.), *The psychology of learning and motivation* (Vol. 22). Orlando, FL: Academic Press.

Henry, F. M., & Harrison, J. S. (1961). Refractoriness of a fast movement. *Perceptual and Motor Skills, 13,* 351–354.

Jennings, J. R., van der Molen, M. W., Brock, K., & Somsen, R. J. M. (1992). On the synchrony of stopping motor responses and delaying heartbeats. *Journal of Experimental Psychology: Human Perception and Performance, 18,* 422–436.

Jennings, J. R., & Wood, C. C. (1977). Cardiac cycle time effects on performance, phasic cardiac responses and their intercorrelation in choice reaction time. *Psychophysiology, 13,* 297–307.

Kornblum, S. (1973). Sequential effects in choice reaction time: A tutorial review. In S. Kornblum (Ed.), *Attention and performance IV* (pp. 259–288). New York: Academic Press.

Kornblum, S., Hasbroucq, T., & Osman, A. (1990). Dimensional overlap: Cognitive basis for stimulus–response compatibility—A model and taxonomy. *Psychological Review, 97,* 253–270.

Kramer, A. F., Humphrey, D. G., Larish, J., Logan, G. D., & Strayer, D. L. (1992, March). *Aging and inhibition.* Paper presented at the Conference on Cognition and Aging, Atlanta, GA.

Ladefoged, P., Silverstein, R., & Papcun, G. (1973). Interruptibility of speech. *Journal of the Acoustical Society of America, 54,* 1105–1108.

Lappin, J. S., & Eriksen, C. W. (1966). Use of a delayed signal to stop a visual reaction time response. *Journal of Experimental Psychology, 72,* 805–811.

Lashley, K. S. (1951). The problem of serial order in behavior. In L. A. Jefress (Ed.), *Cerebral mechanisms in behavior* (pp. 112–136). New York: Wiley.

Levelt, W. J. M. (1983). Monitoring and self-repair in speech. *Cognition, 14,* 41–104.

Logan, G. D. (1981). Attention, automaticity, and the ability to stop a speeded choice response. In J. Long & A. D. Baddeley (Eds.), *Attention and performance IX.* Hillsdale, NJ: Lawrence Erlbaum.

Logan, G. D. (1982). On the ability to inhibit complex actions: A stop-signal study of typewriting. *Journal of Experimental Psychology: Human Perception and Performance, 8,* 778–792.

Logan, G. D. (1983). On the ability to inhibit simple thoughts and actions: 1. Stop signal studies of decision and memory. *Journal of Experimental Psychology: Learning, Memory and Cognition, 9,* 585–606.

Logan, G. D. (1985). On the ability to inhibit simple thoughts and actions: 2. Stop-signal studies of repetition priming. *Journal of Experimental Psychology: Learning, Memory and Cognition, 11,* 675–691.

Logan, G. D. (1990). Repetition priming and automaticity: Common underlying mechanisms? *Cognitive Psychology, 22,* 1–35.

Logan, G. D., & Burkell, J. (1986). Dependence and independence in responding to double stimulation: A comparison of stop, change, and dual-task paradigms. *Journal of Experimental Psychology: Human Perception and Performance, 12,* 549–563.

Logan, G. D., & Cowan, W. B. (1984). On the ability to inhibit thought and action: A theory of an act of control. *Psychological Review, 91,* 295–327.

Logan, G. D., Cowan, W. B., & Davis, K. A. (1984). On the ability to inhibit responses in simple and choice reaction time tasks: A model and a method. *Journal of Experimental Psychology: Human Perception and Performance, 10,* 276–291.

Logan, G. D., Kantowitz, B. H., & Riegler, G. L. (1986). *On the ability to inhibit selectively: Mechanisms of response interdiction in choice reaction time.* Unpublished manuscript, Purdue University.

Long, J. (1976). Visual feedback and skilled keying: Differential effects of masking the printed copy and the keyboard. *Ergonomics, 19,* 93–110.

Lowe, D. G. (1979). Strategies, context, and the mechanism of response inhibition. *Memory & Cognition, 7,* 382–389.

Megaw, E. D. (1972). Directional errors and their correction in discrete tracking task. *Ergonomics, 15,* 633–643.

Neill, W. T. (1977). Inhibitory and facilitatory processes in selective attention. *Journal of Experimental Psychology: Human Perception and Performance, 3,* 444–450.

Ollman, R. T. (1973). Simple reactions with random countermanding of the "go" signal. In S. Kornblum (Ed.), *Attention and performance IV* (pp. 571–581). New York: Academic Press.

Osman, A., Kornblum, S., & Meyer, D. E. (1986). The point of no return in choice reaction time: Controlled and ballistic stages of response preparation. *Journal of Experimental Psychology: Human Perception and Performance, 12,* 243–258.

Osman, A., Kornblum, S., & Meyer, D. E. (1990). Does response programming necessitate response execution? *Journal of Experimental Psychology: Human Perception and Performance, 16,* 183–198.

Pashler, H. (1984). Processing stages in overlapping tasks: Evidence for a central bottleneck. *Journal of Experimental Psychology: Human Perception and Performance, 10,* 358–377.

Pashler, H. (1989). Dissociations and dependencies between speed and accuracy: Evidence for a two-component theory of divided attention in simple tasks. *Cognitive Psychology, 21,* 469–514.

Posner, M. I., & Cohen, Y. (1984). Components of visual orienting. In H. Bouma & D. Bouwhuis (Eds.), *Attention and performance X.* Hillsdale, NJ: Lawrence Erlbaum.

Posner, M. I., & Snyder, C. R. R. (1975). Attention and cognitive control. In R. L. Solso (Ed.), *Information processing and cognition: The Loyola symposium* (pp. 55–85). Hillsdale, NJ: Lawrence Erlbaum.

Rabbitt, P. M. A. (1978). Detection of errors by skilled typists. *Ergonomics, 21,* 945–958.

Reason, J. T., & Myceilska, K. (1982). *Absent minded: The psychology of mental lapses and everyday errors.* Englewood Cliffs, NJ: Prentice Hall.

Riegler, G. L. (1986). *Are stop and go processes independent in the stop-signal paradigm?* Unpublished master's thesis, Purdue University, West Lafayette, IN.

Rumelhart, D. E., & McClelland, J. L. (Eds.). (1986). *Parallel distributed processing: Explorations in the microstructure of cognition* (Vols. 1 and 2). Cambridge, MA: MIT Press.

Rumelhart, D. E., & Norman, D. A. (1982). Simulating a skilled typist: A study of skilled cognitive-motor performance. *Cognitive Science, 6,* 1–36.

Salthouse, T. A. (1986). Perceptual, cognitive, and motoric aspects of transcription typing. *Psychological Bulletin, 99,* 303–319.

Schachar, R. J., & Logan, G. D. (1990a). Impulsivity and inhibitory control in normal development and childhood psychopathology. *Developmental Psychology, 26,* 710–720.

Schachar, R. J., & Logan, G. D. (1990b). Are hyperactive children deficient in attentional capacity? *Journal of Abnormal Child Psychology, 18,* 493–513.

Schachar, R. J., Marriott, M., Tannock, R., & Logan, G. D. (submitted). *Control of response processes in attention deficit hyperactivity disorder.*

Shiffrin, R. M., & Schneider, W. (1977). Controlled and automatic human information processing: 2. Perceptual learning, automatic attending, and a general theory. *Psychological Review, 84,* 127–190.

Sternberg, S. (1969). Discovery of processing stages: Extensions of Donders' method. *Acta Psychologica, 30,* 276–315.

Tannock, R., Schachar, R. J., Carr, R. P., Chajczyk, D., & Logan, G. D. (1989). Effects of methylphenidate on inhibitory control in hyperactive children. *Journal of Abnormal Child Psychology, 17,* 473–491.

Tannock, R., Schachar, R. J., & Logan, G. D. (submitted). *Methylphenidate and cognitive flexibility: Dissociated dose effects on behavior and cognition in hyperactive children.*

Tipper, S. P. (1985). The negative priming effect: Inhibitory priming by ignored objects. *Quarterly Journal of Experimental Psychology, 37A,* 571–590.

Treisman, A., & Sato, S. (1990). Conjunction search revisited. *Journal of Experimental Psychology: Human Perception and Performance, 16,* 459–478.

Vallacher, R. R., & Wegner, D. M. (1987). What do people think they're doing? Action identification and human behavior. *Psychological Review, 94,* 3–15.

Vince, M. A. (1948). The intermittency of control movements and the psychological refractory period. *British Journal of Psychology, 38,* 149–157.

Welford, A. T. (1952). The "psychological refractory period" and the timing of high-speed performance. *British Journal of Psychology, 43,* 2–19.

Wickens, D. D. (1970). Encoding categories of words: An empirical approach to meaning. *Psychological Review, 77,* 1–15.

Zbrodoff, N. J., & Logan, G. D. (1986). On the autonomy of mental processes: A case study of arithmetic. *Journal of Experimental Psychology: General, 115,* 118–130.

6

Directed Ignoring
Inhibitory Regulation
of Working Memory

Rose T. Zacks and Lynn Hasher

I. INTRODUCTION

Parents of teenage children suffer inordinately at the hands of their children and a key component of this suffering is induced by the adolescent's ability to ignore a wide range of stimulation, from background music, to television noise, to a ringing telephone, to, most irritatingly of all, parental speech. These are all examples of a category of behaviors that we call *directed ignoring.* Sometimes, as for the teenagers of our example, the reason for ignoring information is an internally driven one (in this case, something like intense absorption in self-directed thought). Other times the reason for ignoring information is externally driven, as occurs, for example, when there is a change in topic or a sudden change in stimulation—formerly relevant information must now be ignored and new information attended in order to accommodate the change. The importance of directed ignoring for a coherent mental life and for organized behavior is considerable and in this chapter we begin to make this argument by providing a number of formal examples of internally and externally driven directed ignoring behaviors. We take as our central task, however, to demonstrate the role of an attentional mechanism—inhibition—in fostering or limiting the ability to engage in directed ignoring behaviors. To this end, we report research that compares college-age young adults (who are only a little older than the teenagers of our example) to individuals at the other end of the adult age continuum, old age, an age at which we believe directed ignoring becomes particularly impaired, an impairment which to a large extent can be attributed to a decline in the efficiency with which attentional inhibition operates.

We come at the issue of directed ignoring from a theoretical viewpoint which proposes that inhibitory attentional mechanisms play an essential role in the efficient operation of the cognitive system via their control over the contents of working memory (Hasher & Zacks, 1988). In this chapter, we briefly outline the theoretical framework, highlight some of the evidence that is consistent with the assumption that inhibitory control diminishes with age, and then describe some consequences for attention and memory of a reduced ability to control the contents of working memory, or to put it otherwise, the consequences of a diminished ability to ignore task-irrelevant information. The examples were chosen to demonstrate the fact that the larger theoretical framework itself has wide applicability to individual and group differences across a range of cognitive functions, including language comprehension, speech production, episodic memory, problem solving, and selective attention.

Building on models of attention that emphasize "selection for action" (e.g., Allport, 1989; Keele & Neill, 1978; Navon, 1989; Neumann, 1987), Hasher and Zacks (1988) proposed that there are two basic mechanisms of selective attention: activation and inhibition. Inhibition operates in the service of goals by hindering the access to working memory of goal-irrelevant information that may be activated in parallel with goal-relevant information. A similar argument has been made in a different context by Dagenbach and Carr (this volume), and by Carr et al. (in press). Inhibition also functions to suppress (or remove from working memory) whatever irrelevant information happens to leak in as well as information that is no longer relevant because of a change in goals. We (Stoltzfus, Hasher, Zacks, Ulivi, & Goldstein, 1993) have recently proposed that inhibition has the further function of preventing the return of attention to a previously rejected item, whether that item is an external stimulus event or a thought (a notion analogous to "inhibition of return" in visual search; Klein & Taylor, this volume; Rafal & Henik, this volume). In doing so, inhibition helps to maintain attention to selected information so as to enable the development of a coherent thought stream.

Our assumption, based on a close reading of the cognitive gerontology literature, is that older adults have deficient inhibitory mechanisms. Among the relevant findings are those indicating that older adults show increased rates of irrelevant and personalistic intrusions in speech (Gold, Andres, Arbuckle, & Schwartzman, 1988), increased rates of intrusion in free recall of sentences (Stine & Wingfield, 1987), and increased rates of repeating already produced responses (Koriat, Ben-Zur,

& Sheffer, 1988). Also, analysis of traffic accidents of older drivers (see Charness & Bosman, 1992) shows that they tend to have elevated accident rates primarily in situations where there are many potentially distracting stimuli, such as would occur when making turns at busy intersections or trying to enter a superhighway in heavy traffic. These actuarial data are consistent with self-reports of older drivers about the aspects of driving they find difficult (Kline et al., 1992), as well as with data from laboratory studies of selective attention which indicate that older adults are less able than younger adults to maintain the focus of attention on strictly task-relevant information and are often more easily distracted by the presence of irrelevant information in the environment (e.g., Cremer & Zeef, 1987; Rabbitt, 1965). Further, older adults, unlike younger adults, tend not to habituate to the presence of continuing distraction (McDowd & Filion, 1992). Taken together, this general pattern of findings is suggestive of a deficit in inhibitory attentional mechanisms in older adults.

The study of inhibitory processes in aging has recently become a focus of research in several laboratories, with the result that there is now substantial direct evidence of an age-related deficiency of inhibitory control over attention. For example, we and others (McDowd & Oseas-Kreger, 1991; Tipper, 1991) have found age differences in negative priming, currently taken as a key marker of attentional inhibition (Houghton & Tipper, this volume). The negative priming effect is seen in selective attention tasks when a stimulus that had served as an ignored or selected-against distractor on the preceding trial becomes the target on the subsequent trial. For young adults, responding to the target in this situation is slowed compared to a condition in which completely different stimuli occur on successive trials (e.g., Tipper & Cranston, 1985). Furthermore, we know that young adults show this effect across a range of materials, including letters, words, and pictures, and across different response modes and delays between one trial and the next (see Houghton & Tipper, this volume, for a review). By contrast, several studies have found that older adults do not reliably show the negative priming effect (Hasher, Stoltzfus, Zacks, & Rypma, 1991; McDowd & Oseas-Kreger, 1991; Stoltzfus et al., 1993; Kane, Hasher, Stoltzfus, Zacks, & Connelly, in press; Tipper, 1991). We note that this pattern of behavior is limited to situations in which the task requires response to the identity of the target, rather than its location (see Connelly & Hasher, in press, for indications that older adults show efficient inhibition when responding to target location rather than target identity). Thus, taken as a whole, the data on negative priming provide support for our assumption of reduced inhibitory attentional mechanisms in older adults.

Two aspects of inhibitory control over the contents of working memory are relevant to our concern with directed ignoring. The first centers on the ability to screen out irrelevant stimuli while attending to task-relevant ones. The second centers on the ability to switch the focus of attention in response to changes either in goals or in the structure of information. Consider goals. When a particular goal is satisfied, the recent past may no longer be relevant and, if that is the case, then abandoning the sustained activation of ideas that were connected with the no longer relevant information becomes appropriate. Similarly, suppressing no longer relevant ideas is beneficial in situations in which there is a dramatic change in the structure of information. One such change occurs for "garden path" sentences or passages, in which an initial interpretation (either semantic or syntactic) proves to be incorrect and therefore irrelevant. Inhibition, as a key mechanism for influencing what is active in working memory, has a major role to play in such situations; its function is to eliminate from working memory those ideas connected to the satisfied goal or to the misleading information in the front end of a garden path sentence or passage. Basically, our argument is as follows: Inhibition plays a role in situations in which the recent past is no longer relevant. The appropriate response to this, in many situations, is to discontinue maintenance of activation toward that information or to ignore it. Inhibition is a key aspect of successfully ignoring, at least on a momentary basis, the no longer relevant past. Insofar as older adults are deficient at inhibition, disrupted patterns of learned ignoring should be seen.

In this chapter, we point to five lines of work that are consistent with an age-related reduction in the ability to optimize directed ignoring. We note that although in each case our comparison is between younger and older adults, there may well be circumstances in which younger adults also show such inhibitory deficits,[1] however this has not been extensively explored to date. In all the experiments we summarize here, the young subjects were college students and the old subjects were healthy, community-dwelling individuals with a mean age of 67–68 years. In addition, all the participants were given a vocabulary test; in the few cases where the two age groups differed in average vocabulary score, it was the older group who had the higher scores.

II. IGNORING CONCURRENT ENVIRONMENTAL DISTRACTION

The first line of research we consider is one that examines the ability to ignore stimuli that are presented along with target stimuli but which are explicitly designated as irrelevant. Certainly, the literature on aging

[1]Indeed, even adolescents may show an inability to ignore the recent past, even if relatively restricted to only those instances in which their parents have just said no.

contains many findings that are at least superficially consistent with our prediction about this situation. These come from studies on visual search, categorization, and Stroop tasks, among others. Although the size of age differences is dependent on many factors, the clear trend is for older adults to be more negatively impacted by a given amount of environmental distraction than younger adults. A recent study of ours will serve as an example.

In this study (Connelly, Hasher, & Zacks, 1991), subjects read aloud short texts which, in the experimental conditions, had distracting material interspersed among the text words. The target and distracting materials were in different fonts and subjects were instructed to read all the words in one font and to ignore all the words in the other font. In the first experiment of this study, the distracting material consisted of repetitions of four different words or short phrases that were meaningfully related to the texts. In the second experiment, three different types of distracting materials were used: strings of X's, words and short phrases that were unrelated (on the basis of meaning) to the to-be-read passage, and, as in the first experiment, words and short phrases that were meaningfully related to the to-be-read passage. On average, and in irregular places, an interruption occurred every four to five words of the target text.

In both of the Connelly et al. experiments, reading time was increased by distraction for younger as well as older adults, but the effects were substantially larger for the older groups. Furthermore, in Experiment 2 (see Figure 1), whereas the young participants were equally slowed by text-unrelated and text-related irrelevant verbal material, the older participants were more affected by text-related verbal distraction than by text-unrelated verbal distraction. Consistent with a considerable literature, the two Connelly et al. studies indicate that older adults have more difficulty ignoring distracting material than do younger adults. This difference is particularly true for distraction of the same category as the target material (here, words), and is even more the case when those distracting words are meaningfully related to the target material. The fact that the age difference was largest in the text-related condition is consistent with attentional findings previously summarized indicating that it is the inhibition of distractor identity which is particularly affected by aging.

III. IGNORING TO-BE-FORGOTTEN MATERIAL: DIRECTED FORGETTING STUDIES

The next line of research explores the directed ignoring of recently presented stimuli that have been designated as irrelevant by being

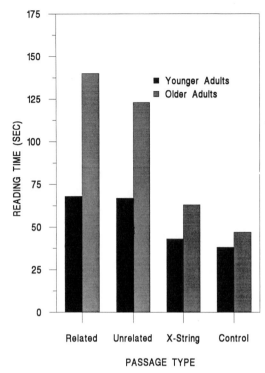

FIGURE 1

Reading times of younger and older adults as a function of different kinds of distraction. From "Age and reading: The impact of distraction" by S. L. Connelly, L. Hasher, and R. T. Zacks, 1991, *Psychology and Aging, 6*, 533–541, Figure 3. Copyright 1991 by the American Psychological Association. Adapted by permission.

marked as to be forgotten. Our reasoning here was that a diminished ability to comply with an instruction to ignore certain stimuli should be seen not only in relation to actually present stimuli, but also in relation to recently presented ones. To explore this idea, we have investigated directed forgetting in older adults (Zacks, Radvansky, & Hasher, 1993).

Research on directed forgetting is predicated on the intuition that active forgetting processes serve important functions. That is, it is frequently the case that being able to forget information that turned out to be wrong or that is no longer relevant is as important to attaining performance goals and maintaining emotional health as is being able to remember information that is correct and still relevant. Memory researchers have used a variety of procedures to study the ability to forget some inputs while remembering others presented in the same context and near the same time. The common feature of these procedures is that the cueing as to which items are to be remembered (TBR items) and which ones are to be forgotten (TBF items) occurs *after* the items have been presented for study, so that subjects cannot afford not to study each item as it is presented. The cueing can occur after each item, or after a group of items has been studied, or after the whole list has been presented. Regardless of the cueing procedure used, successful compliance with forget cueing is demonstrated by three phenomena. First, it can be seen in the absence of interference on the recall of TBR items from the inclusion of TBF items in the presentation list. That is, recall of TBR items is the same whether none, a few, or many TBF items have been presented prior to the TBR items. Second, successful directed forgetting is seen in the small number of intrusions of TBF items when subjects are instructed to recall only TBR items. Third and finally, successfully directed forgetting is seen in the poor recall or recognition of TBF items when, on a final memory test, participants are asked to recall or recognize all presented items. In general, young adults commonly show all these findings (see Bjork, 1989, for a review).

Current theories (Bjork, 1989; Geiselman & Bagheri, 1985; MacLeod, 1989) propose that multiple mechanisms underlie directed forgetting effects. These include stopping the rehearsal of an item following a forget cue, segregation of TBR and TBF items into distinct sets in memory, and inhibition of retrieval of TBF items. Together, these processes are thought to keep TBF items from interfering with the retrieval of TBR items on memory tests on which they *are not* to be retrieved and to produce low retrieval rates of TBF items on memory tests on which they *are* to be retrieved. It seems likely that attentional inhibition is centrally involved in these proposed mechanisms of directed forgetting effects, especially the first (ceasing to rehearse) and third (inhibition of retrieval); and so, our prediction was that older adults would be less successful in complying with directed forgetting instructions than younger adults.

We have completed several experiments on directed forgetting in older adults with fairly consistent results (Zacks et al., 1993). Here, we summarize the findings of two very similar experiments that used a procedure based on an experiment reported by Woodward and Bjork (1971, Experiment 2). In this procedure, subjects studied lists of 24 words, presented one at a time for 5 sec each. At the offset of each word, the subject was given a cue as to whether the *preceding* word should be remembered or forgotten. In each list there were 12 words of each type. Once the entire list had been presented, the subject tried to recall the remember words without intruding any of the forget words. This task was made harder by the fact that the 24 words in a list consisted of 4 words from each of 6 categories, presented in random order. And furthermore, within each category, forget cues were associated with 0,

1, 2, 3, or all 4 words, and remember cues with the rest. In one experiment, half of the items in each list were from exhaustive categories that have only four members each (e.g., north, south, east, and west), and half were high typicality members of nonexhaustive categories. In the other experiment, all the items were from nonexhaustive categories. In both experiments, following the presentation and immediate recall of six lists, participants attempted to recall all of the words, TBF words as well as TBR words. In the second experiment, this was followed by a yes/no recognition test for all TBR and TBF items on which the distractors came from categories that had been included on the presentation lists.

Performance on the immediate recall tests of both experiments is shown in Figure 2. Older adults recalled fewer TBR items than younger adults, but they *included* more TBF items in their recall (both differences are significant). On the final recall test (see Figure 3), younger adults outperformed older adults overall, and both groups produced more TBR than TBF items. One finding of particular interest is that the difference in recall of TBR and TBF items is smaller for the elderly as compared to the young subjects. To put this another way, especially in the second experiment, the older adults recall almost as many TBF items as the younger adults, but the older adults recall considerably fewer TBR items than the young. (In both experiments, the interaction between age and item type—TBR vs. TBF—is significant.) Similar findings were obtained on the final recognition test in the second experiment. This pattern of findings suggests that forget items receive more rehearsal at encoding and are less effectively blocked at retrieval for older, as compared to younger, adults. Taken together, the data from these directed forgetting studies and others we have done suggest that the elderly have a reduced ability to comply with the instruction to forget some of the presented items. This, we suggest, is due to deficient inhibitory mechanisms, mechanisms which, as Stoltzfus et al. (1993) suggest, ordinarily serve to cut off the past from continued consideration.

IV. IGNORING NO LONGER RELEVANT MATERIAL

A. Sentences with Unexpected Endings

Another situation in which we have studied older adults' difficulty suppressing no longer relevant information (Hartman & Hasher, 1991) involved the use of high-cloze sentence frames (e.g., *She ladled the soup into her* _____). Subjects read the sentence frames and tried to predict the ending for each. Because norms had established that each sentence frame elicited a particular ending with high probability, and because for

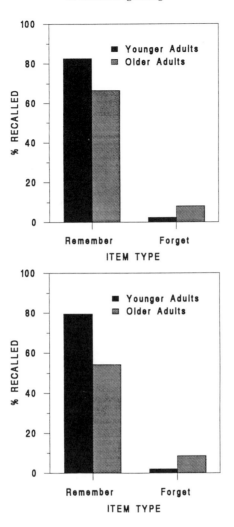

FIGURE 2

Younger and older adults' correct recall of TBR items and intrusions of TBF items on the immediate tests of two directed forgetting studies. The data in the top panel are from the experiment that used both exhaustive and nonexhaustive categories (Experiment 1); those in the bottom panel are from the study that used only nonexhaustive categories (Experiment 2). Both sets of data are from Zacks et al. (in preparation).

half of the frames (the filler items) the expected endings were confirmed, we assume that, for the most part, subjects predicted the high-cloze endings. For critical items, however, the predicted final word (*bowl*) was not shown. Instead, an unexpected but acceptable ending (*lap*) was provided as the target. Thus, in this task, subjects were asked to think of

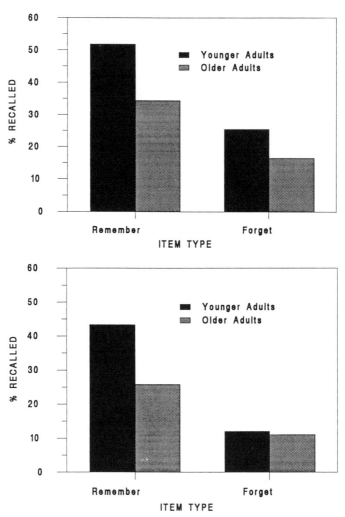

FIGURE 3

Younger and older adults' recall of TBR and TBF items on the delayed tests of two directed forgetting studies. The data in the top panel are from the experiment that used both exhaustive and nonexhaustive categories (Experiment 1); those in the bottom panel are from the study that used only nonexhaustive categories (Experiment 2). Both sets of data are from Zacks et al. (in preparation).

the last word of a sentence and then they were told the "correct," at least for experimental purposes, ending word. They were also told to remember the final words (the ones we provided) for a memory test of an unspecified sort.

The actual memory task (at least in the eyes of the experimenters, if not in those of most participants) was an indirect or implicit memory test in which subjects provided sentence completions for sentence frames of moderate cloze value. For each critical sentence in the first part of the experiment, there were two different frames included among the sentence completion materials: One of these was moderately predictive of the expected (but disconfirmed) ending (*bowl: Scotty licked the bottom of the* _____); the other was moderately predictive of the actual ending that had been presented (*lap: The kitten jumped on the owner's* _____). Control values for the probability of producing the experimental endings were obtained from subjects who had not been previously exposed to the relevant critical sentence. An increase from the control value for a particular test frame (i.e., a priming effect) was taken as evidence that the particular experimental word still had enhanced accessibility in memory.

The two test frames for each critical study sentence allowed us to assess memory for the ending that the subject had presumably originally thought about but should have suppressed when the correct one was given, as well as memory for the correct ending. The data were clear (see Figure 4): The young adults showed no priming effect for the disconfirmed endings; that is, *bowl* was no more accessible than if it had never been thought about in the context of the experiment. The older adults, by contrast, showed priming effects for both endings; that is, both *bowl* and *lap* were more accessible than if they had not been presented in the experimental context. Apparently, for older adults, being told that it was her *lap* not her *bowl* that "she" ladled her soup into does not result in the inhibition of *bowl*, whereas for younger adults, it does result in the inhibition of *bowl*. Another way to describe this situation is that older adults seem to have "richer" memory representations of the study sentences than do younger adults, in that they are more likely to maintain both the ending they initially thought about and the one given by the experimenter. In other words, older adults are not successfully ignoring endings that they generated but that proved irrelevant to the task.

B. Passages with Unexpected Twists

Another study (Hamm & Hasher, 1992) has implications similar to that of the Hartman and Hasher findings, but this time arrived at in the context of requiring participants to encode more elaborate texts, texts that again include garden path twists in the interpretation process. Thus, in this study, younger and older subjects were induced to encode material in a way that later turned out to be wrong. Here, too, a final

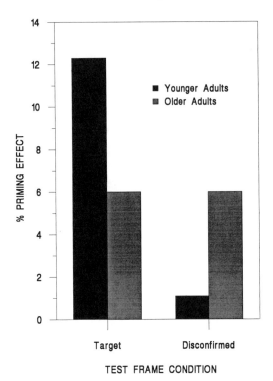

FIGURE 4

Priming effects shown by younger and older adults for the target and disconfirmed words.
Data are from Hartman and Hasher (1991).

correct interpretation was arrived at, this time by the participants themselves. One interest in this study was in the ability of the two groups to
access their initial interpretation (pre-garden-path twist) as well as their
final interpretation.

This study used a set of paragraph-length narrative passages modeled
on materials used in several earlier studies (Alba, 1984; Zacks & Hasher,
1988; Zacks, Hasher, Doren, Hamm, & Attig, 1987). Each passage has
two versions which differ in the degree to which there is contextual
support throughout the passage for the final correct interpretation of the
central situation described in the narrative. In the *expected* version, the
final interpretation is well supported from the beginning of the passage,
whereas in the *unexpected* version, an erroneous initial interpretation
is invited, and it is only after this interpretation has been established
that information is given which shows it to be wrong (i.e., the unexpected versions are actually garden path passages). For example, in the
expected version of "The Artist" passage, the opening sentences make

it clear that the artist has been waiting for a telephone call from his doctor about which he is very concerned. Consequently, it is no surprise when toward the middle of the passage, the doctor tells him the bad news indicating that he only has "three more months" to live. By contrast, the opening sentences of the *unexpected* version of the artist passage omit any mention of the artist's concern about an awaited call from his doctor, and instead imply that he is concerned about finishing the painting he is working on. Consequently, the initial interpretation of the "three more months" mentioned in the telephone call is that this is the amount of time the artist has to finish his painting. It is only when the bad news from the doctor is described that there is a clue that the initial interpretation is wrong.

Our earlier research with these materials involved delayed memory tests following encoding of the passages under different presentation modes. Consider, for example, an experiment (described in Zacks & Hasher, 1988) in which young and old subjects read these passages, displayed one sentence at a time on a computer screen, at their own rate. At the end of groups of six passages, they were given a cued recall memory test for the preceding six passages. Included among the questions asked about each passage was one that tested the subject's interpretation and memory for the central situation in the passage. For "The Artist" passage, that question was *The artist was told he had three more months to do what?* The answer we were looking for was that the artist had three more months to live.

The major finding in this experiment (see Figure 5) was that there was an age difference (favoring the young adults) in retrieval of the critical information for the unexpected but not for the expected passages. Our original interpretation of these data relied on the notion that older adults have a reduced working memory capacity. We argued that the effects of being able to maintain only a reduced amount of information in working memory should be especially apparent when demands on working memory capacity are high. We thought that encoding of the unexpected passages qualified as a situation placing high demands on working memory because, to reach the final correct interpretation of one of these passages, memory for the preceding text had to be consulted and additional general knowledge might need to be activated. By contrast, because the expected passages provided redundant cueing of the correct interpretation and thus low demands on working memory, we felt that older adults would not necessarily be at a disadvantage on these passages.

However, an alternative account of these data is now available, an account consistent with an inhibitory frame. Older adults are especially disadvantaged with the unexpected passages because they are unable to suppress their original interpretation of the situation. Inferences and

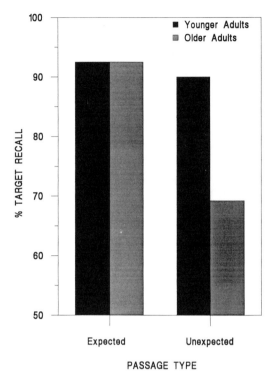

FIGURE 5

Younger and older adults' target recall for expected and unexpected passages. Data are from Zacks and Hasher (1988).

elaborations relevant to that interpretation remain activated and inter-fere with the encoding of a well-structured and coherent representation of the entire passage. The Hamm and Hasher (1992) study provides di-rect evidence for this new formulation.

Hamm and Hasher altered the basic procedure of our previous exper-iments with these passages by including a speeded judgment task which occurred either in the middle of a passage, before the first cue of the final interpretation in the unexpected passages, or at the end. The sub-jects had to judge whether each of a series of words was consistent with their *current* interpretation of the passage. Included among these words was one which referred to correct final passage interpretation (e.g., *live*) or one which referred to the original interpretation in the unexpected version (e.g., *finish*). When the test word was related to the final inter-pretation of the passage, the pattern of "yes" judgments was quite simi-lar in younger and older adults (see Figure 6). The interesting data come from those trials in which the test word was related to the original inter-

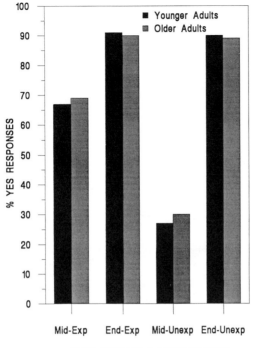

FIGURE 6

Percentage of "yes" responses given by younger and older subjects to test words consistent with the *final* passage interpretations. The results are shown for both the mid (Mid) and end (End) of passage test locations and for expected (Exp) and unexpected (Unexp) passages. Data from Hamm and Hasher (1992).

pretation of the unexpected passage (i.e., *finish*; see Figure 7): In three of four comparison points, older adults said yes to these words more frequently than young adults. That is, except at the midpoint of the unexpected passages, they more often said that *both live* and *finish* were consistent with their interpretation of the passage. For example, older adults' judgments at the end of the unexpected passages indicated that they maintained the original interpretation 48% of the time, although 88% of the time, they had also encoded the correct final interpretation. Another way to describe these data is that older adults were much less likely than younger adults to abandon their original interpretation of the unexpected passages; once they generate an interpretation, they tend to maintain it even in the face of subsequent contrary information.

Thus, in contrast to the idea of *less* information in working memory for older adults, these data suggest an *excess* of information in working

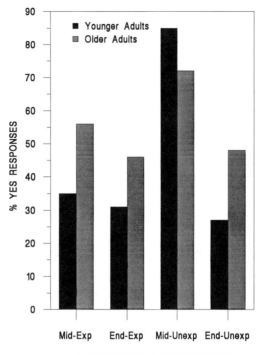

FIGURE 7

Percentage "yes" responses given by younger and older subjects to test words consistent with the *original* passage interpretations. The results are shown for both the mid (Mid) and end (End) of passage test locations and for expected (Exp) and unexpected (Unexp) passages. Data from Hamm and Hasher (1992).

memory, an excess that is the result of difficulty in suppressing original interpretations. One effect of maintaining both interpretations might well be a less coherent memory representation of the passage as a whole for older adults, and consequently poorer performance on a delayed recall test. The latter result was found in the experiment from Zacks and Hasher (1988), as already mentioned.

V. "ENRICHED" WORKING MEMORY CONTENTS AND RETRIEVAL FROM LONG-TERM MEMORY: THE FAN EFFECT

As we see it, the general pattern that emerges from these different lines of research is that older adults have a decreased ability to inhibit the processing of irrelevant stimuli and to quickly suppress irrelevant thoughts inadvertently activated by goal-relevant materials. The last research area we describe explores the impact that this relative inability to ignore irrelevant stimuli and thoughts might have on the speeded retrieval of information from long-term memory. Presumably, older adults' deficiencies in suppressing irrelevant information would operate both during attempts to encode information into long-term memory and also during attempts to retrieve the information from long-term memory, with predictable consequences at both stages. For encoding, one sort of consequence would follow from the notion that simultaneously activated thoughts tend to get associated with each other. With prolonged activation of irrelevant thoughts, more spurious associations between critical and irrelevant thoughts are likely to be stored; these spurious associations could later interfere with retrieval of task-relevant information.

This kind of reasoning led us to explore age-related differences in the "fan effect." In fan effect experiments (e.g., Anderson, 1974, 1983), subjects first learn a set of target facts, such as the following examples from Gerard, Zacks, Hasher, and Radvansky (1991): *The doctor took the car for a short test drive, The judge cut the apple pie into six pieces.* In a subsequent speeded recognition test, they are asked to distinguish between the target facts and unstudied foil facts constructed from repairings of the subject and predicate phrases of the target facts (e.g., *The doctor cut the apple pie into six pieces.*) The fundamental finding is that performance is tied to fan size: The more facts learned about a particular concept (e.g., *the doctor*), the longer it takes to retrieve any one of those facts and usually the more errors are made. This outcome is termed the "fan effect."

We predicted that the relative inefficiency of older adults' inhibitory mechanisms would result in their showing a larger fan effect than younger adults. Our reasoning went as follows: Because of compromised inhibitory attentional mechanisms, older adults should have increased difficulty in focusing on a single set of mental contents, both at learning and retrieval. Consider first what might happen during the learning of the experimental facts. Older adults will be less able to suppress irrelevant thoughts activated by the experimental materials. Such thoughts might include those tied to personal experience with the concepts (*their* doctor, *their friend*, the judge) and facts they are studying. Also, older adults may have a harder time constraining practice to a single experimental item. So when they are supposed to be studying *The doctor took the car for a short test drive*, they might also be prone to rehearse *The doctor danced the night away at the faculty ball.* In essence, the argument is that at any experimental or nominal fan size, the *functional* or *effective* fan size will be larger for older adults than for younger adults. This will then enable any single cue at retrieval (e.g., *the doctor*) to activate a larger number of connected ideas, thus slowing the retrieval of any particular target fact, and also setting the stage for more errors. At the time of retrieval, diminished inhibitory mechanisms will also create problems for older adults. They will be less able to focus their attention on the probed-for fact, because they will be less able to suppress the activation of any non-probed-for facts, whether experimentally related or self-generated.

In one of our fan effect experiments (Gerard et al., 1991), subjects learned lists of 18 facts having the form "The person (type of professional) performed an activity." Each person and each activity appeared in one to three facts. The critical items on the recognition test represented fan sizes 1-1, 2-2, and 3-3, where the first number indicates the number of facts for a particular person and the second the number of facts for a particular activity.

The recognition test reaction time data confirmed all our expectations (see Figure 8): Both groups showed a significant fan effect, which was larger for foil than for presented test items. Importantly, there was also a significant Age × Fan interaction, reflecting the fact that the difference

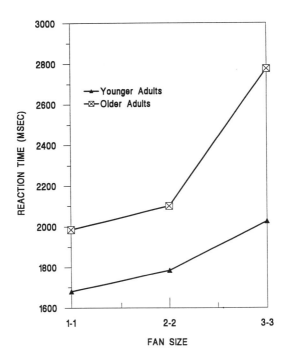

FIGURE 8

Younger and older adults' reaction times for correct recognition judgments as a function of fan size. Data are from Gerard et al. (1991).

between 1-1 and 3-3 fan sizes was almost twice as big for older as for younger adults. Because there were similar findings in the error data, the reaction time results do not reflect a difference between the two groups in speed-accuracy trade-offs.

What these data suggest to us is that the retrieval of well-learned memories can, for older adults, be slowed by the *enrichment* of target information with *irrelevant* associations. In the case of the fan paradigm, the enrichment stems from the older adults' difficulty in suppressing irrelevant associations to the probe concepts, both when they are memorizing the experimental facts and when they are doing the retrieval test. The latter type of effect can impair the retrieval of any well-learned information, with negative consequences for the many cognitive and social tasks that require timely access to information in long-term memory. Therefore, our claim would be that older adults might have trouble when trying to remember the names of acquaintances to make introductions, not because of the loss of access to the relevant memories, but because irrelevant ones are likely to be activated as well, which slows retrieval of the target memories.

The picture may be quite different when the enrichment of target information involves primarily *relevant* or *situationally natural* associations. In such cases, older adults may look no different than younger adults, or may even look in some sense "better." Evidence regarding the first possibility is provided by a fan effect study (Zacks, Radvansky, Hasher, & Gerard, 1990, Experiment 2) using materials that readily evoke elaborations which permit nominally interfering associations to be integrated into unified representations based on mental models. Both younger and older adults showed equal benefit from the availability of these elaborations in the form of a reduced fan effect. One piece of evidence supporting the second possibility comes from a study by Boswell (1979) in which it was found that older adults' interpretations of metaphors were deemed by judges to be more integrative and synthetic than those of younger adults. This finding is consistent with the notion that metaphors activate a broader range of associations for older, as compared to younger, adults. Indeed, there is evidence that older individuals consider a broader range of candidates as completions for incomplete sentences than do younger individuals (Stoltzfus, 1992).

VI. BROADER IMPLICATIONS AND CONCLUSIONS

We believe that the several areas of research we have reviewed in this chapter are all consistent with our central assumption that as a consequence of a decline in the efficiency of inhibitory attentional mechanisms, older adults are less able than young adults to ignore stimuli and thoughts currently irrelevant to the task at hand. Because of this, such information is more likely to enter working memory and to remain there longer if it is does enter. Of course, no one of the experiments we have considered in this chapter is definitive, but taken together we feel the story they tell is quite compelling. This is especially true because the consistency in outcome comes from experiments involving a wide range of procedures, materials, and time frames over which processing is measured.

One general implication of our research relates to the repeated pattern of findings suggesting that older adults have "richer" interpretations and memory encodings of target material than do younger adults. This is particularly obvious in the Hartman and Hasher (1991) and Hamm and Hasher (1992) studies, but it is also quite consistent with the fan effect and directed forgetting data (e.g., the increased rate of intrusions of TBF items on the immediate recall tests). This pattern of findings is particularly of interest in relation to an alternate, widely held account of cognitive aging deficits, namely, an account that ties aging declines in cognitive performance to a decrease in the capacity of some central resource, frequently working memory capacity (cf. Light, 1991). Although this alternative view is appealing in some ways (note its consistency with Just & Carpenter's, 1992, recent account of individual differences in comprehension skill among young adults), and although as previously indicated we (Zacks et al., 1987) have held to this view in the past, our data suggesting that older adults hold more, not less, information in working memory than younger adults argue against such a view.

Of course, there are some data that seem to suggest that older adults do have less capacity for holding task-relevant information in working memory (e.g., Salthouse, Mitchell, Skovronek, & Babcock, 1989). However, such findings are not necessarily contrary to our view. We speculate that working memory sometimes *appears* to be reduced in older adults precisely because they have trouble eliminating from working memory information that is irrelevant to the task at hand. To the degree that measurement of working memory capacity taps only task-relevant information, capacity will be underestimated for older adults. That is, we make the tentative suggestion that a smaller measured working memory capacity may be a *result* of the underlying mechanisms of cognitive aging deficits not their cause.

Though highly speculative, this line of argument has the advantage of possibly being able to handle the divergence of results in studies relating working memory capacity to age-related differences in cognitive performance. For example, it has been reported both that older adults have lower average working memory capacities than younger adults (e.g., Light & Anderson, 1985) and that they do not (e.g., Hartley,

1988). Similarly, some data suggest that age differences in working memory capacity can account for the obtained age difference on the target task (e.g., Stine & Wingfield, 1987), whereas other results do not confirm such a trend (e.g., Light & Anderson, 1985; see Light, 1991, for a review). These conflicting findings would not be surprising if the tasks used to measure working memory capacity (e.g., Daneman & Carpenter, 1980) and the target tasks differed in the presence of distracting stimuli and in their potential for eliciting irrelevant ideas that older adults would have trouble suppressing. In addition, if valid, these conjectures would sidestep the thorny issues of how best to conceptualize working memory and to measure its capacity (Daneman, 1987), and the issue of whether working memory capacity is even the most important central resource to consider in accounting for cognitive aging declines (Light, 1991).

In closing, we note that theoretical views quite similar to ours have been offered in a number of different areas, including as accounts of cognitive developmental changes in children (Bjorklund & Harnish-feger, 1990; Dempster, 1992) and of individual differences in language comprehension skill among young adults (Gernsbacher & Faust, 1991). There have also been tentative claims that deficient inhibitory attentional mechanisms may account for some of the cognitive symptoms associated with certain psychopathologies, including schizophrenia (Beech, Powell, McWilliams, & Claridge, 1989). At the least, the increasing popularity of the general viewpoint, and the associated growing body of evidence it has generated, encourage us to continue exploring the impact on cognitive performance of differences in the ability to inhibit the processing of task-irrelevant information, or in other words, differences in the efficiency of directed ignoring.

ACKNOWLEDGMENTS

Much of the research reported in this chapter was supported by a series of grants from the National Institute on Aging (#RO1 AGO4306). We gratefully acknowledge this support. We are also indebted to the many students and colleagues who contributed in numerous ways to this work.

REFERENCES

Alba, J. (1984). Nature of inference representation. *American Journal of Psychology, 97,* 215–233.
Allport, A. (1989). Visual attention. In M. I. Posner (Ed.), *Foundations of cognitive science* (pp. 631–682). Cambridge, MA: MIT Press.

Anderson, J. R. (1974). Retrieval of propositional information from long-term memory. *Cognitive Psychology, 6,* 451–474.

Anderson, J. R. (1983). *The architecture of cognition.* Cambridge, MA: Harvard University Press.

Beech, A., Powell, T., McWilliams, J., & Claridge, G. (1989). Evidence for reduced "cognitive inhibition" in schizophrenia. *British Bulletin of Clinical Psychology, 28,* 109–116.

Bjork, R. A. (1989). Retrieval inhibition as an adaptive mechanism in human memory. In H. L. Roediger, III & F. I. M. Craik (Eds.), *Varieties of memory and consciousness: Essays in honour of Endel Tulving* (pp. 309–330). Hillsdale, NJ: Lawrence Erlbaum.

Bjorklund, D. F., & Harnishfeger, K. K. (1990). The resources construct in cognitive development: Diverse sources of evidence and a theory of inefficient inhibition. *Developmental Review, 10,* 48–71.

Boswell, D. A. (1979). Metaphoric processing in the mature years. *Human Development, 22,* 373–384.

Carr, T. H., Dagenbach, D., Van Wieren, D., Carlson-Radvansky, L. A., Alejano, A. R., & Brown, J. S. (in press). Acquiring general knowledge from specific episodes of experience. In C. Umilta & M. Moscovitch (Eds.), *Attention and performance XV: Conscious and nonconscious information processing.*

Charness, N., & Bosman, E. A. (1992). Human factors and age. In F. I. M. Craik & T. A. Salthouse (Eds.), *The handbook of aging and cognition* (pp. 495–551). Hillsdale, NJ: Lawrence Erlbaum.

Connelly, S. L., & Hasher, L. (1993). Aging and the inhibition of spatial location. *Journal of Experimental Psychology: Human Perception and Performance, 19,* 1238–1250.

Connelly, S. L., Hasher, L., & Zacks, R. T. (1991). Age and reading: The impact of distraction. *Psychology and Aging, 6,* 533–541.

Cremer, R., & Zeef, E. J. (1987). What kind of noise increases with age? *Journal of Gerontology, 42,* 515–518.

Daneman, M. (1987). Reading and working memory. In J. R. Beech & A. M. Colley (Eds.), *Cognitive approaches to reading* (pp. 57–86). New York: Wiley.

Daneman, M., & Carpenter, P. A. (1980). Individual differences in working memory and reading. *Journal of Verbal Learning and Verbal Behavior, 19,* 450–466.

Dempster, F. (1992). The rise and fall of the inhibitory mechanism: Toward a unified theory of cognitive development and aging. *Developmental Review, 12,* 45–75.

Geiselman, R. E., & Bagheri, B. (1985). Repetition effects in directed forgetting: Evidence for retrieval inhibition. *Memory & Cognition, 13,* 57–62.

Gerard, L., Zacks, R. T., Hasher, L., & Radvansky, G. A. (1991). Age deficits in retrieval: The fan effect. *Journal of Gerontology: PSYCHOLOGICAL SCIENCES, 46,* P131–136.

Gernsbacher, M. A., & Faust, M. E. (1991). The mechanism of suppression: A component of general comprehension skill. *Journal of Experimental Psychology: Learning, Memory and Cognition, 17,* 245–262.

Gold, D., Andres, D., Arbuckle, T., & Schwartzman, A. (1988). Measurement and correlates of verbosity in elderly people. *Journal of Gerontology: PSYCHOLOGICAL SCIENCES, 43,* P27–33.

Hamm, V. P., & Hasher, L. (1992). Age and the availability of inferences. *Psychology and Aging, 7,* 56–64.

Hartley, J. T. (1988). Aging and individual differences in memory for written discourse. In L. L. Light & D. H. Burke (Eds.), *Language, memory, and aging* (pp. 36–57). New York: Cambridge University Press.

Hartman, M., & Hasher, L. (1991). Aging and suppression: Memory for previously relevant information. *Psychology and Aging, 6,* 587–594.

Hasher, L., Stoltzfus, E. R., Zacks, R. T., & Rypma, B. (1991). Age and inhibition. *Journal of Experimental Psychology: Learning, Memory and Cognition, 17*, 163–169.

Hasher, L., & Zacks, R. T. (1988). Working memory, comprehension, and aging: A review and a new view. *The Psychology of Learning and Motivation, 22*, 193–225.

Just, M. A., & Carpenter, P. A. (1992). A capacity theory of comprehension: Individual differences in working memory. *Psychological Review, 99*, 122–149.

Kane, M. J., Hasher, L., Stoltzfus, E. R., Zacks, R. T., & Connelly, S. L. (in press). Inhibitory attentional mechanisms and aging. *Psychology and Aging.*

Keele, S. W., & Neill, W. T. (1978). Mechanisms of attention. In E. C. Carterette & M. P. Friedman (Eds.), *Handbook of perception* (Vol. 9, pp. 3–47). New York: Academic Press.

Kline, D. W., Kline, T. J. B., Fozard, J. L., Kosnik, W., Scheiber, F., & Sekuler, R. (1992). Vision, aging, and driving: The problems of older drivers. *Journal of Gerontology: PSYCHOLOGICAL SCIENCES, 47*, P27–34.

Koriat, A., Ben-Zur, H., & Sheffer, D. (1988). Telling the same story twice: Output monitoring and age. *Journal of Memory and Language, 27*, 23–39.

Light, L. L. (1991). Memory and aging: Four hypotheses in search of data. *Annual Review of Psychology, 42*, 333–376.

Light, L. L., & Anderson, P. A. (1985). Working-memory capacity, aging, and memory for discourse. *Journal of Gerontology, 40*, 737–747.

MacLeod, C. M. (1989). Directed forgetting affects both direct and indirect tests of memory. *Journal of Experimental Psychology: Learning, Memory and Cognition, '15*, 13–21.

McDowd, J. M., & Filion, D. L. (1992). Aging, selective attention, and inhibitory processes: A psychophysiological approach. *Psychology and Aging, 7*, 65–71.

McDowd, J. M., & Oseas-Kreger, D. M. (1991). Aging, inhibitory processes, and negative priming. *Journal of Gerontology: PSYCHOLOGICAL SCIENCES, 46*, P340–345.

Navon, D. (1989). The importance of being visible: On the role of attention in a mind viewed as an anarchic intelligence system: 1. Basic tenets. *European Journal of Cognitive Psychology, 1*, 191–213.

Neumann, O. (1987). Beyond capacity: A functional view of attention. In H. Heuer & A. F. Sanders (Eds.), *Perspectives on perception and action* (pp. 361–394). Hillsdale, NJ: Lawrence Erlbaum.

Rabbitt, P. M. A. (1965). An age decrement in the ability to ignore irrelevant information. *Journal of Gerontology, 20*, 233–238.

Salthouse, T. A., Mitchell, D. R., Skovronek, E., & Babcock, R. L. (1989). Effects of adult age and working memory on reasoning and spatial abilities. *Journal of Experimental Psychology: Learning, Memory and Cognition, 15*, 507–516.

Stine, E. L., & Wingfield, A. (1987). Process and strategy in memory for speech among younger and older adults. *Psychology and Aging, 2*, 272–279.

Stoltzfus, E. R. (1992). *Aging and breadth of availability during language processing.* Unpublished doctoral dissertation, Duke University.

Stoltzfus, E. R., Hasher, L., Zacks, R. T., Ulivi, M. S., & Goldstein, D. (1993). Investigations of inhibition and interference in younger and older adults. *Journal of Gerontology: PSYCHOLOGICAL SCIENCES, 48*, P179–188.

Tipper, S. P. (1991). Less attentional selectivity as a result of declining inhibition in older adults. *Bulletin of the Psychonomic Society, 29*, 45–47.

Tipper, S. P., & Cranston, M. (1985). Selective attention and priming: Inhibitory and facilitatory effects of ignored primes. *Quarterly Journal of Experimental Psychology: Human Experimental Psychology, 37A*, 591–611.

Woodward, A. E., & Bjork, R. A. (1971). Forgetting and remembering in free recall. Intentional and unintentional. *Journal of Experimental Psychology, 89*, 109–116.

Zacks, R. T., & Hasher, L. (1988). Capacity theory and the processing of inferences. In L. L. Light & D. M. Burke (Eds.), *Language, memory, and aging* (pp. 154–170). New York: Cambridge University Press.

Zacks, R. T., Hasher, L., Doren, B., Hamm, V., & Attig, M. S. (1987). Encoding and memory of explicit and implicit information. *Journal of Gerontology, 42,* 418–422.

Zacks, R. T., Radvansky, G. A., & Hasher, L. (in preparation). *Studies of directed forgetting in older adults.*

Zacks, R. T., Radvansky, G. A., Hasher, L., & Gerard, L. (1990, March). *Age-related differences in retrieval interference: The fan effect in younger and older adults.* Paper presented at the Third Cognitive Aging Conference, Atlanta, GA.

7

Mechanisms of Inhibition in Long-Term Memory
A New Taxonomy

Michael C. Anderson and Robert A. Bjork

The existence of forgetting has never been proved: We only know that some things don't come to mind when we want them.

Friedrich Nietzsche

I. INTRODUCTION

Most of us have forgotten things that we were sure we knew: The name of a friend or the location in which we safely stowed our airline tickets may, to our embarrassment or horror, simply elude reinstatement. Later exposure to the name or discovery of the errant tickets frequently prompts an *aha!*, because we recognize the name or the event of storing the tickets. Clearly such information often remains in long-term memory, but has been rendered inaccessible. When these retrieval failures are caused by other memory activities, such as the encoding or retrieval of related information, we say that accessibility of the affected items has been inhibited by those activities. More simply, we say the items have undergone *retrieval inhibition.* In this chapter, we consider theoretical mechanisms that might cause retrieval inhibition in episodic memory, with particular emphasis given to the issue of whether inhibitory mechanisms are responsible for impaired recall.

At least two characteristics motivate the choice of the term *inhibition* to describe these memory failures. First, impairment is thought to arise from an active process—such as the learning or strengthening of related items—that affects specific materials; this impairment contrasts with retrieval failures arising from more global, passive processes, such as changes in the availability of retrieval cues (e.g., as might occur with a change in environmental context) or passive decay. The active, specific nature of these mechanisms can be illustrated with the retroactive interference paradigm employed in classical verbal learning research. In this paradigm, subjects typically learn a first list of verbal paired associates (e.g., Dog–Rock), followed by a second list in which the stimulus terms are the same, but the responses paired with them differ (e.g., Dog–Lamp). On a later cued-recall test, subjects are asked for both responses associated to a given stimulus (e.g., Dog _____ _____). Recall of first-list responses is typically impaired by acquisition of the interpolated list (see, e.g., Postman, 1971; Postman & Underwood, 1973; Crowder, 1976, for excellent reviews). This impairment is dramatically reduced, however, when first-list associates (e.g., Road–Rock) do not share stimulus terms with the second-list associates (e.g., Dog–Lamp). Thus, subsequent memory activity seems to impair recall of earlier responses, and this activity affects some materials much more than others.

Similar impairment can be induced with other procedures, such as part–set cuing. In a common version of this procedure, subjects study a categorized word list (e.g., containing fruits, trees, etc.) and receive an immediate category-cued episodic memory test. Interestingly, if several earlier studied exemplars (e.g., Lemon, Orange) are given along with the category label as cues to help in recalling the remaining words (Cherry, Banana), performance on those remaining words *suffers* rather than benefits, relative to the performance of subjects receiving only the category label (see, e.g., Nickerson, 1984; Roediger & Neely, 1982, for reviews of these and related phenomena). Mere retrieval of information from long-term memory (e.g., Retrieving Orange, given the cue Fruit–Or_____) has also been shown to impair related items (but not unrelated items) in both speeded semantic retrieval tasks (Blaxton & Neely, 1983) and in episodic tasks with delays of 20 min (Anderson & Bjork, 1990; Anderson, Bjork, & Bjork, in press). Classic work in repression (Freud, 1952; Erdelyi & Goldberg, 1979), directed forgetting (Bjork, 1972; Epstein, 1972; Roediger & Crowder, 1972), and posthypnotic amnesia (Kihlstrom, 1983) even suggests that subjects can consciously apply such processes, provided that the to-be-forgotten information is in a clearly demarked episode. The important point, for present purposes, is that retrieval inhibition can be induced by activities such as encoding new similar memories or restudying or retrieving existing competitors.

A second characteristic motivating the use of the term inhibition is that subjects' knowledge of the forgotten items can often be clearly demonstrated with recognition tests. In retroactive interference, impairment of first-list responses is dramatically reduced when a multiple choice recognition test is administered (see, e.g., Postman & Stark, 1969; however, see Chandler, 1989, 1993, for reviews of studies in which recognition deficits have been found). In part–set cuing, recall deficits for cued items are small to nonexistent when recognition probability is tested (Slamecka, 1975; Todres & Watkins, 1981), although they can appear with more sensitive recognition procedures (e.g., recognition time—see Neely, Schmidt, & Roediger, 1983; for a related phenomenon, see the fan effect of Anderson, 1974). List strength effects, or the tendency for the strengthening of some items on a study list to impair free recall of the remainder, disappear or even reverse in recognition tests (Ratcliff, Clark, & Shiffrin, 1990). Our own preliminary investigations with retrieval-induced forgetting corroborate all of the preceding findings. Clearly then, much of the impairment in these paradigms is not permanent, because if it were, recognition memory for impaired items would suffer as well. Thus, in retrieval inhibition, learning or strengthening some information inhibits the *accessibility* of related items, but leaves their absolute *availability* unaffected (Tulving & Pearlstone, 1966).

But what exactly does it mean for items to have inhibited accessibility? In its most theoretically neutral sense, this expression simply describes the fact that some activity caused a decrease in recall performance that would not otherwise have occurred. For example, Bjork (1989) emphasized that the term *inhibition* is often used in the memory literature simply "as a descriptor for empirical effects that are the opposite of facilitation" (p. 309). Clearly, these characteristics justify the use of inhibition in this weak sense. However, if what is meant by retrieval inhibition is that an item's representation is suppressed—that is, *the representation's level of activation is reduced by the action of an inhibitory mechanism*—then the term is not clearly justified. As we will illustrate, most empirical phenomena exhibiting retrieval inhibition in the weaker, descriptive sense can be explained adequately without assuming the existence of retrieval inhibition in this stronger, mechanistic sense. The growing interest in inhibitory mechanisms as theoretical constructs (evidenced, for example, by this volume) has made it crucial to have a means of establishing whether inhibitory phenomena truly reflect inhibition in the strong sense.

Assessing whether impaired performance reflects inhibitory processes requires both a familiarity with inhibitory and noninhibitory mechanisms that might produce it, and an empirical criterion for deciding among those mechanisms. This chapter answers these demands by considering such mechanisms and by offering such a criterion. First, we construct a new taxonomy of the various noninhibitory and inhibitory models we have either encountered in the literature or generated on the basis of logical considerations. It is our hope that vivid illustrations of the many theoretical alternatives will be useful as a tool for interpreting empirical findings and will encourage cross-comparison of the reviewed models. Next, we describe a minimal criterion—cue-independent impairment—developed by Anderson and Spellman (1991a, 1991b, 1993) for establishing an effect as inhibitory. Although developed in the context of episodic memory research, the criterion of cue-independent impairment is quite general and may be adapted to most of the domains concerned with the study of inhibition. To illustrate this criterion, we describe a study by Anderson and Spellman demonstrating cue-independent forgetting. This study argues that inhibitory mechanisms produce retrieval inhibition, at least in the case of retrieval-induced forgetting. The final section advances three challenges to those interested in developing theories of the role of inhibition in long-term memory.

For ease of exposition and cross-comparison of models in our taxonomy, we first develop each class of mechanisms in terms of a common experimental paradigm: the retrieval-practice procedure (Anderson & Bjork, 1990; Anderson et al., in press). We discuss other "inhibitory" paradigms as well if results from those paradigms have been offered as evidence for an instance of a given model type. In the next section we describe the retrieval-practice paradigm and the phenomenon that it produces: retrieval-induced forgetting.

II. RETRIEVAL-INDUCED FORGETTING AS A PARADIGM CASE OF RETRIEVAL INHIBITION

In most of the investigations of retrieval inhibition just reviewed, impairment is induced by the learning or strengthening of materials related to the affected items. However, an interesting prediction that follows from current theories of forgetting is that the act of remembering or recalling an item, itself, ought to be a cause of forgetting. It is not that the remembered item should become more susceptible to forgetting; in fact, recalling an item increases the likelihood that it can be recalled again at a later time. Rather, it is *other* items—items that are also associated to the cue or cues guiding retrieval—that should be put in greater jeopardy of being forgotten. Anderson et al. (in press) refer to this possibility as *retrieval-induced forgetting.*

The prediction of retrieval-induced forgetting follows from three assumptions underlying what Anderson et al. call strength-dependent competition models of interference:

(1) The *competition assumption*—Memories associated to a common retrieval cue compete for access to conscious recall when that cue is presented.

(2) The *strength-dependence assumption*—An item's cued-recall performance decreases with increases in the strengths of its competitors' association to the cue.

(3) The *retrieval-based learning assumption*—The act of retrieval is a learning event in the sense that it enhances subsequent recall of the retrieved item.

According to these assumptions, repeated retrievals should strengthen the association of an item to its retrieval cue, rendering other items associated to that cue less accessible. Thus, remembering some things should cause forgetting of others.

To explore the prediction of retrieval-induced forgetting, Anderson et al. devised a new paradigm intended to maximize the negative side effects of retrieval. The procedure, called the *retrieval-practice procedure*, involves three phases: a study phase, a retrieval-practice phase, and a final test phase. In the study phase, subjects study several categories, each composed of several exemplars in category–exemplar format (e.g., Fruit–Orange). After the study phase, subjects engage in directed "retrieval practice" on half of the items from half of the studied categories (three items from each of four categories). Subjects practice retrieving exemplars by completing category-plus-exemplar stem cue tests (e.g., Fruit–Or_____) three times for each exemplar, each test interleaved with practice trials on other items. After a retention interval (e.g., 20 min), a final and unexpected category-cued recall test is administered; subjects are cued with each category name and asked to free recall any exemplars of that category that they remember having seen at any point in the experiment.

Of crucial interest in this paradigm is the impact of retrieval practice on the episodic recall of the remaining unpracticed exemplars of the practiced category. According to strength-dependent competition, practiced items should be greatly strengthened, increasing competition for unpracticed exemplars of practiced categories. This increase in competition can be assessed on the delayed cued-recall test for each category in terms of the following logic: If repeated retrieval of competitors impairs remaining unpracticed exemplars, performance on those items should be worse than performance on unpracticed exemplars from baseline categories in which no items were practiced. This outcome is indeed what Anderson et al. found; whereas performance on practiced items improved (as expected) relative to the baseline condition (practiced, $M = 74\%$, as compared to the baseline, $M = 49\%$, an improvement of 25%), such facilitation came only at the cost of performance on unpracticed exemplars of practiced categories (unpracticed exemplars of practiced categories, $M = 38\%$, as compared to the baseline, $M = 49\%$, an impairment of 11%). Thus, incidental strengthening due to retrieval can cause substantial retrieval inhibition. Interestingly, impairment was much greater for (and in some experiments, restricted to) categories composed entirely of high taxonomic frequency (strong) exemplars, than for categories composed of low taxonomic frequency (weak) exemplars.

Two aspects of these findings are worth emphasizing in light of our earlier discussion of retrieval inhibition. First, it is clear from these results that retrieval-induced forgetting is materials-specific in the sense that it is greater for (if not entirely restricted to) unpracticed members of practiced categories than for baseline items which are not in those practiced categories. If retrieval practice inhibited both the critical within-practiced-category items and our within-subjects baseline category items equally, negative effects would be obscured, and we would have no evidence for inhibition. Thus, competition occurs primarily among similar items within a category. Second, these findings appear to illustrate the strength-dependent nature of the competition; as practice enhances performance on practiced items, it impairs performance on the remaining members of the category. Based on these considerations, it seems reasonable to propose an inhibitory process that implements the competitive dynamics among category members.

Although it is natural to suppose that competitive relationships are implemented with inhibitory mechanisms—as they often are in connectionist models—it must be emphasized that the notion of strength-dependent competition is strictly neutral with respect to the implementation of competition. Strength-dependent competition models merely state that there is a quantitative relationship among items sharing a common cue: As some get stronger, *performance* on the others decreases. It is not stated how these performance decrements occur. The mere fact that we obtained the expected retrieval-induced forgetting, and that these findings are consistent with an inhibitory model, does not suffice to demonstrate that such effects are the result of an inhibitory process— especially if a noninhibitory process can be shown to produce the same quantitative relationship. In the next section, we highlight this ambiguity by discussing the many classes of mechanisms, both inhibitory and noninhibitory, by which empirical "inhibitory" effects can be produced. Through this classification, we hope to clarify the differences between inhibitory and noninhibitory models so that they may be distinguished empirically.

III. MODELS OF RETRIEVAL INHIBITION: A NEW TAXONOMY

To decide if a phenomenon truly reflects inhibitory mechanisms, we must have a good characterization of the theoretical alternatives. In this section we consider diverse theoretical approaches to retrieval inhibition, integrating them into a new taxonomy that clarifies the differences between inhibitory and noninhibitory models.

The new taxonomy divides theoretical approaches according to the component of the memory representation that is presumed to have the greatest weight in causing impairment. Although the models that appear in our taxonomy vary in their representational assumptions, all include at least three components: (1) a cue representation, at which memory search begins; (2) one or more target representations, at which memory search may end; and (3) associative links, through which target representations are connected to cue representations. In general, one or more associative links may diverge from a cue representation or converge on a target item. On the basis of these three components, three general sources of impairment may be distinguished, as illustrated in the diagram of our taxonomy in Figure 1: impairment arising from dynamics of the cue representation, the associative links, and the target representation.

In this taxonomy, differing emphases on these three representational components motivate three general classes of approaches, which we will refer to as the *cue bias*, *associative bias* (left side of figure), and *target bias* (right side of figure) models, respectively. This division

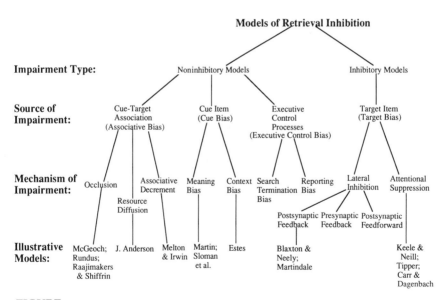

FIGURE 1

A taxonomy of models of retrieval inhibition, organized around the source of impaired performance.

of models into the locus of impairment emphasizes the feature that we argue distinguishes inhibitory models from noninhibitory models: whether the process that causes impairment subtracts activation from the item representation itself. Following this division, Figure 1 depicts target bias models as inhibitory, whereas it depicts cue bias and associative bias models as noninhibitory. An additional noninhibitory source of impairment, *executive control bias*, stems from the manner in which subjects control memory search (middle of figure). Beyond the general locus at which impairment arises, models are further subdivided according to the type of mechanism underlying impairment. For example, associative bias models might attribute impairment to occlusion due to increased associative strengths of competitors, diffusion of finite activational resources across competing items, or to decreased associative strengths between the retrieval cue and the target. Within each of these subclasses, one or more particular instances of that model are depicted.

Although the taxonomy depicted in Figure 1 is concerned with retrieval inhibition in episodic memory, we must emphasize that most of the models considered here are based on general computational strategies that can be applied across many domains. In fact, these models have roots in diverse contexts, including research on classical conditioning (e.g., occlusion and associative decrement models), attention (e.g., resource diffusion, attentional suppression), perception (e.g., lateral inhibition), motor skills (e.g., lateral inhibition), and semantic memory (e.g., lateral inhibition, occlusion). To reflect this generality, we have simplified application of these mechanisms to retrieval inhibition by excluding discussion of particular elements not essential to illustrate a model's basic mechanisms. For example, the representation of temporal context is normally crucial in modeling episodic memory performance, but we exclude it in most cases because it does not contribute to the process being emphasized (with the context bias model as a notable exception).

To emphasize that not all that impairs is inhibitory, we begin discussion of our taxonomy by considering noninhibitory mechanisms. As will be seen, each class of noninhibitory models has phenomena supporting it, suggesting that it is simplistic to seek a unifactor theory of retrieval inhibition that will be able to explain all phenomena. We then complete our taxonomy by discussing inhibitory mechanisms, and how, in some instances, ostensibly noninhibitory models may in fact disguise inhibitory mechanisms.

A. Noninhibitory Accounts of Retrieval Inhibition

Although the term inhibition suggests the operation of inhibitory processes, a surprisingly broad range of noninhibitory mechanisms can accommodate retrieval inhibition. In this section, we describe three general classes of such mechanisms: associative bias, cue bias, and executive control bias models. We review the general logic of each class, distinguish its relevant subtypes, and, when possible, we discuss particular models that illustrate the application of the mechanism to specific inhibitory paradigms.

1. Associative Bias Models   One of the most popular styles of explanation for effects of interference and inhibition ascribes the failure to recall an item to decreased efficacy of the retrieval route normally used to access the item. The heavy emphasis of such models on the role of the retrieval route—or the cue–target association—in producing impairment finds its conceptual heritage in traditional verbal learning research and, ultimately, in behaviorist learning theory. In both of these areas the phenomena of crucial interest involve the acquisition and loss of associations between stimuli and responses. Because impaired recall is purported to arise from dynamics in cue–target associations, and not from a subtractive process acting on the item itself, these models are not, by our definition, truly inhibitory.

Many mechanisms could alter the effectiveness of a retrieval route into a given memory item. In this section, we distinguish three types of such mechanisms: occlusion, resource diffusion, and associative decrement. Interestingly, occlusion and resource diffusion models appeal to the positive effects of strengthening related memory items—with no special impairment process—as a means of explaining impaired access to nonstrengthened targets. Associative decrement models, in contrast, assert that strengthening competitors weakens the cue–target associative links for impaired items. For each of these types of model, we illustrate how the effectiveness of the retrieval route into the critical target memory gets reduced, ultimately impairing recall. We then relate each general model to existing theories that, in our view, instantiate them. Where relevant, we describe related empirical phenomena that lend plausibility to the existence of the hypothetical processes.

a. Occlusion   The dynamics of occlusion models are vividly illustrated by analogy to the phenomenon of perseveration in monkeys with lesions to the prefrontal cortex. Monkeys with prefrontal lesions often perform acceptably in simple discrimination tasks. When the experimenter reverses the discrimination by reinforcing the previously irrelevant stimulus, however, the lesioned animal persists in selecting the inappropriate stimulus for a duration that varies positively with the amount of training on the original discrimination (Butter, 1969). This perseveration, or the persistent repetition of an inappropriate response, occurs despite lack of reinforcement for that response (Fuster, 1989) and despite previous training on discrimination reversals involving those

same stimuli (Butter, 1969). A fairly general phenomenon, perseveration occurs in humans with damage to the prefrontal cortex, and in a
variety of other syndromes, in many different forms (Sandson & Albert,
1984). Such phenomena illustrate how competence on a target behavior
can be occluded if the organism cannot disengage response production
mechanisms from strong alternative response tendencies (e.g., Mishkin,
1964). A similar perseverative process forms the basis for the way in
which occlusion models predict effects of retrieval inhibition; failure
to recall a target memory occurs because the persistent intrusion of
stronger memory targets obstructs production of the target response.
Thus, cue–target associations for critical items lose effectiveness not
because they are weakened, but because strengthening of competing
pathways overfacilitates alternative targets.

To see how occlusion might operate in the context of our retrieval-
practice paradigm, consider the simple model of category exemplar retrieval illustrated in Figure 2. In this model, activation spreads from the
category retrieval cue to exemplars at a rate that increases with the
strength of the category–exemplar association. When an item exceeds a
certain threshold level of activation, that node wins access to a limited
capacity response production mechanism. In the example illustrated
in Figure 2, Orange has been practiced frequently, strengthening the
Fruit–Orange associative link (denoted by the thicker black line connecting Fruit and Orange). Because activation spreads more quickly to
Orange than to Banana, Orange reaches threshold earlier than Banana

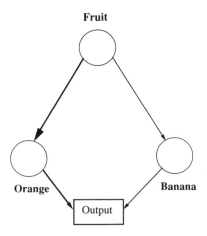

FIGURE 2

Illustration of a simple occlusion model of retrieval-induced forgetting. Strengthening of
the Fruit–Orange associative link (designated by the darkened line) leads to capture of a
limited capacity output channel.

and seizes control of the response production mechanism. As long as Orange's greater cue–target associative strength and its heightened activation persist, subsequent attempts to recall Banana will be thwarted by the perseveration of Orange, unless we add a mechanism by which the system can disengage response production (output) from stronger items. Though Banana remains uninhibited (indeed, it may be very active), and though its category–exemplar association remains intact, recall of Banana is impaired.

What reason is there to believe that perseveration underlies retrieval failure in verbal memory, which seems somewhat remote from perseveration in frontal-lobe syndrome? A closer relationship may be found with the perseverative experience that often occurs when we suffer "tip of the tongue" (hereafter, TOT). The analogy between retrieval inhibition and the TOT state is vivid and compelling, and has been espoused both by researchers in the part–set cuing inhibition literature (Reason & Lucas, 1984; Roediger, 1974; Roediger & Neely, 1982) and by advocates of the blocking theory of the TOT state (see, e.g., Brown, 1991, for a review). The subjective experience of TOT includes a feeling that we know the word we seek and, often, that our failure to produce the word stems from the persistent intrusion of a similar, interfering word. Empirical studies of TOT show that subjects rate these persistent alternates as being either more frequently or recently experienced than the target word (Reason & Lucas, 1984). Because the intruding word usually resembles the target, we examine it closely, which seems to make it harder to ignore, further impairing access to the target word. When we engage our attention in some diversionary activity, the correct response often seems to "pop up" (Reason & Lucas, 1984) at a later time. This phenomenon would be consistent with an occlusion mechanism were we to suppose that time and distraction allow us to disengage our attention from the blocking item. If we accept these subjective analyses of TOT, it appears that the characteristics of the TOT experience illustrate the working of an occlusion mechanism in verbal memory.

Though expressed in different terms, variants of this occlusion model have been proposed to account for retroactive inhibition as far back as in the classic work of McGeoch (1936). According to McGeoch's theory of retroactive interference, previously learned responses to a stimulus (e.g., the response Rock to the stimulus Dog) suffer *reproductive inhibition* as a consequence of the acquisition and strengthening of new responses to that stimulus (e.g., the new response Sky to the stimulus Dog). That is, at the time of the testing, response competition from the new, strengthened item (Sky) impairs the reproduction of the earlier learned target response (Rock). Although test performance on the earlier response was said to be inhibited, McGeoch did not believe that the forgotten item was altered or lost. In his terms:

> Inhibition is not thought of as a separate process, but as a function of competition among responses, with a resultant momentary dominance, at least, of one response over another. Responses thus inhibited are not necessarily lost from the subject's repertoire, but are kept by other responses from appearing. (McGeoch, 1942, p. 495)

McGeoch, like modern theorists in TOT research, cited the occurrence of overt intrusions (see McGeoch, 1942, p. 490), as well as the frequency of subjects' reports of covert intrusions as evidence that response competition impaired performance. Thus, the core assumptions of McGeoch's theory of reproductive inhibition—that stronger responses displace weaker responses, though weaker responses remain intact— make it a clear example of an occlusion model.

The basic dynamics of occlusion have also been included in more recent relative strength models of retroactive interference and part–set cuing inhibition. In their extension of the SAM (search of associative memory; Raajimakers & Shiffrin, 1981) model to findings in the interference domain, Mensink and Raajimakers (1988) account for retroactive interference with an occlusion mechanism. In the SAM model, recalling an item requires locating that item in memory (or "sampling" that item, in the language of the model), followed by production of the appropriate response (or "response recovery" of that item). The probability of sampling an item is a function of the strength of association of that item to the current retrieval cue, relative to the strengths of all other memory items associated to that cue (i.e., Strength [Target]/Strength [all associates]). When the cue–target associative strength of an item increases, the relative strengths of all other items associated to that cue decrease, resulting in decreased sampling probability ratios for the non-strengthened items. According to Mensink and Raajimakers' account of retroactive interference, additional learning trials on the second list strengthen the associations of those new responses to their stimuli, increasing the chances that those new responses will be sampled mistakenly when the older, first-list responses are desired. If subjects mentally perseverate second-list responses when first-list responses are sought, they will ultimately abandon the search, moving on to the next test trial. Essentially the same process model was proposed earlier by Rundus (1973) to account for inhibition from part–set cuing. According to Rundus, presentation of several members of a studied category as retrieval cues strengthened the association of those items to their respective categories. Because the category–exemplar associative strengths of the cue items is presumed to increase, the probability of successfully recalling noncue exemplars should decrease, owing to their weakened relative strength. As in the occlusion model sketched earlier, recall of an item can be impaired simply by increasing the accessibility of competitors.

From the preceding characterization of SAM, it may be difficult to see when and how a limited capacity output channel produces impairment in the model—after all, SAM predicts recall deficits at the stage of *memory sampling*. The stage of *response recovery* is never directly implicated (indeed, the assumption of a limited capacity output channel is rarely made explicit in occlusion models). SAM's status as an occlusion model depends on the interpretation of the sampling process. If sampling is composed of the *activation* of memory targets according to their absolute cue–target associative strengths (as in the model sketched earlier), followed by the *selection* (sampling) of one of those activated targets according to its relative strength of activation, then SAM is a limited capacity output channel (occlusion) model. In this interpretation, the analogue to the capture of the limited capacity output channel by an exemplar (see Figure 2) would be the selection of (sampling) only *one* of the activated targets on which to focus the recovery process. Presumably, this sampling limitation indirectly derives from the restriction that the recovery process can only focus on one response at a time. Thus, if the ratio-rule equation for sampling governs only the *selection* of one among many activated targets, then SAM is an occlusion model.[1]

Although occlusion models are intuitively appealing, especially when illustrated with the subjective experience of TOT states, evidence for such theories warrants caution for at least two reasons. First, there is a tendency to interpret *correlations* between persistent alternates and TOTs as if they were evidence that persistent alternates caused TOTs. It is entirely possible, however, that the reverse is true: A strong correlation between persistent alternates and TOTs is equally good evidence that TOT states cause the generation of such close matches. Given that partial knowledge of the sought-after item often accompanies TOTs (see Brown, 1991, for a review), it is not surprising that the search process often generates close matches, especially when we consider the extreme persistence of people experiencing TOTs. Analogously, subjects in retrieval inhibition paradigms may perseverate in producing strengthened competitors precisely because active inhibition has rendered the desired targets unavailable. Second, even if we grant that occlusion plays a role in causing TOT or retrieval inhibition, we must be cautious not to overextend its explanatory power. For example, it seems likely that blocking cannot be the sole process behind TOT experiences for the simple reason that persistent alternates do not accompany a large

---

[1]As will be seen in our discussion of the resource diffusion model, the ratio rule can be used instead to determine the spread of activation from the cue to the targets, rather than to select targets after they have been activated. Thus, SAM might be interpreted as a resource diffusion model. Because no mention of limited resources is made in discussions of SAM, and because perseveration is stressed, we classified it as an occlusion model.

proportion of the reported incidences in TOT studies. Indeed, whereas the frequency of TOT experiences has been found to increase with age, the incidence of persistent alternates decreases (Burke, MacKay, Worthley, & Wade, 1991). Although occlusion is intuitively appealing, and may be supported by phenomena such as TOT, the empirical case for the role of occlusion processes is not clearly established.

It should be emphasized that in the occlusion model impairment occurs at the stage of final output; limitations on the response channel impede the report of target responses, even though the ability to activate those responses remains intact. If activation of the category cue still activates nonrecalled exemplars, any processing involving the nonrecalled item's representation prior to response production should be unaffected by the strengthening of competitors. For example, nonpracticed exemplars should still be primed by presentation of the category cue, because the amount of activation that spreads to nonpracticed items does not change as a consequence of strengthening competitors (see Yaniv & Meyer, 1987, for work on the TOT state that may support this prediction). This property of occlusion may allow it to be distinguished from the next two classes of noninhibitory mechanisms: resource diffusion and associative decrement.

   b. Resource Diffusion   The occlusion model asserts that strengthened exemplars impair competitors by seizing control of a limited capacity response–production mechanism. Occlusion requires no special processes that inhibit representations of impaired items or that diminish their cue–target associative strengths. Thus, there should be no decrease in the amount of activation spread to nonstrengthened competitors, despite an increase in the amount received by strengthened exemplars. Indeed, connectionist architectures typically assume that the amount of activation spread by a source node to a particular target is not modulated by the amount spread to other associates. However, other spreading activation mechanisms are possible.

Suppose that activation is a finite resource to be divided among the connections emanating from a node. As the number of elements to which a node connects increases, the amount of activation spread to any given associate should decrease. Furthermore, strengthening the associative links of some of the associates should rob the remaining items of activation because strengthened items should receive more of the total activation. Such decreases in the amount of activation received by nodes should reduce their recall probability, despite the absence of an inhibitory mechanism acting on them. Figure 3 illustrates these effects with our category–exemplar materials. In this example, the rate at which activation spreads along a pathway is determined by the strength of that category–exemplar association, *relative* to the strengths of all associations emanating from the category cue. For this reason, resource

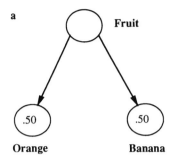

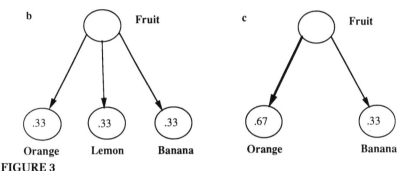

FIGURE 3

Illustration of a resource diffusion model of retrieval-induced forgetting. Strengthening of Fruit–Orange (c) robs Fruit–Banana of activation [note the reduction in percentage activation received by Banana—.33—relative to that received in (a)], as does the addition of a third exemplar (b).

diffusion and occlusion mechanisms (Mensink & Raajimakers, 1988; Rundus, 1973) can behave similarly in that the pattern of recall produced by each obeys a general ratio-rule formulation of memory retrieval (Raajimakers & Shiffrin, 1981; see also Luce, 1959, for a more general treatment of "choice" models). Figures 3a through 3c illustrate how resource diffusion produces this behavior. Note that, assuming equally weighted links, the amount of activation received by any given node decreases from .5 of the total in case (a) to .33 of the total in case (b) because activation must be spread among more links. An increase in the associative strength of an existing item results in similar effects, as illustrated in case (c). It must be emphasized that the absolute associative weights linking cues to targets remain unchanged for nonstrengthened items. Decrements in the potential to activate those items arise strictly from the manner in which activation is divided at the source node, enabling the model to capture interference effects without postulating special weight decrement processes. Essentially this mechanism is embodied in the spreading-activation assumptions of Anderson's (1983) ACT* cognitive architecture.

Perhaps the most relevant body of work supporting the notion of activation as a finite resource is Anderson's own work on the fan effect in fact retrieval. The *fan effect* refers to the increase in reaction time that results from an increase in the number of facts associated to a concept. For example, in an early study by Anderson (1974), subjects studied a set of facts until they knew the facts perfectly. Facts took the form of "Person x is in location y" (e.g., subjects might have studied *The lawyer is in the church*). Subjects were then timed to see how quickly they could judge whether they had seen a sentence in the original study phase. Trials with previously studied facts—to which subjects were to respond "Yes"—were interspersed with new facts composed of the same characters and locations, paired differently—to which subjects were to respond "No." Anderson found that subjects took longer to respond "Yes" if they had studied another fact involving the same character or location (e.g., *The lawyer was in the park* or *The doctor was in the church*). Later studies (Lewis & Anderson, 1976) showed that the delay increased with the number of related facts studied (but see also Radvansky & Zacks, 1991, for restrictions on the generality of this finding). Anderson used these findings to argue that the capacity of a concept, such as *lawyer*, to activate associated material is finite and that adding new associates to a concept should diminish its effectiveness in activating any of its associates. Anderson makes this interpretation of the fan effect explicit in his model of that phenomenon (Anderson, 1976).

Various other findings in both short-term and long-term memory, characterized by the cue-overload principle (Watkins, 1978), are broadly consistent with a resource diffusion model. The cue-overload principle states that as a memory retrieval cue becomes associated to more events, the probability of retrieving any one of those events declines—that is, the retrieval cue becomes "overloaded." For example, it is well known that as the number of items on a study list increases, the proportion of items recalled from that list decreases (Murdock, 1960). According to Watkins (1978), recall performance worsens as lists get longer because more items get associated to a general list retrieval cue, overloading it. Consistent with this notion, lists composed of several semantic categories result in dramatically increased recall proportions, presumably because subjects use the less overloaded category names as retrieval cues. Similar characterizations can be given to a variety of the phenomena of interest in this chapter, such as part–set cuing inhibition and retroactive interference, as well as the buildup of proactive interference in short-term memory.

Although a range of data seems consistent with a resource diffusion model of retrieval, those same data can be modeled by most of the other mechanisms described in this chapter. For example, an occlusion model can explain the list length effect if it is assumed that retrieving list items strengthens the associations of those items to the list-context representation. Longer lists, then, by virtue of having more items to be recalled, will have a larger number of previously strengthened (recalled) competitors against which a nonstrengthened remainder must compete. Thus, though it may seem as though the mere presence of additional associates reduces the effectiveness of a list retrieval cue, performance may be impaired because of a higher incidence of retrieval-induced competitor strengthening.

   c. Associative Decrement   Although it is natural to think that associations both increase and decrease in strength, as they do in connectionist learning schemes, memory theorists frequently assume that associations never go away once learned (see, e.g., the assumptions of Raajimakers & Shiffrin's, 1981, SAM model). This assumption follows from the more general notion that memories are never truly lost, but are merely made inaccessible (e.g., Tulving, 1974; see also, Hintzman, 1978, pp. 297–304; Loftus, 1979; Loftus & Loftus, 1980, for contrasting views). Nonetheless, within the framework of classical associationist learning theory, it is often presumed that decrements in associative strength underlie phenomena such as the extinction of conditioned responses. Recent inquiries into the cellular mechanisms of conditioning render such a decremental mechanism plausible on the neurophysiological level: Synapses in the hippocampus—a brain structure associated with memory storage—demonstrate *associative long-term depression* (the counterpart of long-term potentiation; e.g., Nicoll, Kauer, & Malenka, 1988), a property whereby synaptic efficacy decreases with negative correlations between inputs from that synapse and postsynaptic activity (Stanton & Sejnowski, 1989; see also Levy & Steward, 1983). To the extent that we take such changes in synaptic efficacy to be the neurological underpinnings of associative learning on more complex levels, neural mechanisms exist for both learning through associative increment and *associative decrement.*

   Mechanisms of associative decrement can capture the general character of retrieval inhibition. Suppose, as we have for previous models, that learning Banana and Orange results in an associative structure in which the cue (or stimulus) Fruit is linked to the exemplars (or responses). Successful retrieval practice of Fruit–Orange should reinforce that associative link, increasing the probability that Orange will be given again on presentation of Fruit. However, because Banana is also associated to Fruit, there is some probability that it will be retrieved mistakenly (but not reported, because it is inconsistent with the category stem cue Fruit–Or_____). The critical assumption for an associative decrement process would be that such nonreinforced retrieval of Banana would cause a decrease in the associative link between Fruit and Banana, akin to the decrease hypothesized to underlie extinction in conditioning studies. This decrease in associative strength would cause later category-cued recall of Banana to be impaired.

The most widely known example of an associative decrement mechanism—unlearning—was proposed by Melton and Irwin (1940) as part of their two-factor theory of retroactive interference. Prior to Melton and Irwin, the dominant account of retroactive interference was McGeoch's theory of reproductive inhibition (McGeoch, 1936)—a theory that ascribes impaired performance to response competition at test. A natural prediction following from the response competition view is that increases in overt intrusions of stronger, interpolated material should accompany increases in retroactive interference. Melton and Irwin discovered, however, that as the number of learning trials on an interpolated list was increased to extreme levels (e.g., 10, 20, or 40 learning trials), retroactive interference increased, whereas the frequency of intrusions from the interpolated list *decreased*. This dissociation prompted Melton and Irwin to propose an additional factor contributing to interference, a factor "X," tentatively identified as unlearning of the impaired association: "Available alternative hypotheses regarding Factor X identify it with some process which occurs during the learning of the interpolated responses and weakens the original S-R relationships" (Melton & Irwin, 1940, p. 199). Thus, Melton and Irwin's Factor X constitutes an associative decrement model of retroactive interference.

Associative decrement accounts of retrieval inhibition, such as that proposed by Melton and Irwin, can be given more precise computational expression in terms of error-correction learning algorithms currently popular in connectionist modeling (Rumelhart, Hinton, & Williams, 1986; Sutton & Barto, 1981). The learning rule employed by this class of models, generically referred to as the delta rule (Rumelhart, Hinton, & Williams, 1986), specifies the change to an associative weight—either positive or negative—on a given learning trial. Figure 4 provides a simple version of the delta rule for two-layer associative networks, along with an illustration of how this mechanism can be applied to the retrieval-practice paradigm. The learning procedure for these models requires presentation of a set of pairs of input and output patterns to the network. Figure 4a specifies the initial input pattern, which, for simplicity, is an activation input of 1.0 (in a range of 0.0–1.0). This input causes the spread of activation to both Orange and Banana, the weights of which we have (arbitrarily) set to be equal and .5. The spread of activation from Fruit generates an output pattern on the units of the output

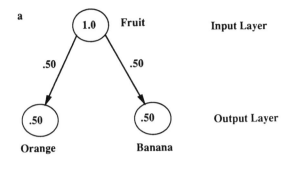

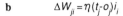

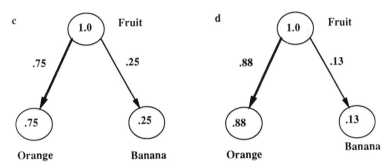

FIGURE 4

Illustration of an associative decrement model of retrieval-induced forgetting. In these examples, the weights into Orange and Banana are written alongside the links, the input ($i = 1.0$) is written in the category node at the input layer, and the result of spreading activation (the output, o) is written at the output layer exemplars. Weights are set to be equal in (a), and the network is trained for two trials in (c) and (d) to produce (practice) the exemplar Orange by punishing the activation of Banana and rewarding the activation of Orange. This is done according to the equation given in (b), the desired output pattern $t = [1,0]$ and the learning rate, $\eta = .5$.

layer (Orange and Banana), a pattern which, in this case, is [.5, .5]. Generation of output is crucial to the learning algorithm, which compares the actual output to the *desired output.* In our example, the model is retrieving Orange, so our desired output pattern has Orange active and Banana inactive: [1, 0].

With these parameters, the delta rule changes weights in a manner that reduces the difference between the actual and desired output: Links decrease for nodes that are too active, whereas links increase for nodes that are not sufficiently active. Changes occur according to the equation in Figure 4b, in which the change of a weight between an item (j) and the category (i), (ΔW_{ji}), is a function of the difference between the target output activation (t_j) and the actual output (o_j), weighted by both a learning rate parameter (η) and the input activation of the sending unit on the input layer (i_j). Figures 4c and 4d illustrate the result of applying this rule to two retrieval practices on the initial representation in 4a, assuming a learning rate parameter, $\eta = .5$. Because Banana is too active (the actual output for Banana in example 4a is .5, not the desired output, 0), its associative weight is decreased, and, because Orange is not active enough, its weight is increased. The same effects occur in 4d, though the magnitude of the changes decreases as actual output gets closer to the target output (changes of .125 as opposed to .250). As in traditional formulations of conditioning, the Fruit–Banana association is punished for causing inappropriate activation of Banana, whereas Fruit–Orange is rewarded.

Although the analogy between extinction and retrieval inhibition is appealing, there are difficulties with interpreting impaired recall performance as reflecting true decreases in stimulus–response (S–R) bonds. If the associative bond between the category and the exemplars were truly damaged, one would expect impaired performance on any task dependent on the integrity of that bond. For instance, the ability to recognize that a response was paired with a given stimulus in a multiple-choice recognition task hinges on the associative bond linking the stimulus to the particular response; according to associative decrement models, recognition memory for items suffering retrieval inhibition should be substantially impaired in this task. Yet, as alluded to in the introduction to this chapter, a central characteristic of retrieval inhibition is impaired recall with relatively intact recognition probability (see, e.g., Slamecka, 1975; McCloskey & Zaragoza, 1985). In those instances in which impaired recognition has been demonstrated (in retroactive interference, see Postman & Stark, 1969; Chandler, 1989, 1993; in part–set cuing inhibition, see Todres & Watkins, 1981), the effects are quite small relative to those observed for cued recall. Enhanced relearning after retrieval inhibition would also seem to cause trouble for the associative decrement approach (although, see Hinton & Plaut, 1987, for an exception)—an observation made even by Melton and Irwin when discussing the merits of the unlearning notion:

> The question remains . . . whether this unlearning factor could be expected to have the functional characteristics assigned to Factor X. . . . [T]he rapid dissipation of the inhibition . . . during relearning requires the assumption that the unlearning of the original responses . . . disappears very rapidly when they are again rewarded. There is no independent evidence on this point. (Melton & Irwin, 1940, p. 201)

Thus, even Melton and Irwin, the progenitors of the associative decrement approach to retroactive interference accepted this hypothesis only tentatively.

In response to such criticisms, one might argue that associations must be decremented more to impair recognition than to impair cued recall. Ignoring the post hoc nature of this rebuttal, more general theoretical analyses of error-correction learning algorithms render such parametric arguments moot. Recent theoretical work by Ratcliff (1990; see also, McCloskey & Cohen, 1989) analyzes the ability of back-propagation (a generalization of the delta rule for multilayer networks) models of learning to capture performance in standard episodic recognition memory tasks. Using a sequential learning procedure (e.g., learn item 1 to criterion, then learn item 2, etc.), Ratcliff (1990) found that error correction models such as back-propagation greatly overpredict the degree of retroactive interference that should be observed in recognition memory tasks. Such catastrophic interference (McCloskey & Cohen, 1989) resulted despite experimentation with a variety of different architectures and learning protocols. In general, these models were best at recognizing the last item trained, and when items trained prior to that were tested, they generated a pattern similar to the final item. Ratcliff (1990) summarizes vividly: "This is like studying the word cat 100 times, studying the word table 100 times, and then finding that cat is not recognized and that when cat is presented for recognition, table is retrieved" (p. 293). Based on the work of McCloskey and Cohen (1989) and Ratcliff's explorations, it appears that such catastrophic interference is a general problem with the ability of error correction algorithms to capture performance in sequential learning tasks. Although there has been some success in reducing catastrophic interference in distributed models of cued recall (see, e.g., Lewandowsky, 1991; Sloman & Rumelhart, 1992), it remains unclear whether these approaches can also model the minimal interference (and occasional facilitation—e.g., Ratcliff et al., 1990; Shiffrin, Ratcliff, & Clark, 1990) observed in recognition memory. To the extent that such algorithms represent the general class of associative decrement models, they fail to provide an adequate account of retrieval inhibition.

2. Cue Bias Models A second major class of noninhibitory models, depicted in Figure 1, focuses on biases in the cues with which subjects search memory. The logic behind these *cue bias* models is simple, and contrasts with that of the associative bias models just reviewed. In both classes of models, retrieval involves activating episodes linked to a specific retrieval cue. According to associative bias models, the efficacy of the link between the cue and the target is diminished; according to cue bias models, the crucial dynamics occur in the *selection of the units or cues* at which activation is initiated: If inappropriate cues are used, retrieval failure will occur. Again, because no special subtractive process acting on target items is proposed, we consider cue bias models to be noninhibitory.

Like occlusion, cue bias might occur in a variety of ways. In this section, we review two types of models in which the cue set is altered to produce retrieval-induced forgetting in the absence of inhibition: meaning bias and context bias models.

a. Meaning Bias   In meaning bias models, facilitation of practiced items and impairment of nonpracticed items arise from changes in the representation of the retrieval cue. Specifically, the features constituting the retrieval cue may change either when that cue is used to access certain targets or when it is repeatedly presented with those items. For example, suppose that subjects learned the items Orange, Pineapple, Lemon, and Banana as part of a list of fruits and subsequently performed retrieval practice on the items Orange and Lemon. Such additional practice could bias the representation of the cue, Fruit, toward *Citrus Fruit*. This possibility is illustrated in Figure 5a. Figure 5a depicts a simple semantic network representation of subjects' knowledge of Fruits, including the subcategories Tropical and Citrus. If, during practice of

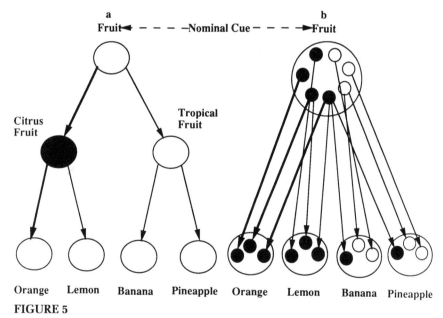

FIGURE 5

Illustrations of meaning bias models of retrieval-induced forgetting. In (a), a localist model, practice of Fruit–Orange shifts subjects' default conception of Fruit to Citrus Fruit (denoted by the darkened node). In (b), a distributed model, practice of Fruit–Orange increases the weights given to citrus features in the retrieval cue (denoted by darkened feature nodes and feature-to-feature-instance links).

Fruit–Orange and Fruit–Lemon, subjects' default conception of Fruit changed to Citrus Fruit, provision of the nominal cue, Fruit, at test would not allow recall of Tropical Fruit. Using an inappropriate retrieval representation would impair performance on all noncitrus exemplars, not because those items get inhibited, but because they are simply not associated to the functional cue—that is, the cue as it is represented by the subject.

Figure 5b depicts a feature-based model that exhibits behavior similar to that exhibited by the model in 5a. In 5b, the concept of Fruit is represented as a constellation of the many features that are associated with Fruit, weighted by their frequency of occurrence in that category. Particular exemplars of Fruit are represented as subsets of instances of those features, associated to their respective features in the general representation. Note that, whereas Tropical and Citrus Fruits do share a common featural element, many more elements are unique to the Tropical and to Citrus subcategories. Retrieval practice would bias the cue representation by increasing the weights of the Citrus features in the general conceptual representation and perhaps by incorporating features unique to practiced items into that representation. An interesting feature of the model in 5b is that it predicts facilitation of nonpracticed items composed of the more heavily weighted features. We will return to this aspect of the meaning bias model at the end of this section.

The meaning bias model asserts that context and the recent processing history of a retrieval cue change the meaning represented for that word on subsequent presentations. This view of the representation of word meaning contrasts with that espoused by traditional theories of natural language semantics, in which the meaning of a word is always represented as a constant set of features (Katz & Postal, 1964; see Barsalou, 1982, for a discussion). An abundance of work, however, illustrates the dynamic, unstable nature of conceptual representations. The overlap in the set of category properties generated by subjects between two sessions separated by a mere week was found to be only slightly more than half (.55—Barsalou, 1987); the speed with which subjects verify whether a property characterizes a category varies significantly as a function of whether an item appears in a neutral or biasing context (Barsalou, 1982) and subjects' typicality ratings for category exemplars vary significantly with linguistic context (Roth & Shoeben, 1983). Such fluctuations in the conceptual representations of words may endure for a long time, as illustrated in an example by Barsalou (1989). Under normal circumstances, seeing the word *frog* may bring to mind the dominant features green and hops. A recent visit to a French restaurant in which frog's legs were consumed, however, may cause one, over the next few days, to encode the property edible upon encountering *frog* because the edibility of frogs has been made salient. Thus, a constant set of features does not enter into the meaning of a word; rather, a word's functional representation varies according to its recent processing history and context. The effectiveness of a retrieval cue, therefore, ought to depend on how previous use changes that cue's meaning.

An early example of how meaning bias could produce impairment is Martin's encoding theory of retroactive interference (Martin, 1971). In Martin's theory, stimulus terms in the typical paired-associate paradigm (e.g., the word *Soap* in the paired associate Soap–Clothes) are assumed to be represented by features varying in saliency to subjects. According to the theory, the features entering into the representation of a stimulus term can change across encodings, depending on how the stimulus term has been used; retroactive interference arises not from response competition, but because the acquisition and strengthening of new responses (e.g., Soap Hand) change which features are salient in the stimulus term, biasing its subsequent encoding at test toward the new response, and away from the original response (in this example, Soap is biased toward bathroom soap and away from detergent). Because, at test, subjects use a different functional encoding of the nominal stimulus term, recall performance on older items is impaired relative to the control group, whose functional encodings of the stimulus terms have not been altered by interpolated learning. Thus, Martin's encoding theory of retroactive interference constitutes a meaning bias model.

Recently, meaning bias has been proposed as a mechanism underlying part–set cuing inhibition (Sloman, Bower, & Roher, 1991). According to Sloman et al., rearranging cues from their original study order changes their interpretation, impairing recall performance on remaining noncue items. Sloman et al.'s view, similar to the earlier strategy-disruption theory of part–set cuing (Basden, Basden, & Galloway, 1977), asserts that this impairment reflects an "incongruency principle"— namely, the more incongruent a "retrieval framework" is with that employed during study, the greater the impairment caused by cuing. Although expressed in different language, Sloman et al.'s (1991) incongruency principle amounts to the dual assertions that (1) recall depends on the overlap between cues at test and the cues during study (encoding specificity) and (2) word meaning depends on context, the latter being evidenced by their application of the incongruency principle to part–set cuing with categorized word lists: "Incongruency could play a role if . . . the interpretation of a category label could be influenced by the presence of category instances that could, for example, make certain attributes of a category more or less salient" (p. 981). Thus, Sloman et al. propose what essentially amounts to a meaning bias model, similar to that outlined here, and by Martin.

Sloman et al. (1991) make the interesting argument that meaning bias can be distinguished from blocking (occlusion) on the basis of the "order-invariance assumption." According to Sloman et al., blocking models such as those proposed by Rundus (1973) and Raajimakers and Shiffrin (1981) predict that the order of presentation of part–set cues should not influence the degree of impairment (order invariance of inhibition). Rearranging cues should not affect the magnitude of impairment because the degree to which cues are strengthened (the crucial determinant to blocking) should not be influenced by their order. In contrast, according to the incongruency principle, cue order should affect interpretation of the cues themselves, enhancing inhibition. To test these predictions, Sloman et al. had subjects listen to a tape-recorded list presenting 36 common names in the order: first name, last name, first name, last name (e.g., Jackie, Smith, Tom, Johnson, Steve, Nelson . . .). Subjects in the congruent cuing condition were presented at test with all of the first names from the first half of the list and all of the last names from the second half (e.g., Jackie, Tom, Steve, . . . Jones, Martin, Robinson) in exactly the same order in which they appeared during study. Subjects in the incongruent order received precisely the same names as did the congruent group, but rearranged so as to form the names of famous persons not on the list (e.g., Jackie, Robinson, Tom, Jones, Steve, Martin . . .). In support of meaning bias, Sloman et al. showed part–set cuing inhibition for recall in the incongruent group, but not for the congruent, although the congruent group showed a trend toward impairment. Order invariance seems to be violated.

Although these results appear to support meaning bias as the mechanism underlying part–set cuing inhibition, the case is unfortunately not clear. First, the property of order invariance applies only to simplistic formulations of blocking processes that ignore the role of interitem associations. The argument for the role of interitem associations in producing blocking is simple. When a cue is presented, subjects retrieve other list items to which that cue was associated during study. If cues are rearranged from the order in which they were originally studied, subjects may acquire new interitem associations among cues that interfere with the use of the previously acquired interitem retrieval routes. Sloman et al.'s materials vividly illustrate how this interitem interference might occur during part–set cuing. Suppose that instead of merely associating items to a general list retrieval cue, subjects in Sloman et al.'s experiment formed interitem associations such that they segmented the study list into first-name–last-name chunks (e.g., the four-item list—Jackie, Smith, Tom, Spellman—would be segmented into two first-name, last-name chunks). When cued with first names from the first half of the list and last names from the second half of the list (e.g., Jackie, Tom, Steve, . . . Jones, Martin, Robinson), subjects probably attempted to retrieve the other name associated to each cue. However, because scrambled cues appeared in first-name last-name format (e.g., Jackie,

Robinson, Tom, Jones, Steve, Martin . . .), subjects arguably formed new
first-name last-name associations during the cuing process that interfered with recall of previously learned first-name last-name pairs—an
occurrence that seems likely because Sloman et al. designed rearranged
cues to form names of famous people (e.g., retrieving the item Smith,
given the cue Jackie was probably much harder given the cue order
"Jackie, Robinson," than the order "Jackie, Tom"). Thus, Sloman et al.'s
results are perfectly consistent with a blocking account of inhibition
that does not ignore the contribution of interitem associations to recall.
The order invariance assumption, therefore, does not distinguish meaning bias from blocking models.

Although order-invariance may not distinguish meaning bias from
blocking models, the positive side effects of meaning bias might. As
noted earlier, meaning bias models predict enhanced performance for
noncued items sharing features with cued items. For example, in the
distributed meaning bias model described earlier, practice of Orange
and Lemon strengthens Citrus Fruit feature weights, increasing the activation spread to both practiced and nonpracticed items sharing those
features. This contrasts with the impairment to nonstrengthened items
predicted by both occlusion and resource diffusion models. Sloman
et al. (1991) noted the facilitatory prediction of meaning bias models as
well: "the extent of part-list inhibition in a category will be negatively
correlated with the degree of consensus concerning the set of instances
that comprise that category" (p. 981). This prediction must be qualified,
however, by the possibility that features of practiced items may also
have greater associative strengths to practiced exemplars (as illustrated
in Figure 5b by darkened lines). To the extent that feature–exemplar
associations get strengthened, feature-level occlusion might offset the
benefit to similar, unpracticed items.

b. Context Bias   A second subclass of cue bias models, context bias,
gives more explanatory weight to fluctuations in retrieval context than
to changes in experimenter-provided retrieval cues. Although the meaning of context can be vague, the term generally refers to any feature of a
subject's experience, other than the nominal stimulus, that may have
occasion to be associated with, and fluctuate independently of the nominal stimulus. For example, thoughts or feelings that a subject may experience while studying a list of words are likely to be incidental to that
particular episode, and may well get associated to the study material.
Other aspects of context include the subject's environment, sensations
(noises, smells), and the subject's understanding of the task. Although
difficult to define and control precisely, some notion of context is essential if we are to account for the ability to access items from particular
episodes.

A context bias account of retrieval inhibition asserts that recall performance will suffer if the contextual representation used to conduct memory search does not match the one present at encoding. For such a bias to explain part–set cuing inhibition, retroactive interference, and retrieval-induced forgetting, it must further be assumed (1) that the task used to strengthen competing items (e.g., cuing, interpolated learning, retrieval practice) differs enough from the one used at learning to generate a new contextual representation to which only strengthened items become associated; (2) that for the experimental group, the test context matches the context formed during the strengthening process more closely than the learning context; and (3) that the test context for the control group matches the one formed during learning. That is, the test context should be biased toward the strengthening phase, reducing recall of nonstrengthened items relative to the recall for those same items in the nonbiased control condition.

Figure 6 illustrates two variations of context bias applied to our retrieval-induced forgetting task. The model illustrated in Figure 6a is what we call a strategic context bias model; a model in which impairment occurs because the subject actively selects the wrong context in

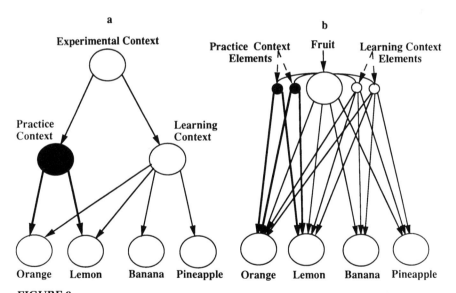

FIGURE 6

Illustrations of context bias models of retrieval-induced forgetting. In (a), a localist model, practicing Fruits biases subjects to use the practice context during search (denoted by darkened context node), causing them to miss items not appearing in that context. In (b), a distributed model, practice context features receive greater weight in the search process (denoted by darkened feature nodes and feature-to-feature-instance links).

which to search. The model assumes that subjects have a representation of the general experimental context, which is further divided into learning and retrieval practice subcontexts. As can be seen in Figure 6a, all experimental items are associated to the learning context, but only those categories and items that were practiced are associated to the practice context. Impaired performance on unpracticed members of practiced categories at final test can then be explained if (1) on seeing a category label, a decision is made about which context to search; (2) selection of context occurs on the basis of familiarity with the category, such that more familiar categories direct search to the practice context and less familiar categories direct search to the learning context; and (3) a switch in context does not occur within a particular category search. On seeing a practiced category, such as Fruit, subjects would search for fruits associated with the practice context, missing items presented only in the learning phase. On seeing an unpracticed category, however, subjects would search with the learning context; because all six items are associated to the learning context, recall should be superior. Thus, according to strategic context bias, impairment results not from inhibition, but from subjects' tendency to look for the right items in the wrong "location."[2]

The strategic context bias model presumes that subjects distinguish among experimental contexts and include these contexts in their conscious search strategies. But if the context to be searched is under the subjects' control, why do they not switch to another context when all items in one have been exhausted? If subjects switched from the practice to the learning context while searching practiced categories, they might retrieve nonpracticed items, eliminating impairment. It is unnecessary, however, to assume that context bias is strategic. Figure 6b illustrates how context bias might impair recall, unbeknownst to the subject. According to automatic context bias, subjects spontaneously associate materials to contextual features with the result that when a category cue is presented at test, the context to which it was most strongly associated is automatically reinstated. Assuming that strengthening phases of inhibitory paradigms associate many additional, unique contextual features to the retrieval cue, presenting a practiced category at test should automatically reinstate the practice context, enhancing recall of practiced items and harming recall of unpracticed items. Unpracticed categories, in contrast, reinstate the learning phase only, enabling access to all exemplars. As in the strategic context bias model, performance is impaired not because items are inhibited, but because the retrieval cues at test are not associated to nonstrengthened items.

---

[2]The authors would like to acknowledge Glen Russ and Andrea Aguiar for the localist context bias argument.

The notion that context is composed of a set of features that automatically fluctuate in saliency was first formalized in Estes's stimulus sampling theory (Estes, 1955). In Estes's theory, the stimulus situation is represented as a population of independently variable components or contextual elements, only a subset of which are active or available at any moment. The set of active elements varies randomly at a rate corresponding to variability in the physical environment and to changes within the organism. To account for performance in learning experiments, the theory asserts that each contextual element is conditioned or associated in an all-or-none fashion to a single response. On a given learning trial, the probability of emitting a particular response is determined by the proportion of the sampled contextual elements associated to the response. When a response is emitted and reinforced, the entire set of sampled elements becomes associated to that response. Other responses previously conditioned to those elements lose their associations.

Stimulus sampling theory accounts for retroactive interference in the following manner. During acquisition of the initial list of paired associates, the currently active contextual elements (including the sampled elements of the stimulus and of the context) become associated to responses. Acquisition of the interpolated list is then accompanied by three types of changes: first, newly active contextual elements get associated to items on the new list; second, some elements associated to first-list items fluctuate out of the available set; and third, contextual elements associated to first-list responses that remain active during interpolated learning are unlearned. If memory tests for first-list responses immediately follow interpolated learning, performance is impaired because most of the active contextual elements are associated to the interpolated list. As time passes, however, and more contextual elements fluctuate in and out of the active set, first-list responses spontaneously recover because some associated contextual elements are reinstated. Thus, as in the model outlined earlier, impairment occurs because the test context is more related to that active in the strengthening phase. Recent accounts of interference phenomena (Mensink & Raajimakers, 1988) have used similar fluctuation mechanisms, although these theories do not stress contextual fluctuation as the primary mechanism underlying retroactive interference.

Although automatic context bias models stress different aspects of the stimulus situation in their explanation of inhibitory phenomena, they may rely on the more basic blocking or finite resource assumptions discussed earlier. This dependence can be illustrated by examining the two ways in which automatic context bias might impair nonstrengthened items. First, it can be assumed—as it often is in stimulus sampling theory—that the number of contextual features in the active set must be a constant size. The strengthening phase of an inhibitory paradigm might then impair nonstrengthened items by adding many new unique features to the active set, forcing out the contextual elements most useful in retrieving nonstrengthened items. Such an approach constitutes a finite resource model of retrieval inhibition, where the size of the active set is the limited resource and where the greater number of contextual elements for strengthened items is like a strengthened association. Second, the number of elements that may be part of a retrieval cue may vary. Practicing some items would then add new, unique elements to the active set, increasing recall probability for strengthened items. For the recall probability of nonstrengthened items to decrease as a result of an increase for strengthened items, some form of occlusion mechanism must be assumed. Thus, context bias may not be a basic mechanism underlying retrieval inhibition in the sense that it may be derivable from other mechanisms.

3. Executive Control Bias   The third major class of noninhibitory models illustrated in Figure 1—executive control bias—emphasizes biases in the manner in which subjects execute the search process. So far, all explanations of retrieval inhibition have attributed decreases in recall to impaired item access. However, performance impairments can also result from decisions the subject makes, such as when to start or stop searching, what cues to emphasize and for how long, and whether or not to report a retrieved item overtly. In this section we sketch two ways that impaired recall might result from such executive control biases: search termination bias and reporting bias.

   a. Search Termination Bias   Subjects' final performance on a recall task depends on when they choose to terminate memory search. The choice of a stopping criterion might lead to impairment of nonstrengthened items in several ways. The first, and perhaps most obvious way would be if subjects underestimate the number of items in the experimental condition, or if they overestimate the number in the control condition. If subjects underestimate the number of items in the experimental condition, search may terminate before all accessible targets have been retrieved. Conversely, if subjects overestimate the number of items in the control condition, search may proceed longer than normal, enabling subjects to retrieve more difficult targets. In either case, recall differences will arise that are not the result of inhibitory mechanisms.

   Set-size underestimation seems especially likely in assessments of part–set cuing inhibition in semantic memory. Unless the target set has a well-known size (e.g., the 50 states), subjects' estimates of it may vary considerably, depending on their conception of how the set is defined. For example, the target set size estimate for the category Soaps might be smaller given the examples Ivory, Dial, and Dove, relative to the estimate given the examples, Ivory, Tide, and Joy, because the latter example set broadens the target set definition to include laundry and dish soaps. To the extent that provision of part-set cues narrows subjects' conception of the target set relative to that ordinarily generated without cues, performance will be impaired in the cued condition. Although this example of set-size bias can be regarded as a form of meaning bias, the bias in the meaning of the set has its impact on the point at which subjects voluntarily terminate search rather than on subjects' ability to retrieve exemplars at all.

Set-size estimates might also cause impairment if subjects underestimate the target set size in both the baseline and the experimental conditions. For example, suppose subjects studied 20 exemplars from a category, but one subject estimated the total number of items as having been 15. Consider what might happen in an experimental condition in which 10 of the 20 exemplars are strengthened in some way. If the subject estimates there to be 15 items in total and recalls all of the strengthened subset, search will terminate after retrieving only 5 items of the nonstrengthened subset, although some of the remaining 5 nonstrengthened items may be accessible. When no additional strengthening occurs, subjects may be equally likely to retrieve exemplars from each of the two subsets of the category. If subjects again only retrieve the estimated 15 items, an average of 7.5 items should be recalled from the noncued subset, yielding an advantage of 2.5 items over the experimental condition. Thus, the manner in which subjects control search processes can yield patterns that appear to reflect inhibition, though they do not.

b. Reporting Bias A second executive control factor that might contribute to an apparent inhibitory effect is the nature of the reporting criterion adopted by the subject. It is clear that recalling items in an episodic memory experiment requires the discrimination of items actually presented in the target episode from similar items that did not appear. For example, an episodic memory experiment using categorized word lists requires the exclusion of exemplars not studied. It seems reasonable to expect that subjects often recall more than they report, and that a certain proportion of items recalled, but not reported, are items that were presented in the experiment that have been inappropriately classified as nonpresented items (see, e.g., Tulving & Thomson, 1973, for a demonstration of the phenomenon of recognition failure of recallable words). If such discrimination failures occur more frequently in the experimental condition than in the control, the result might appear to be inhibition.

There are many ways that reporting bias might arise. For example, suppose that the strengthening phase of an inhibition experiment induced a bias in the contextual representation similar to that outlined in our discussion of context bias models, but that context bias was not sufficiently potent to cause retrieval access failures. Nonetheless, subjects may rely on the match between contextual information stored with a memory item and that which is present in the retrieval cue to assess whether an item was presented. If the category cue is biased toward the strengthening context, nonstrengthened items may not be reported because mismatches in contextual information may lead subjects to be underconfident in their assessment of list membership. Such difficulties would not arise for baseline categories, for which the match between the contextual information present in the retrieval cue and that present in the item would be much stronger. Thus, an apparent inhibitory effect might arise merely from biases in subjects' inclination to report retrieved items.

Reporting bias might also produce false inhibitory effects if the recall test directs (either explicitly or implicitly) subjects to retrieve a smaller number of responses than are actually available. Limitation on the number of responses forces subjects to choose which are the most appropriate to report, and depending on subjects' criteria, false inhibitory effects may result. For example, this factor may contribute to the much debated misleading information effect (Loftus, 1979) in eyewitness memory experiments. In the misleading information paradigm, subjects choose which of two photographic slides they recognize as having been presented earlier. One is the originally viewed slide and the other is a similar slide with a detail altered (e.g., if the original slide depicted a car running through a stop sign, the altered slide may depict the same car running through a yield sign). The misleading information effect refers to subjects' tendency to choose the altered slide if, after viewing the slides, they received a verbal summary containing misleading information (e.g., including the inaccurate detail that the car ran through the yield sign). Loftus interprets the misinformation effect as evidence for alteration of the original memory trace, but critics have argued that the effect can arise even when subjects remember both the original slide and the misleading information (Lindsay, 1993; McCloskey & Zaragoza, 1985). This might occur because (1) the task implies that there is only one right answer, and (2) subjects choose the wrong answer because they assume that the experimenters would not make a mistake about their own materials. Thus, apparent memory deficits can arise purely on the basis of what subjects choose to report. Similar arguments about response competition at test motivated the switch from modified free recall tests (MFR tests—recall tests which required that only one response be given to the stimulus term of a paired associate) to modified-modified free recall tests (MMFR—recall tests which required that all previously learned responses be given to the stimulus term of a paired associate) in classical verbal learning research (Barnes & Underwood, 1959).

B. Inhibitory Models of Retrieval Inhibition

As the previous section demonstrates, most long-term memory phenomena described as inhibition can be explained without recourse to theoretical inhibitory processes. These models are attractive in part because of their theoretical parsimony, capturing "inhibitory" behavior without additional mechanisms. The existence of noninhibitory alternatives, however, does not rule out the possibility that inhibitory mechanisms are the primary cause of retrieval inhibition, nor does it nullify the value of considering how true inhibitory mechanisms might generate such effects. In this section, we consider how inhibitory mechanisms might produce retrieval inhibition.

1. Target Bias Models   As emphasized in the introduction to this chapter, we reserve the theoretical term *inhibition* for performance impairments produced by decreases in the level of activation of the target item arising from the action of an activation-reducing (inhibitory) mechanism. Because the target item representation is affected, inhibitory models can be classified as *target bias* models according to the taxonomy depicted in Figure 1. Although it is common for researchers to appeal to such target inhibition in discussions of retrieval inhibition, relatively few explicit inhibitory models have been proposed. In this section, we explore and elaborate on two broad classes of inhibitory models of retrieval inhibition: lateral inhibition and attentional suppression. Although each class of model captures the core phenomena using decrements in activation to the target, the approaches are sufficiently distinct so as to lead to different ways of thinking about retrieval inhibition.

a. Lateral Inhibition   The mechanisms of lateral inhibition, as they are employed in computational models of cognitive processes, are based on an analogy to the ubiquitous mechanism of lateral inhibition in the nervous system. *Lateral inhibition* refers to phenomena whereby one neuron, A, inhibits another neuron, B, usually via a third (inhibitory) interneuron connecting the two. The circuitry is referred to as lateral inhibition because the neurons that inhibit one another usually are elements of pathways that run in parallel. In computational modeling, lateral inhibition is used to ensure that two processing elements do not remain active simultaneously, if, for reasons of physical or logical incompatibility, their concurrent action is undesirable (e.g., if two elements require a common effector system, paralysis might result if one of the elements were not disabled). Lateral inhibition has been used to model a variety of phenomena, including interference in selective attention (Walley & Weiden, 1973), lexical disambiguation in language comprehension (McClelland & Rumelhart, 1981), phrasal disambiguation in parsing (Waltz & Pollack, 1985), the recall of sequences of items from short-term memory (Estes, 1972), and the production of letter sequences in typing (Rumelhart & Norman, 1982).

Before we consider specific applications of the concept of lateral inhibition to retrieval inhibition, it is useful, as a source of theoretical analogies, to consider the different ways in which lateral inhibition is manifested physiologically. On a physiological level, lateral inhibitory circuits can be classified according to several orthogonal dimensions. First, inhibitory circuits can either be feedback (Figures 7a and 7c) or feedforward (Figures 7b and 7d) in form. Figures 7a and 7c illustrate a feedback circuit in which inhibition occurs between elements in the

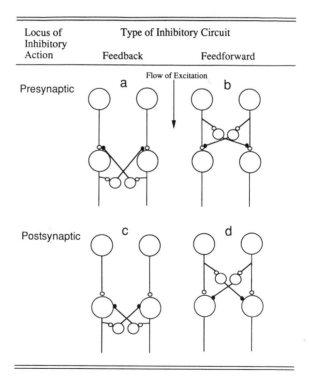

FIGURE 7

Lateral inhibitory circuits, classified according to whether they operate presynaptically (a and b) or postsynaptically (c and d), and to whether they are feedforward (b and d) or feedback (a and c) in design. Solid circles indicate inhibitory synapses and open circles indicate excitatory synapses.

parallel pathways. The term *feedback inhibition* is used because the inhibitory interneuron acts on a prior point (or at the same point) in the neuronal pathway. Figures 7b and 7d illustrate *feedforward inhibition*, in which inhibition acts on elements further ahead in the pathway. The second dimension along which circuits may be classified concerns whether or not inhibition occurs presynaptically or postsynaptically. In postsynaptic inhibition (Figures 7c and 7d), the inhibitory interneuron synapses on the postsynaptic cell itself, hyperpolarizing or inhibiting it, making it less responsive to any excitatory input. Such postsynaptic inhibition contrasts with presynaptic inhibition (Figures 7a and 7b) in which the interneuron synapses on the axon of the presynaptic cell, rather than on the postsynaptic neuron. This axo-axonic (axon-to-axon) synapse reduces the ability of the excitatory synapse to depolarize the postsynaptic cell, effectively gating the input to that cell from that particular connection. It is important to emphasize that the postsynaptic cell remains uninhibited, which, unlike in postsynaptic inhibition, leaves that neuron largely unaffected with respect to excitation from other synaptic connections. So, in considering lateral inhibitory architectures for retrieval inhibition, reference can be made to at least four basic circuits.

In this section, we sketch three simple models of retrieval inhibition based on analogies to the circuitry just reviewed. In all cases, we use our retrieval practice paradigm to illustrate the operation of the lateral inhibitory mechanism, but the functional properties of these as memory models are not restricted to this paradigm. The first model applies the postsynaptic feedback circuit and entails linking category exemplars with lateral inhibitory connections. It is essentially this model that is mentioned by the few authors who have explicitly proposed (or at least, alluded to) inhibitory models of retrieval inhibition (Blaxton & Neely, 1983; Martindale, 1981; Roediger & Neely, 1982). The remaining two models are based on presynaptic feedback and postsynaptic feedforward circuits. To our knowledge, no one has proposed anything like these models in the domain of retrieval inhibition. They are sketched mainly to illustrate how inhibitory models might capture the behavior of ostensibly noninhibitory mechanisms such as occlusion and resource diffusion.

i. Postsynaptic Feedback Model of Retrieval Inhibition In the preceding postsynaptic feedback circuit, neurons at the same level in parallel pathways inhibit one another via inhibitory interneurons. A similar lateral inhibitory circuit can model the negative interdependencies among category exemplars in retrieval inhibition. Figure 8 illustrates this circuit with our retrieval inhibition stimuli. As in the noninhibitory models reviewed previously, categories and exemplars are represented hierarchically. Retrieval occurs by a spread of activation

Fruit

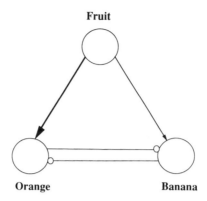

Orange   **Banana**

FIGURE 8

A postsynaptic feedback model of retrieval-induced forgetting. Links ending with circles represent inhibitory connections between units; links ending with arrows represent excitatory connections.

from the category cue to exemplars, ending with the production of a single response from the set of activated alternatives. Like the occlusion model reviewed earlier, only one item can be reported per retrieval attempt because of a limited capacity output channel. Unlike the occlusion model, however, simultaneous activation of many alternatives causes difficulty in response resolution. Lateral inhibition enters the scene to resolve this response competition, providing feedback to enhance differences in activation across exemplars. For instance, given a slight activation advantage of the exemplar Orange over Banana, more inhibition will flow from Orange to Banana than from Banana to Orange. As Banana gets inhibited, its ability to inhibit Orange decreases further, increasing the competitive advantage enjoyed by Orange. Thus, a small amount of evidence in favor of one item is self-reinforcing. After one alternative reaches threshold, a response is produced and the recall process begins again.

Inhibition of the item Banana caused by additional retrieval practice of Orange can be modeled in a number of ways. The simplest approach would assert that Orange, because of its strengthened category–exemplar association, gains a consistent early activation advantage over Banana. As detailed previously, negative feedback via lateral inhibitory links would magnify this advantage, causing the strongest items, such as Orange, to be recalled early. Remaining items would have an order and probability of recall corresponding to their strength of association to the category cue. A more complex approach would assert that retrieval practice has a lasting impact on unpracticed items. For example, repeated inhibition via lateral inhibition might decrease the resting level of activation for unpracticed exemplars, or alternatively, increase response threshold. In either case, the inhibited state of unpracticed exemplars would diminish the effect of activation spread from the category cue, decreasing recall probability for as long as such changes were in force. We discuss the issue of the durability of inhibitory effects further in the final section of this chapter.

ii. Variants of the Lateral Inhibitory Model Although lateral inhibition among category exemplars is the most straightforward inhibitory model of retrieval inhibition, other architectures can achieve similar ends. In this section, we sketch two models based on two of the alternative circuitries reviewed previously: presynaptic feedback and postsynaptic feedforward circuits. These alternative models illustrate how many ostensibly noninhibitory models may be recast in terms of lateral inhibition.[3]

The observant reader may have noted during our discussion of presynaptic inhibition that presynaptic inhibition has properties similar to those presumed in a resource diffusion model of retrieval inhibition. In presynaptic inhibition, the ability of a pathway or axon to activate its postsynaptic neuron is disabled, though the pathway itself is not damaged. The postsynaptic neuron is not hyperpolarized, leaving that neuron free to be activated by alternative excitatory connections. Similarly, impaired recall in the resource diffusion model results from decreased activation flow into the impaired item from a particular link. The link itself is not damaged or unlearned, nor does the exemplar node suffer a subtractive effect. Thus, the behavior of a resource diffusion model can be captured by a presynaptic feedback circuit, such as that illustrated in Figure 9.

In Figure 9, the elementary representation used in many of the models reviewed thus far has been augmented to form the computational analogue of a presynaptic feedback circuit. First, the simple connections between the cue and the target have been replaced by link nodes that, like other nodes in the network, can be activated or inhibited. These link nodes play a role similar to that of the synaptic button in presynaptic inhibition. Second, links emanating from the same retrieval cue compete with one another via lateral inhibitory links. These lateral inhibitory links, like axo-axonic synapses in presynaptic inhibition, reduce the transmission ability of competing associative pathways. During retrieval, activation spreads from the retrieval cue through link nodes to the targets. Meanwhile, link nodes inhibit one another,

[3]The models discussed in this section do not fit the current definition of target bias because structures other than the item representation (e.g., link nodes and response nodes) are inhibited. These models are discussed in this section primarily for convenience. However, a more general notion, such as "node bias" might categorize these accounts together with the current target bias models.

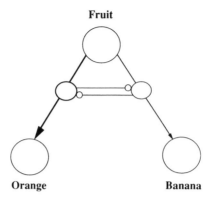

FIGURE 9

A presynaptic feedback model of retrieval-induced forgetting. Links ending with circles represent inhibitory connections; links ending with arrows, excitatory connections. Smaller circles on links between the cue and the target represent "link" or relational nodes that compete with each other through lateral inhibition. Inhibition of the Fruit–Banana link node impairs the spread of activation to Banana.

reducing their effectiveness at propagating activation. This gating mechanism captures cue-overload effects as well as the negative effects of strengthening competitors: as the number of items associated to a retrieval cue goes up, the inhibitory input transmitted to a link node from other link nodes increases, reducing the ability to activate targets. Furthermore, as practice strengthens a link, that link node's ability to inhibit competitors increases, reducing the ability of those competitors to activate their targets. As with the resource diffusion model, however, the targets themselves remain accessible from other retrieval routes. Thus, the circuitry of lateral inhibition can be used in a gating fashion to accomplish the functions of a resource diffusion model.

Like the resource diffusion model, lateral inhibition can capture the behavior of the occlusion model. In occlusion, nonstrengthened items are not themselves impaired, nor are they less capable of receiving activation from the category retrieval cue. Instead, performance on nonstrengthened items is impaired because stronger competitors seize control of a limited capacity output channel. Although such a model appears to be noninhibitory, this claim may be criticized in that it glosses over exactly how a response channel comes to have limited capacity. That is, it can be argued that such an assumption merely disguises or renames an inhibitory mechanism at the level of response production. To illustrate this point, Figure 10 shows how a postsynaptic feedforward network might implement a limited-capacity response channel. In the model illustrated in Figure 10, activation of a category

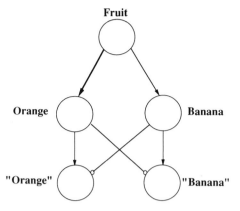

FIGURE 10
A postsynaptic feedforward model of retrieval-induced forgetting. Lexical units representing the verbal response for each exemplar have been added to the model. Feedforward inhibitory links to these lexical units implement a limited capacity output channel.

exemplar excites the response associated to that exemplar and inhibits those responses associated to competing memory targets. This feedforward inhibition from exemplars to competing responses implements a limited-capacity output channel. This circuitry has the effect that items more strongly associated to a retrieval cue will be more effective at inhibiting responses for competing items. Like the occlusion model, the memory target itself may remain active, despite impairment of its associated response. Thus, a feedforward lateral inhibitory model can allow strong responses to exhibit behavior resembling the capture of a limited-capacity output channel.

  b. Attentional Suppression A second class of memory inhibition models draws on an analogy between selective attention and memory retrieval. Selective attention and memory retrieval tasks are similar in that both require the production of a response, the appropriateness of which depends on the isolation of a mental representation of one object or piece of information from among a set of activated alternatives. For example, in the Stroop task—a classic paradigm for investigating selective attention—subjects must produce the name of the color in which a word is printed, ignoring the word itself. If the printed word denotes a color, subjects must isolate which of the two activated color names refers to the ink color in order to give the correct response. In memory retrieval, the cues provided—because they tend to be underspecified—may activate many candidate items before the final target is selected for report. Retrieving the appropriate item requires the discrimination of that item from inappropriate competitors, as in the Stroop task. Thus, isolating a target memory from among a set of activated alternatives requires the solution of computational problems similar to those encountered in isolating the memory representations of task-relevant objects in selective attention. In the selective attention domain, it has been proposed that attentional processes assist response selection both by enhancing a target's activation and by decreasing the activation of alternatives through inhibition (Keele & Neill, 1978; Neely, 1977; Neill, 1989; Neill & Westberry, 1987; Neumann & DeSchepper, 1992; Tipper, 1985; see also Gernsbacher, Barner, & Faust, 1990, for a similar mechanism applied in the context of language comprehension). If retrieval can be regarded as the internal focus of attention on memory items and if inhibition deactivates nontargets in selective attention tasks, inhibition may deactivate memory competitors, resulting in retrieval inhibition.

To see how attentional suppression could produce retrieval inhibition, consider how suppression might occur in our retrieval-practice procedure. During retrieval practice, subjects are cued, one at a time, with the name of a category and the first two letters of one of its exemplars. It can be argued that presentation of a category cue activates associated exemplars, particularly those studied recently. To produce the correct response, however, the activated set must be narrowed to the one item that fits the stem cue. The crucial assumption is that focusing search onto the target memory occurs by mechanisms similar to those proposed for attentional focusing: active enhancement of the target exemplar coupled with active inhibition directed at interfering nontarget exemplars. Because, over successive practices, unpracticed exemplars of practiced categories appear repeatedly in the set of rejected alternatives, they are inhibited on later tests of recall. Exactly such a mechanism was proposed by Blaxton and Neely (1983) as one account of their semantic inhibition findings, and by Anderson, Bjork, and Bjork (in press).

The role of inhibitory attentional mechanisms in retrieval was recently emphasized in work by Dagenbach, Carr, and Barnhardt (1990) and Carr and Dagenbach (1990) on retrieval from semantic memory. Dagenbach et al. exposed subjects to the definitions of extremely low-frequency English words for 15 sec each. Of crucial interest was subjects' performance in a priming task that followed the vocabulary acquisition phase. The newly learned vocabulary words served as primes for well-known target words that were either semantically related or unrelated. Subjects were instructed to try to recall the prime's meaning when it appeared, and then to respond to the target as quickly as possible. When subjects succeeded in recalling the prime's definition, as determined by performance on a recall task administered after the lexical decision phase, lexical decisions on related target words were faster relative to performance on trials in which the prime and target were semantically unrelated; surprisingly, when subjects failed to recall the definition, they were slower to make a lexical decision on the related target. Dagenbach et al. attributed impairment of semantically related targets to the action of an attentionally based center-surround retrieval mechanism, analogous to the center-surround mechanisms proposed in theories of attention (e.g., Walley & Weiden, 1973). As suggested in Dagenbach et al., and detailed by Carr and Dagenbach (1990), this mechanism assists retrieval of weakly activated items by enhancing desired targets (the center) while inhibiting more strongly activated items in the surrounding semantic space (the surround). Thus, Dagenbach and Carr's center-surround mechanism, like the attentional suppression process sketched previously, attributes impairment to an active attentional process that enhances discriminability of items in memory.

One might ask whether attentional suppression truly differs from lateral inhibition, because both emphasize the deactivation of interfering competitors. Lateral inhibitory theories have the further advantage, over attentional suppression, of expression as an explicit computational mechanism. There are virtues, however, to viewing retrieval inhibition in terms of attentional suppression. The metaphor of retrieval as the internal focus of attention brings to retrieval processes all of the characteristics that attention has in its original theoretical context. First, it has an active, goal-directed character, diverging from the automaticity implied by traditional spreading activation theories of retrieval (see, Bjork, 1989, for a related argument). Lateral inhibitory mechanisms are also often taken as a passive, noneffortful, automatic form of competition among similar units (e.g., Norman & Shallice, 1980). However, if retrieval inhibition results from an active attentional suppression process, we might expect less impairment for special populations whose deficits supposedly arise from a decreased ability to apply attentional inhibition (e.g., frontal lobe damaged patients: Fuster, 1989; Luria, 1966, pp. 218–295; Mishkin, 1964; Shallice, 1988; schizophrenics: Beech, Powell, McWilliams, & Claridge, 1989; senior citizens: Hartman & Hasher, 1991; Hasher and Zacks, 1988; Hasher, Stolzfus, Zacks, & Rypma, 1991; see also Dempster, 1991, for a discussion of the role of controlled inhibition in general intelligence).

Second, related to its goal-directed character, attentional suppression can be applied flexibly to the internal representation of any object or signal that interferes with the coherent performance of a task. The case for flexibility in the inhibitory component of attention is nicely illustrated in work by Tipper (1985) in the context of his negative priming paradigm. On a typical trial, subjects view a stimulus, such as a drawing or a letter, colored in red ink, superimposed over a second, to-be-ignored stimulus, colored in green ink. Subjects are instructed to produce the name associated with the stimulus in red ink, and to ignore the stimulus in green ink, supposedly included to make the task more difficult. If the red item on the subsequent trial is the to-be-ignored stimulus from the previous trial, subjects are slower to provide the appropriate name than if an irrelevant stimulus had been ignored on the previous trial—a phenomenon known as negative priming. Interestingly, negative priming does not depend on the existence of a priori semantic relationships between the attended and ignored items: attending to a saxophone while ignoring a picture of a dog results in substantial negative priming, despite their dissimilarity. The effect suggests a general inhibitory mechanism that can be directed at any representation impeding the coherent production of a response, regardless of previously established positive or negative associations in memory. Such an inhibitory mechanism might be regarded as a basic component of executive control of thought and action (Logan, 1985; Logan & Cowan, 1984). Indeed, Tipper has argued that, depending on the goals of the task, inhibitory mechanisms can be directed to different points in the information processing chain, such as at the stage of semantic representation or response production (Tipper, 1992). If inhibitory mechanisms in selective attention are truly this flexible, perhaps the same applies for retrieval inhibition. Such flexibility in the direction of inhibition seems at odds with the lateral inhibitory approach, insofar as we take lateral inhibition as an automatic process operating among items with established similarity relations.[4]

If a flexibly directed inhibitory mechanism causes retrieval inhibition, then any item interfering with the production of a memory target ought to be subject to inhibition, regardless of whether the interfering item is similar or shares a common retrieval cue with the target. An example of this flexibility may be the retroactive interference that occurs in the version of the paired associate paradigm in which stimuli are not shared across the two lists. Most of the factors proposed to underlie retroactive interference (e.g., response competition, unlearning, lateral inhibition) predict the greatest interference between lists with identical stimulus terms (Dog–Rock, Dog–Sky), with no interference predicted to occur between lists with completely distinct stimulus terms (Dog–Rock, Ball–Sky). Yet, although lists with shared stimuli display the greatest interference, lists with differing stimuli also show interference. This finding has been used to argue for a general response-set suppression mechanism (Postman, Stark, & Fraser, 1968), the characteristics of which resemble attentional suppression mechanisms. According to Postman et al., retroactive interference results from a mechanism of response selection that suppresses the entire class of first-list re-

---

[4]This argument makes it unclear whether Carr and Dagenbach's (1990) center-surround theory of semantic retrieval is a pure attentional suppression mechanism. Carr and Dagenbach speculate that their center-surround inhibitory mechanism may employ lateral inhibitory mechanisms such as those used in Walley and Weiden's (1973) theory of attention.

sponses as a whole, rather than individual stimulus–response associations. This process, occurring during the acquisition of second-list responses, involves a response selector mechanism that activates newly prescribed responses and inhibits earlier ones. Thus, Postman et al.'s response selector mechanism performs the functions that attentional mechanisms purportedly achieve in selective attention tasks: the activation of the target representation and the inhibition of activated competitors. Though not expressed in attentional terms, Postman et al.'s proposal of a response-set selection mechanism can be regarded as an early instance of an attentional suppression theory in the domain of memory.

Perhaps more direct evidence for a flexibly controlled attentional suppression mechanism producing retrieval inhibition in long-term memory comes from work on directed forgetting (e.g., Bjork, 1972; Coe, Basden, Basden, & Fikes, 1989; Epstein, 1972; Geiselman & Bagheri, 1985; Roediger & Crowder, 1972). In the typical directed forgetting paradigm, subjects learn a list of 10 unrelated nouns, after which they are either told to forget that list (the "forget" group) because the wrong words had been given to them, or to remember that list (the "remember" group). Both groups then receive a second list of nouns. After a brief retention interval, both groups are tested on their memory for both lists. Typically, forget subjects' recall of the first list is impaired relative to remember subjects' recall of that list, whereas forget subjects' recall of the second list is facilitated. Such impairment occurs even to incidentally encoded items on the first list, indicating that the effect does not merely reflect a deficit in rehearsal on the first list for forget subjects (Geiselman, Bjork, & Fishman, 1983). As in the negative priming paradigm discussed previously, there need exist no a priori semantic relationships between items on the first list and items on the second list for impairment to occur. Because there are no preexisting competitive relationships among items, and because impairment only occurs when subjects are directed to forget the earlier list, it is difficult to see how automatic lateral inhibitory mechanisms could be invoked to account for this effect. Bjork (1989) argues that directed forgetting may arise from the action of a suppression mechanism that subjects can actively direct at memory representations to alleviate effects of proactive interference. This interpretation is supported by recent work showing that directed forgetting effects are greatly attenuated in elderly populations thought to have a deficit in attentional inhibition (Radvansky, Zacks, & Hasher, 1991).

Although treating retrieval as the internal focus of attention may be interesting, and is likely to be a fruitful source of empirical predictions, it is not clear that all forms of retrieval inhibition can be accounted for within this framework. In particular, directed inhibitory mechanisms seem most applicable in cases in which there are right and wrong responses to be given on retrieval attempts—as is the case in our retrieval-practice paradigm and in the retroactive interference procedure. In our retrieval-practice paradigm, the category-stem retrieval cues require subjects to retrieve particular exemplars; activation of competitors is likely to impede report of the appropriate item. In retroactive interference, study-test trials on second-list items require subjects to give only the most recent response, rendering first-list items as errors. In part–set cueing inhibition, however, subjects may report any item at any time. Activation of competing items is not inappropriate, because the report of any is a correct response. It is not clear, then, why retrieval inhibition should be necessary in this task.

IV. A CRITERION FOR INHIBITION IN LONG-TERM MEMORY

Most of the "inhibitory" phenomena reviewed in the introduction can be caused by the variety of associative and cue bias mechanisms outlined in the noninhibitory section of our taxonomy. Although each of these processes, from the standpoint of someone researching the causes of retrieval failure, is a potentially interesting source of forgetting (deserving investigation in its own right), these alternative mechanisms pose a problem for anyone interested in exploring the properties of inhibitory processes: How can genuine inhibition be differentiated from occlusion, resource diffusion, associative decrement, or biases in retrieval cues? For any inhibitory paradigm, some unknown mixture of these mechanisms may contribute to impairment. This ambiguity makes it difficult not only to assess the quantitative and qualitative properties of inhibition, but also to establish the contribution of inhibitory mechanisms at all. Criteria for what constitutes evidence for an inhibitory mechanism are clearly needed.

The previous section reviewed several theoretical mechanisms that might produce genuine inhibition of memory items. When we say an item is inhibited in the theoretical sense, we assert that the representation of that item has suffered a decrease in its activation. The difficulty in believing that the performance impairments reviewed in the introduction reflect inhibition arises because it is never clear that anything has truly happened to the representations of the nonretrieved items. In this section, we review a minimal criterion (i.e., one that is necessary, but may not be sufficient) that a phenomenon must meet to be convincingly established as inhibitory—a criterion referred to as *cue-independent impairment*. We then review the independent probe method, a technique developed by Anderson and Spellman (1991a, 1991b, 1993) for establishing cue-independent forgetting. We present evidence using this paradigm that despite our skepticism has led us to believe that inhibitory mechanisms do produce forgetting in long-term memory.

Anderson and Spellman (1991a, 1991b, 1993) noted that an appropriate test for inhibition must measure changes in the target representation separately from changes to associations and cues. Although associative and cue bias factors seem hopelessly confounded with target inhibition in current paradigms, these factors may be separated if we consider the implication of one crucial observation: Whereas inhibitory models localize impairment to the item itself, factors such as associative bias and cue bias are extrinsic to the target. The fact that extrinsic factors cause impairment implies that changes in the retrieval cue by which an item is accessed should eliminate impairment arising from noninhibitory mechanisms. Any remaining impairment, therefore, should reflect changes in the state of the target, presumably caused by retrieval-based inhibitory processes. For example, if retrieval practice of Fruit–Orange truly inhibits the representation of Banana, recall of Banana should decrease regardless of whether subjects are cued with the category Fruit or with an independent cue such as Monkey. Thus, associative bias and cue bias models predict cue-dependent forgetting (Tulving, 1974), whereas target bias (inhibitory) models predict that forgetting should be independent of the cue used to test the impaired item. If we observe impairment when recall is tested with a cue that is unrelated to the strengthened item, we have a measure of inhibition free from the influences of the noninhibitory mechanisms outlined in this chapter.

To determine whether impairment caused by an inhibitory paradigm is cue independent, independent probes must be used to test recall of impaired items—that is, recall must be tested with probes sufficiently related to impaired items to be effective cues, but that are both (1) unrelated to strengthened competitors and (2) unrelated to the cue shared by the impaired item and its strengthened competitor. For instance, in the preceding example (cuing Banana with Monkey, given that Fruit–Orange was practiced), Monkey is related to Banana, but not to Orange, so it is likely to activate Banana selectively. Because Monkey is not strongly related to Fruit, the common cue linking Orange and Banana, its presentation will not activate Fruit, avoiding the indirect activation of Orange. Thus, Monkey serves as an independent probe for Banana. Following Anderson and Spellman (1991a, 1991b, 1993), we will refer to the use of such an independent cue to assess the activational state of an item as the *independent probe method*.

Anderson and Spellman (1991a, 1991b, 1993) applied the independent probe method to determine whether retrieval-induced forgetting (Anderson, Bjork, & Bjork, in press) is caused by occlusion or by genuine inhibitory processes. They reasoned that if impairment in the retrieval-practice paradigm resulted from lateral inhibitory processes among category exemplars, impairment should be cue independent. To test this prediction, Anderson and Spellman used Anderson et al.'s procedure, but with one crucial change: Unlike Anderson et al.'s work, in which categories were as unrelated as possible, Anderson and Spellman designed their materials so that items from some pairs of categories were similar to one another. Specifically, when two categories were members of the *related category condition*, three members of each category were unique to that category and three members could be categorized under the paired category. Figure 11 illustrates their stimulus materials (with only two items per category, for simplicity). In the example illustrated in Figure 11, the items Blood and Bread are unique to their respective categories, Red and Food, in the sense that they are not categorizable under each other's category label (e.g., Blood is not usually considered

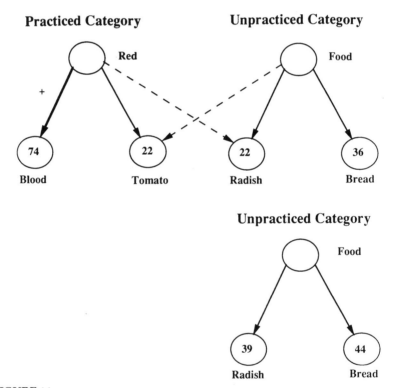

FIGURE 11

Design and results from a study by Anderson and Spellman (1991a, 1991b, 1993). The top materials illustrate the related-category condition, in which two categories with semantic overlap (one category—Red—partially practiced, the other unpracticed) are studied. The bottom illustrates the unrelated-category condition in which only one of the above paired categories is studied; it serves as the control against which to measure inhibition in the related-category condition. Recall percentages for each condition appear in the nodes for the relevant item.

a Food). In contrast, Tomato and Radish, though appearing under the categories Red and Food, respectively, within the context of the experiment, may equally well be categorized under each other's experimental category (e.g., Tomatoes are also Food); that is, strong a priori associations exist between these exemplars and another category name (depicted by dotted lines). Anderson and Spellman used these materials to distinguish occlusion from genuine inhibition in the following manner. If Red–Blood is practiced, then, according to lateral inhibition, Tomato should suffer because of its membership in the Red category. Because Radish is also subsumed under the Red category (though only in semantic memory), it should also be impaired by practicing Red–Blood, even though Radish was studied and tested under the Food category (an independent probe). If occlusion causes retrieval-induced forgetting, studying and testing Radish under the Food category should provide a retrieval route to Radish uninfluenced by the practice of Red–Blood; Blood is not usually Food, so Blood should not intrude given the cue Food. Thus, occlusion predicts that practicing Red–Blood should impair Red–Tomato, but not Food–Radish.

Figure 11 displays results from a representative study by Anderson and Spellman. Mean recall scores are aligned with example items from the various experimental conditions. Replicating Anderson, Bjork, and Bjork (in press), retrieval practice significantly improved performance on unique items (e.g., Red–Blood) relative to the comparable baseline items (e.g., Food–Bread), but only at the expense of performance on other items in the practiced category (e.g., Red–Tomato). Of greater interest for present purposes is the impaired performance on Red items studied and tested under the Food category (e.g., Food–Radish), relative to those same items when Red things were not studied by subjects. Interestingly, impairment on these cross-categorizable items does not seem lessened by their encoding under an independent category context. This basic finding was replicated several times using different materials. Thus, Anderson and Spellman's results support the notion that retrieval practice impairs nonpracticed items via active inhibitory processes, not because of associative or cue bias mechanisms. Impairment can occur even when memory is tested with an independent retrieval cue.[5]

Models other than occlusion can also be ruled out with this demonstration of cue-independent impairment—at least with respect to cross-

---

[5]It should also be noted that the remaining items such as Food–Bread, which are not categorizable under the practiced category, Red, were also impaired (8%) by practicing Red–Blood, but not as much as the critical items (17%). Because Bread cannot fall under the Red category, its impairment appears to be inconsistent with a lateral inhibitory model. Subsequent experiments by Anderson and Spellman replicated this unusual finding and established the conditions necessary for it to occur. Careful analysis reveals that this finding is indeed predicted by lateral inhibitory models as well as by certain distributed models of retrieval inhibition (Anderson & Spellman, 1993).

category inhibition. To see this, consider what models, such as resource diffusion, associative decrement, meaning bias, and context bias, would predict in the independent probe paradigm. According to resource diffusion, practicing Red–Blood should decrease the flow of activation for Red–Tomato, because Blood and Tomato compete for activational resources from a common cue. Furthermore, such practice might decrease the flow of activation across the semantic link connecting Red and Radish, even though Radish was studied as a Food. Because Radish was tested using the Food cue, however, decreased efficacy of the Red–Radish semantic link is irrelevant to recall performance. Also, because the rate at which activation spreads across the Food–Radish link should be unaffected by practice of Red–Blood, performance on Radish should be unaffected. Similar logic applies to associative decrement and meaning bias models. As long as performance is tested with an independent cue, such as Food, bias of the Red cue, or associative decrement of the Red–Radish semantic link should be irrelevant. Finally, because Food was an unpracticed category, subjects ought to use the original learning context to search memory; thus, performance on Food–Radish should be unimpaired, according to context bias models.

This example illustrates the usefulness of the cue independence criterion for establishing inhibition. Because inhibitory mechanisms focus on the state of the item itself, rather than on the associations or the cue, they predict impairment where there should be none, according to noninhibitory models. Furthermore, there is nothing in the logic of cue-independent impairment that restricts the criterion to episodic memory recall; thus it should apply to inhibitory phenomena across a variety of domains. If a given phenomenon can be shown to meet this criterion, then, in most cases, all models on the left branch of the taxonomy in Figure 1 can be ruled out as necessary causes of the impairment. It should be emphasized, however, that we believe cue independent to be a minimal criterion for the establishment of a phenomenon as inhibitory. Further elaboration of the properties of items demonstrating cue-independent impairment may render the inhibitory interpretation unsatisfactory. However, given the inadequacy of the noninhibitory alternatives at explaining the results of Anderson and Spellman, and the plausibility of the functional role of inhibitory processes in retrieval, we interpret the results of Anderson and Spellman as evidence for the existence of inhibitory mechanisms in long-term memory.

V. THREE CHALLENGES FOR A THEORY OF RETRIEVAL INHIBITION

The previous sections emphasized the variety of mechanisms that may contribute to so-called inhibitory effects in long-term memory.

Clearly, empirical work must be done to clarify the relative contributions of such mechanisms in inhibitory paradigms. As we have indicated, however, we believe there is good reason to think that true inhibitory mechanisms at least play a role in some cases of retrieval inhibition—particularly where impairment is demonstrated to be cue independent. But even if impairment in a variety of retrieval inhibition paradigms is shown to be cue independent, there remain many theoretical issues regarding the specific nature of this inhibition. In this section, we present three theoretical challenges for those interested in understanding retrieval inhibition and its function in long-term memory.

A. Explain Why Retrieval Inhibition Lasts So Long

The notion of a "true" inhibitory process underlying retrieval inhibition rests on a theoretical comparison to inhibition on the neuronal level. Frequently, it is unclear whether this comparison implies that retrieval inhibition genuinely reflects the consequences of neuronal inhibition, or whether inhibition is to be taken metaphorically. Although it is clear that retrieval inhibition does not represent hyperpolarization of individual neurons, as connoted in the simple network diagrams used throughout the chapter, it can be argued that it reflects inhibition of a population of neurons, the relationships among which represent the item. If the aggregate behavior of this system of neurons reflects that of its component neurons, retrieval inhibition may behave like neuronal inhibition. If retrieval inhibition is shown to behave similarly to neuronal inhibition, a neuronal interpretation of the phenomenon will become more convincing.

One characteristic of retrieval inhibition that seems at odds with a neuronal interpretation is the difference in the durability between the two phenomena. Whereas the result of an inhibitory impulse into a neuron is quite brief (between a few milliseconds and a few seconds; see Kandel & Schwartz, 1991), retrieval inhibition appears to last far longer. For example, in a classic series of studies, Postman, Stark, and Fraser (1968), demonstrated that retroactive interference lasts as long as 26 min. In our retrieval-induced forgetting paradigm, we still observed impairment after a 20-min retention interval (Anderson & Bjork, 1990; Anderson et al., in press; Anderson & Spellman, 1991a, 1991b, 1993). How can retrieval inhibition last so long if it is caused by neuronal inhibitory mechanisms? Although many researchers consider inhibitory mechanisms a viable interpretation of retrieval inhibition, little attention has been devoted to this glaring inconsistency with the properties of neuronal inhibition.

Although we will not attempt to answer this question here, we will suggest three alternatives that can explain why retrieval inhibition endures as long as it does. The first interpretation is that it does not truly endure throughout the retention interval; rather, it may be the dominance of strengthened exemplars over nonstrengthened competitors that endures. An enduring facilitation of strengthened exemplars may, at test, recreate inhibitory effects on nonstrengthened items because of the propensity for strengthened items to be reported first. Thus, the apparent discrepancy in the durability of inhibitory effects may not truly exist. Results from a study by Anderson et al. (in press), however, argue that such output interference is not the sole source of inhibitory effects. Anderson et al., employing the retrieval-practice procedure reviewed earlier, controlled the order in which subjects reported category exemplars by substituting a category-plus-stem completion test for the normal category-cued free recall procedure. By testing practiced items after unpracticed items in a category, Anderson et al. removed output interference as a potential cause of inhibition. Inhibition on unpracticed items was still observed, though decreased in magnitude relative to the condition in which practiced items were reported first. These findings were replicated using a somewhat different paradigm (Anderson & Spellman, 1991a, 1991b, 1993), reinforcing the interpretation that inhibitory effects are, in fact, quite durable. Thus, although persisting dominance of strengthened items may produce new inhibitory effects on each subsequent test, they appear only to compound an existing inhibitory effect.

A second approach to explaining the durability of retrieval inhibition is to recognize that such inhibitory effects represent the aggregate behavior of complex systems of neurons. Although the behavior of these systems might reflect that of its component neurons, it seems at least plausible that the behavior of the complex system will vary in quantitative if not qualitative respects from the behavior of its constituents. Thus, inhibition of the higher level system may behave like inhibition on the neuronal level, but it may be manifested on a larger time scale. Though underspecified, this class of possibilities cannot truly be ruled out in the absence of a characterization of the relevant neuronal circuitry.

Finally, inhibitory processes may be actively sustained throughout the retention interval. Recall performance should be impaired if inhibition is continuously applied to the representation. Sustained inhibition might be mediated by the sustained preparation of practiced responses during the retention interval via lateral inhibitory links, perhaps to prevent rebound effects from disrupting performance. However, it is not clear why sustained preparation should be necessary in many of the tasks in which enduring inhibition is observed. For example, in our retrieval-practice paradigm, subjects perceive the retrieval-practice phase as the final test; thus, they should not be actively maintaining practiced responses in a state of preparedness throughout the retention interval. Any such theory of the durability of inhibitory effects should be accompanied by a theory of response preparedness.

B. Specify the Relationship between Attentional Inhibition and Retrieval Inhibition

As alluded to in our discussion of inhibitory mechanisms, retrieval inhibition may bear an interesting relationship to phenomena in selective attention. At a minimum, attentional suppression and retrieval inhibition appear functionally analogous: tasks in both domains require the isolation of a target representation from among a set of active alternatives to produce a response. Even granting this functional analogy, however, the specific relation between these phenomena remains unclear. We believe that clarification of the relation of these two areas is theoretically important and would yield interesting empirical ideas. We next consider several interpretations of the relationship between these phenomena.

First, the computational problems in selective attention and memory retrieval may not merely be similar—they may be exactly the same problems solved with the same attentional focusing mechanisms. Focusing attention to a target item may, in some circumstances, result in long-term suppression of distractors similar to what we observe in retrieval inhibition paradigms. A common inhibitory mechanism underlying both retrieval inhibition and attentional suppression does not seem far-fetched when we step away from the traditional divisions made between these domains. For example, the color–word responses inhibited in the Stroop version of the distractor suppression effect (Neill, 1977) are clearly stored in memory—thus, impairment in naming the color on subsequent trials might just as well be referred to as retrieval inhibition. Similarly, the interfering quality of distractors in selective attention arises from their activation of memory representations that disrupt focusing processes. It seems a relatively simple extension to allow activation of distractors to arise internally through spreading activation from other memory representations. Thus, resolving competition during memory retrieval might be regarded as selectively attending to memory items. Although memory researchers often focus on the process of recall for its own sake, it is perhaps more general and realistic to consider memory as having evolved in service of action and perception. When considered in this light, a common mechanism underlying these phenomena should not seem surprising.

A second possibility is that attentional suppression and retrieval inhibition may be produced by similar mechanisms at different levels in the nervous system. To understand this possibility, consider an example of inhibition in motor control. When the flexor muscle of a limb receives an impulse, inhibitory signals are normally sent to the corresponding extensor muscles, preventing them from contracting during flexor contraction. The reverse occurs when the extensor is contracted. Mutual inhibition prevents the paralysis that might result if the opposing muscles were employed in parallel for physically conflicting actions. This mechanism might be functionally similar to that occurring in retrieval inhibition; in retrieval practice, for example, the task requires that one response be given, although many incompatible responses become activated. Because one response must be produced, others might be inhibited. Even the most steadfast supporter of a comparison between motor and retrieval inhibition, however, would never suggest that the same specific circuitry (i.e., circuitry at the same physical location in the nervous system) underlies both processes. At best, these might be functionally analogous mechanisms at two levels of organization in the nervous system—that is, they may both be instances of the way the nervous system solves the problem of selection (see Allport, 1987; Neumann, 1987; Tipper, 1985, for discussions of the role of inhibition in selection). Similarly, although attentional suppression and retrieval inhibition may involve similar inhibitory circuitry, they may occur in functionally distinct systems, or at different levels of organization in the nervous system.

Third, it is possible for attentional suppression and retrieval inhibition to be functionally analogous, yet mechanistically distinct. This would be especially plausible given the discovery of both qualitative and quantitative differences between the inhibitory phenomena. However, differences in implementation should not necessarily lead to the abandonment of the functional analogy; it may still be appropriate to view the two mechanisms as different ways of achieving the selection of a single response from among a set of distracting competitors.

Finally, attentional suppression and retrieval inhibition may be functionally distinct, but mechanistically analogous. We include this possibility because we wish to emphasize that all cases of inhibition need not reflect functionally similar circumstances. The assumption of functional similarity between retrieval inhibition and attentional suppression seems plausible because impairment in the two cases appears precipitated by circumstances in which a response selection must be made. It is possible, however, that similar inhibitory circuitry might serve different functions across the domains of selective attention and memory retrieval. For example, one can acknowledge that selection of the appropriate memory trace is a necessary component of retrieval without accepting the premise that inhibitory mechanisms subserve that function. Impairment of related memory traces during selection may represent the consequence of some functional demand that is merely correlated with selection of the memory trace. Though this logical possibility should be considered, its advocates need to (1) specify a theory of the function of inhibition in memory retrieval that is not based on selection, and (2) specify how selection in memory retrieval, unlike selection in attention, can occur without the aid of inhibition.

C. Provide a Computational Mechanism That Can Capture the Flexibility of Inhibition

In our discussions of the relationship between attentional suppression and retrieval inhibition, we speculated that both phenomena may be produced by a flexibly controlled inhibitory mechanism. The active character of this hypothetical process is motivated by two aspects of attentional suppression. First, effects such as negative priming occur when subjects attempt to ignore a distracting stimulus while attending to a target. Subjects know they must ignore the distracting image and seem able to wield control over the process. Second, it seems implausible that an automatic lateral inhibitory process underlies negative priming because such processes are usually thought to occur between computational units with some a priori competitive relationship (e.g., logical or physical incompatibility of responses, similarity). That negative priming occurs to the semantic representation of a distracting item that is semantically unrelated to the target (e.g., a saxophone and a dog) leads one to question whether lateral inhibition is a good model of negative priming. Thus, it seems plausible that negative priming results from a controlled, goal-directed inhibitory process.

These speculations about a controllable inhibitory process, though intriguing, are relatively vague about the mechanism's functional characteristics and how they might be implemented on a computational level. Exactly how flexible might such a mechanism be? Could any representation be inhibited at any time, or must that representation be actively interfering with the processing of some other stimulus or response? If this process can inhibit any representation, how is this possible on a mechanistic level? Normally, inhibition is thought to spread from one computational unit across inhibitory connections to the to-be-inhibited unit. Must we assume that there exists some unit or inhibitory circuit that has inhibitory links to all possible representations? How would such a structure inhibit items selectively in coordination with patterns of controlled activation? Might such focusing of attention on internal representations operate by principles similar to those employed by thalamic gating mechanisms thought to underlie visual selective attention (Crick, 1984; Laberge, 1990; Scheibel, 1981; Yingling & Skinner, 1977)? If we are to make empirical and theoretical progress in differentiating controlled from automatic forms of inhibition, a clearer theory of how controlled inhibition occurs must be developed.

VI. SUMMARY AND CONCLUSIONS

A central mission of this volume has been to examine the extent to which empirical evidence justifies the postulation of inhibitory mechanisms in the variety of domains in which they have become popular: selective attention, memory retrieval, and language processing. This question arises because, for many empirical phenomena, theories proposing an excess of facilitation on opposing responses can account for performance impairments as effectively as inhibitory models. Such ambiguity renders use of inhibitory constructs a matter of theoretical taste. The present chapter discusses an instance of this issue arising in research on forgetting from long-term memory: the issue of whether retrieval inhibition—impaired accessibility to demonstratably available memory items—is produced by inhibitory or noninhibitory mechanisms. We addressed this issue through two contributions: (1) a review and integration (in the form of a taxonomy) of the noninhibitory and inhibitory mechanisms that might underlie retrieval inhibition, and (2) an empirical criterion by which these models might be distinguished.

In our view, noninhibitory models are those models that do not appeal to a subtractive process reducing the level of activation of impaired items. Noninhibitory models of retrieval inhibition can be grouped into three general classes according to the source of bias in performance. Associative bias models emphasize the role of associations linking the retrieval cue and the target memory; cue bias models attribute retrieval inhibition to biases in the meaning of the functional retrieval cue toward features of frequently used items; and executive control models assert that impaired performance arises from biases in executive control factors such as the point of search termination and the familiarity threshold for reporting items. Much of the data on retrieval inhibition are consistent with at least some of these noninhibitory mechanisms, making them difficult to distinguish from inhibitory models, and, indeed, from each other.

Inhibitory models are those models that attribute performance impairment to a decrease in the activation of the affected item as a result of an activation-reducing mechanism. At least two general classes of inhibitory models may be distinguished: lateral inhibitory and attentional suppression models. Lateral inhibitory models normally presuppose a priori competitive relationships among items bearing certain characteristics (e.g., similarity, logical incompatibility)—competition that is built into the structure of memory in the form of inhibitory connections linking incompatible items. Such competitive processes are often thought to be automatic. Attentional suppression models, on the other hand, propose flexible, goal-directed inhibitory processes that can be applied to any representation whose activation interferes with ongoing processing. Though less developed computationally, such models suggest an interesting link between inhibitory phenomena in selective attention and long-term memory.

From the standpoint of theoretical parsimony, it seems unnecessarily complex to postulate inhibitory processes such as those in lateral inhibition and attentional suppression to account for data that can be explained adequately by ostensibly simpler, noninhibitory models. However, as stressed in our discussion of lateral inhibitory models, many noninhibitory models propose additional processes, that although not labeled as inhibitory, may disguise or rename an inhibitory process. For example, both occlusion (e.g., McGeoch, 1942; Raajimakers & Shiffrin, 1981; Rundus, 1973) and resource diffusion (e.g., Anderson, 1976, 1983) models, as summarized earlier, make limited capacity assumptions with respect to an output channel and activational resources, respectively. Yet, it is never explained how those capacities come to be limited (see also, Neumann, 1987, for a related critique of limited resource theories of attention in general). In our section on lateral inhibitory models, we developed lateral inhibitory circuits illustrating how the behavior of such noninhibitory processes might be modeled via inhibitory mechanisms. To the extent that limited-capacity assumptions are necessary to implement noninhibitory mechanisms, and to the extent that those assumptions bury inhibitory processes, noninhibitory models may not be more parsimonious.

But theoretical parsimony is not the only basis on which to prefer one class of models over another. We argue that inhibitory processes may be distinguished from noninhibitory alternatives by a general criterion developed by Anderson and Spellman (1991a, 1991b, 1993): cue-independent impairment. Applied to episodic recall paradigms, cue-independent impairment requires that recall deficits of an item be measurable from a separate retrieval cue (i.e., separate from the one associated to both the strengthened competitor and the target), something which should occur if the representation of the item is truly less active. We review a study by Anderson and Spellman demonstrating cue-independent impairment. This finding cannot be explained by any of the noninhibitory models in our taxonomy and suggests that inhibitory mechanisms play an important role in retrieval-induced forgetting. Many challenges remain, however, in the theoretical characterization of this inhibition (e.g., how does it last so long?) and how it might relate to other inhibitory phenomena such as attentional inhibition.

Although retrieval inhibition should generally be regarded as a descriptive label, we believe that evidence of cue-independent impairment warrants the use of the term in its stronger mechanistic sense—at least in the case of retrieval-induced forgetting. The functional conditions under which this impairment occurs mirror those present in attentional suppression, suggesting an exciting computational principle—and perhaps a common mechanism—mediating the phenomena.

ACKNOWLEDGMENTS

Preparation of this chapter was supported in part by Contract MDA 903-89-K-0179 from the Army Research Institute to Keith J. Holyoak. The authors gratefully acknowledge John Hummel and Tom Wickens for extensive comments on early drafts of this chapter, and Laura Da Costa for editorial assistance on the final version. We also wish to thank Dale Dagenbach and Tom Carr for insightful comments and recommendations.

REFERENCES

Allport, A. (1987). Selection for action: Some behavioral and neurophysiological considerations of attention and action. In H. Heuer & A. F. Sanders (Eds.), *Perspectives on perception and action* (pp. 395–420). Hillsdale, NJ: Lawrence Erlbaum.

Anderson, J. R. (1974). Retrieval of propositional information from long-term memory. *Cognitive Psychology, 6,* 451–474.

Anderson, J. R. (1976). *Language, memory and thought.* Hillsdale, NJ: Lawrence Erlbaum.

Anderson, J. R. (1983). *The architecture of cognition.* Cambridge, MA: Harvard University Press.

Anderson, M. C., & Bjork, R. A. (1990, November). *Category-specific retrieval inhibition.* Paper presented at the annual conference of the Psychonomic Society, New Orleans, LA.

Anderson, M. C., Bjork, R. A., & Bjork, E. L. (in press). Remembering can cause forgetting: Retrieval dynamics in long-term memory. *Journal of Experimental Psychology: Learning, Memory, and Cognition.*

Anderson, M. C., & Spellman, B. A. (1991a, June). *Retrieval practice inhibits similar memories, regardless of whether common cues are shared.* Poster presented at the annual conference of the American Psychological Society, Washington, D.C.

Anderson, M. C., & Spellman, B. A. (1991b, July). *Does genuine inhibition occur in long-term memory?* Paper presented at the International Conference on Memory, Lancaster, England.

Anderson, M. C., & Spellman, B. A. (1993). *On the status of inhibitory mechanisms in cognition: Memory Retrieval as a Model Case.* Manuscript submitted for publication.

Barnes, J. M., & Underwood, B. J. (1959). "Fate" of first-list associations in transfer theory. *Journal of Experimental Psychology, 58,* 95–105.

Barsalou, L. W. (1982). Context dependent and context independent information in concepts. *Memory & Cognition, 10,* 82–93.

Barsalou, L. W. (1987). The instability of graded structure: Implications for the nature of concepts. In U. Neisser (Ed.), *Concepts and conceptual development: Ecological and intellectual factors in categorization* (pp. 101–140). Cambridge: Cambridge University Press.

Barsalou, L. W. (1989). Intraconcept and interconcept similarity. In S. Vosniadou and A. Ortony (Eds.), *Similarity and analogical reasoning*. New York: Cambridge University Press.

Basden, D. R., Basden, B. H., & Galloway, B. C. (1977). Inhibition with part-list cuing: Some tests of the item strength hypothesis. *Journal of Experimental Psychology: Human Learning and Memory, 3*, 100–108.

Beech, A., Powell, T., McWilliams, J., & Claridge, G. (1989). Evidence of reduced "cognitive inhibition" in schizophrenia. *British Journal of Clinical Psychology, 28*, 110–116.

Bjork, R. A. (1972). Theoretical implications of directed forgetting. In A. W. Melton & E. Martin (Eds.), *Coding processes in human memory*. Washington, DC: Winston & Sons.

Bjork, R. A. (1989). Retrieval inhibition as an adaptive mechanism in human memory. In H. L. Roediger & F. I. M. Craik (Eds.), *Varieties of memory and consciousness: Essays in honour of Endel Tulving* (pp. 309–330). Hillsdale, NJ: Lawrence Erlbaum.

Blaxton, T. A., & Neely, J. H. (1983). Inhibition from semantically related primes: Evidence of a category-specific inhibition. *Memory & Cognition, 11*, 500–510.

Brown, A. S. (1991). The tip of the tongue experience: A review and evaluation. *Psychological Bulletin, 109*, 204–223.

Burke, D. M., MacKay, D. G., Worthley, J. S., & Wade, E. (1991). On the tip of the tongue: What causes word finding failures in young and older adults? *Journal of Memory and Language, 30*, 542–579.

Butter, C. M. (1969). Perseveration in extinction and in discrimination reversal tasks following selective frontal ablations in *Macaca Mulatta*. *Physiology and Behavior, 4*, 163–171.

Carr, T. H., & Dagenbach, D. (1990). Semantic priming and repetition priming from masked words: Evidence for a center-surround attentional mechanism in perceptual recognition. *Journal of Experimental Psychology: Learning, Memory and Cognition, 16*, 341–350.

Chandler, C. C. (1989). Specific retroactive interference in modified recognition tests: Evidence for an unknown cause of interference. *Journal of Experimental Psychology: Learning, Memory and Cognition, 15*, 256–265.

Chandler, C. C. (1993). Accessing related events increases retroactive interference in a matching recognition test. *Journal of Experimental Psychology: Learning, Memory and Cognition, 19*, 967–974.

Coe, W. C., Basden, B. H., Basden, D., & Fikes, T. (1989). Directed forgetting and posthypnotic amnesia: Information processing and social contexts. *Journal of Personality and Social Psychology, 56*, 189–198.

Crick, F. (1984). The function of the thalamic reticular complex: The searchlight hypothesis. *Proceedings of the National Academy of Sciences of the U.S.A., 81*, 4586–4590.

Crowder, R. G. (1976). *Principles of learning and memory*. Hillsdale, NJ: Lawrence Erlbaum.

Dagenbach, D., Carr, T. H., & Barnhardt, T. M. (1990). Inhibitory semantic priming of lexical decisions due to failure to retrieve weakly activated codes. *Journal of Experimental Psychology: Learning, Memory and Cognition, 16*, 328–340.

Dempster, F. N. (1991). Inhibitory processes: A neglected dimension of intelligence. *Intelligence, 15*, 157–173.

Epstein, W. (1972). Mechanisms in directed forgetting. In G. H. Bower (Ed.), *The psychology of learning and motivation* (Vol. 6, pp. 147–192). New York: Academic Press.

Erdelyi, M. H., & Goldberg, B. (1979). Let's not sweep repression under the rug: Toward a cognitive psychology of repression. In J. F. Kihlstrom & F. J. Evans (Eds.), *Functional disorders of memory* (pp. 355–402). Hillsdale, NJ: Lawrence Erlbaum.

Estes, W. K. (1955). Statistical theory of spontaneous recovery and regression. *Psychological Review, 62*, 369–377.

Estes, W. K. (1972). An associative basis for coding and organization in memory. In A. W. Melton & E. Martin (Eds.), *Coding processes in human memory* (pp. 161–191). New York: Wiley.

Freud, S. A. (1952). *A general introduction to psychoanalysis* (J. Riviere, trans.). New York: Washington Square Press. (Originally published, 1920.)

Fuster, J. M. (1989). *The prefrontal cortex: Anatomy, physiology, and neuropsychology of the frontal lobe.* New York: Raven Press.

Geiselman, R. E., & Bagheri, B. (1985). Repetition effects in directed forgetting: Evidence for retrieval inhibition. *Memory & Cognition, 13*, 51–62.

Geiselman, R. E., Bjork, R. A., & Fishman, D. (1983). Disrupted retrieval in directed forgetting: A link with posthypnotic amnesia. *Journal of Experimental Psychology: General, 112*, 58–72.

Gernsbacher, M. A., Barner, K. R., & Faust, M. E. (1990). Investigating differences in general comprehension skill. *Journal of Experimental Psychology: Learning, Memory and Cognition, 16*, 430–445.

Hartman, M., & Hasher, L. (1991). Aging and suppression: Memory for previously relevant information. *Psychology and Aging, 6*, 587–594.

Hasher, L., Stoltzfus, E. R., Zacks, R. T., & Rypma, B. (1991). Age and inhibition. *Journal of Experimental Psychology: Learning, Memory and Cognition, 17*, 163–169.

Hasher, L., & Zacks, R. T. (1988). Working memory, comprehension and aging: A review and a new view. In G. H. Bower (Ed.), *The psychology of learning and motivation* (Vol. 22, pp. 193–225). New York: Academic Press.

Hinton, G. E., & Plaut, D. C. (1987). Using fast weights to deblur old memories. *Proceedings of the Ninth Annual Conference of the Cognitive Science Society* (pp. 177–186). Hillsdale, NJ: Lawrence Erlbaum.

Hintzman, D. L. (1978). *The psychology of learning and memory* (pp. 297–304). San Francisco: W. H. Freeman.

Kandel, E. P., & Schwartz, J. H. (1991). *Principles of neural science.* New York: Elsevier.

Katz, J. J., & Postal, P. (1964). *An integrated theory of linguistic descriptions.* Cambridge, MA: MIT Press.

Keele, S. W., & Neill, W. T. (1978). Mechanisms of attention. In E. C. Carterette & M. P. Friedman (Eds.), *Handbook of perception IX.* (pp. 3–47). New York: Academic Press.

Kihlstrom, J. F. (1983). Instructed forgetting: Hypnotic and nonhypnotic. *Journal of Experimental Psychology: General, 112*, 73–79.

Laberge, D. (1990). Thalamic and cortical mechanisms of attention suggested by recent positron emission tomographic experiments. *Journal of Cognitive Neuroscience, 2*, 358–372.

Levy, W. B., & Steward, O. (1983). Temporal contiguity requirement for long-term associative potentiation/depression in the hippocampus. *Neuroscience, 8*, 791–797.

Lewandowsky, S. (1991). Gradual unlearning and catastrophic interference: A comparison of distributed architectures. In W. E. Hockey and S. Lewandowsky (Eds.), *Relating theory and data: Essays in honor of Bennet B. Murdock* (pp. 445–476). Hillsdale, NJ: Lawrence Erlbaum.

Lewis, C. H., & Anderson, J. R. (1976). Interference with real world knowledge. *Cognitive Psychology, 7*, 311–335.

Lindsay, D. S. (1993). Eyewitness suggestibility. *Current Directions in Psychological Science, 2*, 86–88.

Loftus, E. F. (1979). The malleability of memory. *American Scientist, 67*, 312–320.

Loftus, E. F., & Loftus, G. R. (1980). On the permanence of stored information in the human brain. *American Psychologist, 35*, 409–420.

Logan, G. D., & Cowan, W. B. (1984). On the ability to inhibit thought and action: A theory of an act of control. *Psychological Review, 91*, 295–327.

Logan, G. D. (1985). Executive control of thought and action. *Acta Psychologica, 60*, 193–210.

Luce, R. D. (1959). *Individual choice behavior.* New York: Wiley.

Luria, A. R. (1966). *Higher cortical functions in man.* London: Tavistock.

Martin, E. (1971). Verbal learning theory and independent retrieval phenomena. *Psychological Review, 78*, 314–332.

Martindale, C. (1981). *Cognition and consciousness.* Homewood, IL: Dorsey Press.

McClelland, J. L., & Rumelhart, D. E. (1981). An interactive activation model of context effects in letter perception: Part 1. An account of basic findings. *Psychological Review, 88*, 375–407.

McCloskey, M., & Cohen, N. J. (1989). Catastrophic interference in connectionist networks: The sequential learning problem. In G. H. Bower (Ed.), *The psychology of learning and motivation* (pp. 109–164). San Diego: Academic Press.

McCloskey, M., & Zaragoza, M. (1985). Misleading postevent information and memory for events: Arguments and evidence against memory impairment hypotheses. *Journal of Experimental Psychology: General, 1*, 1–16.

McGeoch, J. A. (1936). Studies in retroactive inhibition: VII. Retroactive inhibition as a function of the length and frequency of presentation of the interpolated lists. *Journal of Experimental Psychology, 19*, 674–693.

McGeoch, J. A. (1942). *The psychology of human learning.* New York: Longmans, Green.

Melton, A. W., & Irwin, J. M. (1940). The influence of degree of interpolated learning on retroactive inhibition and the overt transfer of specific responses. *American Journal of Psychology, 3*, 173–203.

Mensink, G. J. M., & Raajimakers, J. G. W. (1988). A model of interference and forgetting. *Psychological Review, 95*, 434–455.

Mishkin, M. (1964). Perseveration of central sets after frontal lesions in monkeys. In J. M. Warren & K. Akert (Eds.), *The frontal granular cortex and behavior.* New York: McGraw-Hill.

Murdock, B. B. (1960). The immediate retention of unrelated words. *Journal of Experimental Psychology, 60*, 222–234.

Neely, J. H. (1977). Semantic priming and retrieval from lexical memory: Evidence for facilitatory and inhibitory processes. *Memory & Cognition, 4*, 648–654.

Neely, J. H., Schmidt, S. R., & Roediger, H. L. (1983). Inhibition from related primes in recognition memory. *Journal of Experimental Psychology: Learning, Memory and Cognition, 9*, 196–211.

Neill, W. T. (1977). Inhibitory and facilitatory processes in selective attention. *Journal of Experimental Psychology: Human Perception and Performance, 3*, 444–450.

Neill, W. T. (1989). Lexical ambiguity and context: An activation-suppression model. In D. S. Gorfein (Ed.), *Resolving semantic ambiguity* (pp. 63–83). New York: Springer-Verlag.

Neill, W. T., & Westberry, R. L. (1987). Selective attention and the suppression of cognitive noise. *Journal of Experimental Psychology: Learning, Memory and Cognition, 13*, 327–334.

Neumann, E., & DeSchepper, B. G. (1992). An inhibition-based fan effect: Evidence for an active suppression mechanism in selective attention. *Canadian Journal of Psychology, 46*, 11–50.

Neumann, O. (1987). Beyond capacity: A functional view of attention. In H. Heuer & A. F. Sanders (Eds.), *Perspectives on perception and action* (pp. 361–394). Hillsdale, NJ: Lawrence Erlbaum.

Nickerson, R. S. (1984). Retrieval inhibition from part–set cuing: A persisting enigma in memory research. *Memory & Cognition, 12*, 531–552.

Nicoll, R. A., Kauer, J. A., & Malenka, R. C. (1988). The current excitement in long-term potentiation. *Neuron, 1*, 97–103.

Norman, D. A., & Shallice, T. (1980). Attention to action: Willed and automatic control of behavior. In R. J. Davidson, G. E. Schwarts, & D. Shapiro (Eds.), *Consciousness and self-regulation: Advances in research and theory* (Vol. 4, pp. 1–18). New York: Plenium Press.

Postman, L. (1971). Transfer, interference and forgetting. In J. W. Kling & L. A. Riggs (Eds.), *Woodworth and Schlosberg's: Experimental psychology* (3rd ed.). New York: Holt, Rinehart & Winston.

Postman, L., & Underwood, B. J. (1973). Critical issues in interference theory. *Memory & Cognition, 1*, 19–40.

Postman, L., & Stark, K. (1969). The role of response availability in transfer and interference. *Journal of Experimental Psychology, 79*, 168–177.

Postman, L., Stark, K., & Fraser, J. (1968). Temporal changes in interference. *Journal of Verbal Learning and Verbal Behavior, 7*, 672–694.

Raajimakers, J. W., & Shiffrin, R. M. (1981). Search of associative memory. *Psychological Review, 88*, 93–134.

Radvansky, G. A., & Zacks, R. T. (1991). Mental models and the fan effect. *Journal of Experimental Psychology: Learning, Memory and Cognition, 17*, 940–953.

Radvansky, G. A., Zacks, R. T., & Hasher, L. (1991, May). *Directed forgetting and aging.* Paper presented at the meeting of the Midwestern Psychological Association, Chicago, IL.

Ratcliff, R. (1990). Connectionist models of recognition memory: Constraints imposed by learning and forgetting functions. *Psychological Review, 97*, 285–308.

Ratcliff, R., Clark, S. E., & Shiffrin, R. M. (1990). The list-strength effect: I. Data and discussion. *Journal of Experimental Psychology: Learning, Memory and Cognition, 16*, 163–178.

Reason, J. T., & Lucas, D. (1984). Using cognitive diaries to investigate naturally occurring memory blocks. In J. E. Harris & P. E. Morris (Eds.), *Everyday memory actions and absent-mindedness* (pp. 53–70). London: Academic Press.

Roediger, H. L. (1974). Inhibiting effects of recall. *Memory & Cognition, 2*, 261–269.

Roediger, H. L., & Crowder, R. G. (1972). Instructed forgetting: Rehearsal control or retrieval inhibition (repression)? *Cognitive Psychology, 3*, 244–254.

Roediger, H. L., & Neely, J. H. (1982). Retrieval blocks in episodic and semantic memory. *Canadian Journal of Psychology, 36*, 213–242.

Roth, E. M., & Shoeben, E. J. (1983). The effect of context on the structure of categories. *Cognitive Psychology, 15*, 346–378.

Rumelhart, D. E., Hinton, G. E., & Williams, R. J. (1986). Learning internal representations by error propagation. In D. E. Rumelhart & J. L. McClelland (Eds.), *Parallel distributed processing: Explorations in the microstructure of cognition: Vol. 1. Foundations.* Cambridge, MA: MIT Press.

Rumelhart, D. E., & Norman, D. A. (1982). Simulating a skilled typist: A study of skilled cognitive-motor performance. *Cognitive Science, 6*, 1–36.

Rundus, D. (1973). Negative effects of using list items as retrieval cues. *Journal of Verbal Learning and Verbal Behavior, 12,* 43–50.

Sandson, J., & Albert, M. L. (1984). Varieties of perseveration. *Neuropsychologia, 22*(6), 715–732.

Scheibel, A. B. (1981). The problem of selective attention: A possible structural substrate. In O. Pompeiano & C. Marsen (Eds.), *Brain mechanisms and perceptual awareness.* New York: Raven Press.

Shallice, T. (1988). *From neuropsychology to mental structure.* Cambridge: Cambridge University Press.

Shiffrin, R. M., Ratcliff, R., & Clark, S. E. (1990). The list-strength effect: II. Theoretical mechanisms. *Journal of Experimental Psychology: Learning, Memory and Cognition, 16,* 179–195.

Slamecka, N. J. (1975). Intralist cueing of recognition. *Journal of Verbal Learning and Verbal Behavior, 14,* 630–637.

Sloman, S. A., Bower, G. H., & Roher, D. (1991). Congruency effects in part–list cuing inhibition. *Journal of Experimental Psychology: Learning, Memory and Cognition, 17,* 974–982.

Sloman, S. A., & Rumelhart, D. E. (1992). Reducing interference in distributed memories through episodic gating. In A. Healy, S. Kosslyn, and R. M. Shiffrin (Eds.), *From learning theory to connectionist theory: Essays in honor of William K. Estes* (pp. 227–248). Hillsdale, NJ: Lawrence Erlbaum.

Stanton, P. K., & Sejnowski, T. J. (1989). Associative long-term depression in the hippocampus induced by Hebbian covariance. *Nature, 339,* 215–218.

Sutton, R. S., & Barto, A. G. (1981). Toward a modern theory of adaptive networks: Expectation and prediction. *Psychological Review, 88,* 135–170.

Tipper, S. P. (1985). The negative priming effect: Inhibitory priming and ignored objects. *Quarterly Journal of Experimental Psychology, 37A,* 571–590.

Tipper, S. P. (1992). Selection for action: The role of inhibitory mechanisms. *Current Directions in Psychological Science, 1,* 105–109.

Todres, A. K., & Watkins, M. J. (1981). A part-set cueing effect in recognition. *Journal of Experimental Psychology: Human Learning and Memory, 7,* 91–99.

Tulving, E. (1974). Cue-dependent forgetting. *American Scientist, 62,* 74–82.

Tulving, E., & Pearlstone, Z. (1966). Availability versus accessibility of information in memory for words. *Journal of Verbal Learning and Verbal Behavior, 5,* 381–391.

Tulving, E., & Thomson, D. M. (1973). Encoding specificity and retrieval processes in episodic memory. *Psychological Review, 80,* 352–373.

Walley, R. E., & Weiden, T. D. (1973). Lateral inhibition and cognitive masking: A neuropsychological theory of attention. *Psychological Review, 80,* 284–302.

Waltz, D. L., & Pollack, J. B. (1985). Massively parallel parsing: A strongly interactive model of natural language interpretation. *Cognitive Science, 9,* 51–74.

Watkins, M. J. (1978). Engrams as cuegrams and forgetting as cue-overload: A cueing approach to the structure of memory. In C. R. Puff (Ed.), *The structure of memory* (pp. 347–372). New York: Academic Press.

Yaniv, I., & Meyer, D. E. (1987). Activation and metacognition of inaccessible stored information: Potential bases for incubation effects in problem solving. *Journal of Experimental Psychology: Learning, Memory and Cognition, 13,* 187–205.

Yingling, C. D., & Skinner, J. E. (1977). Gating of thalamic input to cerebral cortex by nucleus reticularis thalami. In J. E. Desmedt (Ed.), *Attention, voluntary contraction and event-related cerebral potentials: Progress in clinical neurophysiology* (Vol. 1, pp. 70–96). Basel: Karger.

8

Inhibitory Processes in Perceptual Recognition
Evidence for a Center-Surround Attentional Mechanism

Dale Dagenbach and Thomas H. Carr

I. INTRODUCTION

Many models of cognitive processes maintain a resolute agnosticism regarding the relative contributions of facilitation and inhibition to observed or predicted effects—making a choice but clearly stating that the choice is arbitrary and could have been made the other way. Although this creates a certain ambiguity, it is a reasonable stance when the model can accomplish its ends using either process and there is no strong evidence to argue in favor of one or the other. Moreover, this stance has the advantage of sidestepping the thorny problems associated with distinguishing empirically between inhibition and facilitation (see Anderson & Bjork, this volume, for discussion of this issue). However, in recent years experimental evidence has begun to provide compelling arguments for specifically invoking inhibitory or facilitatory processes, or a combination of both, in at least some situations. One such situation may occur during the retrieval of information from memory when the sought after information is highly susceptible to interference. In this chapter, we present evidence that attempting to retrieve perceptually activated information from semantic memory under such circumstances is accompanied by active inhibition of related information that is producing the interference. We further suggest that this inhibition reflects the operation of a center-surround attentional mechanism, and summarize the results of experiments bearing on this hypothesis. The term *center-surround* is intended to capture the essence of the mechanism's operating principles. As will be seen, we believe the mechanism works to facilitate a semantic code on which it is focused or "centered" while inhibiting "surrounding" codes, codes that are similar to but different from the desired code and are competing with it for retrieval.

Most of the inhibitory effects that we describe result from semantic priming of lexical decision judgments under circumstances where the prime's semantic representation is not strongly activated. Obtaining inhibition in this context is of interest for at least two reasons. First, there is a voluminous literature documenting facilitation of lexical decision performance by semantically related primes under a wide range of conditions. Indeed, facilitation from semantic priming is so ubiquitous that even its absence is of potential theoretical importance (see, e.g., Friedrich, Henik, & Tzelgov, 1991). Clearly, then, inhibition due to semantic priming is a particularly interesting anomaly deserving of further attention. Second, and more importantly, most accounts of lexical decision performance suggest that it involves the retrieval of information from semantic memory (see, however, Shelton & Martin, 1992, for a different interpretation). As will be discussed, the retrieval of weakly activated information from a system with the characteristics attributed, in most theories, to semantic memory may illustrate one of the basic situations where there are principled reasons for invoking inhibitory processes.

II. SEMANTIC MEMORY AND MODIFICATIONS

A. Network Models

Semantic memory is generally defined as a memory system containing overlearned world knowledge, such as the meanings of words and basic arithmetic facts, embedded in a highly structured associative or relational system (Collins & Loftus, 1975; Tulving, 1972, 1983). Many models describe this system as a networklike structure with interlinked nodes that represent concepts or features. Models of this sort typically characterize the process leading to the retrieval of information as one of activation of the relevant nodes and invoke the concept of automatic spreading activation to explain a variety of findings (e.g., Anderson, 1983; Collins & Loftus, 1975). According to spreading activation theory, transient activation spreads automatically and quickly from one strongly activated node to other associated nodes, thus rendering them more accessible to subsequent retrieval operations.

Much of the evidence used to support the conception of semantic memory as an associative network system with automatic spreading activation between nodes comes from priming studies (see McKoon & Ratcliff, 1992, and McNamara, 1992a, 1992b, for discussions of the role of priming effects in theories of semantic memory). In general, priming studies entail the presentation of pairs of stimuli on a trial, either simultaneously or, more often, sequentially. The relationship between the first item (the prime) and the second (the target) is systematically manipulated, and the consequences of prime–target relatedness for the speed and accuracy of some form of speeded decision about the target are then assessed. In investigations of semantic memory, the speeded decision is often one requiring a judgment about category membership or whether the stimuli are real words. In the latter case, the lexical decision task, responses to word targets are typically faster and more accurate when they are preceded, or primed, by a related word. Thus, *butter* would be identified as a real word more quickly, and would be less likely to be rejected, when it is primed by a word such as *bread* compared to when it is primed by a word such as *house*.

Experimental manipulations of variables such as the stimulus onset asynchrony (SOA) between the prime and target, and the probability of prime–target relatedness, have provided evidence suggesting that these priming effects are due to at least two distinct mechanisms (e.g., Carr, 1986; Neely, 1977, 1991; Posner & Snyder, 1975a, 1975b). One mechanism reflects the operation of automatic processes. It produces facilitation even with very short prime–target SOAs (e.g., less than 250 msec), and seems relatively unaffected by manipulations of subjects' expectations about prime–target relatedness. The second mechanism, termed strategic, produces priming effects that build up more slowly and change in magnitude in response to manipulations of subjects' expectations.

These ideas are especially well illustrated in the results of Neely's (1977) widely cited study in which subjects were required to make category judgments about words. They were informed that if the prime was from one category (e.g., body parts), the probability was very high that the target item would be from another (e.g., building parts). With a long prime–target SOA (approximately 2000 msec), subjects were faster when the expected pattern obtained—when *arm* was followed by *window*, for example—and slower when the target item was from the same category as the prime, relative to when the prime was a neutral cue. However, with short prime–target SOAs (approximately 200 msec), subjects were faster on trials when the prime and target were from the same category, even though the probability of these trials was low and their occurrence ran counter to the subjects' expectations. The standard, two-process theory interpretation of these results would be to attribute the facilitation found at short prime–target SOAs for semantically related items to automatic spreading activation, whereas the facilitation and inhibition found with longer SOAs reflects the operation of strategic processing. These results also suggest that one distinguishing characteristic of strategic priming might be the production of inhibition relative to a neutral condition when a strategic expectation is not met by the target item. However, it should be noted that subsequent studies have pointed out difficulties in determining exactly what constitutes a "neutral" cue that can be used to provide a baseline against which facilitation and inhibition can be accurately assessed (e.g., Jonides & Mack, 1984).

B. Issues in Modifying Semantic Memory

For present purposes, the important part of the preceding theory is the claim that presentation of a word produces automatic processing of it, including activation of its representation and the representations of related or associated words in semantic memory. An interesting question to consider when thinking of semantic memory in such a framework, and one that has been little addressed, is how such a stable, overlearned system of knowledge could get modified in a way that allows new information to be added and provides relatively effective access to the new information as it is being incorporated into the system. A full account of semantic memory must include mechanisms that can modify the system, but in principle it is also desirable to constrain these mechanisms in some way so that the stability of the system is maintained. A system that is unmodifiable would be clearly maladaptive because no new learning could occur. On the other hand, a system that is extremely easy to modify would also be maladaptive because knowledge obtained from past experience would then be easily overturned by a discrepant example. The fine line that must be walked between these two extremes is illustrated in work by Jacoby and Hollingshead (1990) and Brown (1988) showing that erroneous instances can sometimes have quite noticeable impacts on what ought to be well-learned knowledge. These studies report pronounced effects of encountering incorrect spellings on the ability to ascertain correct spellings. Nevertheless, despite the fact that single instances can sometimes cause noticeable impacts, training experiments by Dagenbach, Horst, and Carr (1990) indicate that learning in semantic memory involving the addition or reorganization of word meanings does take place rather slowly, making the system conservative in how it implements long-lasting or permanent change.

In the framework of a semantic memory system with automatic spreading activation, such slow learning is potentially problematic in the following sense: Assuming that new codes entered into the system will be inherently weaker in their activation than older, well-established codes, what is there to prevent the more easily activatable older codes from interfering with attempts to access the weaker new information, especially if the activation levels of the old codes are raised due to automatic spreading activation along the well-learned network connections in which they are embedded?

C. Possible Solutions

There may be a number of plausible solutions to this potential problem. One solution might be to invoke an asymmetric pattern of activation between old and new items in semantic memory such that new items are capable of receiving activation from old items, but the reverse becomes true only gradually. This account would predict that automatic "primability" of new items would be observed after relatively little learning in a semantic task, but automatic priming from the new items to related old items would require much more learning. Little research has addressed this question, but extrapolating from two relevant studies suggests that it is possible. Dagenbach, Horst, and Carr (1990) examined the amount of learning necessary to enable newly learned vocabulary words to produce automatic semantic priming effects for well-known targets and found that it was quite extensive—a 1-week study regimen was insufficient, whereas 5 weeks was sufficient. Potts, St. John, and Kirson (1989) found some evidence for automatic semantic priming of newly learned vocabulary word targets by well-known words with much less study. However, it is unclear whether these findings reflect actual differences in priming versus primability, or are a consequence of procedural differences between the studies. It would be informative to track simultaneously the development of the ability of new items to produce and receive priming within a single study under conditions where the potential primes and targets are studied in exactly the same way.

Another possible solution involves assuming that the initial activation for the new information would be very strong due to the recency of processing, thus offsetting the strength of the older, more established codes. This would allow successful access of the information immediately following an initial encoding into semantic memory. There are, however, potential problems with this solution over a period of time. Say, for example, that one is learning a new member of some category such as birds and that this member is relatively obscure. Repeated encounters with the item should lead to its becoming incorporated into semantic memory structures (see Dagenbach, Horst, & Carr, 1990, and Tulving, Hayman, & MacDonald, 1991, for illustrations of this process). However, presumably one would also encounter more typical members of the bird category over any given period of time, increasing their activation due to recency of processing as well as negating any advantage that the new item might have.

An interesting variation on this might be to invoke constraints on activation parameters, such as an asymptote on the activation level obtainable by well-established items. With this constraint, the baseline activation of new members would increase with repeated exposure, whereas the activation of items already at ceiling would not increase further. This would allow eventual incorporation of new information into the semantic system, with the new information ultimately attaining the same degree of accessibility as the old. This would not seem to solve the problem of accessing the new information during the early stages of its incorporation into the semantic system, but it might be the case that new information is not accessible in semantic memory until it has become well incorporated. This solution accomplishes the desired goal of having a semantic system that is modifiable, but not easily so. New information might be accessible via nonsemantic representations in the interim period. Testing this possibility requires developing good criteria for determining whether performance with newly learned information is based on semantic or nonsemantic—perhaps episodic?—representations (see Carr et al., in press, for a discussion).

Still another plausible solution is to incorporate a search or retrieval mechanism that is able to suppress the activation of related codes while not suppressing the activation of the target code. Such a mechanism might be functionally similar to the mechanism of lateral inhibition in the visual system, and has precursors in many classic theories of attention (e.g., Pillsbury, 1908; Wundt, 1902). A more recent variation on this notion can be found in a neuropsychological theory of attention described by Walley and Weiden (1973). Walley and Weiden suggested that encoding one stimulus actively interferes with the encoding of other stimuli, and that this interference is due to lateral inhibition between neurons in associative cortex that varies as a function of arousal. In their account, the lateral inhibition is proportionately greater for similar stimuli than dissimilar, although stimuli that share the same ultimate perceptual representations do not inhibit each other.

The last 15 years or so have produced a rapid increase in the number of inhibition-oriented proposals for selection among competing codes. In particular, inhibitory processes involving the active suppression of potential distractor items have been invoked extensively in studies of selective attention (Houghton & Tipper, this volume; Keele & Neill, 1978; Neill, 1977; Neill & Westberry, 1987; Tipper, 1985; Tipper & Cranston, 1985; Tipper & Driver, 1988). Many of these studies report inhibition for responses to targets that are identical to, or share qualities with, the distractor items of a preceding trial—negative priming, to use Tipper's (1985) term. Thus, selection of the target in a selective attention task seems to be accomplished in part by active inhibition of distractor items, or at least of the accessibility of their representations to decision and response mechanisms. This inhibition persists over time and can spread from representations of the distractor items to related items.

The importance of such inhibitory processing is underscored by studies of individual differences. Negative priming effects seem to vary inversely across groups of subjects in relationship to the likelihood of successful suppression of potential interference. Populations that are known to be less successful at inhibiting distractor information, such as the elderly or children with attention deficit disorders, show correspondingly less negative priming. Thus, inhibition may have wide utility as a functional means of isolating target items from distractors under conditions in which the distractors work against successful access of the target or successful deployment of information about it. Houghton and Tipper (this volume) summarize these negative priming effects and describe a computational model of an attentional mechanism capable of producing them.

D. Retrieving Weakly Activated Semantic Codes

The situation of interest to us, in which a perceiver attempts to retrieve a weakly activated code from semantic memory under conditions where the code is in danger of being obscured by more strongly activated related codes, seems analogous to that encountered in selective attention studies in at least some respects. An attentional mechanism that is able to enhance the items on which it is focused while suppressing related items (see Figure 1) would clearly be useful in extracting weakly activated codes. It is tempting to speculate that a mechanism similar to that described for selective attention, or perhaps even the same mechanism, might be directed toward perceptual or semantic codes in memory under such circumstances (see Anderson & Bjork, this volume, for a similar suggestion). This center-surround mechanism would enhance the accessibility of a sought-for code by inhibiting neighboring codes, and perhaps by increasing the activation of codes in the center region as well. We will present evidence that we think is consistent with the operation of such a mechanism, after consideration of some recent theoretical developments that challenge the models of semantic memory and priming effects described thus far.

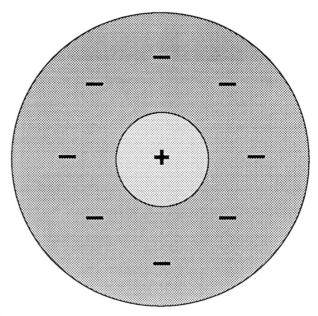

FIGURE 1

A hypothetical center-surround mechanism, with inhibition of related items and activation of the item it is directly focused on.

III. ALTERNATIVE ACCOUNTS OF SEMANTIC MEMORY AND PRIMING

The preceding account of semantic memory and priming effects suggests that there might be a need to invoke inhibitory processes when attempting to retrieve weakly activated codes from a networklike semantic memory system with automatic spreading activation between nodes. However, this account fails to consider other theoretical arguments that could conceivably remove the need for inhibitory processes by doing away with automatic spreading activation. Theorists such as Jacoby and Brooks (1984) and Hintzman (1986) have suggested that the preceding characterization of semantic memory is fundamentally flawed in its assumption that abstractions of experience are stored in a separate system. Instead, they suggest that what is stored are individual episodes of experience, and that abstracted qualities are computed by retrieval processes applied across the individual stored episodes. Instance-based theories of this type have garnered considerable attention in recent years, and the debate between instance theories and abstractionist accounts seems likely to continue for some time to come.

A similar debate characterizes current theories of priming effects. The operation of abstractionist network models of semantic memory has often been characterized in terms of the language of spreading activation, and, as noted earlier, certain kinds of automatic priming effects provide some of the evidence used to justify such accounts. However, the concept of automatic spreading activation has also been called into question by what might be referred to as retrieval-based theories of priming (e.g., Ratcliff & McKoon, 1988; Dosher & Rosedale, 1989). In general, these theories suggest that priming effects, including those attributed to automatic spreading activation, can be interpreted in terms of the prime and target joining together to form a compound cue in short-term memory. Facilitation for responding to the target item is due to higher familiarity of the compound when the prime and target are related instead of to transient activation of long-term memory representations. This debate also seems likely to continue (see McKoon & Ratcliff, 1992, vs. McNamara, 1992b, for a current version of the debate).

Although adding new information to an abstractionist system with automatic spreading activation between nodes might be problematic and require inhibitory processes, or one of the other solutions proposed earlier, to allow successful access of that information, it is less clear that this is inherently true for instance-based theories of semantic memory or retrieval-based theories of priming effects in terms of their predictions. It should be noted that an attempt to model semantic memory effects in at least one instance-based model (Hintzman, 1986) accomplishes this by assuming events are represented as a vector of feature loadings. Retrieval of an item from memory is produced by a retrieval cue or probe that activates stored memory traces simultaneously, producing an echo that is a composite of activated traces. Depending on the assumptions made about the activation of instance vectors from stored events sharing features with a presented event, and how the activated instance vectors might combine in the echo to determine the final retrieved code, the same kind of selection problem ascribed to network models might apply here as well. More generally, we note that any model of semantic memory ultimately has to account for the possible addition of new information to the system, to have the new information share in the processes or mechanisms that give rise to the various kinds of effects attributed to spreading activation in abstractionist models, and to allow it to remain accessible for retrieval. The appropriate tack here, we believe, is to describe the effects that we have observed that appear to bear on these issues, and to allow theorists working with these models to explain how the effects might arise within such a system. In this vein, Neill and Valdes (1992) have proposed an episodic retrieval theory of negative priming effects where inhibition arises as a function of the subject retrieving a past episode in which the present target was associated with a nonresponse.

IV. EMPIRICAL STUDIES OF INHIBITORY SEMANTIC PRIMING

A. Inhibitory Semantic Priming from Pattern-Masked Primes

As noted earlier, studies of semantic priming effects in the lexical decision task have shown them to be a highly robust phenomenon, with facilitation from prime–target relatedness obtained under a wide range of experimental conditions. One of the more provocative claims about this phenomenon is that it can be obtained even when the prime is followed by a pattern mask that renders it inaccessible to conscious perception (e.g., Marcel, 1983; Balota, 1983; Fowler, Wolford, Slade, & Tassinary, 1981). Such reports, if accurate, would bear on a number of issues including the locus of selective attention effects and the occurrence of automatic spreading activation in memory.

However, the reality of subthreshold semantic priming effects has been extensively debated (see Holender, 1986, and associated commentaries for reviews). Many of the arguments regarding the reality of subthreshold priming have hinged on methodological issues, and in particular on whether the threshold setting procedures used were adequate to ensure that subjects had no conscious knowledge whatsoever regarding the primes that might be responsible for producing any observed facilitation. For example, Cheesman and Merikle (1985) suggested that some reports of subthreshold semantic priming were flawed by the use of inadequate threshold setting procedures. In particular, they argued that studies that failed to use rigorous forced-choice procedures to bring subjects to chance performance levels during threshold setting were likely to underestimate the amount of information visible to subjects. In their work they showed that semantic priming effects could be obtained from stimuli presented under conditions in which subjects claimed not to see them but were still above chance performance levels in a forced-choice threshold setting procedure, but not under conditions in which performance in the forced-choice procedure had been brought to chance. The forced-choice procedure involved presenting subjects with a masked word, then having them guess from a set of alternatives which word had been presented. Cheesman and Merikle termed the first condition the *subjective threshold*, and the latter the *objective threshold*, and argued that priming effects could be obtained below subjective, but not objective threshold.

This argument is complicated by variations across experiments in the kind of judgment that subjects have been asked to make. For example,

Marcel (1983) had subjects make a presence–absence judgment in which they indicated whether a word or a blank field preceded the mask. Cheesman and Merikle's forced-choice procedure required subjects to judge which of a set of alternatives had been presented, and thus required identification of at least some specific perceptual or semantic information. On the face of it, the task used by Marcel actually might have resulted in a more stringent threshold, because answers could have been generated on the basis of any partial information, even though a forced-choice procedure was not used. The contradiction between the nature of the procedure (forced choice or not) and the specific judgment (detection vs. identification) makes it quite difficult to draw any firm conclusion from a comparison between Marcel's experiments and those of Cheesman and Merikle.

To address such questions, Dagenbach, Carr, and Wilhelmson (1989) opted to examine subthreshold priming effects in subjects following a variety of different threshold-setting judgments administered under similar conditions. In the first experiment, two thresholds were set for each subject. The first of these was based on a presence–absence judgment similar to that used by Marcel (1983): Subjects were asked to discriminate between trials on which a word or a blank field had preceded a pattern mask. The second threshold judgment varied between subjects and involved one of three forced-choice judgments based on more specific knowledge of the stimulus than would be logically necessary for the presence–absence judgment. These were called "informed choice" judgments. For one group of subjects, the second threshold was an informed choice analogue of the presence–absence procedure. They were shown a specific word after each trial, and asked to indicate whether that word or a blank field had preceded the mask. For the second group of subjects, the informed-choice procedure required identification, analogous to the procedure used by Cheesman and Merikle. A word was presented prior to the mask on each trial. After each trial, the subject was shown two words, and asked to indicate which word had been presented on the preceding trial. For the third group of subjects, a novel threshold measure was explored. These subjects were asked to introspect directly on the kind of information that presumably would drive priming effects in the subsequent lexical decision experiment: semantic information about the masked prime. A word was presented prior to a pattern mask on each trial, after which subjects were asked to indicate which member of a pair of clearly visible words was semantically related to the masked word.

The initial presence–absence threshold was determined using short blocks of trials and a descending staircase procedure until performance fell to approximately chance levels. Subjects were informed that words would be present on half of the trials in each block, and were

TABLE 1
Design of the Masked Priming Experiment

Event: Threshold setting task using presence–absence detection judgment

Event: Threshold setting task using one of three informed choice judgments:
    (a) Informed-choice version of presence–absence judgment
    (b) Forced-choice identification judgment
    (c) Forced-choice semantic judgment

Event: Primed lexical decision trials with prime–mask SOA equal to the SOA determined in the detection judgment threshold task

Event: Primed lexical decision trials with prime–mask SOA equal to the SOA determined in the informed-choice judgment threshold task

encouraged to use this knowledge in their guessing. After the initial presence–absence threshold was determined, the appropriate informed-choice threshold was then assessed. The stimulus–mask SOA on the second threshold measure began at the level determined by the initial presence–absence procedure. If performance on the initial block of trials using the second threshold judgment was above chance, the SOA was shortened further until it fell to chance levels. If performance was already at chance, the SOA was lengthened until it exceeded chance, and the SOA setting just below that was taken to be the threshold.

Immediately after the two threshold judgment tasks, subjects experienced two blocks of primed lexical decision trials using words as stimuli that were different from any of the words seen during threshold setting but comparable to them in length, frequency, and the like. In the first block, the primes were presented at the prime–mask SOA determined in the initial detection threshold judgment, and in the second block, at the prime–mask SOA determined in the second informed-choice threshold judgment. A summary of the design of the experiment is shown in Table 1.

We turn now to the results. Overall, the threshold setting procedures produced a coherent pattern, shown in Table 2, with the initial detection threshold producing the shortest prime–mask SOAs. Among the

TABLE 2
Mean Prime-Mask SOAs (msec) as a Function of Threshold Judgment

Forced-choice judgment	Presence–absence threshold	Forced-choice threshold
Presence–absence	15.6	16.8
Identification	18.5	24.0
Semantic similarity	17.3	22.6

TABLE 3
Mean Priming Effects (msec) for Lexical Decision Experiment

Forced-choice judgment	Presence–absence threshold	Forced-choice threshold
Presence–absence	+32	−5
Identification	+39	+14
Semantic similarity	−23	−7

informed choice thresholds, the informed choice version of the detection task produced the shortest stimulus–mask SOA, and the forced choice identification procedure produced the longest.

The data from the lexical decision trials are shown in Table 3. These data are from only those subjects who remained at chance performance on a threshold recheck administered at the conclusion of the lexical decision trials, and whose second forced-choice threshold measure resulted in a longer prime-mask SOA than the original presence–absence measure—in other words, those subjects who were most likely to have had the least possible conscious knowledge of the masked primes when those primes were presented at the detection-threshold SOA. The data showed significant priming effects in the initial detection-threshold condition for all threshold groups, and no effect in the second informed-choice threshold condition for any of the groups. Of particular interest for our work is that the priming obtained in the detection-threshold condition appeared to vary *in direction* as a function of which threshold group the subject was in: Subjects whose informed-choice threshold judgment required either a presence–absence or a forced-choice identification decision showed significant facilitation from semantically related primes presented under threshold conditions established by the initial presence–absence judgment, but the subjects who had been asked to make semantic judgments about the masked primes showed significant *inhibition* under the threshold conditions established by the initial presence–absence judgments.

B. Interpretations of Masked Priming Effects

These rather complex results were puzzling in a variety of ways. First, to obtain significant priming under the more stringent conditions with the shorter prime–mask SOA, and no effect under the less stringent conditions with the longer prime–mask SOA, appears anomalous, although other studies of unconscious perception have referred to similar phenomena (see Dixon, 1981). Dagenbach, Carr, and Wilhelmson suggested that there may be a "window" in which subthreshold priming effects can be obtained. At prime–mask SOAs below this window, priming effects diminish as the prime provides less and less useful input capable of activating semantic memory. As SOAs rise above the window, the prime's semantic code becomes active enough to attract conscious retrieval attempts that sometimes succeed and sometimes fail, with the successful and unsuccessful retrievals obscuring one another's impact on subsequent target processing.

Clearly, this is a speculative account of a problematic result. Even more problematic was the inhibitory effect shown by the group of subjects whose informed-choice threshold task required semantic judgments. The inhibition was produced from primes presented under the initial presence–absence threshold conditions. Subjects from the other two groups showed significant facilitation from primes presented under the same conditions. The only difference between the subjects in the third group and those in the other two groups was the second threshold setting procedure that they underwent, and the only way in which it seemed possible for the second threshold setting procedure to influence performance in the priming task would be if it had altered the way in which the subjects intentionally processed the masked stimuli, inducing a particular strategy for trying to perceive the masked primes that carried over from the last task of the threshold setting session to the primed lexical decision task.

If the inhibition was not a spurious result, and the preceding interpretation of it is correct, it poses serious questions for interpretations of masked priming effects. In general, it has been assumed that masked priming effects, when obtained, reflect the operation of automatic encoding mechanisms. Evidence that these effects are modifiable by the way in which subjects try to process the masked stimuli would be problematic for such accounts (see Dagenbach, Carr, & Wilhelmson, 1989, for extended discussion of this issue).

A second experiment was conducted to replicate this finding using a within-subjects design. A detection threshold was set for subjects as in the first experiment, followed by a block of primed lexical decision trials with masked primes presented at the prime–mask SOA determined by that threshold judgment. An informed-choice threshold based on semantic judgments was then set, followed by a second block of primed lexical decision trials with primes again presented at the initial detection threshold prime–mask SOA. Thus, the only difference between the two blocks was the preceding threshold judgment—physical prime presentation conditions were identical. The same pattern of results was obtained. There were 13 msec of facilitation from semantically related primes in the first block of trials, and 13 msec of inhibition from semantically related primes in the second block of trials. A control experiment in which no semantic similarity judgments were interposed between blocks of trials yielded facilitation in both blocks, arguing against interpretations of the inhibition as a consequence of fatigue or some other artifactual cause unrelated to performing the semantic threshold judgment.

Thus, the inhibitory effect appears to be a replicable phenomenon, but not one for which there is any straightforward theoretical account. One possible interpretation is that it might reflect a laboratory analogue to the everyday experience where thinking about, or introspecting on, skilled activities interferes with performance. More specifically, the long and laborious threshold setting procedure might have trained subjects to direct their attention toward semantic codes when they saw a masked prime. In general, the effect of attending to semantic information is to increase semantic priming effects, and therefore this would not seem to be a likely explanation of the observed inhibition. However, the increased facilitation from semantic priming that accompanies attending to semantic information occurs under conditions where the semantic information is easily accessible and subjects do become aware of it. In the experiments described here, the attentional processes were unsuccessful in the attempt to retrieve information about the weakly activated prime. According to this hypothesis, such unsuccessful retrieval attempts leave an inhibitory signature in performance on the immediately following related target.

V. TESTS OF THE FAILED RETRIEVAL HYPOTHESIS IN VOCABULARY ACQUISITION STUDIES

The preceding interpretation points to an interesting possibility. It suggests that unsuccessful attempts to retrieve information from memory may have discernible consequences other than the obvious one of failure to extract the desired information, such as the inhibition of related items in memory. Exploring such effects may provide new insight into the operation of perception and memory, as has the study of priming effects following successful retrieval attempts.

However, the wide array of methodological issues that complicate the interpretation of studies of subthreshold priming makes it desirable to determine if the same phenomenon can be observed in a different paradigm. Dagenbach, Carr, and Barnhardt (1990) pursued this goal in a series of studies involving the acquisition of new vocabulary words. In the masked priming studies, the retrieval failure for information about the prime presumably stemmed from impoverished perceptual input— there was too little clear input to activate a well-known prime word's semantic code enough for it to be retrieved successfully into working memory. In the vocabulary acquisition studies, the degree of learning, rather than clarity of perceptual input, was manipulated as an alternative means of creating conditions under which retrieval failures would be likely to occur.

Subjects were asked to learn new vocabulary words and their definitions. These new vocabulary words then served as primes for well-known related targets in a subsequent lexical decision task. The study conditions for the new vocabulary words were chosen to make it likely that the words and their meanings would be encoded into memory, but in such a way that it was also likely that intentional attempts to retrieve information about the meanings would frequently result in failure. This was done by providing subjects with a fairly large set of words and definitions in a short span of time.

In the first experiment, which was intended to develop the methodology to see if it had any promise, subjects saw new vocabulary words and their definitions, for example, "accipiter: a hawk," for 15 sec each on a computer monitor. After this, a block of lexical decision trials was administered in which the new vocabulary words served as primes for well-known targets. On one-third of the trials, the prime–target pairs were related (i.e., *accipiter* as a prime for *eagle*). The prime appeared for 5 or 15 sec, followed 2 sec later by the target. The idea here was to provide subjects with sufficient time to actively attempt to retrieve information about the prime. Subjects were instructed to verbally recall the meaning of the prime if they could retrieve it, but to give priority to responding to the target after prime offset.

The resulting data were categorized according to whether the prime and target were related on a given trial, and according to whether or not the subject was successful in retrieving the meaning of the prime as indicated by verbal report. This resulted in four categories of data: (1) recalled and related, (2) recalled and unrelated, (3) not recalled and related, and (4) not recalled and unrelated. An obvious problem with this approach was that there was no way of guaranteeing which stimuli would fall into which categories, or even that some would fall into all of the categories. Therefore, only data from subjects who had at least three data points in each of the categories were used.

The results of prime–target relatedness were highly variable in this exploratory experiment, but they did hint at a difference between priming from recallable and unrecallable primes. A substantial, but only marginally significant, facilitation effect was obtained overall, and the interaction between prime–target relatedness and prime recall success was also marginally significant. This interaction reflected 86 and 67 msec of facilitation from recalled primes in the 5- and 15-sec study conditions respectively, and essentially no effect at all from the unrecalled primes (2 and 0 msec, respectively). Thus, while unrecalled primes produced no facilitation, no hint of the sought-for inhibition was obtained, either. One possible reason for this might be that having subjects attempt to orally define the prime when it appeared interfered with the mechanisms that produce semantic priming. This procedure also resulted in rather long prime–target SOAs compared to the 2 sec SOAs used in the masked priming studies. Although it is not clear at this time that the inhibitory effects observed in our various experiments are due to the same processes that produce negative priming, work on negative priming by Neill and Valdes (1992) showed that negative priming effects dissipate quickly over time. Their finding is consistent with the possibility that the long SOAs used here obscured the inhibition effect.

In an attempt to make the conditions of prime processing more analogous to those in the masked priming studies, a second experiment looked at priming from new vocabulary words using much shorter prime–target SOAs and no requirement for verbal recall of the prime's definition during the lexical decision trials. In this experiment, primes appeared for 1800 msec, followed 200 msec later by the target. Subjects were instructed to recall the prime's meaning when they could, and to try to use it to anticipate or predict the target; they were not required to define the prime aloud.

Determination of recall success during the lexical decision trials depended on diagnostic memory tests administered after the lexical decision experiment was completed. The first measure was a free recall test in which the subject was given each of the studied vocabulary words and asked to recall its definition. The second measure was a four-choice recognition memory test in which the subject was given the vocabulary word, then asked to pick out its definition from four alternatives. One of the alternatives was the studied definition, one was the definition of another studied word, and two were definitions of words not used in the study. It was assumed that items whose definitions could be recalled subsequently were those for which recall was likely to have been successful during the lexical decision task. In contrast, those items whose definitions could be recognized but not recalled were the ones for which some learning had taken place (supporting successful recognition), but for which recall failure was likely to have occurred during the lexical decision task, just as it definitely occurred during the recall test.

The lexical decision data were categorized on the basis of whether the prime's definition was subsequently recognized correctly (83% were). These data were further subdivided on the basis of prime–target relatedness and whether recall of the definition had been successful. This resulted in four prime categories as before: (1) recalled and related, (2) recalled and unrelated, (3) not recalled and related, and (4) not recalled and unrelated. Again, there was no way of guaranteeing which stimuli would fall into which of these categories, or that data would

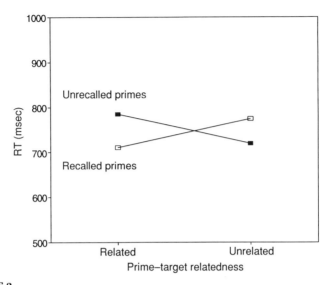

FIGURE 2

Crossover interaction showing effects of prime–target relatedness as a function of whether definitions of primes were correctly recalled or not in diagnostic memory tests administered at the end of Experiment 2, Dagenbach, Carr, and Barnhardt (1990).

be present in all of them for any given subject. Therefore, as before, only data from subjects with at least three responses in each category were used.

The resulting response time data are shown in Figure 2. As can be seen, when the definition of the prime was recalled successfully, targets preceded by a related prime were responded to 64 msec faster than those preceded by an unrelated prime. More importantly, when the definition of the prime was not recalled, targets preceded by a related prime were responded to 64 msec *slower* than those preceded by an unrelated prime. Thus, the inhibitory effect originally obtained with masked primes was obtained again in this vocabulary acquisition study under conditions where the prime was clearly visible, but its meaning was not accessible due to low levels of learning.

These results seemed to confirm the presence of inhibition subsequent to unsuccessful attempts to retrieve weakly activated semantic information. As noted earlier, this phenomenon is of interest given the novelty of obtaining inhibitory semantic priming effects in any situation. However, the data described thus far do not really tell much about the functional properties of the inhibitory processes observed—how they arise and what purpose they serve. One possibility is that the inhibition reflects a general refractory period in memory, where after an unsuccessful search attempt in a given semantic "neighborhood," further searches there are not possible for some period of time. Such a phenomenon might be akin to the "inhibition of return" described for visual attention to locations in space by Posner and his colleagues (e.g., Posner & Cohen, 1984; see also Tipper, Driver, & Weaver, 1991; Klein & Taylor, this volume). Another possibility, as suggested earlier, is that this inhibition reflects the operation of a center-surround attentional mechanism used to access weakly activated codes that are surrounded by more easily activatable related items.

VI. TESTS OF THE CENTER-SURROUND THEORY

A. Repetition versus Semantic Priming

To begin to address these possibilities, Carr and Dagenbach (1990) employed a variation of the masked priming paradigm in which repetition priming effects were examined along with those from semantic priming. The center-surround theory would predict inhibition for semantically related items when retrieval of the prime fails due to the masking procedure. Different variations of this theory may predict either activation of the prime itself (this is the possibility illustrated in Figure 1), or a lack of inhibition, but without corresponding facilitation. That is, responses to a subsequent target should be slower when the target is a word that is semantically related to the prime compared to when the target is unrelated. Responses to a target that is the *same* as the prime should be either faster than, or the same as, when the prime is an unrelated word, depending on what occurs in the center region—if facilitation occurs in the center, responses will be faster. In contrast, the alternative refractory period theory—the analogue to "inhibition of return"—would predict slower responses on trials on which the target is the same as the prime, as well as when it is semantically related to the prime, compared to unrelated trials, because the entire semantic neighborhood is inhibited, including the prime itself which has now become the target.

In a baseline experiment, masked repetition and semantic priming were compared after setting a threshold based on presence–absence detection judgments. As shown in Figure 3, significant and approximately equal amounts of facilitation were obtained from masked repetition and masked semantic priming—26 and 24 msec, respectively. In the second and key experiment, a semantic similarity threshold was determined for each subject as in Dagenbach, Carr, and Wilhelmson (1989). After this, a block of lexical decision trials was administered using pattern-masked primes that were either unrelated, semantically related, or identical to

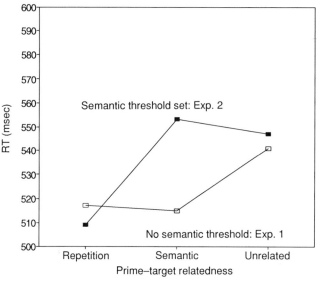

FIGURE 3

Semantic and repetition priming effects after a detection threshold setting procedure (Exp. 1), and a semantic similarity threshold setting procedure (Experiment 2, Carr & Dagenbach, 1990). Note that the prime presentation conditions are the same across the two experiments.

the target on word trials. The prime–mask SOA was set at 70% of the semantic similarity threshold, which, based on previous work, would be approximately equal to the presence–absence threshold SOA. Thus, physical prime presentation conditions were again similar or identical, as in Dagenbach et al. (1989), with the difference between experiments lying in the type of threshold judgment task performed just before the primed lexical decision task.

The resulting response time data from the lexical decision task, also shown in Figure 3, revealed that repetition priming produced 38 msec of facilitation, slightly more than occurred in the repetition condition of the initial experiment, whereas semantic priming produced 6 msec of inhibition. Although the inhibition effect was not significantly less than zero when tested by itself, it was significantly less than the 24 msec of semantic facilitation found in the initial experiment. Overall, then, the pattern of results of this experiment was generally consistent with our previous studies, and it followed the predictions of the center-surround theory quite well.

There is one possible complication for interpreting the results of this experiment in this way. The complication comes from work suggesting that subthreshold priming effects might be due to a "backwards" priming mechanism, where having a related target actually makes the prime more visible, even though the target appears after the prime (e.g., Bernstein, Bissonnette, Vyas, & Barclay, 1987; Briand, den Heyer, & Dannenbring, 1988; Dark, 1988). This is problematic because during threshold setting, primes are typically not followed by a related target (and they were not in the present study). Therefore, primes actually may be more visible in the context of a lexical decision experiment than in the context of the threshold setting procedure, and subthreshold priming effects may not really be due to imperceptible stimuli. Such reinstatement of the prime by the target typically is found at shorter prime–target SOAs than those used in the present experiments. Other studies using longer SOAs, more comparable to these experiments, have failed to find reinstatement effects.

Nevertheless, there is a variant of the prime reinstatement notion that remains problematic. It is possible that the backward priming effect might be even stronger for repetition priming than semantic priming, and that it might be obtained at longer prime–target SOAs. Thus, one could argue that the stimulus presentation conditions were sufficiently stringent to eliminate the backward priming effect for semantically related items, but not stringent enough to eliminate the backward repetition priming effect. To date, we know of no work bearing on the relative magnitudes of backward semantic versus repetition priming effects, so the implications of this remain unresolved.

B. Artificial Semantic Memories and the Center-Surround Mechanism

In all of the previously described studies, the evidence for inhibition of semantically related items when a prime with weak activation was processed was obtained in lexical decision experiments. The next study (Carr et al., in press; Dagenbach & Carr, 1993) attempted to determine if this effect could be obtained in a different context. This question was pursued as a subset of a larger body of issues concerning the development of semantic memory and priming effects in general. In an effort to gain greater precision in assessing priming effects, a priming experiment was conducted that reverted in part to the verbal learning tradition. In this experiment, artificial semantic memory structures were created using novel, or relatively novel, visual stimuli. The stimuli were selected from the extended keyboard set of characters and were arbitrarily assigned to two categories: "fleps" and "gleps." The two sets of stimuli that were used are shown in Figure 4.

FIGURE 4

Characters assigned to be "fleps" and "gleps" in experiments examining the development of priming effects with novel stimuli.

The general logic was to have subjects become fluent at classifying individually presented fleps and gleps through extensive practice. After this, the fleps and gleps became prime and target items in subsequent sessions in which prime–target SOAs and the proportion of related trials were manipulated. One issue of interest was whether automatic priming effects would be obtained, as evidenced by facilitation from related primes at short prime–target SOAs and with a low proportion of related trials. A second issue of interest, directly relevant to the present work, involved the consequences of adding new exemplars once stable priming effects were attained. The addition of these new exemplars provided an opportunity to simulate the addition of new vocabulary words to preexisting structures investigated in the vocabulary acquisition studies already described.

Subjects were initially given 5 min to study the first five fleps and five gleps. This was followed by 10 blocks of categorization trials to firm up their learning of the stimuli. In these trials, a fixation point appeared briefly, followed by a single stimulus that was either a flep or a glep. Subjects indicated which kind it was by pressing the corresponding assigned keys. Errors in categorization were followed by a loud beep. Each item appeared 10 times in each block. Subjects then returned for a second session of categorization trials on a different day. The same stimuli were again presented for 10 blocks of trials, so that by the end of the second session each flep and glep had been seen 200 times. The response time data shown in Figure 5 suggests that subjects were quite adept at flep and glep recognition by the end of Session 2. (And some subjects were starting to dream about them, or so they reported.) Overall accuracy was 96% on both days.

In the third session, primes were added to the classification trials. Subjects continued to classify the target item as a flep or a glep, but these were now preceded by a prime that appeared for 150 msec, with

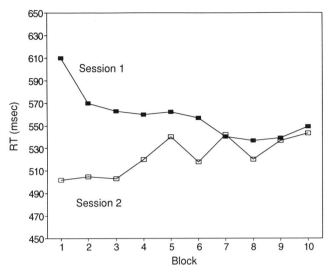

FIGURE 5

Mean response times across blocks for classification of fleps and gleps in the unprimed trials of Sessions 1 and 2.

the target appearing 50 msec after the prime's offset. The short prime–target SOA was chosen in an effort to limit the effects observed to the products of automatic encoding mechanisms. The primes were the already familiar fleps, gleps, or the fixation point that preceded the earlier classification task stimuli. The fixation point was chosen as an approximation to a neutral cue against which facilitation and inhibition effects could be estimated.

The session had four blocks of trials. Each block had 120 trials on which the prime and target came from the same category (both fleps or both gleps), 40 trials on which the prime was the neutral fixation cross, 28 trials on which the prime and target came from opposite categories, and 4 catch trials that occurred at the end of the block.[1] Subjects were informed that there was a high probability that the target would be from the same category as the prime when the prime was a flep or glep. The related pairs consisted of four pairings from each category rather than all possible combinations in an attempt to promote the development of specific associations.

[1]The catch trials constituted tests for mediated or multiple-step priming and effects of backward versus forward associations, which are phenomena relevant to debates on the underlying organization and operating characteristics of semantic memory (e.g., McNamara, 1992a, 1992b; Ratcliff & McKoon, 1988). These results are not discussed in this chapter.

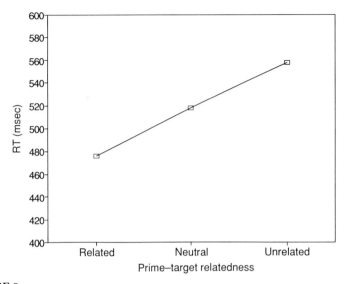

FIGURE 6

Effects of prime–target relatedness in Session 3, with a 200 msec prime–target SOA and a high proportion of related trials.

The resulting priming data are shown in Figure 6. Clear evidence for priming effects was found, with related trials responded to significantly faster than neutral trials, which in turn were responded to significantly faster than unrelated trials. These effects appeared to be roughly symmetric around the "neutral" prime. Session 3's short prime–target SOA of 200 msec constituted a weak test for whether automatic priming was occurring because of the high proportion of related trials. In Session 4, the prime–target SOA was lengthened to 2 sec to allow subjects to think more actively about prime–target pairings and to observe the effect of expected relationships. Session 5 returned to the shorter SOA of Session 3. In Session 6, the prime–target SOA remained at 200 msec, but the proportion of related trials was decreased dramatically from 70% to 32%. Finally, in Session 7, a long SOA and high proportion of related trials were used to reestablish any connections that might have become weakened during preceding sessions with short SOAs and low proportions of related trials. The data from Sessions 4 through 7 are shown in Figure 7.

These data presented few surprises. In Session 4, response times were significantly faster on the related trials than the neutral trials, which in turn were significantly faster than on the unrelated trials. This was not surprising given that subjects had time to actively develop expectations, and that significant priming effects had already been ob-

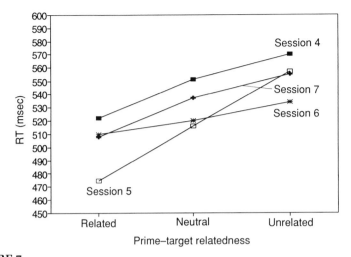

FIGURE 7

Effects of prime–target relatedness across Sessions 4 through 7. In Sessions 4 and 7, the prime–target SOA was 2 sec, and there was a high proportion of related trials. Session 5 had a 200 msec SOA and a high proportion of related trials. Session 6 had a short prime–target SOA (200 msec), and a low proportion of related trials.

tained with a much shorter prime–target SOA in Session 3. Session 5, which was analogous to Session 3, also produced analogous results. In Session 6, the proportion of related trials was low. If the prime–target associations established in the previous sessions had resulted in connections sufficient to drive completely automatic priming, one would expect priming effects to persist despite the short SOA and low proportion of related trials. The results of Session 6 were roughly consistent with that prediction: Response times on related trials were marginally faster than on neutral trials, and response times on unrelated trials were significantly slower than on neutral trials. Finally, in Session 7, where the goal was to restrengthen any learning that might have been weakened during the preceding session, significant facilitation and inhibition relative to the neutral condition were obtained once again.

Session 8 was the critical session with respect to the center-surround hypothesis. In this session, new exemplars of fleps and gleps were introduced into the experiment. Five new fleps were presented for a total of 5 sec, followed by five new gleps presented for 5 sec. This short study period was used to ensure that learning of the new items would be weak to begin with. The new exemplars then became primes in the classification task, along with the old primes that had been used previously. The target items were always old, well-learned exemplars. A 2-sec prime–target SOA was used, and subjects were instructed to try to remember the prime's category when it appeared. This procedure was roughly analogous to the vocabulary word learning experiments in which inhibition had been previously observed. If an analogous process was at work, the old primes should produce facilitation, whereas the new primes should produce inhibition in at least some cases. In particular, those new primes that were learned least well ought to have an inhibitory effect, whereas those that were learned better might produce facilitation.

To determine which items among the new exemplars were learned well and which were not, a test block of unprimed categorization trials for the new stimuli occurred after the block of primed categorization trials. The new stimuli were presented one at a time, and subjects classified them as fleps or gleps, with feedback provided. The new stimuli that were categorized correctly were then subjected to a median split based on their test block response times. We assumed that items that were classified more rapidly were better learned and would be less likely to require the center-surround attentional mechanism to help retrieve their category memberships during the primed classification trials. Items that were classified more slowly were less well learned, and therefore they would be more likely to engage the center-surround mechanism. This procedure was repeated three more times for a total of four pairs, each pair consisting of a block of primed categorization trials and a test block. Because of the feedback provided during the test blocks, each pair represented a higher level of learning of the new items, and indeed by the second block, performance in the test block was nearly perfect and differences in response time across items were small. We focus here on data from the first pair of blocks only, representing the conditions most likely to expose the center-surround retrieval mechanism's operation.

Priming results from the first pair were as follows: Related *old* primes still produced faster responses than neutral primes (49 msec), whereas unrelated old primes produced slower responses than neutral primes (25 msec), for a total facilitatory priming effect of 74 msec.

More importantly, the comparison of priming effects from the new stimuli as a function of the speed with which they were categorized in the test block (Figure 8) showed the same pattern observed in the earlier work with newly learned vocabulary words. The new primes that were rapidly categorized produced facilitation—related targets were responded to 53 msec faster than unrelated targets. The new primes that were classified slowly produced inhibition—unrelated targets were responded to 28 msec faster than related targets. The resulting pattern replicates the crossover interaction obtained in the studies using new vocabulary words. This pattern cannot be explained in terms of devoting more processing effort or resources to the less well learned primes

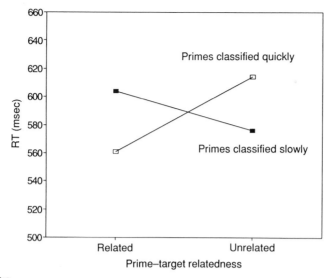

FIGURE 8

Effects of prime–target relatedness on target classification RT for trials with new primes as stimuli in Block 1 of Session 8. These primes were classified as fleps or gleps at the end of the block and a median split was performed on the items based on classification time. The RT for targets primed by items quickly classified forms one function on the graph; the RT for targets primed by items slowly classified forms the other.

because that would produce a slowdown for all targets, both related and unrelated, rather than the content-specific reverse or inhibitory relatedness effect actually observed.

VII. CONCLUSIONS

The studies described in this chapter comprise a rather long odyssey in pursuit of what was originally assumed to be a spurious result in a masked priming experiment. The persistence of the inhibition effect across the different studies in which it was sought suggests that it was not spurious after all. Instead, inhibition of related items when attempting to retrieve weakly activated information appears to occur in a variety of different paradigms and procedures.

We have suggested that this inhibition reflects the operation of an attentional mechanism used to help retrieve weakly activated codes. Numerous questions remain regarding this mechanism and the interpretation of these effects offered here. Among the more notable are questions about how pervasive is the inhibitory effect, and what are the exact conditions that trigger the deployment of the attentional mechanism.

Thus far, the inhibition effect has been obtained when subjects are required to make semantic judgments about meaning or category membership. Would the same effect be obtained for other kinds of memory decisions, such as episodic recognition memory? Results consistent with automatic spreading activation in episodic memory have been reported (Ratcliff & McKoon, 1981), and thus the functional utility of the inhibitory process might apply across different memory domains.

The results of the fleps and gleps categorization study are particularly important in illuminating the conditions under which the attentional mechanism might be deployed and when its inhibitory effects might be observed in performance. In the masked priming and vocabulary acquisition studies, inhibitory priming was obtained under conditions in which the attempt to retrieve the prime's meaning had *failed*. In the fleps and gleps study, the items giving rise to the inhibition were not ones for which retrieval failure was likely to have occurred. Instead, their categorization was ultimately correct, indicating that retrieval was likely to have succeeded rather than failed, but access to the category information was demonstrably slower or less efficient. Items for which access was demonstrably faster or more efficient produced facilitatory priming rather than inhibition. These results suggest that the attentional mechanism might be triggered dynamically, as a function of the rate of growth of differential activation levels among codes (Carr et al., in press). According to this account, if activation of several similar or related codes in a region of semantic space occurs, and one does not begin to increase in activation more rapidly than the others within a relatively short period of time, the attentional mechanism is elicited. Its facilitatory and inhibitory inputs combine with the continuing bottom-up activation arriving via perceptual pathways to produce the differential levels of activation that are needed for one code to be more active than any of the others and hence retrievable. Sometimes bottom-up activation is insufficient for this to happen even with the help of the center-surround mechanism. Presumably this is what occurred in the masked priming and vocabulary acquisition studies that were described. Other times, the combination is successful and retrieval occurs that would not have been possible without the center-surround mechanism's help. Presumably this is the situation that occurred in the fleps and gleps study.

This account predicts that the same kinds of newly learned words that generate inhibition of related items with relatively long prime–target SOAs (on the order of 2 sec) might actually give rise to facilitation at much shorter SOAs, during the initial period of multiple activation that eventually elicits the center-surround mechanism's application. For example, suppose that simultaneous and approximately equal activation of many related codes in response to the newly learned word is the condition that triggers the center-surround mechanism. If one could tap into the system before the mechanism has had a chance to operate, then one might observe facilitatory priming from newly learned words consistent with such early multiple activation. This possibility is being pursued in ongoing vocabulary acquisition studies.

Questions also remain regarding the center region of the center-surround mechanism. The benefit found from masked repetition priming in Carr and Dagenbach (1990) under conditions that yielded inhibition for semantically related items suggests that the center region is facilitated. However, as noted earlier, masked priming experiments are always controversial. Therefore, we are conducting vocabulary acquisition studies in which newly learned words serve as targets as well as primes, and in which semantic and repetition priming are contrasted. It is hoped that these studies will enable a more confident choice between the center-surround conceptualization in which the center is facilitated at the same time the surround is inhibited, and the alternative possibility, suggested by Wundt quite some time ago for selective attention in general, according to Pillsbury (1908), that the enhancement of the sought-after code might occur solely through inhibition of related items.

REFERENCES

Anderson, J. R. (1983). *The architecture of cognition.* Cambridge, MA: Harvard University Press.

Balota, D. (1983). Automatic semantic activation and episodic memory encoding. *Journal of Verbal Learning and Verbal Behavior, 22,* 88–104.

Bernstein, I. H., Bisonnette, V., Vyas, A., & Barclay, P. (1989). Semantic priming: Subliminal perception or context? *Perception and Psychophysics, 45,* 153–161.

Briand, K. A., den Heyer, K., & Dannenbring, G. L. (1988). Retroactive semantic priming in a lexical decision task. *Quarterly Journal of Experimental Psychology, 40A,* 341–360.

Brown, A. S. (1988). Encountering misspellings and spelling performance: Why wrong isn't right. *Journal of Educational Psychology, 80,* 488–494.

Carr, T. H. (1986). Perceiving visual language. In K. Boff, L. Kaufman, & J. Thomas (Eds.), *Handbook of perception and human performance* (pp. 19-1–19-92). New York: Wiley.

Carr, T. H., & Dagenbach, D. (1990). Semantic priming and repetition priming from masked words: Evidence for a center-surround attentional mechanism in perceptual recognition. *Journal of Experimental Psychology: Learning, Memory and Cognition, 16,* 341–350.

Carr, T. H., Dagenbach, D., Van Wieren, D., Carlson-Radvansky, L. A., Alejano, A. R., & Brown, J. S. (in press). Acquiring general knowledge from specific episodes of experience. To appear in C. Umilta & M. Moscovitch (Eds.), *Attention and performance XV.* Hillsdale, NJ: Lawrence Erlbaum.

Cheesman, J., & Merikle, P. M. (1985). Word recognition and consciousness. In D. Besner, T. G. Waller, & G. E. MacKinnon (Eds.), *Reading research: Advances in theory and practice* (Vol. 5, pp. 311–352). New York: Academic Press.

Collins, A. M., & Loftus, E. F. (1975). A spreading-activation theory of semantic processing. *Psychological Review, 82*, 407–428.

Dagenbach, D., & Carr, T. H. (in preparation). *The development of automatic priming from novel stimuli and categories: Studies in the ontogeny of semantic structures.*

Dagenbach, D., Carr, T. H., & Barnhart, T. (1990). Inhibitory semantic priming of lexical decisions due to failure to retrieve weakly activated codes. *Journal of Experimental Psychology: Learning, Memory and Cognition, 16*, 328–340.

Dagenbach, D., Carr, T. H., & Wilhelmson, A. (1989). Task-induced strategies and near-threshold priming: Conscious influences on unconscious perception. *Journal of Memory and Language, 28*, 412–443.

Dagenbach, D., Horst, S., & Carr, T. H. (1990). Adding new information to semantic memory: How much learning is enough to produce automatic priming? *Journal of Experimental Psychology: Learning, Memory and Cognition, 16*, 581–591.

Dark, V. J. (1988). Semantic priming, prime reportability, and retroactive priming are interdependent. *Memory & Cognition, 16*, 299–308.

Dixon, N. F. (1981). *Preconscious processing.* New York: Wiley.

Dosher, B. A., & Rosedale, G. (1989). Integrated retrieval cues as a mechanism for priming in retrieval from memory. *Journal of Experimental Psychology: General, 118*, 191–211.

Fowler, C. A., Wolford, G., Slade, R., & Tassinary, L. (1981). Lexical access with and without awareness. *Journal of Experimental Psychology: General, 110*, 341–362.

Friedrich, F. J., Henik, A., & Tzelgov, J. (1991). Automatic processes in lexical access and spreading activation. *Journal of Experimental Psychology: Human Perception and Performance, 17*, 792–806.

Hintzman, D. (1986). Schema abstraction in a multiple trace memory model. *Psychological Review, 93*, 411–428.

Holender, D. (1986). Semantic activation with and without conscious identification in dichotic listening, parafoveal vision, and visual masking: A survey and appraisal. *Behavioral and Brain Sciences, 9*, 1–23.

Jacoby, L. L., & Brooks, L. R. (1984). Nonanalytic cognition: Memory, perception, and concept learning. In G. H. Bower (Ed.), *The psychology of learning and motivation: Advances in research and theory* (Vol. 18). New York: Academic Press.

Jacoby, L. L., & Hollingshead, A. (1990). Reading student essays may be hazardous to your spelling: Effects of reading incorrectly and correctly spelled words. *Canadian Journal of Psychology, 44*, 345–358.

Jonides, J., & Mack, R. (1984). On the cost and benefit of cost and benefit. *Psychological Bulletin, 96*, 29–44.

Keele, S. W., & Neill, W. T. (1978). Mechanisms of attention. In E. C. Carterette & M. P. Friedman (Eds.), *Handbook of perception* (Vol. 9, pp. 3–47). San Diego: Academic Press.

Marcel, A. J. (1983). Conscious and unconscious perception: Experiments on visual masking and word recognition. *Cognitive Psychology, 15*, 197–237.

McKoon, G., & Ratcliff, R. (1992). Spreading activation versus compound cue accounts of priming: Mediated priming revisited. *Journal of Experimental Psychology: Learning, Memory and Cognition, 18*, 1155–1172.

McNamara, T. P. (1992a). Priming and constraints it places on theories of memory and retrieval. *Psychological Review, 99*, 650–662.

McNamara, T. P. (1992b). Theories of priming: I. Associative distance and lag. *Journal of Experimental Psychology: Learning, Memory and Cognition, 18*, 1173–1190.

Neely, J. H. (1977). Semantic priming and retrieval from lexical memory: Roles of inhibitionless spreading activation and limited-capacity attention. *Journal of Experimental Psychology: General, 106,* 226–254.

Neely, J. H. (1991). Semantic priming effects in visual word recognition: A selective review of current findings and theories. In D. Besner & G. Humphreys (Eds.), *Basic processes in reading: Visual word recognition.* Hillsdale, NJ: Lawrence Erlbaum.

Neill, W. T. (1977). Inhibitory and facilitatory processes in attention. *Journal of Experimental Psychology: General, 106,* 226–254.

Neill, W. T., & Valdes, L. A. (1992). Persistence of negative priming: Steady state or decay? *Journal of Experimental Psychology: Learning, Memory and Cognition, 18,* 565–576.

Neill, W. T., & Westberry, R. L. (1987). Selective attention and the suppression of cognitive noise. *Journal of Experimental Psychology: Learning, Memory and Cognition, 13,* 327–334.

Pillsbury, W. B. (1908). *Attention.* New York: Macmillan.

Posner, M. I., & Cohen, Y. A. (1984). Components of visual orienting. In H. Bouma and D. G. Bouwhuis (Eds.), *Attention and performance X* (pp. 531–554). Hillsdale, NJ: Lawrence Erlbaum.

Posner, M. I., & Snyder, C. R. R. (1975a). Attention and cognitive control. In R. L. Solso (Ed.), *Information processing and cognition: The Loyola Symposium* (pp. 55–85). Hillsdale, NJ: Lawrence Erlbaum.

Posner, M. I., & Snyder, C. R. R. (1975b). Facilitation and inhibition in the processing of signals. In P. M. A. Rabbitt & S. Dornic (Eds.), *Attention and performance V* (pp. 669–682). New York: Academic Press.

Potts, G. R., St. John, M. F., & Kirson, D. (1989). Incorporating new information into existing world knowledge. *Cognitive Psychology, 21,* 303–333.

Ratcliff, R., & McKoon, G. (1981). Automatic and strategic priming in recognition. *Journal of Verbal Learning and Verbal Behavior, 20,* 204–215.

Ratcliff, R., & McKoon, G. (1988). A retrieval theory of priming in memory. *Psychological Review, 95,* 385–408.

Shelton, J. R., & Martin, R. C. (1992). How semantic is automatic semantic priming? *Journal of Experimental Psychology: Learning, Memory and Cognition, 18,* 1191–1210.

Tipper, S. P. (1985). The negative priming effect: Inhibitory priming by ignored objects. *Quarterly Journal of Experimental Psychology, 37A,* 571–590.

Tipper, S. P., & Cranston, M. (1985). Selective attention and priming: Inhibitory and facilitatory effects of ignored primes. *Quarterly Journal of Experimental Psychology, 37A,* 591–611.

Tipper, S. P., & Driver, J. (1988). Negative priming between pictures and words: Evidence for semantic analysis of ignored stimuli. *Memory & Cognition, 16,* 64–70.

Tipper, S. P., Driver, J., & Weaver, B. (1991). Object-centered inhibition of return of visual attention. *Quarterly Journal of Experimental Psychology, 43A,* 289–298.

Tulving, E. (1972). Episodic and semantic memory. In E. Tulving and W. Donaldson (Eds.), *Organization of memory* (pp. 381–403). New York: Academic Press.

Tulving, E. (1983). *Elements of episodic memory.* New York: Oxford University Press.

Tulving, E., Hayman, C. A. G., & Macdonald, C. A. (1991). Long-lasting perceptual priming and semantic learning in amnesia: A case experiment. *Journal of Experimental Psychology: Learning, Memory and Cognition, 17,* 595–617.

Walley, R. E., & Weiden, T. D. (1973). Lateral inhibition and cognitive masking: A neuropsychological theory of attention. *Psychological Review, 80,* 458–466.

9

Inhibitory Processes in the Recognition of Homograph Meanings

Greg B. Simpson and Hyewon Kang

I. INTRODUCTION

Since the early 1970s, researchers concerned with language comprehension have actively investigated the processes of word recognition
and, in particular, how those processes are affected by the context in
which a word appears (e.g., Meyer & Schvaneveldt, 1971; Stanovich &
West, 1983). There are several reasons that word recognition has become
such a growth industry (Besner & Humphreys, 1991). One is that word
recognition is seen as a foundation on which higher language comprehension processes are built. Second, it is often implied that context
effects in word recognition serve as a model for such effects at other
processing levels. A third reason stems not from interest in language
comprehension per se, but rather from questions about the structure of
semantic memory. Because the relationships between words can be nor-
matively cataloged, they serve as an ideal medium for studying memory
structure (e.g., Rosch, 1975).

All of these reasons have also motivated a subset of studies of word
recognition, namely, those concerned with the processing of words with
multiple meanings. From the standpoint of semantic memory, it is interesting to question the relations between concepts tied to a common
word. With regard to language processing, lexical ambiguity has played
a central role in the debate over the modularity of comprehension sub-
processes (Fodor, 1983; Forster, 1979). According to the modularity

hypothesis (at least, as it concerns word recognition processes), the lexical processor is an autonomous, informationally encapsulated module, impervious to input from higher processes (e.g., syntactic and semantic constraints). Particularly in the last decade, research on lexical ambiguity has focused on this single issue: whether sentence context is able to constrain processing only to the meaning that is appropriate in the context, or whether the multiple meanings of an ambiguity become activated in memory in all contexts. The latter view has received considerable support in recent years, and these data are frequently cited as evidence for the modularity of lexical processing (e.g., Lucas, 1987; Onifer & Swinney, 1981; Seidenberg, Tanenhaus, Leiman, & Bienkowski, 1982; Swinney, 1979; Tanenhaus, Leiman, & Seidenberg, 1979). However, other recent research has found evidence that context can constrain access to one meaning (e.g., Paul, Kellas, Martin, & Clark, 1992; Simpson, 1981; Simpson & Krueger, 1991; Tabossi, 1988; Tabossi, Colombo, & Job, 1987; Van Petten & Kutas, 1987), a result more in line with an interactive conception of language processes (McClelland, 1987).

It is not the intent of this chapter to add to the box score of either side of this debate. Rather, we report on some recent studies that are concerned with the fate of meanings *after* the processing of an ambiguous word has presumably run its course. It is necessary, however, to set the stage for these studies with an abbreviated review of ambiguity research. We then report several studies showing that one meaning of an ambiguous word may be suppressed following the selection of the other for a response. Finally, we discuss the results of these studies in terms of their implications for word processing in discourse, individual and developmental differences in language comprehension, and the modularity debate.

II. CONTEXT EFFECTS AND AMBIGUITY: A BRIEF REVIEW

As just mentioned, ambiguity research has been aimed principally at the role that context plays in the activation and selection of an appropriate ambiguous word sense. In an earlier review of ambiguity research, Simpson (1984) identified three fundamental models of the effects of context. According to a context-dependent view, context acts immediately to activate only a single meaning. In an early study supporting this view, Schvaneveldt, Meyer, and Becker (1976) presented subjects with series of three words, the second word of which was ambiguous. The first and third words varied in their relations to the ambiguity. Lexical decision responses to the critical third word were fastest when it was related to the same meaning as that cued by the first word (e.g., as in the triple SAVE–BANK–MONEY). Some more recent sentence-context studies have found compatible results, with the processing of a target being facilitated if it is related to the same meaning of an ambiguity as that biased by the sentence (e.g., Paul et al., 1992; Simpson, 1981; Simpson & Krueger, 1991; Tabossi, 1988; Tabossi et al., 1987).

The remaining models contend that context does not have any effect until after the initial activation processes have occurred. According to one version of this view, activation is driven by the frequency of the meanings. Only the most common meaning is retrieved initially: This meaning is tested for coherence with the context, and only if it fails is a second meaning retrieved. This model finds support in studies in which the subject is required to decide whether a word that ends a sentence has more than one meaning. Subjects respond more quickly when the ambiguous word is biased by the sentence toward its less frequent meaning, presumably because the more common meaning is retrieved automatically regardless of the context (Hogaboam & Perfetti, 1975). However, more recent research by Neill, Hilliard, and Cooper (1988) has yielded results in which context does appear to contribute to initial meaning activation in the ambiguity-detection paradigm, and so undermines the purest form of a model that attributes activation entirely to meaning frequency.

Finally, the multiple- or exhaustive-access model contends that *all* meanings of an ambiguous word are always activated, regardless of the context. A number of sentence priming studies have shown that immediately after an ambiguous word is presented in a sentence, responses to targets related to either meaning of that word are facilitated, regardless of the meaning biased by the sentence (Conrad, 1974; Lucas, 1987; Onifer & Swinney, 1981; Seidenberg et al., 1982; Swinney, 1979; Tanenhaus et al., 1979; Till, Mross, & Kintsch, 1988). It is this result that is taken as strong evidence for the autonomy of lexical processing. If a meaning of a word is activated, despite its inappropriateness in the context, then it is reasonable to conclude that context has not constrained the initial meaning activation process.

These models have been described mainly in their strongest versions. A number of mixed models have been proposed as well (Gorfein & Bubka, 1989; Neill, 1989; Duffy, Morris, & Rayner, 1988; Simpson, 1984). Most of these models hypothesize partial constraints from context and frequency, such that all meanings may be activated, but the strength or the speed of this activation will vary with the frequency of the meaning and/or the bias of the context.

It is still the case, then, that despite two decades of investigation, the issue of single versus multiple access of ambiguous word meanings remains unsettled. Controversy has continued to revolve around several methodological issues, the most critical of which concerns the timing of stimulus presentation. All models of ambiguity agree that the outcome of the processing of an ambiguous word in context is the integration of the single meaning that is appropriate with that context. The controversy concerns the processes whereby this one meaning is chosen: whether the initial activation is itself selective, or rather whether the selection takes place after more than one meaning is activated. Consequently, researchers have recognized the importance of evaluating processing as soon as possible following the presentation of an ambiguous word. Only in this way can we hope to capture the earliest stages of processing, and separate those operations that take place before lexical access (i.e., the initial activation processes) from those that occur after access (i.e., selection of a single meaning).

Because it is difficult with any method to ensure that the earliest stages have been captured (Kellas, Paul, Martin, & Simpson, 1991; Simpson, 1994; Simpson & Krueger, 1991), a number of experiments have directly manipulated the amount of time that elapses between presentation of the ambiguity and the target. Many of these timecourse studies have drawn, implicitly or explicitly, on the two-stage model proposed by Posner and Snyder (1975) and applied to word recognition by Neely (1976, 1977) and Stanovich and West (1979, 1981). That model is characterized by a fast-acting automatic spreading activation component, and a slower attentional component. Applied to lexical ambiguity, such a model might suggest that all meanings are automatically activated initially. A selection process subsequently focuses limited-capacity processing resources on the contextually appropriate meaning. As these resources are given to one meaning, they are withdrawn from others, resulting in slower responses to an inappropriate meaning at longer, but not shorter, context–target intervals. Several of these time-course studies have found evidence that the initial activation process is exhaustive, with all meanings activated originally. After a delay, however, only one meaning remains, suggesting that a postaccess selection process is the locus of the context effects (Lucas, 1987; Onifer & Swinney, 1981; Seidenberg et al., 1982; Swinney, 1979; Tanenhaus et al., 1979; Till et al., 1988). Other studies, on the other hand, have shown selective activation even at the earliest prime–target intervals (Paul et al., 1992; Simpson & Krueger, 1991; Tabossi & Zardon, 1993).

In short, not even careful examination of the timecourse of processing has resolved the discrepant results in this area. As previously mentioned, another attempt at such a resolution is not the intent of this chapter. Indeed, we have argued elsewhere (Simpson, in press) that it probably will never be possible to resolve the issue of modularity versus interactionism in any universally satisfying way with any set of ambiguity studies, because clearly there are experimental parameters (e.g., type and strength of context, timecourse manipulations, etc.) that are not well understood. Rather, we have presented this summary in order to provide a background for introducing an issue of context that has previously been neglected, in hopes that we may achieve a better understanding of how ambiguous words are processed in discourse.

III. THE CONTEXT OF REPETITION

As active and informative as the research on lexical ambiguity has been, there is a sense that it has addressed only part of the story. The research has been concerned exclusively with what we might call "local" context, that is, the context of the immediate sentence in which the ambiguity occurs. The universal practice in the existing studies is to present a sentence containing a particular ambiguous word, and then to present a target word for the subject's response. After the subject has responded to the target, the next trial presents a new context and a new ambiguous word. In discourse, however, the activation of concepts follows a very different path. Here, concepts are raised and typically maintained over several sentences. For example, in a typical ambiguity experiment, a sentence such as (1) would be followed by a completely unrelated new sentence, such as (2).

(1)   *I opened a checking account at the bank.*

(2)   *The men were told to mop the deck.*

In written or spoken discourse, however, such sentences would virtually never occur in succession. On the other hand, we would not be surprised to find sentence (1) followed by a sentence such as (3).

(3)   *I'm using that new bank near our office.*

In other words, in discourse the context of a word extends well beyond the boundaries of the particular sentence that contains it, and that extended context will likely include prior processing of the word itself. Prior processing should certainly qualify as relevant context, but it has been completely ignored in research on lexical ambiguity. The research that we describe in this chapter represents our initial attempts to understand the context of repeated processing of an ambiguous word.

We began this research with the apparently simple question of what might happen to the processing of a particular homograph if one of its meanings has been emphasized in a previous processing episode. Most simply, the possibilities can be broken down into two categories: The first encounter with an ambiguity has an effect on later processing, or it does not. A strong modularity view would take the latter position. If the processing of an ambiguous word is governed strictly by bottom-up information provided by the word itself, then we would expect lexical access to proceed in exactly the same manner each time the word was presented. On the other hand, it has been suggested that, following the exhaustive access of a homograph's meanings, one of those meanings is suppressed as the other is selected and enhanced (Lucas, 1987; Tanenhaus et al., 1979). It is not unreasonable to ask how long lived such effects may be, if they occur at all.

Therefore, we conducted an experiment in which each trial presented a single homograph prime (without sentence context), followed after 200 msec by a target for a naming response. The target was a word related to the more frequent (dominant) meaning of the ambiguity, the less frequent (subordinate) meaning, or was unrelated to the homograph. However, unlike previous studies using this method (e.g., Simpson & Burgess, 1985; Simpson & Foster, 1986), we presented each homograph prime on two trials, separated by lags of 0, 1, 4, or 12 intervening trials. On the second presentation of a prime, the target was either the same as that shown on the first presentation, or (in most instances) a new target. If the target was new, it could be related to the same meaning as that represented by the earlier target, or another meaning. These conditions and sample stimuli are shown in Table 1.

We were interested primarily in the naming times for targets following the second presentation of a prime, as a function of what was shown on the first presentation. If the prior processing of one homograph meaning has an impact on later processing, this should be reflected in the naming time to targets on the second prime presentation. That is, if one

TABLE 1
Sample Stimuli from Experiment 1

Condition	Presentation 1		Presentation 2	
	Prime	Target	Prime	Target
Same	bank	save	bank	money
	bank	stream	bank	river
Different	bank	stream	bank	money
	bank	save	bank	river
Unrelated	calf	save	calf	money
	calf	stream	calf	river
Repeated (R)[a]	bank	money	bank	money
	bank	river	bank	river
Repeated (U)[a]	calf	money	calf	money
	calf	river	calf	river

[a]R and U for repeated conditions stand for Related and Unrelated, respectively.

meaning remains activated for some time after the initial processing episode, this should be realized as an increase in facilitation of that meaning and inhibition (or at least a lack of facilitation) for the other meaning, relative to an unrelated control.

The results showed an unexpected pattern. Although a meaning that was repeated from the first presentation to the second was facilitated relative to the control (i.e., the Same vs. the Unrel conditions in Figure 1), this facilitation was actually less than is typically seen with no prior presentation (e.g., Simpson, 1981; Simpson & Burgess, 1985). Instead, the effect manifested itself almost entirely in terms of inhibited responses to words related to the meaning other than that shown on the earlier trial (the Diff vs. the Unrel conditions in Figure 1). Although we have found in earlier research (Simpson & Burgess, 1985) that once activated, a meaning's activation may be dampened to the level of unrelated words, this is the first time that we have found a target related to its prime to be responded to more slowly than an unrelated word.

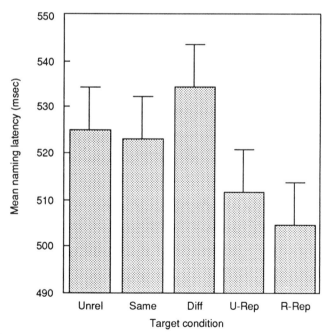

FIGURE 1

Mean naming latencies (+1 standard error) to targets following the second presentation of the prime in Experiment 1. "Diff" indicates stimuli in which the target represented a different meaning on the two presentations. "U-Rep" indicates the condition in which the target was repeated exactly, but was unrelated to its prime. "R-Rep" indicates a repeated target that was related to the prime.

Furthermore, this effect was symmetrical with respect to the frequency of the meanings of the homograph. That is, inhibition of the dominant meaning was as strong as that of the subordinate, given that the other meaning had been presented on an earlier trial. In addition, the effect did not diminish across the range of intervening trials tested. That is, the suppression of a meaning was as strong after 12 trials as it was immediately following the first presentation.

These results indicate that context in the form of an earlier processing episode does indeed have a profound impact on subsequent processing of a homograph. However, this context effect is clearly quite different from that which arises from sentence processing. These studies, whether or not they show immediate access of all meanings, invariably show an eventual advantage for the appropriate meaning. It is *not* customarily found, however, that the other meaning actually leads to slower responses than do completely unrelated words.

As previously discussed, the timecourse of ambiguous word processing has frequently been discussed in terms of the Posner and Snyder (1975) two-process model of context effects (see also Neely, 1976, 1977; Stanovich & West, 1979, 1981). Simpson and Burgess (1985) tested a two-stage account explicitly in their study of meaning frequency effects. When an ambiguous word was presented in isolation, only responses to targets related to the more frequent meaning were initially facilitated. After 300 msec, however, both meanings were activated. At still longer intervals, facilitation was again shown only for the dominant meaning; activation for the subordinate meaning had declined to a level equal to that of unrelated words. Simpson and Krueger (1991) obtained the same results for homographs that completed ambiguous sentences (i.e., sentences that were not biased toward either meaning). In the present case, however, the responses to a different meaning (i.e., a target on the second presentation that was incompatible with the meaning shown on the first) were considerably slower than those to unrelated words. The inhibition here is more than a straightforward withdrawal of resources.

Also unique to these results is the symmetry with respect to meaning frequency. Previously, we have found the meaning frequency effect to be remarkably robust (Burgess & Simpson, 1988; Simpson & Burgess, 1985). Here, however, it is completely reversed—with the dominant meaning showing as much inhibition as the subordinate as long as it is incompatible with the meaning cued on a prior trial.

Consequently, the existing views of lexical ambiguity processing that were reviewed earlier do not provide a sufficient account of these results. The repetition factor alters the availability of a meaning from the usual frequency-based ordering (Duffy et al., 1988; Simpson & Burgess, 1985) and it shows an inhibition-dominant, rather than facilitation-dominant, pattern of contextual influence. The pattern of results appears instead to be more reminiscent of inhibitory or negative priming effects reported in research in attention (e.g., Neill, 1979; Neill & Valdes, 1992; Neill & Westberry, 1987; Neumann & DeSchepper, 1992; Tipper, 1985; Tipper & Cranston, 1985). Although theoretical accounts of the basis of inhibitory attentional mechanisms vary (see Neill & Valdes, 1992, for a recent discussion), the general finding is that when one stimulus must be ignored in deference to a competing stimulus, the ignored item is actively inhibited. If on a subsequent trial the previously ignored stimulus becomes relevant, responses to it are slowed relative to a control stimulus that was not presented previously. For example, in a Stroop color-naming task (Neill, 1977), if a word to be ignored on trial n (e.g., *green* written in red ink) becomes the required response on trial $n + 1$ (*blue* written in green ink), that response is inhibited relative to the control (i.e., if *green* had not been the ignored word on trial n).

Applied to the case of ambiguous words, it appears that an inhibitory mechanism operates to suppress one meaning of a homograph when its competitor (i.e., the other meaning) has previously been processed for a response. Our hypothesis, that this active inhibitory process requires a *response* to be made to the competitor, is based on earlier research that did not include the repetition of primes (Simpson & Burgess, 1985). In that research, it was shown that, once activated, a meaning may decline in activation until it is at the same level as unrelated words. To reach a level that is lower than unrelated, therefore, requires more than simply having been activated previously. Rather, we suggest that the suppressed meaning is one that has been selected against in favor of a response to another meaning.

At this point, the precise nature of the inhibitory mechanism is unclear. We hypothesize that as the homograph is shown on the first presentation, activation immediately begins to build for each of a set of mutually exclusive semantic codes (i.e., one code associated with each of the homograph's meanings). When the target is presented, attention is drawn to one of those codes, enhancing it and inhibiting the competitors. At the time of the response, the differences in the activation levels between the meaning indicated by the target and the competing meanings is maximal, and the response "sets" that difference for some period of time. When the prime is presented again, therefore, this difference in activation is still in force, and a response to a word related to one of the competing meanings is very difficult.

We also hypothesize that this inhibitory effect is a rather specific one. That is, the inhibition is restricted to those codes that are direct competitors of the one called on for a response on the first presentation. There are both empirical and ecological reasons for this suggestion. Neill (1979) has shown in a matching task that inhibitory effects are greater when an unexpected stimulus comes from the same category as an expected stimulus (e.g., numbers) than when it comes from a different category (letters when numbers are expected). In the word recognition domain, Carr and Dagenbach (1990) have proposed a center-surround mechanism for enhancing weakly activated codes. They have found inhibitory priming from related primes under some conditions (see Carr & Dagenbach, 1990; Dagenbach, Carr, & Barnhardt, 1990; Dagenbach, Carr, & Wilhelmson, 1989) in which the code activated by the prime does not reach threshold for entry into working memory, but does call on attentional resources to boost the activation to threshold. If there are related codes that are also partially activated, those will be inhibited. In the case of ambiguous words, the competing codes are initially close in activation level, but the processing of the target serves to increase the difference in activation, and this difference is clear when another meaning must be processed later.

It also seems reasonable from the standpoint of natural language processing that the inhibition should be quite specific. In discourse, a wide variety of concepts may be active at any time. A widespread inhibitory effect, therefore, would pose a problem for comprehension, as many potentially relevant concepts might be inhibited. For example, in a conversation in which the financial sense of BANK is activated, it would not be prudent to have inhibited such concepts as *car, house, robbery*, and so forth. The only concept that poses a serious threat to comprehension if activated is the other meaning of BANK. That is, competitor meanings of the homograph are more likely to represent a potential hindrance to understanding, and therefore should be inhibited.

A. The Scope of Inhibition

We performed two experiments, therefore, to test the scope of the inhibitory effect. The first of these was similar to the earlier experiment in that homograph primes were presented twice with different targets. In the original experiment, however, the unrelated control stimuli against which the inhibitory effects of a meaning change were tested consisted of two unrelated words, effected by re-pairing targets with unrelated homographs. For example, the BANK–MONEY, BANK–RIVER pairs were tested for inhibition against pairs in which the target was unrelated to the prime on *each* presentation (e.g., CALF–MONEY, CALF–RIVER). In the second study, we included two additional control conditions (see Table 2). One of these conditions displayed a related pair on the first presentation (e.g., BANK–MONEY) and a new, unrelated target on the second (BANK–CHAIR). If the inhibitory mechanism is a very general one, then the response to CHAIR should be slowed (as we found RIVER to be slowed in the first experiment). In other words, under

TABLE 2
Sample Stimuli from Experiment 2

Condition	Presentation 1		Presentation 2	
	Prime	Target	Prime	Target
Same	bank	save	bank	money
	bank	stream	bank	river
Different	bank	stream	bank	money
	bank	save	bank	river
U-U[a]	calf	save	calf	money
	calf	stream	calf	river
U-R[a]	bank	chair	bank	money
	bank	heat	bank	river
R-U[a]	bank	money	bank	chair
	bank	river	bank	heat

[a] U-U = Unrelated-Unrelated control pairs (i.e., unrelated targets on both prime presentations, the same unrelated condition as used in Experiment 1); U-R = Unrelated-Related stimuli (i.e., unrelated on first presentation, related on second); R-U = Related-Unrelated stimuli (i.e., related on first presentation, unrelated on second).

a broad-based inhibition, any information that diverges from the meaning activated earlier will show the inhibitory effect. On the other hand, if the inhibitory process is a very specific one, we would anticipate that this control would not differ from other unrelated targets. On this view, only the incompatible meaning of the homograph is suppressed, as only this meaning is a competitor with the previously activated one.

Similar reasoning underlies the second control, which reversed the order of the related and unrelated pairs. In this case, a pair such as BANK–MONEY was *preceded* by BANK–CHAIR. This control was included to inform us about the kind of information that must be activated in order to lead to inhibition of a meaning. Again, if the process is a general one, we might expect that any stimulus pair that is not related to the same meaning as the second-presentation target will lead to inhibition of that target. In this case, the response times to MONEY following BANK should be equivalent if the first pair is either BANK–RIVER or BANK–CHAIR, and both of these conditions should be slower than a condition in which both prime–target pairs are unrelated. However, we hypothesize that the suppression is very specific, and a meaning (BANK–MONEY) is only inhibited if its direct competitor (BANK–RIVER) is required for a response on a prior trial. Although the results of the first experiment have led us to focus on the inhibitory effects for the different-meaning condition, we also included same-meaning pairs

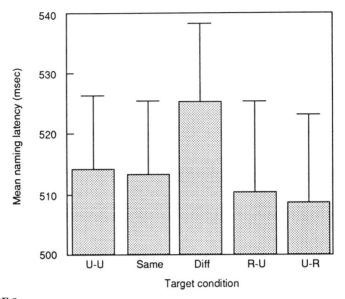

FIGURE 2

Mean naming latencies (+1 standard error) to targets following the second presentation of the prime in Experiment 2.

in this experiment to examine again the possibility that facilitation may arise when a meaning is maintained from one homograph presentation to another.

The results (see Figure 2) showed that the inhibitory effect is indeed very specific. Only the condition displaying competing meanings of a homograph on its two presentations led to suppression. Such a result is consistent both with results reported by Neill (1979) and with our intuition that in discourse, the mechanism should serve to assist comprehension by inhibiting a competing meaning. As in the first experiment, the same-meaning condition did not show significant facilitation in comparison to unrelated pairs. This result indicates, again, that in word priming, the homograph repetition effect is principally an inhibitory one.

The compatibility of these results with those found in attention research, and the role that inhibitory processes may play in language comprehension, suggest that this is not a phenomenon that is likely restricted to the competing meanings of ambiguous words. Rather, we would expect such a mechanism to operate in any case where activation of one concept is likely to interfere with the comprehension of an appropriate competing concept. Such an effect has been found in research on the activation and suppression of competing antecedents to a pronoun

(Gernsbacher, 1989). Gernsbacher tested subjects on sentences in which a pronoun was ambiguous with respect to its referent (e.g., as in *Ann predicted that Pam would lose the track race, but **she**. . .*). When the antecedent was identified later in the sentence (*. . .came in first very easily.*), Gernsbacher found that recognition of the competitor (in this case, *Ann*) was slowed relative to the antecedent (*Pam*), and relative to its accessibility immediately following the pronoun. Such a result is consistent with the present pattern indicating inhibitory processing when the competitors are mutually exclusive.

This hypothesis of the specificity of inhibitory processes also suggests cases in which these processes should *not* operate. In short, they should be less apparent in any case in which two or more domains of information, though they may be quite different, are not exclusive of one another. There are, of course, numerous demonstrations that processing can be made to emphasize one aspect of a concept over others. To take one prominent example, cued-recall research has shown that a retrieval cue will be successful only if it cues the information that was emphasized at the time of encoding. For example, a recall cue "something musical" is a good retrieval cue for the sentence. *The man **tuned** the piano,* but a poorer cue for *The man **lifted** the piano.* "Something heavy," on the other hand, is a better cue for the second sentence than for the first (Barclay, Bransford, Franks, McCarrell, & Nitsch, 1974). We would predict, however, that this kind of contrasting information, if used in our repetition paradigm, would *not* lead to inhibitory effects of the kind that we have found with homograph meanings. This is because the attributes of pianos concerning their weight and their musical nature, though very different, are not exclusive. That is, a particular instantiation of the piano category is *both* a musical instrument and a heavy object, and it is not at all implausible that both characteristics could be relevant in a single discourse episode. However, a particular bank can not be both a financial institution and a land formation, so the activation of the inappropriate meaning poses a threat to comprehension here that is not seen in the piano example.

To test this hypothesis, we conducted a third experiment, this time using as primes nonhomographs, and as targets, words representing different aspects or different features of the prime's meaning (see Table 3). Again, the prime occurred twice, with a different target on each presentation. Two control conditions were used. The first (U-U) presented unrelated targets on both trials. The second (U-R) presented the related pair following an unrelated pair. This control allowed us to assess the degree to which a target might be facilitated by having a different related target presented earlier. We hypothesized that in comparison to the control condition using unrelated prime–target pairs, the related (R-R) stimuli would not show the negative priming effect (i.e., responses to

TABLE 3
Sample Stimuli from Experiment 3

	Presentation 1		Presentation 2	
Condition[a]	Prime	Target	Prime	Target
R-R	piano	heavy	piano	music
	apple	pie	apple	tree
U-U	apple	heavy	apple	music
	piano	pie	piano	tree
U-R	piano	pie	piano	music
	apple	heavy	apple	tree

[a] R-R = related pairs (i.e., different related targets on the two presentations); U-U = Unrelated-Unrelated control pairs; U-R = Unrelated-Related stimuli.

MUSIC would not be slowed for having followed a pair emphasizing the weight feature of pianos).

It is clear from the results shown in Figure 3 that this hypothesis was confirmed. In fact, these pairs, which were intended to activate very different aspects of the primes (and which therefore were intended to serve as analogues of our different–meaning pairs in the first two experiments), led to facilitated rather than inhibited responding. The fact that there was no difference between related targets that followed a related pair and those following an unrelated pair suggests that the particular aspect of a word's meaning called for on the second presentation was not primed by an earlier related pair. These results support our contention that inhibitory processes should be seen not simply when different domains of information are presented, but only when those domains are competitors in the sense in which homograph meanings compete—that is, when the appropriateness of one sense precludes the appropriateness of the other.

B. Inhibition in Sentence Comprehension

We have now demonstrated the semantic suppression effect in two experiments, and identified one of its principal characteristics: that it appears to be restricted to cases in which two candidates for activation are direct competitors of one another. In the discussion of the first experiment, we suggested a second characteristic. This concerned the necessity that a meaning be processed to the level of a *response* before suppression of the other meaning will be seen. We have shown (Simpson & Burgess, 1985; Simpson & Foster, 1986) that simply having been

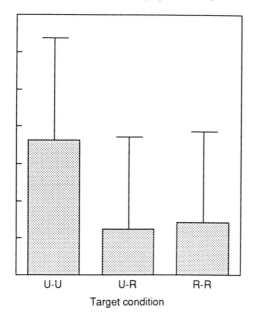

Target condition

FIGURE 3

Mean naming latencies (+1 standard error) to targets following the second presentation of the prime in Experiment 3. "R-R" indicates the condition in which different related targets were presented and is analogous to the "Diff" conditions of Experiments 1 and 2. "U-R" indicates a condition showing an unrelated target on the first presentation, and a related target on the second.

activated (but being activated no longer) is not enough for a meaning to be inhibited. Instead, it appears necessary that the subject's processing becomes committed to a single meaning by making a response on its basis. We might liken the activation and response processes to the development of a photographic image. When a sheet of photographic paper is exposed, it is first placed in a developing solution. At this point, the latent image on the paper emerges, visibly changing over the space of some seconds, the darker portions of the images appearing first. It is still fragile, however, until placed in a fixing bath that stops further development and sets the image permanently. When first presented, the meanings of the ambiguous word begin to "develop." When the target appears, that meaning is accessed fully for a response. The speed of the process to this point may depend on the dominance of the meaning and/ or its context. That is, it may take longer for a less frequent or an inappropriate meaning to become activated fully, and therefore responded to. Once the response is made, however, the "image" of a single selected meaning is fixed, and other meanings are retrieved only with great difficulty.

Our final experiment had two goals. The first was to test the inhibitory effect in a task requiring a less overt response. In all of the preceding experiments, the response was the overt naming of a target following the prime. We are trying to argue for a discourse-based role for the inhibitory mechanism, but we are using a response very different from the "response" that is made to a word during normal language comprehension. Indeed, it is not easy even to identify a word recognition response during comprehension. Obviously, however, the generality of the phenomenon requires a demonstration beyond overt naming. The second goal was a related one: to examine whether the inhibitory effect is restricted to the rather artificial priming paradigm, or whether it extends to the case of sentence comprehension.

In the final experiment, a sentence-verification paradigm was used (Krueger, 1990). On each trial, a single sentence was presented and the subject judged whether the sentence was semantically acceptable or anomalous. Each sentence contained a homograph and was clearly biased toward one meaning of that homograph. A later trial (separated from the first by 0, 1, or 6 sentences) repeated the homograph in a new sentence, this biased either toward the same meaning as the prior sentence, or the other meaning (see sample sentences in Table 4). As in the priming experiments, we were interested in the response times on the second presentation of a homograph as a function of its relation to the meaning processed in the earlier sentence.

The location of the homograph within the sentence varied across sentences, so the critical word was not highlighted for the subject in any way. In addition, in this case *no* explicit response was required to the homograph or to any single associate. Rather, the "response" being made to the homograph itself consisted of whatever operations are nor-

TABLE 4
Sample Sentences from Experiment 4

Condition	Sentences[a]
Same meaning	
First sentence	*She learned to play the* **organ** *while in school.*
	She learned to play the **piano** *while in school.* (Control)
Second sentence	*The keys to the* **organ** *were splintered and broken.*
Different meaning	
First sentence	*The man had to have an* **organ** *transplant.*
	The man had to have a **liver** *transplant.* (Control)
Second sentence	*The keys to the* **organ** *were splintered and broken.*

[a] Homographs and their control words are set bold-faced here for clarity but were not so distinguished when presented to the subjects.

mally carried out in the process of retrieving a word's meaning for comprehension of a sentence.

It is clear from Figure 4 that the inhibitory effect obtains in sentence comprehension as well as in lexical priming. Although attention was not drawn explicitly to the homograph, and despite the lack of an overt response to a target representing one of the homograph's meanings, we still see much slower processing of a sentence when the meaning is changed than when it remains constant over sentences. A difference between these results and those of the word priming experiments is that here, in addition to the inhibition of sentences representing a different meaning from that shown in the first sentence, verification of sentences maintaining the same meaning across presentations was facilitated. This result suggests that in comprehension of discourse, the role of the repetition of concepts is a dual one of enhancement of relevant concepts along with inhibition of the irrelevant (Gernsbacher, 1990).

We believe that the results of this experiment provide evidence for our contention that the inhibitory mechanism operates in service of discourse comprehension. It goes beyond priming, and includes cases

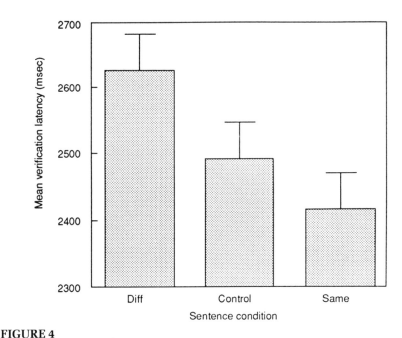

FIGURE 4

Mean sentence verification latencies (+1 standard error) following the second sentence containing a homograph (Experiment 4). "Control" indicates the condition in which the homograph was replaced by a control word for the first sentence.

in which the only response to be made to the homograph's meaning are those normal covert responses made in the process of understanding a sentence.

IV. SUMMARY AND CONCLUSIONS

Processing one meaning of a homograph, and responding to that meaning, results in the active and specific inhibition of competing meanings. Our studies so far suggest two characteristics of this inhibitory process. First, it is quite specific. Unrelated information that is not in specific competition with the previously processed meaning is not inhibited. Even closely related information, if it is not mutually exclusive of the information processed earlier, will not show the inhibitory effect. Likewise, a meaning of a homograph will not show inhibition unless it has been preceded by its competitor—simply seeing the homograph with an unrelated word will not lead to the effect. This result is also informative as to the second characteristic of the semantic inhibition effect: the requirement that the processing of a meaning run its full course, that is, that it be carried to the point of a response. In the case in which an unrelated target has appeared on the first presentation, we assume that the meanings of the homograph nevertheless become at least partly activated. However, when one of those meanings later appears as a target, the inhibitory effect will not be seen. Unless the subject makes a commitment to a meaning by a response on an earlier occurrence, the competitor will not be inhibited.

The sentence verification experiment shows, however, that this response need not be overt naming of a target. Normal word-processing operations in service of sentence comprehension are powerful enough to slow understanding of a sentence that requires a new homograph meaning for comprehension. This experiment also shows that suppression generalizes beyond the word priming paradigm to conditions that come closer to matching the kinds of processing that words undergo in discourse. We believe that these results are compatible with the hypothesis that the inhibitory effect serves the discourse-processing role of eliminating competitors from the pool of those concepts that may have discourse relevance. These competitors represent a threat to comprehension in a way that other information does not, and therefore must be specifically inhibited to prevent an intrusion that could greatly disrupt comprehension.

Although the modularity issue has not been the focus of this research, some points of relevance to that issue may be raised. Heretofore, work on lexical ambiguity has concentrated exclusively on the processes leading up to the response to some target stimulus, that is, the stages prior to lexical access. The present research, however, with its emphasis on the processing of a homograph that has been presented previously, focuses on the fate of an unselected meaning *after* access of the other meaning is complete. If we consider this prior processing to be a part of the context on the homograph's second presentation, then we are inclined to say that this represents a case of contextual influence on lexical processes. Under a strong view of lexical autonomy, the priming process is set by the relationships among entries in the internal lexicon, and priming operations should unfold in the same manner each time a word is presented. These results, however, suggest that the priming pattern for a word can be changed dramatically (if temporarily), and that this change is achieved through the context of a prior processing episode. On the other hand, the results are no more supportive of a strong context-dependent view than they are of a strong modularity position.

It seems necessary that in order to be identified as a potential competitor, a meaning must undergo some degree of activation (see also Tipper & Driver, 1988). We might go so far as to say that an inhibitory effect is diagnostic of prior activation. It may be that although some level of activation may be too low to show itself with the usual word- or sentence-priming methods (e.g., Simpson & Krueger, 1991), it can be manifested as inhibition on a later trial. Our continued research is aimed partly at examining this possibility. At the present, the results are compatible with our view of ambiguity processing generally (Simpson, 1984; Simpson & Krueger, 1991), that when a homograph is encountered, all of its meanings undergo some activation, but that the speed or degree of activation may still be influenced by the frequencies of the meanings and their context. The present research, however, suggests a new kind of context that although it has been ignored experimentally, must be extremely common in normal language comprehension.

Finally, a brief comment may be made about the possible relevance of this research to issues in developmental and individual differences. It has been suggested that one of the hallmarks of developmental change in cognitive processes is an increase through childhood in the efficiency of inhibitory processes (Dempster, 1992). A reversal of this trend is also held to underlie cognitive declines during adult senescence (Dempster, 1992; Hasher, Stoltzfus, Zacks, & Rypma, 1991; Hasher & Zacks, 1988). Likewise, it has been suggested that individual differences in language comprehension skill can be traced partly to the relative efficiency of inhibitory processes. Indeed, Gernsbacher and her colleagues (Gernsbacher, Varner, & Faust, 1990) have shown that subjects scoring low on a language comprehension test fail to show inhibitory effects. They found that shortly after reading sentences containing an ambiguous word, good comprehenders were more likely than poor comprehenders to show suppression of the contextually inappropriate meaning of the homograph. Clear predictions emerge, therefore, concerning the performance of these groups in the homograph repetition paradigm. We might anticipate that young children, older adults, and poorer comprehenders would show "better" performance than our college subjects (i.e., they would not show slowed responses to a changed meaning across presentations). In fact, this "better" performance would reveal the failure of what appears to be a powerful and important component of language comprehension.

ACKNOWLEDGMENTS

This research was supported in part by U.S. Department of Education Grant G008630072 to the Kansas Bureau of Child Research and the Learning Disabilities Institute of the University of Kansas, and in part by a Summer Fellowship to the first author from the University Committee on Research of the University of Nebraska at Omaha. We are grateful to Kelly Lyons, Merilee Krueger, and Robin Beyer for their help in conducting the experiments, and to George Kellas, Joseph S. Brown, Tram Neill, Dale Dagenbach, and Tom Carr for a number of helpful discussions on the ideas contained herein.

REFERENCES

Barclay, J. R., Bransford, J. D., Franks, J. J., McCarrell, N. S., & Nitsch, K. (1974). Comprehension and semantic flexibility. *Journal of Verbal Learning and Verbal Behavior*, *13*, 471–481.

Besner, D., & Humphreys, G. W. (1991). Basic processing in word recognition and identification: An overview. In D. Besner & G. W. Humphreys (Eds.), *Basic processes in reading: Word recognition* (pp. 1–9). Hillsdale, NJ: Lawrence Erlbaum.

Burgess, C., & Simpson, G. B. (1988). Cerebral hemispheric mechanisms in the retrieval of ambiguous word meanings. *Brain and Language*, *33*, 86–103.

Carr, T. H., & Dagenbach, D. (1990). Semantic priming and repetition priming from masked words: Evidence for a center-surround attentional mechanism in perceptual recognition. *Journal of Experimental Psychology: Learning, Memory and Cognition*, *16*, 341–350.

Conrad, C. (1974). Context effects in sentence comprehension: A study of the subjective lexicon. *Memory & Cognition*, *2*, 130–138.

Dagenbach, D., Carr, T. H., & Barnhardt, T. M. (1990). Inhibitory semantic priming of lexical decisions due to failure to retrieve weakly activated codes. *Journal of Experimental Psychology: Learning, Memory and Cognition*, *16*, 328–340.

Dagenbach, D., Carr, T. H., & Wilhelmson, A. (1989). Task-induced strategies and near-threshold priming: Conscious influences on unconscious perception. *Journal of Memory and Language*, *28*, 412–443.

Dempster, F. N. (1992). The rise and fall of the inhibitory mechanism: Toward a unified theory of cognitive development and aging. *Developmental Review*, *12*, 45–75.

Duffy, S. A., Morris, R. K., & Rayner, K. (1988). Lexical ambiguity and fixation times in reading. *Journal of Memory and Language*, *27*, 429–446.

Fodor, J. A. (1983). *Modularity of mind.* Cambridge, MA: MIT Press.

Forster, K. I. (1979). Levels of processing and the structure of the language processor. In W. E. Cooper & E. C. T. Walker (Eds.), *Sentence processing: Psycholinguistic studies presented to Merrill Garrett* (pp. 27–85). Hillsdale, NJ: Lawrence Erlbaum.

Gernsbacher, M. A. (1989). Mechanisms that improve referential access. *Cognitive Psychology, 32,* 99–156.

Gernsbacher, M. A. (1990). *Language comprehension as structure building.* Hillsdale, NJ: Lawrence Erlbaum.

Gernsbacher, M. A., Varner, K. R., & Faust, M. (1990). Investigating differences in general comprehension skill. *Journal of Experimental Psychology: Learning, Memory and Cognition, 16,* 430–445.

Gorfein, D. S., & Bubka, A. (1989). A context-sensitive frequency-based theory of meaning achievement. In D. S. Gorfein (Ed.), *Resolving semantic ambiguity* (pp. 84–106). New York: Springer-Verlag.

Hasher, L., Stoltzfus, E. R., Zacks, R. T., & Rypma, B. (1991). Age and inhibition. *Journal of Experimental Psychology: Learning, Memory and Cognition, 17,* 163–169.

Hasher, L., & Zacks, R. T. (1988). Wording memory, comprehension, and aging: A review and a new view. In G. H. Bower (Ed.), *The psychology of learning and motivation* (Vol. 22, pp. 193–225). San Diego: Academic Press.

Hogaboam, T. W., & Perfetti, C. A. (1975). Lexical ambiguity and sentence comprehension. *Journal of Verbal Learning and Verbal Behavior, 14,* 265–274.

Kellas, G., Paul, S. T., Martin, M., & Simpson, G. B. (1991). Contextual feature activation and meaning access. In G. B. Simpson (Ed.), *Understanding word and sentence* (pp. 47–71). Amsterdam: North Holland.

Krueger, M. A. (1990). *Sentence priming effects on the processing of ambiguous words.* Unpublished masters thesis, University of Nebraska at Omaha.

Lucas, M. M. (1987). Frequency effects on the processing of ambiguous words in sentence context. *Language and Speech, 30,* 25–46.

McClelland, J. L. (1987). The case for interactionism in language processing. In M. Coltheart (Ed.), *Attention and performance XII: The psychology of reading* (pp. 3–36). Hillsdale, NJ: Lawrence Erlbaum.

Meyer, D. E., & Schvaneveldt, R. W. (1971). Facilitation in recognizing pairs of words: Evidence of a dependence between retrieval operations. *Journal of Experimental Psychology, 90,* 227–234.

Neely, J. H. (1976). Semantic priming and retrieval from lexical memory: Evidence for facilitatory and inhibitory processes. *Memory & Cognition, 4,* 648–654.

Neely, J. H. (1977). Semantic priming and retrieval from semantic memory: Roles of inhibitionless spreading activation and limited-capacity attention. *Journal of Experimental Psychology: General, 106,* 226–254.

Neill, W. T. (1977). Inhibitory and facilitatory processes in attention. *Journal of Experimental Psychology: Human Perception and Performance, 3,* 444–450.

Neill, W. T. (1979). Switching attention within and between categories: Evidence for intracategory inhibition. *Memory & Cognition, 7,* 283–290.

Neill, W. T. (1989). Lexical ambiguity and context: An activation-suppression model. In D. S. Gorfein (Ed.), *Resolving semantic ambiguity* (pp. 63–83). New York: Springer-Verlag.

Neill, W. T., Hilliard, D. V., & Cooper, E. (1988). The detection of lexical ambiguity: Evidence for context-sensitive parallel access. *Journal of Memory and Language, 27,* 279–287.

Neill, W. T., & Valdes, L. A. (1992). Persistence of negative priming: Steady state or decay? *Journal of Experimental Psychology: Learning, Memory, and Cognition, 18,* 565–576.

Neill, W. T., & Westberry, R. L. (1987). Selective attention and the suppression of cognitive noise. *Journal of Experimental Psychology: Learning, Memory and Cognition, 13*, 327–334.

Neumann, E., & DeSchepper, B. G. (1992). An inhibition-based fan effect: Evidence for an active suppression mechanism in selective attention. *Canadian Journal of Psychology, 46*, 11–50.

Onifer, W., & Swinney, D. A. (1981). Accessing lexical ambiguities during sentence comprehension: Effects of frequency of meaning and contextual bias. *Memory & Cognition, 15*, 225–236.

Paul, S. T., Kellas, G., Martin, M., & Clark, M. B. (1992). The influence of contextual features on the activation of ambiguous word meanings. *Journal of Experimental Psychology: Learning, Memory and Cognition, 18*, 703–717.

Posner, M. I., & Snyder, C. R. R. (1975). Attention and cognitive control. In R. L. Solso (Ed.), *Information processing and cognition: The Loyola symposium* (pp. 55–85). Hillsdale, NJ: Lawrence Erlbaum.

Rosch, E. H. (1975). Cognitive representations of semantic categories. *Journal of Experimental Psychology: General, 104*, 192–233.

Schvaneveldt, R. W., Meyer, D. E., & Becker, C. A. (1976). Lexical ambiguity, semantic context, and visual word recognition. *Journal of Experimental Psychology: Human Perception and Performance, 2*, 243–256.

Seidenberg, M. S., Tanenhaus, M. K., Leiman, J. M., & Bienkowski, M. (1982). Automatic access of the meanings of ambiguous words in context: Some limitations of knowledge-based processing. *Cognitive Psychology, 14*, 489–537.

Simpson, G. B. (1981). Meaning dominance and semantic context in the processing of lexical ambiguity. *Journal of Verbal Learning and Verbal Behavior, 20*, 120–136.

Simpson, G. B. (1984). Lexical ambiguity and its role in models of word recognition. *Psychological Bulletin, 96*, 316–340.

Simpson, G. B. (1994). Context and the processing of ambiguous words. In M. A. Gernsbacher (Ed.), *Handbook of psycholinguistics* (pp. 359–374). New York: Academic Press.

Simpson, G. B., & Burgess, C. (1985). Activation and selection processes in the recognition of ambiguous words. *Journal of Experimental Psychology: Human Perception and Performance, 11*, 28–39.

Simpson, G. B., & Foster, M. R. (1986). Lexical ambiguity and children's word recognition. *Developmental Psychology, 22*, 147–154.

Simpson, G. B., & Krueger, M. A. (1991). Selective access of homograph meanings in sentence context. *Journal of Memory and Language, 30*, 627–643.

Stanovich, K. E., & West, R. F. (1979). Mechanisms of sentence context effects in reading: Automatic activation and conscious attention. *Memory & Cognition, 7*, 77–85.

Stanovich, K. E., & West, R. F. (1981). The effect of sentence context on ongoing word recognition: Tests of a two-process theory. *Journal of Experimental Psychology: Human Perception and Performance, 7*, 658–672.

Stanovich, K. E., & West, R. F. (1983). On priming by a sentence context. *Journal of Experimental Psychology: General, 112*, 1–36.

Swinney, D. A. (1979). Lexical access during sentence comprehension: (Re)consideration of context effects. *Journal of Verbal Learning and Verbal Behavior, 18*, 645–659.

Tabossi, P. (1988). Accessing lexical ambiguity in different types of sentential context. *Journal of Memory and Language, 27*, 324–340.

Tabossi, P., Colombo, L., & Job, R. (1987). Accessing lexical ambiguity: Effects of context and dominance. *Psychological Research, 49*, 161–167.

Tabossi, P., & Zardon, F. (1993). Processing ambiguous words in context. *Journal of Memory and Language, 32*, 359–372.

Tanenhaus, M. K., Leiman, J. M., & Seidenberg, M. S. (1979). Evidence for multiple stages in the processing of ambiguous words in syntactic contexts. *Journal of Verbal Learning and Verbal Behavior, 18,* 427–440.

Till, R. E., Mross, E. F., & Kintsch, W. (1988). Timecourse of priming for associate and inference words in a discourse context. *Memory & Cognition, 16,* 283–298.

Tipper, S. P. (1985). The negative priming effect: Inhibitory priming by ignored objects. *Quarterly Journal of Experimental Psychology, 37A,* 571–590.

Tipper, S. P., & Cranston, M. (1985). Selective attention and priming: Inhibitory and facilitatory effects of ignored primes. *Quarterly Journal of Experimental Psychology, 37A,* 591–611.

Tipper, S. P., & Driver, J. (1988). Negative priming between pictures and words in a selective attention task: Evidence for semantic processing of ignored stimuli. *Memory & Cognition, 16,* 64–70.

Van Petten, C., & Kutas, M. (1987). Ambiguous words in context: An event-related potential analysis of the timecourse of meaning activation. *Journal of Memory and Language, 26,* 188–208.

10

Phonological Inhibition in Auditory Word Recognition

Kathleen M. Eberhard

I. INTRODUCTION

Models of speech comprehension are constrained by real-time operation and the high rate of accuracy with which their processes must
perform their functions. Real-time operation is reflected in the fact that
a normal speech rate ranges from 150–200 words per minute (Levelt,
1992). This translates into about 2 to 4 words, or 12 to 50 phonemes, per
second. Despite this rapidity, the processes of speech comprehension
are quite accurate. Findings from fast reaction-time tasks (e.g., shadowing and phoneme monitoring) have shown that correct recognition for
one- and two-syllable content words heard in normal utterance contexts
can occur as early as 200 msec from the onset of the word (Marslen-
Wilson, 1987). This suggests that, given contextual constraints, some
spoken words may be correctly recognized before their corresponding
signal has been completely processed. Clearly, auditory word recognition is a result of highly efficient processing mechanisms.

As in other domains of cognitive inquiry, several theoretical models
of auditory word recognition have chosen the activation metaphor as
the appropriate one for meeting the constraints of this high efficiency. It
has been estimated that an average adult speaker has about 30,000
known words in his or her mental lexicon (Levelt, 1989). Therefore, one
way of meeting the efficiency constraints of language comprehension is
to provide a mechanism that will delimit the lexicon so that only a
subset is considered as possible matches to the acoustic input. The
activation metaphor does this by creating a candidate set of highly

activated word representations whose membership depends on the degree to which they match the sensory input.

More specifically, many activation models (e.g., Morton, 1969; McClelland & Elman, 1986; Marslen-Wilson, 1987) assume that stored word representations connect to lower level sublexical representations, for example, phonemes. The process of word recognition begins when sensory input activates these lower level representations. They, in turn, activate the word representations that they are connected to. So, for example, the initial acoustic input *pe* of the word *pet* may be assumed to activate the phonemes /p/ and /e/. These phonemes then activate all corresponding word representations such as *pet, pen, peg*, and so on, thereby creating an activated candidate set at the word level.

Many models adopting the activation metaphor assume that the activated candidate set is inherently competitive: The word representations compete via their activation levels, which numerically represent their goodness-of-fit with the sensory input, until one achieves a level that discriminates it from the rest (e.g., McClelland & Rumelhart, 1981; Marslen-Wilson, 1990; McClelland & Elman, 1986). In the preceding example, the processing of the final phoneme /t/ provides additional activation to the word representation *pet* which helps it achieve an activation level that can be discriminated from its competitors.

Although activation models share these processing assumptions, there is a difference among them that concerns the manner in which the correct lexical item emerges from the competing set. Specifically, some activation models assume that the correct item's activation level becomes discriminable as a result of both the continued bottom-up activation from its constituent phonemes and the decay (over time) of its competitors' levels. The activation levels of competitors are assumed to begin to decay once they no longer share connections to phonemes activated by the input. Other activation models, however, assume that the emergence of the correct lexical item is also aided by a mechanism of mutual inhibition, that is, active suppression. Although this is a less parsimonious approach to the resolution of the competitive process, Houghton and Tipper (this volume) argue that the addition of an inhibitory mechanism increases the efficiency (i.e., rate and accuracy) of the processing within a system. Because, as stated previously, the processes of speech comprehension are highly efficient, their efficiency may be a result of the operations of an inhibitory mechanism.

Following Bard (1990), I will argue that the general class of activation models that incorporate a mechanism of mutual inhibition makes predictions concerning competitor effects on auditory word recognition that contrast with the predictions made by activation models that do not contain such a mechanism. I will present the argument for the contrasting predictions by comparing two activation models of auditory word recognition that share many common processing assumptions, but which differ in this important respect. One model, the most recent version of Cohort (Marslen-Wilson, 1987, 1990), does not include an inhibitory mechanism; the other, TRACE (McClelland & Elman, 1986), does. I will then examine the empirical evidence on the basis of the contrasting predictions to see if it warrants the inclusion of an inhibitory mechanism that operates on phonological representations during auditory word recognition.

Although a similar issue has been actively explored in the domain of visual word recognition, where it is translated into one about recognition of orthographic representations (e.g., Colombo, 1986; Segui & Grainger, 1990; Grainger & Segui, 1990; Grainger, 1990), only evidence from investigations of auditory word recognition is examined here. It is plausible that the processes underlying visual word recognition may to some extent parallel those underlying auditory word recognition (e.g., Bradley & Forster, 1987); however, because the nature of the stimulus input is very different (i.e., spoken words are temporal, transient, and continuous both from one word to the next and from phoneme to phoneme within each word; visual words are none of these things), the processes in these two modalities must differ at some level. Thus, evidence that supports the operation of an inhibitory mechanism during visual word recognition does not necessarily imply that a parallel mechanism operates during auditory word recognition. This chapter, therefore, addresses whether there is evidence of inhibition specifically within the domain of spoken word recognition.

II. COHORT AND TRACE MODELS OF AUDITORY WORD RECOGNITION

According to the most recent version of the Cohort model (Marslen-Wilson 1987, 1990; Marslen-Wilson & Tyler, 1980), because the speech signal is temporally distributed, membership in the activated set, or cohort, crucially depends on shared initial phonological segments with the target input. For example, the words *brake* and *braid* would be competitors for the target word *brain*, but *train, crane,* or *drain* would not. Without support, the activation levels of the cohort members are assumed to decay back to a resting level; therefore, maintaining membership in the cohort depends on continued bottom-up activation from the sensory input.

Selection of a target item from the cohort occurs when its activation level is a criterial amount greater than that of its nearest competitor. Thus, the rate of the recognition process will reflect the time it takes for a target to achieve an activation level that allows it to be discriminated from its competitors (Marslen-Wilson, 1990). Although the most important factor affecting activation levels is incoming bottom-up information, or sensory input, the model may allow context to increase the activation levels of cohort members that fit the developing context. Nevertheless, the enhancement of activation from contextual information cannot override the level of activation that results from clear or unambiguous sensory input.

McClelland and Elman's (1986) model, TRACE, is an interactive activation model that is derived from McClelland and Rumelhart's (1981; Rumelhart & McClelland, 1982) model of visual word recognition. The model consists of a lexical network containing three levels of representation that consist of feature, phoneme, and word units, respectively. As shown in Figure 1, the levels of units are hierarchically organized and are aligned with moments in time referred to as slices. A complete set of phonetic feature units is duplicated at each time slice. Each phoneme unit at the next level spans six of these feature time slices (i.e., one phoneme time slice equals six feature time slices). Furthermore, there is a copy of each phoneme unit that begins every three feature slices. In other words, there are overlapping copies of phonemes. A similar alignment occurs at the word level where there is a copy of each word unit that begins whenever a copy of a phoneme unit begins. The word units span the range of time slices that its constituent phonemes span. This organization attempts to capture the coarticulatory effects that result from the continuous and temporal nature of speech.

There are facilitatory connections between units at adjacent levels and inhibitory connections between units within levels. Sensory input activates the appropriate feature units which activate phoneme units. The phoneme units, in turn, activate all words that they are connected to regardless of the position in the word where the phoneme appears. Unlike the Cohort model, TRACE places no restrictions on the parts of the speech signal that may activate candidate units. Without restrictions, the size of the candidate set is greatly increased, and TRACE's inhibitory mechanism allows the model to meet the constraints of high efficiency by effectively narrowing down the large set of candidates to the correct target item. The inhibitory connections do this by exaggerating the differences in activation levels of units within a candidate set so that the strong competitors quickly become stronger and suppress the weaker ones.

Similar to the Cohort model, correct selection of a target item from an activated set in TRACE occurs when the target unit's activation level is criterially higher than that of the other units. "Criterially higher" is determined by the Luce (1959) decision rule, which converts the target unit's activation level into a response probability that is based on the ratio of its response strength to that of all the other units at a particular

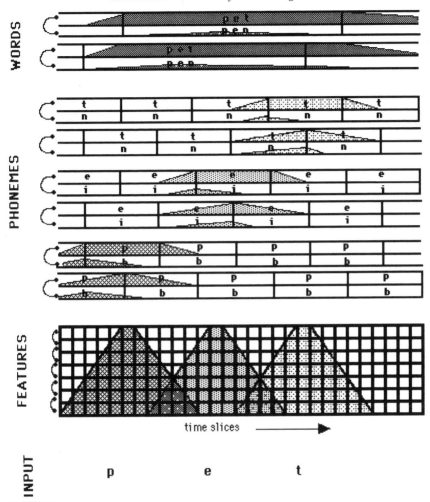

FIGURE 1

A simplified diagram of TRACE. Only a subset of the features, phonemes, and word units are depicted. Each column of squares at the feature level represents a time slice. Each square in a column represents a different feature unit. The complete set of features is duplicated at each time slice; thus, each row of squares represents the same feature. Each phoneme unit at the next level spans six feature time slices and there are overlapping copies of each phoneme unit which begin every three time slices. Likewise, at the word level, there is a copy of every word unit that begins whenever a set of phoneme copies begin, and each word unit spans the range of time slices that its constituent phonemes span. There are connections between units on adjacent levels (not depicted) which are bidirectional and excitatory. There are also inhibitory connections between units within levels, some of which are depicted in the figure by the lines terminating in dots. The shaded units in the figure are some of the units that would become activated by the presentation of the spoken word *pet*. The degree of activation is represented by the amount of shading. The pattern of shading represents the activation from particular sets of features that become activated by the phonemes in the input.

time. As in the Cohort model, the recognition rate of a target depends on the time it takes it to reach an activation level that allows it to be discriminated from its competitors.

In addition, both models assume that the intrinsic properties of candidates, such as their frequency of occurrence, will influence activation levels. Specifically, a high frequency candidate is assumed to have a higher resting level of activation than a low frequency candidate. This assumption is supported by evidence of faster lexical decision and repetition or shadowing times for high frequency spoken words presented in isolation (e.g., *street*) than for low frequency spoken words (e.g., *streak*; Marslen-Wilson, 1987, 1990; Connine, Mullennix, Shernoff, & Yelen, 1990). The implication of this assumption is that because the processing within the candidate set is competitive, the frequencies of the candidates within the set should affect the time it takes a target candidate to achieve an activation level that is discriminable from the other candidates. Therefore, targets that have high frequency competitors should have greater difficulty achieving a discriminable level of activation than targets that have low frequency competitors.

Some support for this comes from recognition threshold and gating task studies that involve auditorily presented words (Savin, 1963; Grosjean, 1980; Tyler, 1984). Both types of studies have found that when a spoken word is presented for recognition in a manner that does not allow it to be unambiguously identified (e.g., it is presented in white noise, as in the threshold task, or it is clearly presented but its presentation is incomplete, as in the gating task), the erroneous guesses that are given by the listeners in the task are often phonologically related to the target word and are higher in frequency. This type of support, however, is attenuated by the inability to separate the effects of perceptual processing from those of production.

A different source of evidence for competitor frequency effects comes from a cross-modal priming task by Marslen-Wilson, Brown, and Zwitserlood (cited in Marslen-Wilson, 1987). In this study, subjects were presented with auditory words such as *captive* or *captain*. Concomitant with the auditory word was the presentation of a related visual probe such as *guard* or *ship* for a lexical decision. The timing of the onset of the visual probe was varied so that it occurred either at an early or late position in the auditory word presentation. The early position was at a point before a sufficient amount of the auditory word was heard that would allow it to be unambiguously identified from other possible candidates. For example, an early probe was presented before the offset of /t/ in the auditory words *captive* and *captain*. The late position probe occurred at the end of the auditory word presentation. Findings from the early probe positions showed greater facilitatory priming for probes that were related to the higher frequency candidate than for probes that were related to the lower frequency candidate. For example, there was greater facilitation for *ship*, which is related to the higher frequency word *captain*, than for *guard*, which is related to the lower frequency word *captive*. Findings from the late probe positions showed only facilitatory priming for the probe that was related to the actually presented auditory word.

Marslen-Wilson (1987) interpreted these findings to mean that early in the processing of spoken words, high frequency candidates have higher activation levels than low frequency candidates. However, the findings from the late probe position suggest that the effects of competitor frequency dissipate once disambiguating sensory information arrives.

Because both Cohort and TRACE assume that the recognition process is a competitive one, and that frequency of occurrence is reflected in the activation levels of word representations, findings of competitor frequency effects are consistent with both models. However, as argued by Bard (1990), because Cohort and TRACE differ according to whether they incorporate a mechanism of mutual inhibition to resolve the competition, they make contrasting predictions concerning the nature of the effects of competitor and target frequency. In particular, in auditory word recognition tasks that require the recognition of spoken words presented without context, Cohort predicts both main effects of target and competitor frequency and no interaction. In contrast, TRACE predicts an interaction between these two frequency effects.

The contrasting predictions are demonstrated in Figures 2a–d, which contain activation curves from simulations that replicated the ones conducted by Bard (1990). The simulations were run on two simplified versions of TRACE. Specifically, the versions were single-layer systems that ran according to the activation functions given in McClelland and Rumelhart (1981, 1988) and the parameter values used by Bard (1990). Both versions had identical parameter settings except for gamma—the strength of inhibition. Gamma was set to 0 for the simulations that were run on a system without inhibition (corresponding to Cohort) and to .50 for the simulations that were run on a system with inhibition (corresponding to TRACE). The function containing γ is

$$net_i = e_i - \gamma(a_k)$$

Where net_i is the net input to unit i, e_i is the amount of excitatory input to unit i, and a_k is the positive activation level of a neighboring unit k. Thus, a γ value greater than zero essentially scales the strength of the inhibition that is sent from a unit k to a unit i, such that the more activated unit k is the greater its inhibitory strength is on unit i. The end

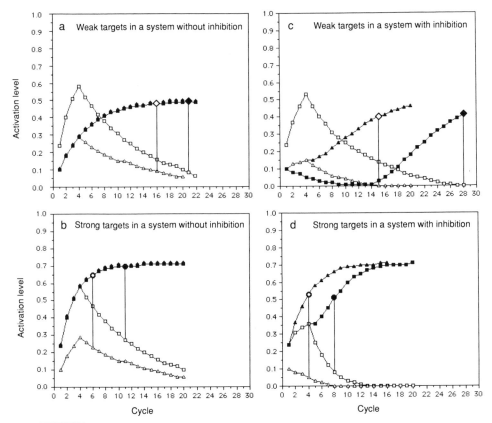

FIGURE 2

Results of simulations run on two single layer systems that differed in whether they contained mutual inhibition. (a) and (b) contain results from a system without inhibition (corresponding to Cohort); (c) and (d) contain results from a system with inhibition (corresponding to TRACE). In both system versions the recognition points for targets that have strong (high frequency) competitors versus weak (low frequency) competitors were examined. The contrasting competitor strengths were examined for targets that were, themselves, either weak (a and c) or strong (b and d) competitors. Key to symbols: For (a) and (c), –■–, weak target with strong competitor (♦, recognition point); –▲–, weak target with weak competitor (◇, recognition point); –□–, strong competitor with weak target; –△–, weak competitor with weak target; for (b) and (d), –■–, strong target with strong competitor (●, recognition point); –▲–, strong target with weak competitor (○, recognition point); –□–, strong competitor with strong target; –△–, weak competitor with strong target.

result of this is the "rich get richer effect" (McClelland & Rumelhart, 1988, p. 15), in which strong units receiving positive input rapidly surpass the rest of the units in total activation. Minimum and maximum activation values in both system versions were set to 0 and +1, respectively. The resting level for all units was 0, and the decay rate was set to .10.[1]

Competitor and target frequency effects were examined in the two system versions by varying the amount of input to the units. Units representing high frequency targets and competitors received an excitatory input value that was 2.5 times greater than the input value that units representing low frequency targets and competitors received (the input values were .62 and .25, respectively).[2] Thus, units that received the larger input value became strongly activated and units that received the smaller input value became weakly activated. This permitted an examination of the effects of the strength of competition on the recognition rate of targets that are, themselves, either strong or weak competitors.

The x-axis in Figure 2a–d represents processing time in cycles. Two processing routines were executed during each cycle: getnet and update. The getnet routine determined the net input to each unit based on the excitatory and inhibitory inputs to the unit. The update routine then incremented the activation of each unit on the basis of the net input and the existing activation value. As in Bard's simulations, the target and competitor units received constant excitatory input until the fourth processing cycle; thereafter, only the target continued to receive excitatory input. Thus, the fifth processing cycle represents the point where the target word and the competitor diverge.

Four simulations were run in each system version. Two simulations examined the recognition of weakly activated targets and two examined the recognition of strongly activated targets. The simulations for each target type differed according to whether the target had a strongly or weakly activated competitor to overcome in order to achieve recognition. Figures 2a and 2b give the results of the four simulations that were run in a system that has only positive activation (e.g., Cohort). Figures 2c and 2d give the results of the simulations that were run in a system that has both positive activation and mutual inhibition (e.g., TRACE).

In all four figures there are two recognition points: One recognition point is for targets that have only weak competitors and the other is for targets that have strong competitors. Each recognition point represents the time (in cycles) when the target's activation level reaches a criterial amount greater than its competitor's level (i.e., an amount that would

[1]The parameter values adopted for these simplified simulations differed from the original parameter settings given by McClelland and Rumelhart (1988). Their parameter settings were as follows: $\gamma = .21$, minimum activation $= -.20$, maximum activation value $= 1.00$, and decay $= .07$.

[2]These input values differ from the ones Bard (1990) chose. In her simulations, the input value for strong units was 1.5 times greater than the input value for weak units. This difference between our two simulations did not change the pattern of results.

allow it to be discriminated from the closest competitor). The value for the criterial amount was arbitrarily chosen and was the same for all targets. In the figures presented here, each recognition point is the earliest processing cycle when the target's activation level (a_t) reaches an amount that is at least .40 greater than its competitor's activation level (a_c). This is indicated by the vertical line that connects the target's activation curve to its competitor's.

Bard calculated the recognition points in her simulations using both this simple rule (i.e., $a_t = a_c + .40$) and the Luce (1959) decision rule. She compared the results of these two rules and found that although the actual points differed between them, the pattern of the recognition points was the same. Because it is the pattern of recognition points that is important for the argument underlying the contrasting predictions, only the simple recognition rule of $a_t = a_c + .40$ was computed for the simulation results presented here.

In all four figures, the recognition points for targets with strongly activated competitors (represented by the solid diamond and circle points) are delayed relative to the recognition points for targets with weakly activated competitors (represented by the open diamond and circle points). This demonstrates both models' prediction of competitor frequency effects. The comparison between the recognition points for weak and strong targets within the same system version (i.e., Figures 2a,b and Figures 2c,d) shows that the weak target recognition points (represented by diamonds) are delayed relative to the strong target recognition points (represented by circles). This demonstrates both models' prediction of target frequency effects.

Notice, however, that in Figures 2a and 2b, which contain curves from a system without inhibition, the increase in recognition time that is caused by a strong competitor relative to a weak competitor is the same for both strong and weak targets. This demonstrates the Cohort model's prediction of no interaction between the effects of competitor and target frequency. Because the Cohort model does not contain mutual inhibition, the activation levels of competitors cannot affect the activation levels of targets and vice versa. Thus, reaching an activation level that is discriminable from strong competitors as opposed to weak competitors will be equally difficult for strong and weak targets (Bard, 1990).

In contrast, Figures 2c and 2d, which contain the activation curves from a system with inhibition, show that the increase in recognition time that is caused by strong competitors relative to weak competitors is not equal for weak and strong targets. Furthermore, the curves for targets that have weak competitors reach higher activation levels faster than the curves for targets that have strong competitors. Both of these effects are consequences of mutual inhibition: Mutual inhibition allows the activation levels of targets to affect the activation levels of competitors and vice versa. Targets that have strong competitors receive more inhibition than targets that have weak competitors, and so they are slower to achieve as high an activation level. However, the strength of the competitors interacts with the target's strength. When a target is itself a strong competitor, it is also a strong source of inhibition. As a result, a strong target is able to quickly overcome the inhibition it receives from weak or strong competitors. This is the rich get richer effect referred to earlier. When the target is a weak competitor it has greater difficulty overcoming the inhibition it receives from its competitors, particularly the inhibition it receives from strong competitors. Thus, TRACE predicts an interaction between the factors of competitor and target frequency.

Bard points out that the specific quantitative predictions concerning the main effects and interaction of competitor and target frequency would depend on the values assigned to the set of parameters, as well as on the choice of the particular decision rule that determines the recognition points. Furthermore, neither these simulation results nor hers included the effects of processing at lower sublexical levels. Such effects would be expected also to affect the specific quantitative predictions. The simplified single-layer simulations, therefore, only demonstrate the contrasting qualitative predictions that activation models with and without mutual inhibition make.

Recently, Jacobs and Grainger (1992) reported the results of a simulation that was conducted on the complete multilayer version of McClelland and Rumelhart's interactive activation model of visual word recognition (McClelland & Rumelhart, 1981, 1988). They examined recognition times (in cycles) for low and medium frequency words that had either high or low frequency competitors. Their simulations results (1992, Simulation Study 1, p. 1178) for the complete model with all three lexical levels, including both mutual inhibition within levels and facilitatory feedback between levels, demonstrated the interaction that is predicted by Bard from the simplified single-layer version of TRACE previously described. Although there are important differences between the visual and auditory versions of the interactive activation model of word recognition, the functions underlying the activation and inhibition processes are the same (McClelland & Elman, 1986, p. 20); therefore, it seems reasonable to assume that the multilayer version of TRACE would produce similar results with respect to these particular factors.

Thus, with TRACE and Cohort's contrasting predictions in mind, as illustrated by the simulations inspired by Bard (1990), I examine the empirical evidence to see if it warrants the inclusion of an inhibitory mechanism in an activation-based model of auditory word recognition.

III. AN EXAMINATION OF THE EMPIRICAL EVIDENCE

Marslen-Wilson (1990) investigated the effects of competitor frequency on the recognition times for high and low frequency targets in several auditory word recognition tasks. He constructed four sets of stimuli. Two sets had high frequency target words and two had low frequency target words. One of the high frequency target word sets consisted of words that have low frequency competitors (e.g., the high frequency target word *book* has only low frequency competitors such as *bush* and *bull*); the other set consisted of words that have high frequency competitors (e.g., the high frequency target word *light* has the high frequency competitor *like*). The two sets of low frequency target words contrasted target and competitor frequency in the same manner (e.g., the low frequency target word *flock* has low frequency competitors *flog* and *flop* and the low frequency target item *streak* has the high frequency competitor *street*). All target words were monosyllabic and became disambiguated only when their final consonant was heard.

Marslen-Wilson examined the mean correct recognition times for each of the four sets of target words in both an auditory lexical decision task and an auditory repetition task. The recognition times were measured from the vowel offset in each of the words; that is, a point that was considered to be informationally equivalent across the words in the four sets. The findings from both tasks demonstrated significant effects of target frequency such that the two high frequency target sets had faster recognition times than the two low frequency target sets. However, contrary to the predictions from both Cohort and TRACE, there was no evidence of a competitor frequency effect, and contrary to the predictions of TRACE, there was no interaction between competitor frequency and target frequency.

Marslen-Wilson then presented the four sets of stimuli in a gating task. Subjects received successive fragments of each word at increments of 50 msec (the "gate") until the entire word was heard. After each gate, subjects attempted to guess what the word was and indicated how confident they were of their guess. Two measurements from the vowel offset of each of the words were made. The first was the isolation point, which is the point where subjects began to correctly identify the word regardless of their confidence level. The second measurement was the recognition point, which is the average point in the word where subjects began to identify it correctly with a confidence level of 80%. Thus, the isolation points typically precede the recognition points.

The findings from the recognition point measurements showed a weak effect of target frequency and no effect of competitor frequency. However, the findings from the isolation point measurements showed not only a significant effect of target frequency, but also a significant effect of competitor frequency. High frequency target words had a mean isolation point that was less than the mean for the low frequency target words. Within the high frequency target word sets, targets that have high frequency competitors had a mean isolation point that was greater than that for targets that have low frequency competitors. The same direction of competitor effects was observed in the sets of low frequency target words; that is, low frequency targets that have high frequency competitors had a greater mean isolation point than low frequency targets that have low frequency competitors. Furthermore, the difference between the mean isolation points of the two high frequency target sets was about equal to the difference between the two mean isolation points of the two low frequency target sets (24 and 20 msec, respectively). Thus, competitor frequency did not interact with target frequency.

These findings favor a model that does not contain an inhibitory mechanism that operates on a neighborhood of competing phonological word representations. However, this is only one piece of evidence, and the lack of findings of any competitor frequency effects in the other recognition tasks appears to be inconsistent with the predictions of both Cohort and TRACE.

Marslen-Wilson suggested that competitor frequency effects were only evident in the isolation point measurements because the effects are transient. They may only be detected when listeners respond at a point before sufficient sensory information discriminates the target from its competitors. As stated earlier, both Cohort and TRACE assume that the bottom-up sensory information is the most important factor that influences activation levels. Thus, according to Marslen-Wilson, the competitive advantage of high frequency neighbors rapidly becomes subsidiary to the dominant effects of the sensory input. The lexical decision task may have failed to detect competitor frequency effects because the task requires listeners to wait until all sensory information has been analyzed (i.e., the offset of the target presentation), and the listener is certain that the information corresponds to a real word. This point of certainty may be past the transient period when the competitors' activation levels delay the target's achievement of the criterial difference.

Because only real words were presented in the repetition task, the responses should have been made at an earlier point in the identification process when the effects of competitor frequency can be detected. However, Marslen-Wilson claimed that the listeners in this task may have also delayed their responses until a later point when they were certain what the word was. In support of this, he found that both the lexical decision and the repetition response times correlated much more strongly with the gating task's recognition point measurements (the point where subjects were at least 80% confident of their guesses) than with its isolation point measurements (average point where subjects correctly guessed the word). Thus, it appears that only when listeners respond at a point when the sensory information is still ambiguous will competitor frequency effects be observed.

Because the gating task is not a timed recognition task, it is not a direct measure of the rate of the recognition process. Therefore, additional empirical evidence should be examined before drawing any conclusions concerning the nature of the effects of competitor and target frequency.

IV. ADDITIONAL SOURCES OF EMPIRICAL EVIDENCE

One possible source of additional empirical evidence is to examine how the prior processing of a competitor influences the recognition of a following target. In other words, Cohort and TRACE may make contrasting predictions concerning the nature of phonological priming effects in auditory word recognition tasks. I will once again argue that the consequences shown in Figure 2a–d of including mutual inhibition versus not including inhibition result in contrasting predictions. After presenting this argument, I will examine the evidence to see if it provides insight into the nature of the underlying mechanisms.

A. Phonological Priming Predictions

Some researchers (e.g., Slowiaczek and Hamburger, 1992; Slowiaczek and Pisoni, 1986) have argued that the Cohort model predicts facilitatory phonological priming effects because targets that share word initial phonemes with primes would become activated during prime processing. The boost in the target's activation level from the processing of the prime may be expected to facilitate its subsequent recognition. Slowiaczek and Hamburger (1992) also claimed that inhibitory or interfering phonological priming effects are consistent with connectionist models that incorporate mutual inhibition (e.g., TRACE). However, deriving contrasting predictions concerning the nature of phonological priming effects from models such as Cohort and TRACE may not be as straightforward as these researchers suggest. This is because, as explicated, both TRACE and Cohort assume that the recognition process is a competitive one and that the rate of recognition depends on the degree of competition between a target and the other activated candidates.

In the case of the Cohort model, when a target that is phonologically related to a prime is presented for recognition, its recognition time will not only be affected by the amount of residual activation it may have from being a member of the preceding prime's cohort, but the time will also be affected by the amount of residual activation that the prime has. It is reasonable to assume that if a prime was recognized (i.e., fully processed), then the amount of residual activation that it will have from its own processing will be greater than the amount that any of its cohort members will have. This is because the prime will have achieved a higher activation level than any of its cohort members, and will have been the last in its cohort to begin to decay from the cessation of bottom-up support. Furthermore, the lack of any findings of competitor frequency effects in several nonpriming word recognition tasks previously discussed, suggests that the activation levels of competitors in a cohort rapidly decay once disambiguating information arrives (Marslen-Wilson, 1990). Thus, contrary to Slowiaczek and Hamburger's claim (1992), a target unit that was a competitor in a preceding prime's cohort may not be expected to have any residual activation when it is presented for recognition. The prime may be the only word unit that can be expected to have a heightened or boosted activation level due to its processing at the point of target presentation.

When we consider the frequency factors that are assumed to affect activation levels, we can make the assumption that low frequency primes will be the most likely primes to have activation levels that will not have fully decayed by the time a target is presented for recognition— at least when stimuli are presented at constant interstimulus intervals. This is because low frequency primes take longer to be recognized than high frequency primes, and so will begin to decay at a later point in the interstimulus interval that separates the prime and target (see Goldinger, Luce, & Pisoni, 1989; Goldinger, Luce, Pisoni, & Marcario, 1992; Luce, Pisoni, & Goldinger, 1990, for a similar argument). Because a phonologically related prime will be part of a target's cohort, it will receive bottom-up activation from the shared phoneme segments during target processing. If a high frequency related prime has decayed to its resting level during the prime–target interstimulus interval, then the bottom-up activation it receives from the target processing will not make it any more competitive than it usually is. However, if a low frequency prime has not fully decayed to its resting level during the interstimulus interval then the bottom-up activation from the target processing will continue to support the prime's undecayed activation level and cause it to be a stronger competitor for the target than it might ordinarily be.

Thus, depending on the decay rate, a low frequency prime may be a strong competitor for a related target. The Cohort model, therefore, predicts that if the interstimulus interval between a prime and a target is constant, and short enough to tap into the effects of residual activation from complete prime processing, then low frequency related primes will delay target recognition. In contrast, high frequency related primes may be expected to cause no delay. Furthermore, the delay in target recognition that is caused by low frequency related primes, relative to low frequency unrelated primes, may be expected to be the same for both high and low frequency targets. This is because, as depicted in Figures 2a and 2b, without mutual inhibition, strong competitors delay the recognition of strong and weak targets, relative to weak competitors (or in this case, noncompetitors, i.e., unrelated primes), to the same extent.

B. TRACE

The account of phonological priming effects in TRACE is similar to Cohort's. The recognition of a prime should leave its word unit with the highest level of activation. The competitors of the prime will have had their activation levels inhibited to a level that allowed the prime to achieve the criterial difference for recognition. If one of those competitors is subsequently presented as a target for recognition, then its strongest competitor should be the prime. Because a related prime shares phonological segments with the target, its strength will continue to be supported during target processing. Thus, the prime's competition should delay the recognition time for a related target rather than facilitate it.

As in the Cohort model, the most likely prime to have an activation level that will not have decayed to its resting level during a constant prime–target interval will be one that is low in frequency. Thus, TRACE also predicts that low frequency related primes will delay target recognition relative to unrelated controls. Furthermore, TRACE makes the contrasting prediction that the interfering effects of low frequency related primes will interact with target frequency. This prediction arises from the rich get richer effects of mutual inhibition. As depicted in Figures 2c and 2d, mutual inhibition causes weak targets to have greater difficulty than strong targets overcoming strong competitors. Thus, the interaction should reflect greater interference effects for low frequency targets than for high frequency targets because it is assumed that low frequency targets are weak targets.

Once again, the specific quantitative predictions would depend on the assignment of values to the complete set of parameters. Nevertheless, the mechanism of mutual inhibition in TRACE causes it to make qualitative predictions concerning phonological priming effects that contrast with those from the Cohort model. These contrasting qualitative predictions provide an additional basis for examining the empirical evidence to see if it supports the inclusion of an inhibitory mechanism.

It should be noted, however, that the contrasting predictions apply to quite specific circumstances. Specifically, both TRACE and Cohort predict phonological priming effects only when the interval between the prime and target is constant and sufficiently short to tap into the residual activation from the complete processing (recognition) of a prime. Only low frequency related primes are predicted to cause priming effects, and these effects are relative to the effects of low frequency unrelated primes. Finally, the contrasting predictions from TRACE and Cohort can only be evaluated by observing whether the effects of low frequency related primes interact with target frequency.

V. AN EXAMINATION OF THE EVIDENCE FROM PHONOLOGICAL PRIMING STUDIES

There are a number of studies, employing a variety of recognition tasks, that have examined phonological priming in auditory word recognition. All possible priming effects have been found: inhibitory or interference effects (Goldinger, Luce, & Pisoni, 1989; Goldinger et al., 1992; Slowiaczek & Pisoni, 1986; Radeau, Morais, & Dewier, 1989), facilitatory effects (Jakimik, Cole, & Rudnicky, 1985; Slowiaczek, Nusbaum, & Pisoni, 1987; Slowiaczek & Hamburger, 1992), and null effects (Slowiaczek & Pisoni, 1986; Radeau et al., 1989; Goldinger, Luce & Pisoni, 1989). None of these priming studies have included all the factors that are needed for a convincing evaluation of Cohort and TRACE's contrasting predictions. Nevertheless, by examining the factors that have been included in the various studies, it may be possible to determine the degree of consistency of the evidence with the predictions from Cohort and TRACE.

Most of the priming studies have not included both the factors of prime and target frequency. This may be part of the reason for the findings of null priming effects in timed recognition tasks that have otherwise included the necessary factors that are predicted to produce effects. For example, no significant priming effects were found in two separate auditory lexical decision studies (Slowiaczek & Pisoni, 1986; Radeau et al., 1989) in which phonologically related and unrelated prime–target word pairs were presented at short interstimulus intervals. Although Slowiaczek and Pisoni (1986, Experiment 2) examined the effects of target frequency, they did not include prime frequency as a factor. Radeau et al. (1989, Experiment 2) did not include either frequency factor. The prime–target interval in Slowiaczek and Pisoni's experiment was fixed at 50 msec. Although short, the interstimulus interval in Radeau et al.'s experiment was not constant. The targets in their experiment were presented 850 msec from the onset of the prime, which created an interstimulus interval that varied according to the duration of the prime. Thus, the nonsignificant priming effects in

Radeau et al.'s experiment may in part be due to the variable prime–target interval. However, because prime frequency was not a factor in either Radeau et al.'s or Slowiaczek and Pisoni's experiments, both experiments' findings of null effects may be explained by Cohort and TRACE as simply reflecting an averaging of the effects from low and high frequency related primes.

The findings of null priming effects are not confined to the auditory lexical decision task. Radeau et al. (1989, Experiment 2) presented the same stimuli employed in their lexical decision task in an auditory word repetition task. The prime–target stimulus onset asynchrony (SOA) was also 850 msec, and subjects responded only to the target. The results showed no effects on repetition times for target words that were preceded by phonologically related prime words relative to those that were preceded by phonologically unrelated prime words. Again, this may reflect the averaging of prime frequency effects.

Recently, Slowiaczek and Hamburger (1992) claimed that they found evidence of both facilitation and interfering priming effects in their auditory word repetition task. In one experiment (Experiment 2A), they presented subjects with auditory prime–target pairs that had initial overlaps of zero, one, two, or three phonemes. Subjects did not respond to the primes and the interstimulus interval was 500 msec. The results showed that the mean repetition time for targets that shared one phoneme with a prime was significantly faster than the mean repetition time for targets that shared no phonemes with a prime (i.e., unrelated controls). In addition, the mean repetition time for targets that shared three phonemes with a prime was significantly slower (35 msec) than the mean repetition time for targets that shared only one phoneme with a prime. Slowiaczek and Hamburger labeled this finding an interference effect. However, relative to the unrelated baseline, which is the baseline Slowiaczek and Hamburger used to determine the facilitatory effect, the interference effect in the three-phoneme overlap condition was a much smaller 16 msec. Slowiaczek and Hamburger did not report whether this effect was significant. Despite this, the direction of the effect is consistent with the predictions from both Cohort and TRACE.

The significant facilitatory effect, however, appears to be inconsistent with the predictions from both models. This apparent inconsistent finding may be attributed to the length of the interstimulus interval that was employed in Slowiaczek and Hamburger's study. Their interval was a somewhat long 500 msec. This may be too long for tapping into the effects of residual activation from prime processing. Furthermore, it may have been sufficient time to allow for the emergence of the effects of strategic processing.

Semantic priming studies have shown that subjects can use the prime to develop expectations about following targets (Neely, 1977, 1991). As a result, responses to expected targets are facilitated, and responses to unexpected targets are inhibited. It is assumed that prime-induced expectations (de Groot, 1984) take time and will only be observed when the interval between the prime and target is long enough to allow the expectations to develop (Posner & Snyder, 1975). Neely's (1977) investigation of semantic priming effects showed evidence of expectancy effects at a SOA of 700 msec for visually presented prime–target pairs. Thus, the 500 msec interstimulus interval in Slowiaczek and Hamburger's experiment could feasibly have permitted expectations to influence the priming effects. In addition, it is claimed that the proportion of related trials in an experiment will determine whether and to what extent subjects develop prime-induced expectations (e.g., Neely, 1977; de Groot, 1984). Because 75% of the experimental pairs in Slowiaczek and Hamburger's experiment contained prime–target pairs that shared at least the first phoneme, subjects could have detected this relationship and developed a strategy based on it.

Other findings of facilitatory priming effects have also been attributed to possible strategic processing. For example, Jakimik et al. (1985) presented phonologically related prime–target pairs in an auditory lexical decision task that had a long, 2-sec interstimulus interval. They found facilitation for monosyllabic target words that were preceded by bisyllabic primes whose first syllable was identical in both sound and spelling to the target (e.g., *dollar–doll*). However, there was no facilitation for targets when their preceding primes had initial syllables that were identical in sound but different in spelling (e.g., *definite–deaf*). Jakimik et al. suggested that the results may be due to a spelling strategy adopted by the subjects because most of them reported noticing the priming relationship.

Strategic processing may also account for the seemingly contradictory facilitatory priming and interference effects that have been found in two separate studies employing a perceptual identification task. Slowiaczek et al. (1987, Experiments 1 & 3) found that the correct identification of target words presented in white noise was significantly better when they were preceded by prime words that shared two or three phonemes than when they were preceded by prime words that shared only one or no phonemes. In contrast, Goldinger, Luce, and Pisoni (1989) found that the correct identification of targets presented in white noise was significantly worse when they were preceded by phonetically related primes than when they were preceded by phonetically unrelated primes.

The contradictory findings do not appear to be attributable to any procedural differences between the two studies. Both studies clearly presented the primes before the degraded targets and did not require the subjects to respond to the primes. In addition, both studies employed a constant interstimulus interval of 50 msec. Although this interval may be considered too short for strategic processing to exert its influence, because the speed of target identification was not emphasized or measured, subjects may have engaged in such processing (Radeau, Morais & Dewier, 1989; Goldinger et al., 1992). This concern led Goldinger et al. to employ related prime–target pairs that were constructed on the basis of their phonetic confusability rather than on the basis of their shared phonemes. Their related pairs did not share any phonemes; instead, they shared phonetic features (e.g. *veer–bull*). Goldinger et al. claimed that their phonetically related prime–target pairs prevented the use of guessing strategies, and so their findings of interference effects were reflective of the automatic processes involved in auditory word recognition. Because Slowiaczek et al. employed related prime–target pairs that shared phonemes (e.g., *stiff–still*), their stimuli may have induced the use of guessing strategies, and this could have contributed to their findings of facilitation in accuracy of identification. Specifically, subjects may have used the phonological structure of the primes to make inferences about the phonological structure of the degraded targets.

Recently Goldinger et al. (1992) examined this explanation in a series of experiments in which they manipulated variables that are assumed to influence the magnitude and direction of strategic processing. Their experiments employed several recognition tasks that presented unrelated prime–target pairs and either phonemically related pairs (i.e., pairs that shared the initial phoneme) or phonetically related pairs. One manipulation decreased the proportion of related pairs in the experimental list in order to reduce the effects that are attributable to biases or expectations. Goldinger et al. found that when only 10% of the experimental trials consisted of *phonemically* related prime–target pairs, the facilitatory priming effect was significantly attenuated in a perceptual identification task, and reversed to an interference effect in an auditory lexical decision task. In contrast, the magnitude of the interfering *phonetic* priming effect was unaffected by the proportion of related trials in either task.

These results were found when the interstimulus interval in both tasks was 50 msec. Furthermore, the priming effects in the auditory lexical decision task were only found when the primes were clearly presented and the targets were presented in white noise. When the targets were also clearly presented, no priming effects were observed (either from phonemically or phonetically related primes). To the extent that the interference effects are due to competition within an activated cohort, it appears that, once again, competitor effects are only observed when the target word cannot be unambiguously identified. In other words, the competitor effects that arise from priming may also be quite transient. They may only be detected when the sensory information is ambiguous or when subjects are encouraged to respond at the earliest point of target identification. Due to the nature of the auditory lexical decision task, subjects must wait to respond until they are certain that the complete sensory input corresponds to a real word.

In addition to manipulating the proportion of related trials, Goldinger et al. manipulated the length of the interstimulus interval. They found that when the prime–target interval in an auditory lexical decision task was either 500 or 1500 msec, the interference effect from phonetically related primes was eliminated. In contrast, the facilitatory effect from phonemically related primes was still significant at both the longer intervals. Based on these findings, Goldinger et al. argued that the facilitatory effects of phonemic priming are due to biases, whereas the interference effects of phonetic priming are due to the transient competition that occurs automatically from the residual activation of prime processing.

This argument is consistent with the predictions from both TRACE and Cohort. Furthermore, the related primes that were employed in all of Goldinger et al.'s (1992) experiments were low in frequency. These are precisely the primes that are predicted to cause interfering effects by both Cohort and TRACE. Although target frequency was controlled in their studies, it was not a manipulated factor. Thus, it is not possible to examine whether the interference effects from low frequency related primes interact with target frequency as predicted by TRACE, but not by Cohort.

Goldinger et al. (1992) restricted their related primes to only low frequency words because of the previous findings by Goldinger, Luce, and Pisoni (1989), who found that the interference effects in their perceptual identification task only occurred when the related primes were low in frequency. This finding is consistent not only with the predictions of TRACE and Cohort, but also with the predictions from the neighborhood activation model (NAM; Goldinger, Luce, & Pisoni, 1989) of auditory word recognition.

Unlike Cohort and TRACE, the predictions from NAM most directly apply to the perceptual identification task because it incorporates a specific rule, referred to as the neighborhood probability rule, that determines the probability of correct identification for targets presented under conditions of low signal-to-noise ratios. The rule essentially computes the probability of identifying a target word by dividing the probability of the target by the probability of the target plus the sum of the probabilities of its neighbors. The probabilities for the target and individual neighbors are computed from phonetic confusion matrices. Each of the individual probabilities are frequency weighted in favor of high frequency words.

The system in NAM is similar to that in the logogen model (Morton, 1969, 1982). The presentation of a stimulus causes the activation of acoustic-phonetic patterns. These activated patterns activate word decision units. The word decision units are similar to logogens in that they monitor the information coming from the lower sensory level (i.e., the acoustic patterns) as well as the information coming from higher lexical levels (e.g., frequency or contextual information). The word decision units compute a probability value for correct recognition according to the preceding rule. Unlike the logogen model, in which the probability of correct recognition is independent of the activation values of neighboring logogens, the probability of correct recognition in NAM depends on the overall activity within the system. Specifically, the more highly activated the neighboring units of a target are, the lower its recognition probability will be. To the extent that the probability of correct recognition can be translated into the rate of correct recognition, NAM predicts that target recognition will be delayed when its competitors have high activation levels. Furthermore, because NAM does not incorporate a mechanism that directly suppresses the activation levels of the competitors (S. Goldinger, personal communication, February 18, 1993), its predictions concerning the effects of low frequency related primes are the same as Cohort's.

The experiments in Goldinger, Luce, and Pisoni's (1989) perceptual identification study included both the factors of prime and target frequency. Despite the task not being a timed recognition task, the factors in their Experiment 1 created the circumstances that permit the evaluation of the contrasting predictions from Cohort and TRACE. As previously mentioned, the results of their experiments showed interference effects (in terms of correct target identification) only when targets were preceded by low frequency related primes, relative to unrelated primes. Furthermore, there was a slight trend toward high frequency targets experiencing more interference from low frequency related primes than low frequency targets. This is not consistent with either TRACE or Cohort's predictions. However, in Experiment 1B, which was a complete replication of Experiment 1A, this trend was much less evident, with the magnitude of the interference effects for low and high frequency targets being about equal. Thus, the results of Experiments 1A and 1B together do not allow any strong conclusions to be drawn concerning whether there is reason to include an inhibitory mechanism that operates on phonological representations during auditory word recognition, but they certainly do not constitute support for such inclusion.

VI. SUMMARY AND CONCLUSIONS

The intent of this chapter was to survey the empirical evidence to see if there is support for the inclusion of a mechanism of inhibition that operates on phonological representations during auditory word recognition. It was necessary to first determine what evidence would be considered as supportive of such a mechanism. Because even activation models that do not incorporate inhibition assume that the processes underlying recognition are competitive, evidence of interference effects in auditory word recognition is not sufficient for concluding that a mechanism of inhibition is involved. Instead, it is necessary to examine more closely the nature of the interference effects. This same point is made by Dell and O'Seaghdha (this volume) in the context of studies of speech production, and Anderson and Bjork (this volume) in the context of studies of memory retrieval.

Following Bard (1990), I argued that activation models that incorporate a mechanism of mutual inhibition as a means of resolving competition (e.g., TRACE) predict an interaction between either competitor frequency or related prime frequency and target frequency. This prediction contrasts with that from activation models that do not incorporate mutual inhibition (e.g., Cohort). These models predict no interaction between these two frequency factors.

Armed with these contrasting predictions, I surveyed the empirical evidence. The results of this survey did not offer compelling evidence for either prediction. Nevertheless, evidence was found that suggests that the processes underlying auditory word recognition are competitive. However, the effects of competition appear to be quite transient, and it is because of this that the evaluation of the contrasting predictions is difficult. The difficulty was particularly evident in the examination of the evidence from nonpriming auditory word recognition tasks, where even the effects of competition were elusive.

Future research employing phonological priming tasks may permit a more successful evaluation of the contrasting predictions. However, the contrasting predictions from activation models with and without mutual inhibition need to be evaluated under quite specific priming circumstances. These circumstances include: (1) a direct measure of the rate of auditory word recognition (such as response time measurement), (2) prime–target intervals that are short (e.g., 50 msec as suggested by the results of Goldinger et al.'s, 1992, study), (3) both phonologically or phonetically related and unrelated prime–target pairs, and (4) the inclusion of both the factors of prime and target frequency. The results of future research that includes all the factors needed for a convincing evaluation of the contrasting predictions will provide additional insight into the nature of the mechanisms that underlie auditory word recognition.

ACKNOWLEDGMENTS

I thank Kay Bock, Tom Carr, Dale Dagenbach, and Steven Goldinger for their helpful comments and suggestions on earlier versions of this chapter.

REFERENCES

Bard, E. G. (1990). Competition, lateral inhibition, and frequency: Comments on the chapters of Frauenfelder and Peeters, Marslen-Wilson, and others. In G. T. M. Altmann (Ed.), *Cognitive models of speech processing: Psycholinguistic and computational perspectives* (pp. 85–210). Cambridge: MIT Press.

Bradley, D. C., & Forster, K. I. (1987). A reader's view of listening. *Cognition, 25,* 103–134.

Colombo, L. (1986). Activation and inhibition with orthographically similar words. *Journal of Experimental Psychology: Human Perception and Performance, 12,* 226–234.

Connine, C. M., Mullennix, J., Shernoff, E., & Yelen, J. (1990). Word familiarity and frequency in visual and auditory word recognition. *Journal of Experimental Psychology: Learning, Memory and Cognition, 16,* 1084–1096.

de Groot, A. M. B. (1984). Primed lexical decision: Combined effects of the proportion of related prime–target pairs and the stimulus onset asynchrony of prime and target. *Quarterly Journal of Experimental Psychology, 36A,* 253–280.

Goldinger, S. D., Luce, P. A., & Pisoni, D. B. (1989). Priming lexical neighbors of spoken words: Effects of competition and inhibition. *Journal of Memory and Language, 28,* 501–518.

Goldinger, S. D., Luce, P. A., Pisoni, D. B., & Marcario, J. K. (1992). Form-based priming in spoken word recognition: The roles of competition and bias. *Journal of Experimental Psychology: Learning, Memory and Cognition, 18,* 1211–1238.

Grainger, J. (1990). Word frequency and neighborhood frequency effects in lexical decision and naming. *Journal of Memory and Language, 29,* 228–244.

Grainger, J., & Segui, J. (1990). Neighborhood frequency effects in visual word recognition: A comparison of lexical decision and masked identification latencies. *Perception and Psychophysics, 47,* 191–198.

Grosjean, F. (1980). Spoken word-recognition processes and the gating paradigm. *Perception and Psychophysics, 45,* 267–283.

Jacobs, A. M., & Grainger, J. (1992). Testing a semistochastic variant of the interactive activation model in different word recognition experiments. *Journal of Experimental Psychology: Human Perception and Performance, 18,* 1174–1188.

Jakimik, J., Cole, R. A., & Rudnicky, A. I. (1985). Sound and spelling in spoken word recognition. *Journal of Memory and Language, 24,* 165–178.

Levelt, W. J. M. (1989). *Speaking: From intention to articulation.* Cambridge, MA: MIT Press.

Levelt, W. J. M. (1992). Accessing spoken words in speech production: Stages, processes and representations. *Cognition, 42,* 1–22.

Luce, R. D. (1959). *Individual choice behavior.* New York: Wiley.

Luce, P. A., Pisoni, D. B., & Goldinger, S. D. (1990). Similarity neighborhoods of spoken words. In G. T. M. Altmann (Ed.), *Cognitive models of speech processing: Psycholinguistic and computational perspectives* (pp. 122–147). Cambridge: MIT Press.

Marslen-Wilson, W. D. (1987). Functional parallelism in spoken word-recognition. *Cognition, 25,* 71–102.

Marslen-Wilson, W. D. (1990). Activation, competition, and frequency in lexical access. In G. T. M. Altmann (Ed.), *Cognitive models of speech processing: Psycholinguistic and computational perspectives* (148–171). Cambridge: MIT Press.

Marslen-Wilson, W. D., & Tyler, L. K. (1980). The temporal structure of spoken language understanding. *Cognition, 8,* 1–71.

McClelland, J. L., & Elman, J. L. (1986). The TRACE model of speech perception. *Cognitive Psychology, 18,* 1–18.

McClelland, J. L., & Rumelhart, D. E. (1981). An interactive activation model of context effects in letter perception: I. An account of basic findings. *Psychological Review*, *88*, 375–407.

McClelland, J. L., & Rumelhart, D. E. (1988). *Explorations in parallel distributed processing: A handbook of models, programs, and exercises.* Cambridge: MIT Press.

Morton, J. (1969). The interaction of information in word recognition. *Psychological Review*, *76*, 165–178.

Morton, J. (1982). Disintegrating the lexicon: An information processing approach. In J. Mehler, E. C. T. Walker, & M. Garrett (Eds.), *Perspectives on mental representation.* Hillsdale, NJ: Lawrence Erlbaum.

Neely, J. H. (1977). Semantic priming and retrieval from lexical memory: Roles of inhibitionless spreading activation and limited-capacity attention. *Journal of Experimental Psychology: General*, *106*, 226–254.

Neely, J. H. (1991). Semantic priming effects in visual word recognition: A selective review of current findings and theories. In D. Besner & G. Humphreys (Eds.), *Basic processes in reading: Visual word recognition* (pp. 264–336). Hillsdale, NJ: Lawrence Erlbaum.

Posner, M. I., & Snyder, C. R. R. (1975). Facilitation and inhibition in the processing of signals. In P. M. A. Rabbitt & S. Doring (Eds.), *Attention and performance V* (669–682). London: Academic Press.

Radeau, M., Morais, J., & Dewier, A. (1989). Phonological priming in spoken word recognition: Task effects. *Memory and Cognition*, *17*, 525–535.

Rumelhart, D. E., & McClelland, J. L. (1982). An interactive activation model of context effects in letter perception: 2. The contextual enhancement effect and some tests and extensions of the model. *Psychological Review*, *89*, 60–94.

Savin, H. B. (1963). Word-frequency effect and errors in the perception of speech. *Journal of the Acoustical Society of America*, *35*, 200–206.

Segui, J. & Grainger, J. (1990). Priming word recognition with orthographic neighbors: Effects of relative prime-target. *Journal of Experimental Psychology: Human Perception and Performance*, *16*, 65–76.

Slowiaczek, L. M., & Hamburger, M. (1992). Prelexical facilitation and lexical interference in auditory word recognition. *Journal of Experimental Psychology: Learning, Memory and Cognition*, *18*, 1239–1250.

Slowiaczek, L. M., Nusbaum, H. C., & Pisoni, D. B. (1987). Phonological priming in auditory word recognition. *Journal of Experimental Psychology: Learning, Memory and Cognition*, *13*, 64–75.

Slowiaczek, L. M., & Pisoni, D. B. (1986). Effects of phonological similarity on priming in auditory lexical decision. *Memory & Cognition*, *14*, 230–237.

Tyler, L. K. (1984). The structure of the initial cohort: Evidence from gating. *Perception and Psychophysics*, *36*, 417–427.

Inhibition in Interactive Activation Models of Linguistic Selection and Sequencing

Gary S. Dell and Padraig G. O'Seaghdha

I. INTRODUCTION

The term *inhibition* is increasingly used in the recent literature on language production and comprehension. It is used in at least two distinct senses which we will label *molecular* and *molar*. In interactive activation models of language processing, inhibition is a molecular, quasi-neural process by which representational units send inhibitory signals to one another, or regulate their own activation by self-inhibition. In the experimental psycholinguistic literature, inhibition applies to a molar level of behavioral description that is often synonymous with interference. Molar inhibition may or may not entail inhibition at an underlying molecular level. For example, selection and decision processes involve competition, but they do not require that the competing elements inhibit one another. In this chapter, we focus on the use of the concept of inhibition in the interactive activation literature, but we will also examine the implications of our analysis for the interpretation of experimental data. We survey the wide range of functions served by inhibitory mechanisms in language processing and examine the question of whether inhibition is an identifiable process in language production and comprehension.

409

Inhibition, in the molecular sense, pertains to actual neural processes, or, in behavioral psychology, to hypothesized neural processes, such as lateral inhibition, that are seen in simple tasks involving the orientation of attention, the identification of simple stimuli, or the selection of a response. For basic processes such as these, there is a relatively close relation between psychology and neuroscience, or at least a prospect of integration between the two. In contrast, the study of language processes appears to be rather remote from the neural level. In the first place, language is not a basic process in cognition. It comprises several very different sorts of knowledge—phonological, syntactic, semantic, and pragmatic—and this knowledge is put to use in a variety of tasks: speaking, listening, reading, and writing. Moreover, even a relatively simple component of language processing, the retrieval of a word in production, is a complex multistep event in which many kinds of linguistic knowledge must be coordinated (e.g. Bock, 1982; Levelt et al., 1991). Given this complexity, it is not surprising that most psycholinguistic researchers have not shown much concern about whether a given phenomenon is, at core, based on excitation or inhibition. Of course, language processing models must have devices that select among alternatives or remove unwanted linguistic units, functions that suggest inhibition. But, in traditional psycholinguistic circles, the details of these devices have seemed secondary to questions regarding the nature of linguistic representations and the overall architecture of the processing system (e.g., Garrett, 1975; Fodor, Bever, & Garrett, 1974; Forster, 1976).

Another reason that inhibitory mechanisms in language processing have until recently not received much scrutiny is that the potential for bringing neural evidence to bear on putative inhibitory devices for linguistic functions has appeared slim. Although we can correlate language functions with brain areas through the study of aphasia and measures of brain metabolism, our ability to link such functions to particular inhibitory or excitatory neural processes is limited for obvious reasons. Experimental animals do not use language—and if they did, we would certainly be less inclined to use them as experimental animals.

Despite these considerations, two relatively recent developments in psycholinguistic theory have suggested the need for an examination of inhibitory mechanisms in language models. The first is the incursion of interactive activation, connectionist, neural-net, or parallel-distributed-processing models into word recognition (e.g., Elman & McClelland, 1986; Kawamoto & Zemblidge, 1992; McClelland & Rumelhart, 1981; Seidenberg & McClelland, 1989) and other aspects of psycholinguistics (Bates & Elman, 1992; Dell, Juliano, & Govindjee, 1993; Elman, 1990; MacKay, 1987; MacWhinney & Leinbach, 1991; Plunkett & Marchman,

1991; Rumelhart & McClelland, 1986a; Stemberger, 1985; St. John & McClelland, 1990). Because these models make claims about behavioral data and compute by means of quasi-neural elements, including excitatory and inhibitory connections, they begin to provide a bridge between psycholinguistic phenomena and neural processes.

The second development in language research that requires a consideration of inhibitory processes is the explosion of research using priming techniques to study language comprehension and production. In a priming experiment, a subject either comprehends or produces a priming sentence, phrase, or word. At some point in this process, a target stimulus such as a written word is presented and the subject responds. For example, the subject might simply be required to read to word aloud as quickly as possible. The relation between the target and the linguistic prime is manipulated and the response time to the target indexes the processing of the sentence, phrase, or word. This method was originally used to study the activation of isolated words (e.g., Meyer & Schvaneveldt, 1971), was later extended to the study of lexically ambiguous words in context (Swinney, 1979; Tanenhaus, Leiman, & Seidenberg, 1979), and has recently been applied to a wide variety of questions in both language production and comprehension (for reviews, see Dell & O'Seaghdha, 1992; McKoon & Ratcliff, 1992; Kawamoto, 1993). Because the effects of a related prime on the target are sometimes facilitatory (e.g., Meyer & Schvaneveldt, 1971; Tanenhaus et al., 1979), sometimes inhibitory (e.g., Blaxton & Neely, 1983; Colombo, 1986; Levelt et al., 1991), and sometimes both (e.g., Levelt et al., 1991; Schriefers, Meyer, & Levelt, 1990), a theory of inhibitory and excitatory mechanisms is required in order to interpret the data. In particular, we will consider how strongly the finding of behavioral inhibition between a prime item A and a target item B suggests a theory in which there is an explicit inhibitory connection from A to B. We will return to a consideration of the priming data after we examine the role of inhibition in interactive activation models.

Although most interactive activation models employ a combination of excitation and inhibition, we focus in this chapter on the role of inhibitory mechanisms in fulfilling psycholinguistic functions. In addition, we will emphasize language production, although issues in comprehension and word recognition will frequently arise.

II. INTERACTIVE ACTIVATION

Before we turn to psycholinguistic issues, we briefly outline the nature of interactive activation models. An interactive activation model is a specific kind of connectionist or neural network model, the classic examples being Grossberg's (1978) adaptive resonance theory, and McClelland and Rumelhart's (1981) word recognition model. As Mc-Clelland (1987) describes the prototype of this type of model, computation takes place in a network of excitatory and inhibitory connections among simple units. These units represent hypotheses about input in the case of a perceptual system, and they represent potential actions in the case of a production system. Each unit has an activation level that is a function of the excitatory and inhibitory inputs it receives, and is often also influenced by its own recent activation level. The units are arranged in layers, most commonly in an abstraction hierarchy, with units representing more peripheral information occupying lower layers. For example, in a lexical network, one might find phonetic or articulatory features at the lowest level, followed by phonological segments (phonemes) at the next level, combinations of segments such as syllables and words at the next level, and semantic features or concept nodes at the highest level. The network computes by activating an outside layer, the lowest one in the case of perception and the highest in the case of production, and activation spreads throughout the network. The units typically connect only to other units in the same and adjacent layers. Connections within a layer are usually inhibitory, and those between layers are usually excitatory. Processing is often assumed to be interactive, in the sense that later levels can influence earlier levels. This occurs because connections run in both directions between levels, that is, there are both top-down and bottom-up connections.

It is important to keep in mind that not all interactive activation models have all of the preceding features. Rather, the models share a family resemblance, most exhibiting many of these characteristics and some manifesting additional features that we have not listed.

III. FUNCTIONS OF INHIBITION IN INTERACTIVE ACTIVATION MODELS OF LANGUAGE PRODUCTION

Saying a sentence involves making a great many decisions—decisions about lexical items (Should I say *dime* or *coin*?), about sentence structure (Should the active or passive be used? Which noun phrases should be expressed as pronouns?), about optional arguments (Do I need to say *with a bat* when I say *The girl hit the ball*?), about constituent order not determined by sentence structure (Is it *boys and girls* or *girls and boys*?), about intonational phrasing, pausing, and many other features. The informational sources and principles that guide these decisions are the primary objects of study in the field of language production (Levelt, 1989). Recently, models of production have adopted activation-based approaches to decision making (e.g. Berg, 1988; Berg & Schade, 1992; Bock, 1982, 1986b; Bock, Loebell, & Morey, 1992; Dell, 1986, 1988; Dell et al., 1993; Dell & Reich, 1981; Eikmeyer & Schade, 1991; Harley, 1984, 1990; Houghton, 1990; Levelt, 1989; Levelt et al., 1991; MacKay, 1982, 1987; Martin, Weisberg, & Saffran, 1989; Martin & Saffran, 1992; Meyer & Gordon, 1985; Meyer, 1991; O'Seaghdha, Dell, Peterson, & Juliano, 1992; Peterson, Dell, & O'Seaghdha, 1989; Roelofs, 1992; Schade, 1992; Stemberger, 1985, 1990, 1991). In these models, constraints on production decisions are translated into excitatory and inhibitory inputs to units representing the options open to the system. The inputs modulate the activation level, or the probability of being active, of these units. Thus, decisions are, to a large extent, a function of the inputs to units as determined by the structure of the network.

The activation-based models of language production must make two distinct kinds of decisions: selection decisions and sequence decisions. Using standard linguistic terminology (cf. Eikmeyer and Schade, 1991), we label these paradigmatic decisions and syntagmatic decisions, respectively. *Paradigmatic decisions* involve selection for a particular role from a set of candidate units in the relevant linguistic category. For example, the system may need to choose *dog* rather than *cat*, or *eat* instead of *drink* when selecting lexical items, or /k/ instead of /d/ when choosing, say, the initial consonant of the syllable /kæt/. Another example is a choice of syntactic structure, such as a double object construction (*Mary gave John the ball*) versus a prepositional dative (*Mary gave the ball to John*).

In contrast to paradigmatic decisions, *syntagmatic decisions* involve the selection of the correct elements of sequences at the right time. When producing *big dogs*, the activation of *big* must initially dominate that of *dogs*, and then the relative activations must quickly flip-flop. Likewise, in the production of a particular word, for example *dog*, /d/ must initially dominate, then /ɔ/, and then /g/.

Both paradigmatic and syntagmatic decisions often depend on inhibitory processes in activation-based language models. In both cases, the correct unit must prevail over its competitors. Many models employ a combination of excitation and inhibition to achieve the desired patterns of activation, but because the nature of the competition among units is different in the paradigmatic and syntagmatic cases, the configurations of excitation and inhibition in the two cases must also differ. There are two principal differences between paradigmatic and syntagmatic decisions. First, for paradigmatic decisions, the relation between correct and competing units can be partly specified in advance, and to this extent is independent of the intended utterance. Units in the same linguistic categories are competitors. At the syntactic level, nouns compete with other nouns. At a phonological level, vowels compete with vowels.

Although the categorical structure may be complex, including subcategories and multiple membership, the structure of language tells us, beforehand, which items have the potential to incorrectly replace other items. We can see this paradigmatic principle at work in noncontextual speech errors, slips of the tongue in which a linguistic unit from outside the intended utterance replaces an intended unit. Most of the time, the replacing unit is a member of the same linguistically defined category as the replaced one (Fromkin, 1971; Garrett, 1975; MacKay, 1972).

In contrast, for syntagmatic decisions, the set of competitors depends not on categorical structure but on the content of the intended utterance. We subdivide syntagmatic decisions into two classes: noncreative and creative. In noncreative syntagmatic decisions, those involving a well-known sequence, for example, an idiom or the sounds that make up a familiar word, the competing elements are already stored in memory. In the case of saying the word *cat*, the segments /k/, /æ/, and /t/ are in competition, and the structure of the word determines how that competition should evolve over time. However, in the case of creative language use, such as the construction of novel sentences or phrases, the syntagmatic competition pattern is not so easily specified (see MacKay's, 1987, discussion). The same system that can store the ordering relations in the familiar phrase *Venetian blind*, must also be capable of producing and understanding the novel phrase *blind Venetian*.

The second critical difference between syntagmatic and paradigmatic decisions is that in the syntagmatic case, the problem is not what items to output but rather one of outputting the items in the correct serial order. Each competitor has to win the competition at some point. For example, although the /ɔ/ in *dog* must lose to /d/ initially, it must quickly become the winner of the next competition. Unlike the paradigmatic case, in which the unwanted competitors can be unceremoniously dispatched, rejected items must often be immediately resuscitated in syntagmatic processing.

Both of these differences suggest that syntagmatic decisions are more complex than paradigmatic ones. As we shall see, syntagmatic decisions, particularly creative syntagmatic decisions, require complex excitatory and inhibitory systems in activation-based models of production. We therefore consider the simpler paradigmatic case first.

IV. PARADIGMATIC CHOICES AND LATERAL INHIBITION

Interactive activation models of production and comprehension have, for the most part, used some kind of lateral inhibition in paradigmatic decisions. Units that represent mutually exclusive options send inhibition to one another with the result that the single option with the

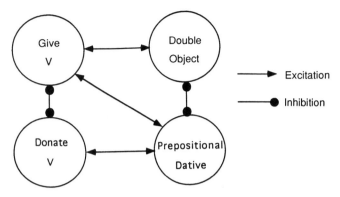

FIGURE 1

Lateral inhibition among competing verbs and competing syntactic structures, and excitation between compatible verbs and structures allows for lexical–syntactic interaction.

strongest support is eventually selected. This configuration is a potent decision-making system, one that the brain clearly adopts (Feldman & Ballard, 1982; Grossberg, 1978; Ratliff & Hartline, 1959). Interactive activation models of language production that use lateral inhibition among linguistic units at the same level include Berg (1988), Eikmeyer and Schade (1991), Harley (1984, 1990), Houghton (1990), Schade (1992), and Stemberger (1985, 1990, 1991). The decision to incorporate inhibition in these models was largely inspired by the success of visual and auditory word-recognition models (e.g., Elman & McClelland, 1986; McClelland & Rumelhart, 1981; Rumelhart & McClelland, 1982) and typing models (e.g., Rumelhart & Norman, 1982), all of which made extensive use of within-level inhibition. Specifically, these models proposed that nodes for sublexical (letters, phonemes) and lexical units inhibited others at the same level.[1]

To illustrate lateral inhibition in language production, Figure 1 shows a small network of units representing two verbs, *give* and *donate*, and two syntactic options coded as single nodes, one for a double-object construction and one for a prepositional dative. The configuration embodies the approach to lexical–syntactic interactions present in the work of Bock (1982) and Stemberger (1985). Such a network will settle to a state in which a single verb and a single syntactic structure that is appropriate for that verb are active. The network uses lateral inhibition between the verbs and between the syntactic options along with

[1]Because nodes for letters in the McClelland and Rumelhart visual model were duplicated for each serial position within a word, and all nodes in the Elman and McClelland auditory model were duplicated for each temporal position or "time slice," lateral inhibition only occurred between nodes that dealt with the same spatial or temporal positions. That is, the inhibition was used to resolve paradigmatic competition within a given position.

excitatory connections that specify the syntactic subcategorizations of the verbs. Note that an alternative network might have each verb inhibiting the syntactic structures that are not appropriate for it, rather than exciting the appropriate ones. For this problem, the excitatory solution would, in a complete model, use fewer connections, because there are fewer appropriate than inappropriate structures. The excitatory solution is also implicitly assumed in psycholinguistic theories that emphasize automatic activation of subcategorization (e.g., Boland, Tanenhaus, & Garnsey, 1990), but, aside from the number of connections, there is no compelling computational reason to prefer one over the other. A third possible configuration would have both excitatory connections from each verb to its appropriate structures and inhibitory connections to inappropriate structures, combined with lateral inhibition at each level.

Although many activation-based models have used lateral inhibition to aid decision making, several models of production use only excitation. However, when lateral inhibition is not present, there are other mechanisms for enhancing the activation of intended units, or otherwise setting them apart from competing units. For example, MacKay (1982) defined priming as a process by which nodes representing options within a given linguistic category (e.g., verb) gradually build up their activation levels. Eventually, one node reaches a threshold and becomes "activated." When a node is activated, its activation level becomes much greater and is sustained over a period of time. Thus, in MacKay's model, the decision mechanism is an absolute threshold and does not use lateral inhibition, but it achieves the desired result: a distancing of the winner of the race from the competition. Likewise, in Dell's (1986, 1988) language production model, the most highly activated node within a category is "selected" and linked to a particular slot in the production plan. Because linkage eventually entails a large boost of activation, the effect is somewhat similar to what obtains in MacKay's model when the threshold is reached. Roelof's (1992) model of lexical retrieval in production incorporates two selection mechanisms: a critical difference threshold, in which a target word node becomes available for selection when its activation is greater than that of all of its competitors by a certain amount, and a stochastic mechanism, in which the probability that the available target is selected is a function of the ratio of its activation level to the total activation of all competitors (see Luce, 1959). Again, the effect is similar to lateral inhibition, in that the most activated word ends up being selected.

A feature of lateral inhibition in some of the production models is that it applies within all pairs of units at a linguistic level (e.g., Eikmeyer & Schade, 1991; Harley, 1990; Stemberger, 1985). So all words inhibit all other words, all segment nodes inhibit all other segment nodes, and so on.[2] Earlier however, we suggested that paradigmatic decisions might be profitably restricted, perhaps by linguistic category. For example, vowels would inhibit other vowels, but not consonants. In addition, paradigmatic competition might be further narrowed if the extent of lateral inhibition were related to similarity, with inhibition reserved for or more potent among similar units. This idea is implicit in the following literature on retrieval inhibition, in which tokens from the same semantic category appear to inhibit one another under certain conditions (e.g., Brown, 1981; Blaxton & Neely, 1983; Wheeldon, 1989). Likewise, Meyer and Gordon (1985) and MacKay (1970) have suggested that lateral inhibition occurs primarily between speech sounds that share features. Finally, the idea of similarity-based competition is inherent in many models of auditory and visual word recognition (see, e.g., Colombo, 1986; Forster & Davis, 1991; Marslen-Wilson & Tyler, 1980).

A. Similarity-Based Inhibition

The question of the role of similarity or neighborhood in determining the strength of lateral inhibition can be illuminated by considering the function of such inhibition and by examining how inhibitory connections might be acquired. A paradigmatic decision is, by definition, one in which a single unit is chosen from a predetermined set of potential competitors for a linguistic role; for example, the role of subject noun of a sentence. If only the members of the appropriate set, say nouns, are highly activated at the time the subject noun is being chosen, then lateral inhibition might be limited to that set. But even within the category of nouns, it makes sense that some nouns would be more potent competitors for a given role than others. In attempting to find the appropriate name for a particular aquatic mammal (*dolphin*), the noun *pencil* should not be much competition. It might, therefore, be useful to have *dolphin* inhibit semantically similar nouns such as *porpoise* to a greater extent than *pencil*.

On first consideration, such "smart" inhibition might seem unlikely. How could the semantic system allow inhibition among closely related competitors while retaining the ability to activate relevant information in a sufficiently wide-ranging manner? However, examination of the operation of error-correcting learning procedures suggests that such selective inhibition could indeed by learned. Similarity-dependent lateral

---

[2]Part of the reason that these models have such wide-ranging lateral inhibition is that it plays a role in their treatment of serial order as well as in paradigmatic decision making. Because any word has the potential to appear in a sentence with any other word, all words may have to inhibit one another if lateral inhibition is an important mechanism in creative syntagmatic decisions. See our discussion of the Eikmeyer and Schade model.

inhibition would result from the application of error-based algorithms (e.g., back-propagation; Rumelhart, Hinton, & Williams, 1986) in an interactive-activation architecture. These procedures change connection weights in response to feedback regarding target activation levels that is delivered while a model is being trained to produce a particular input–output mapping.

Consider the task of mapping from a semantic unit or set of units representing a particular concept to a single unit representing the corresponding word or lemma (e.g., Levelt, 1989; Roelofs, 1992). Further, let us suppose that there are potential connections from the semantic units to the word units, and potential lateral connections among word units, and that the excitatory or inhibitory character of these connections is set by the learning process. Under such conditions, lateral inhibition will develop between semantic neighbors roughly in proportion to their relatedness.

To see how this happens, consider the case of two word units, *dog* and *cat*. The word *dog* is connected to the features *canine* and *pet*, and *cat* to the features *feline* and *pet*. Assume that there are top-down excitatory connections from the semantic unit to the appropriate word units, such that the correct word is more activated by its two features than the other word. But, as of yet, there is no lateral inhibition. Now, when *pet* and *canine* are input to the network, both *dog* and *cat* are activated, let us say, *dog* = .75 and *cat* = .25, on a range of [0,1]. The target activation levels, provided by external feedback, however, are 1 for *dog* and 0 for *cat*. That is, the network wants *dog* fully active and *cat* completely inactive. Hence, there would be an error signal of .25 (target activation − actual activation) on *dog* and a signal of −.25 on *cat*. The weight change from unit i to unit j with error-based learning algorithms is in proportion to the activation of unit i and the error signal on unit j. So, some lateral inhibition (.75 × −.25 = −.1875) would grow from *dog* to *cat*.[3] In addition, a smaller amount of lateral excitation (.25 × .25 = .0625) would grow from *cat* to *dog*. However, when *cat* is the intended word, the reverse effects occur (large growth of inhibition from *cat* to *dog*, with a smaller growth of excitation from *dog* to *cat*). The net result over the long run is that the two words inhibit one another.

B. Modularity or Interdependence of Perception and Production

If lateral inhibition is a function of similarity and error correction, the extent to which linguistic units inhibit should be related both to

[3]This assumes a learning constant of 1, and an activation function in which activation of a node equals its net input.

similarity and to the linguistic task being performed. We have just seen how semantically related words might come to inhibit one another in the task of mapping from concepts to words. When the task involves word perception, either visual or auditory, the same considerations would lead to formally similar, instead of semantically similar words inhibiting each other. Hence, in production, *dog* and *cat* would mutually inhibit, whereas in perception, *cat* and *can* would inhibit one another. This logic suggests a number of possible configurations when the full architecture of the mental lexicon is considered. Figure 2 presents three of the possibilities.

The first possibility, which we call a *fully modular* architecture, has two characteristics: There are separate units and connections for perception and production, and there is no feedback or reverse flow of activation. In such a system, what we call *task-dictated lateral inhibition* would grow from an error-correction learning procedure: The *dog*-production and *cat*-production units would inhibit one another, as would the *cat*-perception and *can*-perception units. Because of the separateness of production and perception, and the fact that activation only flows in the task-dictated direction, each task's network does not experience the similarity relations governing competition in the other task.

In contrast, a *half-modular* architecture retains the separate production and perception networks, but allows a two-way flow of activation in each. In this case, the task-dictated pattern of similarity-based lateral inhibition would occur as before, but there would also be a *reverse* pattern pertaining to the other task—the *cat* and *can* production units would inhibit, and the *dog* and *cat* perception units would inhibit. This reverse pattern would arise from feedforward and feedback within each network. During production, when the target word is *cat*, not only *dog* but also *can* is a competitor because of the flow of activation from *cat* to its phonological units (/k/,/æ/, and /t/) and back to formally related words. Likewise, during perception, the target *cat* activates semantic units that then activate *dog*. The result, in both perception and production, is that a target word encounters both semantic and form-related competitors, and needs to inhibit them. However, with the half-modular architecture, the task-dependent lateral inhibition connections should be much stronger than the reverse ones because the task-dictated competitors (*dog* for *cat* in production, *can* for *cat* in perception) would be activated earlier and to a greater extent than the competitors activated by feedback (*can* for *cat* in production, and *dog* for *cat* in perception).

The third possibility we consider is a *fully interactive* architecture (see Figure 2). This configuration involves a single network for production and perception and consequently must allow activation to flow in both directions (e.g., MacKay, 1987). In this situation, a given word unit would develop lateral inhibition to both semantic competitors (from

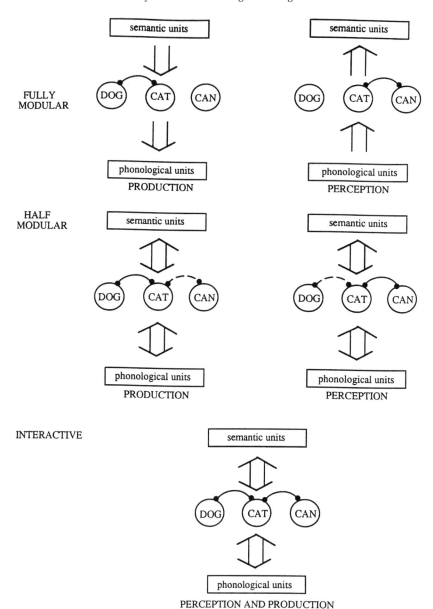

FIGURE 2

Three architectures and their associated patterns of lateral inhibition, assuming that lateral inhibition reflects experienced competition.

production and, to a smaller extent, from feedback during perception) and formally related competitors (primarily from perception, and secondarily from production). So, the fully interactive architecture resembles the half-modular one in that an error-correction learning rule creates the reverse pattern of lateral inhibition as well as the task-dictated pattern. In the fully interactive case, however, the reverse pattern would be as strong as the task-dictated one because the same nodes are used in both tasks. Any tendency for *cat* to inhibit *dog* in production should also be observed in perception.

C. Empirical Status of Paradigmatic Inhibition

We now turn to an evaluation of the experimental evidence for paradigmatic lateral inhibition. As we indicated earlier, priming procedures provide the major source of data on facilitation and inhibition in language processing. Therefore, this is where we will look for evidence concerning the prevalence of inhibition.

Several obstacles stand in the way of a straightforward evaluation of the evidence concerning lateral inhibition. Chief among them is the fact we alluded to earlier—that we do not have direct access to inhibitory mechanisms in language processing. Further, if inhibition exists, it may well be obscured by concurrent excitatory activation. To take one example, the fully interactive configuration we have just considered suggests the possibility that lateral inhibition exists between semantically related words in perception. Behaviorally, it is well known that *cat* facilitates *dog* in perception, but is this effect purely excitatory, or is it possible that semantic facilitation merely dominates lateral inhibition? Another obstacle to the evaluation of inhibition in priming data is that experimental tasks are not purely perceptual or productive. Rather, they involve some mixture of these processes. For example, responses in perceptual priming experiments are productive, and eliciting displays in production experiments necessarily entail perception. As we shall see, the mapping between tasks and levels of processing is very difficult to specify.

Keeping these concerns in mind, our strategy will be to first look for inhibition in the most clearcut cases, the task-dictated cases for which all configurations in Figure 2 predict lateral inhibition. Therefore, we will look for evidence of semantic inhibition in production and for form-related inhibition in perception. Interestingly, both the possibility of semantic inhibition in production and of form-related inhibition in perception have emerged in the literature as counterintuitive phenomena, which goes against the grain of facilitation-based theories of similarity effects. Where we do find evidence of task-dictated inhibition, we will consider whether processes other than lateral inhibition might account for it. Our analysis suggests that if we do not find lateral inhibition in the task-dictated cases, we should not find it elsewhere. We will keep this in mind in evaluating the status of reverse effects—semantic inhibition in perception and form-based inhibition in production.

1. Semantic Inhibition in Production   There is now considerable evidence that inhibition may occur between related concepts in the process of semantic retrieval. The experimental literature on this topic may be traced at least as far back as the category-instance experiments of Loftus and associates (e.g., Loftus, 1973; Loftus & Loftus, 1974). These experiments measured latency to retrieve the appropriate instance (e.g., APPLE) given a category label and a letter restrictor (e.g., FRUIT–A). Though these early studies found that the second retrieval from the same category (e.g., FRUIT–A; FRUIT–P vs. VEHICLE–C; FRUIT–P) was facilitated, later studies found that repeated retrievals from the same category led to inhibition (e.g., Blaxton & Neely, 1983; Bowles & Poon, 1985; Brown, 1979, 1981; Roediger, Neely, & Blaxton, 1983; Wheeldon, 1989; and see Roediger & Neely, 1982, for a review of other retrieval inhibition effects). Blaxton and Neely (1983) found inhibitory effects when subjects generated the names of four category instances prior to a critical retrieval trial, but not when they read them. This suggests that prelexical retrieval processes must be engaged for inhibition to occur. In fact, this rather than the number of retrievals may be the critical factor. Studies using definition tasks that involve difficult retrieval show inhibition effects following a single retrieval (see Bowles & Poon, 1985; Wheeldon, 1989).

Although the evidence suggests that retrieval inhibition in production is a real phenomenon, the nature of the effect is not evident. First, the evidence that prelexical retrieval is involved suggests that the effect may not be due to inhibition among lexical units. We explore this question further in the subsection on reverse effects. Second, the molar inhibition is not necessarily mediated by molecular lateral inhibition. Earlier, we contrasted models of language production with lateral inhibition (e.g., Eikmeyer & Schade, 1991; Stemberger, 1985) and models that eschew it (Dell, 1986; MacKay, 1987; Roelofs, 1992). In the latter models, the activation of conceptually related items creates a situation in which they may compete for selection. The models need only assume that the decision process is more difficult when more than one exemplar is highly activated to account for retrieval inhibition. We note that models that incorporate a differential selection criterion (e.g., Roelofs, 1992) are better equipped for this purpose.

In fact, Roelofs (1992) provides one clear case where molar semantic inhibition in production likely is *not* solely due to molecular lateral inhibition. Roelofs found that picture naming was inhibited by a super-imposed semantically related word. For example, producing *dog* to a picture of a dog was slowed by the word *fish* printed on the picture. This result cannot be due to hardwired inhibition between pairs of animal words, however, because the inhibitory effect is present only when the interfering word is known to be a potential response in the task. When *fish* is *not* a potential response, semantically related words facilitate picture naming. Thus, in this case, the competitive relations are dynamic rather than hardwired. We suggest that this characterization may apply generally to semantic inhibition. Similarity-based behavioral inhibition in production may be a real phenomenon, but we think it unlikely that the effect is mediated by fixed inhibitory connections among semantically related words.

2. Form-Related Inhibition in Word Recognition   We turn now to the possibility of lateral inhibition among formally similar words in word recognition. The notion of lateral inhibition is used in interactive activation models of visual and auditory word recognition, including those listed earlier (e.g., McClelland & Rumelhart, 1981; Elman & McClelland, 1986). In addition, the potential for similarity-based competition of the kind we are considering is directly related to the distributional properties of lexical neighborhoods (e.g., Andrews, 1989; Coltheart, Davelaar, Jonasson, & Besner, 1977; Glushko, 1979; Luce, Pisoni, & Goldinger, 1990; Marslen-Wilson & Tyler, 1980; and see Forster & Davis, 1991; Segui & Grainger, 1990; Slowiaczek & Hamburger, 1992; Taraban & McClelland, 1987). Although the models proposed in these references differ in many important respects, all of them conceive of auditory or visual word recognition as a discrimination problem. From the point of view of our analysis of similarity, such discrimination is more difficult in the more highly populated lexical neighborhoods that are inhabited by many formally similar words. Therefore, independent of other considerations, the potential exists for the growth of similarity-based lateral inhibition as a function of neighborhood density.

Although we have identified a basis for the existence of similarity-based lateral inhibition, it is difficult to assess the status of neighborhood density effects for some of the reasons outlined earlier. In particular, interactive activation models accommodate both lexical facilitation due to feedback from sublexical representations and inhibition due to lexical competition, and these effects may be modulated by other lexical characteristics such as frequency. Therefore, it is difficult to isolate inhibitory and facilitatory effects of neighborhood structure. In any case, the empirical picture on this issue is incomplete (but see Andrews, 1989; Forster, Davis, Schoknecht, & Carter, 1987; Forster & Davis, 1991). For the most part, priming experiments on form similarity have not directly addressed neighborhood structure but have concentrated on the related though simpler question of whether formally similar words (e.g., *cat–can*) inhibit one another in perception.

As in the category retrieval literature, similarity effects in visual word recognition were, until recently, viewed as facilitatory (e.g., Hillinger, 1980; Meyer, Schvaneveldt, & Ruddy, 1974; see O'Seaghdha et al., 1992, for a review). However, Colombo (1986) found that high frequency words were inhibited by similar primes, whereas low frequency words were facilitated, and this phenomenon is now well established (see Lupker & Williams, 1987; Peterson et al., 1989).

Although interactive activation models have the potential for modeling frequency-dependent, similarity-based inhibition, models such as McClelland and Rumelhart (1981) do not. Rather, they postulate across-the-board, within-level lateral inhibition, which serves the function of segregating relevant words from competitors. Modifications of interactive activation models that could account for frequency-dependent inhibition between similar words can, however, be easily envisaged. Colombo (1986) proposed that lateral inhibition only applies between words that exceed a certain level of activation. However, this suggestion is rather ad hoc and undercuts the role of lateral inhibition in promoting perceptual sharpening (O'Seaghdha et al., 1992). Our earlier formal analysis suggests a simpler alternative. If lateral inhibition among similar words is learned, then the relation of inhibition to word frequency is a natural result. A high frequency word is more likely to be activated when it should not be, promoting the growth of inhibition. This analysis is compatible with Segui and Grainger's (1990) discussion of relative prime and target frequency effects and also comports with the evidence that low frequency but not high frequency words show net facilitation in high density neighborhoods (Andrews, 1989). The benefits of having congenial neighbors are balanced by the need to build fences in the case of high frequency words.

However plausible this scenario may be, the evidence suggests that acquired inhibitory connections may not in fact account for the empirically observed inhibition of high frequency words. Peterson et al. (1989) showed that when primes are forward masked, high frequency target words are facilitated rather than inhibited. If lateral inhibition between *cat* and *can* were acquired through experience, it should not be affected by a display manipulation such as masking. Peterson et al. also found that nonhomographic homophones (e.g., *mussel–muscle*) produce facilitation rather than inhibition. Learned similarity-based inhibition would dictate that homophones should accrue more lateral inhibition than other words, but in fact they produce facilitation rather than inhibition. Both results suggest that something other than lateral lexical inhibition—for example, competition for selection at the phonological level (Peterson et al., 1989)—determines when behavioral inhibition is observed. If so, the differential receptivity of high and low frequency words to their neighbors (Andrews, 1989) may have a simpler explanation, such as that high frequency words are quickly recognized and therefore do not benefit from orthographic feedback.

Before leaving this topic, we briefly consider one other case, the inhibitory effect of phonetic similarity in auditory word perception recently discovered by Goldinger et al. (Goldinger, Luce, & Pisoni, 1989; Goldinger, Luce, Pisoni, & Marcario, 1992). In these studies, phonetically similar words are closest neighbors (defined in terms of a global index of the confusability of their segments); however, they do not share any phonological segments (e.g., *bull–veer*). Goldinger et al. contrast this kind of similarity with the kind of componential phonological similarity previously discussed (e.g., *bull–beer*). In auditory word identification and lexical decision, they find what appears to be a genuine inhibition effect for the phonetically related words but not for the phonologically related words. This is an interesting result, but we do not consider it to be compelling evidence for lateral inhibition. First, like other inhibitory effects, it could be accounted for by decision processes rather than by lateral inhibition (see Goldinger et al., 1992, p. 1233). That is, interactive activation models without lateral inhibition could easily account for the effect. Second, the effect appears to be specific to the auditory modality, and it is evident only when the words are presented in noise. This suggests that the effect may be due to the confusability of the phonological constituents of primes and targets rather than to the proximity of the words in an amodal lexical neighborhood.

Thus far, we have found good behavioral evidence for task-dictated competition based on similarity. This suggests that the conditions for the growth of lateral inhibition are present. However, we have found little unqualified support for the existence of lateral inhibition, itself, in language processing. In production, lateral inhibition may occur in the mapping from concepts to words, but effects of lateral inhibition can also be accounted for as competition for selection. The case for lateral inhibition among formally similar words in perception, as we have just discussed, is also weak. Our conclusions do not, of course, rule out the existence of lateral inhibition, but we suggest that its role in explaining similarity-based behavioral inhibition is limited.

In general, resolution of the status of intralevel lateral inhibition depends on the ingenuity of experimenters in defining experimental tests that both address identifiable levels and test directly for inhibitory mechanisms. For example, Frauenfelder, Segui, and Dijkstra (1990) conducted a direct test of lateral inhibition at the phonemic level of Elman and McClelland's (1986) TRACE model of speech perception. Their conclusions were negative. Likewise, Marslen-Wilson (in press) reports a test of lexical-level inhibition in auditory word recognition as a function of the density of lexical neighborhoods. Marslen-Wilson argues that the evidence speaks against lateral inhibition, but in favor of bottom-up inhibition. We cannot evaluate these studies in detail here. Rather, we cite them as examples of the kind of work that may eventually resolve the status of lateral inhibition.

3. Reverse Effects   In the absence of strong evidence of task-dependent lateral inhibition in production or perception, the status of the reverse effects we considered earlier is even more difficult to evaluate. The reverse effects are semantic inhibition in perception and form-related inhibition in production. We now consider each of these in turn.

To our knowledge, the work of Dagenbach and Carr (Dagenbach, Carr, & Wilhelmsen, 1989; Carr & Dagenbach, 1990; Dagenbach & Carr, this volume) provides the only well-documented case of semantic inhibition in perception. Briefly stated, Dagenbach et al. made the nonintuitive discovery that the nature of the task used during a threshold-setting procedure influenced the effect of masked semantically related primes in subsequent priming trials. Specifically, when semantic similarity judgments were made during the threshold setting procedure, semantically related masked primes subsequently produced inhibition (see Dagenbach & Carr, this volume). This is not the kind of reverse effect our theoretical analysis requires however. According to Dagenbach et al. (1989), it is more akin to the kind of retrieval inhibition we discussed in the context of production than to the kind of hardwired lexical inhibition that might arise in a shared architecture for perception and production. The threshold-setting procedure appears to influence the operation of early retrieval processes, the same retrieval processes that are involved in mapping from concepts to words in language production, and the inhibitory effect appears to take place at this level rather than at the level of word representations. In addition, the effect, like other inhibitory effects on retrieval we have considered, is dynamic and transient rather than hardwired.

The other reverse case we are interested in is form-related inhibition in production. Given our negative conclusions with regard to form-related lateral inhibition in perception, it would be surprising to find clear evidence in production. However, there are several relevant cases to consider.

Meyer and Gordon (1985) found that similar phonemes inhibit in production, a potential instance of reverse similarity-based inhibition. They attributed the effect to lateral inhibition between similar phonemes that arises from bottom-up feedback from features to phonemes. When planning to produce a particular segment, say /b/, one needs to inhibit similar segments such as /d/ that are activated by feedback from shared features. Thus, they suggest that the effect is due to feedback at the phonological level. In this sense, Meyer and Gordon are opting for true lateral inhibition and, particularly, for an explanation of reverse effects as in our half-modular architecture, where the relevant levels are the phonological feature and the phonological segment, rather than segments and words. This is an appealing account and is, as well, the only instance in the literature of an explanation of molar-level reverse inhibition in terms of lateral inhibition needed to overcome bottom-up feedback. However, as with other simple molar effects of inhibition, there is no compelling need to postulate acquired inhibitory connections.

Sevald and Dell (submitted) have shown that the production of phonologically similar word pairs has an inhibitory component if the similar sounds are word-initial. However, they attribute the inhibition to competition at the phonological level (in the spirit of Peterson et al's, 1989, explanation of form-related priming), rather than to lateral inhibition between formally similar word nodes. There are several other examples of form-related inhibition in production. For example, it has been suggested that tip-of-the-tongue states may be induced by form-related competitors (Jones & Langford, 1987; Woodworth, 1938), but Meyer and Bock (1992) and Perfect and Hanley (1992) have shown that this conclusion may be premature. Bock (1987), Levelt et al. (1991), and Dell and O'Seaghdha (1992) discuss several more complex cases. However, the examples we have considered are sufficient to demonstrate that there is little basis for attributing behaviorial form-based inhibition in production to lateral inhibition.

Overall, our review of paradigmatic inhibition reduces to two key points. An abstract analysis shows that, in principle, similarity-based lateral inhibition could be acquired from experience. A survey of experimental studies, however, finds no clear-cut demonstration of the existence of such inhibition. The cases of molar or behavioral inhibition we have reviewed either have an alternative explanation or can be accounted for by interactive activation models that do not involve lateral inhibition. Lateral inhibition is still a viable candidate explanation in the latter cases. Demonstration of its existence, however, remains a challenge for experimenters.

V. SYNTAGMATIC PROCESSES

Syntagmatic decisions involve the serial order of linguistic items. In activation-based models of production, these decisions require the activation in correct sequence of the units representing the items. First, we consider noncreative syntagmatic decisions in which the sequence is already known; for example, the order of the sounds in a word or the order of words within a formulaic or idiomatic phrase. Then, we turn to the more complex issues of creative sequencing.

A. Noncreative Syntagmatic Decisions

The earliest accounts of sequencing, *chain associative* models, used forward excitatory associations. Each item in a sequence excited its successor. For example, in producing the word *cat*, /k/ excites /æ/, which then excites /t/. The problems with the simplest kind of chain association are well known (Lashley, 1951; see MacKay, 1987, for review). If all of the sequences make use of the same elementary units, the associative chains are completely lost: /k/ not only has an association to /æ/, but to lots of other sounds as well. As a result, there is no way to choose which association to follow. Hence, there has to be some kind of plan or goal that controls which associations are followed, or which units are considered. We consider two proposals for how such plans might be represented, Estes' (1972) hierarchical scheme and Jordan's (1986) recurrent network.

1. Estes' Hierarchical Model   Estes (1972) based his theory of the long-term representation of serial order on a hierarchical organization. Contiguous elementary response units form chunks, and contiguous chunks form higher level chunks (see Figure 3). A chunk unit such as *cat* tends to excite its constituents, /k/, /æ/, and /t/. Each constituent unit inhibits all of the others that follow it, for example, /k/ inhibits /æ/ and /t/.

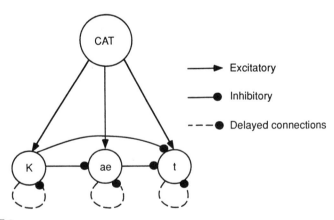

FIGURE 3

The Estes model of the long-term storage of serial order. CAT is the chunk or plan unit. Its activation triggers the sequential production of its three sounds.

Moreover, each unit enters a period of self-inhibition after it has become sufficiently active to be produced.

Let us consider how serial order is regulated by this scheme. First, *cat* begins to activate /k/, /æ/, and /t/; /t/, and to a lesser extent /æ/, are inhibited by earlier units and, hence, initially only /k/ sustains its activity. After /k/ reaches a predetermined threshold and is produced or promoted to the next level of processing, it undergoes self-inhibition. As a result /æ/is disinhibited, becomes the most active constituent, and is in turn selected. Finally, /t/ is selected in the same manner.

The Estes scheme is admirably simple and can explain a number of findings in serial learning. In particular, it offers an account of why chunk sizes of three lead to better retention than others. Organizing a sequence into chunks of three requires fewer connections within and between the chunks.

2. Jordan's Recurrent Network   Another general solution to representing stored syntagmatic relations was offered by Jordan (1986). The scheme includes both a plan and a context that changes throughout the execution of the plan, and allows the plan and the context to combine in a nonlinear fashion in determining what unit is to be produced next. Figure 4 shows the design of the system, which contains three layers: an input layer, which includes the plan and the context, a hidden layer, and an output layer. As in many models of this sort, the activation value of each node is a sigmoidal function of its inputs. The figure shows an illustrative network with three possible plans, the words *cat*, *act*, and *tack*, each associated with a single input unit. There are three output units, one for each segment. Connections can be either excitatory or inhibitory and run from the plan units, through the hidden units, to the output units. There are no within-level connections and no interactive feedback connections in the conventional sense, so the architecture is at least superficially very different from an interactive activation network. The connection weights are set by a learning algorithm such as back-propagation. The novel component of Jordan's approach is the addition of a set of context or state units that serve, technically, as input, but are actually derived from the previous output of the network (see Figure 4). Each context unit's activation is a function of that of a corresponding output unit and its own previous level of activation.

Serial order is produced because the pattern of activation among the context units changes as the sequence is produced, and this pattern can combine nonlinearly with the plan to control the output. When the plan is to produce *cat*, the plan units are activated appropriately, say 1 unit of activation for *cat*, and none for the other plan units, and the context units have no activation. Under these circumstances, the model's connection weights are tuned by the learning process, so that activation

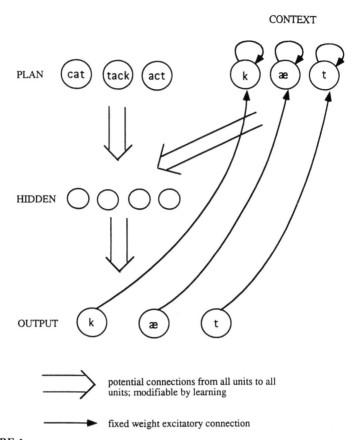

FIGURE 4
A Jordan network for producing *cat*, *tack*, or *act*.

flows from the input to the /k/ output unit. Having produced the first sound, each output unit sends activation to its corresponding context unit. Assuming that the output was in fact /k/, the context unit for /k/ acquires some activation. At this point, there is another forward spread of activation from input to output. Although the plan has not changed (the *cat* plan unit is still active), the context is different from what it was at the beginning of the word. The network "knows" that it has just produced /k/, and therefore it now learns to produce /æ/. Thus, as long as the context keeps changing, the network knows where it is in the sequence.[4]

[4] Even if there are repeated items in the sequence, no problem arises because the context is not just a copy of the previous output, it is a function of the previous output and the previous context.

The Estes and Jordan systems are similar in that both embody mechanisms for relating a stored plan to a sequence by means of spreading activation through excitatory and inhibitory connections. Also, both embody a hierarchical organization. An element produced in a sequence can, itself, be a plan for another constituent of the sequence—an essential feature for a language production model. In the Estes model, there are two particular kinds of inhibition: asymmetric lateral inhibition, in which each output unit inhibits those following it, and delayed self-inhibition, the tendency for each node to turn itself off after it has been fully activated. These two functions are accomplished in Jordan's model by the way the activation on the context units combines with that of plan units. But the actual mechanisms—for example, the extent to which inhibition is used—are not stipulated in the model. The learning process determines the configuration of excitation and inhibition. Therefore, the extent to which inhibition is used depends heavily on the structure of the set of sequences that is learned.

3. The Generalized Estes Model   Let us consider the relation between the two models in more detail. Figure 5 shows a three-unit network that illustrates what we call the generalized Estes model. It consists of a plan unit for the sequence AB, a response unit A, and a response unit B. The network has top-down connections from the plan unit to each response unit, and has two kinds of lateral and self-connections—immediate and

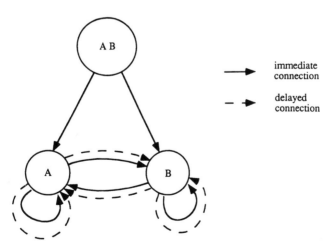

FIGURE 5

The generalized Estes model. Activation of the plan AB results in the activation of A and the inhibition of B, then the activation of B and inhibition of A, and finally the inhibition of both A and B. Excitation versus inhibition is not specified.

TABLE 1
List of Connections in the Generalized Estes Model

AB→A	Chunk to first unit
AB→B	Chunk to second unit
A→A	Immediate self-connection for first unit
B→B	Immediate self-connection for second unit
A→B	Immediate forward lateral
B→A	Immediate backward lateral
A→A(d)	Delayed self-connection for first unit
B→B(d)	Delayed self-connection for second unit
A→B(d)	Delayed forward lateral
B→A(d)	Delayed backward lateral

delayed. Immediate connections send activation at time step t, based on the activation of the source node at $t - 1$. Delayed connections send their activation based on the source node's activation at some earlier time step. The entire scheme has 10 potential connections, which are listed and labeled in Table 1.

The serial order of a two-unit chunk can be produced in several ways using this generalized model. For example, a simple forward chain association model might have excitatory connections AB→A and A→B(d), and delayed self-inhibition A→A(d) and B→B(d). Assuming that the delayed connections have a lag of four time steps, and that one starts by activating AB, this configuration will activate A and then after four time steps, turn A off and activate B, which will, itself, turn off after four time steps. At this point, the plan has been executed and AB is turned off.

The original Estes approach can be characterized by the following constraints on the connections: AB→A and AB→B are excitatory and equal in strength (symmetric chunk connections); A→B is inhibitory (immediate forward inhibitory connection); and A→A(d) and B→B(d) are inhibitory (delayed self-inhibition). It is also in the spirit of Estes' discussion that activation tends to persist in a node over time. This can be represented by immediate self-excitation (A→A and B→B are excitatory). All other connections are null. We can make this more concrete by working through an example. Assume that at each time step, each node i possesses an activation value $A(i)$ between 0 and 1 with a resting level of .5, and that the activation of a node is a sigmoidal function of its input. Specifically, for each time step,

$$A(i) = 1/(1 + \exp(-input\ i))$$

and

$$input\ (i) = \sum_j A(j)w_{ij}$$

where w_{ij} is the connection strength from node j to node i.

TABLE 2
Production of a Two-Item Sequence by the Generalized Estes Model

Time step	Activation of A	Activation of B
1	.88	.88
2	.88	.18
3	.94	.10
4	.94	.07
5	.18	.03
6	.09	.72
7	.04	.90
8	.03	.93
9	.55	.94
10	.30	.07
11	.51	.09
12	.57	.03
13	.10	.02
14	.20	.37

Connection weights: $AB{\rightarrow}A, AB{\rightarrow}B = 2$
$A{\rightarrow}B = -5$
$A{\rightarrow}A, B{\rightarrow}B = 1$
$A{\rightarrow}A(d) = -5$
$B{\rightarrow}B(d) = -1$

Suppose that the goal is to turn on A and then B, where "turn on" means that a node has an activation of greater than .6 for four time steps in a row. If we assume that the chunk node is given an activation level of 1 for nine time steps and that the delay connections send activation after a lag of four time steps, the set of connection weights shown in Table 2 will achieve the goal: A is activated for steps 1 to 4, and B is activated for steps 6 to 9. After that, nothing turns on, but the activation levels continue to oscillate with diminishing amplitude.

The generalized Estes model can be shown to be a kind of Jordan network by placing the nodes in the Jordan configuration shown in Figure 6. The AB node is a plan unit, A and B are output units, and a, b, a(d), and b(d) are context units. As in the basic Jordan network, the context units derive their activation from the output and they then serve as input during the next time step. The a and b context units copy the activations of the A and B units, respectively, and the a(d) and b(d) context units store the activations of the A and B units four time steps earlier. A further characteristic of this network is that there are no hidden units—each input unit (the plan and context units) has a potential direct connection to each output unit. Thus, the network's 10 input–output connections correspond to the 10 connections presented in Table

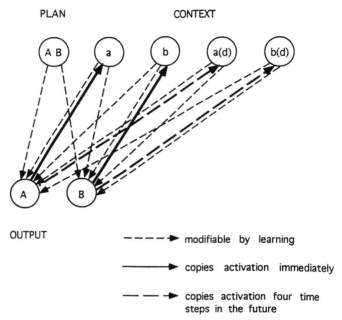

FIGURE 6
The generalized Estes model expressed as a Jordan network with both immediate and delayed context units. Excitation versus inhibition is not specified.

1 and Figure 5. The connections from the a and b context units represent either immediate lateral connections (as in a→B or b→A) or immediate self-connections (a→A or b→B). Those from the a(d) and b(d) context units to the output units are the analogous delayed connections. The two configurations are computationally equivalent when it is further stipulated that a single time step involves the spread of activation from input to output and the updating of the context units' activations.

4. Learning in the Generalized Estes Model   We are now in a position to use the learning aspect of the Jordan network to investigate how the inhibitory configuration of the Estes approach might be acquired. In the section on paradigmatic decisions, we speculated that lateral inhibition might grow in response to an error-correcting learning rule. Jordan's network sets connection weights by this kind of rule. We will use the simplest version of an error-correcting rule: The change in weight from an input unit i to an output unit j is

$$\epsilon(t_j - a_j)a_i$$

where ϵ is the learning rate, t_j is the target activation of an output unit,

a_j is its actual activation, and a_i is the input unit's activation. We set ϵ to 0.1, a moderately small value. Small values are associated with a greater probability of eventual success in learning but have, of course, the disadvantage of requiring many trials.

The original Estes model used immediate forward lateral inhibition and delayed self-inhibition. To find out if these inhibitory relations would be learned, we started by giving the network in Figure 6 the task of learning to produce A for four time steps (target activation of A = 1 and B = 0), B for four time steps (A = 0 and B = 1), and then neither for four more steps (A = 0 and B = 0). The AB unit was turned on for the first eight time steps. The network was required to fit the original Estes mold in that its AB→A and AB→B connections were fixed at a weight of +2.0 and it could have no lateral delayed connections [a(d)→B and b(d)→A were fixed at 0]. Further, each output node was given a small persistence of activation by means of fixed immediate self-excitation; a→A and b→B were fixed at 1.0. Only the immediate lateral connections and delayed self-connections were modifiable by the learning process. After 200 trials, the network learned to produce the sequence about as well as the generalized Estes network configuration shown in Table 2, and it did, indeed, use asymmetric lateral inhibition (a→B = −4.25 and b→A = −2.55), and delayed self-inhibition [a(d)→A = −7.30 and b(d)→B = −.83].

Would the model discover the original Estes configuration if it were not constrained to have identical top-down connections and no delayed lateral connections? The answer to this question is negative. If all connection weights are initialized to zero and are modifiable by learning, the network becomes extremely accurate, much more so than in the constrained case, and its weight configuration exhibits the following variety of serial order devices (see Table 3):

1. Asymmetric top-down connections: The chunk node favors the first item by exciting it and inhibiting the second item.
2. Immediate lateral inhibition: Each response node tends to turn the other off.
3. Excitatory chaining: The first response tends to turn on the second one at a delay.
4. Backward delayed inhibition: The second response turns the first one off at a delay.
5. Delayed self-inhibition: This device is the same as in the original Estes model.

One other important feature of the unconstrained model is that the weight pattern shown in Table 3 is stable. That is, regardless of the initial values of the weights, the learning process arrives at a similar configuration. For example, if the weights are initialized to the same

TABLE 3

Results of Learning to Produce a Two-Unit Sequence

Time step	Activation of A	Activation of B
1	.90	.29
2	.94	.06
3	.96	.07
4	.96	.07
5	.13	.82
6	.03	.95
7	.02	.95
8	.02	.96
9	.01	.06
10	.02	.07
11	.02	.07
12	.02	.07

Connection weights (after 100 trials):
Plan to output: AB→A = 2.17; AB→B = −0.93;
Immediate self-connections: a→A = 1.10; b→B = − 1.19
Immediate lateral connections: a→B = −1.66; b→A = −1.76;
Delayed self-connections: a(d)→A = −4.42; b(d)→B = −2.78
Delayed lateral connections: a(d)→B = 5.58; b(d)→A = −3.84

magnitudes but are assigned to the opposite directions to those shown in Table 3, learning still brings them back close to the configuration shown in the table.

5. Different Orders of the Same Elements   We have shown that the Estes model can be expressed as a special kind of constrained Jordan network. In addition, some of the features of an Estes model, particularly its use of inhibition, can be acquired by the kind of learning that characterizes a Jordan network. We now turn to the real challenge for serial order models: Can these networks handle the serial order relations required in a model of language production? It turns out that neither the original nor the generalized Estes model is capable of storing the noncreative syntagmatic relations required to produce the phonological segments of words.

If we assume that phonological segments are response units, there are many cases where anagramlike permutations of the same elements comprise several different words. As MacKay (1987) pointed out, Estes' original model fails in these cases. For example, in the case of the words *oat* and *toe*, the order of /t/ and /o/ is indeterminate. The problem can be understood by recalling that the plan unit in the Estes model only activates a set of constituents, leaving the constituents, themselves, to sort out their order. Consequently, if there is more than one order associated with the set, the model fails. When /o/ and /t/ are activated, each desperately tries to inhibit the other: /t/ attempts to inhibit /o/ because of the existence of *toe*, and /o/ does the same to /t/ because of *oat*. One might think that the problem could be solved by relaxing the constraint that the plan signal each constituent equally (identically weighted top-down connections), as we did with the generalized Estes model. So, for example, perhaps the connection from *toe* to /t/ would be stronger than that from *toe* to /o/, and the reverse would be true for *oat*. Unfortunately, this will not work either. If we attempt to learn a set of weights in the generalized framework from two plans, AB and BA, to the sequences, A B stop, and B A stop, respectively, the weight changes never make progress toward a solution. It is not difficult, though, to learn weights to store other pairs of sequences, such as AA and BB, or AB and BB. It is the anagram case that presents the problem.

The difficulty that both the original and the generalized Estes models experience with storing different sequences of the same elements is related to the well known intractability of the exclusive OR (XOR) problem in a two-layered network (Minsky & Papert, 1969; Rumelhart el al., 1986). The XOR problem is the classic example of a mapping that requires the computation of an interaction or nonlinear combination of inputs. The expression p XOR q is false when p is false and q is false, and when p is true and q is true. If one identifies "true" with an activation of 1 and "false" with 0, and sets up a network of two inputs, one each for the truth values of p and q, and one output unit that is supposed to compute p XOR q, one cannot find a set of weights that performs the computation (assuming that output activation is monotonically related to net input). This can be illustrated geometrically by imagining an input plane whose dimensions are the activation of the input units p and q. Two points in the plane (0,0) and (1,1) require an output of 0, and two points (0,1) and (1,0) require an output of 1. The intractability of the problem is seen in the fact that the points associated with an output of 0 are not in a region of the plane that can be separated by a straight line from the region associated with an output of 1. When inputs requiring different output values of the same output unit can be separated by a straight line (or plane or hyperplane in higher dimensional input spaces) and this is true of all outputs, the problem is *linearly separable*. Problems such as XOR are therefore not linearly separable. In general, two-layered networks can only store sets of input–output pairs in which similar inputs lead to similar outputs. The input patterns that should turn on a given output unit must fall in a region of input space that is linearly separable from the ones that should turn that unit off.

The difficulty of the generalized Estes model with anagrams arises because it is a two-layered model—it has no hidden units—and the task of dealing with both AB and BA is not, as we have defined it, linearly

TABLE 4
The Problem with Anagrams[a]

	Input units			
	AB	BA	a(d)	b(d)
Output unit for B should be				
ON				
Beginning of BA	0	1	0	0
Middle of AB	1	0	1	0
OFF				
Beginning of AB	1	0	0	0
Middle of BA	0	1	0	1
End of AB	0	0	0	1
End of BA	0	0	1	0

| | *Solution with hidden unit* | | | | | |
	AB	BA	a(d)	b(d)	ABa(d)	Net input to B
Connection weights to B	−	+	−	− −	+ + +	
Output for B should be						
ON						
Beginning of BA	0	1	0	0	0	+
Middle of AB	1	0	1	0	1	+
OFF						
Beginning of AB	1	0	0	0	0	−
Middle of BA	0	1	0	1	0	−
End of AB	0	0	0	1	0	− −
End of BA	0	0	1	0	0	−

[a] Beginning = prior to time step 1; middle = prior to step 5; end = prior to step 9.

separable. Table 4 provides some insight into the task. We can specify the input space in terms of four dimensions corresponding to the two plan units, AB and BA, and the two context units a(d) and b(d).[5] We focus only on the output unit B and consider when it should be on. The table presents six moments defined by three locations in the input patterns AB and BA. To illustrate the difficulty, let us attempt to determine which connections from the input units to B should be excitatory and which should be inhibitory. First, the connection BA→B must be excitatory because BA is the only input unit on at the start of a BA sequence. Similarly, AB→B must be inhibitory to turn B off at the beginning of AB. Finally, both a(d)→B and b(d)→B must be inhibitory to turn B off at the

[5] For simplicity, we are not considering the a and b immediate context units. Only certain key times in the production of the sequences are being examined and, at these times, the activation of a equals a(d), and b equals b(d). Consequently, the immediate context units are redundant and do not expand the input space.

end of BA and AB sequences, respectively. However, these connections don't work for the middle of AB, where the net input from the connections that we have specified thus far is strongly inhibitory and it should be excitatory, and for the middle of BA where the net input is neutral and it should be inhibitory. The latter difficulty can be fixed by making b(d)→B doubly inhibitory so that the excitatory contribution of BA→B is overwhelmed. But there is no such quick fix for the middle of AB. In essence, this is the multidimensional analogue of the XOR problem.

The problem can be solved by adding another unit, one that only turns on when AB and a(d) are on. Then, a triply strong excitatory weight from the new unit to B will permit B to correctly turn on in the middle of an AB sequence and, generally, will allow B to be turned off and on when it should. This new unit thus must obtain activation from the input units and, in turn, send activation to the output unit B. So, it is effectively a *hidden* unit. Adding one or more hidden units to a two-layered model is the only way to implement a mapping that is not linearly separable.

The standard Jordan network, unlike the generalized Estes model, is set up with a layer of hidden units just so that complex sets of sequences can be stored. Although the actual use of hidden units will be determined by the patterns to be learned and architectural constraints, the hidden units will come to encode nonlinear combinations of inputs. It is as if the plan unit in the Estes model not only signals which items are in the sequence, but also tells which particular connections among the items should be followed for a particular plan.

One very interesting way that an extra layer of units can be used is as a competitive filter. Houghton's (1990) competitive cueing model uses three layers of units: plan and response units analogous to what we have discussed thus far, and a third layer that uses very strong lateral inhibition to resolve competition. Specifically, suppose that there are two plan units, AB and BA, connecting to two response units, A and B. In Houghton's model, the plan units use asymmetrical top-down excitatory connections to simultaneously retrieve all of the responses for a given plan, such that response activation is a function of position in the plan. For example, the first response is more active than the second. The activation from the response units is then passed on to the competitive filter layer, which, for our simple example, would contain units A' and B'. A' would receive excitatory input from A, and B' from B. In the filter layer, A' and B' strongly inhibit each other so that only one of these units, the one whose response unit had the most activation, is activated and the other is inhibited. This constitutes the selection of the first unit. Then, the single activated filter node strongly inhibits its corresponding response unit with the effect that it is no longer activated. At this point, the most highly activated response unit is the one that was next most strongly signalled by the top-down connections and so the competitive filter will then select this next unit, and so on.

Notice how the model solves the anagram problem. AB would initially excite both A and B, but A would be more activated. There is no need for either A or AB to inhibit B because this is accomplished in the filter layer, where A' ends up with all the activation and B' is inhibited. Then, after A' inhibits A, B' will win in the filter, leading to the production of B. Finally, B is inhibited by B' shutting everything down. If BA is the plan, everything works the same way except that the top-down connections favor B over A. In general, the competitive cueing model works because it separates the competitive interactions (in the filter) from the retrieval of the items of the plan (in the response units). This makes it possible for order to be stored in the connection weights from plan to responses. Although the competitive cueing model is very different from Jordan's model (e.g., it uses different learning rules), there is, we believe, also a deep similarity. Both allow for the storage of any order because the decision to output an item at a particular time is determined by a nonlinear combination of plan information (plan-to-response connections in Houghton's model) and contextual information (context units in Jordan's model, the activated state of the response and filter units in Houghton's model).

Variations on Jordan's network, particularly those developed by Elman (1989, 1990), have been used with some success in accounting for the facts associated with the storage of phonological sequences, facts about coarticulation (Jordan, 1986), phonological speech errors (Dell et al., 1993), and other linguistic patterns (e.g., Corina, 1991; Gasser & Lee, 1990; Hare, 1990). As we turn to creative syntagmatic relations, however, we will see that the applicability of these kinds of networks to language is controversial.

B. Creative Syntagmatic Relations

A central feature of any language production model is that it must allow for the production of novel sequences. The creative component to language is most obvious in the need to combine words to produce novel sentences, although the ability to build new words out of existing morphemes and phonological segments is an important part of the creativity in many languages.

Activation-based systems that retrieve order from chunks, such as the generalized Estes model, are limited to reproducing learned orders and, hence, are not equipped to create novel orders. As we have just discussed, the problem is that these systems attempt to order content directly by stipulating connections in advance. For example, the chunk *big–dog* must be stored in memory if *big* and *dog* are to be produced in sequence. To overcome this restriction, the schemata, rules, or structures that regulate order must be represented separately from the content items that they operate on. So, rather than directly storing the sequence *big–dog*, there needs to be an independently represented rule that says that things in the category ADJECTIVE come before things in the category NOUN. Then, it is possible to produce both familiar (*big dog*) and unfamiliar (*tiny aardvark*) content sequences. The only serial order that need be stored is the order of the linguistic categories.

The separation of linguistic rules or structures, which bear the primary responsibility for order, from linguistic content is a major tenet of linguistic and psycholinguistic theory. Every model of language production, including those that are based on spreading activation, employs structural frames or other generalizations that operate on linguistic categories, not individual items (see Levelt, 1989, for a review). These frames enable the system to order items creatively. To illustrate, we now consider two related activation-based models. The first is MacKay's (1982, 1987) model and the other is a model that has emerged from the recent work of Berg, Schade, and Eikmeyer (e.g., Berg & Schade, 1992; Eikmeyer & Schade, 1991). The latter model is similar in many respects to the earlier model of Stemberger (1985).

1. MacKay's Model   MacKay's use of structural and content nodes in production is illustrated in the top of Figure 7. Although we focus only on MacKay's treatment of creative syntagmatic processes in language production, it should be recognized that the entire theory deals with perception as well as production, learning as well as performance, and, moreover, applies to nonlanguage phenomena as well. The model is a network with nodes organized along two dimensions. First, there are levels of processing corresponding to conceptual (including the word and phrase level), phonological, and motor levels. The figure shows only the conceptual level. Second, there is a distinction between *content nodes*, which are organized hierarchically and represent particular phrases, words, syllables, syllabic constituents, segments, and so on, *structural nodes*, which represent linguistic categories and ordered relations among the categories, and *timing nodes*, which control the rate of activation of the structural nodes. The figure shows only content and structural nodes.

The production of a sequence such as *the girl* starts with the activation of the content node for the entire phrase. One can think of this phrasal content node as representing the complex concept of GIRL (singular, definite). Many such complex concepts will already be in memory. Others, such as *green cows* will be the product of inferential processes (e.g., what happens when you drop a load of green paint from

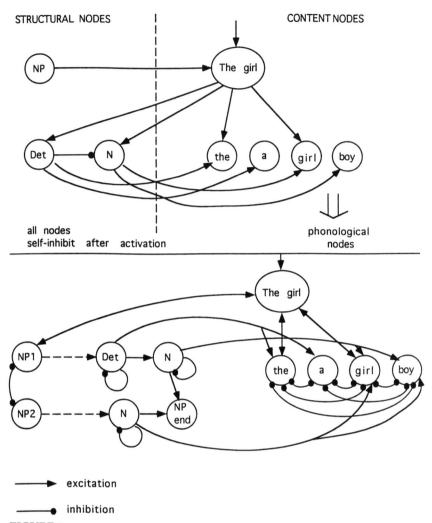

FIGURE 7

Models of creative syntagmatic decisions in production. MacKay (1982) top and Eikmeyer and Schade (1991) bottom.

a plane onto a dairy farm?) or perceptual processes (e.g., from the un-likely event of seeing green cows). Thus phrasal nodes are assumed to exist prior to the sequencing of their words. For our example, we will label the phrasal node as "the girl," even though it is not, itself, a se-quence of words. When *the girl* is activated, it primes the content nodes for *the* and *girl*, and the structure nodes det and N. Recall that, as pre-viously mentioned, MacKay distinguishes between the activation of a node, which is characterized by a sustained and very high level of activation, and priming, which involves lower levels of activation. The structure nodes also receive priming from a timing node. Because det inhibits N, the net result is that priming builds up most quickly on the structure node det and it becomes activated. The activation of det primes the content nodes for all possible determiners and, in the case of *the*, the summation of priming from det and *the girl* is sufficient to activate it. After each node is activated, it enters a period of self-inhibition. So after det is activated, it is inhibited, and now the structure node for N can become activated when the timing node primes it. The activated N node then primes all the content nodes that it connects to, that is, all nouns, and *girl* becomes activated because of its extra source of priming from *the girl*.

There are several important characteristics of MacKay's approach from our perspective. One is that the relation between *the girl* and det and N in the model is just like that in the Estes model. Serial order is controlled by a hierarchical chunk and by immediate forward inhibition. Moreover, each node undergoes self-inhibition after it is activated. Does the model, then, experience the same difficulties that the Estes model does when there are different orders involving the same items? MacKay avoids this problem by means of additional features in his model. First, ordered relationships are not marked on the content nodes, but rather on the structural nodes. It turns out that there is much less need to worry about different orders of the same nodes at the structural level. For example, the only ordering involving determiners and nouns is det, N. However, this cannot be the entire solution because there are cases in which different orders of the same linguistic categories do occur. At the phonological level, for example, there are syllables composed of the categories C (consonant) followed by V (vowel), as well as the reverse. MacKay's solution is to treat the structural nodes not as strict linguistic categories such as vowel, consonant, adjective, or noun, but rather as sequentially defined categorical domains. For example, the category of C in the case of a CV syllable would belong to the domain onset, whereas the C in a VC syllable would belong to the domain coda.[6] Hence, the same response units are not used. Some evidence that categories are sequentially defined comes from the fact that phonological speech errors tend to involve onsets replacing other onsets, and codas replacing codas (MacKay, 1970). So, although MacKay makes use of the Estes configuration, he does so in a way that avoids the difficulties.

The absence of lateral inhibition among competing alternatives at the content level is another feature of MacKay's model. As we mentioned

---

[6]MacKay's use of rhyme units intervening between syllables and segments also helps to avoid the problem; a rhyme unit dominates a coda, but not an onset.

earlier in our discussion of paradigmatic selection, this is compensated for by MacKay's notion of activation. When priming builds up in several nodes within the same categorical domain (e.g., *girl, boy*), it is stipulated that only the first one to reach an activation threshold becomes activated. And when a node achieves activated status, it is given an activation level much greater than what can be achieved by mere priming. To make this more concrete, assume that priming can build up to a level of 50 units of excitation. The first node in a domain to get to 50 becomes activated and immediately ups its excitation level to 100 units. Furthermore, every other node in the domain is then prevented from being activated and, hence, cannot exceed 50 units of excitation. The effect of this is very similar to what might be achieved by lateral inhibition within a domain. In general, MacKay's model, like models with lateral inhibition, has the property that few nodes can be highly active at once. Only one node from a domain can achieve an activated state and the sequential nature of the structure nodes largely ensures that nodes in only one domain at a time are building up appreciable levels of priming.

In sum, MacKay's model deals with creative syntagmatic decisions by a combination of noncreative syntagmatic mechanisms, such as the Estes sequencing schema, that operate on structurally defined categories, paradigmatic decisions among competing content items, and links between the two mechanisms. This solution is, in gross terms, quite similar to that adopted by other activation-based models. The model of Eikmeyer and Schade (1991) presented in the bottom of Figure 7 can be used to illustrate some dimensions of difference.

2. The Eikmeyer and Schade Model   The first difference between Eikmeyer and Schade's (1991) model and that of MacKay (1982, 1987) is that the structural nodes are ordered by forward associative chains rather than by the Estes configuration. The content node for *the girl* excites the content nodes for *the* and *girl*, and it also excites an appropriate syntactic node for NP1. The syntactic node then excites the first category of the sequence, Det. Det sends activation to all possible determiners (as in the MacKay model) and to the next category N, and so on until a special NP-end node is reached. The sequencing of categories is achieved via a combination of forward excitatory connections and self-inhibition. The higher level structure nodes (e.g., noun phrases) do not stand in a hierarchical relation to their sequential constituents, but rather serve as starting states (see Dell, 1988, for a similar configuration). As we showed earlier, this kind of serial order device will not work when units participate in more than one chain. Eikmeyer and Schade, therefore, used different units for different chains, as shown in Figure 7 for det N and N.

Another difference between the two models concerns lateral inhibition. Eikmeyer and Schade use lateral inhibition between competing sequential chains, as shown in the figure by the lateral inhibition between NP1 and NP2, and between all content units at a particular level, as shown in the lateral inhibition among the word units. This inhibition ensures that only one sequence at a time controls behavior and that only one content item becomes highly activated. It gives lateral inhibition a role in both planning and producing a sentence. Not only do *girl* and *boy*, traditional paradigmatic competitors, inhibit one another, but also *girl* and *the* inhibit one another because they are words in the intended utterance. According to Berg and Schade (1992), this kind of arrangement allows for the planning or subthreshold activation of all of the words in an utterance. During planning, lateral inhibition keeps the activation of each intended word low, but during production inhibition is overcome when the syntactic nodes activate in sequence.

Thus, Eikmeyer and Schade's use of lateral inhibition serves the same functions that MacKay addresses by distinguishing between priming and activation, and by allowing only one node in a domain to become activated. Berg and Schade (1992) suggest that one can tell whether certain production decisions are truly implemented by inhibition or by other means, by attempting to model atypical production such as that of aphasic patients or children. The idea is that it may be possible to attribute certain phenomena to a general problem with inhibition, given a model that treats inhibition in a particular fashion. We agree that such data and modeling efforts would provide useful constraints on theory, but our earlier conclusion concerning the difficulty of identifying lateral inhibition in experimental data suggests that the attribution of a cluster of behavioral effects to an inhibitory problem will be quite difficult.

3. Evaluation of the Models   Both MacKay and Eikmeyer and Schade use serial order devices for storing the order of sequences of categories that are less powerful than mechanisms capable of storing any orders (e.g., Jordan networks with hidden units), and both solve the problem by using different units for the same categories when they have different sequential functions. Which is better? The MacKay system has the advantage that it does not require a separate chain for every order. Moreover, it supports its use of categories by pointing to the speech error literature, in which sequentially defined domains account for what units replace one another. The forward chaining system of Eikmeyer and Schade, though, has the virtue of a clear implementation, one that does not require anything other than spreading activation.

We suggest that for the most part the two systems make similar empirical predictions. However, one may be able to distinguish between them by testing whether two related syntactic structures use common nodes. The Eikmeyer and Schade system uses, for example, different chains for Det N and Det adj N, whereas in MacKay's system the same Det and N nodes could be used. The hierarchical nature of the Estes configuration would supply the Adj when it is part of the sequence. Syntactic persistence effects (e.g., Bock, 1986) could, at least in principle, reveal whether these related sequences use common sequential resources. For example, one could have subjects produce a particular priming syntactic structure and then see if there is any benefit or cost to later using other target structures. The idea is that phrases or sentences that are assumed to use the same structural nodes may exhibit a priming effect. By examining pairs of prime–target structures which one theory says use common nodes and the other theory says use distinct nodes, one could conceivably discriminate between the theories.

4. PDP Models   To complete our discussion of creative syntagmatic relations in activation-based models, we briefly consider a quite different approach—an approach that questions the need for an explicit distinction between content and structural nodes. Researchers who adopt a parallel-distributed-processing (PDP) approach to connectionist modeling have developed models of language processing in which rules or other structural generalizations are not built into the architecture, but rather emerge from the superimpositional storage of the linguistic sequences that comprise the set of training items (e.g., Corina, 1991; Elman, 1989, 1990; Hare, 1990; Gasser & Lee, 1990; MacWhinney & Leinbach, 1991; Rumelhart & McClelland, 1986b; Seidenberg & McClelland, 1989; St. John & McClelland, 1990). In short, these models use networks that can store sequences, as a Jordan network does, but because of the use of distributed representations, the sequences are stored in such a way that the network has some ability to extend itself to novel sequences. Rumelhart and McClelland's (1986b) model of English past tense allomorphy is the classic example. The network learns a set of paired root and past tense forms of verbs. Each verb is associated with a distributed representation involving many nodes and connections that are shared with other verbs. Consequently, the weight changes associated with the learning of a particular verb are mingled with those associated with other verbs. The superimposition of the weight changes allows the network to act as if it has extracted general rules. When given a novel verb, the network can, to some extent, form the correct past tense. Yet there is no rule that is stored separately from the storage of the trained verbs. The network is able to create new output, that is, to generalize to novel forms, without an explicit structure–content distinction.

At present, it is too early to say whether the creative syntagmatic relations required for language production can be exhibited by this kind of PDP model. The issues are quite complex and the work done in the area is still preliminary. One model of this type was specifically developed to account for psycholinguistic data in production (Dell et al., 1993). That model used a variant of a Jordan network to store the phonological forms of English words as sequences of phonological features. Because the network had hidden units it had no trouble storing the sequences, that is, it could effectively deal with the required noncreative syntagmatic relations. However, Dell et al. wished to see if the model could exhibit structural effects that in other models have been ascribed to structural nodes or frames. These effects involved two characteristics of phonological speech errors. First, speech errors can create novel phonological strings, but only novel strings that obey the phonotactic constraints of the language being spoken. Second, there are syllable structure effects whereby errors tend to involve sets of features that comprise syllabic constituents. After the model stored sets of English words, its performance was degraded by noise added to the connection weights to simulate interference from surrounding words and other processing losses. The noise resulted in the model producing "speech errors" and the errors did, indeed, exhibit the structural effects. Dell et al. concluded that at least some of the effects attributed to phonological frames or structural nodes may, instead, reflect the combined influence of the stored vocabulary. For our purposes, this raises the possibility that powerful noncreative syntagmatic mechanisms may, when combined with distributed representations, deal with creative effects. Of course, Dell et al.'s efforts apply only to phonology, the least creative aspect of language production. It remains to be seen whether syntax can be similarly treated.

VI. SUMMARY AND CONCLUSIONS

Inhibition serves many purposes in interactive activation models of language production. Some models use lateral inhibition to aid in paradigmatic selection, others use inhibition only to regulate sequencing (e.g., MacKay, 1987), and others use inhibition in the service of both selection and sequencing (e.g., Eikmeyer & Schade, 1991). Our survey found good evidence for molar-behavioral inhibition in paradigmatic selection. However, the mapping of these effects to molecular lateral inhibition was unclear. In most cases, alternative mechanisms could also account for the data. Therefore, it appears that experiments that are specifically designed to test for the presence of lateral inhibition will be required to constrain models and theory in this area.

Whereas the status of lateral inhibition in tasks such as lexical retrieval is unresolved, inhibitory mechanisms appear to be essential to the complex sequencing requirements of language production. We explored the range of these requirements and of the inhibitory mechanisms that serve them in a variety of different models. Although the functional requirement for inhibition in syntagmatic processing is clear, there are no specific processes analogous to lateral inhibition that the models mimic. The models serve the purpose of clarifying functional requirements and thus supporting theory building. Thus, for example, we were able to identify the difficulty some models have with the requirements of being able to represent different sequences of the same items. Interactive activation models like MacKay's and Eikmeyer and Schade's address this problem by a variety of means including a separation of structure and content representations. These models employ a range of inhibitory and excitatory devices that should in principle be susceptible to empirical evaluation. Finally, the development of PDP models that dissolve the distinction between content and structure presents a new challenge to interactive activation models. The PDP approach suggests that at least some effects that have been ascribed to structure may instead be emergent from content. To the extent that this is the case, the division of structure and content in activation-based models must be modified, and this in turn will have implications for the role of inhibition in these models. The need for the variety of inhibitory processes we have discussed remains. However, it may be difficult to justify assigning particular inhibitory devices to content nodes, and others to a separate set of structural nodes.

ACKNOWLEDGMENTS

This work was supported by NSF-89-10546 and DC-00191 (NIH). The authors wish to thank Ulrich Schade, David Adams, Vic Ferreira, Anita Govindjee, Scott McGurrin, and Chris Sevald for helpful suggestions and Linda May for work on the manuscript.

REFERENCES

Andrews, S. (1989). Frequency and neighborhood effects on lexical access: Activation or search? *Journal of Experimental Psychology: Learning, Memory and Cognition, 15,* 804–814.

Bates, E. A., & Elman, J. L. (1992). *Connectionism and the study of change.* CRL Technical Report 9202. Center for Research on Language, University of California, San Diego.

Berg, T. (1988). *Die Abbildung des Sprachproduktionprozess in einem Aktivationsflussmodell.* Tübingen: Max Niemeyer.

Berg, T., & Schade, U. (1992). The role of inhibition in a spreading activation model of language production: 1. The psycholinguistic perspective. Unpublished manuscript, University of Oldenburg, Germany.

Blaxton, T. A., & Neely, J. H. (1983). Inhibition from semantically related primes: Evidence of category specific inhibition. *Memory & Cognition, 11,* 500–510.

Bock, J. K. (1982). Toward a cognitive psychology of syntax: Information processing contributions to sentence formulation. *Psychological Review, 89,* 1–47.

Bock, J. K. (1986). Syntactic persistence in language production. *Cognitive Psychology, 18,* 355–387.

Bock, J. K. (1987). An effect of the accessibility of word forms on sentence structure. *Journal of Memory and Language, 26,* 119–137.

Bock, J. K., Loebell, H., & Morey, R. (1992). From conceptual roles to structural relations: Bridging the syntactic cleft. *Psychological Review, 99,* 150–171.

Boland, J. E., Tanenhaus, M. K., & Garnsey, S. M. (1990). Evidence for the immediate use of verb control information in sentence processing. *Journal of Memory and Language, 29,* 413–432.

Bowles, N. L., & Poon, L. W. (1985). Effects of priming on word retrieval. *Journal of Experimental Psychology: Learning, Memory and Cognition, 11,* 272–283.

Brown, A. S. (1979). Priming effects in semantic memory retrieval processes. *Journal of Experimental Psychology: Human Learning and Memory, 5,* 65–77.

Brown, A. S. (1981). Inhibition in cued retrieval. *Journal of Experimental Psychology: Human Learning and Memory, 7,* 204–215.

Carr, T. H., & Dagenbach, D. (1990). Semantic priming and repetition priming from masked words: Evidence for a center-surround attentional mechanism in perceptual recognition. *Journal of Experimental Psychology: Learning, Memory and Cognition, 16,* 341–350.

Colombo, L. (1986). Activation and inhibition with orthographically similar words. *Journal of Experimental Psychology: Human Perception and Performance, 12,* 226–234.

Coltheart, M., Davelaar, E., Jonasson, J. T., & Besner, D. (1977). Access to the internal lexicon. In S. Dornic (Ed.), *Attention and Performance VI.* New York: Academic Press.

Corina, D. P. (1991). *Toward an understanding of the syllable: Evidence from linguistic, psychological, and connectionist investigations of syllable structure.* Doctoral dissertation, University of California, San Diego.

Dagenbach, D., Carr, T. H., & Wilhelmsen, A. (1989). Task-induced strategies and near-threshold priming: Conscious effects on unconscious perception. *Journal of Memory and Language, 28,* 412–443.

Dell, G. S. (1986). A spreading activation theory of retrieval in language production. *Psychological Review, 93,* 283–321.

Dell, G. S. (1988). The retrieval of phonological forms in production: Tests of predictions from a connectionist model. *Journal of Memory and Language, 27,* 124–142. Reprinted (1989). In W. Marslen-Wilson (Ed.), *Lexical representation and process* (pp. 136–165). Cambridge, MA: MIT Press.

Dell, G. S., Juliano, C., & Govindjee, A. (1993). Structure and content in language production: A theory of frame constraints in phonological speech errors. *Cognitive Science, 17,* 149–195.

Dell, G. S., & O'Seaghdha, P. G. (1992). Stages of lexical access in language production. *Cognition, 42,* 287–314.

Dell, G. S., & Reich, P. A. (1981). Stages in sentence production: An analysis of speech error data. *Journal of Verbal Learning and Verbal Behavior, 20,* 611–629.

Eikmeyer, H.-J., & Schade, U. (1991). Sequentialization in connectionist language production models. *Cognitive Systems, 3*(2), 128–138.

Elman, J. L. (1989). Structured representations and connectionist models. *Proceedings of the 11th Annual Conference of the Cognitive Science Society,* Ann Arbor, MI.

Elman, J. L. (1990). Finding structure in time. *Cognitive Science, 14,* 213–252.

Elman, J. L., & McClelland, J. L. (1986). The TRACE model of speech perception. *Cognitive Psychology, 18,* 1–86.

Estes, W. K. (1972). An associative basis for coding and organization in memory. In A. W. Melton & E. Martin (Eds.), *Coding processes in human memory* (pp. 161–190). Washington, DC: Winston.

Feldman, J. A., & Ballard, D. H. (1982). Connectionist models and their properties. *Cognitive Science, 6,* 205–254.

Fodor, J. A., Bever, T. G., & Garrett, M. F. (1974). *The psychology of language.* New York: McGraw-Hill.

Forster, K. I. (1976). Accessing the mental lexicon. In R. J. Wales & E. Walker (Eds.), *New approaches to language mechanisms.* Amsterdam: North Holland.

Forster, K. I., & Davis, C. (1991). The density constraint in the naming task: Interference effects from a masked prime. *Journal of Memory and Language, 30,* 1–25.

Forster, K. I., Davis, C., Schoknecht, C., & Carter, R. (1987). Masked priming with graphemically related forms: Repetition or partial activation? *Quarterly Journal of Experimental Psychology, 39A,* 211–251.

Frauenfelder, U. H., Segui, J., & Dijkstra, T. (1990). Lexical effects in phonemic processing: Facilitatory or inhibitory? *Journal of Experimental Psychology: Human Perception and Performance, 16,* 77–91.

Fromkin, V. A. (1971). The nonanomalous nature of anomalous utterances. *Language, 47,* 27–52.

Garrett, M. F. (1975). The analysis of sentence production. In G. H. Bower (Ed.), *The psychology of learning and motivation* (pp. 133–177). San Diego: Academic Press.

Gasser, M., & Lee, C.-D. (1990). Networks that learn about phonological feature persistence. *Connection Science, 2,* 265–278.

Glushko, R. (1979). The organization and activation of orthographic information in reading aloud. *Journal of Experimental Psychology: Human Perception and Performance, 5,* 674–691.

Goldinger, S. D., Luce, P. A., & Pisoni, D. B. (1989). Priming lexical neighbors of spoken words: Effects of competition and inhibition. *Journal of Memory and Language, 28,* 501–518.

Goldinger, S. D., Luce, P. A., Pisoni, D. B., & Marcario, J. K. (1992). Form-based priming in spoken word recognition: The roles of competition and bias. *Journal of Experimental Psychology: Learning, Memory and Cognition, 18,* 1211–1238.

Grossberg, S. (1978). A theory of visual coding, memory, and development. In E. L. J. Leeuwenberg & H. F. M. Buffart (Eds.), *Formal theories of visual processing.* New York: Wiley.

Hare, M. (1990). The role of similarity in Hungarian vowel harmony: A connectionist account. *Connection Science, 2,* 125–152.

Harley, T. A. (1984). A critique of top-down independent levels of models of speech production: Evidence from non-plan-internal speech errors. *Cognitive Science, 8,* 191–219.

Harley, T. A. (1990). Paragrammatisms: Syntactic disturbance or breakdown of control? *Cognition, 34,* 85–91.

Hillinger, M. L. (1980). Priming effects with phonemically similar words: The encoding bias hypothesis reconsidered. *Memory & Cognition, 8,* 115–123.

Houghton, G. (1990). The problem of serial order: A neural network model of sequence learning and recall. In R. Dale, C. Mellish, & M. Zock (Eds.), *Current research in natural language generation* (pp. 287–319). London: Academic Press.

Jones, G. V., & Langford, A. S. (1987). Phonological blocking in the tip of the tongue state. *Cognition, 26,* 115–122.

Jordan, M. I. (1986). Attractor dynamics and parallelism in a connectionist sequential machine. In *Proceedings of the Eighth Annual Conference of the Cognitive Science Society* (pp. 531–546). Hillsdale, NJ: Lawrence Erlbaum.

Kawamoto, A. H. (1993). Nonlinear dynamics in the resolution of lexical ambiguity: A parallel distributed processing account. *Journal of Memory and Language, 32,* 474–516.

Kawamoto, A. H., & Zemblidge, J. H. (1992). Pronunciation of homographs. *Journal of Memory and Language, 31,* 349–374.

Lashley, K. S. (1951). The problem of serial order in behavior. In L. A. Jeffress (Ed.), *Cerebral mechanisms in behavior* (pp. 112–136). New York: Wiley.

Levelt, W. J. M. (1989). *Speaking: From intention to articulation.* Cambridge, MA: MIT Press.

Levelt, W. J. M., Schriefers, H., Vorberg, D., Meyer, A. S., Pechmann, T., & Havinga, J. (1991). The timecourse of lexical access in speech production: A study of picture naming. *Psychological Review, 98,* 122–142.

Loftus, E. F. (1973). Activation of semantic memory. *American Journal of Psychology, 86,* 331–337.

Loftus, G. R., & Loftus, E. F. (1974). The influence of one memory retrieval on a subsequent memory retrieval. *Memory & Cognition, 2,* 467–471.

Luce, P. A., Pisoni, D. B., & Goldinger, S. D. (1990). Similarity neighborhoods of spoken words. In G. T. Altmann (Ed.), *Cognitive models of speech processing* (pp. 122–147). Cambridge, MA: MIT Press.

Luce, R. D. (1959). *Individual choice behavior.* New York: Wiley.

Lupker, S. J., & Williams, B. A. (1987). *When do rhyming primes inhibit target processing?* Paper presented at the 28th Annual Meeting of the Psychonomic Society, Seattle, WA.

MacKay, D. G. (1970). Spoonerisms: The structure of errors in the serial order of speech. *Neuropsychologia, 8,* 323–350.

MacKay, D. G. (1972). The structure of words and syllables: Evidence from errors in speech. *Cognitive Psychology, 3,* 210–227.

MacKay, D. G. (1982). The problems of flexibility, fluency, and speed–accuracy trade-off in skilled behaviors. *Psychological Review, 89,* 483–506.

MacKay, D. G. (1987). *The organization of perception and action: A theory for language and other cognitive skills.* New York: Springer.

MacWhinney, B., & Leinbach, J. (1991). Implementations are not conceptualizations: Revising the verb learning model. *Cognition, 40,* 121–157.

Marslen-Wilson, W. (in press). Issues of process and representation in lexical access. In G. Altmann & R. Shillcock (Eds.), *Cognitive models of language processes: The Sperlonga Meeting II.* Hillsdale, NJ: Lawrence Erlbaum.

Marslen-Wilson, W., & Tyler, L. (1980). The temporal structure of spoken language understanding. *Cognition, 8,* 1–71.

Martin, N., & Saffran, E. M. (1992). A computational account of deep dysphasia: Evidence from a single case study. *Brain and Language, 43,* 240–274.

Martin, N., Weisberg, R. W., & Saffran, E. M. (1989). Variables influencing the occurrence of naming errors: Implications for a model of lexical retrieval. *Journal of Memory and Language, 28,* 462–485.

McClelland, J. L. (1987). The case for interactionism in language processing. In M. Coltheart (Ed.), *Attention and performance XII.* Hillsdale, NJ: Lawrence Erlbaum.

McClelland, J. L., & Rumelhart, D. E. (1981). An interactive activation model of context effects in letter perception: 1. An account of basic findings. *Psychological Review, 88,* 375–407.

McKoon, G., & Ratcliff, R. (1992). Inference during reading. *Psychological Review, 99,* 440–466.

Meyer, A. S. (1991). The timecourse of phonological encoding in language production: Phonological encoding inside a syllable. *Journal of Memory and Language, 30,* 69–89.

Meyer, A. S., & Bock, K. (1992). The tip-of-the-tongue phenomenon: Blocking or partial activation? *Memory & Cognition, 20,* 715–726.

Meyer, D. E., & Gordon, P. C. (1985). Speech production: Motor programming of phonetic features. *Journal of Memory and Language, 24,* 3–26.

Meyer, D. E., & Schvaneveldt, R. W. (1971). Facilitation in recognizing pairs of words: Evidence for a dependence between retrieval operations. *Journal of Experimental Psychology, 90,* 227–234.

Meyer, D. E., Schvaneveldt, R. W., & Ruddy, M. G. (1974). Functions of graphemic and phonemic codes in visual word recognition. *Memory & Cognition, 2,* 309–321.

Minsky, M., & Papert, S. (1969). *Perceptrons.* Cambridge, MA: MIT Press.

O'Seaghdha, P. G., Dell, G. S., Peterson, R. R., & Juliano, C. (1992). Models of form-related priming in comprehension and production. In R. G. Reilly & N. E. Sharkey (Eds.), *Connectionist approaches to natural language processing* (pp. 373–408). Hillsdale, NJ: Lawrence Erlbaum.

Perfect, T. J., & Hanley, J. R. (1992). The tip-of-the-tongue phenomenon: Do experimenter-presented interlopers have any effect? *Cognition, 45,* 55–75.

Peterson, R. R., Dell, G. S., & O'Seaghdha, P. G. (1989). A connectionist model of form-related priming effects. *Proceedings of the 11th Annual Conference of the Cognitive Science Society* (pp. 196–203). Hillsdale, NJ: Lawrence Erlbaum.

Plunkett, K., & Marchman, V. (1991). U-shaped learning and frequency effects in a multi-layered perceptron: Implications for child language acquisition. *Cognition, 38,* 43–102.

Ratliff, F., & Hartline, H. K. (1959). The response of Limulus optic nerve fibers to patterns of illumination on the receptor mosaic. *Journal of General Physiology, 42,* 1241–1255.

Roediger, H. L., & Neely, J. H. (1982). Retrieval blocks in episodic and semantic memory. *Canadian Journal of Psychology, 36,* 213–242.

Roediger, H. L., Neely, J. H., & Blaxton, T. A. (1983). Inhibition from related primes in semantic memory retrieval: A reappraisal of Brown's (1979) paradigm. *Journal of Experimental Psychology: Learning, Memory and Cognition, 9,* 478–485.

Roelofs, A. (1992). A spreading-activation theory of lemma retrieval in speaking. *Cognition, 42,* 107–142.

Rumelhart, D. E., Hinton, G. E., & Williams, R. J. (1986). Learning internal representations by error propagation. In D. E. Rumelhart & J. L. McClelland (Eds.), *Parallel distributed processing: Explorations in the microstructure of cognition* (Vol. 1). Cambridge, MA: MIT Press.

Rumelhart, D. E., & McClelland, J. L. (1982). An interactive activation model of context effects in letter perception: 2. The contextual enhancement effect and some tests and extensions of the model. *Psychological Review, 89,* 60–94.

Rumelhart, D. E., & McClelland, J. L. (Eds.). (1986a). *Parallel distributed processing: Explorations in the microstructure of cognition* (Vol. 1). Cambridge, MA: MIT Press.

Rumelhart, D. E., & McClelland, J. L. (1986b). On learning the past tenses of English verbs. In J. L. McClelland & D. E. Rumelhart (Eds.), *Parallel distributed processing: Explorations in the microstructure of cognition* (Vol. 2, pp. 216–271). Cambridge, MA: Bradford Books.

Rumelhart, D. E., & Norman, D. A. (1982). Stimulating a skilled typist: A study of skilled cognitive motor performance. *Cognitive Science, 6,* 1–36.

Schade, U. (1992). *Konnektionismus - Zur Modellierung der Sprachproduktion.* Opladen: Westdeutscher Verlag.

Schriefers, H., Meyer, A. S., & Levelt, W. J. M. (1990). Exploring the timecourse of lexical access in production: Picture–word interference studies. *Journal of Memory and Language, 29,* 86–102.

Segui, J., & Grainger, J. (1990). Priming word recognition with orthographic neighbors: Effects of relative prime–target frequency. *Journal of Experimental Psychology: Human Perception and Performance, 1,* 65–76.

Seidenberg, M. S., & McClelland, J. L. (1989). A distributed developmental model of visual word recognition and naming. *Psychological Review, 96,* 523–568.

Sevald, C., & Dell, G. S. (submitted). *Planning units in speech production: Evidence for sequential activation of units inside the syllable.*

Slowiaczek, L. M., & Hamburger, M. (1992). Prelexical facilitation and lexical interference in auditory word recognition. *Journal of Experimental Psychology: Learning, Memory and Cognition, 18,* 1239–1250.

Stemberger, J. P. (1985). An interactive activation model of language production. In A. W. Ellis (Ed.), *Progress in the psychology of language* (Vol. 1, pp. 143–186). Hillsdale, NJ: Lawrence Erlbaum.

Stemberger, J. P. (1990). Wordshape errors in language production. *Cognition, 35,* 123–158.

Stemberger, J. P. (1991). Apparent antifrequency effects in language production: The addition bias and phonological underspecification. *Journal of Memory and Language, 30,* 161–185.

St. John, M. F., & McClelland, J. L. (1990). Learning and applying contextual constraints in sentence comprehension. *Artificial Intelligence, 46,* 217–257.

Swinney, D. A. (1979). Lexical access during sentence comprehension: (Re)consideration of context effects. *Journal of Verbal Learning and Verbal Behavior, 18,* 545–569.

Tanenhaus, M. K., Leiman, J. M., & Seidenberg, M. A. (1979). Evidence for multiple stages in the process of ambiguous words in syntactic contexts. *Journal of Verbal Learning and Verbal Behavior, 18,* 427–441.

Taraban, R., & McClelland, J. L. (1987). Conspiracy effects in word pronunciation. *Journal of Memory and Language, 26,* 608–631.

Wheeldon, L. (1989). *Priming of spoken word production,* Unpublished doctoral dissertation, University of Cambridge.

Woodworth, R. S. (1938). *Experimental psychology.* New York: Holt.

Index